CRIMINAL PROCEDURE AND EVIDENCE

Sue Strickland-Lord

TAP

Toronto Academic Press

CRIMINAL PROCEDURE AND EVIDENCE

Sue Strickland-Lord

Toronto Academic Press
4164 Lakeshore Road
Burlington ON L7L 1A4
Canada
www.tap-books.com

Email: orders@arclereducation.com

ISBN: 978-1-77956-928-8

ABOUT THE AUTHOR

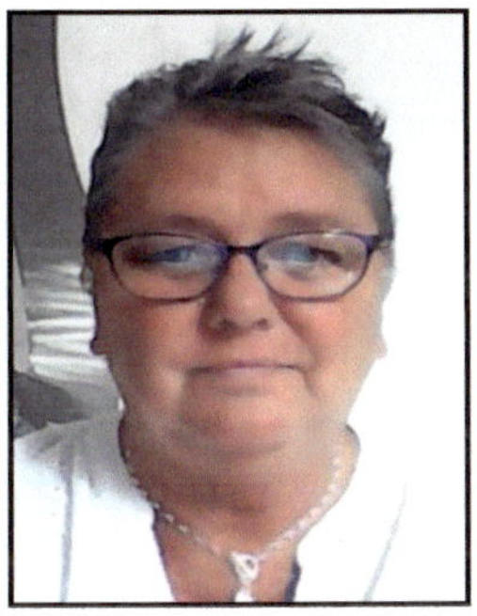

Sue Strickland-Lord is a college lecturer in Social Sciences, lecturing for over twenty years in several UK colleges. She specialises in Criminology and has a 1st Class degree in Criminology from the University of Winchester and a MSc in Criminal Justice, with merit from the University of Portsmouth. Sue achieved particularly high grades in her dissertations with pass percentages at 85% and she has been able to pass on those skills to many of her students who have excelled in their educational achievement. Sue works hard to introduce students to the world of Criminology and inspires students to research the subject thoroughly and understand it fully to support their own academic writing. Many of her students have gone on to gain their educational aspirations and go on to work in areas such as criminal justice, policing, law and prison services. Her own career as also included working with vulnerable victims and writing educational programmes within prison reform.

Brief Contents

1. Introduction to Criminal Procedure and Evidence 1
2. The Criminal Justice System and Procedural Roles 39
3. Investigation and Pre-trial Procedures of Criminal Procedure 73
4. Search, Seizure, and Surveillance in Criminal Procedure 109
5. Bail and Remand Procedures in Criminal Procedure 143
6. Initiation of Proceedings and Charge Framing in Criminal Procedure 177
7. Criminal Trial Process 211
8. Evidence: Meaning, Types, and Admissibility in Criminal Procedure 245
9. Examination of Witnesses in Criminal Procedure 281
10. Confessions, Statements, and Burden of Proof in Criminal Procedure 313
11. Appeals, Revisions, and Post-Trial Remedies of Criminal Procedure and Evidence 347
12. Emerging Issues and Reforms in Criminal Procedure and Evidence 383

Index 419

Table of Contents

List of Figures *xv*

Preface *xxi*

1

INTRODUCTION TO CRIMINAL PROCEDURE AND EVIDENCE 1

Introduction **1**

1.1. The Criminal Justice System **6**

1.1.1. Structure of the Criminal Justice System 7

1.1.2. Roles of Key Participants 8

1.1.3. Interaction between Law Enforcement and the Judiciary 9

1.2. Sources of Criminal Procedure Law **11**

1.2.1. Constitutional Provisions 12

1.2.2. Statutory Law 13

1.2.3. Case Law and Judicial Precedents 14

1.3. The Role of Evidence in Criminal Proceedings **15**

1.3.1. Definition of Evidence 15

1.3.2. Types of Evidence 16

1.3.3. Importance of Evidence in Proving Guilt 17

1.4. The Exclusionary Rule **19**

1.4.1. Definition and Purpose 20

1.4.2. Exceptions to the Rule 20

1.4.3. Impact on Law Enforcement Practices 21

1.5. Search and Seizure **23**

1.5.1. Fourth Amendment Protections 24

1.5.2. Types of Searches 25

1.5.3. Legal Standards for Search Warrants 26

1.6. Trial Procedures **27**

1.6.1. Pre-Trial Motions and Hearings 28

1.6.2. The Trial Process 28

1.6.3. Sentencing and Appeals 29

Summary **31**

References **34**

2

THE CRIMINAL JUSTICE SYSTEM AND PROCEDURAL ROLES 39

Introduction **39**

2.1. Historical Context of the Criminal Justice System **43**

2.1.1. Evolution of Legal Systems 43

2.1.2. Key Milestones in Criminal Justice History 45

2.1.3. Impact of Historical Events on Current Practices 45

2.2. Components of the Criminal Justice System **47**

2.2.1. Law Enforcement Agencies 47

2.2.2. Judicial System 48

2.2.3. Correctional Institutions 49

2.3. Roles of Law Enforcement **51**
2.3.1. Responsibilities of Police Officers 51
2.3.2. Investigative Procedures 52
2.3.3. Community Policing Initiatives 53
2.4. The Judicial Process **55**
2.4.1. Structure of the Court System 56
2.4.2. Roles of Judges and Prosecutors 57
2.4.3. The Importance of Defense Attorneys 58
2.5. Correctional System Functions **59**
2.5.1. Types of Correctional Facilities 60
2.5.2. Rehabilitation vs. Punishment 60
2.5.3. Challenges in the Correctional System 61
2.6. Procedural Justice **63**
2.6.1. Definition and Principles of Procedural Justice 64
2.6.2. The Role of Fairness in Legal Proceedings 65
2.6.3. Impact of Procedural Justice on Public Perception 66
Summary **67**
References **70**

3

INVESTIGATION AND PRE-TRIAL PROCEDURES OF CRIMINAL PROCEDURE 73

Introduction **73**
3.1. The Role of Law Enforcement in Investigations **77**
3.1.1. Initial Response to a Crime Scene 78
3.1.2. Collection of Evidence 79
3.1.3. Interrogation of Suspects and Witnesses 80
3.2. Types of Evidence in Criminal Investigations **82**
3.2.1. Physical Evidence 82
3.2.2. Testimonial Evidence 83
3.2.3. Digital Evidence 84
3.3. Legal Standards for Searches and Seizures **86**
3.3.1. Fourth Amendment Protections 87
3.3.2. Search Warrants and Exceptions 87
3.3.3. Exclusionary Rule 88
3.4. The Process of Charging a Suspect **90**
3.4.1. Role of the Prosecutor 91
3.4.2. Grand Jury Proceedings 91
3.4.3. Filing of Charges 92
3.5. Pre-trial Motions and Hearings **94**
3.5.1. Motion to Suppress Evidence 95
3.5.2. Motion for Change of Venue 95
3.5.3. Pre-trial Conferences 96
3.6. The Importance of Discovery in Pre-trial **98**
3.6.1. Disclosure of Evidence by Prosecution 99
3.6.2. Defense's Right to Discovery 99
3.6.3. Impact of Discovery on Trial Preparation 100
Summary **102**
References **105**

4

SEARCH, SEIZURE, AND SURVEILLANCE IN CRIMINAL PROCEDURE 109

Introduction **109**
4.1. Historical Context **114**
4.1.1. Origins of Search and Seizure Laws 115
4.1.2. Key Supreme Court Cases Shaping the Doctrine 115
4.1.3. Evolution of Privacy Rights in the United States (U.S.) 117
4.2. The Fourth Amendment **118**
4.2.1. Text and Interpretation of the Fourth Amendment 118
4.2.2. Reasonable Expectation of Privacy 119
4.2.3. Exceptions to the Warrant Requirement 120
4.3. Search Warrants **122**
4.3.1. Requirements for Obtaining a Search Warrant 123
4.3.2. Execution of Search Warrants 124
4.3.3. Challenges to the Validity of Search Warrants 125

4.4. Exclusionary Rule **126**

4.4.1. Definition and Purpose of the Exclusionary Rule 127

4.4.2. Key Cases Establishing the Exclusionary Rule 127

4.4.3. Limitations and Exceptions to the Exclusionary Rule 128

4.5. Surveillance Techniques **130**

4.5.1. Types of Surveillance Used in Criminal Investigations 131

4.5.2. Legal Standards Governing Electronic Surveillance 132

4.5.3. Impact of Technology on Surveillance Practices 133

4.6. Balancing Security and Privacy **134**

4.6.1. Tensions Between Law Enforcement and Individual Rights 135

4.6.2. Public Perception of Surveillance and Privacy 136

4.6.3. Legislative Responses to Privacy Concerns 136

Summary **138**

References **141**

5

BAIL AND REMAND PROCEDURES IN CRIMINAL PROCEDURE 143

Introduction **143**

5.1. Historical Context of Bail **147**

5.1.1. Evolution of Bail Laws 147

5.1.2. Key Legal Cases Influencing Bail Practices 149

5.1.3. Historical Perspectives on Remand Procedures 149

5.2. Types of Bail **151**

5.2.1. Cash Bail 152

5.2.2. Surety Bail 153

5.2.3. Personal Recognizance 154

5.3. Factors Influencing Bail Decisions **155**

5.3.1. Flight Risk Assessment 156

5.3.2. Severity of the Offense 156

5.3.3. Criminal History of the Accused 157

5.4. Remand Procedures **159**

5.4.1. Definition and Purpose of Remand 160

5.4.2. Legal Standards for Remand 160

5.4.3. Differences Between Remand and Bail 161

5.5. Rights of the Accused **163**

5.5.1. Right to a Fair Hearing 164

5.5.2. Right to Legal Representation 165

5.5.3. Right to Appeal Bail Decisions 166

5.6. Criticisms and Challenges **167**

5.6.1. Inequities in Bail Practices 167

5.6.2. Impact of Bail on Marginalized Communities 168

5.6.3. Calls for Reform in Bail and Remand Systems 169

Summary **171**

References **174**

6

INITIATION OF PROCEEDINGS AND CHARGE FRAMING IN CRIMINAL PROCEDURE 177

Introduction **177**

6.1. The Concept of Initiation of Proceedings **181**

6.1.1. Legal Framework Governing Initiation 182

6.1.2. Types of Proceedings in Criminal Law 182

6.1.3. Role of Law Enforcement in Initiation 184

6.2. The Role of the Police in Initiating Proceedings **185**

6.2.1. Investigation and Evidence Collection 186

6.2.2. Filing of First Information Report (FIR) 187

6.2.3. Discretionary Powers of Police 187

6.3. The Role of the Prosecution in Charge Framing **189**

6.3.1. Responsibilities of the Prosecutor 190

6.3.2. Evaluation of Evidence for Charge Framing 191

6.3.3. Decision-Making Process in Charge Framing 191

6.4. Legal Standards for Charge Framing **193**

6.4.1. Threshold for Framing Charges 194

6.4.2. Types of Charges: Felonies vs. Misdemeanors 194

6.4.3. Impact of Charge Framing on the Accused 196

6.5. Judicial Oversight in Charge Framing **197**

6.5.1. Role of the Courts in Reviewing Charges 198

6.5.2. Pre-Trial Hearings and Their Significance 199

6.5.3. Judicial Discretion in Charge Framing 199

6.6. Challenges in Initiation of Proceedings and Charge Framing **201**

6.6.1. Issues of Misuse of Power 202

6.6.2. Impact of Public Opinion and Media 203

6.6.3. Legal Reforms and Recommendations 203

Summary **205**

References **208**

7

CRIMINAL TRIAL PROCESS 211

Introduction **211**

7.1. Pre-Trial Procedures **215**

7.1.1. Arrest and Booking 216

7.1.2. Initial Appearance and Bail Hearings 217

7.1.3. Preliminary Hearings and Grand Jury Indictments 217

7.2. The Role of Key Participants **219**

7.2.1. The Judge's Responsibilities 219

7.2.2. The Prosecutor's Role in the Trial 220

7.2.3. The Defense Attorney's Duties 221

7.3. Jury Selection **223**

7.3.1. Importance of an Impartial Jury 224

7.3.2. The Voir Dire Process 225

7.3.3. Challenges and Strikes During Jury Selection 226

7.4. Trial Phases **228**

7.4.1. Opening Statements 228

7.4.2. Presentation of Evidence 229

7.4.3. Closing Arguments 230

7.5. Deliberation and Verdict **231**

7.5.1. Jury Deliberation Process 232

7.5.2. Types of Verdicts (Guilty, Not Guilty, and Hung Jury) 233

7.5.3. Impact of the Verdict on the Defendant 233

7.6. Post-Trial Procedures **235**

7.6.1. Sentencing Options and Considerations 235

7.6.2. Appeals Process and Grounds for Appeal 236

7.6.3. Role of Post-Conviction Relief 237

Summary **239**

References **242**

8

EVIDENCE: MEANING, TYPES, AND ADMISSIBILITY IN CRIMINAL PROCEDURE 245

Introduction **245**

8.1. The Concept of Evidence **249**

8.1.1. Historical Background of Evidence in Legal Systems 249

8.1.2. The Role of Evidence in Establishing Facts 250

8.1.3. Distinction Between Direct and Circumstantial Evidence 251

8.2. Types of Evidence **253**

8.2.1. Physical Evidence and Its Significance 254

8.2.2. Testimonial Evidence and Its Reliability 255

8.2.3. Documentary Evidence and Its Role in Court 256

8.3. The Rules of Evidence **259**

8.3.1. Overview of the Federal Rules of Evidence (FRE) 259

8.3.2. State-Specific Variations in Evidence Rules 260

8.3.3. The Purpose of Rules Governing

Evidence 261

8.4. Admissibility of Evidence 263

8.4.1. Criteria for Admissibility in Criminal Trials 263

8.4.2. The Role of Relevance and Materiality 264

8.4.3. The Impact of Prejudicial Versus Probative Value 265

8.5. Exclusions and Exceptions 267

8.5.1. Overview of Hearsay and Its Exceptions 267

8.5.2. The Exclusionary Rule and Its Implications 268

8.5.3. Exceptions to the Exclusionary Rule 269

8.6. The Role of Judges and Juries 271

8.6.1. Judges' Responsibilities in Determining Admissibility 271

8.6.2. Juries' Role in Evaluating Evidence 272

8.6.3. The Impact of Judicial Decisions on Jury Perceptions 273

Summary 275

References 278

9

EXAMINATION OF WITNESSES IN CRIMINAL PROCEDURE 281

Introduction 281

9.1. Types of Witnesses 285

9.1.1. Eyewitnesses 286

9.1.2. Expert Witnesses 287

9.1.3. Character Witnesses 288

9.2. The Role of Witnesses in Criminal Trials 289

9.2.1. Establishing Facts of the Case 289

9.2.2. Influencing Jury Perception 291

9.2.3. Providing Credibility to the Prosecution or Defense 291

9.3. Pre-Trial Procedures 293

9.3.1. Witness Interviews 294

9.3.2. Subpoenas and Legal Obligations 294

9.3.3. Disclosure of Witness Information 296

9.4. Examination Techniques 297

9.4.1. Direct Examination 297

9.4.2. Cross-Examination 298

9.4.3. Re-Direct Examination 299

9.5. Challenges in Witness Examination 301

9.5.1. Memory Reliability 301

9.5.2. Witness Bias 302

9.5.3. Legal Objections During Examination 303

9.6. Legal Standards and Guidelines 304

9.6.1. Rules of Evidence 305

9.6.2. Admissibility of Witness Testimony 306

9.6.3. Ethical Considerations for Attorneys 306

Summary 308

References 311

10

CONFESSIONS, STATEMENTS, AND BURDEN OF PROOF IN CRIMINAL PROCEDURE 313

Introduction 313

10.1. The Role of Confessions in Criminal Procedure 317

10.1.1. Legal Definition and Types of Confessions 318

10.1.2. Historical Context and Evolution of Confession Laws 319

10.1.3. Impact of Confessions on Case Outcomes 320

10.2. The Admissibility of Confessions 321

10.2.1. Legal Standards for Admissibility in Court 322

10.2.2. The Role of Miranda Rights in Confession Admissibility 323

10.2.3. Exceptions to the Exclusionary Rule 323

10.3. Statements vs. Confessions 325

10.3.1. Distinction Between Statements and Confessions 326

10.3.2. Legal Implications of Each in Criminal Cases 327

10.3.3. Examples of How Statements Can Influence Investigations 328

10.4. The Burden of Proof in Criminal Cases 329

10.4.1. Definition and Significance of the Burden of Proof 330
10.4.2. Differences Between Civil and Criminal Burden of Proof 331
10.4.3. The Presumption of Innocence and Its Implications 332
10.5. The Impact of Coerced Confessions 334
10.5.1. Psychological Factors Leading to Coerced Confessions 335
10.5.2. Legal Ramifications of Admitting Coerced Confessions 336
10.5.3. Case Studies Highlighting the Consequences of Coercion 336
10.6. The Role of Technology in Confessions and Statements 338
10.6.1. Use of Recording Devices and Their Legal Implications 339
10.6.2. The Impact of Social Media on Confessions and Statements 340
10.6.3. Emerging Technologies and Their Influence on Evidence Gathering 341
Summary 342
References 345

11 APPEALS, REVISIONS, AND POST-TRIAL REMEDIES OF CRIMINAL PROCEDURE AND EVIDENCE 347

Introduction 347
11.1. The Appeals Process 351
11.1.1. Types of Appeals in Criminal Cases 352
11.1.2. Grounds for Filing an Appeal 353
11.1.3. The Role of Appellate Courts 354
11.2. Standards of Review 356
11.2.1. De Novo Review 357
11.2.2. Abuse of Discretion Standard 358
11.2.3. Harmless Error Analysis 359
11.3. Revisions in Criminal Procedure 361
11.3.1. Legislative Changes and Amendments 362
11.3.2. Judicial Interpretations and Precedents 363
11.3.3. Impact of Revisions on Case Law 364
11.4. Post-Trial Remedies 365
11.4.1. Motion for a New Trial 366
11.4.2. Writs of Habeas Corpus 367
11.4.3. Sentencing Modifications 367
11.5. The Role of Defense Attorneys 369
11.5.1. Responsibilities During the Appeals Process 370
11.5.2. Strategies for Effective Representation 371
11.5.3. Ethical Considerations in Appeals 371
11.6. The Impact of Technology on Appeals 373
11.6.1. Digital Evidence and Its Implications 373
11.6.2. Online Resources for Legal Research 374
11.6.3. Virtual Courtrooms and Remote Hearings 375
Summary 377
References 380

12 EMERGING ISSUES AND REFORMS IN CRIMINAL PROCEDURE AND EVIDENCE 383

Introduction 383
12.1. Technological Advancements in Evidence Collection 388
12.1.1. Use of Digital Evidence in Criminal Cases 389
12.1.2. Impact of Surveillance Technology on Privacy Rights 390
12.1.3. Challenges of Cybercrime and Digital Forensics 391
12.2. The Role of Artificial Intelligence (AI) in Criminal Justice 392
12.2.1. Artificial Intelligence (AI) in Predictive Policing and Risk Assessment 393
12.2.2. Ethical Concerns Surrounding Artificial Intelligence (AI) Decision-Making 394
12.2.3. Potential for Bias in Artificial Intelligence (AI) Algorithms 395

12.3. Reforms in Search and Seizure Laws **397**

12.3.1. Changes in Legal Standards for Warrants 397

12.3.2. The Exclusionary Rule and Its Implications 399

12.3.3. Impact of Recent Supreme Court Decisions 399

12.4. The Right to Counsel and Access to Justice **401**

12.4.1. Challenges Faced by Public Defenders 402

12.4.2. Innovations in Legal Aid and Representation 402

12.4.3. The Role of Technology in Enhancing Access 403

12.5. Issues of Racial and Socioeconomic Disparities **405**

12.5.1. Disparities in Sentencing and Conviction Rates 405

12.5.2. The Impact of Socioeconomic Status on Legal Outcomes 407

12.5.3. Reforms Aimed at Reducing Discrimination 407

12.6. Legislative Changes and Policy Reforms **409**

12.6.1. Recent Legislative Initiatives in Criminal Procedure 409

12.6.2. The Role of Advocacy Groups in Reform Efforts 411

12.6.3. Future Directions for Policy Changes 411

Summary **413**

References **416**

INDEX 419

List of Figures

Figure 1.1. The criminal procedure
Figure 1.2. The historical development of criminal procedure
Figure 1.3. Criminal justice system
Figure 1.4. The criminal justice system serves as a complex structure designed to uphold societal laws
Figure 1.5. Roles of key participants
Figure 1.6. The interaction between law enforcement and the judiciary
Figure 1.7. Sources of criminal procedure law
Figure 1.8. Statutory law
Figure 1.9. The concept of case law and judicial precedents
Figure 1.10. The judicial evidence
Figure 1.11. Types of evidence
Figure 1.12. Importance of evidence in proving guilt
Figure 1.13. The exclusionary rule serves as a pivotal mechanism within the framework of criminal procedure and evidence
Figure 1.14. Exceptions to the rule
Figure 1.15. Search and seizure
Figure 1.16. The concept of searches in criminal procedure
Figure 1.17. Trial procedures stand at the foundation of criminal justice
Figure 1.18. The trial process
Figure 2.1. The examination of the criminal justice system and procedural roles
Figure 2.2. The importance of procedural roles within the criminal justice system
Figure 2.3. The evolution of legal systems
Figure 2.4. Impact of historical events on current practices
Figure 2.5. The law enforcement agencies
Figure 2.6. Correctional institutions
Figure 2.7. Responsibilities of police officers
Figure 2.8. Community policing initiatives

Figure 2.9. The judicial process
Figure 2.10. The structure of the court system
Figure 2.11. The roles of judges and prosecutors in the criminal justice system
Figure 2.12. The correctional system serves multiple critical functions
Figure 2.13. Rehabilitation vs. punishment
Figure 2.14 The procedural justice within the framework of the criminal justice system
Figure 2.15. The concept of procedural justice
Figure 2.16. The role of fairness in legal proceedings
Figure 3.1. Investigation and pre-trial procedures
Figure 3.2. The role of law enforcement in investigations
Figure 3.3. The initial response to a crime scene
Figure 3.4. The collection of evidence
Figure 3.5. Interrogation of suspects and witnesses
Figure 3.6. The concept of physical evidence
Figure 3.7. Testimonial evidence
Figure 3.8. The integration of digital evidence
Figure 3.9. The legal standards governing searches and seizures
Figure 3.10. The search warrants and exceptions
Figure 3.11. Process of charging a suspect
Figure 3.12. Grand jury proceedings
Figure 3.13. Pre-trial motions and hearings represent critical components in the criminal procedure landscape
Figure 3.14. The motion for a change of venue
Figure 3.15. Importance of discovery in pre-trial
Figure 4.1. The search and seizure
Figure 4.2. Importance of surveillance in criminal procedure
Figure 4.3. The foundations of constitutional protections
Figure 4.4. The historical context of search, seizure, and surveillance
Figure 4.5. Key supreme court cases shaping the doctrine
Figure 4.6. The evolution of privacy rights in the United States
Figure 4.7. Text and interpretation of the Fourth Amendment
Figure 4.8. The concept of reasonable expectation of privacy
Figure 4.9. Exceptions to the warrant requirement
Figure 4.10. Search warrants
Figure 4.11. The execution of search warrants
Figure 4.12. The exclusionary rule

Figure 4.13. Key cases establishing the exclusionary rule
Figure 4.14. Surveillance techniques
Figure 4.15. The legal standards governing electronic surveillance
Figure 4.16
Figure 4.17. Public perception of surveillance and privacy
Figure 5.1. The concepts of bail and remand
Figure 5.2. The importance of bail in the criminal justice system
Figure 5.3. The evolution of bail laws
Figure 5.4. Historical perspectives on remand procedures
Figure 5.5. Types of bail
Figure 5.6. Cash bail
Figure 5.7. The concept of surety bail
Figure 5.8. Factors influencing bail decisions
Figure 5.9. The severity of the offense
Figure 5.10. Remand procedures
Figure 5.11. Legal standards for remand
Figure 5.12. Rights of the accused
Figure 5.13. The right to a fair hearing
Figure 5.14. The right to appeal bail decisions
Figure 5.15. Inequities in bail practices
Figure 6.1. Initiation of proceedings
Figure 6.2. The concept of initiation of proceedings
Figure 6.3. Types of proceedings in criminal law
Figure 6.4. The police play a crucial role in the initiation of criminal proceedings
Figure 6.5. The filing of a First Information Report (FIR)
Figure 6.6. The role of the prosecution in charge framing
Figure 6.7. Responsibilities of the prosecutor
Figure 6.8. Decision-making process in charge framing
Figure 6.9. The legal standards for charge framing in criminal procedure
Figure 6.10. The classification of criminal offenses into felonies and misdemeanors
Figure 6.11. Judicial oversight is a fundamental aspect of charge framing in criminal procedure
Figure 6.12. The significance of pre-trial hearings within the framework of criminal procedure
Figure 6.13. The initiation of proceedings and charge framing in criminal procedure is fraught with various challenges
Figure 6.14. Impact of public opinion and media
Figure 7.1. Illustration of courtroom

Figure 7.2. The criminal trial process
Figure 7.3. Pre-trial procedures
Figure 7.4. A man arrested by police
Figure 7.5. Initial court appearances
Figure 7.6. Preliminary hearings and grand jury indictments
Figure 7.7. The role of a judge in the criminal trial process
Figure 7.8. The prosecutor serves as a central figure within the criminal trial process
Figure 7.9. The defense attorney's duties
Figure 7.10. Jury selection
Figure 7.11. The concept of an impartial jury serves as a crucial pillar of the criminal trial process
Figure 7.12. Voir dire process
Figure 7.13. The presentation of evidence in criminal trials
Figure 7.14. The process of deliberation within a jury
Figure 7.15. Impact of the verdict on the defendant
Figure 7.16. The sentencing phase of the criminal trial process
Figure 7.17. Post-conviction relief
Figure 8.1. The evidence in the context of criminal law
Figure 8.2. The significance of evidence in the judicial process
Figure 8.3. Historical background of evidence in legal systems
Figure 8.4. The distinction between direct and circumstantial evidence
Figure 8.5. Types of evidence
Figure 8.6. Physical evidence and its significance
Figure 8.7. Testimonial evidence and its reliability
Figure 8.8. Documentary evidence and its role in court
Figure 8.9. Overview of the federal rules of evidence
Figure 8.10. The purpose of rules governing evidence
Figure 8.11. Criteria for admissibility in criminal trials
Figure 8.12. The impact of prejudicial versus probative value
Figure 8.13. Overview of hearsay and its exceptions
Figure 8.14. The exclusionary rule serves as a fundamental principle in American criminal procedure
Figure 8.15. Judges' responsibilities in determining admissibility
Figure 9.1. The witness examination
Figure 9.2. The examination of witnesses in criminal procedure
Figure 9.3. Eyewitness testimony remains a pivotal element in the context of criminal procedure
Figure 9.4. The role of character witnesses in criminal proceedings

Figure 9.5. Establishing facts in criminal cases
Figure 9.6. Providing credibility to the prosecution or defense
Figure 9.7. The pre-trial procedures
Figure 9.8. Subpoenas and legal obligations
Figure 9.9. The practice of disclosing witness information
Figure 9.10. Direct examination
Figure 9.11. Cross-examination
Figure 9.12. Witness bias
Figure 9.13. The legal standards and guidelines governing the examination of witnesses in criminal procedure
Figure 9.14. Admissibility of witness testimony
Figure 10.1. Key terms: confessions, statements, burden of proof
Figure 10.2. The Role of confessions in criminal procedure
Figure 10.3. The historical context of confession laws
Figure 10.4. The admissibility of confessions in criminal procedure
Figure 10.5. The legal standards for admissibility in court
Figure 10.6. Exceptions to the exclusionary rule
Figure 10.7. The distinction between statements and confessions
Figure 10.8. Distinction between statements and confessions
Figure 10.9. The burden of proof in criminal cases
Figure 10.10. The significance of the burden of proof
Figure 10.11. The presumption of innocence and its implications
Figure 10.12. The phenomenon of coerced confessions significantly undermines the integrity of the criminal justice system
Figure 10.13. The legal ramifications of admitting coerced confessions
Figure 10.14. The role of technology in confessions and statements
Figure 10.15. The impact of social media on confessions and statements
Figure 11.1. The system of appeals and revisions
Figure 11.2. The appeals process
Figure 11.3. Types of appeals in criminal cases
Figure 11.4. Grounds for filing an appeal
Figure 11.5. The role of appellate courts
Figure 11.6. The concept of standards of review
Figure 11.7. The essential components of the appellate process
Figure 11.8. Abuse of discretion standard
Figure 11.9. Harmless error analysis plays a pivotal role in the context of criminal procedure
Figure 11.10. Revisions in criminal procedure

Figure 11.11. Judicial interpretations and precedents
Figure 11.12. The realm of post-trial remedies in criminal procedure
Figure 11.13. Writs of Habeas Corpus
Figure 11.14. Role of defense attorneys
Figure 11.15. The ethical considerations in appeals
Figure 11.16. Digital evidence and its implications
Figure 12.1. The role of evidence in legal proceedings
Figure 12.2. An overview of emerging issues and reforms
Figure 12.3. Technological advancements in evidence collection
Figure 12.4. Use of digital evidence in criminal cases
Figure 12.5. Impact of surveillance technology on privacy rights
Figure 12.6. The role of artificial intelligence (AI) in criminal justice
Figure 12.7. Ethical concerns surrounding artificial intelligence (AI) decision-making
Figure 12.8. Potential for bias in artificial intelligence (AI) algorithms
Figure 12.9. The evolution of legal standards for warrants
Figure 12.10. Impact of recent supreme court decisions
Figure 12.11. Challenges faced by public defenders
Figure 12.12. The role of technology in enhancing access
Figure 12.13. Disparities in sentencing and conviction rates are significant issues within the criminal justice system
Figure 12.14. Reforms aimed at reducing discrimination
Figure 12.15. Recent legislative initiatives in criminal procedure

PREFACE

Evidence law and criminal procedure are the engine room of criminal justice. They determine how the state may investigate, charge, and ultimately prove guilt, but leave the accused with actual tools of resistance to prevent overreach. Rules on arrest, search, disclosure, admissibility, and burden of proof are not niceties; they are the safeguards that distinguish between a show trial and a fair trial. When these standards are clear and applied uniformly, the public may have assurance that convictions are based on reliable evidence and acquittals are not the products of gamesmanship in procedure but of the inability of the state to fulfill its obligation.

But procedure and proof are never static. Advances in crime investigation technology, shifting social expectations, and evolving constitutional dogma keep courts and practitioners in a watchful stance. Questions that had seemed settled—such as when a confession is voluntary, how to verify digital evidence, or whether preventive detention is appropriate—recur whenever law enforcement technology or societal expectations change. Competence in this field therefore requires more than rote memorization of sections and precedents; it requires understanding of the reasoning behind the rules and the policy judgments they reflect.

Criminal Procedure and Evidence has been so written. The book offers a transparent path from first principles to high-level applications, combining statutory provisions with contemporary leading cases and examples. Each chapter balances doctrinal accuracy with procedural flowcharts, checklists, and illustrations that mirror real decision points. The emphasis is on empowering readers to see how rules connect across stages—investigation, charging, trial, and review—to apply them confidently in practice, exams, or research.

Chapter 1 sets out the conceptual premises: what criminal process is trying to achieve, why evidence law matters, and how fairness, efficiency, and pursuit of truth are balanced. It sets out definitions, introduces due process and fair trial protection, and sketches the stages of a general case from suspicion through to final judgment.

Chapter 2 examines the institutions and actors that must implement the process—the police, prosecution, defence counsel, judiciary, and ancillary agencies. It summarizes statutory and ethical requirements, decision-making thresholds (from reasonable suspicion to proof beyond reasonable doubt), and checks and balances within their respective roles.

Chapter 3 covers inquiry and pre-trial actions, including FIR/complaint registration, arrest standards, custodial safeguards, disclosure of the evidence, plea bargaining, and committal procedures. Timelines, custody rules, and accused individuals' rights at the early stages are indicated with procedural flowcharts.

Chapter 4 considers search, seizure, and surveillance. Warrants, warrant exceptions, electronic forensics, chain of custody, and norms of privacy are all treated in depth. Covert operations, communications interception, and judicial controls needed to prevent abuse are also discussed in the chapter.

Chapter 5 addresses the process of bail and remand and defines the test for release, the conditions which can be imposed, and the significance of anticipatory, regular, and default bail. It also addresses preventive detention, speedy trial issues, and remedies against illegal custody.

Chapter 6 explains how cases are initiated and charges are framed. Jurisdictional questions, courts taking cognizance, joinder and separation of charges, amendment of charges, and the consequences of defects are explained through illustration and leading judgments.

Chapter 7 outlines the criminal trial process from opening addresses to judgment. It states the order of evidence, accused's rights in trial, results of plea bargaining, judge versus jury (or assessors) cases where applicable, and safeguards like presumption of innocence and right to silence.

Chapter 8 describes evidence in all its forms—oral, documentary, electronic, and real evidence—and the law of admissibility. Relevancy tests, exclusionary rules, privileges, and doctrines such as res gestae or similar fact evidence are addressed along with practical steps to authentication and proof.

Chapter 9 is dedicated to examination of witnesses. It addresses competency, compellability, requirement of oath, examination-in-chief, cross-examination, re-examination, leading questions, impeachment of credibility, and protection to vulnerable witnesses.

Chapter 10 is concerned with confessions, statements, and the burden of proof. It distinguishes between voluntary and involuntary confessions, statements made before police as contrasted with magistrates, effect of retracted confessions, and probative value of accomplice evidence. Burdens of proof for different matters and shifting of the burden of presumptions under statutes are considered.

Chapter 11 deals with appeals, revision, and post-trial remedies. Ways of appeal, grounds for interference, jurisdiction of appellate and revisional courts, review of sentence, compensation for malicious prosecution, and extraordinary remedies like habeas corpus are dealt with in a rational way.

Chapter 12 canvasses upcoming issues and reforms. Some issues discussed are digital evidence management, restorative justice projects, victim engagement, expansions of plea bargaining, artificial intelligence policing, and debates over exclusionary rules that continue to rage. The chapter invites critical reflection on how procedure and the law of evidence ought to address issues of the day.

This book is aimed at law students sitting for procedural law and evidence examinations, bar exams, and mooting problems; new lawyers and judicial trainees seeking a sure-footed companion to take to court; police and prosecution trainees requiring an explication of procedural thresholds; and scholars investigating doctrinal change and reform. Policy analysts, paralegals, and criminal justice accountability campaigners will also find something here to hold practice to principle.

Chapter

1

INTRODUCTION TO CRIMINAL PROCEDURE AND EVIDENCE

Contents

Introduction..1
1.1. The Criminal Justice System..6
1.2. Sources of Criminal Procedure Law..11
1.3. The Role of Evidence in Criminal Proceedings..15
1.4. The Exclusionary Rule..19
1.5. Search and Seizure..23
1.6. Trial Procedures..27
Summary..31
References...34

INTRODUCTION

An understanding of criminal procedure is needed in order to cope with the complexities of the legal system as it governs the procedures under which criminal cases are determined. Criminal procedure outlines the rules and principles that must be followed by law enforcement agencies, prosecutors, and judges to dispense justice while protecting the constitutional rights of each person. The overall objective of these procedures is to balance the need for public safety with the rights of the accused, which are safeguarded by the Constitution. For instance, the right to a fair trial, the exclusionary rule, and the presumption of innocence are some of the key components of this regime. As these practices evolve, they also reflect the social consensus on crime and justice, adapting to new challenges such as technological advancement and shifting standards of justice. An awareness of this evolution is necessary for comprehending the interaction between judicial decision and law enforcement practice. In recent years, there has been a significant evolution toward greater consideration of claims of innocence on conviction, which has gained national focus. Previously, the legal system attached great significance to the finality of convictions so that it was difficult for individuals to appeal their convictions due to previously unknown evidence. Such strictness has drawn controversy around the adequacy of present procedures that settle post-trial claims. Several scholars contend that the legal system must advance to allow the accused with more alternatives to prove their innocence effectively. With more jurisdictions adopting broader remedies for post-conviction claims, this change implies an expanding recognition of wrongful convictions and the manner in which they affect justice. This change would then contribute to greater understanding of the essential interplay between procedural safeguards and the pursuit of true justice, unveiling the way the system can better respond to long-standing issues related to wrongful convictions and the rights of the accused (Garrett et al., 2017). Second, the interplay between federal and state law works to serve an important role in the evolution of criminal procedure within the U.S. legal framework. The Supreme Court frequently looks back at state and local laws to inform its interpretation of the Constitution, understanding that localized legal tradition shapes more general constitutional norms. This tension has specific implications for a wide range of criminal prosecutions, including the enforcement of capital punishment and other severe punishments. Inequalities at the local level can have a significant effect on judicial rulings, as shown in Supreme Court cases, where geographic variation raised issues of impartiality and justice. The use of local data and practices not only enhances constitutional jurisprudence but also casts light on the diverse realities prevailing in different jurisdictions. The use of local law and practices is thus necessary in developing a rich insight into criminal procedure and ensuring justice to be equal and consistent (Garrett et al., 2018).

Definition and Importance

The criminal procedure is pivotal to the understanding of the mechanisms through which justice is administered within the judiciary. It is the body of law that defines the norms that govern the investigation, prosecution, and determination of criminal offenses. The intricate mechanism not only delineates the rights of the accused but also identifies the responsibilities of law enforcement and the judiciary. In this procedural framework, the principles of due process, presumption of innocence, and burden of proof become critical. Observance of these principles in a correct manner ensures that justice is not only an illusion but a reality for the accused. With evolving systems of justice complying with society's norms and values, the meaning of criminal procedure remains of continued importance both in theory and practice to guarantee equal treatment before the law. An understanding of the importance of criminal procedure is not only beyond theoretical constructs, but it discloses serious implications for individual rights and the integrity of the system of justice. If criminal procedure is strictly applied, it protects against arbitrary power and miscarriage of justice as a bulwark against discrimination and abuse. For example, the requirements specified by constitutional safeguards require legal authorities to follow due procedure in criminal proceedings so that individuals are given fair trials and adequate representation. Such protections are essential in the preservation of public trust in legal institutions. The interplay between the statutory provisions and the procedural guarantees reflects the dedication of the legal system to safeguarding fundamental rights, thereby ensuring the highest possible effectiveness and legitimacy of law enforcement mechanisms and judicial decisions. Additionally, the study of criminal procedure is indissolubly connected with the evolution of legal doctrines and the adaptability of justice systems to changing societal needs. As testified by Priester's analysis, the Constitution provides necessary limits on parliamentary powers, such that certain facts must be established in order to warrant any criminal charge (Priester et al., 1998).

Figure 1.1. The criminal procedure.

Source: https://encrypted-tbn0.gstatic.com/images?q=tbn:ANd9GcSZw4NLia1jYr592rWYcTeprIMwKID5DovdNQ&s.

Such analysis not only highlights the importance of evidence in criminal trials but also signifies the necessity for balance between parliamentary powers and human rights. Moreover, comparative examination of different systems of law, such as English and Scots law, illustrates that the study of their differences offers an insight into more universal legal principles relevant to other jurisdictions (Cockburn et al., 1999). Such considerations ultimately enrich the argument surrounding criminal procedure, emphasizing its pivotal role in organizing equitable and effective legal practice as well as addressing emerging challenges to justice (Figure 1.1)..

Historical Development

Historical development of criminal procedure and evidence indicates fundamental shifts in standards of law throughout history, motivated primarily by the ethical and philosophical premises of various cultures. The appearance of legal codes, such as the Code of Hammurabi and Roman law, provided minimum standards of justice with an emphasis on preeminence of equitable treatment and rules of evidence. As societies developed, so did their legal systems, influenced by the attitudes towards authority, rights, and the freedom of individuals. The process shows that procedural justice and admissibility of evidence have not remained constant but are the product of intricate interactions between legal systems and the societal norms they exist within, and the end result is always in favor of justice and balancing state powers with individual freedom. The comparative analysis of interrogation techniques between jurisdictions is a true reflection of the diverse directions of criminal procedural development. Chinese techniques of interrogation, for instance, have never been similar to those of European ones as evidenced through the divergent legal traditions that emerged from Greek and Chinese civilizations throughout history. This historical context illuminates current debate over the universality of fairness during interrogation and illustrates the challenge faced by legal reformers in implementing practices that might lack resonance in their respective cultural realities. These differences highlight the need to consider history and institutional setting when evaluating contemporary-day interrogation practices and suggest that the evolution of such processes is by no means linear but is instead punctuated by clear national characteristics (Beken et al., 2012). In examining admissibility of evidence in criminal trials, it is apparent that the historical background plays a significant role in the comprehension of its use in contemporary times. Admissible evidence definitions have shifted with various legal philosophies and historical events, and hence various jurisdictions have varying approaches. For instance, in Ukraine, the development of historical evidence admissibility shows an ongoing debate on procedural guarantees and rights of accused individuals. Law scholars have debated the origins and implications of classifying evidence as inadmissible, with a focus on procedural justice as a vital component of fair trials (Basai et al., 2012). This discussion of historic practice and its applicability to modern procedural rules emphasizes the necessity for continuous reform and calibration based on domestic as well as international standards (Figure 1.2).

Figure 1.2. The historical development of criminal procedure.

Source: https://blog.ipleaders.in/wp-content/uploads/2021/01/Criminal-Law.jpg.

Key Principles and Concepts

The arena of criminal procedure and evidence is governed by fundamental principles that ensure justice and fairness throughout the legal process. Underlying it all are the principles of presumption of innocence, which holds that a defendant shall be presumed innocent until guilt is established beyond reasonable doubt. Such a simple concept is a safeguard against mistaken convictions, and it puts the burden of proof squarely on the prosecution. Furthermore, the right to a fair trial is of utmost importance and encompasses the notion that defendants must be given an opportunity to have their case heard as a whole and to contest the evidence placed against them. These are fundamental rules in maintaining public trust in the legal system through protecting individual rights while upholding the need for public order and safety. Evidence relevance and admissibility constitute another crucial element of criminal procedure.

The rules of evidence are designed to ensure that only evidence supporting the facts of the case is placed before a court. Degrees of reliability, probative value, and credibility are major considerations in deciding whether or not evidence can be admitted at trial. This is used to draw a line between admissible evidence, such as witness testimony and documentary evidence, and hearsay, which typically is not admissible because it lacks reliability. But the application of these rules can get more complicated when dealing with war crimes or international tribunals where other standards of evidence may be varied to suit the particular circumstances met with, as it was in debates regarding trials such as Nuremberg and others when making the conclusion that an accessible justice system is needed (Halpern et al., 2018). Secondly, an understanding of the similarities and differences between legal traditions is needed in order to comprehend criminal procedure principles. Even while common law tradition, as in the United States and England, has a tendency to stress singular methods of evidence, comparative studies can improve our perception of criminal law. For instance, the analysis of Scottish criminal law against the backdrop of English law identifies concurrent principles that denote a homogeneous yet rich legal framework. Alongside identifying the significance of contextual determinants in applying legal principles, this kind of analysis serves to foster a general understanding of the impact of jurisdiction on justice as well as evidence concerns (Cockburn et al., 1999). As legal scholars and academics wrestle with these complexities, the pursuit of a thorough grasp of criminal procedure and evidence remains essential to the just administration of justice.

1.1. THE CRIMINAL JUSTICE SYSTEM

The foundation of the criminal justice system is the principles of justice, fairness, and accountability. In criminal procedure, these ideals endeavor to protect the rights of individuals while enhancing public safety. The process has several stages, including investigation, prosecution, defense, and appeal, that the law uses to address human activity complexities and societal values. An effective criminal justice system is crucial in ensuring respect for the rule of law since it provides mechanisms for addressing crime, thereby enhancing community confidence. Furthermore, the functioning of such systems can be subjected to testing against international standards, which uphold defendants' rights and put a high value on due process—principles that continue to be of paramount relevance in contemporary discourse over criminal justice reform, spurring nations to align national practices with international human rights norms.

Figure 1.3. Criminal justice system.

Source: https://media.licdn.com/dms/image/v2/C4D12AQFbWgDQuxAiMA/article-cover_image-shrink_720_1280/article-cover_image-shrink_720_1280/0/1628615351143?e=2147483647&v=beta&t=Vy798ffXEbf4v-2w5QRP25pavIlTWbyYKInT0gDyuN4.

The pursuit of justice in criminal procedure is often marred by problems that need to be remedied. For instance, China's criminal justice system has undergone significant reforms in an attempt to align its practices with international human rights standards. Although improvement has been registered since the implementation of the Criminal Procedure Law of 1996, much obstruction still exists. These are ideological cultures that are antithetical to established principles, insufficient legal staff training, as well as structural deficits leading to human rights violations in pre-trial proceedings. The need for a balance between crime control and the protection of human rights is most urgent, especially since China is undergoing overarching social change and rising crime. With ongoing reform mechanisms, there is an increasing necessity to look back at the accommodation of legal advances with traditional morals, thereby making it possible for a better justice system for all parties involved (LU and YANBIN, 2010). Similarly, Mexicos transition to an adversarial model of criminal justice following the 2008 constitutional reforms reflects a stark move towards ensuring a fair trial and safeguarding defendants' rights. Historically plagued by an inquisitorial system afflicted with inefficiencies and abuses, reforms aim to introduce new guarantees in line with international human rights standards. The role of the United States as a border representative of a different tradition of law has been pivotal. It has facilitated financing and educational initiatives aimed at promoting legal acumen and procedural skill among Mexican legal professionals. However, despite successive reforms, there are still problems, most significantly the delicate balancing act between protecting defendants' rights on the one hand while simultaneously dealing with serious problems of organized crime. Thus, it is crucial that Mexico enacts rules of evidence as built-in protections under this new system so as to develop a just and transparent criminal justice system (Dang et al., 2014) (Figure 1.3).

1.1.1. Structure of the Criminal Justice System

The criminal justice system is a systematized framework established to uphold societal laws, enhance public safety, and ensure justice. This intricate system contains a series of significant components like law enforcement agencies, judicial courts, and prisons. The law enforcement agencies are tasked with initial investigation and arrest of accused criminals and act as the frontline defenders of social order. The judicial machinery, on the other hand, through the judiciary courts, evaluates the presented evidence, implements the law, and determines the innocence or guilt of a defendant person. Lastly, the prison system enforces sentences through punishment and rehabilitation. All of these work in conjunction with one another, reflecting a system attempting to balance individual rights and public needs, working its way through procedural safeguards that underlie criminal procedure. There has been a change over the last several years regarding the victim's role in this formalized system. Historically marginalized, victims themselves were typically viewed more as witnesses than complete parties to the criminal justice system. That perception has shifted with time, with more emphasis placed on hearing and valuing victims' voices in the courtroom. As legal systems change and victims' rights are advanced, there is greater recognition that their presence can enrich justice. Academics would argue that making the victims more participatory in hearings will allow healing and present a counter-narrative for the processes, moving towards a broad-based understanding of criminal justice in keeping with public norms (Doak et al., 2005). Additionally, the advent of risk assessment tools has added another dimension in the criminal justice system architecture, impacting decision-making at numerous stages ranging from policing to parole. These tools attempt to reduce incarceration rates by predicting recidivism and informing judges at sentencing. Their implementation, however, has not been without controversy. Critics say that risk assessments can serve to reinforce bias built into the system and make it harder to look for equal outcomes. Even with all their promise of effectiveness, the issue remains how to ensure decisionmakers utilize these tools in a fair and consistent manner since inconsistency in use can take the form of enormous disparities in justice. This recognizes the need for ongoing regulation and reform in the system, in a way that gains from developments in technology are aligned with the ultimate values of fairness and responsibility in criminal procedure and evidence (Garrett et al., 2020) (Figure 1.4).

Figure 1.4. The criminal justice system serves as a complex structure designed to uphold societal laws.

Source: https://www.iasgyan.in//ig-uploads/images//image00940.png.

1.1.2. Roles of Key Participants

In criminal procedure and evidence, it is crucial to understand the roles of key actors in the legal system in a comprehensive way. Some of the most critical actors are law enforcement officials, who are the immediate agents responsible for investigating crimes and upholding the law. Their work extends beyond mere apprehension of suspects; they must also obtain evidence and draft reports that will serve as the foundation of subsequent legal proceedings. Whether or not a case succeeds usually hinges on the quality of work that these officers undertake, with considerable emphasis placed on their pivotal role towards maintaining justice. In addition, the relationship among them and other stakeholders, such as prosecutors and defense attorneys, controls the direction of the judicial process, necessitating effective communication and coordination among all stakeholders in the criminal justice system. Prosecutors' work is also essential because they must represent the state in criminal trials. Their responsibility is to review evidence presented by police, making charging decisions, and ensuring cases are presented equitably at trial. Unlike defense attorneys, whose only responsibility is to advocate for their clients, prosecutors have the responsibility to respond ethically as well as advocate justice and public security. This is complicated when considering the implications of controversial issues such as gun control and community violence. For instance, when Indiana's gun-withdrawal law is considered, prosecutors need to cross the thin line separating community safety and individual rights, reflecting the intricate dance of law enforcement and public policy (Alanis-Hirsch et al., 2019). Thus, their critical thinking and decision-making are crucial factors influencing outcomes within the criminal justice system. Defense attorneys serve as a check on prosecutorial discretion, ensuring the accused have their rights protected during the process. They do more than advise legally; they represent their clients and try to challenge the prosecutions strategy and evidence. This is particularly important in an ever-changing environment where recent legislative reforms may influence defense and prosecutorial approach, for example, as highlighted in debate regarding criminal justice professional training in Ireland (Conway et al., 2019). With continual evolution of the platform for criminal procedure and evidence, defense attorneys must stay current with new legal precedent and practices. This ongoing adjustment reiterates the importance of their role in safeguarding civil liberties as well as contributing towards the bigger picture of justice and accountability under the legal system (Figure 1.5).

Figure 1.5. Roles of key participants.

Source: https://www.conferencecalling.com/static/ee744cefd1cae427c5732ca41cec8396/084e2/meeting-participant-responsibilities.png.

1.1.3. Interaction between Law Enforcement and the Judiciary

Interaction of law enforcement with the judiciary is a deciding criterion for the efficacy of the criminal justice system. It is the main responsibility of law enforcement agencies to conduct investigations and provide evidence, which is the foundation for court proceedings. The interaction involved here is essential because the quality of the evidence generated by law enforcement can influence judicial decisions and how justice is handed down. For instance, when law enforcement uses effective investigation techniques while adhering to procedural law, they enhance the possibility of successful prosecution. Nevertheless, incompetent or illicit techniques can lead to evidence that is relevant being precluded, undermining the judiciary's ability to make impartial rulings and hence protecting the aspect of due process embedded in the right to a fair trial. The dynamic between these two actors also becomes more complicated due to the existence of various procedural safeguards designed to protect the accused's rights. Judiciary serves as a check on the authority of law enforcement to ensure the constitutional rights at every level of the criminal process. It is governed by rules of evidence and criminal procedure that decide the admissibility of the evidence and thereby set the boundaries of the actions of the law enforcement. Judicial review process is very important in determining if the practices of the law enforcement, such as searches and seizures, are at the constitutional standards. As a result, judicial precedents significantly influence the way law enforcement conducts investigations, creating a necessary interaction with a goal of effective crime control and protection of individual rights. Moreover, the complementary role of settlements in criminal procedure evidently demonstrates the multifaceted interaction between law enforcement and the judiciary. Settlements, such as plea bargains or negotiated settlements, represent a practical way of disposing of cases in an economic manner and minimizing the cost of lengthy litigation. Under this model, law enforcement agencies may utilize settlements as a tool for eliciting cooperation or information from defendants in exchange for reduced charges or sentences. However, the judiciary must ensure that these settlements do not undermine the greater interests of justice, particularly in high-profile cases of public interest. The Brazilian experience of settlement policies in cartel cases is a proper reflection of this balance, where judicial intervention can aid the authenticity of the process while addressing resource limits as well as the necessity of finality in legal proceedings (Azevedo et al., 2025). This intricate interaction between the judiciary and law enforcement emphasizes the importance of possessing a comprehensive and clear criminal justice system (Richman et al., 2012) (Figure 1.6).

Law Enforcement
VS
Criminal Justice
Comparison Table

Characteristics	Law Enforcement	Criminal Justice
Definition	The activity or process of compelling members of the society to adhere to the laws of the land	The process of delivering justice to ofernders and victims of a criminal activity
Purpose	Implementing the law and ensuring members of the society comply with and observe it	Administering and serving justice to lawbreakers and offering moral support to the victims
Composition	Made up of the police and other agencies as the jurisdiction may constitute	Made up of law enforcement agencies, courts priosons and probation facilities juries, the prosecutors' and defense lawyers' offices

Figure 1.6. The interaction between law enforcement and the judiciary.

Source: https://www.differencebetween.net/wp-content/uploads/2019/02/Law-Enforcement-vs-Criminal-Justice.jpg.

1.2. SOURCES OF CRIMINAL PROCEDURE LAW

The sources of criminal procedure law encompass a wide array of legal instruments, judicial decisions, and statute laws that provide the guidelines governing criminal justice procedures. Underlying all of these sources are state and federal constitutions, which have fundamental rights and safeguards for alleged criminals. The U.S. Constitution, particularly the Bill of Rights, enshrines significant doctrines such as the right to a fair trial, immunity from self-incrimination, and exclusion from unreasonable searches and seizures. In addition, legislatures enact statutes that specify certain procedures law enforcement officers and courts must employ, further outlining the character of criminal procedure law.

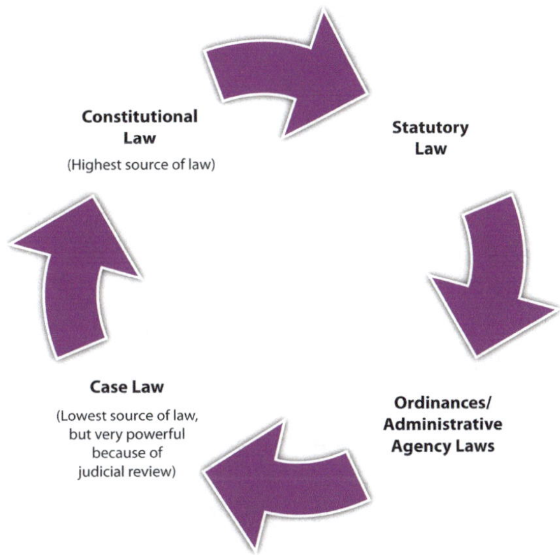

Figure 1.7. Sources of criminal procedure law.

Source: https://slcc.pressbooks.pub/app/uploads/sites/70/2015/11/93398fa1b6e90e3c53bfc4e30fa49fb6.jpg.

Those statutory frameworks are ordinarily developed in response to temporal contexts and the evolving character of public norms, emphasizing the dynamic tension between law and public understanding of justice. Judicial interpretation plays a crucial role in the development of criminal procedure law. Courts also construe constitutional provisions and statutes and form legal precedents that govern the application of criminal procedure. Lower courts are obligated by higher court rulings by virtue of the doctrine of stare decisis, a practice which ensures consistency and predictability in outcomes. Landmark cases also typically portray the conflict between individual rights and states interest in maintaining public order, producing the rich appreciation of criminal procedure.

For instance, the varying handling of rights in interrogation rooms—conflicting approaches in disparate cultures, by classical analysis—demonstrates the complexity of implementing procedural rules under varying legal traditions. Judicial decisions thus have a very important role and define the procedural system as they resolve contemporary legal questions and societal needs. Another essential source of law that regulates criminal procedure derives from administrative regulations that manage police and prosecutorial conduct. Institutions such as the Department of Justice establish guidelines and rules in line with legislative needs so that procedural standards are practiced. The rules are supposed to fill gaps that may exist within statutory law, addressing actual issues encountered by the criminal justice system. Additionally, the interaction between civil and criminal procedural systems has drawn scholarly attention, with some examining the potential for harmonizing the two. The ancient recommendation of a unified code of procedure, highlighted in Federal Rules of Criminal Procedure debates, reflects the evolving nature of legal thought regarding the interrelationship between civil and criminal proceedings (Beken et al., 2012; Meyn et al., 2017). This development corroborates that criminal procedure law is not static; rather, it develops due to a combination of past history, litigation needs, and reform attempts to achieve more justice (Figure 1.7).

1.2.1. Constitutional Provisions

The constitutional provisions in the area of criminal procedure are the bedrock upon which the rights of the individual are safeguarded and the legitimacy of the legal process maintained. The framework established by the Constitution regulates the boundaries and limitations under which the police operate, and therefore protects citizens from potential abuses of power. The Fourth Amendment, for instance, avoids unreasonable searches and seizures by requiring law enforcement to obtain warrants on probable cause. This amendment not only represents a reverence for personal privacy but also underscores the balance attempted among public security and individual freedoms. Such protective provisions under the constitution are necessary in maintaining the rule of law and ensuring that the rights of the defendant are protected throughout the judicial process. Additionally, constitutional protections do not only encompass the procedural protection but also the substantive rights of criminal accused individuals.

The Fifth Amendment protects against self-incrimination and also prevents any individual from being put in double jeopardy. These rights serve to safeguard the underlying mandate that the burden of proof be held by the prosecution, a rule that applies the presumption of innocence until proven guilty. Furthermore, the Sixth Amendment contains such fundamental rights as counsel and a speedy trial. Such provisions are key in guaranteeing an equal trial environment in which defendants are able to adequately defend themselves against charges and hence instill trust in the judicial process and enhance democratic values within society. Constitutional provisions regarding exclusion of improperly obtained evidence also show assurance in upholding individual rights in the face of law enforcement conduct. For example, Article 177 para. 2 of the Greek Code of Penal Procedure provides that evidence derived from illegal sources automatically cannot be taken into account by the court. This strict rule is characteristic of a rights-based approach, as it can also be seen in the constitutional system which strongly underlines the protection of citizens' rights against admissibility of evidence. The significance of the right to privacy is enshrined in article 19 para. 3 of the Constitution, which prohibits the admission of evidence that is obtained in violation of this right. Omitting such evidence not only promotes the integrity of the judicial process but also preserves the public's faith in the criminal justice system, and justice is dispensed in accordance with constitutional dictates.

1.2.2. Statutory Law

Statutory law is a cornerstone in the criminal procedure and evidence framework and refers to legislations passed by assemblies that dictate the conduct of society. Statutory law differs from common law, which is developed by court decisions since statutory law is codified and depicts explicit legislative intent to solve particular issues in society. Statutory law governs, in criminal justice, how the authorities investigate crimes, arrest suspects, and conduct trials, thus stipulating procedural rules to be followed by the judiciary and the police. Moreover, the availability and simplicity of statutory law facilitate the more consistent application of justice, which is critical in protecting the rights of defendants and the integrity of the legal process.

This formal process of legislation reduces the vagariness prevalent in case law, as statutes provide a clear-cut legal regime that guides practitioners in interpreting and enforcing the law in criminal procedure and evidence. The enactment of statutory law also decidedly treats new social issues, demonstrating this responsiveness through legislating intervention into crimes with prejudiced nature. For instance, the Criminal Justice (Scotland) Act 2003 is a case of an ongoing legislative response to addressing religious intolerance-motivated crime. This and similar legislative responses illustrate the malleability of statute law, as social needs evolve. This responsiveness is once more highlighted by the Hate Crime Working Groups report through to gender aggravation provisions debates, showing the legislatures ongoing activity in responding to complicated social issues. Statute development, which is determined by both public policy rhetoric and empirical reality, suggests that statutes must not only react to the current crime environment but also anticipate emerging challenges as society's values shift (Burman et al., 2010). However, the integration of statutory law into criminal procedure is not without controversy, as controversy over the effectiveness of such legislation mirrors deeper societal cleavages. Critics have alleged that while legislative action may identify and define particular crimes, it can fall short in introducing significant changes in police action or citizen relations.

Figure 1.8. Statutory law.

Source: https://idole.in/img/service/6.png.

The efficacy of laws, such as the gender violence legislations, has stirred debate among advocacy organizations and law scholars alike, often focusing on whether legal safeguards truly lead to positive results or merely provide a cosmetic facade of legal protection. In addition, ongoing controversies surrounding the adequacy of these laws also pose important questions on how criminal justice practitioners can better utilize statutory frameworks for enhancing justice and transcending legal process biases. Hence, as statutory law continues to evolve progressively, its critical assessment of effectiveness continues to be relevant to the maintenance of ensuring that it plays the purposeful role of justice and equity in the criminal justice system (Bean et al., 2016) (Figure 1.8).

1.2.3. Case Law and Judicial Precedents

The subject of case law and judicial precedents is key to the operation of the legal system, especially if considered against the context of criminal procedure and evidence. Judicial precedents are instances where superior courts develop legal maxims through their rulings, which inferior courts are required to follow. This practice provides predictability and consistency of application of the law and therefore people's confidence in the judicial process. The process not only assures similar cases being dealt with similarly but also facilitates evolution of standards in the law as morals in society change. In criminal law, where stakes are individually very high, dependence on established precedent serves to safeguard individual rights and ensure impartial administration of justice. Hence, knowing precedents is required for legal practitioners who need to navigate the complex realm of criminal procedure. Besides the purpose of making the law consistent, too, is the function that judicial precedents perform in actively constructing justice in the legal system. The common law system is constructed substantially on the doctrine of precedents to make sure that there are fair outcomes since it is through such highly regarded decisions that courts interpret and apply the law. As noted, the practice of issuing non-precedential opinions not only demeans constitutional requirements and creates practical problems for the appellate process; deviation from precedent undermines justice itself (Bader et al., 2011). By providing a tool whereby courts can draw on past decisions, the system not only maintains integrity but also strengthens the rule of law. This interconnectedness of precedents brings into perspective the relevance of factoring in prior decisions during the settlement of criminal cases, ensuring that justice remains at the forefront of legal practice. At a broader scale, the intersection of judicial duty and international criminal law demonstrates the extensive ramifications of precedents and case law. As has been pointed out, court decisions may have long-term implications for practices that may amount to international crimes and thus challenge the ethical function of judges (Neugebauer et al., 2019). In such a scenario, the danger of judges' accountability over their decisions acts as a much-needed check to counterbalance the authority exercised by them. When judges make precedents that would lead to egregious violations of human rights or international law, it not only affects the immediate parties but can have an effect that ripples through the entire legal system and eventually influence future cases and cultural norms overall. Thus, the study of case law and their precedents must consider their international significance within a broader framework of things so that justice is not only pursued domestically but also internationally (Figure 1.9).

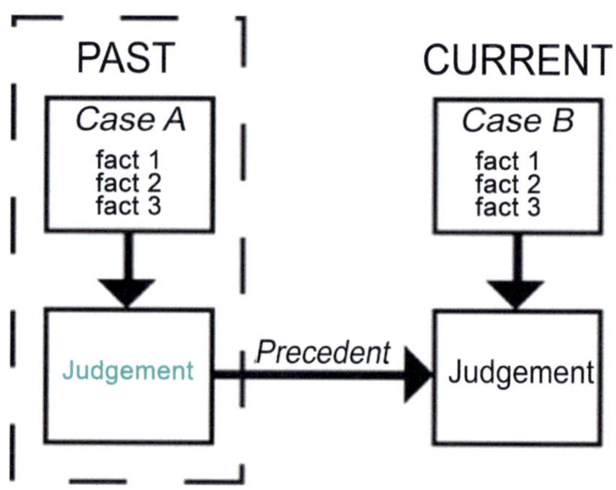

Figure 1.9. The concept of case law and judicial precedents.

Source: https://lawsisto.com/images/category images/1588449302Precedent.png.

1.3. THE ROLE OF EVIDENCE IN CRIMINAL PROCEEDINGS

The role of evidence in criminal proceedings is the most critical, as evidence is the cornerstone on which justice is founded. Evidence essentially determines how information is utilized by courts to adjudge the guilt or innocence of a defendant. In adversarial systems, there are two aspects to an argument—the prosecution and defense—and each has to employ evidence to advance their argument. This competitive framework ensures that thorough scrutiny of the facts occurs so that judges or juries can make informed judgments. Second, the credibility and weight of evidence are frequently challenged, as they are the key to solving a case. The mixture of various types of evidence, which can be either testimonial, documentary, or physical, also proves the complexity that comes with criminal trials, each having a significant impact on the adjudication process. The use of evidence to secure defendants' rights is perhaps one of the most significant functions of evidence in criminal law. A good requirement of evidence protects allegations from being made needlessly, and which is key in ensuring that individuals are not convicted unjustly. For instance, the need to prove beyond a reasonable doubt not only emphasizes the prosecution's burden but also fortifies the defendants' standing in the judiciary. A study of standards of evidence indicates the manner in which courts balance effective law enforcement and ensuring the accused's rights. Legal culture elsewhere, as revealed through the comparative analysis of prosecutorial roles, exhibits contrasting orientations to evidence process and recognizes the primacy of these dynamics to contemporary criminal justice institutions (Montana et al., 2012). Further, rules and standards of evidence can influence the criminal procedure landscape in a significant manner. In the majority of states, evidence collection and presentation reforms to enhance integrity have caused extensive debate across legal professionals and scholars. The ongoing debate regarding the evaluation of evidence by courts is a manifestation of implied concerns over fairness and impartiality in the judiciary. As illustrated in Schwarzes depiction of administrative procedures, the need for crystallized guidelines ensures evidence is scrutinized with the intention of upholding the legitimacy of judicial proceedings (Schwarze et al., 2004). These innovations not only affect the current context but also set precedents for practice in evidence law in the future, pointing to the dynamic interplay between legal norms and social needs in criminal justice.

1.3.1. Definition of Evidence

Evidence in criminal procedure is of maximum importance, as it is the foundation for the determination of criminal cases. Evidence is all the material and information brought before the court that assist in proving the facts of a case. These are physical objects, eyewitnesses, and documentary materials, each of which must meet specific legal requirements in order to be admissible. Notably, evidence not only confirms accusations presented at court trials but also sets the direction of directions for the legal cases. The credibility and authenticity of evidence come under continuous scrutiny since the prosecution and defense attempt to validate or nullify it as a means of securing justice. Thus, comprehending the complex definition and classification of evidence is imperative for legal practitioners as well as researchers. Moreover, evidence in general can be classified into two categories: direct and circumstantial. Direct evidence gives a definite demonstration of fact, such as eyewitness testimony, while circumstantial evidence requires inference to establish a conclusion regarding a fact. Clinical and toxicological evidence of impairment, for example, can be extremely useful in drive-under-the-influence cases. With codified laws like the mooted regulations on car homicide that emphasize the requirement of trustworthy evidence, the legal process addresses the intricacies of how the identification and admission of such evidence work.

Figure 1.10. The judicial evidence.

Source: https://i0.wp.com/iasnext.com/wp-content/uploads/2023/07/INDIAN-EVIDENCE-ACT.jpg?fit=1200%2C675&ssl=1.

This case emphasizes the intricate interplay between emerging laws and the evidentiary thresholds upon which they are constructed, posing major issues in contemporary legal practice, particularly around issues of public safety and liability (Cociani et al., 2015). Furthermore, the concept of evidence is not just confined to forms; it encompasses more general models and legal principles, including relevance and materiality. Relevance deals with how much evidence can contribute towards establishing or refuting a matter in issue, and materiality deals with importance in the context of law. In current discussion, particularly in that which contrasts legal systems, say, English law and Scots law, it seems that a complete comprehension of evidence is generally capable of illuminating criminal law similarities in approach, thus enriching law theory. By examining these relationships, researchers can make significant observations concerning current legal issues and the evolution of standards of evidence, developing a more consistent and principled knowledge of criminal justice across jurisdictions(Cockburn et al., 1999) (Figure 1.10).

1.3.2. Types of Evidence

The classification of evidence is at the heart of the process of adjudication in criminal procedure since it dictates what information will be admissible in court. The evidence can be collectively categorized into two types: circumstantial and direct. Direct evidence is evidence which points one directly to a person as the crime's perpetrator without the need for inference, such as a recording of the crime being committed or eyewitnesses' testimonies. Circumstantial evidence, on the other hand, has to be reasoned out to link it to the criminal act, normally by a chain of facts, which, collectively, are able to carry the weight of implication of guilt. The fine nuances between these types of evidence are essential to legal professionals, determining the way case-construction is carried out and the way that arguments are being presented before a judge or jury. Complicating further the landscape of evidence are types such as testimonial, physical, documentary, and digital evidence, each with its own body of rules and considerations. Testimonial evidence, a lot of which is gathered from witnesses, can be tested for reliability and credibility, physical evidence like fingerprints or weapons must be recovered and maintained under very stringent procedures so that its integrity is not impaired, documentary evidence ranges from letters to contracts, and digital evidence encompasses data from electronic devices, which is gaining a lot of prominence in contemporary jurisprudence. It is significant that legal professionals should comprehend these various forms of evidence since they affect court tactics and assumptions regarding the outcome of cases. Additionally, the institutional and cultural environment in which evidence is to be analyzed may heavily affect its significance and relevance. For instance, differences in legal structures, as explained in the West versus other countries like China comparison, demonstrate how cultural standards impact the acceptability and value of some evidence. Studies show that legal procedures have differed based on differing historical paths, e.g., influences of ancient cultures on current legal systems (Beken et al., 2012). Similarly, Scots and English law interactions showcase the role of comparison in facilitating a more thorough understanding of evidence assessment (Cockburn et al., 1999). Comparative thoughts in such a manner provide crucial information on the types of evidence and their application across different jurisdictions, noting the significance of adaptability in legal proceedings (Figure 1.11).

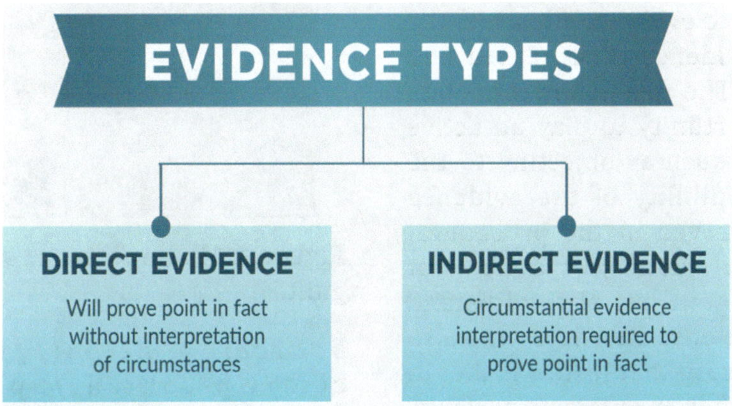

Figure 1.11. Types of evidence.

Source: https://pressbooks.bccampus.ca/criminalinvestigation/wp-content/uploads/sites/162/2017/05/Img-01-1024x501.png.

1.3.3. Importance of Evidence in Proving Guilt

The significance of evidence in determining guilt within the criminal justice system cannot be overstated. Evidence is the keystone upon which legal proceedings are based, determining the direction of a case and ultimately the fate of the accused. Evidence plays an essential role in establishing the elements of an offense and fulfilling the requirement of burden of proof, which is the sole burden borne by the prosecution. Without admissible and credible evidence, the foundation of a criminal case is undermined, which may lead to wrongful acquittals or convictions. As mandated by rules of evidence procedurally established, each piece must not just be pertinent but also imbued with sufficient credibility to validate the charges against a defendant. This also points to the important role of evidence, not only in the court of law but generally in bringing fairness and integrity to the broader justice system, in line with key values of defendant interaction emphasized in Faber et al. (2018). Furthermore, evidentiary principles that establish what can be admitted in court serve to protect the rights of the accused individual as well as the foundations of justice. Each jurisdiction develops guidelines about admissibility, relevance, and weight of evidence to protect the courts from admitting only evidence that fulfills certain legal criteria to assist a judgment.

Law centers on the central role of verifiable facts in determining guilt beyond reasonable doubt. The Constitution, as argued by Priester et al. (1998), requires that some elements of fact must be established to validate an offense, bolstering the view that the burden imposed on the prosecution is not procedural but in ensuring a fair trial. By requiring some levels of evidence to be met prior to the delivery of a verdict, the court upholds its integrity as well as protects individual rights, thereby supporting public faith in judicial rulings. Lastly, the defendant's participatory rights, such as right to counsel and freedom to object to evidence, illustrate the complexity of how evidence is presented and is accepted in court. The defendants ought to be accorded the opportunity to play an active role in their defense, such as objecting to the admissibility and credibility of the evidence against them. As observed in the procedural traditions of criminal justice, evidence not only needs to prove guilt but also withstand interrogation by the defense attorneys, who also have a vital role to ensure that justice is met in its entirety. Denial of these participatory rights, as provided in Faber et al. (2018), can affect the adversarial systems fairness and effectiveness. Thus, evidence, accused participation, and lawyer representation are important to attaining a balance that is respectful of both the pursuit of truth and the protection of individual rights in the criminal justice system (Figure 1.12).

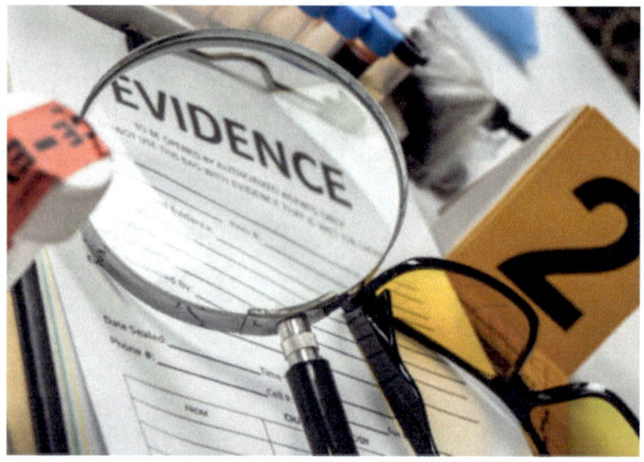

Figure 1.12. Importance of evidence in proving guilt.

Source: https://www.gslawyers.com/wp-content/uploads/2023/09/AdobeStock_270266244-1-500x356.jpeg.

1.4. THE EXCLUSIONARY RULE

The exclusionary rule is a landmark tool in the sphere of criminal procedure and evidence. Essentially founded on the Fourth Amendment, this doctrine mandates that evidence, which has been acquired unlawfully—i.e., through unreasonable searches and seizures—is not to be utilized during criminal proceedings. The overarching purpose of the exclusionary rule is to discourage law enforcers from going forward with illicit acts that infringe on personal rights. Whenever judges exclude such evidence, they are not only safeguarding constitutional protection but also upholding the dignity of the judicial process by ensuring that the government does not benefit from its own misconduct. This rule has therefore developed into a pillar of American law, exercising a deep impact on the conduct of police investigations and procedures followed in criminal trials. Despite its importance, the exclusionary rule has generated a great deal of controversy as to whether it is working and what its impacts are.

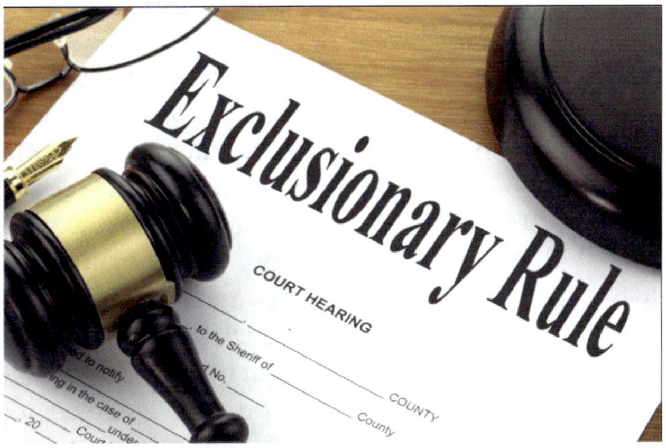

Figure 1.13. The exclusionary rule serves as a pivotal mechanism within the framework of criminal procedure and evidence.

Source: https://pix4free.org/assets/library/2021-01-21/originals/exclusionary_rule.jpg.

The rule, some writers aver, can lead to the exclusion of pertinent evidence, and the guilty could thus go free. Others assert that requiring police to follow rigorous procedures could stifle their ability to conduct good-quality investigations. Moreover, the evolving dynamics of criminal procedure are further complicated by a range of different interpretations and applications of the rule across various courts in different jurisdictions. More precisely, the United States Supreme Court's decisions have set the boundaries of the exclusionary rule, oftentimes underlining its character as a judicially created remedy rather than a constitutional right per se. This strategy has led to ongoing discussion about the likelihood of legislative adjustments or reinterpretation of the rule as societal attitudes towards crime and law enforcement shift. Throughout the world, the exclusionary rule is argued in terms of varying systems of law, prompting re-examination of whether it can be applied beyond national jurisdictions. Article 69(7) of the Rome Statute provides an exclusionary rule for the ICC, reflecting the need to apply customary exclusionary principles to the international civil law context. This is due to the fact that the international community has a challenge in ensuring fair trials as against the inherent idiosyncrasies of international crimes. Observation of various national systems of justice serves to understand how the exclusionary doctrine operates differently in practice. The comparative framework does not only help in comprehending the possible application of exclusionary rules around the world but also emphasizes the need to have a careful understanding of how such rules must adjust to global needs for justice (Hessler et al., 2000; Madden et al., 2014) (Figure 1.13).

1.4.1. Definition and Purpose

In defining and ascertaining the purpose of criminal procedure and evidence, it should be noted that they have a primary function in the justice system. Criminal procedure pertains to the rules and regulations that define how the law enforcement agencies and the courts operate when prosecuting offenses. The general aim is to enhance fairness, uphold the rule of law, and guarantee the rights of the citizens during the judicial process. By defining the respective roles of various factors such as the police, prosecutors, and lawyers, such processes create an institutional setting that governs the pursuit of justice and therefore inspires public trust in legal institutions. To this end, an integrated understanding of criminal procedure not only leads to legal convictions but reduces wrongful charges, making the criminal justice system more valid. The purpose in putting strict criteria on evidence is equally significant, as it gives credence to the purity of the legal process. Evidence forms the factual basis upon which cases are built, determining guilt or innocence for defendants. Evidence admissibility and credibility are contingent on specific requirements, aimed at preventing the presentation of irrelevant or prejudicial evidence in court. This ensures liability or punishment determinations are made upon objective and factual examination rather than subjective or emotional deliberation. By submitting evidence to the interpretive authority of established law principles, legal jurisdictions like English law and Scots law illuminate procedural intricacies. All these similarities and nuances in legal traditions point towards the importance of context in ascertaining evidences role in criminal trials (Cockburn et al., 1999). Additionally, contextual analysis of the criminal procedure and purpose of evidence provides a better understanding of its socio-economic impact. The efficiency of the systems in managing crime ultimately transcends individual cases, as it impacts the welfare of society. For instance, ineffective criminal management can escalate economic costs, like in the case of violence against women, which is expending the EU EUR 226 billion annually in missed economic output and associated services (Olive et al., 2013). This highlights the way procedural shortcomings have far-reaching implications that spread throughout society, indicating the necessity of exercising vigilance in ensuring adherence to legal norms. Therefore, the understanding of the definition and purpose of criminal procedure and evidence is imperative as it outlines their purpose not only to continue justice but also for encouraging overall stability in society and economic progress.

1.4.2. Exceptions to the Rule

Exceptions to the exclusionary rule are a significant factor within the realm of criminal procedure that impacts the admissibility of evidence. The exclusionary rule is primarily to deter police wrongdoing by excluding such evidence procured through unreasonable searches and seizures as guaranteed by the Fourth Amendment. Over time, however, courts have established some exceptions to the rule allowing the admission of some evidence despite potential constitutional violations. Such judicial flexibility is required to balance the demand for efficacious law enforcement and individual rights. Recognition of the necessity of some exceptions provides for a reminder of the nicety of navigating legal concepts as applied to the evolving context of criminal justice within the United States, in which societal order and individual rights are precariously weighed. A major exception is the inevitable discovery rule, which allows evidence that would have otherwise been discovered lawfully to be admitted even if it was initially obtained illegally. The principle acknowledges the truth that, despite the illegality of the search, the evidence in question would inevitably have been discovered through proper investigative procedures. Here, the courts are concerned with the admissibility of the evidence based on its reliability and not the process of how it was acquired. Additionally, the good faith exception preserves evidence that was acquired by police officers with the belief that they were legally entitled to do so, even if follow-up decisions establish otherwise. Such exceptions are crucial to the integrity of the law in the sense that they advance law enforcement's operational ability while at the same time affording constitutional protection against unreasonable intrusion into personal rights. Broadening such exceptions is normally contentious, with the critics arguing that they invade civil liberties and advance a beneficial position for law enforcement. The historical evolution of the exclusionary rule has illustrated this tension in practice, most notably in such cases as Mapp v. Ohio, in which the applicability of the exclusionary rule to state courts was solidified. Exceptions like those listed, including the good faith and inevitable discovery doctrines, illustrate ongoing discussion regarding the topic of balancing personal rights and the ability of law enforcement to function effectively. Understanding of these nuances is necessary for all those who are studying criminal procedure and evidence because it does not only enlighten us about the machinery of the law but also provokes further thought on values in society towards justice and enforcement practices (Leverick et al., 2015; Oliver et al., 2018) (Figure 1.14).

Figure 1.14. Exceptions to the rule.

Source: https://www.legalserviceindia.com/legal/uploads/majorexp onentsofnaturalschoolofjurisprudenceinanutshell_1187611878.jpg.

1.4.3. Impact on Law Enforcement Practices

The evolution of policing practice has been influenced significantly by various frameworks that govern policing practice, particularly in the context of wrongful convictions. Policymakers are particularly concerned with misidentification, and its high miscarriages of justice have raised significant concerns. For instance, the Commonwealth of Virginia passed a law mandating police agencies to create written eyewitness identification policies following a series of DNA exonerations that were caused by such misidentifications. Lacking this legislative measure, the absence of uniform procedure left agencies to make their own way through policy-making, often with limited guidance. The next production of a model policy by the Virginia Department of Criminal Justice Services (DCJS) in 2011 is illustrative of an attempt at improved practices. But the slow adoption by most agencies of these standards is illustrative of ongoing issues within law enforcement that demonstrate a fragmented policymaking practice that has immediate repercussions for the validity of eyewitness testimony (Persson et al., 2011). The impacts of unjust convictions have prompted an increased scrutiny of police practice, specifically in terms of the procedural safeguards afforded to defendants. Exonerated individuals usually file civil lawsuits that identify systemic failures within the law enforcement apparatus, most prominently on matters of evidence management and integrity of criminal procedure. Of special concern are the civil rights cases that challenge dominant models of harmless error rules that more or less regularly apply to criminal cases. The Supreme Court's allowance in constitutional rights cases such as the right of effective representation and protection against suggestive identification techniques underscores the interest in law enforcement imposing practice which fosters procedural integrity. These wrongful conviction cases not only expose the consequences of government abuse but also spur reforms, prompting law enforcement authorities to re-examine and refine their actions in order to ensure that the values of justice are upheld (Garrett et al., 2005). With law enforcement agencies now beginning to recognize the fallout of wrongful convictions, greater emphasis has been given to procedural reforms that move in the direction of safeguarding the rights of defendants and enhancing the justice system in general. The adoption of best practices for eyewitness identifications is a case in point; only with some reluctance did the majority of Virginia agencies adopt the DCJS model policy, which allows for better training and use of proper procedures. These reforms represent a significant step toward greater accountability and transparency in policing, filling the holes of past errors that resulted in wrongful convictions. Besides, the overall recognition of the need for these reforms has the ability to alter the character of police procedures nationwide. The call for systemic policy adjustments not only enhances the credibility of the law enforcement bodies but also restores public confidence, crucial to the effective functioning of the criminal justice system (Persson et al., 2011).

1.5. SEARCH AND SEIZURE

Search and seizure law is at the heart of criminal procedure, encapsulating the balance between police power and individual rights. The United States Constitution's Fourth Amendment plays a pivotal role in safeguarding citizens from unreasonable searches and seizures, ensuring that any invasion of privacy is justified and legal. Police officers typically have to get a warrant under probable cause, but there are exceptions under which one can search without a warrant in exigent circumstances or through the consent of the parties involved.

Figure 1.15. Search and seizure.

Source: https://upload.wikimedia.org/wikipedia/commons/f/fb/Vehicle_drug_search_australia.jpg.

These nuances capture the complex interplay between legal guidelines and practical police realities, necessitating a careful evaluation of each case by which to measure the constitutionality of a search. Furthermore, the evolution of interpretations given to the Fourth Amendment has resulted in ongoing judicial scrutiny, particularly as technology has developed and privacy expectations have changed. The emergence of DNA analysis as a cornerstone of criminal investigation has significantly influenced the search and seizure debate. The courts have increasingly approved the application of DNA evidence to both convict and exonerate the innocent, evidencing broader acceptance of scientific practice within the realm of criminal procedure. This has created subtle legal challenges and varying readings of Fourth Amendment protections. In Maryland v. King, the Supreme Court convened to determine whether taking DNA samples from arrestees is constitutional, particularly before a conviction has been attained. While some argue such practices infringe the right to the presumption of innocence, others think that they are serving a necessary public interest, truly balancing law enforcement needs against individual rights. The case highlights the contested conflict about how modern policing practices interact with constitutional protections and how the courts reconcile competing interests. Over the past several years, the debate concerning search and seizure has extended to the application of new legislation permitting the taking of DNA from individuals who have been merely arrested on major crimes. The courts have revealed a division of opinion regarding whether the actions are in accordance with provisions against unreasonable searches in the constitution. Critics contend that taking DNA samples without conviction crosses the threshold of the individualized suspicion requirement fundamental to Fourth Amendment jurisprudence. Conversely, several states have endorsed such policies, justifying the same in terms of maintaining public safety and law-enforcement effectiveness. The fine line which the courts have to walk between balancing personal liberty and the necessity of effective policing suggests the complexity of contemporary criminal procedure. As this conversation comes further to the fore, it continues to be important for scholars and practitioners of law to remain in line with evolving innovation dynamics in technologies and traditional constitutional norms, particularly search and seizure (Figure 1.15).

1.5.1. Fourth Amendment Protections

The Fourth Amendment of the United States Constitution is critical in ensuring the privacy rights of individuals and the limitation of government power. It prohibits unreasonable searches and seizures, hence compelling law enforcement agencies to first obtain a warrant based on probable cause before violating an individual's rights. This policy tries to reconcile the interests of the government to have society be crime-free and in order with individuals' rights to privacy. Significantly, procedural rights enshrined in the Fourth Amendment not only safeguard private spaces but also ensure a legal framework upon which evidence can be obtained and introduced in court. In this case, the amendment is crucial to criminal procedure integrity, basically setting forth how evidence is obtained and what can be introduced in trials so that there would be a fair court proceeding. Fourth Amendment protections that emerged reflect both cultural change and available technology to police. As police policy evolved and technological innovation improved, the boundaries of what constitutes a search have expanded, raising new legal questions that challenge traditional conceptions of privacy. Issues related to electronic surveillance, such as extracting information from smart phones or cloud storage, present a special challenge to the privacy rights of individuals. The Stored Communications Act, which regulates access to cloud data, illustrates the conflicting needs between safeguarding personal data and enabling law enforcement to effectively carry out investigations. The implications of such cases as United States v. Microsoft prove the inadequacy of existing law to cope with such new challenges, suggesting a pressing need for legislative amendment that ensures Fourth Amendment protections keep abreast of the realities of a hyper-connected, global and technologically advanced world (Kirschenbaum et al., 2018). Apart from being paramount to addressing the dilemmas created by modern technology, the Fourth Amendment is also a paramount issue of argument regarding issues of immigration enforcement within the US. Encouragement of additional procedural protections for immigrants emphasizes an essential element of Fourth Amendment rights, especially in view of the increasing overlap between immigration enforcement and criminal law. Most notably, calls for greater procedural rights reflect a broader concern with the moral integrity of imposing criminal procedures on immigration cases. Detractors claim, however, that these safeguards alone will not provide actual reform to the system. Without an actual shift towards a broader understanding of immigration justice, they claim, merely expanding procedural rights will fail to confront the underlying ills borne by vulnerable communities (McLeod et al., 2016). This disparity reflects a complex interaction between constitutional safeguards and day-to-day experiences of marginalized communities, which requires a reevaluation of the mechanisms through which the legal system discerns and enforces Fourth Amendment rights in the contexts of multicultural societies.

1.5.2. Types of Searches

The criminal procedure definition of searches encompasses various methodologies and settings through which police may pursue suspected criminal conduct. A critical difference is made between general and specific searches, with the former referring to broad searches that may violate Fourth Amendment protection if conducted without probable cause or warrant. Specific searches are, by contrast, precisely bound by the terms of a warrant. This is particularly relevant as applied to modern challenges of technology, such as electronic communication. Courts have increasingly had to contend with the issues of electronically stored information, and this has led to a two-step process for carrying out search warrants under Federal Criminal Procedure Rule 41. This system is intended to balance the need for effective law enforcement with the privacy expectations of citizens, particularly in instances of nonresponsive material that are encountered during the course of a search (Dennis et al., 2018). In addition, the evolving technology has led to the formulation of the mosaic theory that holds that the aggregations of information compiled under government watchfulness might be deemed a search within the Fourth Amendment's meaning. The doctrine is of particular import in the Internet age, considering the various volumes of personal data found on social media, email, and other websites. The Supreme Court decision in United States v. Jones represents a turning point, recognizing the possibility that grouping together the monitoring of a person's movements can be an invasion of privacy rights. The portent of mosaic theory therefore extends beyond physical eavesdropping to encompass the government's increasing utilization of data-mining techniques combined that cumulatively construct a creeping picture of individuals' lives.

Figure 1.16. The concept of searches in criminal procedure.

Source: https://www.criminallawyer-nj.com/wp-content/uploads/2023/10/police-searching-car-1.jpg.

By establishing a more precise legal standard, lawmakers can provide necessary guidance to police officers while remaining sensitive to constitutional rights (Slobogin et al., 2012). Finally, familiarization with the different types of searches is not only necessary for legal practitioners but also for the public to know their rights. The fineness of warrant requirements, including probable cause and specificity, can have direct impact on the admissibility of evidence in criminal cases. As legal precedents are continually being shaped, especially as a response to ongoing technological advances, it is important that courts revisit and adapt clear standards for searches to the realities of our times. Debates on procedures for the warrant's execution, and what this says about privacy, need to be ongoing to be able to balance good policing with safeguarding civil liberties. By encouraging dialogue between scholars, legislators, and judges, a more principled approach towards searches can be developed, one that can reconcile the ongoing tensions between governmental interests and individual rights (Dennis et al., 2018) (Figure 1.16).

1.5.3. Legal Standards for Search Warrants

Legal warrant standards for search are at the core of safeguarding individual rights under the context of criminal procedure. Enshrined in the Fourth Amendment, these standards give highest priority to the need for probable cause, which must be based on reliable information. This requirement serves as a bar to unreasonable searches and seizures, reflecting the Framers' intention to limit government intrusion. In particular, the doctrine holding that probable cause can support a criminal search developed long after the ratification of the Bill of Rights, inferring a considerable shift in legal practice and interpretation. As Davies points out, this was a move away from what was believed to have been upheld in the creation of the United States in terms of standards of procedure, referencing how legal standards are dynamic in addressing evolving social and governmental needs (Davies et al., 2010). Legal standards in granting search warrants have become more complex with the advancement of contemporary technologies. The introduction of electronic communication altered daily life and criminal investigation, necessitating new considerations for law enforcement agents. Electronic evidence usually presents itself in humongous volumes, necessitating the introduction of procedures, such as those legislated under Federal Criminal Procedure Rule 41. This two-step process of issuing search warrants considers the complexities of dealing with electronically stored information, distinguishing the treatment of responsive and nonresponsive information. It is this kind of framework that attempts to balance the government's investigatory needs with individual privacy rights, a perpetual predicament in modern jurisprudence (Dennis et al., 2018). In the midst of courts and scholars still grappling with the issues that electronic evidence poses, some proposals have been presented on simplifying search warrant execution procedures. The threats posed by blanket general searches have prompted arguments regarding the best means to oversee retention and utilization of nonresponsive materials collected during investigations. These arguments highlight the need to enhance Rule 41 with improved standards designed to protect individuals' privacy while permitting law enforcement officers to execute effective searches. By examining the strengths and limitations of methods throughout the spectrum of justification for search warrant execution, stakeholders can advocate for reforms that are attuned to contemporary values and technological realities and maintain the system for search warrants as sound and equitable in a more dynamic world. To maintain privacy rights and investigation efficiency in balance in today's world, legal standards need to be revisited in this regard (Dennis et al., 2018).

1.6. TRIAL PROCEDURES

Trial procedures form the core of criminal justice, where legal process never infringes on the rights of both the defendant and the state. The procedures offer a well-structured environment where evidence is listened to and scrutinized, with the aim of upholding fairness and justice during court processes. The basis of this system lies in the observation of code-based laws, such as the Criminal Procedure Code, which determine the function and role of various stakeholders involved in the trial. Evidentiary principles such as the presentation of evidence, witness examination, and jury deliberation are basic components of procedure in trials. Without such a systematic procedure, arbitrary judgments would have more opportunities, and citizens' faith in the judiciary would be lost. Thus, an orderly methodology of trial procedure not merely safeguards the rights of the individual but also serves the legitimacy of the entire judicial process as a safeguard against miscarriage of justice.

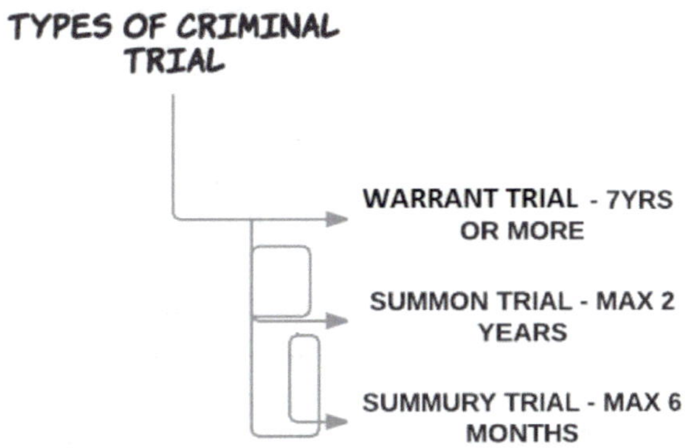

Figure 1.17. Trial procedures stand at the foundation of criminal justice.

Source: https://blog.ipleaders.in/wp-content/uploads/2017/02/1.png.

The integrity of trial procedure is further illustrated in the relationship between evidential standards and judicial judgment. For a conviction to hold, it is imperative that the judges embrace the established rules of evidence, which necessitate the demand for sound evidence, as provided for in Article 184 of the Criminal Procedure Code. Disobedience of the established norms could lead to incorrect judicial judgments, as seen in current criticism of some court decisions. For example, in Court Decision Number 10/PID.B/2021/PN.PLK, the judge is purportedly supposed to have issued a verdict with insufficient evidence behind it, and thus there is concern for the trial's overall equity. Article 183 of the Code mandates that a judgment should be based upon at least two sound items of evidence, and this indicates the crucial importance of stringent evidentiary requirements in validating judicial findings. With this, the enthusiasm with which a trial is prosecuted according to these criteria of evidence lies at the heart of making judicial decisions sound. As societal attitudes towards criminal justice evolve, the role of victims in trial proceedings has also seen cataclysmic transformation. Having been traditionally placed in the role of passive witnesses, the victim increasingly stands recognized today as a central stakeholder in the judicial process. This change is in tune with newer methods that promote victim participation, like the plans used in the majority of European legal systems. This change eliminates the traditional dichotomy between private and public interests in criminal cases and encourages a more participatory justice. The recognition of victims' rights to actively participate in criminal trials not only fulfills their pursuit of justice but also enhances the openness and comprehensiveness of the legal process. Ultimately, this shift in paradigm recognizes that victim participation can enrich the trial proceedings, providing courts with new factors to consider that have the potential to impact decisions and ensure the legitimacy of the justice system, e.g., Doak et al. (2005) (Figure 1.17).

1.6.1. Pre-Trial Motions and Hearings

Pre-trial hearings and motions in the criminal justice process are necessary components that decide the direction in which a case is moving. Both prosecution and defense can present specific points of law before the trial in such processes, which can significantly affect the admission of evidence and the overall strategy adopted thenceforth. The primary goals of pre-trial motions are to resolve legal matters in advance of trial, i.e., motions to suppress evidence, motions for discovery, and motions for change of venue, among others. In addition to guaranteeing a fair trial, pre-trial motions also enhance judicial efficiency by resolving possible controversies in advance so that the court's workload during the trial process is kept to a minimum. The significance of pre-trial motions is also reinforced by the potential consequences they have for prosecutors and defendants. A successful motion to suppress, for instance, can lead to the exclusion of critical evidence and thus invalidate the prosecution's case and, potentially, lead to acquittal or reduced charges. Meanwhile, where the defense motion for dismissal of the charges is granted, the case may never reach the trial stage at all, precluding the possibility of conviction. These movements are significant as they not only rely on the construction of legal criteria but also on the provision of corroborative evidence typically in the form of affidavits and pleadings that take place in pre-trial hearings, where judges use their discretion and set precedents which can shape future cases. Criminal procedure development has only served to highlight the importance of such pre-trial practices in that they reaffirm the importance of a refined understanding of the interface between criminal and civil procedures. Historically, as seen in Meyn et al. (2017), the difference between the rules of criminal and civil procedures has been debated, and it impacts how motions are framed and moved through court hearings. The processual obstacles of these pre-trial motions shed light upon the fundamental principles that guide criminal procedure today. Moreover, while tools created under civil procedure can be observed in the criminal realm, substantial obstacles persist—particularly with respect to discovery, which continues to be notoriously restrictive by comparison. This lacuna prompts ongoing debate on the future of procedural unification, and the consequences that would result for fair trial rights and evidence standards in criminal justice.

1.6.2. The Trial Process

The trial process is a key component of the criminal justice system, serving as the arena in which charges are formally tested. Essentially, the trial offers a framework in which both the prosecution and defense are able to put before the court their case supported by evidence and witness testimony. The rights of the accused are always of paramount concern at every stage, with various protections available to ensure fairness. This includes innocence until proven guilty, the right to be represented, and the opportunity to challenge the evidence presented by the prosecution. Furthermore, the trial format provides the opportunity to seriously deliberate facts, where the jurors play a key role in rendering a judgment based on the evidence submitted. Thus, the trial process entails the justice and due process needed for a sound legal system. Overarching the trial process is the role of witnesses whose testimony can actually determine the outcome of a case. In the various categories of witnesses, a crown witness is unique because such individuals can be suspects or co-defendants in a criminal charge. The legal standing of crown witnesses, as analyzed in recent research, points to the complexity entailed when they provide evidence against their collaborators and are rewarded with lessened charges or immunity in return. This dynamic raises important questions about the reliability of their testaments and potential coercion since these witnesses play their dual roles in the criminal justice framework. The authenticity of their testimonies matters, and the police have to guarantee that their role as witnesses does not violate human rights or reduce the fairness of the trials, in harmony with the standards of justice that must be applied in criminal trials (ari anzari et al., 2024). Additionally, the rising demands for active engagement by defendants at the trial level have raised immense controversy around their involvement in the process. The law has increasingly demanded greater active engagement by defendants in their defense, with profound implications for the adversarial character of trials. Critics argue that it is coercive to require defendants to cooperate and turns the trial into an apparatus capable of punishing non-cooperation. This perspective believes that the primary focus of the criminal process is to hold the state accountable for its accusations, granting defendants autonomy to choose their participation. With an understanding of the significance of establishing a balance of equitable rights to trial, there is a need to maintain the dignity and autonomy of the accused via trials, as per normative theories that focus on a fair and equitable criminal process (Owusu-Bempah et al., 2016) (Figure 1.18).

Figure 1.18. The trial process.

Source: https://galballyparker.com.au/wp-content/uploads/2023/05/Preparing-for-trial-what-to-expect.jpg.

1.6.3. Sentencing and Appeals

In criminal procedure, the process of sentencing forms a critical component of the process that encompasses so much more than only the imposition of punishment. It is the subtle balance of justice, fairness, and legislature to make sure that the punishment has relevance and proportion for the crime committed. Sentencing is based on numerous varied factors such as the defendant's background in crime, the type of the crime, as well as the statute guidelines. Significantly, any error in this phase may have severe implications for the accused. It is for this purpose that knowledge of the nature of sentencing errors is important because these have the capability to violate aspects of justice or constitute disproportionate punishment and therefore deserve re-examination of the standard process in our courts (Aleklett et al., 2009). The appeal process is a critical right for defendants who are dissatisfied with their sentencing outcomes, providing a vehicle for disputing potential mistakes within the court process. Sentence appeals typically hinge on an argument that the trial court legally erred or misunderstanding facts. Appeals may range from charges of improper enhancements in sentence to assertions of ineffective assistance of counsel at the first trial. But appellate courts do not retry the cases in their entirety but instead see whether the original court made legal errors significant enough to warrant a reversal of the decision. The process not only serves as a check on the judiciary but also ensures that it highlights how significant it is to adhere to legal standards throughout the process of sentencing (Aleklett et al., 2009). In capital punishment cases, for instance, the intricacies of sentencing and post-trial appeals are compounded further. The controversy over the death penalty raises questions on morality, effectiveness, and constitutional legitimacy, especially in states like New York, where legislative bids have resulted in the invalidation of capital punishment statutes as unconstitutional. The ongoing debate with regard to capital punishment requires a critical appraisal of how such sentencing judgments may be appealed and ultimately reversed. This complex interplay between practices of sentencing and the appellate mechanism throws into sharp relief important issues relating to the function of finality in the administration of justice. As discussion progresses, so also must our comprehension of how legal systems can provide avenues for appeal in the context of extreme ethical challenges to severe sentences, hence enhancing an even more just justice system.

SUMMARY

The pursuit of criminal procedure and evidence, it is essential to appreciate the delicate balance between upholding justice and being efficient in the legal system. A successful understanding of the dynamic is required in order to grasp better the complexities faced by defense attorneys and defendants of a similar nature. New structural changes to the fee-remuneration of defense attorneys, particularly towards fixed fees, have raised significant questions regarding the impact they have on the progression of criminal trials. As revealed by research, these reforms inadvertently affect the way lawyers handle cases, negotiate with prosecutors, and advise clients, ultimately establishing the overall justice delivered in the justice system (Stephen et al., 2007). Secondly, the implications of altering legal systems have grave consequences for defendants and their right to a fair trial. Structural changes in legal aid are not just financial administration changes within the system but have consequent impacts on client experience and results. Theoretical efficiency of fixed payment structures can give rise to unanticipated difficulties, and these can be an indication of policy intention and actual implementation. It is for this reason, therefore, that it becomes necessary to rethink such reforms critically and their broader implications, so that the rights of clients are not second-order considerations in the scenario of structural change (Bean et al., 2016). Lastly, examining the interface between criminal procedure and evidence demonstrates the need for ongoing scrutiny and adaptation within legal frameworks. As legislation evolves to address the issues and demands of society, it is important that stakeholders take note of assessing the impacts of such changes to the administration of justice. The pursuit of efficiency should not compromise the underlying principles of fairness and due process, which are the foundation of the criminal justice system. By establishing a framework supportive of these values, stakeholders can move toward a more equitable legal system, where the rights and interests of both sides are considered in the criminal process.

The intricacy of evidence and criminal procedure is the basis of the justice system, underscoring the importance of due process and the rights of the accused. Fundamental to understanding such concepts is the study of legal aid structures, which have an important role to play in terms of shaping how criminal cases proceed. The most recent developments concerning criminal defense remuneration, such as the move toward fixed fees in Scotland, is designed to highlight the influence of legal systems on case evolutions. Promoting efficiency in the criminal process, such developments aim to optimize overall performance in legal representation. However, as the study has documented, such adjustments would most probably have unforeseen outcomes that act against the initial intentions, say, in impacting attorney-client negotiations and decision-making in plea bargaining (Stephen et al., 2007). Thus, the legal aid architecture does not only impact individual cases but also highlights greater system implications in criminal justice. In the evidence field, the interconnection between science and law remains crucial, particularly in international criminal proceedings. Forensic science-based expert evidence is crucial for guiding judicial outcomes and allocating responsibility for war crimes and serious offenses. For instance, forensic archaeology analysis of mass graves illustrates the pivotal role scientific information plays in legal process. This strategy highlights both theoretical constructs and working realities that arise within the context of international law. The admissibility and use of expert evidence remain nevertheless made difficult by the existence of few guidelines emanating from legal standards. Courts have to depend upon the adversarial process, either in the form of cross-examination and generation of counter-expertise, in determining the reliability and relevance of forensic conclusions (Klinkner et al., 2009). Thus, the use of scientific evidence in court proceedings is odd challenges and opportunities for justice. Lastly, the chart of the highlights on criminal procedure and evidence informs us of the interdependent dynamics among law, science, and human rights. As the law changes, the impact of reforms on legal aid and the role of forensic evidence in the courtroom becomes ever more pertinent. Legal professionals are required to make sense of these developments keeping clients' rights and the integrity of the judicial process in mind. The changing strategies of legal defense in response to remuneration trends and the delicate balance in the introduction of expert testimony to trials suggest a broader movement toward a more effective but more just legal system. Moving forward to explore these trends, it becomes essential to consider how reforms impact not only the machinery of justice but also the principles on which the rule of law is maintained and the rights of individuals are protected under the criminal justice system.

KEY TERMS

Admissibility of Evidence	Arraignment
Arrest	Bail
Beyond a Reasonable Doubt	Burden of Proof
Chain of Custody	Circumstantial Evidence
Confession	Criminal Procedure
Cross-Examination	Custodial Interrogation
Direct Evidence	Due Process
Exclusionary Rule	Expert Witness
Hearsay Rule	Indictment
Judicial Notice	Miranda Rights

A LOOK TO THE FUTURE

THE FUTURE OF CRIMINAL PROCEDURE

Criminal procedure is significantly impacted by the use of technology, particularly in the way evidence is presented and assessed in court. New approaches such as video recorded evidence are a milestone towards ensuring that legal proceedings are made more accessible to intimidated and vulnerable witnesses (VIW). Special measures have been introduced through the Youth Justice and Criminal Evidence Act (YJCEA, 1999) to reduce the intimidating nature of the legal process for them. Through the facility of video recorded cross-examination, section 28 provisions of the YJCEA reduce delays in first giving of evidence and subsequent questioning where the case is not guilty. Not only does this innovation make it easier to access justice, it also ushers in a more supportive setting that is respectful and dignified of individuals' mental well-being. As the world evolves, the interface between technology and legal regimes will play a key role in shaping the direction of criminal procedure. However, notwithstanding the adoption of advanced technologies such as video recording, challenges remain in internalizing the schemes in a beneficial manner. Research demonstrates large knowledge gaps on identification of vulnerable witnesses who can benefit from protection under the YJCEA, particularly in how effectively the Intermediary service operates. The service aims to facilitate smooth communication between vulnerable witnesses and legal professionals, but its implementation and design should be further strictly analyzed. The criminal procedure of the future will largely be based on the development of interdisciplinarity-based research centered on best interview practices, enhancing witness protection procedures, and appropriate verification of testimony. Closing these gaps is vital to the formulation of an inclusive criminal justice system where the needs of all the actors are addressed without compromising procedural integrity. In addition, inter-disciplinary collaborations will be necessary in addressing the new challenges of criminal procedure within the justice framework. As criminal cases continuously become more sophisticated, combining insights from fields such as linguistic psychology and communication studies can yield significant improvement in presentation of evidence as well as witness questioning techniques. Future research has to be oriented towards the development of general guidelines that not only cover technological developments but also witness testimony-related psychological concerns. In facilitating a deeper understanding of the ways in which various elements affect communication within the courtroom, the legal system can better provide for the needs of vulnerable witnesses. This integrative overhaul of criminal procedure benefits not only the quality of evidence presented but also enhances public faith in the legal process with a more balanced and fair treatment of all parties involved, hence building a stronger criminal justice system.

REFERENCES

1. Alanis-Hirsch, K., Belden, C. M., Easter, M. M., Frisman, L., et al. (2019). Criminal justice and suicide outcomes with Indiana's risk-based gun seizure law. https://core.ac.uk/download/322846892.pdf (accessed on 13th August 2025).
2. Aleklett, K., Höök, M., Jakobsson, K., Söderbergh, B., et al. (2009). Accuracy in sentencing. https://core.ac.uk/download/213020452.pdf (accessed on 13th August 2025).
3. Anzari, A. (2024). Analisis yuridis kedudukan saksi mahkota sebagai alat bukti dalam persidangan. https://core.ac.uk/download/12141477.pdf (accessed on 13th August 2025).
4. Azevedo, P. F. de, & Henriksen, A. L. (2025). Cartel deterrence and settlements: The Brazilian experience. https://core.ac.uk/download/pdf/6485357.pdf (accessed on 13th August 2025).
5. Bader, W. D., & Cleveland, D. R. (2011). Precedent and justice. https://core.ac.uk/download/144551123.pdf (accessed on 13th August 2025).
6. Bean, D., Cooper, P., Creaby-Attwood, A., Grubin, D., et al. (2016). Unfitness to plead. Volume 1: Report. https://core.ac.uk/download/41075001.pdf (accessed on 13th August 2025).
7. Burman, M., de Haan, J., Johnstone, J., Macleod, N., et al. (2010). Responding to gender-based violence in Scotland: The scope of the gender equality duty to drive cultural and practical change. https://core.ac.uk/download/10387.pdf (accessed on 13th August 2025).
8. Cociani, L., Fattorini, P., Moratti, M., Santangelo, A., et al. (2015). Omicidio e lesioni personali da incidenti della strada in stato di ebbrezza e di alterazione psico-fisica. Criticità e problematiche. Considerazioni medico-legali. https://core.ac.uk/download/84675968.pdf (accessed on 13th August 2025).
9. Cockburn, H., Lacey, N., & Farmer, L. (1999). Debatable land: An essay on the relationship between English and Scottish criminal law. https://core.ac.uk/download/1422349.pdf (accessed on 13th August 2025).
10. Conway, V., & Daly, Y. M. (2019). From legal advice to legal assistance: Recognizing the changing role of the solicitor in the Garda station. https://core.ac.uk/download/286779063.pdf (accessed on 13th August 2025).
11. Dang, C. (2014). Admissible or inadmissible: The role of formally codified rules of evidence as a safeguard in Mexico's developing adversarial system. https://core.ac.uk/download/157727504.pdf (accessed on 13th August 2025).
12. Davies, T. Y. (2010). How the post-framing adoption of the bare-probable-cause standard drastically expanded government arrest and search power. https://core.ac.uk/download/62553055.pdf (accessed on 13th August 2025).
13. Dennis, S. J. (2018). Regulating search warrant execution procedure for stored electronic communications. https://core.ac.uk/download/216957632.pdf (accessed on 13th August 2025).
14. Djerf, H., & Hy, J. (1990). Rights of the criminally accused. https://core.ac.uk/download/62554233.pdf (accessed on 13th August 2025).
15. Doak, J. (2005). Victims' rights in criminal trials: Prospects for participation. https://core.ac.uk/download/30635564.pdf (accessed on 13th August 2025).

16. Evans, J., Khan, H. T. A., & Kubascikova, J. (2018). Video recorded cross-examination or re-examination: A discussion on practice and research. https://core.ac.uk/download/158372846.pdf (accessed on 13th August 2025).
17. Ewin, R. (2018). Video recorded cross-examination or re-examination: A discussion on practice and research. https://core.ac.uk/download/158372846.pdf (accessed on 13th August 2025).
18. Faber, S. R. (2018). Competency, counsel, and criminal defendants' inability to participate. https://core.ac.uk/download/213019928.pdf (accessed on 13th August 2025).
19. Garrett, B. L. (2005). Innocence, harmless error, and federal wrongful conviction law. https://core.ac.uk/download/213020502.pdf (accessed on 13th August 2025).
20. Garrett, B. L. (2017). Towards an international right to claim innocence. https://core.ac.uk/download/213020519.pdf (accessed on 13th August 2025).
21. Garrett, B. L. (2018). Local evidence in constitutional interpretation. https://core.ac.uk/download/213020399.pdf (accessed on 13th August 2025).
22. Garrett, B. L., & Monahan, J. (2020). Judging risk. https://core.ac.uk/download/213021325.pdf (accessed on 13th August 2025).
23. Giannoulopoulos, D. (2007). The exclusion of improperly obtained evidence in Greece: Putting constitutional rights first. https://core.ac.uk/download/6113204.pdf (accessed on 13th August 2025).
24. Grossman, S. P. (2014). Using the DNA testing of arrestees to reevaluate Fourth Amendment doctrine. https://core.ac.uk/download/144552234.pdf (accessed on 13th August 2025).
25. Halpern, M. (2018). Trends in admissibility of hearsay evidence in war crime trials: Is fairness really preserved? https://core.ac.uk/download/213020809.pdf (accessed on 13th August 2025).
26. Hessler, S. E. (2000). Establishing inevitability without active pursuit: Defining the inevitable discovery exception to the Fourth Amendment exclusionary rule. https://core.ac.uk/download/232710215.pdf (accessed on 13th August 2025).
27. Huffman, D. N. (2008). To act or not to act: Will New York's defeated death penalty be resurrected? https://core.ac.uk/download/144227799.pdf (accessed on 13th August 2025).
28. Hungan, F. C. (2024). Jumping conclusion dalam putusan pengadilan nomor 10/PID.B/2021/PN.PLK. https://core.ac.uk/download/12139261.pdf (accessed on 13th August 2025).
29. Johansson, H., & Pillai, A. K. M. (1988). Mechanical applications of the harmless error rule in cases of prosecutorial grand jury misconduct. https://core.ac.uk/download/62549741.pdf (accessed on 13th August 2025).
30. Kirschenbaum, A. (2018). Beyond *Microsoft*: A legislative solution to the SCA's extraterritoriality problem. https://core.ac.uk/download/216957567.pdf (accessed on 13th August 2025).
31. Klinkner, M. J. (2009). Forensic science expertise for international criminal proceedings: An old problem, a new context and a pragmatic resolution. https://core.ac.uk/download/4897045.pdf (accessed on 13th August 2025).
32. Leverick, F. (2015). "Legal history" in the making: HM Advocate v Sinclair and the Double Jeopardy (Scotland) Act 2011. https://core.ac.uk/download/42365747.pdf (accessed on 13th August 2025).

33. Lu, Y. (2010). A critique of human rights protection for suspects in the Chinese criminal justice system: An examination of the extent to which there is and could in future be compatibility between Chinese law and practice and international human rights norms. https://core.ac.uk/download/85570.pdf (accessed on 13th August 2025).
34. Madden, M. (2014). The exclusion of improperly obtained evidence at the International Criminal Court: A principled approach to interpreting Article 69(7) of the Rome Statute. https://core.ac.uk/download/337414051.pdf (accessed on 13th August 2025).
35. McLeod, A. M. (2016). Immigration, criminalization, and disobedience. https://core.ac.uk/download/70375543.pdf (accessed on 13th August 2025).
36. Meyn, I. (2017). Why civil and criminal procedure are so different: A forgotten history. https://core.ac.uk/download/144232643.pdf (accessed on 13th August 2025).
37. Montana, R. (2012). Adversarialism in Italy: Using the concept of legal culture to understand resistance to legal modifications and its consequences. https://core.ac.uk/download/9559363.pdf (accessed on 13th August 2025).
38. Neugebauer, K. (2019). Holding domestic judges accountable under international criminal law – A useful step to foster the international rule of law? https://core.ac.uk/download/225124777.pdf (accessed on 13th August 2025).
39. Olive, P., & Walby, S. (2013). The European added value of a directive on combatting violence against women: Annex 2 economic aspects and legal perspectives for action at the European level. https://core.ac.uk/download/187717984.pdf (accessed on 13th August 2025).
40. Oliver, W. M. (2018). Prohibition's anachronistic exclusionary rule. https://core.ac.uk/download/232978484.pdf (accessed on 13th August 2025).
41. Owusu-Bempah, A. (2016). Introduction: Participatory requirements and rights. https://core.ac.uk/download/82917151.pdf (accessed on 13th August 2025).
42. Persson, A. C., Kak, K., Stierstorfer, M., Bazalova, P., Joseph, W., & Schneider, X. L. (2011). Self-policing: Dissemination and adoption of police eyewitness policies in Virginia. https://core.ac.uk/download/286540208.pdf (accessed on 13th August 2025).
43. Priester, B. J. (1998). Sentenced for a "crime" the government did not prove: Jones v. United States and the constitutional limitations on factfinding by sentencing factors rather than elements of the offense. https://core.ac.uk/download/62568597.pdf (accessed on 13th August 2025).
44. Richman, D. (2012). Federal white collar sentencing in the United States: A work in progress. https://core.ac.uk/download/62559791.pdf (accessed on 13th August 2025).
45. Schwarze, J. (2004). Judicial review of European administrative procedure. https://core.ac.uk/download/62553540.pdf (accessed on 13th August 2025).
46. Slobogin, C. (2012). Making the most of United States v. Jones in a surveillance society: A statutory implementation of mosaic theory. https://core.ac.uk/download/62560000.pdf (accessed on 13th August 2025).
47. Stephen, F., & Tata, C. (2007). When paying the piper gets the 'wrong' tune: The impact of fixed payments on case management, case trajectories and 'quality' in criminal defense work. https://core.ac.uk/download/9018154.pdf (accessed on 13th August 2025).

48. Sussmann, M. A. (1999). The critical challenges from international high-tech and computer-related crime at the millennium. https://core.ac.uk/download/62547637.pdf (accessed on 13th August 2025).

49. Vander Beken, T., & Wu, W. (2012). Relativism and universalism in interrogation fairness: A comparative analysis between Europe and China. https://core.ac.uk/download/55853450.pdf (accessed on 13th August 2025).

Chapter 2

THE CRIMINAL JUSTICE SYSTEM AND PROCEDURAL ROLES

Contents

Introduction 39
2.1. Historical Context of the Criminal Justice System 43
2.2. Components of the Criminal Justice System 47
2.3. Roles of Law Enforcement 51
2.4. The Judicial Process 55
2.5. Correctional System Functions 59
2.6. Procedural Justice 63
Summary 67
References 70

INTRODUCTION

The introduction to the Criminal Justice System and Procedural Roles study is a vital portal to a multi-dimensional and complex subject. The system uses a chain of procedures from arrest through prosecution, which impacts the delivery and perception of justice in society. The procedural roles in this arrangement include various actors, including the police, attorneys, and magistrates, each contributing to the general integrity of the justice system. It is important to know these roles because they not only establish the procedural mechanisms of justice provision but also arise from deeper ethical and cultural values in the legal ecosystem. Through an exploration of these dimensions, the introduction aims to lay a basis for further discussion on the interlinkage between procedural integrity and legal fairness and societal expectations. In addition, an examination of the historical development of procedural roles helps advance the evolution of interrogation and legal methods throughout history across societies. Of particular interest, comparative analysis shows remarkable differences in interrogation methods across regions, particularly between Western and Eastern societies. For instance, the advent of interrogation rules in ancient China and Greece explains how various legal cultures shape criminal process (Beken et al., 2012). The comparative analysis provides an insight into issues experienced in current reform efforts. Societies strive for justice reforms while, at the same time, understanding such historical antecedents is required in order to have contextually informed debate. The introduction, therefore, not only situates the topic of the procedural roles but also places emphasis on the relevance of historical knowledge towards encouraging equitable legal practice. Lastly, the introduction emphasizes the need for urgency in the ethical challenges faced within the criminal justice system, most prominently the dual roles many practitioners fill. The tension between client advocacy and public safety has a tendency to emerge in complex form, generating ethical dissonance among forensic and correctional professionals (Andrews et al., 2015). The early exploration of this study incites reflective examination of the possibility of restorative justice frameworks offering resolutions for these ethical concerns. Positioning restorative justice within the consideration of procedural roles, the introduction sets the stage for an in-depth consideration of non-conventional conflict resolution and offender rehabilitation mechanisms. As such, this analysis advocates for a progressive consideration of how moral concerns are interwoven with procedural integrity, thereby underscoring the necessity for reformist debates in criminal justice (Figure 2.1).

Figure 2.1. The examination of the criminal justice system and procedural roles.

Source: https://blog.ipleaders.in/wp-content/uploads/2019/12/estate-litigation-lawyer.jpg.

Definition of the Criminal Justice System

The criminal justice system is a central framework established to uphold social order and administer justice in society. In general terms, it encompasses various institutions, customs, and policies directed towards regulating crime, enforcing law and order, and protecting the rights of the citizens. It typically comprises police forces, judiciary courts, and jails, each adding a specialized role to the justice system. The prime objective is not only to punish criminal behavior but also to resocialize criminals and rehabilitate them and provide reparation to victims. As the societies evolve and adapt to meet new challenges, the criminal justice system must similarly redefine its role and terms so that it can adequately cope with new trends in criminality and societal perception of justice, equity, and retribution. The complexity of the crime in recent times has spurred a re-evaluation of the traditional definition of the criminal justice system. All of these factors, including advancements in technology and increased global mobility, have resulted in new types of criminal behavior and the need for a more comprehensive understanding of crime beyond conventional confines. As an example, the creation of the FIDUCIA project is helpful to emphasize the need for a policy model based on trust that incorporates public opinion and institutional legitimacy into the equation on crime and punishment. These perspectives place emphasis on establishing community trust alongside addressing challenges like human trafficking and cybercrime, thus transforming the role of the criminal justice system in contemporary society (Bradford et al., 2013). Along the way, stakeholders must contend with the intricate relationship between applying law and forming society values. Furthermore, increasing awareness of the everyday rights of victims has begun to shift the profile of criminal justice. Traditionally, victims were relegated to the background in an adversary system where the accused person's rights were given priority. However, more recent innovations such as the 'Victims Focus Scheme' in England and Wales look to give greater voice to the victim in court, a change of course in everyday administration of justice. This evolution provokes critical discourse regarding the dynamic interplay between victim rights and due process rights afforded to defendants. Throughout the debate, the toughness of procedural justice and the overall integrity of the criminal justice system remain at the forefront, while the close-knit web of interests and ethical concerns at the base of contemporary justice procedures are noted (Mitchell et al., 2009).

Importance of Procedural Roles

In researching the functions of procedural roles in the criminal justice system, it is evident that the procedural roles are very central to maintaining fairness and justice. Procedural roles refer to the established procedures and guidelines that govern how judicial process functions. The procedural roles are central to maintaining the protection of the rights of individuals throughout the legal system, thereby making the criminal justice system legitimate. For instance, the players in this system, such as police officers, lawyers, and judges, are bound by certain rules of procedure that guide them in their interaction with defendants and victims as well. By adhering to such procedures, the system tries to prevent miscarriages of justice and hence gain the public's confidence and trust. The impact of procedural roles is not limited to the short-term environment of the courtroom, but it finds its way into societal attitudes toward justice and legal integrity. An open and fair judicial process is of fundamental significance in a democratic society, as it enforces the rule of law and encourages adherence to the law by the community. And beyond this, procedural standards mature and advance, transforming over time in response to cultural, technological, and societal changes. For example, advances in forensic technology and global migration of populations have opened the floodgates to new procedural challenges. In this regard, Legal reformers have to constantly argue with these shifting procedural standards in a bid to address new problems in an effective manner (Bradford et al., 2013). How investigations and trials are carried out ultimately reflects the expectations placed in society upon justice and thus procedural roles constitute the bedrock of public trust. In addition, the uneven handling of procedural functions across legal systems brings into focus the imperative of constant dialogue and potential reform. Comparative research on criminal procedure across jurisdictions reveals stark disparities in protecting rights, particularly with respect to interrogation policies (Beken et al., 2012). Such disparities can create problems for global cooperation in criminal matters and reiterate the necessity of universal procedural fairness standards. These variations not only show the richness of legal practices but also the complex play between modernity and tradition in judicial and police practices. Ultimately, determining the significance of procedural roles alters methodologies in justice administration, maintaining the fundamental principles that secure social order and protect individual rights (Figure 2.2).

Figure 2.2. The importance of procedural roles within the criminal justice system.

Source: https://law.yale.edu/sites/default/files/styles/content_half_width/public/area/center/justice/new_pj_image.png?itok=0kAiCeCa.

2.1. HISTORICAL CONTEXT OF THE CRIMINAL JUSTICE SYSTEM

The development of the criminal justice system is deeply embedded in historical contexts that shaped its foundation and procedural aspects. A significant aspect of this background is how ancient civilizations shaped legal practices. Ancient Greece and China both had unique legal traditions in addressing criminal interrogation and trial procedures. For instance, the procedural mores of ancient Greek societies required public discussion and charged rights, while Chinese civilizations established a more coercive and hierarchical position. This type of divergence over history is the foundation for modern conflicts about legal rights universality and procedural justice among multicultural societies, which speaks to how entrenched practices may be immune to transformation (Beken et al., 2012). The acknowledgment of these underlying differences is important to appreciating the current complexion of criminal justice systems across the globe and the procedural roles that define them. Over time, the criminal justice system remained reflective of and responsive to societal values and political atmospheres. The 20th century witnessed the coming together of cultural narratives and legal practices that shaped public attitudes regarding justice. Television programs like The Defenders in the 1960s and in the 1990s served as a prism through which social concern regarding crime and legislation was articulated. These representations belied the stark, dichotomous perceptions of law and justice and revealed the contradictions of legal representation, particularly of defense lawyers operating in and beyond the borders of formal law (Classen et al., 2007). These popular tales not only expressed contemporary fears but also served to feed the ongoing debate about the humanistic aspects of legal practice, demanding a blend of compassion and the severity of law. The historical record of the criminal justice system also reveals the impact of reform movements aimed at improving procedural fairness. Over time, various social movements have emerged in agitating for rights such as presumptions of innocence and the right against self-incrimination. These social movements are usually drawn from historical scenarios from prevailing legal orders across the globe, from evolving guidelines on interrogations. The ghoulish divide between coercive practices and rights-based approaches speaks volumes of the persistent tension over humane treatment within the justice system. Furthermore, on-going demands for reform suggest that having strict adherence to established legal systems may not be sufficient to engage with the complex nature of criminal processes (Beken et al., 2012). By an examination of such background circumstances and their implications for procedural roles, it is possible to realize that the quest for justice is a constantly developing dialogue shaped by cultural, political, and societal forces.

2.1.1. Evolution of Legal Systems

The evolution of legal systems itself proves the pervasive influence of cultural origins and historical outlook on criminal justice procedures. For instance, Chinese and ancient Greek civilizations' interaction has developed distinct legal systems in both nations. The division proves that legal systems are not only functional but also indicative of social values and norms. Considering modern-day interrogation practices, one sees radical differences based on these premise principles. Even as contemporary argument upholds universal rights, like the right to remain silent, practice indicates that these principles are realized in varying forms across disparate jurisdictions with distinct histories, meaning hopes for change in the law have to meet institutional and cultural conditions. They are reminders that all attempts at change in legal systems must bear in mind their roots in tradition and society for the purposes of efficient and fair justice delivery, according to Beken et al. (2012). Through this review of the structural differences of legal systems, comparisons between American and French models identify the varying functions within their judicial systems. Both have a three-tiered court system but differ in aim and focus. In the United States system, the separation between trial courts and appellate courts provides the possibility of a clear distinction between findings of fact and interpretation of law. The French system, on the other hand, intermixes findings of fact and legal consideration at various levels, with limited opportunity to appeal factual disputes at the last court. This disparity emphasizes the way philosophies and procedural roles shape legal outcomes and justice access. These structural variations within the appeals process impact each system's overall effectiveness and fairness considerably, shaping the citizens experience on the criminal justice landscape, as outlined by Blockx et al. (2018). Legal system advancement is also put into context when considering pursuing procedural fairness across jurisdictions. Legal changes that have been sought in many countries have consisted in unearthing a developing argument between entrenched traditions and current ethical demands. In China, traditional norms of interrogation are quite different from simultaneous calls for a right against self-incrimination. Although past precedents remain to inform modern practices, reform potential remains based upon embracing cooperative interviewing methods for reducing coercive treatment. This discussion proves that while global legal norms exercise powerful influences, the ability of a system to create room to accommodate indigenous legal principles is essential. Therefore, as legal systems evolve, they must walk the thin line between respecting established tradition and advocating for advancement in procedural justice, inclusive of both the past context and the aspiration for current fairness, just like Beken et al. (2012) (Figure 2.3).

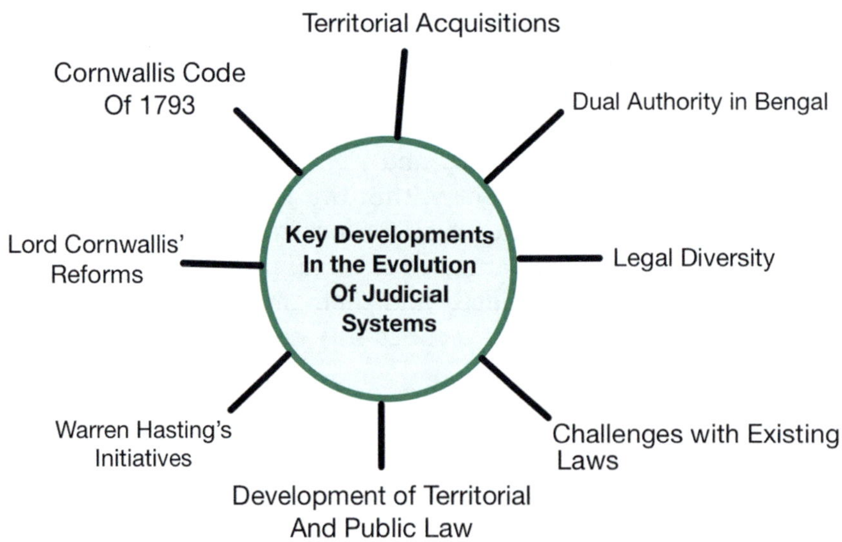

Figure 2.3. The evolution of legal systems.

Source: https://pwonlyias.com/wp-content/uploads/2024/09/unnamed-5-1-2.webp.

2.1.2. Key Milestones in Criminal Justice History

The trajectory of criminal justice history has been shaped essentially by significant landmarks that have defined the practices and rules of the system. One of the landmarks was the development of the Magna Carta in 1215, which defined a number of legal principles employed nowadays, like the right to due process. This document not only restricted the powers of the monarchy but also established the principle that no one is beyond the law. Such a principle is essential within the contemporary justice system, ensuring that everyone, irrespective of their status, is accountable to the same legal principles. Consequently, the Magna Carta is a key precursor of contemporary notions of procedural justice, greatly influencing the relationship between state and citizen in terms of legal accountability and citizens' rights. Another significant milestone emerged in the early part of the 20th century with the professional model of policing, in which crime prevention and maintaining public order were promoted through the employment of standardized training for police officers. Before this transformation, the police were usually described as corrupt and inefficient, which contributed to a lack of public confidence. When police academies and intense training programs were introduced, it succeeded in redefining the image of law enforcement as a respected profession. This transformation not only improved police-citizen relations but also set the stage for subsequent criminal justice reforms, emphasizing ethical conduct and procedural justice among law enforcers, which still defines contemporary practices in the justice system. More recent past involves the creation of the My Brothers Keeper Initiative as a critical effort to address systemic injustices that affect vulnerable groups such as those who become involved with the criminal justice system. It focuses on developmental science principles in order to promote positive educational and violence reduction results and ultimately play a role in greater social justice. Moreover, it emphasizes a crucial connection between criminal justice reform and broader civic objectives, i.e., educational success and communal well-being. By interaction with developmental models, policymakers and law enforcers can better understand and tackle the determinants of criminality, supporting the notion that procedural functions within the judicial system must encompass overall strategies towards sustained change and equality of access to justice (Akintoye et al., 2019; Barbarin et al., 2016).

2.1.3. Impact of Historical Events on Current Practices

The historical evolution of the criminal justice system has a deep impact on contemporary practice, particularly in regard to victims' rights. In the last few decades, there has been a powerful trend towards victim-oriented strategies in the law, and this change has been overwhelmingly shaped by increased social awareness of the trauma involved for crime victims. This has produced a trail of reform aimed at overcoming the disadvantage that the victim experiences at every stage of the course of justice. For instance, initiatives to extend advocate services, specialization in police training, and alternative provision for evidence at trial have emerged as backstroke measures to address past failure in the system. These reforms present a revolutionary effort to redefine the procedural roles in the criminal justice context towards easing a more empathetic and better-informed engagement with victims experiences, as noted by Fileborn et al. (2014). Complicating the landscape of the criminal justice system is ongoing debate about the interface between victim rights and the due process rights of the accused. Historical precedent has come to establish strict procedural boundaries favoring the accused due to an initial emphasis on protecting civil liberties. But increasing pressure for victim access in this system now properly challenges the enduring principles of the adversarial process. Policymakers and practitioners are now wrestling with integrating victim-centered reforms without undermining defendants' rights or jeopardizing public justice. Such tensions can be observed in instances such as the introduction of the Victims Focus Scheme, which seeks to reconcile victims' interests with the requirements of positioning within established procedural traditions, as highlighted in Mitchell et al. (2009). The tension between past and current practice at criminal justice is also evident in the evolving roles of various stakeholders, including police, legal representatives, and courts. These actors must adapt and implement reforms that take into consideration and surpass systemic barriers to victims. A survey of criminal justice practitioners emphasizes the need to institutionalize victim-sensitive practices as part of everyday work and surpassing the many factors that can facilitate or weaken these changes. Effective implementation of changes relies on collaboration between the various actors and shifting in culture within the justice system itself. By examining the impact of historical events on the development of procedural roles, we can better understand the process for change towards a more integrated and balanced criminal justice system that is primarily concerned with the needs of all the parties (Figure 2.4).

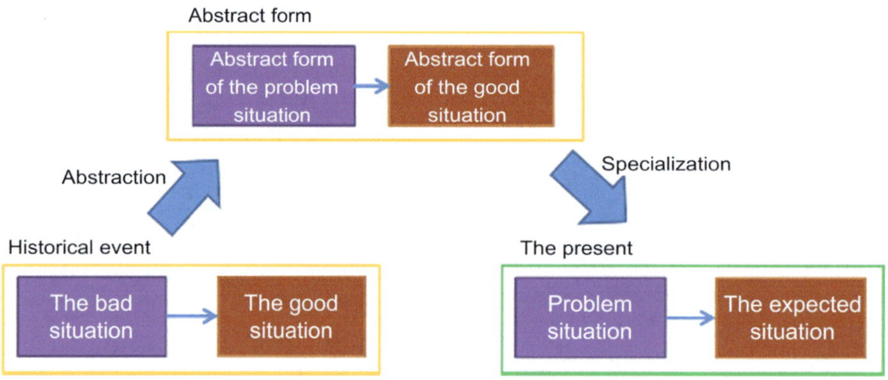

Figure 2.4. Impact of historical events on current practices.

Source: https://www.researchgate.net/publication/281511968/figure/fig1/AS:651875196084229@1532430566935/Application-of-historical-events-to-current-problem.png.

2.2. COMPONENTS OF THE CRIMINAL JUSTICE SYSTEM

The criminal justice system consists of many components, each contributing significantly to maintaining social order and dispensing justice. The core of this system is the law enforcement agencies, who are responsible for crime prevention and crime investigation. Police officers are the initial and frequently best point of contact most citizens will have with the criminal justice system, charged with both the enforcement of laws and exercising their own discretion in enforcing them. That discretion then generates difficult interactions with community, as the effectiveness of efforts at policing are directly tied to public perception and trust. Thus, there needs to be a strong relationship between the law and the community, so there is cooperative participation, which can determine the crime rate and system efficiency. Judicial organizations are also an integral component, which is comprised of courts at varying levels that rule on criminal matters. The judiciary ensures that the legal proceedings are conducted fairly and objectively, interpreting legislations and providing justice in accordance with established procedures. Judges serve the role of presiding over court hearings, providing neutrality and the assurance that rights to all parties are upheld. This is done by ensuring that there is a balance between the rights of the accused and society's interests. The struggle entailed in doing so is reflected in the arguments provided for victims' rights. Contemporary developments, such as the introduction of programs aimed at integrating victims' voices into courtroom processes, highlight the ongoing evolution of the judiciary and their functions and the complexity entailed in attempting to balance the rights of various parties to the criminal justice process (Mitchell et al., 2009). Finally, the correctional system is also a critical component, managing offenders once convicted and facilitating rehabilitation and reintegration back into society. Corrections cover a range of institutions, such as jails, prisons, probation and parole systems, which all focus on the different levels of criminal conduct. The industry works under the policies of rehabilitation and punishment, attempting to lower recidivism while responding to general societal interests. The effectiveness of correctional practice often parallels the difficulty that legal professionals experience in dealing with defendants, particularly in those cases reliant on guilty pleas. The use of pre-sentence reports, for instance, has a significant impact on decision-making within the judiciary and adds strength to the contention that individual circumstances should be considered in the context of court proceedings (Tata et al., 2010). This highlights the fact that all elements of the criminal justice system should work in tandem to promote an equitable and fair result for all parties involved.

2.2.1. Law Enforcement Agencies

The organization of law enforcement agencies is part of the operation of the criminal justice system, as it provides the framework necessary for public safety and enforcing the law. The agencies have operations at various levels, including local, state, and federal levels, with varying jurisdictions and roles. The local police forces are primarily involved in matters at the community level, with roles directed towards crime prevention and reaction. In contrast, federal agencies such as the

FBI and DEA answer calls that transcend state lines, making investigations that require highly specialized assets and expertise. The dynamic among the agencies is critical to the creation of an integrated response to crime, with the need for cooperation between jurisdictions emerging as they grapple with keeping the rule of law and protecting societal interests. In appreciating the procedural roles of law enforcement agencies, one must examine their role and limitations in legal systems. In investigations of crimes, these agencies enjoy extensive discretion, particularly in how they collect evidence, deal with suspects, and respond to the community. Such discretion is necessary as it not only determines the fate of specific cases but also the perceptions of the public on the legitimacy of law enforcements. Because they are the first line of enforcement, police departments must balance their mandates to enforce order and justice with their duty to protect citizens' rights. More transparency and accountability are crucial towards gaining people's confidence since they clear the fears of misuse of authority or indiscriminate use of force that could exist within these agencies. The evolving law enforcement context also necessitates examination of the rising involvement of private resources in government litigation. As organized in recent studies, law enforcement agencies more and more depend on private legal aid, making the line between public and private interests in criminal prosecution obscure. Although the tactic may yield fiscal and operational efficiencies, it raises pertinent questions regarding the preservation of public interest within the criminal justice system. The addition of private lawyers can introduce inherent biases and promote profit-driven litigation as opposed to the welfare of the people, ultimately distorting the integrity of police work. This trend challenges conventional norms of the criminal justice system, bearing witness to an acute need for the reinterpretation of the roles of law enforcement agencies in the context of this trend towards privatization, aimed primarily at the provision of equal and equitable treatment of all citizens (Lemos et al., 2016; Murray et al., 2018) (Figure 2.5).

Figure 2.5. The law enforcement agencies.

Source: https://images.squarespace-cdn.com/content/v1/66140083ebc5ba3f6579eaab/cf773078-d776-49c8-8859-decffcc7642d/shutterstock_699002479.jpg.

2.2.2. Judicial System

The judiciary is a critical element in upholding the rule of law and ensuring justice is administered fairly and equally. It is a system through which the laws are interpreted and enforced, a set of rules under which the adjudication of disputes and criminal behaviour takes place. Central to this role is the adherence to the principle of due process, a term applied to safeguard the individual rights in the course of legal proceedings. This principle serves not just for the safeguard of defendants but also for maintaining public confidence in the justice system. In this context, the effectiveness of interrogation procedures and the rights of the accused become key issues determining the integrity of judicial rulings. As the complexities inherent in other legal systems imply, comparative analysis of such processes reveals how various cultural and historical backgrounds mold dispensation of justice in contemporary societies (Beken et al., 2012). Additionally, trends in judicial systems reveal a great transformation in societal values and norms of rights and obligations. This understanding becomes a requirement when considering reform, particularly in nations that aim to create new judicial systems. For instance, the Western legal model and less institutionalized legal models in terms of principles such as the right to remain silent show the issue at work in broader legal reforming currents. Where coercion by the police continues to be so prevalent in a jurisdiction, the necessity to enforce equitable interrogation practices becomes twofold. These problems highlight the necessity of ongoing legal and institutional innovation that not only reflects international human rights standards but also subscribes to local traditions and expectations of society. Effective reforms must thus achieve this delicate balancing act to enhance the credibility of the justice system to the public (O'Neill et al., 2015). Finally, the reliance of the judiciary and procedural roles on one another highlights the necessity of cooperation among stakeholders like law enforcement, defense attorneys, and the judiciary. The efficiency of these players is essential in maintaining justice without infringing on the rights of individuals. Involvement of international cooperation, particularly in cases of cross-border crime and legal international relations, cannot be circumvented. For instance, frameworks such as the Stockholm Programme highlight the nuances of handling cross-border relationships with compliance to due process rights. With countries venturing into the complexities of globalization, harmonization of disunited legal systems poses challenges as well as opportunities for improvement in judicial efficiency. Under this paradigm, procedure roles must adapt to incorporate best practices in different legal traditions, ultimately making the judicial system more robust in integrity and credibility (Beken et al., 2012).

2.2.3. Correctional Institutions

Correctional institutions form part of the criminal justice system, instilling its procedure roles and grappling with the complexities entailed in mass incarceration. The United States has seen an unprecedented growth of its prisoner base, charting a significant chapter of its penal history. As of late 2014, the country's prison population rose to more than 2,306,100 individuals, supplying proof of the extensive reach of penal establishments in the social framework. The growth has drawn scholars and policymakers toward examining the effectiveness and ramifications of such a broad-based policy of incarceration. As is also evident, recognition is growing that the majority of non-violent offenders, particularly those convicted of drug crimes, may be managed by other means that reduce the deployment of incarceration but also guarantee public safety. The reform debate is reaching a turning point as society begins questioning the role of correctional institutions in rehabilitation rather than the expansion of punitive sanctions (Teague et al., 2016).

The prison processing dynamics also make the function of these prisons in the criminal justice system as a whole more difficult to determine. Over punishment of minor offenses raises immediate moral issues regarding the fairness and efficacy of existing law. Most find themselves experiencing severe consequences beyond official sentencing due to the hidden punishment that accompanies a criminal conviction. These effects habitually lead to decreased social mobility and access to employment, detrimentally impacting marginalized populations disproportionately. The convergence of law enforcement, civil regulatory agencies, and private actors' roles suggests that these agencies frequently employ criminal law for economic gain, which thus entangles their incentive structure to function with punitive measures. This background reveals a troubling dynamic in which the carceral system extends quite beyond its intentional punitive function, provoking calls for reform that account for these sophisticated institutional interests (Jain et al., 2018). As discussion of correctional reform becomes increasingly salient, it is essential to be able to identify institutional incentives driving the persistence of mass incarceration. Today's penal system operates not only under the burden of repressive legislation but also in a context where criminal justice decisions profit various actors. Municipal governments, private probation companies, and employers often take advantage of the presence of a low-level criminal record, which brings in profit streams and serves specific administrative interests. This creates a vicious cycle where the prison dynamics are not amenable to change because they are founded upon a system that is financially rewarding to the majority of actors in the system. It is critical to understand these interdependencies so that comprehensive reform initiatives can be conceptualized that not only tackle punishment excesses but also root out the entrenched systems that perpetuate the prisons' status quo (Jain et al., 2018) (Figure 2.6).

Figure 2.6. Correctional institutions.

Source: https://upload.wikimedia.org/wikipedia/commons/d/da/FCIDanburylarge.jpg.

2.3. ROLES OF LAW ENFORCEMENT

The roles of law enforcement within the criminal justice system are twofold and instrumental in the maintenance of public security and order. The police officers, who dominate and lead the law enforcement, are first to arrive at a crime scene and are responsible for the enforcement of laws, preventing criminals, and arresting offenders. They patrol neighborhoods to deter criminal activity, ensuring that citizens are secure. Moreover, police officers are also required to conduct investigations, such as gathering evidence, interviewing witnesses, and integrating with other agencies in the criminal justice system. This is a pillar for not only the immediate safety of the public but also for the integrity of the entire legal process, focusing on good and sound practice of law enforcement as a part of democracy (Wasem et al., 2004). In addition to the usual policing activities, contemporary police agencies are likely to engage in community-oriented practices with the goal of building a rapport with the public. These involve proactive initiatives, such as community policing, in which police officers undertake collaborative effort with constituents in identifying problems and in finding solutions to crime and safety. With trust and communication, the police can effectively address the real roots of criminality. Programs like the Youth Violence Reduction Partnership (YVRP) are a prime example of such initiatives, aimed at diverting high-risk youth from violence through the synergistic application of coercive monitoring and supportive intervention by probation agents and community organizations (Jucovy et al., 2008). Such positions not only protect the public, but serve as well to promote the broader ends of rehabilitation and reintegrating individuals into society, sounding out an increasingly nuanced conception of crime prevention. In addition, the law enforcers' procedural roles are directly connected to their respect for constitutional norms, which specify how they act in the criminal justice system. Upholding the rule of law requires law enforcers to balance their roles as enforcers and protection of people's rights. For instance, arrest, search, and interrogation procedures are subject to the law's review in order to mitigate abuse of power. Training in ethical conduct and lawful standards is therefore essential to law enforcement officers, having their operations not just compliant with legal mandates but also fostering public trust. As police agencies work more collaboratively with judicial and correctional functions, their role in upholding justice is not just limited to enforcement but a broader obligation toward upholding the rights of all individuals during the course of the criminal justice system (Wasem et al., 2004).

2.3.1. Responsibilities of Police Officers

The responsibilities of police officers are multifaceted and fundamental to the functioning of the criminal justice system. In essence, these officers have the duty of preserving public order and securing citizens in their zones of work. They are tasked with a multitude of activities, from patrolling neighborhoods to respond to emergencies, to investigations and arrests. Moreover, police officers have a mandate to gather and record evidence, thus playing a key role in the prosecution. This all-round role not only calls for physical readiness but also demands officers to exercise sound judgment and uphold high ethical standards. The officers must deal with complex situations and make quick decisions that usually carry dire consequences for people and society at large, thus vindicating the imperative of professionalism and integrity in their policing approach. Apart from the police officers being law enforcers, they are also public servants and have a relationship with members of the community to build cooperation and trust. Establishing cordial relations with members of the community is central to effective policing since it ensures there is an environment where citizens feel safe reporting crimes or requesting assistance. Community policing strategies rest on mutual cooperation between police officers and citizens because they emphasize sharing responsibility for safety and crime prevention. This is a valuable strategy, as it helps to counteract negative police-public images and engenders respect on both sides.

By engaging in joint outreach events and community contact events, officers are in a better position to understand the issues and concerns of the groups they serve and enforce policing strategies more efficiently, with increased support from the population for law enforcement efforts. Furthermore, police officers are expected to exercise ethical obligations to respect the rights of all individuals, upholding justice and fairness principles. This responsibility also extends to enforcing laws without bias on the basis of race, gender, or economic status. Failing to perform these ethical responsibilities not only erodes public confidence but can also have internal issues within the criminal justice system itself. For instance, instances of police coercion, like are evidenced in most studies, raise strong doubts regarding the credibility of evidence generated in the course of investigation (Beken et al., 2012). These issues underscore the importance of training and policy revisions aiming to facilitate procedural justice continually. Moreover, understanding the dynamics of deterrence and compliance can help to inform the best practices for law enforcement and promote a cooperative atmosphere between the police and those communities that they serve (Filteau et al., 2012). By being keen on ethical norms, officers are in a position to make significant progress towards creating a more equitable and just society (Figure 2.7).

Figure 2.7. Responsibilities of police officers.

Source: https://upload.wikimedia.org/wikipedia/commons/e/ee/Very_friendly_MPS_officers_in_London.jpg.

2.3.2. Investigative Procedures

The universe of investigative practices within the criminal justice system is complex and multi-faceted, a balancing act between effective law enforcement and protection of individual rights. Investigative practices are requisite guidelines to direct law enforcement agencies on evidence collection while being mindful of provisions of the constitution. They may vary significantly from one legal system to another based on circumstances of history, culture, and institutions. For example, the difference between European and Chinese interrogations shows how cultural heritages shape legal practices. In China, historically based interrogations have hindered the evolution of rights such as the right to silence, complicating an effort to implement fair interrogations during modern legal reforms (Beken et al., 2012). It is thus of paramount importance to understand these intricacies in order to gauge effectiveness and fairness in investigative practices. Also, an effective investigative process hinges on the balance between collecting vital evidence and maintaining the rights of the accused. In the Egyptian legal system, for instance, the extent of investigative powers garnered by authorities must be carefully studied to prevent chances of abuse, particularly the manner in which private letters between lawyers and firms are dealt with (Greiss et al., 2010). This analysis becomes necessary in identifying the boundaries of legal privilege and that investigation techniques don't breach the rights of the people or organizations. The importance of transparency in the investigation process thus arises with its two-sided role of creating public confidence in the criminal justice system and putting investigative agencies on high alert against accountable behavior. Short of those steps, the integrity of the judicial process is threatened, eventually weakening pursuit of justice. Last but not least, the establishment of investigative procedures reflects broader trends in criminal justice systems worldwide. Because societies are continually confronting new threats like organized crime, terrorism, and cybercrime, the adaptability of investigative structures becomes increasingly vital. That adaptability must constantly be reviewed and reformed on the basis of both national requirements and international best practices. For instance, the global debate on police interrogation practices and protecting human rights echoes across various jurisdictions, which reflects shared values for justice and fairness (Beken et al., 2012). Accordingly, efficient investigation policies are not only expected to adapt to the new paradigm of crime but also prioritize human rights issues first. In doing this, the criminal justice system can seek to maintain an image of legitimacy and public trust, essential for effective law enforcement and cooperation on the part of the community.

2.3.3. Community Policing Initiatives

Community policing initiatives are an innovative paradigm within the broader model of the criminal justice system, centered on the collaboration between law enforcement agencies and the communities that they serve. It tries responding to public safety as a whole by building relationships based on respect and trust. In the process of doing this, police departments engage the community to help identify issues pertinent to the neighborhood and utilize strategies specific to these matters. These programs have the capacity to relax the divide often sensed between police and community, leaving room for citizens to be facilitated to participate actively in crime prevention and solving. The shift from historical, reactive policing to a more proactive, inclusive model not only improves public perceptions of the police but also increases overall community resilience against adversity. The use of restorative justice methods in community policing initiatives is a significant step forward for the criminal justice system. In recent times, 33 police forces within England and Wales have begun applying such methods to their dealing with minor crimes committed by youths and adults. This forward movement recognizes the necessity for different responses that are more centered on healing than on punishment, with a focus on victim experience as well as enabling offender accountability. By working within a policing system through community involvement, restorative justice seeks to respond to not only individual crimes but to the factors that lead to crime. However, there remain obstacles to procedural and cultural adoption of these practices within police agencies that could deter their effective use as part of an integrated community policing approach (Bazemore et al., 2012). In addition, the role of community policing is now more clearly defined within wider policy language at the global level, particularly in terms of external affairs and security arrangements. With European Union being confronted with problematic political environments, community policing practices are deemed essential towards uniting member states as well as neighboring regions to embrace collaborative security strategies. Well-organized legal agreements between police and civil society organizations become critical, particularly due to EU policing provisions as well as procedural justice (O'Neill et al., 2015). These structures ensure that community policing strategies not only work in local contexts but also fit within broader international and structural regulations. Thus, the introduction of community policing programs into the criminal justice system reflects a growing comprehension of public security in recognizing community engagement, procedural justice, and international cooperation (Figure 2.8).

Figure 2.8. Community policing initiatives.

Source: https://officersurvey.com/wp-content/uploads/2023/04/community-policing-.jpeg.

2.4. THE JUDICIAL PROCESS

Judicial process is a key component of the criminal justice system, which consists of the institutions through which justice is administered. This multifaceted process comprises various stages, such as investigation, prosecution, trial, and sentencing, all of which are key to ensuring the rule of law. Through this institution, the interactions between legal actors—judges, prosecutors, defense attorneys, and law enforcement officers—are key. Both discharge special responsibilities working in interdependence of each other to provide a fair trial, protect accused rights, and contribute to public safety. Moreover, the wise application of principles of law at every point affects case judgments and therefore indirectly, public opinion towards justice. As the system evolves, accountability of procedures is necessary to maintain trust and effectiveness in the judicial process. In addition, the evolution of the judicial process is often subject to large-scale cultural and historical factors. Comparative analysis demonstrates differences in judicial processes, particularly when analyzing jurisdictions such as China and Europe.

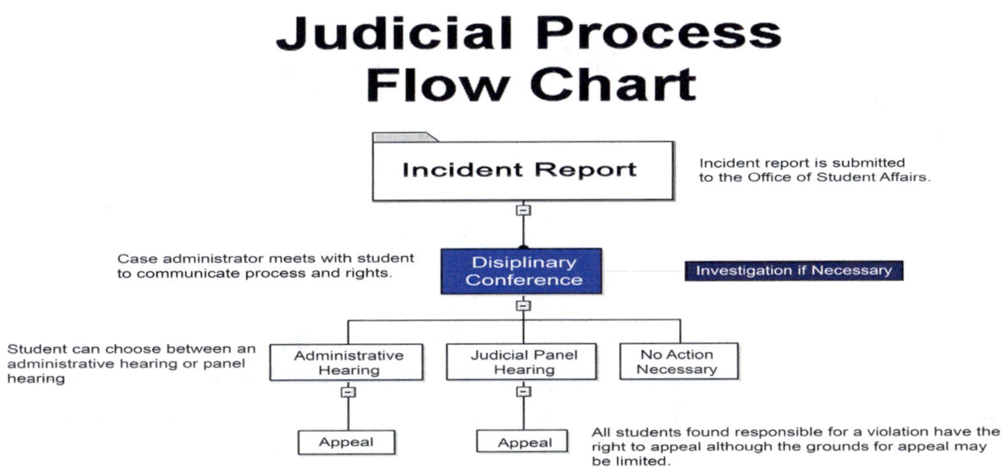

Figure 2.9. The judicial process.

Source: https://www.cotc.edu/sites/main/files/imagecache/lightbox/main-images/judicialflowchart.jpg.

The interrogation procedures in these jurisdictions have developed differently due to different legal traditions. For example, it has been remarked that the absence of an independent right against self-incrimination in China—based on different cultural foundations—is causing difficulties in providing fair interrogation practice. In their involvement with tradition and modem standards, legal reformers underscore the significance of adopting a more cooperative interviewing approach, thus increasing procedural fairness (Beken et al., 2012). Such developments are a reflection of the dynamic nature of the judiciary, demonstrating the need for constant review of legal practice to be in line with evolving social demands. Procedural roles of legal practitioners within the court system are increasingly vital as criminal trial procedures undergo revolutionary changes. China's judicial system, for instance, has undergone significant procedural reform aimed at fostering an adversarial system befitting the expectations of contemporary legal standards. Training institutes, like the China Trial Advocacy Institute, consider very seriously the requirement for judges, prosecutors, and defense attorneys to be highly proficient in trial advocacy and procedure (Lancaster et al., 2006). These training institutions play a vital role in dealing with the dynamics of modern criminal trials and in enhancing the effectiveness of the judiciary. Through enhanced capability, legal practitioners contribute to the establishment of a strong judiciary able to better address the intricate problems of criminal justice while upholding procedural rights. Professional development thus becomes even more significant in emphasizing the pivotal role of procedural knowledge in achieving justice in the judicial process (Figure 2.9).

2.4.1. Structure of the Court System

The structure of the court system is itself the backbone of the criminal justice system, defining the legal framework through which justice is administered. Essentially, the court system is typically made up of a number of levels, each fulfilling different functions. In America, for example, there are state and federal courts, with a hierarchical system comprising trial courts, appeals courts, and a supreme court at each level. This hierarchical system is constructed so that legal issues may be appealed and examined as necessary. Trial courts initially determine cases and determine facts, and the appeals courts review decisions for legal mistake. This division not only guarantees the effective handling of cases but also guarantees the rights of the accused, the procedure being just at all times throughout the judicial process. Further, procedural functions in such courts carry significant influence on the administration of justice. There are specialized procedures at each level of the judicial system that guarantee that the criminal cases are handled effectively. For instance, trial courts follow established rules of procedure to ensure that trials are being conducted in an equitable fashion—avoiding the rights of the defendant and the interests of the state from colliding. Also, the appellate courts are crucial in making lower court judgments available for review, but not again reviewing facts, instead, reviewing legal interpretations and adherence to established law. Such formalistic strictness is needed to help maintain public confidence in the judicial process and prevent arbitrary outcomes. As indicated in most cross-national contexts, the proportionality of the procedural rights is a delicate matter, demonstrated in the comparative examination of criminal questioning procedures across cultures (Beken et al., 2012). Further, looking at the system of the courts and its procedural role shows the necessity for continual reform and adaptation to evolving legal contexts. The biform nature of the system of courts—that is, having both adversarial and inquisitorial traditions—requires innovation in procedural practices to be investigated and, if necessary, integrated. For instance, international criminal justice has emerged as a field where such sensitiveness in balancing these traditions is required under the realities of international crimes. Contemporary scholarly writing prescribes improved institutional architecture and procedural devices that can mobilize the cooperation between the international and the national officials to the extent of enhancing the efficacy of prosecutions (Bibas et al., 2010). As societies respond to the double imperatives of justice and restorative outcomes, the shape and procedures embedded in the court system will unavoidably require responses of adaptation to meet the demands of justice in an increasingly interconnected world (Figure 2.10).

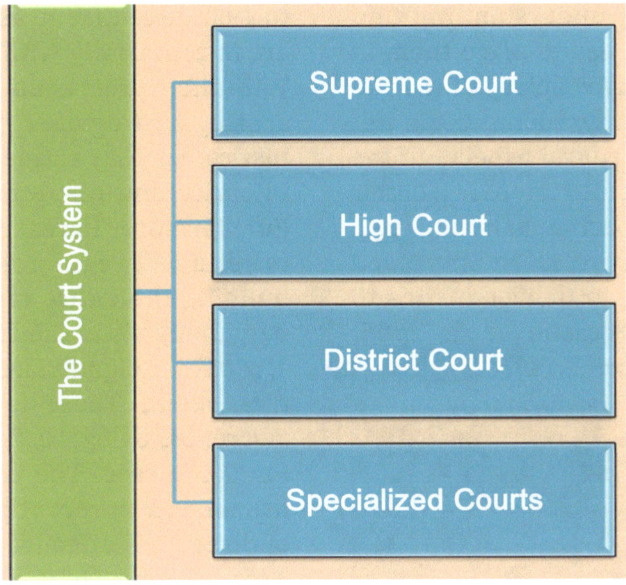

Figure 2.10. The structure of the court system.

Source: https://i0.wp.com/www.managementnote.com/wp-content/uploads/2023/06/Screenshot-2114.png?fit=591%2C487&ssl=1.

2.4.2. Roles of Judges and Prosecutors

The prosecutors and judges' function in the criminal justice process is instrumental to the administration of justice and the maintenance of integrity of legal proceedings. Judges play the role of neutral umpires, facilitating the legal process, making interpretations of laws, and allowing trials to proceed fairly and effectively. Their authority allows them to decide matters of admissibility of evidence, manage jury selections, and decide matters that have substantial effects on the outcome of cases. Moreover, judges have a duty to oversee constitutional protections and avoid the abuse of power by either party. This equilibrium demands a shrewd understanding of procedural and substantive law, thus evidencing the role of judges in shaping the path of justice in any given legal setting. Prosecutors, for their part, carry a twofold burden in that they seek not merely convictions but also an obligation to administer justice. This dual function necessitates them to exercise discretion not only at the pretrial level but also post-conviction, as maintained in recent scholarship on prosecutorial judgment. After the guilt phase is completed, prosecutors must consider strategically such issues as expungement for non-conviction and conviction statistics. This is a reflection of a broader commitment to justice and fairness in the system beyond the utilitarian goal of securing guilty convictions. On this point, the prosecutorial role is not that of an adversary, but as a vital stakeholder in the verification that the judicial system ensures that it performs its ethical mandate to administer justice, hence upholding the integrity of the entire judicial process. Within the framework of global shifts in legal systems, such as are experienced in China, the evolving roles of judges and prosecutors are more vigorously actualized. The fine-tuning of procedural procedures, as is evident in efforts such as that of the China Trial Advocacy Institute, reflects increased sensitivity to the need for legal practitioners to be capable of surviving new adversarial frameworks. Such an adaptation demands that judges and prosecutors across various jurisdictions constantly upgrade their understanding and application of legal principles to place them in the best position to maneuver through intricate criminal cases. Consequently, such growth not only strengthens the procedural aspects in the criminal justice system but also imposes a better moral and equitable approach to handling legal disputes, making sure there is an improved debate on what it means to deliver justice to contemporary society (Lancaster et al., 2006; Murray et al., 2018) (Figure 2.11).

Figure 2.11. The roles of judges and prosecutors in the criminal justice system.

Source: https://assets.aclu.org/live/uploads/2019/09/web17-prosecutorjudge-1160x768.jpg.

2.4.3. The Importance of Defense Attorneys

The criminal defense lawyer's contribution to the criminal justice system is crucial to the protection of the accused criminals' rights. They operate on the basis that every single defendant is entitled to zealous defense, a right well entrenched by the historical decision of Gideon v. Wainwright. This case confirmed that defendants who cannot afford counsel must be given legal representation by the state, hence placing a great significance on proper legal representation during a fair trial. Defense attorneys not only contest prosecution's evidence but also attempt to guarantee that all aspects of the legal process are in conformity with constitutional standards. With their professional expertise, they serve as a safeguard against potential miscarriages of justice, so that the legal system operate with integrity and respect for the accused's rights. Furthermore, defense lawyers' work extends beyond the courtroom; they contribute to building the entire criminal justice system. By bargaining pleas, they negotiate conclusions that can have a significant influence on the lives of their clients. These negotiations also require an awareness of legal concepts and social situations for every case. The criminal defense situation has shifted in recent years because the charge of direct or ineffective assistance of counsel has become prevalent in habeas corpus cases. These claims also support effective representation of the law and greater expectations from defense counsel. Dialogue among defense attorneys and other systemic actors can enable systemic reform, and as the discussion continues, the information being learned by defense attorneys can be invaluable contributions to enhancing the justice process itself (Garrett et al., 2013). Beyond professional obligations as legal professionals, defense attorneys must continually adapt in line with changing legal contexts and developing practices in order to serve their clients suitably. For instance, the focus on adversarial processes has changed the paradigm of legal practice and education globally, putting greater emphasis on skill development for defense practitioners. These cooperative efforts like the China Trial Advocacy Institute reflect greater awareness that successful trial advocacy is essential in today's legal systems. These training programs are aimed at giving lawyers the skills necessary to successfully conduct complex criminal procedures. Defense attorneys grow more competent in representing accused persons as they participate in such programs, hence maintaining the stipulation that everyone is entitled to a fair trial and competent legal assistance (Lancaster et al., 2006).

2.5. CORRECTIONAL SYSTEM FUNCTIONS

The correctional system serves a number of critical functions in the overall criminal justice system, and its core role is managing and treating offenders. At the core of everything, the correctional system serves the role of safeguarding the public from the offenses that have been perpetrated by the offenders by keeping them in seclusion and reducing their harm to society. Concurrently, it tries to provide rehabilitation opportunities that will set the stage for effective reintegration into society. This dual purpose shows the intrinsic contradiction within the correctional system because employees have to manage the competing demands of ensuring public safety while facilitating the rehabilitation of offenders. The ethical complexity of this dual role is more evident as practitioners seek to reconcile the safeguarding of populations with the necessity to treat human beings with dignity, towards a fineness of approach to matters of correction as espoused in contemporary literature (Andrews et al., 2015). Mass incarceration has been the primary challenge confronting the American correction system over recent decades, to the point of receiving broad condemnation and publicity.

Figure 2.12. The correctional system serves multiple critical functions.

Source: https://www.goodwin.edu/enews/wp-content/uploads/2020/05/Types-of-Correctional-Officers-You-Can-Become-with-an-Associate-Degree-1920x768.jpg.

The United States is also accountable for a record proportion of the world's prisoners, with a mind-bogglingly huge population of inmates warehoused inside its prisons. The War on Drugs, in particular, has been directly accountable for this scourge, imprisoning individuals for non-violent offenses, thus fueling the fire of arguments over whether policies are just and effective or not. Several scholars argue that the unbridled expansion of prison buildings has not only fallen short of its promise to reduce crime but has also further entrenched social ills such as poverty and inequality. There is growing public recognition within the political and academic communities that incarceration alternatives, i.e., community-based interventions, could offer a helpful strategy for addressing some forms of crime without wasting criminal justice resources (Teague et al., 2016). The addition of RJ principles to the correctional system has the potential to assist in resolving some of the systemic challenges currently faced. This approach moves toward a more integrated understanding of justice, one that prioritizes the interests of offenders and victims alike and produces accountability and healing. By emphasizing dialogue and restorative action over punishment, RJ models can decrease some of the ethical unease practitioners experience in carceral contexts. Additionally, the implementation of RJ practices can promote stronger community ties and a more supportive setting for rehabilitating offenders. This not only is in keeping with the overall goals of rehabilitation but also counteracts the negative social consequences related to punitive imprisonment. Thus, the inclusion of RJ in correctional processes can offer a powerful way of rethinking the correctional systems role in a more effective and equitable manner (Andrews et al., 2015) (Figure 2.12).

2.5.1. Types of Correctional Facilities

The geography of prisons is diverse and encompasses a variety of types of institutions designed to serve different functions in the criminal justice system. Among the primary categories are federal prisons, state prisons, and local jails. Federal prisons typically hold offenders convicted of federal crimes and are operated by the Federal Bureau of Prisons. State prisons hold offenders convicted of offenses against the state and generally house longer-term inmates. County jails detain individuals in pretrial detention or short-sentence detainees for misdemeanor offenses, and they are most likely to detain individuals serving short sentences for misdemeanor offenses. Each of these institution types has varying regulations and levels of security, highlighting the complexities of imprisonment in a system coping with mass incarceration and its impacts on society (Teague et al., 2016). Another form of correctional facility is the juvenile detention center, which addresses the interests of youths who have found themselves engaged in legal problems. These centers not only aim at detaining youths who commit crimes but also at rehabilitating them from their criminal acts through counseling and education. The system of juvenile justice believes more in rehabilitation than in punishment, since there is greater acknowledgment of distinctions in adolescent and adult development. This policy is one of reform and reintegration into society and places juvenile detention facilities as central elements of an emerging criminal justice system. The contrasting conditions of adult and juvenile institutions emphasize the necessity of unique approaches that meet the distinct challenges and potential of various offender types (Denno et al., 2016). This is also supported by alternative mechanisms to traditional imprisonment, including halfway houses and community corrections programs. Such facilities strive to reintegrate offenders into society in ways that prevent recidivism and promote reentry. Halfway houses provide structured environments that result in responsibility with some degree of freedom preserved. Community corrections work emphasizes probation or parole supervision so that offenders can be integrated into community life while fulfilling legal responsibilities. Such alternatives align with current criminal justice reform movements, which strive to minimize dependence on incarceration as a core punishment mechanism. Diversifying correctional facilities and forms of incarceration helps ensure that the system develops more effective methods for dealing with criminal behavior and maintaining rehabilitation (Teague et al., 2016).

2.5.2. Rehabilitation vs. Punishment

The debate over rehabilitation versus punishment within the criminal justice system highlights the underlying tension between promoting general safety within society and promoting individual transformation. Historically, the punitive perspective has dominated the debate, emphasizing retribution over rehabilitation. This perspective is more likely to emphasize preserving society in the short term through imprisonment, with offender transformation having limited scope. However, there are arguments against such a strategy for failing to address the underlying causes of criminality and leaving us with unrealistically high rates of recidivism. By contrast, rehabilitation is trying to reintegrate individuals into society by addressing psychological, social, and economic reasons for their crime. This philosophical shift reflects a growing recognition that effective criminal justice policy must focus on long-term solutions rather than punitive ones. Besides, the integration of rehabilitative responses into the criminal justice system offers a way of breaking the cycle of crime. Education, vocational rehabilitation, and mental health treatment have shown promising results in reducing recidivism, thereby addressing the needs of both offenders and society. For instance, restorative justice models offer a participatory process that seeks to restore victim-offender relationships, foster accountability and empathy, and maximize benefits. By keeping the healing of individuals and communities as a first priority, these types of programs can balance out the risk of dissonance for practitioners in forensic and correctional environments, as addressed in dual role analysis in rehabilitation and punishment programs (Andrews et al., 2015). Integrating restorative practices creates an ethical context in which both rehabilitation of individuals and public safety are considered important. Secondly, a critical examination of prosecutorial discretion reveals additional nuances in overriding the mere punishment with rehabilitation. After the guilt has been determined by the legal process, many avenues for diminishing the punitive impact of the criminal justice system are available, particularly regarding expungement procedures. As highlighted in recent controversies, the role of the prosecutor is not just confined to convictions during trials, and there is a need for a redefinition of their role in guaranteeing justice on the offenders path post-conviction (Murray et al., 2018). This broadened scope promotes an expansive approach to procedural roles where punishment and rehabilitation are not opposing forces but complementary forces that can increase harmony in society and in human growth. This approach redefines the shared narrative, suggesting a balanced use of both principles as being able to create a more equitable criminal justice system (Figure 2.13).

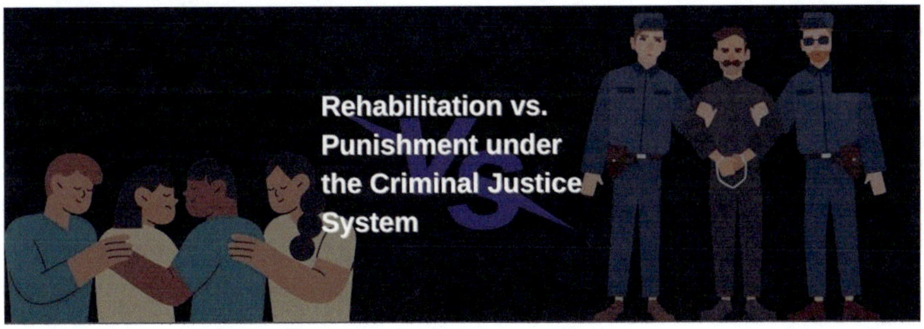

Figure 2.13. Rehabilitation vs. punishment.

Source: https://bnblegal.com/wp-content/uploads/2024/12/Rehabilitation-vs-Punishment-under-the-Criminal-Justice-System.jpg.

2.5.3. Challenges in the Correctional System

The correctional system faces numerous challenges, primarily due to the complexity of handling prison populations while maintaining justice and rehabilitation. It is high recidivism rates that highlight the system's failures when rehabilitation gives way to punishment. Education and vocational training programs, intended to prepare inmates for release, are inadequately funded, providing environments where inmates are ill-equipped for society. Offenders' mental illness, furthermore, is left untreated too frequently, continuing the cycle of incarceration. Effective therapeutic practices might neutralize such issues, but the money to implement them is often lacking in prisons, creating a dilemma between the intent of rehabilitation and the supply of punishment. Such a dilemma necessitates engaging in comprehensive reform, primarily in designing programs that do not solely concern public safety but also the offenders' well-being, potentially reducing recidivism over time. Moreover, ethical problems faced by correctional professionals bring an added dimension of complexity to the correctional process. The dual-role dilemma is one which continually puts the practitioner in a position where he or she must balance the inmates' health with safety concerns for the community. The dilemma is capable of creating dissonance that precludes effective decision-making and degrades the effectiveness of rehabilitation services. Implementation of Restorative Justice (RJ) models in the practice of correction, as the new literature in the field advocates for, presents a viable avenue to the resolution of such ethical challenges. RJ places emphasis on responsibility and harm restoration that can foster positive relationships between victims and offenders, thereby redirecting perceptions of justice. By moving the emphasis from punishment in itself to reconciliation, practitioners are able to engage more ethically and effectively into the intricacies of their role within the justice system (Andrews et al., 2015). Furthermore, management of social order within prisons is significant in presenting challenging issues which increase the troubled context of inmate interactions and institutional stability. The austere rules that govern prison life tend to serve the purpose of ensuring order is maintained, but in so doing, these rules have the propensity to create a vicious cycle of violence and inequality among prisoners. As discussed in the description of social systems in prisons, the rules are aimed at reproducing the given regime rather than towards creating a rehabilitative context. This intense enforcement thus fosters inequality among convicted people, resulting in heightened tensions and conflicts. It is necessary that correctional policymakers and personnel understand the nuanced social processes at work, so that they create a rehabilitative environment supporting good behavior, ultimately for the overall effectiveness and integrity of the correctional system (Bradford et al., 2010).

2.6. PROCEDURAL JUSTICE

In procedural justice analysis of the context of the criminal justice system, balancing the rights of the accused and those of the victims is essential. Procedural justice emphasizes fairness in procedures that lead to consequences, which argues that people should have a say in matters concerning them, particularly in criminal cases. Yet this concept is threatened by the traditional adversary system, in that rigid adherence to due process protections for the accused can deny the victims a chance to contribute positively towards the judicial process. Current evolutions, such as the implementation of the Victims Focus Scheme within England and Wales, signal the emergence of an evolving context in which the focus on victim participation raises critical policy questions about re-adjusting the systems normative parameters. The tension between preserving due process for defendants and providing victims with a voice continues to shape discussion on procedural justice in contemporary legal contexts (Mitchell et al., 2009).

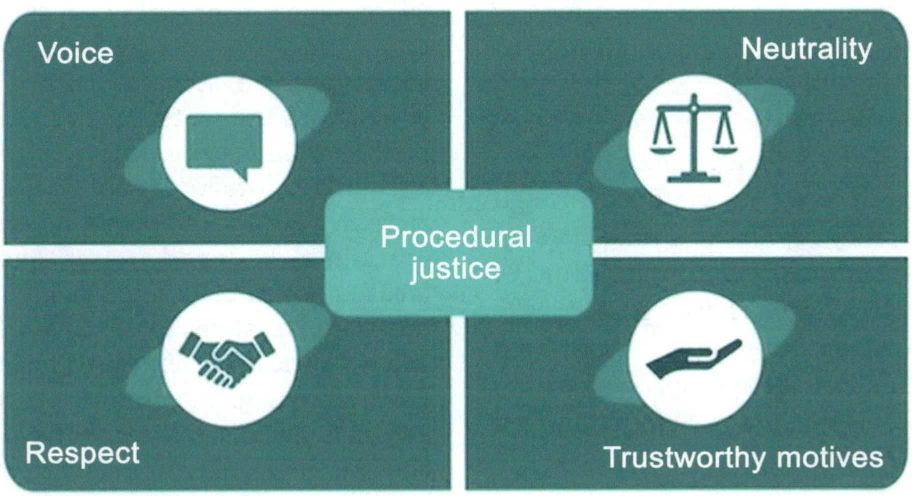

Figure 2.14 The procedural justice within the framework of the criminal justice system.

Source: https://media.licdn.com/dms/image/v2/C4D12AQHPs-Gqf4Z50g/article-cover_image-shrink_600_2000/article-cover_image-shrink_600_2000/0/1622190039640?e=2147483647&v=beta&t=lxW2O63x-GRWCqDlu1ULXRIOD-x_RpjDHu0iBUwW56U.

The subject of order both in society in general and in the specific case of the criminal justice system is similarly significant within the understanding of procedural justice. Hope for order in most societies is likely to shape the behavior and contact in institutions, including prisons. In prison settings, for instance, policy and law strive to maintain an externally imposed order and control hierarchy, but the existing structures can conceal the facts of justice and equality. Procedural justice tends to be implemented as a way of exerting control rather than enforcing rehabilitation, and it challenges how procedural justice can be implemented effectively. Because such systems rigidly adhere to specified norms of acceptable behavior—frequently ignoring individual rights to fairness and agency—the transparency of order is less just and more about maintaining a status quo that quite frequently quiets the voices of the affected (Bradford et al., 2010). Thus, the intersection of procedural justice and the working dynamics of the criminal justice system reveals a complex interplay of interests that must be negotiated through to achieve equity and fairness. Efforts to incorporate victim interests raise essential questions about how such changes impact the due process rights of the accused. As the justice system evolves, stakeholders must critically assess the implications of prioritizing victim voices while safeguarding the foundational rights of defendants. Ultimately, the future of procedural justice rests upon a commitment to fostering dialogue between all parties involved, ensuring that justice is not only administered lawfully but perceived as legitimate and fair by all who engage with the system. Through these dialogues, they represent a valuable step towards more extensive comprehension of justice, where roles are determined procedurally through collaboration and progress is achieved towards solutions that are appropriate for both victims and accused individuals alike (Mitchell et al., 2009) (Figure 2.14).

2.6.1. Definition and Principles of Procedural Justice

Theory of procedural justice is also sustained by ethical principles that compel reasonableness and transparency in judicial processes. Procedural justice, as a norm, is distinguished from the outcomes of judicial verdicts but focuses on the processes through which laws are enforced and adjudicated. The heart of procedural justice is the belief that individuals always tend to perceive the legal system as legitimate if they believe that the procedures are respectful and fair. Being treated with fairness by authorities matters, since individuals are concerned about how decisions are being made just as much as they concern themselves with what decisions are made. This emphasis on just procedures promotes public confidence in the criminal process and causes cooperation and compliance from citizens along with enhanced overall social stability. It is in the heart of procedural justice that the notion of individualized suspicion is considered to be significant, where there needs to be specific evidence available before one can be accused of criminal activity. This principle highlights the importance of less general law enforcement—where, rather than being able to guess, law enforcement officials are required to make decisions based on concrete evidence regarding an individual. As detailed in descriptions of probable cause, individualized suspicion is a central aspect of legal legitimacy, based on which interventions such as detentions or searches are justified. The move away from mass profiling towards evidence-based action not only protects people's rights but also increases public confidence in policing practices. Procedural justice advocates thus demand such focused procedures for ensuring the integrity of the justice system, reminding all that fairness and rights lie at its very core (Taslitz et al., 2010). Furthermore, principles of procedural justice may also differ significantly from one legal and cultural environment to another, as evidenced by differences between Western and Eastern law. In environments in which procedural norms are very much shaped by history and culture, as is the situation with China, perceptions of fairness in interrogatory and trial procedure may also differ significantly from those of Western society. This imbalance comes into clear relief in reflection on the rights of a person in interrogation, where traditional and institutional norms regulate the degree of procedural justice. The legislative reforms needed to enhance procedural justice must remain attuned to these cultural nuances even as they aim for an international benchmark of equity in the criminal justice system. As comparative research illustrates, drawing on traditional legal systems can mean significant improvement in practices such as collaborative interviewing, with the ultimate aim of eliminating coercive methods that degrade trust and integrity in the judicial process (Beken et al., 2012) (Figure 2.15).

Figure 2.15. The concept of procedural justice.

Source: https://www.clio.com/wp-content/uploads/2024/12/Blog_Blog-Procedural-Justice.png.

2.6.2. The Role of Fairness in Legal Proceedings

The concept of fairness during court hearings is a cornerstone of the justice system that rests upon which the people's rights and credibility of judicial outcomes are founded. Fairness ensures the existence of procedural safeguard so that there is impartial treatment regardless of parties.

Central to this is the belief that defendants are to be given a clear understanding of the charges brought against them, transparency of procedure within the law, and access to quality legal representation. As long as these factors are adequately enforced, they pave the way for a system where not just is justice meted out but is perceived to be so too. In so doing, fairness is not only an elementary right but also a watchdog of social order in the juridical arena, reinforcing confidence in the judicial institution as such. Besides, legal fairness is also determined by culture and history, which could result in varying interpretations and uses of fairness in juridical practicability. For instance, while democratic cultures are likely to emphasize the right to remain silent and immunity from self-incrimination, other legal cultures will utilize various techniques drawn from their own backgrounds.

Comparative studies show that fairness is never perceived similarly because, as with differing interrogation rules in Europe and China, there are varying influences from ancient civilizations which have given rise to prevailing legal cultures. According to the findings, a "homegrown autonoeoe" form of rights such as the privilege against self-incrimination may emerge in a variety of ways in various legal systems, thus having an impact on broader social meaning of fairness and justice in legal systems of crime (Beken et al., 2012). Furthermore, within confines of prisons, social order can explain the significance of fairness in legal proceedings. Prisons are highly visible social orders governed by formal rules that guide behavior and accountability. It is necessary to distinguish, however, between maintaining order and maintaining justice because the rules can inadvertently perpetuate injustice if applied properly. Effective legal processes must deliberately do as much as possible to impose individual rights in the face of these prevailing orders, establishing the space in which procedural fairness is dominant. The constantly evolving background of prisons demonstrates the manner in which deeply rooted structures complicate notions of justice, thus bringing into focus the importance of fair legal processes in the preservation of both individual liberty as well as the overall ethical background of the criminal justice system (Bradford et al., 2010) (Figure 2.16).

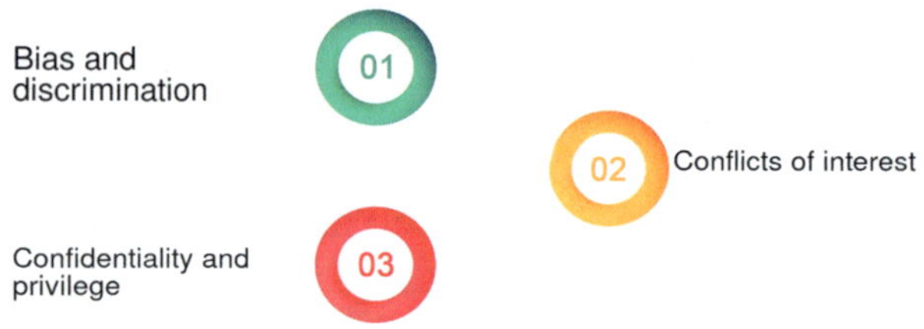

Figure 2.16. The role of fairness in legal proceedings.

Source: https://fastercapital.co/i/Ethical-law--How-to-practice-and-enforce-law-in-a-way-that-is-ethical-and-just--Ensuring-Fairness-and-Justice-in-Legal-Proceedings.webp.

2.6.3. Impact of Procedural Justice on Public Perception

The procedural justice theory is fundamental to how the police are viewed by the public as well as the overall criminal justice system. When police exercise fair and transparent processes in addressing the community, there is an increase in the legitimation of their policing and thereby public trust in the same. This concept is encapsulated in Tylers process-based model of policing, whereby seeing law enforcement as fair makes citizens and groups more inclined to obey the law.

By such displays of impartiality, consistency, and commitment to the protection of legal rights, police can transform encounters into positive reflections on community government. Procedural justice is thus not a theoretical construct but a practical design for policing that unites individuals and law enforcement agencies in collaborative partnerships, ultimately towards social order and civic responsibility (Modise et al., 2024). Additionally, procedural justice not only affects individual attitudes but continues to affect institutional legitimacy and operational performance. Members of the community, having been treated fairly, act in support of law enforcement programs, thereby facilitating crime prevention operations and facilitating participation from the community in safety activities. This is particularly crucial for communities that have previously been underpinned by distrust and strained relations. By emphasizing procedural fairness, law enforcement can reshape their identities as collaborative partners in public safety rather than as mere enforcers. The integration of procedural justice principles into police training and policy can greatly enhance the credibility of law enforcement agencies as being fair and representative of the communities they serve. Public support, in turn, legitimates the functioning capacity of the justice system, suggesting that procedural justice is both a process and outcome within community obedience and approval of the law (Modise et al., 2024). Effects of procedural justice also appear in legal structures like the Canadian Charter of Rights and Freedoms, which reshaped interaction between the police and the public. The Charter introduced essential judicial safeguards and principles requiring police to operate within a framework emphasizing rights, thereby aligning policing practice with democratic values. Contrary to the initial concerns that the Charter would undermine law enforcement, its impact has facilitated a radical shift towards Canadian due process-based policing. This shift not only enhances the effectiveness of police operations but also profoundly impacts public perceptions of legitimacy within the justice system. As citizens witness strict compliance with procedural safeguards, they may perceive the police as more likely to be regarded as guardians of their rights rather than adversaries. This confirms the argument that legal systems' requirement of procedural fairness has a significant impact on public confidence and trust in the criminal justice system.

SUMMARY

In an examination of the intricate dynamics of the criminal justice system and the procedural roles, it is clear that a comprehensive understanding of these facets is crucial towards the protection of individuals' rights. The blending of successful legal representation is a cornerstone of justice, best exemplified by the historical context of Gideon v. Wainwright. The decision established the foundation that the right to counsel was implicit and created the framework of criminal defense and shaped the necessity of effective representation. As procedural functions evolve, ongoing examination is required to meet the precepts of justice, particularly as claims of ineffective assistance of counsel are more and more preeminent in habeas corpus cases. While doing so, the judiciary is not simply required to ensure representation but must indeed react to evolving standards that support effective defense technique (Garrett et al., 2013). In addition, the challenges of the criminal justice system indicate the intersection of law, social science, and historical contingency in shaping procedural norms. The continuing debate over the practice of interrogation refers to the need for legal systems that are culturally and historically attuned. Comparing the development of the procedures of interrogation in different legal cultures, primarily between Europe and China, we observe how different historical trajectories forge contemporary practice. In spite of the constraints on the potential for far-reaching reform in certain circumstances, there is powerful argument for consolidating the classical legal materials into their support of collaborative interrogation methods. This would minimize abuses and enhance the fairness of criminal trials, in direction of the further goal of an equitable system of law (Beken et al., 2012). Finally, the research about the procedural functions of the criminal justice system paints a picture by both promise and problem. As the field sets about to contend with the ramification of inadequate defense, the necessity for a sophisticated understanding of legal representation cannot be overstated. The collaboration of the legal and social science communities can create firmer standards of effective defense sensitive to the evolving demands of society. Establishing an atmosphere that values people's rights while taking care to ensure that procedural systems are dynamic enough to address shifting contexts will be crucial in the process of the ongoing advancement of justice. In accepting these nuances, the criminal justice system can more comfortably situate itself within the concepts of fairness and equality, providing a more equitable legal arena for all people involved.

In learning the complexity of the criminal justice system, it is essential to highlight the roles of the various practitioners, namely those in forensic and correctional work. These roles overlap, reflecting a dissonance between ethical duty to clients and the broader duty of ensuring public safety. Practitioners are frequently haunted by dissonance as they try to balance these competing mandates. This ethical dilemma is also exacerbated by the relationships created between criminals and their victims and it suggests that a broader conceptualization is needed to understand the consequences of dual roles in the system. Restorative Justice (RJ) research can offer a paradigm that satisfies these ethical mandates while allowing for a deeper sense of interconnectedness of individual experience within the justice process, ultimately guiding practitioners toward more holistic practice approaches (Andrews et al., 2015). Procedural roles of criminal justice system also assume significant forms across various cultures. A comparative analysis underscores the historical evolution of the interrogation process in Europe and China, emphasizing cultural and institutional variations for constructing legal processes. An understanding of these differences is central to establishing fair interrogation standards everywhere. Importantly, legal institutions of both the ancient Greek and Chinese civilizations have been influenced by early philosophies, leading to varied approaches to interrogation. In this context of history, any Chinese reforms in the future may be tested by ingrained customs, particularly concerning rights like the right against self-incrimination. Nevertheless, a reflective examination of traditional interviewing traditions might assist in crafting a more cooperative interrogation regime, bringing about more criminal questioning fairness (Beken et al., 2012). Further examination of the roles in the criminal justice system provides the significance of the ongoing ethical debates and how they are influencing procedural practices. Accessing approaches such as Restorative Justice not only deals with the ethical dilemmas experienced by practitioners of justice but also facilitates a victim-focused orientation within the system. Instances in which the double professional roles create ethical dilemmas put into perspective the imperative of structural reform with a view to promoting openness, accountability, and fairness. This harmonization of ethical issues with procedural tools is central to developing a system of justice responsive to safeguarding the rights of all parties involved while effectively maintaining public order. As both researchers and practitioners continue to look ahead and navigate these concerns, the combination of historical context and contemporary ethical standards will be central in shaping the future criminal justice landscape and its procedural mechanisms.

A LOOK TO THE FUTURE

THE FUTURE OF THE CRIMINAL JUSTICE SYSTEM

The evolution of the criminal justice system will be significantly influenced by advances in technology and changes in societal norms. As the world becomes increasingly digital, law enforcement agencies are adopting new technologies such as artificial intelligence and data analytics to enhance their powers of investigation. While these technological advancements make processes easier, they are also accompanied by urgent ethical concerns related to surveillance and privacy. An example is predictive policing, which can give rise to biases in law enforcement, where certain communities are disproportionately picked as targets according to algorithmic decisions. As the European Union develops legal structures that place procedural assurances and core rights first, the challenge would be to balance the efficacy of such mechanisms with the requirement for human rights and civil liberties safeguards, a mandate starkly underscored in the discussions on the AFSJ and how it impacts policing and prosecution under. Moreover, the more widely embraced restorative justice models become, the more the criminal justice system paradigm can shift in a rehabilitative direction and be focused on victims' and offenders' interests. This is in outright contrast to a punitive approach and provides a structure that facilitates accountability and healing. The doubled tasks of practitioners in the corrections and forensic professions necessitate a careful balancing act on the tightrope of ethical dilemmas, as noted in recent critical assessment of criminal justice practice. Pointing to cooperative approaches to justice can demystify tensions between the public safety and the rehabilitation of individuals. Through the integration of restorative justice philosophy with moral acquaintance models, practitioners are better equipped to confront multi-faceted ethical dilemmas.

This shift not only reshapes institutional functions throughout the justice system but also places it in the position to respond to the multifaceted needs of society. In the future, prudent international cooperation will be crucial to charting the course of the criminal justice system. With ongoing globalization across borders, the complexities of transnational crime—ranging from trafficking in persons to cybercrimes—demand a unified response. The role of the European Union in establishing rapport with neighboring nations by using the paradigm of AFSJ proves the importance of cooperative mechanisms while addressing such illegal networks. These relationships, though, have to be developed keeping a clear understanding of the diverse legal frameworks and ethical standards prevailing globally. An assurance that extradition and mutual legal assistance frameworks maintain core principles of justice and human rights will continue to prove to be an issue. The future of the criminal justice system will rest ultimately in how it manages to bring these international subtleties together with a commitment to a principle of fairness and justice for all involved, marking the intricate dance between power and responsibility.

REFERENCES

1. Akintoye, S., & Joshua, A. (2019). Evaluation of the rule of law as a pre-requisite to the right to development in Africa. https://core.ac.uk/download/287585180.pdf (accessed on 13th August 2025).
2. Andrews, D. A., Appelbaum, P. S., Arrigo, B. A., Engelhardt, H. T., Glaser, B., Gutheil, T. G., Johnstone, G., et al. (2015). Restorative justice-informed moral acquaintance: Resolving the dual role problem in correctional and forensic practice. https://core.ac.uk/download/30712423.pdf (accessed on 13th August 2025).
3. Barbarin, O. A., Tolan, P., Graham, S., & McBride Murry, V. (2016). Development of boys and young men of color: Implications of developmental science for My Brother's Keeper Initiative. https://core.ac.uk/download/75761678.pdf (accessed on 13th August 2025).
4. Barry, M., Dignan, J., Duff, R., Faulkner, D., Johnstone, G., Doak, J., Henham, R., et al. (2009). Victims and the sentencing process: Developing participatory rights? https://core.ac.uk/download/30638311.pdf (accessed on 13th August 2025).
5. Bazemore, G., Brain, T., Clamp, K., Crawford, A., Daly, K., Dignan, J., et al. (2012). Exploring recent developments in restorative policing in England and Wales. https://core.ac.uk/download/42539720.pdf (accessed on 13th August 2025).
6. Bibas, S., & Burke-White, W. W. (2010). International idealism meets domestic-criminal-procedure realism. https://core.ac.uk/download/62560142.pdf (accessed on 13th August 2025).
7. Blockx, F. (2018). A comparison of the American model and French (-inspired) appellate model. https://core.ac.uk/download/213020912.pdf (accessed on 13th August 2025).
8. Bradford, B., Gerber, M., Hohl, K., Hough, M., et al. (2013). Trust and legitimacy across Europe: A FIDUCIA report on comparative public attitudes towards legal authority. https://core.ac.uk/download/16379434.pdf (accessed on 13th August 2025).
9. Bradford, B., Jackson, J., Shiner, M., Taylor, G., et al. (2010). Legitimacy and procedural justice in prisons. https://core.ac.uk/download/96325.pdf (accessed on 13th August 2025).
10. Classen, S. (2007). Lawyers not in love, *The Defenders* and sixties TV. https://digitalcommons.georgefox.edu/cgi/viewcontent.cgi?article=1019&context=comm_fac (accessed on 13th August 2025).
11. Denno, D. W. (2016). Foreword. https://core.ac.uk/download/144231725.pdf (accessed on 13th August 2025).
12. Fileborn, B., & Bluett-Boyd, N. (2014). Victim/survivor-focused justice responses and reforms to criminal court practice: Implementation, current practice and future directions. https://core.ac.uk/download/pdf/30674908.pdf (accessed on 13th August 2025).
13. Filteau, M. R. (2012). Deterring defiance: 'Don't give a poacher a reason to poach.' https://core.ac.uk/download/159563657.pdf (accessed on 13th August 2025).
14. Garrett, B. L. (2013). Validating the right to counsel. https://core.ac.uk/download/213020469.pdf (accessed on 13th August 2025).
15. Greiss, M. (2010). Investigative powers of the Egyptian Competition Authority: A guide for companies in the Egyptian market. https://core.ac.uk/download/2710011.pdf (accessed on 13th August 2025).

16. Jain, E. (2018). Capitalizing on criminal justice. https://core.ac.uk/download/213020057.pdf (accessed on 13th August 2025).
17. Jucovy, L., & McClanahan, W. S. (2008). Reaching through the cracks: A guide to implementing the Youth Violence Reduction Partnership. https://core.ac.uk/download/71341367.pdf (accessed on 13th August 2025).
18. Lancaster, R., & Ding, X. (2006). Addressing the emergence of advocacy in the Chinese criminal justice system: A collaboration between a U.S. and a Chinese law school. https://core.ac.uk/download/144226114.pdf (accessed on 13th August 2025).
19. Lemos, M. H. (2016). Privatizing public litigation. https://core.ac.uk/download/62570849.pdf (accessed on 13th August 2025).
20. Modise, J. M. (2024). Increasing community involvement in law enforcement through procedural justice to improve ties with the community. https://core.ac.uk/download/654958947.pdf (accessed on 13th August 2025).
21. Murray, B. M. (2018). Unstitching scarlet letters? Prosecutorial discretion and expungement. https://core.ac.uk/download/216957629.pdf (accessed on 13th August 2025).
22. O'Neill, M. (2015). The development of the external dimension of the AFSJ: New challenges of the EU legal and policy framework. https://core.ac.uk/download/228177580.pdf (accessed on 13th August 2025).
23. Taslitz, A. E. (2010). What is probable cause, and why should we care? The costs, benefits, and meaning of individualized suspicion. https://core.ac.uk/download/62553070.pdf (accessed on 13th August 2025).
24. Tata, C. (2010). A sense of justice: The role of pre-sentence reports in the production (and disruption) of guilt and guilty pleas. https://core.ac.uk/download/9031164.pdf (accessed on 13th August 2025).
25. Teague, M. (2016). Mass incarceration: The juggernaut of American penal expansionism. https://core.ac.uk/download/46171414.pdf (accessed on 13th August 2025).
26. Vander Beken, T., & Wu, W. (2012). Relativism and universalism in interrogation fairness: A comparative analysis between Europe and China. https://core.ac.uk/download/55853450.pdf (accessed on 13th August 2025).
27. Wasem, R. E. (2004). Visa policy: Roles of the Departments of State and Homeland Security. https://core.ac.uk/download/5132260.pdf (accessed on 13th August 2025).
28. Whiting, J. M. (1997). The impact of the Canadian Charter of Rights and Freedoms on law enforcement: A case study on impaired driving and the Winnipeg Police Service. https://core.ac.uk/download/644031198.pdf (accessed on 13th August 2025).

Chapter

3

INVESTIGATION AND PRE-TRIAL PROCEDURES OF CRIMINAL PROCEDURE

Contents

Introduction..........73
3.1. The Role of Law Enforcement in Investigations..........77
3.2. Types of Evidence in Criminal Investigations..........82
3.3. Legal Standards for Searches and Seizures..........86
3.4. The Process of Charging a Suspect..........90
3.5. Pre-trial Motions and Hearings..........94
3.6. The Importance of Discovery in Pre-trial..........98
Summary..........102
References..........105

INTRODUCTION

The investigative process and pre-trial process in today's evolving criminal justice landscape are central doorways to the legal process. These procedures are not only imperative to confirm the prosecution's case, but also essential to uphold the rights of the accused. Proper investigative procedures precondition an open legal process because they determine the admissibility and credibility standards of evidence produced at trial. With shifts in societal norms and law over them, there is a need to analyze how they influence the procedural techniques as well as principles of justice. More is emphasized on the intricacies brought by issues like corruption that are on the rise and the adaptations needed because of atypical circumstances, as illustrated by recent experience in certain legal systems, particularly under martial law circumstances (Gurtieva et al., 2022). The surge in corruption crimes in the context of growing state surveillance has had profound impacts on criminal procedure law. For instance, for purposes of countering rooted corruption during times of political turmoil, lawmakers have sought to enhance methods of investigation and find a balance between requiring expediency and remaining within the confines of dictated legal customs. Procedural change demands a close examination of the way investigatory measures are performed, especially where there is a need for swift action by law enforcement agencies.

This change in pre-trial procedures is not merely a reaction but also a precursor to greater change in terms of public trust and state action legitimacy in civil liberties. Scholars have pointed to the necessity of adapting to these forces to protect individual rights, with the focus tension falling on the discourse between legal transformation and changing societal demands (Gurtieva et al., 2022). In addition, the prosecutorial role is central to the criminal justice process, with an impact on the investigative and pre-trial stages. Discretion on their part decides how evidence is gathered, charges are filed, and defendants' rights are handled. Legal culture significantly impacts prosecutorial behavior, which may in its turn counteract or facilitate legal reforms. Probing the nuances of prosecutorial authority under various legal systems, including comparative analysis of inquisitorial and adversarial systems, scholars offer valuable information about functioning mechanisms of justice. It not only discloses the use of prosecutorial discretion but also requires reconsideration of legal norm construction and enforcement. Therefore, an understanding of transformative processes in pre-trial and investigative procedures requires knowledge of the intricate interdependencies between legal culture, prosecutorial discretion, and the general objectives of justice in contemporary society.

Definition of Criminal Procedure

Criminal procedure is a central element in the justice system that prescribes the manner in which criminal cases progress through the process within the criminal justice system. It encompasses the rules and standards to which law enforcement agencies and legal experts must stick at the investigation, arrest, and prosecution levels of criminal cases. The definition of criminal procedure not only prescribes the actions of officials but also demarcates required protections for defendants' rights to ensure the legal process remains fair and even. The intricate dance between procedural rules and substantive rights necessitates a structured approach in controlling criminal behavior while safeguarding personal freedoms. In addition, an understanding of the definition and scope of criminal procedure is important in considering how well it falls in line with due process standards and rights of fair trial, as deficiencies in these areas lead to miscarriages of justice and reduced public confidence in the system. A fundamental principle of criminal procedure is that it is inquisitorial as opposed to adversarial systems, which has a fundamental impact on the investigation and preliminary stages. In adversary systems prevalent in the United States, defense and prosecution present opposing sides of the argument before a neutral jury or judge, who technically resolves the case. Conversely, inquisitorial systems prevalent in most civil law nations have more active judges investigating cases. The politics of the systems set the tone of investigation behavior, with implications for processes such as evidence collection, witness questioning, and the administration of truth-finding overall. The comparative analysis of such systems presents the variations in levels of powers of prosecutors and procedural safeguards protecting defendants, with the need for robust debate around best practices between jurisdictions (Montana et al., 2012). Pre-trial procedures are the backbone of establishing a criminal case. These procedures address significant aspects like preliminary hearings, arraignments, and pre-trial motions, which serve various roles under the criminal law umbrella. Preliminary hearings establish probable cause, whereby judges are able to decide if sufficient evidence exists to warrant transferring the case to trial. Arraignment, however, permits formal reading of charges against the defendant and potential entry of a plea. The importance of such procedural elements cannot be overstressed, as it is necessary to make the general judicial process more effective and truthful. Moreover, scholars like Gerard E. Lynch have noted the extent to which plea bargaining renders adversarial and inquisitorial approaches indistinguishable, endangering defendants' rights and requiring evaluation of these practices based on their justice concerns (Asrih et al., 2015).

Importance of Investigation and Pre-trial Procedures

The role of investigation and pre-trial procedures in the criminal justice system cannot be overstressed because these initial steps set the stage for the entire legal process. A sound investigation helps identify the facts in a case so that evidence is gathered in a legally valid way. This conscientious collection is required to the integrity of the ensuing proceeding, as it directly affects the quality of the evidence at trial. Investigations not only involve collecting facts but also discovering applicable legal tenets and possible defenses to be on the lookout for when litigation occurs. According to this, the emphasis on these initial procedural steps is important as it puts the spotlight on the doctrine of due process, whose purpose is to protect the rights of suspects and victims alike and see that justice is determined fairly, as explained in some criminal procedure analyses like by Davis et al. (2014). Pre-trial procedures are a necessary protection against sifting cases before the trial process, thus relieving courts of workload and protecting against mistaken convictions. Through preliminary hearings and motions, defense and prosecution can consider the vigor of evidence and whether or not the case will work. Such procedures provide the means of resolving problems prior to trial, with scope for plea bargain and, where necessary, disposal of weak cases.

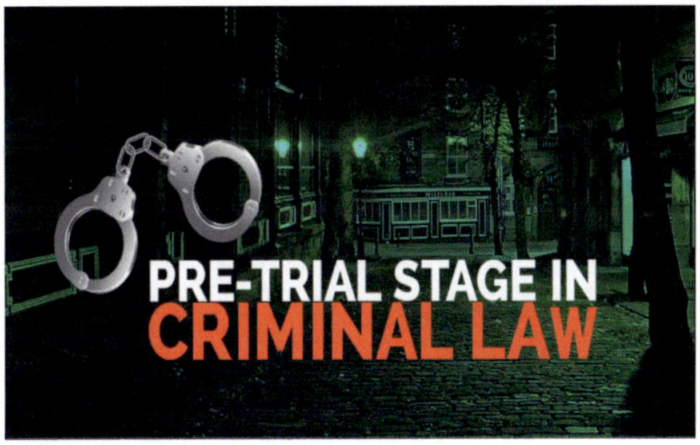

Figure 3.1. Investigation and pre-trial procedures.

Source: https://www.livelaw.in/h-upload/2021/02/24/1500x900_389700-pre-trial-stage-in-criminal-law.jpg.

The involvement of professional experts who clarify complex forensic material, such as the outcome of DNA testing, is significant since such evidence will frequently become impossible for jurors to cope with in the absence of background explanation. The outcomes of juror comprehension studies highlight that pre-trial discussion can help simplify trial presentation of complicated evidence, thus contributing to the jury's comprehension of critical issues in circumstantial cases (Chesterman et al., 2008). Moreover, effective investigation and pre-trial procedures facilitate the eventual goals of justice through rendering the criminal justice system transparent and accountable. These phases provide an in-depth analysis of the situation behind criminal charges, building public faith in the legal process. Investigative practices, if carried out fairly, can expose possible abuse of authority by law enforcement and safeguard the rights of defendants during the legal process. This is especially critical when it comes to the rights of victims, where seeking truth is crucial not just for purposes of accountability but also for healing in communities that have suffered from crime. By integrating the views of victims into investigation and pre-trial processes, the authorities enhance the authenticity of the justice system and the notion that criminal offenses significantly influence people's lives, as argued in victims' rights rhetoric under transitional justice mechanisms (Davis et al., 2014) (Figure 3.1).

3.1. THE ROLE OF LAW ENFORCEMENT IN INVESTIGATIONS

The role played by law enforcement at the time of investigation is at the core because essentially, it is the collection, preservation, and analysis of evidence that plays a critical role in the building of a case against suspected criminals. As soon as police come into the investigatory process, they apply techniques ranging from forensic analysis to interrogating witnesses. These include approaches that are led by compliance with legal standards and practices such that the evidence collected is credible and admissible in court.

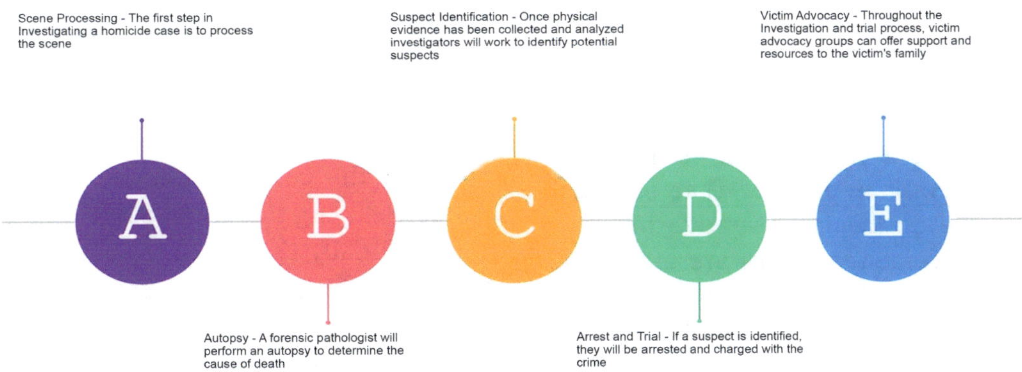

Figure 3.2. The role of law enforcement in investigations.

Source: https://fastercapital.co/i/Homicidal-strangulation--A-Dark-and-Disturbing-Crime--The-Role-of-Law-Enforcement-in-Investigating-Homicidal-Strangulation-Cases.webp.

The comprehensiveness of these investigations is illuminated by Gerard E. Lynch's observation of the implications of plea bargaining on the criminal justice system. Obscurity of adversarial and inquisitorial methods makes the processes by which law enforcement agencies must operate more difficult, not only case determinations but also the inherent fairness the justice system strives to uphold (Asrih et al., 2015). Effective communication and collaboration with various stakeholders, including legal experts and members of society, also define the operations of law enforcement agencies during investigations. The officers are often required to work with other agencies, such as forensic experts, social workers, and even foreign agencies depending upon the nature of the crime. This aspect of police work is especially applicable in cross-jurisdictional investigations when coordination is necessary to ensure that every critical piece of evidence is collected systematically and effectively. Within the European Union, however, the Stockholm Programme system demands a general framework of law over policing and investigation. Police forces must thus be skilled at handling complex legal ground, ensuring that their investigations adhere to both national and international norms of law (O'Neill et al., 2015). The principal challenges faced by police in investigations extend beyond procedural rigidity to ethical aspects. Officers must balance effective crime fighting with the protection of individual rights, which at times can be at variance with pursuit of justice. Investigations through plea bargaining allows pressure towards conviction acquisition to imperil proper investigative practice. Law enforcement must beware that their methods do not compromise the integrity of the judicial process. Watchfulness is crucial in pre-trial procedures where the admissibility of evidence decides case outcomes. Law enforcement's role during investigations is therefore two-faceted, weaving procedural conformity and ethical obligation to promote justice in a democratic country (Figure 3.2).

3.1.1. Initial Response to a Crime Scene

Initial response to a crime scene is a critical phase in the criminal process that sets the direction of the entire investigative process. When law enforcement officers are alerted to a crime, they must take immediate action to secure the crime scene in order to prevent contamination and preserve evidence. This involves creating a perimeter and limiting access to authorized personnel only.

The response of the officers goes a long way in defining the integrity and quality of the evidence collected. The officers also conduct initial interviews of any witnesses or victims present in this initial phase, which can provide critical information on context that can guide the subsequent investigations. In particular, as revealed in discussions surrounding the validity of confession, procedural errors at this stage can have repercussions for future interrogations and the risk of false confessions, again supporting maintaining a clear, unambiguous process from the beginning of a criminal investigation (Garrett et al., 2010). Lastly, officers must carry out a systematic canvass of the scene of the crime where every visible detail is written down meticulously. This may include the recording of photographs or videos of the environment, recovery of physical evidence, documentation of any visible injuries or bloodstains. All of these documents are significant not only for the initial investigatory needs but also for the requirements in the future in the courts. Development of a planned and accurate record helps maintain the chain of evidence, thus preventing controversy over the credibility and reliability of evidence collected. Further, initial findings have to be communicated efficiently between responding officers and detectives detailed for follow-up investigation. This collaboration forms the backbone of constructing a consistent account of events that will direct further questioning. As explained, the nature of initial contacts is able to shape the direction of the investigation, thus pointing towards the contribution of law enforcement officers during the initial stage (Klinkner et al., 2009). Finally, the absolute necessity of training and compliance with set standards during the initial response cannot be overemphasized. It is up to the first responders to apply forensic science principles to the field, striking the delicate balance between the need for speed and due diligence in evidence handling. Anything short of the balance between the two will have far-reaching implications, such as the possible contamination of evidence and making the case for prosecution more difficult. Also, enhanced procedural stringency at initial response can avoid doubts about false confessions through creating a better framework for subsequent interrogations. Contaminations of confessions highlight procedural fidelity because handling evidence must be flawless in order to maintain fair convictions during trials. Hence, the initial response phase serves not merely as a stage for investigative work but also as a safeguard against subsequent legal attacks (Garrett et al., 2010) (Figure 3.3).

Figure 3.3. The initial response to a crime scene.

Source: https://www.seattle.gov/images/OPA/kyr-crimescene-lg.jpg.

3.1.2. Collection of Evidence

Evidence collection is a vital component in the investigation and pre-trial stages of criminal procedure since it provides the foundation on which cases are built. Effective collection of evidence not only establishes facts but is vital in safeguarding the rights of the accused as well. Investigators must adhere to strict procedures so that evidence can be presented in court, with police learning the thin line between proper investigation techniques and the subject's constitutional rights.

Erroneous evidence collection can lead to tainted conclusions, and might violate Fourth Amendment protection against unreasonable search and seizure. This juxtaposition highlights the importance of legal standards that regulate the admissibility of evidence such that the investigative work of law enforcers does not infringe upon the privacy rights of suspects but still work towards finding justice. In the final analysis, evidence collected at the crime scene must be spotless to benefit the judicial process. Also, recent proceedings showcased the evolving nature of evidence collection methods, particularly with the speedy increase in forensic technology. One such excellent example is the case of Maryland v. King in the Supreme Court, challenging the constitutionality of obtaining buccal swabs during arrest for DNA identification. The court's decision in the case would redefine the parameters around admitting evidence obtained through such means, emphasizing the need for law enforcement to balance privacy rights with the ability to effectively conduct investigations. As technology evolves, the legal and ethical implications of evidence collection will increasingly intersect with individuals' rights. Consequently, criminal investigative agencies must stay abreast of changes in legal requirements and judicial precedent to conform, thereby safeguarding the rights of accused individuals while aiding careful investigations. Implications of evidence collection become more than merely short-run concerns for investigations in influencing the whole judicial process, particularly in capital cases.

A study of Virginia capital trials from 2005–2015 discovers a dramatic decline in the imposition of death sentences, linked to enhancement of the quality of defense material available. Capital defense improvements have made significant contributions to the gathering of evidence presented at trial by rendering thorough and accurate accountings of the case, often resulting in life sentences and not death sentences. This change brings into play basic issues about how unequal resource access to resources utilized for defense can affect arbitrariness in death sentencing, and this involves Eighth and Sixth Amendment rights. Through observing these trends, legal stakeholders can gain a fuller understanding of the interconnected relationships between evidence collection, trial outcomes, and broader implications for criminal process justice, and the need for continued reform and support of effective legal defense provision (Heedman et al., 2014; Witanachchi et al., 2013) (Figure 3.4).

Figure 3.4. The collection of evidence.

Source: https://www.azolifesciences.com/image-handler/picture/2021/8/shutterstock_1400087216.jpg.

3.1.3. Interrogation of Suspects and Witnesses

An integral part of the criminal investigation process, suspect and witness interrogation is employed to collect key information required for prosecutorial and defense strategy. This step typically involves complex legal matters, particularly those concerning persons' rights. The techniques employed during interrogation in most jurisdictions can directly impact the admissibility of the evidence and the resulting court case. For example, coercive methods or deception can lead to false confessions, undermining the validity of the justice system. Furthermore, cultural divergence in the application of interrogation measures indicate the need for change and harmonization across different legal systems. The varying development of interrogation methods across geographical regions, more so between Western and Eastern judicial systems, points to the importance of a comprehensive analysis of interrogation ethics and policy in the overall context of criminal procedure (Beken et al., 2012). Legal reforms have been initiated in response to the challenges faced in suspect and witness interrogation in an attempt to offer better protection to the accused while securing effective justice for the victim. Right to counsel, access to information, and safeguard of individual liberties are key to ensuring interrogative procedures are fair and equitable. In the European Union, for instance, there has been effort towards harmonization of interrogation procedures as well as upholding universal standards regarding issues of protection of human rights (Cape et al., 2010). These reforms encourage a transparent and accountable criminal justice process, enabling defendants to possess the rights required to challenge interrogation strategies employed against them. The acknowledgment of the psychological and social forces at play when interrogations are being conducted also underscores the imperative necessity of procedure grounded on the law that respects individual rights while, at the same time, fostering successful law enforcement outcomes. Furthermore, effective witness examination is just as important to the investigative process in that it has the ability to steer a case in a particular direction. Testimony of witnesses must be gathered under conditions that minimize the potential for contamination or coercion. Application of science-based methods, such as the cognitive interview technique, is capable of enhancing the quality of information yielded by witnesses and making them feel comfortable and willing to co-operate. This process establishes the ambiance required for securing sound memories, which is paramount in criminal cases. Legal mechanisms that support witness rights and develop standards for interrogation procedures not only benefit the cause of justice but also guarantee that the entire process of the judicial system is reliable and credible, emphasizing the crucial role of comprehensive interrogation to the broader criminal procedure framework (Figure 3.5).

Figure 3.5. Interrogation of suspects and witnesses.

Source: https://financialcrimeacademy.org/wp-content/uploads/2023/10/697d6d63-bc6b-4eee-a179-1d8b34bc5ff1.png.

3.2. TYPES OF EVIDENCE IN CRIMINAL INVESTIGATIONS

Collection and analysis of evidence are the most important moments in criminal investigations because they influence further legal proceedings significantly. There are numerous different types of evidence, each of which has some unique properties and implications for an investigation. Physical evidence such as fingerprints or DNA has absolute information that directly relates a suspect to a crime scene. Computer evidence is increasingly prevalent, and technology advancements create new areas of pertinent information, including emails and online activity. Presentation of such evidence necessitates stringent procedures to make it admissible in court and respect the rights of everyone involved in the investigation. In addition to physical and digital evidence, testimonial evidence plays a vital role in building a criminal case narrative. Witness statements and expert witness testimony can contextualize and support claims being made in court. This is notwithstanding, as testimonial evidence is continuously subjected to the frailties of human sight and memory. These are stress during the incident, lapse of time, and leading questions. With criminal procedure in constant flux, it is important that investigators and law professionals are aware of the strengths and weaknesses of testimonial evidence so that a fair trial may be based on the full assessment of all the evidence available. As the face of criminal investigations evolves, particularly with the emergence of digital technology, new authenticity and evidence collection challenges face investigators. The investigation and prosecution processes increasingly rely upon obtaining access to and analyzing electronic information, with deep jurisdictional and ethical consequences. For instance, the ability to obtain digital evidence from transborder private firms raises legal hurdles that must be negotiated with caution. Scholars and practitioners are presently debating about what the consequences of expanding provisions for digital evidence as outlined in the current policy discussions on the "E-Evidence" Package are. These considerations serve to illustrate not just the procedural aspects of criminal investigations but also the overall obligation to protect basic rights and respond to victims' rights, even including the right to truth, as outlined in recent research work under (Carrera et al., 2020; Davis et al., 2014).

3.2.1. Physical Evidence

Physical evidence is a central consideration in the investigation and pre-trial phase of criminal procedure. Described in terms of tangible objects that can be identified through the senses, physical evidence includes, among other things, fingerprints, DNA, weapons, and other forensic materials. Physical evidence collection, preservation, and analysis have a significant impact on the outcome of a case because it could corroborate or corroborate against witness testimony. Apart from this, physical evidence also connects the suspect to the crime scene, focusing the investigations. Even though experts gather the evidence with great care, they must adhere to rigid procedures to ensure that it remains intact so that it is admissible in court. The chain of custody established during the investigation process is critical, as lapses raise questions regarding the validity and reliability of the evidences in pre-trial hearings. Additionally, the interface between physical evidence and forensic science enhances the investigative process. Expert witnesses, especially in fields like forensic archaeology, offer unbiased perspectives that can demolish the results of exhumations and crime scene analysis. For instance, the investigation of mass graves relies on reliable methods for ensuring the authenticity and relevance of physical evidence presented in court. This forensic evidence not only contributes to the creation of the factual record of a case but also assists in the verification of credibility necessary for courtroom operations.

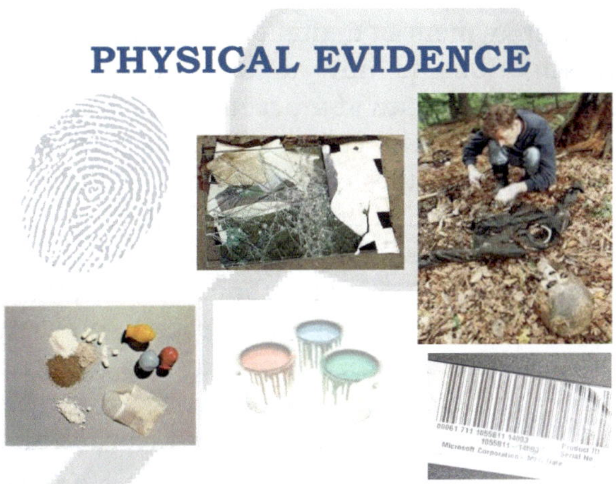

Figure 3.6. The concept of physical evidence.

Source: https://image5.slideserve.com/9299479/physical-evidence-l.jpg.

As has been noted in some ad hoc tribunals, forensic science application to law is difficult and calls for an intense debate on the interplay of law and science. Overcoming these difficulties is fundamental for justice to be efficiently administered within the criminal justice system. Besides, the admissibility of physical evidence becomes of keen interest at the pre-trial stage, where motions to admit or exclude physical evidence are the norm. Judges normally apply rigorous criteria in assessing admissibility, with physical evidence expected to be relevant, reliable, and not highly prejudicial. This is even more complicated once a historical view of police practices is incorporated, enabling what may undermine ethical mandates in the gathering of evidence. Instances of pervasive coercive institutional practices have been reported, and it has also raised issues about their impact on the rights of criminal suspects. As societies seek more compassionate criminal justice, it is important to learn about the place of physical evidence in this system. As one navigates these complex legal environments, the interaction between physical evidence, judicial examination, and existing practices in law enforcement is key to obtaining fair results in criminal investigations and their related trials (Figure 3.6).

3.2.2. Testimonial Evidence

Testimonial evidence plays a vital role in criminal procedure's examination and pre-trial process and is something on which case facts are built. Testimonial evidence tends to be statements by witnesses or victims regarding their first-hand experiences or perceptions in relation to the crime at hand. Such declarations may be determinative in constructing the case for prosecutors, offering invaluable information that is used to support or refute findings collected through other measures, including physical findings or forensic reports. More so in sensitive matters, like abuse of children or rape, the conditions under which testimonial evidence is obtained can strongly determine whether or not it will be admitted to court and viewed as credible throughout the course of a trial. Admissibility of testimonial evidence is also made more complex by legal constructions of the Sixth Amendment's Confrontation Clause. Observing in recent case law, including the landmark Supreme Court decisions, is especially intense scrutiny of the "primary purpose" that invokes victims' statements, particularly when they are not directly testifying at trial. For instance, child reports to different legal agencies of abuse can be quite problematic if the purpose is seemingly more geared towards representing legal cases rather than immediate protection or assistance. In the context of reports to specially trained medical professionals, such as S.A.N.E. nurses, the need to separate medical from legal purpose is crucial. The ongoing debate regarding these complexities depicts how testimonial evidence remains a pivot of pre-trial inquiries while, at the same time, mirroring the evolving legal boundaries established by more recent jurisprudence (Rothstein et al., 2015).

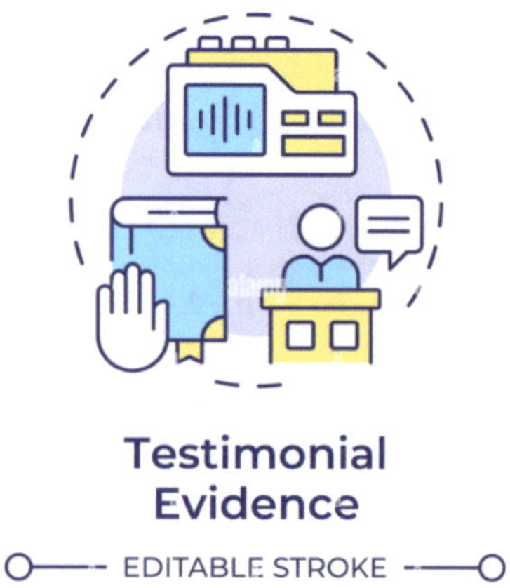

Figure 3.7. Testimonial evidence.

Source: https://c8.alamy.com/comp/2X5D32A/testimonial-evidence-multi-color-concept-icon-2X5D32A.jpg.

Not to be overemphasized is also the importance of context in evaluating testimonial evidence. The contextual elements in regard to the way in which and the time of making a statement can provide invaluable insights into its credibility. For example, if a victim is conversing with a police officer in a situation of emergency, the type of conversation may be more of immediate medical or safety needs, hence making it admissible or not in court. On the other hand, if statements are provided under a more structured setting for legal record purposes, they might fall short of being for purely medical purposes. More recent scholarship on the Confrontation Clause highlights the ongoing ambiguities and emphasizes the necessity of clarification of interactions between law enforcement officials and victims or witnesses during an investigation (Herskowitz et al., 2011). Together, these relationships provide a nuanced picture of testimonial evidence, shedding light upon its essential role in both preliminary proceedings and subsequent trials (Figure 3.7).

3.2.3. Digital Evidence

The employment of digital evidence in criminal investigations is now a key component of contemporary law enforcement. In a time where electronic communication and data storage are ubiquitous, possessing the ability to access, acquire, and utilize digital information is fundamental to effective prosecution. Increased technology has brought about revolutionary changes in the investigative process, and law enforcement organizations have to counter with paradigm shifts in evidence collection encompassing social media interactions, emails, and data archived in cloud services. Defeating challenges that involve the legal and jurisdictional standards that regulate such activities is essential. Such challenges on cross-border access to information necessitate updating the existing guidelines and protocols to guarantee that investigations remain legally sound while effectively taking advantage of the information abundance that exists in digital formats (Carrera et al., 2020). In pre-trial proceedings, the management of digital evidence typically entails elaborate procedures demanding cautious attention from legal practitioners. Prosecutors have to traverse sensitive legal territory relating to the admissibility and integrity of electronic evidence, especially if it is from private companies or foreign sources. Collaboration between law enforcers, legal professionals, and technology experts plays a crucial role in creating guidelines that preserve the integrity of the evidence as well as protecting the rights of individuals to privacy. A structured approach of video evidence, that is, family violence case, reflects the importance of clear rules to manage collection and use of such evidence while conducting investigations. An accurate documentation and maintenance of digital evidence are of utmost significance in making it effective in court (Backes et al., 2019). Moreover, digital evidence problems are not limited to collection and admissibility; they also reflect broader judicial cooperation problems at the national and international levels. As law enforcement agencies increasingly rely on digital data for prosecution, jurisdiction-related problems become significant, particularly with cross-border cases. Legal systems must adjust to the issues of mutual legal assistance and recognition so that digital evidence can easily be incorporated into other legal systems. The ongoing debate regarding the E-Evidence Package in the European Union indicates activity aimed at making procedures less complicated involving access to digital data. It is the duty of policymakers to continue arguing so as to balance the effectiveness of the investigations with protection of fundamental rights to ensure an equitable and fair legal process (Carrera et al., 2020) (Figure 3.8).

Figure 3.8. The integration of digital evidence.

Source: https://advantageinvestigators.com/wp-content/uploads/2023/06/Digital-Evidence-Collection.png.

3.3. LEGAL STANDARDS FOR SEARCHES AND SEIZURES

Legal standards for search and seizure within criminal procedure serve as the foundation for maintaining individual rights protection as in the United States Constitution's Fourth Amendment. The amendment prohibits unreasonable searches and seizures, constituting a crucial balancing act between rights of an individual and law enforcement interests. One of the foundations of such standards is the "probable cause" requirement, under which adequate grounds must be presented to a judge or magistrate by law enforcement before a warrant is issued. The judicial check has the purpose of maintaining public trust in the criminal justice system through preventing random government intrusion into private life.

Figure 3.9. The legal standards governing searches and seizures.

Source: https://slamatlaw.co.za/wp-content/uploads/2021/06/searchandseizures-600x400-1.jpg.

The dynamic development of surveillance techniques also renders the application of these constitutional protections even more difficult. As noted, government authorities are capable of exploiting the "initial use" of surveillance techniques prior to their regulation, leading to the circumstance wherein individuals are subjected to unregulated investigation techniques with inadequate legal restraint. Such an event calls forth fundamental concerns over the social cost of regulatory lags and the attendant impacts on privacy and civil liberties. Underpinning Fourth Amendment extension debates, there is a compelling basis for reading the "to be secure" phrasing more broadly, thus guaranteeing a right to be "protected" against overreaching government surveillance and searches beyond shielding from unreasonable methods (Milligan et al., 2014). Importantly, the doctrine of "qualified immunity" often shields law enforcement officers from liability for constitutional violations in these pre-regulatory periods. This immunity and the good faith exception to the exclusionary rule undermine the deterrent impact of Fourth Amendment criteria. Because investigations are carried forward, government overreach is feasible particularly when these actors are shielded from repercussions for their actions. Thus, there is a necessity to create a firmer basis of individuals' rights to be free from unreasonable searches and seizures. To assume a stance in support of a principle set by the courts over the government's application of uncontrolled investigative methods can present at least if not an overall solution, a step in the right direction of protecting individual freedom from technological and procedural advancement (Djerf et al., 1990) (Figure 3.9).

3.3.1. Fourth Amendment Protections

United States Constitution Fourth Amendment is an important safeguard in criminal process, particularly in investigation and pre-trial processes. The amendment protects individuals from unreasonable seizures and searches, and hence necessitates the police officers to obtain warrants backed by probable cause prior to making searches. The effect of this protection is enormous as it provides that the privacy of individuals is never interrupted despite the exigency of criminal investigations. As policing itself becomes more adept at evolving, so too is the application of the Fourth Amendment tested under the umbrella of technological advancement, most prominently that of DNA analysis. The Supreme Courts forthcoming rulings on matters such as Maryland v. King will continue to determine the boundaries of such protections to be applied to the realities of contemporary environments, most significantly for those who have yet to be convicted, but merely arrested (Witanachchi et al., 2013). Problems with DNA testing illustrate the conflicts between effective law enforcement and Fourth Amendment rights. As authorities become more dependent on DNA evidence to both implicate suspects and clear the innocent, governments have passed legislation that allows for the collection of DNA from arrestees for specific crimes. This legislative trend has significant ethical and constitutional implications, especially regarding the presumption of innocence, because the critics believe that such practices are incompatible with fundamental due process principles. Courts have often declared DNA collection from convicted offenders to be constitutional, but the legal status of arrestees is in dispute. These later decisions are very likely to be struggling with such complexities, pointing to the ongoing controversy over the balance of public interests in security and personal rights under the Fourth Amendment (Grossman et al., 2014). As the Fourth Amendment continues to evolve in court interpretations, the emphasis on individualized suspicion remains a central cornerstone of protection against random governmental intrusions. The Supreme Court has applied a balancing test in ruling on the constitutionality of searches and seizures, weighing government interests against rights of the individual. Such issues have become even more relevant in instances involving new investigative techniques, where the primary purpose test comes into play as well. This test seeks to establish if law enforcers motive for undertaking a search was to seek ordinary criminal activity or if it was meant to address some other legitimate governmental interest. Heightened judicial scrutiny of the practices is a reflection of the necessity of balancing rights against investigation needs, which finally identifies the direction of future Fourth Amendment protections in investigation and pre-trial proceedings (Grossman et al., 2014; Witanachchi et al., 2013).

3.3.2. Search Warrants and Exceptions

Search warrants are valuable tools in law enforcement that allow authorities to search property while defending citizens Fourth Amendment rights against unreasonable searches and seizures. A judge issues a warrant upon a law enforcement officers presentation of probable cause backed by sworn statements or affidavits outlining the evidence warranting the search. The warrant requirement is a critical component of investigation and pre-trial procedures, as it serves the aim of both legitimizing police actions and maintaining public trust in the justice system. The warrant acquisition system is not infallible, and it is challenged in court proceedings. Availability of sufficient evidence, warrant specificity, and rigid following of legal procedures are essential to ensure that a warrant authority search is constitutionally sound and therefore admissible before the court. While the seminal rule requires the utilization of search warrants, there are several legally recognized exceptions that justify law enforcement organizations to search without a warrant. These exceptions arise from the need for expediency in situations where the acquisition of a warrant would be inconvenient or where immediate injury is likely to be inflicted. An outstanding exception is the exigent circumstances doctrine, which authorizes officers to perform a warrantless search where they reasonably believe that a suspect will escape or that evidence will be destroyed. Other exceptions include searches conducted during legal arrests, mutually agreed searches, and searches of vehicles under particular conditions. The safeguards under the law regulating such exceptions are a balancing act between governments' responsibilities to enforce the law and the protection of individuals' liberties. The exceptions are prone to controversy with regard to their application in actual scenarios as they sometimes are wrongly applied or misused by law enforcement officials. The ramifications of being in warrantless or otherwise exceptionally applicable operation affect the evidentiary context of criminal prosecutions. Concededly, evidence gained by unconstitutional search falls under the exclusionary rule, which excludes evidence so obtained from trial. The doctrine not only protects personal rights but also provides a deterrent for law enforcement officers from conducting illegal search operations. The issues of investigative overreach ring familiar in modern debate, especially when considering the changes in the nature of surveillance technology and police procedure. For example, the principle of use comes before control creates problems since unregulated investigation techniques will subject citizens to intrusive investigation (Milligan et al., 2014). In addition, the on-going debate on the Fourth Amendment raises the importance of ensuring search warrants and exceptions are thoroughly explored so that abuses can be prevented during the pre-trial phase of criminal procedures (Djerf et al., 1990) (Figure 3.10).

Figure 3.10. The search warrants and exceptions.

Source: https://capitolcitylawgroup.com/wp-content/uploads/2020/02/shutterstock_333537803-1024x683-1.webp.

3.3.3. Exclusionary Rule

The Exclusionary Rule is a fundamental principle in the criminal procedure scheme, which is in place to maintain the integrity of the judicial process. It mandates that no evidence so obtained in disregard of a defendants constitutional rights may be used in court. This principle finds its primary source in the Fourth Amendment that offers protection from unreasonable searches and seizures. By enforcing the Exclusionary Rule, courts try to deter law enforcement agencies from engaging in unconstitutional acts. This constitutional mandate not only instills compliance with procedural standards but also reinforces the principle that protection of individual rights is supreme in a democratic state. Use of this mandate, however, has generated quite a controversy regarding its impact on the prosecution's power to secure convictions, typically raising questions regarding the potential for guilty defendants to go free due to procedural-level mistakes. Several jurisdictions have adopted varying applications of the Exclusionary Rule, producing a complex paradigm of application. In other countries, for example, Greece, exclusion of unconstitutionally or illegitimately acquired evidence is statutory, as set forth in Article 177 para. 2 of the Code of Penal Procedure. The strict approach manifests a rights-oriented approach, as opposed to regimes such as England and Wales, where discretion plays an active role. Article 19 para. 3 of the Greek Constitution enforces this to the extent that it forbids evidence obtained in disregard of privacy rights. Such disparate systems bring to the fore the balancing act jurisdictions have to undertake between safeguarding constitutional rights and providing effective law enforcement. Therefore, a comparison of the disparate approaches emphasizes the effect of the Exclusionary Rule on large-scale investment in investigative methods and the pursuit of justice in each legal system. As further debate continues around the Exclusionary Rule, it also intersects with civil lawsuits, particularly in cases of wrongful conviction. In cases where defendants are exonerated, often through DNA testing, they may obtain remedy through civil rights litigation that reveals government misconduct in the initial criminal trial. These types of instances show a transformation in dealing with procedural rights; while criminal prosecutions may claim that some breaches are innocuous, civil actions can strip such breaches of their defenses. The Supreme Courts establishment of internal harmless error rules, particularly in the case of milestone cases like Brady v. Maryland, can revolutionize the manner in which wrongful convictions are handled completely. Through the illumination of Exclusionary Rule complexities, it is realized that this doctrine is not only an effective pre-trial safeguard, but also a prevailing issue of debate with respect to justice and responsibility within criminal justice (Garrett et al., 2005; Giannoulopoulos et al., 2007).

3.4. THE PROCESS OF CHARGING A SUSPECT

Charging of a suspect is a critical phase in the criminal justice process, having significant influence on the progression from investigation to pre-trial process. It typically comes after a lengthy investigation in which evidence has been collected and suspects have been identified by the police. After sufficient evidence has been obtained, the prosecutor must determine if the evidence would justify formal charges. The charging determination depends on various factors, including the admissibility of evidence, seriousness of the offense charged, and public safety issues. Charging similarly leads to issues of justice and fairness, since imbalances may exist within racial and economic segments of society, showing the need for scrutiny and overhaul of the charging process (Rudovsky et al., 2015).

Figure 3.11. Process of charging a suspect.

Source: https://i.guim.co.uk/img/media/37ccd4b48d609ba811911a16a27049761c058070/0_281_8192_4918/master/8192.jpg?width=1200&height=900&qualit y=85&auto=format&fit=crop&s=c67c70cf549e5e7b956eb8f37d55e8c2.

Following the intention to bring charges, the prosecutor is required to draft formal charges, which specify the nature of the crime alleged. In most jurisdictions, this entails drafting a complaint, information, or an indictment, based on the scope of the charges and applicable legal systems. Formalization not only notifies the accused but also provides the basis for any subsequent judicial process. How the charges are phrased can frame the suspects' perception of the process and potentially the plea bargaining process that will ensue. Moreover, this stage brings to light the risk of disproportionate impact on marginalized populations and challenges with the motives of charges and how the necessity for systemic reform in order to bring about equality and justice to all accused becomes apparent (Asrih et al., 2015). After charges have been lodged, the suspects' rights are paramount since they are entitled to a fair hearing that examines the merits of the lodged charges against them. The process typically leads to the preliminary arraignment, where defendants are formally read their charges and make a plea. The plea is guilty, not guilty, or no contest, with varying implications for the judicial process. Significantly, the charging process also opens up the way for plea bargaining under which the defense and prosecution can settle their interests to the terms mutually agreeable to both. As has been observed in plea bargain debates, this can lead to disorientation between the adversarial and inquisitorial approaches of justice and thus calls for a critical examination of charging mechanisms in order to prevent unfairness while also enhancing the effectiveness of the criminal justice system (Asrih et al., 2015) (Figure 3.11).

3.4.1. Role of the Prosecutor

The role of the prosecutor is a vital one in the criminal justice system, particularly at investigation and pre-trial stages. Both as a state legal advocate and a justice administrator, the prosecutor has a lot of authority. It entails making decisions about whether or not to prosecute, which determines the direction of a case. The prosecutorial discretion is often informed by what is discovered through the investigation, which captures the combination of legal norms and moral ideals that accompany the office. Furthermore, the prosecutor will be forced to weigh the pursuit of justice against the rights of the defendants, a conflict that has profound implications for the integrity of the criminal justice system. As with a range of legal culture analyses, the entire scope of prosecutorial power often must be balanced with regard to its impact upon defendants' rights and the broader societal interests that are concerned with the administration of justice (Montana et al., 2012). In addition to legal accountability, prosecutors must also deal with the complexities of plea bargaining, an activity which often operates at the heart of pre-trial negotiations. The function of plea bargaining serves to hasten the court process but raises cutting questions concerning fairness and equality within the adversarial system. In highlighting the cutting arguments in adversarial versus inquisitorial models, vagueness in demarcating these models can complicate a prosecutors role. The prosecutor is often tasked with swimming through such complexities in search of a solution that meets the ends of justice while considering the potential consequences for defendants who may be coerced into plea bargains (Asrih et al., 2015). Such a delicate balance supports the prosecutors dual responsibility to serve the state and uphold the principles of fairness and justice. Lastly, the efficiency and ethical integrity of prosecutors have considerable influence both on the investigation and pre-trial process of criminal cases. Their choices not only affect short-term legal consequences but also have an impact on the perception of the public and on the criminal justice system. A prosecutor's compliance with ethical standards and his/her ability to operate transparently can enhance the legitimacy of their role, towards a system where justice is valued more than conviction rates. In addition, the recognition of prosecutors as key actors in the justice system emphasizes the necessity for ongoing reforms and training to enable them to operate within the boundaries of set ethical standards. As systemic problems are dynamic, it also becomes very clear that the prosecutor's role in investigation and pre-trial proceedings must always adapt to keep justice within a dynamic legal system (Montana et al., 2012).

3.4.2. Grand Jury Proceedings

Grand jury proceedings are of utmost significance in the investigation and pre-trial process of the criminal justice system. Unlike initial hearings, grand jury hearings do not include a judge and are in-camera, which allows for a high level of confidentiality regarding sensitive case details. The grand jury examines evidence presented by the prosecution to determine if there is sufficient cause to issue an indictment.

This procedure serves as a check against indiscriminate prosecution, safeguarding the rights of the defendants and ensuring charges have probable cause. The grand juries authority to subpoena witnesses and obtain evidence further underscores its significance because it allows for investigation of the cases to be tried in detail. The equilibrium between the state's interest in prosecuting a crime and the rights of an accused is an integral element in this procedural framework. The grand jury's independence is a principle in U.S. law, which highlights its position as an antidote against prosecutorial abuse of power. The historical significance of the institution is identified in a number of legal critiques, such as Priester et al.'s, which follows the evolution of investigative techniques and their connection to the independent counsel statute. The grand jury serves not just as a charging device for individuals but also as an integral aspect of democratic accountability within the legal system. When people come together to weigh evidence and testimony, their collective judgment verifies societal norms and values. Thus, the process is more than just legal formalities; it reflects the role of the community in deciding what constitutes a legitimate criminal charge, thereby building greater public faith in the justice system. However, grand jury proceedings have been said to lack effectiveness and justice, especially where there are concerns regarding transparency and possible prosecutorial prejudice. The confidentiality attached to grand jury proceedings could make the right of the defendant to challenge evidence brought against them ineffective, which raises concern about the integrity of justice. Such concern is heightened by awareness that prosecutors wield considerable power in these proceedings, often weaving narratives at the expense of defense objection. The tension of managing these dynamics makes an ongoing conversation in legal scholarship a call to order, where grand jury practice is developed against the backdrop of larger societal trends. Ensuring that the grand jury is a fair and impartial institution is an ever-evolving critical issue in the realm of criminal procedure, necessitating watchful overtures and potential reforms to include modern standards of the law (Figure 3.12).

Figure 3.12. Grand jury proceedings.

Source: https://federalcriminallawcenter.com/wp-content/uploads/2016/08/grand-jury.jpg.

3.4.3. Filing of Charges

The filing of charges is the critical juncture in the criminal justice process, bridging investigation and full prosecution. Once the police have completed their investigation of a suspected crime, the prosecutor will examine the evidence and determine if there is sufficient foundation to formally charge an individual with a crime. This relies not just on the amount and integrity of the evidence at hand but also on relevant standards of law for the crime in question. The prosecutor has to fulfill ethical expectations and prosecutorial discretion, whereby a reasonable determination of conviction is established before charges are brought. This step emphasizes the significance of the prosecutors role, as it balances the interests of justice against the accused's rights, setting the stage for the subsequent pre-trial and trial phases. The impacts of these initial charges can then echo throughout the rest of subsequent proceedings, influencing plea bargaining and case results in general. In addition, the charging choice issued by prosecutors carries extensive implications for defendants as well as the overall justice system. When charges are filed, defendants are formally notified of their allegations under law, invoking several protections under law, including counsel access and a speedy trial. The Sixth Amendment guarantees these rights, which have been further fortified by judicial doctrine and legislative enactments. The uncertainty surrounding how to define a speedy trial, as the courts have defined it in their previous decisions, is symptomatic of the complex dynamics between constitutional guarantees and the case-specific variables that arise in prosecution. Furthermore, societal interests in securing a prompt disposition of criminal cases are advanced by statutes like the Speedy Trial Act of 1974, which are meant to define more specific time periods for trials. These mechanisms are not only meant to protect the interests of defendants but also maintain the integrity of the judicial process and uphold public confidence in law enforcement. As the case unfolds, the forum in which charges are filed has a great deal of power to shape the course and tenor of the trial itself. Prosecutors can make decisions on where to bring the most beneficial venue for a prosecution—federal or state courts—depending on the nature of the offense and potential legal strategy. This latitude presents advanced institutional design challenges, particularly given that federal courts possess a strong success rate in litigated matters. As such, charging determinations in one forum over another can present concerns of the fair administration of justice. Notably, as the forum selection can present perceived advantages for prosecutors, so too does it accentuate defendants' rights to seek open and fair trials on diverse judicial forums. Lastly, these aspects of charging underlie the greater issues of the investigation and pre-trial process that are the essence of criminal procedure (Chepiga et al., 1976; Grundfest et al., 2016).

3.5. PRE-TRIAL MOTIONS AND HEARINGS

Pre-trial motions and hearings are fundamental aspects in the realm of criminal procedure that have a significant function in deciding the path of a case. These pre-trial motions serve a number of significant purposes, including determining whether or not evidence should be admissible, making the charges specific, and resolving various procedural issues before a trial. The importance of pre-trial motions is evident in their capacity to address legal issues in an effective way that, otherwise, would make the trial process cumbersome. For instance, motions to suppress evidence challenge the legality of the way in which evidence was seized, potentially excluding highly prejudicial evidence from the case entirely. Through having a clear legal framework in effect and ensuring respect for rights before trial, these motions are not only in the interests of the accused but also in the public interest of judicial efficiency and fairness. Also, the importance of pre-trial hearings cannot be overstated as they allow prosecution and defense to make educated decisions. By means of the hearings, both parties to the dispute present their arguments regarding the motions so that the judge may see which side's interpretation of the law is strongest. This adversarial process results in the creation of a better informed understanding of the case at hand. Besides, it reduces the likelihood of trial surprises since it cultivates a culture in which evidence and arguments are critically examined.

Figure 3.13. Pre-trial motions and hearings represent critical components in the criminal procedure landscape.

Source: https://www.combswaterkotte.com/wp-content/uploads/2024/09/Pre-Trial-Motions-and-Hearings-1024x254.jpg.

Bearing in mind that the pre-trial phase tends to be the most challenging aspect of a criminal process, it actually enhances the predictability and transparency of the judicial process so that the legal representatives and defendants are well prepared. The historical evolution of criminal procedural rules has also created enormous variations in how pre-trial motions and hearings are managed between jurisdictions. Fascinating, as Meyn et al. (2017) illustrates, the evolution of criminal procedure was initially entangled with that of civil procedure, assuming the feasibility of a comprehensive procedural system. But as criminal procedure evolved separately, it established itself deeply in its own distinct rules and traditions. This divergence has serious implications regarding the efficiency and effectiveness of the existing system, most notably in relation to the process of discovery, which is still less rigorous in criminal cases compared to civil cases. The implications of the variations indicate that reform and ongoing discussion are crucial towards enhancing the fairness and effectiveness of pre-trial proceedings by addressing the disparities that exist while maintaining uniform application of justice in cases (Figure 3.13).

3.5.1. Motion to Suppress Evidence

Motion to suppress evidence is a fundamental component in the pre-trial procedures of criminal procedure. It gives defendants an avenue through which they can challenge the admission of evidence gathered by law enforcers, particularly when such evidence is gathered through unconstitutional means. Primarily grounded on the Fourth Amendment's protection against unreasonable searches and seizures, this procedural motion is intended to protect defendants from the ramifications of the aggregation of police violations during investigative activities. This is because the integrity of the judicial system relies on the moral procurement of evidence to ensure that defendants receive a fair hearing. Without the motion to suppress, potentially contaminated evidence from misconduct might unfairly influence jury perceptions in ways that lead to potential miscarriages of justice, especially where confessions' admissibility comes into question (Garrett et al., 2010). Judicial scrutiny of the evidence is important, particularly considering the broadened understanding of the complexities surrounding confessions. The risk of false confessions—most often caused by coercive interrogation strategies—ensures that motions to suppress are used to ascertain not only the method of evidence gathering but also its factual correctness. Empirically, it has been shown that innocent individuals confess incriminatory information under psychological stress, and concerns over the quality of such confessions at trial have arisen (Garrett et al., 2010). Consequently, suppression motions can play a decisive role to remedy such issues by guarding against the judicial admission of tainted evidence. By making it necessary for courts to closely scrutinize the context and circumstances under which confessions are given, the motion has the effect of reaffirming the doctrine of fair trial rights and doing justice to the accused. In pursuit of transformation in pre-trial process, the motion to suppress is a process that requires judicial consideration of nature of evidence presented before courts. The recent debates have increased the appeal to rethink about interrogation and police behavior rules. There are developments, as claimed by advocates, including mandatory videotaping of interrogations to screen against contamination and promote accountability (Garrett et al., 2010). As the law evolves, it is important that reform is enacted to assist the integrity of evidence without undermining fair protection of defendants. Focusing on how evidence received before trials can be guaranteed to be accurate, the motion to suppress allows for a fair legal process that ensures the balance between necessary effective law enforcement and fundamental rights of those within the criminal justice system.

3.5.2. Motion for Change of Venue

The motion for change of venue is a crucial tool in the criminal procedure mechanism, particularly at pre-trial stages. It offers the avenue through which defendants can request a change of venue of their trial, primarily in reaction to the potential for biased jury selection as a result of local media coverage or public opinion. Such a motion is most often predicated on the theory that an impartial trial cannot be had in the current locale and thus insuring the defendants constitutional right of an impartial jury. The validity of such a motion is also substantiated by not only the prejudicial impact of the pre-trial publicity but by the social dynamics of the community opinion regarding the guilt or innocence of the defendant, which can play a strong determining factor regarding juror impartiality. Judicial interest in a motion for a change of venue is multifaceted and long-standing in its concern with upholding fairness in the judicial process. The courts balance the value placed on local opinion against the backdrop of constitutional safeguards, striving to uphold the integrity of the judicial process. For instance, in Alvarado v. State, the Alaska Supreme Court mandated that a jury must be representative of the community in which the case unfolds and thus reiterates the importance of context in ensuring the selection of a jury (May et al., 2011). The application of this rule becomes particularly important in well-known cases, where pre-trial publicity may render the impartiality of a local jury questionable. By allaying such fears with a thought-out motion for change of venue, courts can reduce prejudice and strengthen the public's confidence in the judiciary to enable even-handed justice. The procedural machinery of movant status for a motion for change of venue also reveals intricate judicial practice that emphasizes the utility of this device within the pre-trial process. Defendants, assisted by their lawyers, have to file credible evidence for their claims of bias, including data on media reportage, opinions of the general public, and sentiments among the local populace on the case. Hearings typically take place in courts to determine the merits of such motions, weighing defense and prosecution arguments. While the discretion to grant the motion lies with the presiding judge, there are trends that can provide insight into systemic issues surrounding venue availability, including the potential for perceived bias or overall fair trial unavailability in specific regions (Grundfest et al., 2016). Lastly, the motion for change of venue represents a core point of nexus of criminal procedure and constitutional protection of rights since they guarantee that the principles of justice are observed during the pre-trial process (Figure 3.14).

Figure 3.14. The motion for a change of venue.

Source: https://www.clio.com/wp-content/uploads/2024/05/Blog_Blog-Pre-Trial-Motions-Option-2-750x422.png.

3.5.3. Pre-trial Conferences

Pre-trial conferences serve a significant role in criminal procedure by implementing an orderly discussion between the prosecution and defense prior to the trial. The primary purpose of such conferences is to clarify the issues in question, streamline the process, and provide a fair trial. Through conferences, attorneys can possibly resolve issues of evidence, plea bargaining, and settlement options, which in turn can significantly reduce the need for a complete trial. Such a component of Pre-trial conferences is congruent with the empirically developed research on court process that has been studied in the literature. Specifically, court management practice research, for instance, implementing Pre-trial conferences, is proven to be successful in the management of caseload and increasing the efficiency of the judiciary, report Garth et al. (2010). Thus, Pre-trial conferences improve an underlying process that not only addresses legal complexity but also minimizes judicial bottlenecks. Besides, the efficacy of Pre-trial conferences may be judged in relation to procedural reform with an aim towards enhancing the justice system. Such conferences are a preventive measure for dispute resolution because parties communicate directly with the purpose of negotiating conditions or outlining procedural matters before proceeding to court. This is particularly pertinent in light of the grievances around availability of justice and potential court congestion in litigation. The empirical literature within the field of civil procedure rules emphasizes the usefulness of such mechanisms of alternatives as instruments for facilitating cooperation between litigants and minimizing disputes see Garth et al. (2010). By fostering communication, Pre-trial conferences can also serve as a forum for addressing systemic concerns, like equal access to legal means, and hence increase integrity to the legal proceedings overall. However, the impact of external factors, such as media publicity, should not be overlooked in Pre-trial conferences because it has the potential to alter the public perception of ongoing cases. The doctrine of innocence, a fundamental aspect of criminal law, can be compromised if public opinion is swayed by sensationalized reports disseminated via media outlets. This aspect introduces a level of sophistication in Pre-trial conferences, whereby attorneys will be forced to negotiate pre-trial publicity impacts on jury selection and trial outcomes. As witnessed in legal models of governance debates, understanding the relationship between media and the judicial process is necessary in order to conduct equitable trials (as discussed in). Accordingly, legal practitioners should always be sensitive to such dynamics with the aim of ensuring that the integrity of the court system prevails even in the midst of the invasive nature of public scrutiny that often comes with sensationalized cases.

3.6. THE IMPORTANCE OF DISCOVERY IN PRE-TRIAL

Discovery plays a crucial role in pre-trial procedures in facilitating information exchanges between the prosecution and defense, thus ensuring a fair trial process. In this phase, both sides can gather evidence, assess the strengths and weaknesses of their cases, and formulate strategies that could potentially determine the outcome of the trial. By mandating disclosure of material evidence, the discovery process not only promotes transparency but also minimizes the likelihood of surprise witnesses or 11th-hour evidence being presented in trial, which will undermine the integrity of the judicial process.

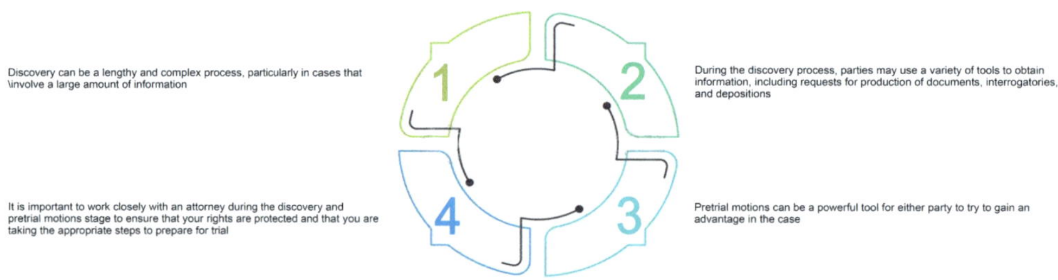

Figure 3.15. Importance of discovery in pre-trial.

Source: https://fastercapital.co/i/Legal-remedies--Seeking-Legal-Remedies-in-Common-Law--A-Step-by-Step-Guide--Discovery-and-Pretrial-Motions.webp.

As succinctly expressed in judicial holdings, this bedrock aspect of criminal procedure delineates the parameters under which justice is to operate, affirming the necessity for a systematic and disciplined process of disclosure ahead of the trial court proceedings (Asrih et al., 2015). Besides, discovery promotes valuable procedural efficiencies that can be employed to accelerate the disposition of cases before trial. A good discovery period permits the determination of undisputed facts, thereby saving time and resources for the parties and the courts. Such efficiency relies on the precision and completeness of information flowing through since its bearing on pre-trial settlement or plea bargaining options. An example is how discovery helps parties make more informed agreements, which generally result in reduced caseloads for the judicial system. Thus, the dynamics generated by discovery serve both prosecutors and defendants as well as advance the general goal of a quicker and more equitable legal process (Kötz et al., 2009). Lastly, the interplay between discovery and the rights of the accused is most significant in the context of criminal procedure. Discovery provides defendants with critical access to evidence that can be beneficial to their case or rebut the charges against them and thus make their right to a fair defense all the stronger. It is nevertheless crucial that this right should be weighed against the prosecutorial duty to uphold justice. Abuse or misuse of the discovery process may have severe implications, not only tainting the integrity of a case but, more importantly, infringing on the rights of parties concerned. Legal regulation of discovery is hence both sword and shield, helping strike a balance of the delicate pendulum between effective legal representation and protection of public safety and justice interests (Asrih et al., 2015) (Figure 3.15).

3.6.1. Disclosure of Evidence by Prosecution

Prosecutor responsibility to disclose evidence is a cornerstone of the criminal justice system, essential to ensuring fair trials and safeguarding defendants' rights. Prosecutors are required to provide access to all pertinent evidence, including incriminating and exculpatory records, to defense counsel at the stage of investigation and pre-trial. The rationale behind this process of revelation is to provide transparency and equity so that the accused party may develop a strong case. As withholding key evidence could lead to wrongful conviction or case dismissals, delineating strict parameters on evidence sharing is of paramount significance to the legal systems.

The nuances of these guidelines reflect the nuance of balancing the prosecutions duty to achieve justice with demands to protect the integrity and confidentiality of the investigation, finally deciding case outcomes definitively. Secondly, the nature of disclosure has been revolutionized in terms of technology, especially with respect to digital evidence. Modern examinations have a tendency to massively rely on electronic data held by non-state agencies, posing jurisdiction and right to privacy concerns that must be addressed with restraint. It is important to prosecutors, as it is specified in existing legislation, for example, those produced in ongoing discussions of the E-Evidence Package, to adapt procedures to effectively acquire access to and utilize digital data. This adaptability is necessary in order to make sure that the quest for justice continues to be in sync with emerging technologies, as well as reacting to associated legal issues. By collaboration between law enforcement agencies across various borders and adapting to new means of obtaining evidence, prosecutors are capable of maximizing their potential for uncovering all relevant information, thereby making the overall integrity of the justice system regarding electronic evidence better. Furthermore, the consequences of disclosure of evidence go beyond the immediate legal situation, having wider impact on society's attitudes towards justice and accountability. When there is transparency from the prosecutorial process, public trust in the legal system is improved because citizens feel there is a care for fairness and due process. Lack of transparency, however, can lead to suspicion and distrust, which destroy confidence in institutions of justice. Thus, the procedural paradigms governing disclosure of evidence must not only be responsive to the operations problems facing prosecutors but also sensitive to their social implications. Getting the balance right is likely to create a fairer legal environment, in which the rights of the accused are maintained without discouraging the prosecution's duty to present a reasonable and effective case to court. The commitment to maintaining both legal and ethical standards in disclosure procedures remains central to ongoing criminal procedure and public trust development.

3.6.2. Defense's Right to Discovery

Right to discovery is a fundamental defense pillar of the criminal justice system, as it provides defendants an opportunity to be fairly presented the means of preparing cases. This right allows the defense to be provided with pertinent evidence that will be introduced against them by the prosecution. Access is necessary for safeguarding due process rights as it enables the defense to adequately challenge the prosecutions allegations and present a comprehensive counter-account. Without an effective discovery process, there is an increased risk of wrongful convictions since defendants may end up being unprepared to counter unexpected evidence. Therefore, the values implicit in the right to discovery reflect the need for transparency and fairness in court proceedings as a safeguard against uncontrolled digression in the application of justice. The history of the development of discovery rights in criminal procedure has been controversial, with changing philosophies about the division of power between prosecution and defense. The criminal procedure had no wide discovery procedures like those in civil cases initially, primarily due to traditional thinking that embraced the prosecution (Meyn et al., 2017). The civil-criminal procedure difference has helped create the impression that rights afforded in civil cases are not applicable directly to criminal cases. Current debate refutes this traditional thinking by advocating for an integrated procedural system encompassing both areas. From a comparison of earlier efforts to harmonize criminal and civil proceedings, it is evident that the integration of coercive discovery methods into criminal law is less a matter of reform than a necessary step toward achieving justice. As the controversy surrounding the defenses right to discovery continues, its pertinence refers to broader controversies surrounding structural injustice and systemic reform. Leading jurist scholars, for example, Gerard E. Lynch, believe that the current adversarial vs. inquisitorial model differences highlight the need to enhance discovery processes according to American law (Asrih et al., 2015). The plea bargaining practice, which has generally been criticized for the unfair disadvantage of defendants, is one such example highlighting the need for reforms to promote transparency and fair treatment. Here, the right of discovery emerges not only as a process but also as a determining factor for providing a fair and efficient criminal justice system. While reformers continue to push for radical changes, the continued investigation of discovery rights in response to pre-trial processes will play a determining role in charting the future of criminal law and its fair application.

3.6.3. Impact of Discovery on Trial Preparation

Trial preparation depends to a great extent on the process of discovery, which is a cornerstone of criminal procedure. Discovery enables the sharing of information between prosecution and defense so that both can be adequately prepared to present cases at trial. This procedure entails numerous instruments such as depositions, interrogatories, and document requests, whereby lawyers can acquire pertinent proof and witness evidence way in advance of the court session. Thus, the discovery process not only enhances legal representation quality but also prevents surprise tactics that would disrupt a trial. Therefore, a good understanding of the process of discovery significantly impacts the way lawyers prepare and organize themselves, hence deciding the direction and outcome of their cases. The implications of discovery extend beyond the sharing of information; they significantly contribute to influencing the pleabargaining dynamics. As Gerard E. Lynch argues, the intersection of adversarial traditions and plea bargaining is relevant when analyzing discovery's role in trial preparation (Asrih et al., 2015). The disclosed materials and evidence can lead to intelligible negotiations on the likely fate of a case, compelling defendants to weigh the pros and cons of accepting or rejecting plea deals. This paper affirms the value of lawyers practicing complete discovery, as the quality and amount of information gathered can impact the strategic decisions made throughout the pre-trial stage. As such, effective discovery not only prepares lawyers for trial but lays the groundwork for negotiations that can avoid lengthy trials altogether. Historical evolution of criminal procedure highlights the central conflict between justice and efficiency in the discovery system. The initial proposals for a unified procedural code, which would have coordinated civil and criminal procedures, highlight the revolutionary potential of discovery in pretrial preparation (Meyn et al., 2017). The eventual differentiation of procedures has ingrained inequalities that continue to shape modern litigation. The absence of a robust discovery mechanism in criminal cases, as opposed to civil cases, poses pertinent issues on trial fairness and transparency. Recognition of this context compels legal experts to agitate for reform that consolidates discovery provisions in criminal process so that the system becomes efficient, not only appreciating efficiency but also emphasizing the accused's rights, thus leading to fair trial outcomes.

SUMMARY

The criminal procedure investigation and pre-trial processes are the backbone of an efficient and fair system of justice. These initial phases are not only important to building the fact-based framework of criminal cases but also to safeguarding defendants' rights in the system of justice. The interplay of tension between investigative action by law enforcement and procedural safeguards built into the legal system is such that it holds a delicate equilibrium between seeking justice and safeguarding individual rights. As criminal case complexities keep up with the march of advancing times, the nuances of these processes are as important to legal practitioners and researchers as they remain subject to continuous re-evaluation and overhaul. Further, the legal culture of the prosecution plays a significant role in informing the effectiveness of pre-trial and investigation practices. As recently interpreted in empirical studies, prosecutors' hesitation regarding certain legal reforms reveals the highly rooted assumptions and traditions that shape their behaviors. This predisposition affects the implementation of investigative techniques and evidence integration within the pre-trial context. Thus, such comprehensive understanding of the legal culture provides an insight into its broader ramifications on prosecutorial discretion and interpretation of defendants' rights, ultimately influencing the trajectory of criminal cases and their outcomes (Montana et al., 2012). Finally, the interaction between forensic expertise and legal procedure highlights the complexities entailed in the collection and interpretation of evidence. The application of scientific methodology to inquiry reflects the face-lift of criminal justice, where the pursuit of 'forensic truth' is paramount. However, as the issues that have been raised with the presentation of forensic evidence in high-stakes court cases, like those within the International Criminal Tribunal for the former Yugoslavia, illustrate, the introduction of forensic information into court may make legal accounts more complex and influence judicial decision-making. Understanding these dynamics is vital to increasing the efficacy of investigations and making pre-trial processes relative to the contemporary scientific advancements (Klinkner et al., 2008). To that end, the on-going debate regarding such issues remains a cornerstone in maintaining the integrity of criminal processes in the attainment of justice.

The investigative phase of criminal procedure is pivotal in setting the ground upon which cases are built. In this period, police units gather evidence, interview witnesses, and pursue tips in attempts to construct a coherent narrative relating to the alleged crime. Effective investigations rely on observance of procedure and adherence to the law so that all gathered evidence can be admissible at trial. Moreover, application of forensic science cannot be overstated; application in the inquiry not only facilitates verification of witness statements but also guarantees overall validity of the findings. For instance, expert evidence is vital in international criminal trials, particularly on mass grave forensic science evidence, and it illustrates the substantial role of evidence in establishing facts in prosecution, such as the existence of mixed legal systems and complexity of expert evidence (Klinkner et al., 2009). Pre-trial is a time when gathered evidence is scrutinized to determine whether it is enough to proceed to trial. This is the phase where the collected evidence are subjected to law to find out if charges can be substantiated. Prosecutors must scrutinize the evidence carefully, paying attention to the relevance and potential issues that may arise at trial. Defense also plays an important role, as it can provide countering expertise or challenge the introduction of evidence. This live dynamic between defense and prosecution not only highlights the need for good legal foundation but also mirrors the pragmatic trends seen in international settings, such as in the cases tried by ad hoc tribunals, where cross-examination and counter-expertise are paramount towards ensuring fairness and justice (Davis et al., 2014). Besides, the theoretical underpinnings of the right to truth bring complexity to investigation and pre-trial procedure. In cases like the International Criminal Court, victim rights to truth institutionalization in law is extremely pragmatic and jurisprudentially challenging. Such calls need to have a nuanced understanding of transitional justice, that is, preservation of how investigation and trial uphold victims' rights and ensuring legality. The conflict between the presentation of truth to victims and procedural fairness that is required in trial calls for innovative solutions in the justice system. With researchers investigating the challenges, understanding derived makes better practice in integrating victims' rights into pre-trial procedures possible, making the justice system legitimate in responding to international crimes (Davis et al., 2014).

KEY TERMS

- Case Diary
- Charge Sheet (Final Report)
- Cognizance of Offence
- Committal Proceedings
- Crime Scene Examination
- Custodial Interrogation
- Forensic Evidence
- Judicial Custody
- Police Custody
- Prima Facie Evidence
- Remand Application
- Search and Seizure
- Witness Statement

A LOOK TO THE FUTURE

FUTURE CONSIDERATIONS IN CRIMINAL PROCEDURE

The criminal procedure of the future will need a serious reconsideration of gathering and employing evidence procedures. Foremost among its concerns is the integration of digital evidence, which poses unique issues due to its nature and susceptibility to exploitation. As legal systems struggle to cope with the digital environment, admissibility concerns regarding electronically obtained evidence must be solved. Jurisdictions have responded widely to the subject, ranging from a strict rights-based approach in Greece, where automatic exclusion of illegally acquired evidence is given prominence, to one of permissiveness, such as in Hungary, where there is no such necessity. Such rigid exclusionary requirements not only try to protect constitutional rights but also place focus on an orderly re-consideration of procedures that control digital evidence collection, with a goal of finding a balance between good law enforcement and safeguarding fundamental rights. Furthermore, increasing reliance on electronic information makes it incumbent upon governments to seek transnational frameworks for cross-border data access and collection. As criminal activity grows more global and traverses borders with greater ease, the role of international cooperation in investigation and pre-trial action grows more crucial. The legal and jurisdictional challenges resulting from accessing and transferring data within possession of private companies present challenging challenges. Whether by means of mutual legal assistance agreements or building frameworks like the "E-Evidence" Package, these barriers need to be tackled with care to both maintain the rule of law and the protection of citizens' rights. Future policy must not only emphasize the importance of judicial cooperation but also seek to apply definite parameters guiding the ethical use of shared data, further enhancing trust among nations and the integrity of the privacy rights of individuals. Criminal procedure reform extends beyond the collection of evidence and access to information to encompass more fundamental systemic changes allowing for developing technology. The future is likely to require more embedding of technology into pre-trial processes, such as the use of artificial intelligence to scan evidence rapidly and efficiently. Such embedding, though, also has a set of difficulties, particularly related to transparency, accountability, and bias in algorithmic decision-making. With such issues coming to the fore, a comprehensive debate should involve diverse stakeholders—lawmen, jurists, technologists, and human rights activists—to come together and address the implications of such technological advancement. By engaging proactively with these issues, stakeholders can better guarantee that criminal procedure development is aligned with democratic ideals and justice is served evenly and judiciously.

REFERENCES

1. Andersson, M., Brun, A., Knutsson, H., Ljung, M., et al. (2008). Dynamic investigative practice at the International Criminal Court. https://core.ac.uk/download/62560488.pdf (accessed on 13th August 2025).
2. Asrih, M., Bautzova, T., Harmening, N., Izsvak, Z., et al. (2015). Our administrative system of criminal justice. https://core.ac.uk/download/144230276.pdf (accessed on 13th August 2025).
3. Backes, B., Grau, K., Kammer-Kerwick, M., LaMotte, A., et al. (2019). Recording victim video statements as evidence to advance legal outcomes in family violence cases (ReVEAL). https://core.ac.uk/download/286367667.pdf (accessed on 13th August 2025).
4. Cape, E., Namoradze, Z., Smith, R., Spronken, T., et al. (2010). *Effective Criminal Defense in Europe. Executive Summary and Recommendations*. https://core.ac.uk/download/pdf/11869692.pdf (accessed on 13th August 2025).
5. Carrera, S., & Stefan, M. (2020). Access to electronic data for criminal investigations purposes in the EU. *CEPS Paper in Liberty and Security in Europe, 2020–01*. https://core.ac.uk/download/287647967.pdf (accessed on 13th August 2025).
6. Chepiga, S. F. (1976). Speedy trials: Recent developments concerning a vital right. https://core.ac.uk/download/144227518.pdf (accessed on 13th August 2025).
7. Chesterman, M., Cunneen, C., Duff, R. A., Findlay, M., et al. (2008). Juror comprehension and the hard case–Making forensic evidence simpler. https://core.ac.uk/download/50973.pdf (accessed on 13th August 2025).
8. Davis, H., & Klinkner, M. J. (2014). A victim's right to truth and the International Criminal Court (ICC): Summary project report. https://core.ac.uk/download/19532319.pdf (accessed on 13th August 2025).
9. Djerf, H., & Hy, J. (1990). Rights of the criminally accused. https://core.ac.uk/download/62554233.pdf (accessed on 13th August 2025).
10. Dohrn, B., Crawford, C., Moss, M. B., Puritz, P., & Geraghty, T. F. (2007). Illinois: An assessment of access to counsel & quality of representation in delinquency proceedings. https://core.ac.uk/download/71352113.pdf (accessed on 13th August 2025).
11. Garrett, B. L. (2005). Innocence, harmless error, and federal wrongful conviction law. https://core.ac.uk/download/213020502.pdf (accessed on 13th August 2025).
12. Garrett, B. L. (2010). The substance of false confessions. https://core.ac.uk/download/213020483.pdf (accessed on 13th August 2025).
13. Garth, B., & Menkel-Meadow, C. (2010). Process, people, power and policy: Empirical studies of civil procedure and courts. https://core.ac.uk/download/70375292.pdf (accessed on 13th August 2025).
14. Grossman, S. P. (2014). Using the DNA testing of arrestees to reevaluate Fourth Amendment doctrine. https://core.ac.uk/download/144552234.pdf (accessed on 13th August 2025).
15. Grundfest, J. A. (2016). Fair or foul? SEC administrative proceedings and prospects for reform through removal legislation. https://core.ac.uk/download/144231809.pdf (accessed on 13th August 2025).

16. Gurtieva, L., Lisitsyna, Y., Lukashchuk, K., Nuriyev, R., et al. (2022). Corruption crimes and peculiarities of their investigation procedure under martial law. https://core.ac.uk/download/568030778.pdf (accessed on 13th August 2025).

17. Heedman, H., & Pärlerstrand, E. (2014). The decline of the Virginia (and American) death penalty. https://core.ac.uk/download/213020423.pdf (accessed on 13th August 2025).

18. Herskowitz, A. (2011). *Bullcoming v. New Mexico*: Revisiting analyst testimony after *Melendez-Diaz*. https://core.ac.uk/download/62559569.pdf (accessed on 13th August 2025).

19. Horowitz, M. A., Priester, B. J., & Rozelle, P. G. (1999). The Independent Counsel Statute: A legal history. https://core.ac.uk/download/62568603.pdf (accessed on 13th August 2025).

20. Johansson, H., & Pillai, A. K. M. (1988). Mechanical applications of the harmless error rule in cases of prosecutorial grand jury misconduct. https://core.ac.uk/download/62549741.pdf (accessed on 13th August 2025).

21. Klinkner, M. J. (2008). Proving genocide? Forensic expertise and the ICTY. https://core.ac.uk/download/4897043.pdf (accessed on 13th August 2025).

22. Klinkner, M. J. (2009). Forensic science expertise for international criminal proceedings: An old problem, a new context and a pragmatic resolution. https://core.ac.uk/download/4897045.pdf (accessed on 13th August 2025).

23. Kötz, H. (2009). Civil justice systems in Europe and the United States. https://core.ac.uk/download/62565990.pdf (accessed on 13th August 2025).

24. Magaloni, B., & Rodriguez, L. (2020). Torture as a method of criminal prosecution: Police brutality, the militarization of security and the reform of inquisitorial criminal justice in Mexico. https://core.ac.uk/download/322310836.pdf (accessed on 13th August 2025).

25. May, J. D. (2011). *Alvarado* revisited: A missing element in Alaska's quest to provide impartial juries for rural Alaskans. https://core.ac.uk/download/62546141.pdf (accessed on 13th August 2025).

26. Meyn, I. (2017). Why civil and criminal procedure are so different: A forgotten history. https://core.ac.uk/download/144232643.pdf (accessed on 13th August 2025).

27. Milligan, L. (2014). The forgotten right "to be secure." https://core.ac.uk/download/186332456.pdf (accessed on 13th August 2025).

28. Montana, R. (2012). Adversarialism in Italy: Using the concept of legal culture to understand resistance to legal modifications and its consequences. https://core.ac.uk/download/9559363.pdf (accessed on 13th August 2025).

29. O'Neill, M. (2015). The development of the external dimension of the AFSJ: New challenges of the EU legal and policy framework. https://core.ac.uk/download/228177580.pdf (accessed on 13th August 2025).

30. Resta, G. (2008). Trying cases in the media: A comparative overview. https://core.ac.uk/download/62553225.pdf (accessed on 13th August 2025).

31. Rothstein, P. F. (2015). Ambiguous-purpose statements of children and other victims of abuse under the Confrontation Clause. https://core.ac.uk/download/70375290.pdf (accessed on 13th August 2025).

32. Rudovsky, D., Owens, E., Mayson, S., & Bibas, S. (2015). Improving fairness and addressing racial disparities in the Delaware criminal justice system. https://core.ac.uk/download/75761612.pdf (accessed on 13th August 2025).

33. Vander Beken, T., & Wu, W. (2012). Relativism and universalism in interrogation fairness: A comparative analysis between Europe and China. https://core.ac.uk/download/55853450.pdf (accessed on 13th August 2025).

34. Witanachchi, S. V. (2013). *Maryland v. King*: The Fourth Amendment spirals down the double helix. https://core.ac.uk/download/62560368.pdf (accessed on 13th August 2025).

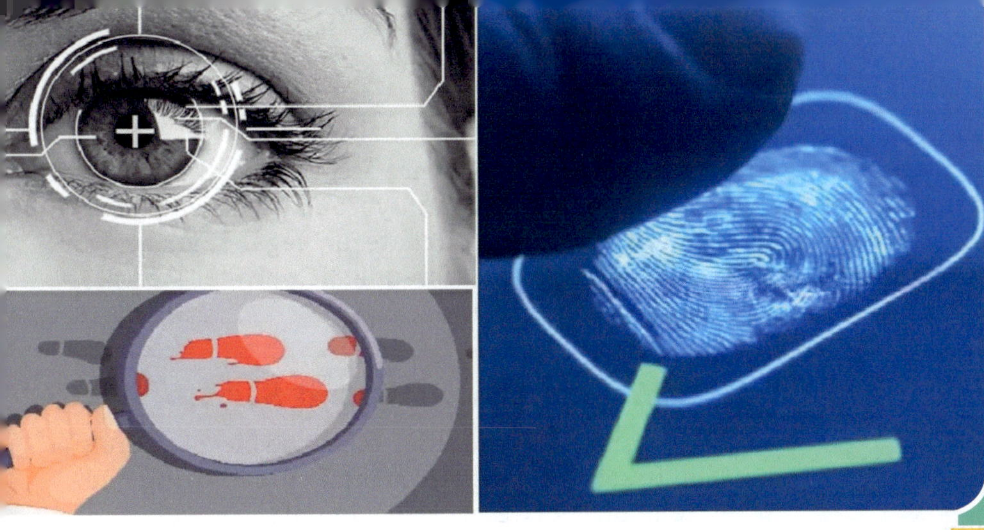

Chapter 4

SEARCH, SEIZURE, AND SURVEILLANCE IN CRIMINAL PROCEDURE

Contents

Introduction....................109
4.1. Historical Context....................114
4.2. The Fourth Amendment....................118
4.3. Search Warrants....................122
4.4. Exclusionary Rule....................126
4.5. Surveillance Techniques....................130
4.6. Balancing Security and Privacy....................134
Summary....................138
References....................141

INTRODUCTION

The intricate body of criminal procedure law governing search, seizure, and surveillance has its roots, actually, in the principles set forth by the Fourth Amendment. The amendment is an important safeguard against arbitrary governmental invasion, reinforcing not just individual privacy but also public confidence in the justice system. As societal norms shift and technology advances, so too does the characterization of reasonable expectations of privacy. This evolution is particularly pertinent with the introduction of computer technology in everyday life, in effect changing the manner in which evidence can potentially be obtained and analyzed in criminal cases. Being aware thus of the historical origins and contemporary traditions of the Fourth Amendment is therefore imperative to adopting the nuances of contemporary legal matters that are concerned with search and seizure. The role of constitutional protection against unreasonable search has been best established by landmark decisions of the Supreme Court. Those cases have established the development of what came to be referred to as the exclusionary rule, a judicial doctrine that serves to exclude evidence found in violation of constitutional rights. By dissecting the nuances of the Courts jurisprudence, the trend seems to be that the equilibrium between developing standards within society and interpretation by the judiciary has led to an extensive array of procedural findings in case law concerning surveillance and investigative steps. Of specific interest is the rise of governmental authority to acquire personal information by way of sophisticated methods, which raises pressing ethical issues about privacy and civil liberties. The consequences of the rulings extend beyond individual cases to imply broader societal impacts that must be carefully examined under the law of criminal procedure. As government agencies increasingly utilize technology to conduct searches and surveillance, particularly on borders, concerns over compliance with the constitution have grown. For instance, the increasing practice of warrantless electronic device searches by institutions like U.S. Customs and Border Protection illustrates the manner in which existing legal precedent is being stretched to its limits. These practices strain the notions of privacy with which the Fourth Amendment is tasked to protect, prompting a constitutional question about the boundaries of reasonable search and seizure. Other scholars contend that the governments rationale for such expanded practices, based on public safety and national security, should be subjected to close examination to make sure that rights of citizens are not unfairly sacrificed. Consequently, this essay attempts to analyze the historical origins and contemporary importance of search, seizure, and surveillance according to the Fourth Amendment with an eye on the urgent need for a continuous debate on legal reforms to protect personal freedom (Doernberg et al., 2006; Donohue et al., 2019).

Definition of Search and Seizure

In criminal procedure, the doctrine of search and seizure is instrumental in capturing the tension between governmental power and privacy rights of an individual. A search refers to an investigation into the person, property, or computer trail of an individual by the police for the purpose of locating evidence of crime. Seizure, on the other hand, is the taking into custody of persons or property by law enforcement officers through direct physical possession of objects believed to be related to a crime. Both definitions are derived from the U.S. Constitution's Fourth Amendment, under which citizens are safeguarded from unreasonable seizures and searches. This constitutional foundation is significant, not merely because it establishes procedural safeguards but also because it gives rise to continuing legal arguments regarding the limits and connotations of these terms in the modern world of policing. The evolution of search and seizure jurisprudence in the United States has increasingly concerned itself with the subtleties of sophisticated technologies. Courts have grappled with physical search vs. electronic surveillance issues, particularly as technology erodes historical models of privacy. A good example is the Supreme Court decision in United States v. Jones, which reflected on the concept of mosaic theory, or that combining surveillance information from various methodologies could be a Fourth Amendment intrusion. This perspective marks a shift from strictly physical notions of search and seizure to a broader conception which recognizes the imperatives of pervasive surveillance in contemporary society. These developments suggest the need for repeated adaptive responses to legal standards in order to protect individual freedom from evolving state practice in the name of security and law enforcement (Slobogin et al., 2012). Moreover, the implications of surveillance techniques on definitions of search and seizure are immense since the social costs incurred in their enforcement are typically overlooked. The use-first policy allows law enforcement agencies to utilize potentially intrusive techniques without express control, which is contentious as it can result in their abuse and, consequently, deprivation of civil liberties. Furthermore, regulatory delay has often discouraged timely action against abusive investigative practices, complicating the terrain for protection under the law on unreasonable searches and seizures. Redrafting the words of the Fourth Amendment can give clearer vision for rights to be safeguarded and without fear, further asserting the necessity of court review of government behavior that would otherwise fall at the fringes of exercised norms. Handling these legal nuances fosters a greater insight into how contemporary frameworks can be reinterpreted in light of contemporary challenges (Milligan et al., 2014) (Figure 4.1).

Figure 4.1. The search and seizure.

Source: https://www.helbraunlaw.com/wp-content/uploads/2013/02/1584386947574.jpeg.

Importance of Surveillance in Criminal Procedure

Surveillance is an indispensable part of the criminal procedure, significantly enhancing the effectiveness of law enforcement in the struggle against crime. Through systematic observation and recording of suspects, authorities can gather precious evidence crucial to prosecution. This ability is particularly relevant in an age of technology when electronic information frequently has the answer to criminal investigations. The Stored Communications Act shows how new surveillance methods face difficulties, especially when trying to access information kept overseas. Courts, by way of statutory limits of limitation and global considerations, can sharpen the standards of surveillance within the realm of criminal procedure in order to ensure the rights of both individuals and the police. Legislative steps towards reformulating current laws to the rapid advancement in technology will also underscore the necessity of surveillance in the establishment and maintenance of public justice and security in a globalized world (Kirschenbaum et al., 2018). Furthermore, the tenet of "use before regulation" underscores the dynamic tension of surveillance practices because law enforcement agencies can often turn to methods not well enough controlled. This trend raises substantive ethical questions regarding the misuse of surveillance methods before the implementation of formal regulations. The effects of late regulation can lead to unwarranted privacy intrusions, undermining public trust in law enforcement agencies. As the methods of surveillance become more advanced, so must the legal framework surrounding them. The fact that previous applications of such methods may go unchecked due to qualified immunity makes it necessary to re-examine how the Fourth Amendment is interpreted. Emphasizing the constitutional protections to be "protected" and "free from fear" of unreasonable searches might afford an equilibrium perspective, enabling courts to scrutinize unregulated surveillance more stringently (Milligan et al., 2014). Aside from enhancing the efficacy of law enforcement, surveillance is at its core inextricably linked to issues of civil liberties and privacy rights of individuals. The more advanced surveillance technology is, the thinner the line becomes between public security and personal freedom. Effective legislation must be sensitive to the social implications that result from widespread surveillance as well as from the regulatory mechanisms charged with governing it. Overreaching government demands a firm resolution to safeguard personal rights with continued surveillance operations that help contribute to solving crimes. By facing such challenges through lawful channels, legislators and the courts can work together to create a surveillance mechanism that not only improves criminal procedure, but guarantees the underlying values of freedom and security in a democratic nation. Thus, the worth of surveillance in criminal procedure demands not only strategic tact from law enforcement, but virtuous oversight from the legal system (Figure 4.2).

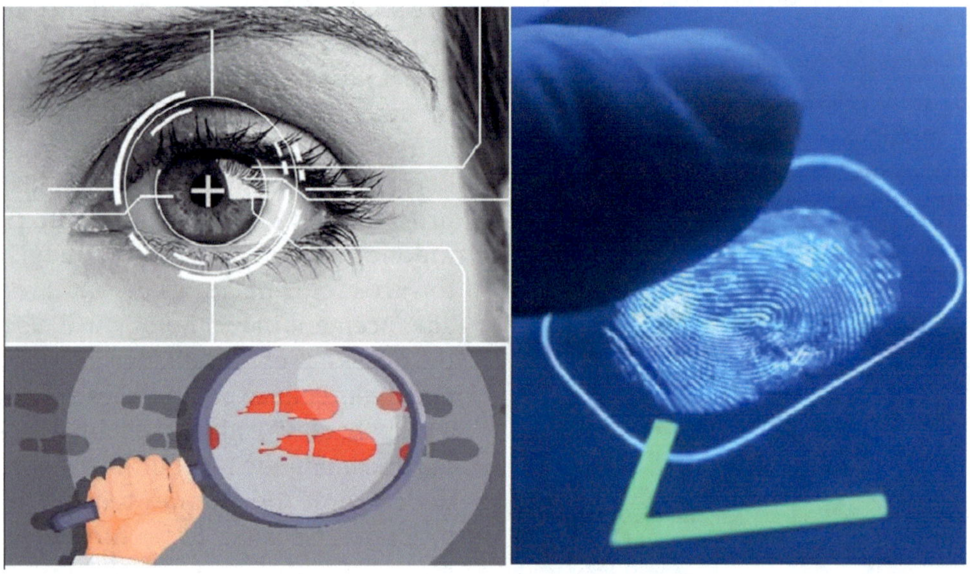

Figure 4.2. Importance of surveillance in criminal procedure.

Source: https://www.indiancurrents.org/files/issue/criminal-procedure-identification-bill-2022.png.

Overview of Constitutional Protections

The foundation of constitutional protection in the United States is firmly grounded in the Fourth Amendment, which enunciates the right of the people to be free from unreasonable searches and seizures in their persons, houses, papers, and effects. This provision aims to safeguard citizens against government arbitrariness and ensures that the police must adhere to legal procedure. The evolution of judicial interpretations regarding this amendment has shaped the terrain of criminal procedure, particularly the balance between individual rights and public safety. With advancing technology and dealing with modern data storage as increasingly complex, the established constructions are strained, as evidenced in ongoing legal battles over electronic privacy and government access to electronic information. The dialogue between warrants and probable cause remains essential, as law enforcement procedures and constitutional protections develop in the new digital world. Since the last decade, the growing popularity of electronic devices has introduced significant issues regarding context and scope of constitutional protections. The Stored Communications Act is the quintessence of such conundrums, since it delineates the limits to law enforcement access to cloud-stored information. But the law has trouble keeping current with technological developments and is beset by fundamental questions of foreign sovereignty issues and extraterritorial warrants. Most commentators call for an even more active legislative response that could provide guidance and instruction, especially as such cases as United States v. Microsoft approach the Supreme Court. Resolution of these issues through particular constitutional norms will not only be helpful to law enforcement agencies but will also preserve citizens' constitutional rights from unnecessary violations of their privacy. Constitutional protections therefore still rely on shifting understandings of how the existing laws work under the auspices of emerging technologies. The border-search exception to the Fourth Amendment is another field where constitutional protections clash with governmental interests. As the recent policies implemented by U.S. Customs and Border Protection (CBP) and Immigration and Customs Enforcement (ICE) illustrate, warrantless searches of electronic devices on travelers have raised considerable privacy concerns. While the government claims these searches as a tool to prevent contraband from entering the country and exert control over immigration, critics argue that such policies intrude on fundamental constitutional freedoms. Electronic device searches differ qualitatively from routine baggage searches in that they potentially disclose vast quantities of intimate information, triggering an advanced discussion about the parameter of government powers at border checkpoints. The exchange identifies a critical need for legislative intervention to ensure that constitutional protection is upheld, protecting individual rights in evolving national security measures (Figure 4.3).

Figure 4.3. The foundations of constitutional protections.

Source: https://i0.wp.com/lawbhoomi.com/wp-content/uploads/2023/07/LawBooks6.jpg?fit=600%2C400&ssl=1.

4.1. HISTORICAL CONTEXT

Historically, search, seizure, and surveillance in American criminal process have entailed an evolving tension between shifting societal values and legal norms. In crafting the Constitution and particularly the Fourth Amendment, the framers of the Constitution tried to establish a balance between preserving personal freedoms on one side and facilitating the state in fostering public security on the other. This early amendment, which safeguards against unreasonable searches and seizures, developed out of early colonial encounters with British privacy rights abuse. By looking at history in this way, it is clear that modern-day interpretations of the Fourth Amendment were shaped by the abuses of previous times, foreshadowing modern debates regarding state surveillance and citizens' rights.

Thus, the past record of search and seizure practice educates the present legal standard and serves to highlight the continuing conflict between governmental authority and individual freedom in a democratic state. With technology, so too has surveillance capability grown, to pose new challenges for the law. The setting of context must be attuned to the touchstone moments of technological advance which have determined legislative and judicial responses to surveillance methods. For instance, the advent of wiretapping in the mid-20th century prompted significant legal scrutiny and the eventual establishment of regulatory frameworks aimed at limiting government overreach. Earlier forms of surveillance, often analog in nature, have since evolved into sophisticated digital techniques capable of extensive data collection. This development has led to the application of the "use precedes regulation" doctrine, where initial use of surveillance technology typically occurs prior to effective regulation, hence causing a regulatory lag that puts pressure on the constitutional safeguards enshrined in the Fourth Amendment (Milligan et al., 2014). Knowledge of this historical evolution is key to appreciating the current legal landscape of surveillance and its implications on civil liberties. The consequences of delayed regulation of surveillance are anything but trivial; they expose citizens to potentially uncontrolled government actions that continue to be of an intrusive nature. An examination of historical gaps in regulation reveals a trend whereby law enforcement agencies obtain new investigative techniques with impunity, as evidenced by the use of qualified immunity and the good faith exception in litigation. Delays in regulation are to blame for the cycle whereby social costs are incurred long prior to legislative remedies being instituted (Taslitz et al., 2009). The delays are compounded by various forms of delaying mechanisms by the police in most instances, which makes it increasingly difficult to seek justice in cases of unreasonable searches leading to problematic admissibility of evidence. A broader interpretation of the Fourth Amendment based on the right to be "protected" from unreasonable searches could hold out the potential for greater judicial control and proactive measures against omnipresent government intrusiveness. According to this perspective, history can serve not just as a guide to solving current challenges but as an argument for calling for a newly conceived system of protection of civil liberties in the face of constantly emergent surveillance technologies (Figure 4.4).

Figure 4.4. The historical context of search, seizure, and surveillance.

Source: https://www.livelaw.in/h-upload/2023/09/28/750x450_495209-search-and-seizure.webp.

4.1.1. Origins of Search and Seizure Laws

The origins of search and seizure laws in America have their roots in the experiences of colonial times involving abusive British practices, the most prominent of which was the issuance of general warrants referred to as writs of assistance. These writs gave authorities general authority to search people and property without specific reason, and this led to a pervasive distrust of unrestrained government power. The American colonial resistance to such unrestrained searches culminated in a desire for constitutional safeguards that would ensure citizens' rights. In response to these abuses in the immediate way, the Fourth Amendment was ratified, which enshrined the philosophy that the citizens should be free from unreasonable searches and seizures and thereby provided a minimum legal structure aimed at protecting individuals' privacy and property rights. In the developing phase of search and seizure laws, the probable cause became the determinative standard for the issuance of warrants. This requirement necessitated police to present sufficient evidence to an unbiased judge before they could conduct searches, thereby instituting a balance against arbitrary governmental intrusion. Additionally, the evolution of case law under the Fourth Amendment has continued shaping the legal world in terms of search and seizure. Important Supreme Court decisions have continued to define what would constitute an unreasonable search, adapting to societal conditions and technological advancements in the process and trying to balance individual rights with the needs of law enforcement. Its emphasis on historical background demonstrates how these laws and underlying case law were drafted as a safeguard against the very abuses colonists had suffered. In contemporary contexts, the use of search and seizure law continues to evolve, especially in the context of emerging digital technology. The law concerning electronic devices' searches reflects an enduring equilibrium between liberty and security. The case of extending border searches by agencies such as U.S. Customs and Border Protection (CBP) is a prime example of how traditional legal principles are being pushed to their limits by modern realities. Based on shifting meanings tracked in discussion of such practices, online searches can activate privacy concerns in dimensions beyond those of real searches, pushing the boundaries of the Fourth Amendment (Donohue et al., 2019). Conversely, the definition of receiving cell site location information points to the complexity of modern surveillance practices and their relative impact on personal privacy (Citron et al., 2017). Thus, the origins of search and seizure statutes do not merely reflect a historical struggle for freedom from too much government control but also signify ongoing debate over privacy rights in our highly computerized age.

4.1.2. Key Supreme Court Cases Shaping the Doctrine

The evolution of Fourth Amendment doctrine on search, seizure, and surveillance has in the headlines highlighted a line of landmark Supreme Court decisions that together shape the doctrine. One of the most influential cases is United States v. Katz, where the Court held that the Fourth Amendment protects persons, not places, thereby affirming citizens' reasonable expectations of privacy. This case broke new ground from prevailing common law perspectives regarding bodily intrusiveness, introducing the concept that electronic monitoring constituted a search within the Amendment. The effect of Katz carried forward into future decisions in that it laid the groundwork for the court to address the complexities generated by modern technology and observation methods, emphasizing the necessity for the court to adapt its interpretation in accordance with prevailing societal expectations and norms of privacy. A further landmark case is United States v. Jones, which explored the privacy right of an individual and the consequences of GPS tracking. The Courts decision identified long-term observation of a person's movements as a search, departing from previous narrow interpretations of governmental incursion. This ruling introduced the mosaic theory, which holds that the accumulation of data collected over time can yield intimate information about a person's life and therefore merit Fourth Amendment protection. Adopting this theory could usher in a significant shift in the judiciary's evaluation of surveillance and data gathering, particularly at a period when government surveillance powers are continually expanding. By laying down the possibility of cumulative surveillance as a potential breach of privacy rights, Jones has far-reaching implications for subsequent case law in digital privacy and police tactics (Slobogin et al., 2012). The Stored Communications Act (SCA) similarly demonstrates the interaction of legislative law and privacy rights in the context of digital surveillance. In cases such as United States v. Microsoft, the Court has to weigh competing interests between law enforcement needs and international standards of privacy. This case looks at whether US warrants can be directed at foreign information, citing gaps in existing law that fails to reflect the nature of the global digital world. Opponents have urged a reinterpretation of the SCA in light of changing times, with its provisions not providing adequate protection for user privacy in the globally networked world today. This tension between changing technology and outdated legislative frameworks underscores the need for legislative adaptation to balance the protection of individual rights with successful law enforcement measures (Kirschenbaum et al., 2018) (Figure 4.5).

Figure 4.5. Key supreme court cases shaping the doctrine.

Source: https://res.cloudinary.com/aenetworks/image/upload/c_fill,ar_2,w_3840,h_1920,g_auto/dpr_auto/f_auto/q_auto:eco/v1/supreme-court-1167833543?_a=BAVAZGDX0.

4.1.3. Evolution of Privacy Rights in the United States (U.S.)

The emergence of privacy rights in the U.S. has been shaped significantly by social change and technological advancements. The Fourth Amendment initially installed an elementary safeguard against unreasonable searches and seizures, reflecting the colonists' experience with authoritarian British rule. Over time, privacy rights' meaning has expanded to embrace new technology and methods of monitoring, which requires a balancing by the courts between government interests in law enforcement and individuals' expectations of privacy. Important legal precedent has emerged on issues such as electronic monitoring, warrantless searches, and applications of new technologies, which have remapped the landscape of privacy rights in contemporary society. Along with advancing technology is the shifting legal realm of privacy, which requires constant reconsideration of what constitutes reasonable expectation in a particular situation. The judiciary's reaction to emerging technology reveals the complexity of defining privacy rights under the Fourth Amendment. The milestone cases have confronted challenges to traditional notions of privacy by the government's application of electronic beepers and GPS tracking devices. In particular, the law of GPS monitoring highlights a basic divide between judges regarding the degree to which individuals should be entitled to a reasonable expectation of privacy over their travels. Of especial focus is whether individuals can expect privacy when they use technology enabling their tracking by service providers. This gray area of the law welcomes scrutiny, observing that developing technologies demand a re-examination of existing privacy norms to make sure that they remain protective against excessive state intrusion and thereby warrant the imposition of a robust legal regime keeping pace with technological change. The role of regulatory regimes and legal norms associated with privacy rights becomes ever more pressing, as surveillance technology saturates society. While the overall principle of "use precedes regulation" has guided the evolution of surveillance practices, it has also come at great social cost and elicited growing calls for greater protection against intrusive investigative tactics. Delay in regulation permits ill practices to diffuse unchecked that undermine citizens' trust in governmental institutions. Emphasizing the need for a more proactive role, some legal analysts are of the opinion that the Fourth Amendment needs to be interpreted so that it confers rights beyond safeguarding against unreasonable searches. By declaring privacy rights to be an element of human dignity, the courts will be able to establish a stronger foundation for citizens to withstand invasive government activity and hence increase the public's ability to defend their privacy against the rising tide of technology-based surveillance (Milligan et al., 2014; Plourde-Cole et al., 2010) (Figure 4.6).

Figure 4.6. The evolution of privacy rights in the United States.

Source: https://cdn.prod.website-files.com/6155ab6c75f4f8744b419dab/67a0eac99eba4bd783f9ddde_a%20history%20of%20privacy.jpeg.

4.2. THE FOURTH AMENDMENT

Fourth Amendment is a central element in upholding privacy rights of the individual in the American criminal procedure. It prohibits unreasonable search and seizure and makes warrants issue only upon probable cause attached with oath or affirmation. Over time, case law has had a significant impact on the definition of what constitutes a "search" or "seizure." The Supreme Court has recognized that actions such as wiretapping, aerial surveillance, and even thermal imaging are likely to trigger Fourth Amendment protection. Such elasticity is predicated on the necessity of safeguarding citizens against the vagaries of developing technology and trends in law enforcement. The ongoing discussion between privacy interests and governmental needs is indicative of the nuance required for the Fourth Amendment's application in a world with expanding surveillance capabilities that increasingly infringe upon personal freedom. Recent legal debates, including that of the mosaic theory set forth in United States v. Jones, reflect a turn in the Fourth Amendment's application to contemporary surveillance techniques. This is the theory that the cumulated data collected on an individual over extended periods of monitoring cannot individually be unreasonable but collectively must be deemed an unreasonable search and hence cause Fourth Amendment protection. This kind of expansion of Fourth Amendments' meaning could overthrow jurisprudence by establishing that aggregating information—especially in data mining contexts—violates citizens' right to privacy (Slobogin et al., 2012). With the police increasingly using more advanced surveillance technologies, there is a need for the legal standards under which they operate to be reviewed in order to ensure the delicate balance between public safety and personal privacy remains intact. In regard to consequences of means of surveillance used prior to being regulated, it is clear that the social costs of such practices can be profound and far-reaching. The "use before regulation" theory highlights that government agencies use investigatory methods without judicial oversight, and thus their powers are more liable to be abused. The pre-regulation era allows techniques to diffuse freely, which jeopardizes individual liberty immensely. Moreover, the expectation of immunity within this hiatus can result in arbitrary methods at the expense of constitutional protections. By holding to the broader Fourth Amendment interpretation, which stresses the individual's right to be "protected" and "free from fear," legislatures and courts can create precedents that encourage people to resist encroaching measures earlier in the regulatory process (Milligan et al., 2014). This preventive step may help safeguard individual rights and prevent workarounds of constitutional protections in the new age of technology.

4.2.1. Text and Interpretation of the Fourth Amendment

The Fourth Amendment's text and meaning have come a long way since its establishment, particularly in relation to changes in technology and law enforcement. Initially meant to protect citizens from unreasonable searches and seizures, the language of the Amendments is relatively wide and, as society's norms and technological environment shift, it has been interpreted in a variety of fashions. Judges often find themselves caught between the need to uphold constitutional protection and the ever-changing nature of the surveillance techniques used today. The result is a dynamic legal landscape, where courts are forced to contend with the implications of new technology on ancient common law precedents. This debate is an ongoing phenomenon that demonstrates the natural conflict within the Fourth Amendment, unveiling the difficulty of making historical precepts applicable to the present situation, especially in criminal procedure and the need for a nuanced judicial attitude towards new practices. With the increasing use of technologies by law enforcement branches, like digital retrieval of data and observation technologies, the Fourth Amendment comes under intense scrutiny for its adequacy in safeguarding the rights of individuals. Professor Orin Kerr's argument that the courts should exercise caution in construing the Amendment against the backdrop of technological advancements raises pertinent issues of legislatures' roles in developing broad paradigms of law enforcement. Kerr argues that legislators would be better placed to make plain and malleable rules, thereby filling the gap heralded by traditional judicial interpretations. But it must be critically examined that this perspective, keeping in view the fact that political processes may lag behind sudden technological advancements, as has been argued in the critiques of Kerr's assertions. The discourse regarding the Fourth Amendment, thus, needs a balanced framework that identifies judicial as much as legislative roles towards developing effective protection. In addition, the modern issues regarding the application of the Fourth Amendments involve questions of jurisdiction and international law, especially as they pertain to cyberspace. The Stored Communications Act is an example of this complexity; it regulates law enforcement access to cloud data but has difficulty dealing with the extraterritoriality of information stored across borders. As the case of United States v. Microsoft particularly emphasizes, the courts then have to decide whether it is legal to use U.S. warrants for data that is stored abroad and raise fundamental issues of sovereignty and right to privacy. The need for legislative action becomes apparent, as fixed legislation cannot possibly cover the complexities involved in communications technologies today. Based on recent legislative bills, it may be critical to build distinct legal procedures that honor user identity and jurisdictional boundaries, such that both individual rights and law enforcement objectives are adequately addressed in the evolving landscape of the Fourth Amendment (Figure 4.7).

Figure 4.7. Text and interpretation of the Fourth Amendment.

Source: https://www.thoughtco.com/thmb/nnHqHWDIdRtTOyHXMSX-6O3zCcU=/1500x0/filters:no_upscale():max_bytes(150000):strip_icc()/sb10069770d-001-56a153023df78cf77269a20a.jpg.

4.2.2. Reasonable Expectation of Privacy

The expectation of reasonableness is now at the heart of contemporary Fourth Amendment rhetoric and its application to forms of police surveillance and data gathering. Evolving through seminal Supreme Court opinions, this doctrine defines the boundaries of privacy rights citizens possess against state invasion. An underlying appreciation of this principle necessitates an awareness that privacy expectations can range from very different based on the given context and in accordance with prevailing societal norms for a particular setting. As technology grows more sophisticated, so too do the complexities of what makes up a reasonable expectation of privacy. The theoretical possibility of applying the mosaic theory, as in United States v. Jones, captures how collective surveillance data can intrude on privacy interests even if individual pieces of data would not typically be classed as intrusive (Slobogin et al., 2012). Additionally, the growing convergence between technology advancements and police practices renders the reasonable expectation standard challenging to apply. Professor Orin Kerr has claimed that Fourth Amendment safeguards are quickly disappearing in the legal sphere due to booming technological innovation, making courts hesitate to adequately decide on privacy matters (Solove et al., 2005).

Such hesitation may result in legislative action being necessary to adopt new legislation that specifically delineates privacy expectations where advanced surveillance technologies currently operate. The inability of courts to keep up with such technological advancements also raises doubts regarding judicial understandings of privacy being satisfactory, subjecting individuals to unrestrained surveillance procedures. While analyzing the implications of the reasonable expectation of privacy, it is also essential to analyze how society's comprehension develops along with legal standards. As people grow more aware of omnipresent surveillance and data mining, they might realign their expectations in terms of privacy. This fluidity in societal norms can impact judicial decision-making, eventually dictating the manner in which cases are resolved in matters of search and seizure. Even as law enforcement tries to strike a balance between public safety and personal rights, comprehension of the reasonable expectation of privacy is vital in assessing the legitimacy of a range of surveillance practices. The potential normalization of broadened surveillance can lead to the degradation of privacy expectations when not critically scrutinized, putting emphasis on the need for ongoing discourse and legislative interventions to protect individual rights in the intricate situations of modern surveillance (Slobogin et al., 2012) (Figure 4.8).

Figure 4.8. The concept of reasonable expectation of privacy.

Source: https://tampacrimeattorneys.com/wp-content/uploads/2024/03/ab34j34ju3u4.png.

4.2.3. Exceptions to the Warrant Requirement

The criminal procedure landscape is marked by broad exceptions to the warrant requirement, and each of these exceptions requires a delicate balance between public safety and individual rights. One such fundamental exception is the "exigent circumstances" doctrine under which police officers may search without a warrant in cases of immediate threat of life, destruction of evidence, or flight of a suspect. This exception emphasizes the necessity for police to act swiftly where delay to secure a warrant would disrupt public safety. This procedure, however, raises substance concerns regarding abuse potential and circumvention of constitutional protections. Critics have argued that this broad definition of exigent circumstances threatens arbitrary police behavior, basically undermining the limits of constitutional protection and potentially expanding government intrusions into private lives past enough checks. The search incident to arrest doctrine is a commonly debated exception that authorizes the police to search an individual and the surrounding area without a warrant upon arrest. This exception is reasonable on grounds that officers should be safeguarded against injury and that evidence should not destroy itself during the process of arrest. The extent of this exception has, however, been altered by a series of leading cases such as Chimel v. California, which reinforced that there must exist a close connection between the searches and the circumstances of the arrest. Although this doctrine is a significant pragmatic tool, it poses significant issues concerning its scope and boundaries, more specifically balancing effective law enforcement and individuals Fourth Amendment rights. The critics hold that such searches could be extended beyond their original purpose and scope and may potentially violate constitutional protections from unreasonable search and seizure. Outside of these exceptions, the automobile exception to the warrant requirement illustrates the complex interplay between law and evolving social norms, particularly for vehicle searches. The exception allows police to search a vehicle without a warrant when there is probable cause to believe that an automobile holds evidence of a crime. The rationale for this exception lies in the mobility of automobiles, which poses a threat that evidence will be lost or destroyed unless swift action is taken. The extensive application of the automobile exception has been condemned, however, along with its abuse potential and high racial profiling rates of traffic stops. This concern reflects broader societal concerns about the fairness and justice of policing operations. The ongoing debate over the appropriate boundaries of this exception demonstrates tensions in balancing technological innovation, like surveillance technologies, with privacy and security rights of individuals under the Fourth Amendment (Milligan et al., 2014; Solove et al., 2005) (Figure 4.9).

Figure 4.9. Exceptions to the warrant requirement.

Source: https://embed-ssl.wistia.com/deliveries/6d0bc42fabfa31e0afb968f0f117d008.jpg?image_resize=750.

4.3. SEARCH WARRANTS

The search warrant law is the cornerstone of Fourth Amendment protection from unreasonable searches and seizures in the United States. A search warrant is a formal order, typically handed down by a judge or magistrate, authorizing police to enter a specific location and take evidence pertaining to an ongoing investigation. The probable cause requirement is paramount; police are required to provide sufficient evidence to the issuing authority that there exists reasonable belief there is evidence of criminality at the specified place. This due process requirement stems from the desire to balance the interest of the government to investigate crime and privacy rights of an individual.

Figure 4.10. Search warrants.

Source: https://taxlawcanada.com/wp-content/uploads/2020/12/Search-Warrant-1200x630-630x630.png.

Neglect of these established procedures can lead to evidence being rendered inadmissible in court, pointing out all the more the critical role that search warrants play in upholding constitutional safeguards against unreasonable governmental invasion. The impact of current technology on the issuance and enforcement of search warrants cannot be overstated. With electronic communications and cloud storage multiplying, law enforcement officers are looking more and more to search warrants to obtain access to electronic data. Current legal frameworks are inadequately designed in many instances to cope with the unique problems generated by these technology advances. For instance, the Stored Communications Act, which governs law enforcement access to cloud data, does not adequately address international matters. Current court proceedings, such as the present U.S. Supreme Court case United States v. Microsoft, is the central question of extraterritorial jurisdiction of search warrants and potential interference with foreign sovereignty. Thus, procedures under search warrants must be thoroughly examined with respect to their adequacy and flexibility to ensure that they protect national security interests as well as privacy rights of individuals in an evolving digital landscape (Kirschenbaum et al., 2018). In addition, growth in surveillance methods has also created serious problems in regulatory terms concerning the regulation of investigative practices used prior to guideline formulation. The use precedes regulation explains how state actors can utilize particular surveillance methods in the lack of immediate regulation, which raises ethical concerns regarding monitoring of these processes.

This lag in regulation can create a world where unsafe investigative techniques are made the norm before they are subject to scrutiny. The critics urge a wider interpretation of Fourth Amendment protections to cover the right to be protected and safe from fear of such intrusiveness. By encouraging strict judicial standards against the use of uncontrolled surveillance methods, the judiciary is in a stronger position to safeguard constitutional protections and allow citizens to obtain timely redress. Overcoming these challenges is vital to ensuring public confidence in the law enforcement and judicial systems (Milligan et al., 2014) (Figure 4.10).

4.3.1. Requirements for Obtaining a Search Warrant

The execution of a warrant of search is a constitutional pillar of enforcing the Fourth Amendment safeguard from unreasonable searches and seizures. Law enforcement must establish probable cause to obtain a warrant, a procedural requirement which requires facts constituting a reasonable belief that the criminal activity is present or criminal evidence can be attained within the premises to be searched. This is a condition for ensuring that the public is not exposed to unnecessary governmental intrusion. The warrant also demands that there must be an affidavit sworn by the requesting officer, which states the facts and the circumstances supporting the conclusion of probable cause. In the absence of such fundamental requirements, legality for the search can be jeopardized and any evidence found excluded, thereby emphasizing the importance of adherence to procedural safeguards in order to protect individual rights. In addition to providing evidence of probable cause, the warrant itself is also to be specific in terms, such as the location to be searched and items to be seized.

This level of specificity serves to prevent overbroad and intrusive searches that could infringe on privacy interests. Judges have insistently demanded that general warrants, which fail to clearly mark the subject of the search, infringe Fourth Amendment protections. This emphasis upon specificity is more than a formality; it is what ensures searches are done upon a definite legal basis and thereby limits abuse of authority by law enforcement. Furthermore, the execution of the warrant must be within the time frames and other conditions listed in the warrant, emphasizing law enforcement to operate within a legally prescribed framework when performing searches. Furthermore, the evolving technology and surveillance context makes it more difficult to define the terms for obtaining a search warrant.

As the Supreme Courts consideration of the mosaic theory and related issues makes clear, there is increasingly widespread acknowledgement that collecting data points can be a Fourth Amendment search, and there are serious questions as to how warrants must be obtained in those circumstances (Slobogin et al., 2012). In addition, experts have also argued that new legislative regulations may be needed to adapt to the increased pace of technology advances, and courts are then asked to practice restraint with respect to emerging technologies in investigative methods (Solove et al., 2005). Therefore, the fundamental needs of warrants remain at the center of maintaining effectiveness in criminal investigations while preserving fundamental individual rights.

4.3.2. Execution of Search Warrants

The issuance of warrants to search is a critical element within the doctrine of criminal procedure to ensure that law enforcement can follow proper legal procedure while safeguarding the rights of citizens. A search warrant is a court-issued permission slip that grants law enforcement officials entry onto privately owned property in order to search for specific things relating to criminal activity. The Fourth Amendment mandates that such warrants must be based on probable cause and clearly state the places to be searched and the things to be seized. This provision serves to limit unthinking governmental incursion and asserts an individual's privacy right. But while the theoretical issuance of these warrants is always easy, the actual application of them tends to be problematic, given that the quick evolution of technology complicates long-held notions of property and privacy, eventually influencing the methods in which the police undertake searches. Proper application of search warrants in modern law enforcement must then address the intricacies brought by the technology environment. For instance, with information booming in the age of technology, warrants may have to extend beyond physical objects to extend to digital information remotely stored, for instance, in cloud storage. This poses very deep legal questions of jurisdiction and constitutional protections, particularly where data is stored within foreign jurisdictions. As evidenced by recent controversies surrounding the Stored Communications Act, recent cases like United States v. Microsoft have sparked discussions surrounding the applicability of warrants to access such information across borders. The legislative reform call runs with the imperative of clear rules that acknowledge current technological realities without sacrificing people's rights to privacy and due process, upholding the significance of lawful implementation of warrant in this new paradigm (Kirschenbaum et al., 2018). Moreover, the regulatory lag for addressing the implementation of search warrants suggests an implicit weakening of constitutional protections. Because government actors tend to exploit restricted windows of lawful search activity in anticipation of regulatory intervention, it is possible that it will create a precedent that has risky investigation methods proliferating without adequate restraints. "Use precedes regulation" means the society's costs that occur as a result of uncontrolled searches may escalate without taking positive steps to restrain such investigations. At a moment when investigative practices evolve rapidly, the judicial construction of the Fourth Amendment becomes increasingly significant, expanding the concept of individuals' rights to be free from unreasonable searches and seizures. By promoting judicially-created rules tackling the longstanding delays in formalized regulation processes, a stronger legal framework would rise, hence protecting citizens effectively from unregulated government intervention in the implementation of search warrants (Milligan et al., 2014) (Figure 4.11).

Figure 4.11. The execution of search warrants.

Source: https://assets.cat5.com/images/tactical-experts/officers-guide-to-preparing-and-executing-a-search-warrant/warrant-execution.jpg.

4.3.3. Challenges to the Validity of Search Warrants

Validity of search warrants is often challenged on diverse grounds, and this has far-reaching implications for criminal procedure. One significant problem involves the probable cause to justify a warrant. Courts have specified that probable cause must be based on something greater than suspicion; it needs to be grounded on a substantial basis upon which to conclude that evidence of an offense most likely will exist. However, the police can occasionally introduce weak or false evidence to create probable cause, and an arguably defective warrant is issued as a consequence. This can be seen as a sign that serious questions exist regarding protections that are afforded under the system to prevent the unreasonable seizure and search of individuals, as the Fourth Amendment requires. Finally, an invalid warrant can render all the evidence obtained in the process of that search ineligible to be used in court, hence impacting the direction of criminal cases and reaffirming the necessity of rigorous judicial criteria when reviewing warrant applications. The second major challenge to the validity of search warrants comes from the execution process itself. Police officers are obligated to execute warrants according to the detailed procedural law, including observing the knock and announce requirement, which entails announcing officers' presence and purpose of entry before forced entry into occupied space. Violation of this rule leads to accusations of unconstitutional conduct, invalidating the search. Additionally, overuse of force or disregard for privacy interests can dramatize public apprehensions about police excesses and possible abuse. Within this scenario, perceptions of civilians concerning the execution of search warrants have the potential to influence discussions at large about police practices' legitimacy. In order to reinforce confidence in the criminal justice system and ensure constitutional protections against unreasonable searches are upheld, these variables are a top priority, as citizens should be entitled to a right to feel secure in their homes and personal communications. Further, the creation of advanced surveillance technology creates new challenges to the validity of search warrants. Because government bureaus increasingly employ unregulated or under-regulated technical equipment to survey individuals, proper policing techniques and invasive techniques become blurred. The Fourth Amendment promise of privacy is also vulnerable to being greatly eroded if police agencies engage in practices infringing on individual freedoms without sufficient judicial supervision. The significance of this shift is wide-ranging, leading to a call that existing legal frameworks around search warrants need to be readdressed. To address these concerns, courts can potentially review the time-tested definitions of unreasonable searches and seizures and reprobe the evolving nature of privacy in the digital age. These measures would result in more definitive rules and greater safeguards against overreaching government, ultimately supporting the constitutional rights safeguarding citizens privacy and autonomy in the eras of ubiquitous surveillance technologies, highlighting the necessity of wholesale reform of the judiciary (Burton et al., 2006; Milligan et al., 2014).

4.4. EXCLUSIONARY RULE

The Exclusionary Rule is a necessary safeguard in the regime of search, seizure, and surveillance in criminal procedure. It mandates that evidence acquired by invasions of constitutional rights, particularly the Fourth Amendment, be excluded at trial. Its intention is to discourage law enforcement authorities from conducting unwarranted searches and seizures and thereby preserve judicial integrity and public confidence in the judicial process. The more sophisticated the methods of governmental investigation and surveillance, the more evident the necessity of the Exclusionary Rule becomes. Without such a rule, there is greater potential for abuse of investigatory techniques and an erosion of civic liberties and human rights with more serious ethical concerns regarding government overreach in policing practices which are unregulated (Milligan et al., 2014). Tension about the Exclusionary Rule is also increased by recent Supreme Court decisions questioning its enforcement.

Figure 4.12. The exclusionary rule.

Source: https://lh4.googleusercontent.com/proxy/2ECkhxbHWUWIO2ZP_MPQQ5u30r3lRD_2i-6BDU6t2gNBkLAjGlGNcrXh1mB_v1jFm-DCL29-A45p_1u2GjXD_xmw5h8A66azwwfzw-w2mVW7rqF5XBAwX-BuOBbmXw.

Of special mention are the Hudson v. Michigan and Herring v. United States cases, whereby there has been a developing rift among the justices regarding the cost-benefit approach to exclusion. Critics argue that the existing practice is excessively preoccupied with the release of guilty individuals, rather than with ensuring that law enforcement is in conformity with constitutional standards. As some judges would put it, excluding evidence would impair the effectiveness of the judicial system, and others would posit that respecting the rule serves to maintain civil liberties and discourage arbitrary authority. The arguments that follow underscore the necessity of balancing government interests against accused rights, and pose the Exclusionary Rule as a paradigm mechanism for keeping those in power accountable (Dripps et al., 2010). Initiatives to improve the Exclusionary Rule are imperative when handling such matters, particularly issues of law enforcement accountability. Proposed strategies, like the virtual deterrence model, advance that the courts can demand unique remedial measures from the police forces before deciding to exclude evidence. The system aims to deter future violations and promote compliance with the constitutional protection, thereby improving the integrity of the legal process. It is the duty of policymakers and law scholars to adjust these evolving dynamics such that the Exclusionary Rule remains effective and authoritative in an era where surveillance technology evolves rapidly. The Exclusionary Rule is a foundational tenet in the pursuit of justice that wards off the balance between security and individual rights within broader criminal procedure (Dripps et al., 2010) (Figure 4.12).

4.4.1. Definition and Purpose of the Exclusionary Rule

The exclusionary rule is a fundamental criminal procedure legal doctrine, whose purpose is to protect the integrity of the judicial process. It is primarily intended to deter the utilization of evidence obtained as a result of unconstitutional searches or seizures, particularly those which violate the Fourth Amendment, which safeguards the people against unreasonable searches and seizures. By implementing this rule, courts wish to deter the police from engaging in illegal activities that infringe on individuals' rights. The overall purpose is not just to protect the defendant but also to preserve public confidence in the administration of justice and the enforceability of constitutional protections. This purpose of the exclusionary rule is in accordance with the view that the legitimacy of the judicial process is most important, ultimately determining society's perception of the neutrality of legal proceedings. The exclusionary rule has been a controversial topic for many years in legal theory. Opponents of the rule commonly argue the rule can hinder the prosecutions from securing convictions, particularly when the key evidence is discovered to be inadmissible due to procedural violations or abuse of rights. In traditional cases like Hudson v. Michigan, the court has revisited and argued over the efficacy of the exclusionary rule, with some judges believing it could potentially hinder justice rather than promote it. Further, in Herring v. United States, dissenting opinions brought up the cost-benefit analysis of applying the rule, deprecating that they dismiss broader issues with judicial integrity and the long-term impacts of police activity. Such controversy signals the complexities and evolving perceptions of the exclusionary rule in contemporary judicial practice, as it navigates a thin line between safeguarding rights and guaranteeing justice. The rationale behind the exclusionary rule runs deeper than simply to ensure taint is excluded from the courtroom; it is an accommodation to system checks and balances that are meant to deter improper government conduct. As there is a shifting landscape of laws, so too shifts discussion about possible reform of the exclusionary rule, e.g., as hinted at by an approach to "virtual deterrence.." This approach encourages open accountability processes prior to evidence suppression being implemented, with emphasis on the obligation of law enforcement bureaus to implement training and remedial action in answer to constitutional violations. These solutions aim to encourage compliance with the law while limiting instances of misconduct, for the least possible risk of culprits escaping justice. The ongoing controversy concerning the definition and purpose of the exclusionary rule is emblematic of a deeper scrutiny of its role in the general design of search, seizure, and surveillance within criminal procedure, ultimately seeking balance between individual rights and the pursuit of effective law enforcement.

4.4.2. Key Cases Establishing the Exclusionary Rule

The exclusionary rule, established with the aim of safeguarding the Fourth Amendment protections, prohibits courts from admitting evidence that has been confiscated in violation of a person's constitutional right against unreasonable searches and seizures. This rule of law was largely established in historic Supreme Court cases. A landmark case is Weeks v. United States (1914), where the Court determined that proof obtained through a Fourth Amendment violation by federal officers was inadmissible in federal prosecutions. This landmark decision not only provided the foundation for the exclusionary rule but also articulated the requirement of government deference to constitutional rights, an essential precursor to later Fourth Amendment precedent. The exclusionary rule seeks to dissuade police departments from engaging in illegitimate searches by removing any incentive to ignore constitutional norms. Subsequent cases refined and bolstered the paradigm of the exclusionary rule. Notably, Mapp v. Ohio (1961) expanded the reach of the exclusionary rule to state courts, ruling that state evidence obtained through illegitimate searches would not be admissible in court. The Courts decision brought to the forefront the necessity to uniformly apply the exclusionary rule across all state and federal jurisdictions, emphasizing that the Fourth Amendment protection should not be determined by the level of government. Mapps contribution depicted the dedication of the judiciary to protecting citizens' rights, essentially wrestling with the greater significance of police practices. This seminal shift in Fourth Amendment theory emphasizes the ongoing tension between state power and personal freedoms, determining the parameters of the arguments over what constitutes a reasonable search. Under contemporary law, the exclusionary rule is still contentious and scrutinized to an unprecedented degree, particularly as it can be seen being applied in decisions such as Hudson v. Michigan and Samson v. California, where the relevance of the rule in various contexts for searches was challenged. The Hudson ruling, which held that knock-and-announce violations do not trigger exclusionary remedies, provoked fundamental questions regarding the integrity of Fourth Amendment protection. Critics contend that such decisions point towards favoring law enforcement interests over the rights of individuals, undermining the Fourth Amendment's original purpose. The evolving court interpretations illustrate the need for a balance between effective policing and safeguarding the constitutional rights of citizens, as evidenced by the recent jurisprudential trends that threaten the very foundations of the exclusionary rule, as deconstructed in critical examinations of such trends (Castiglione et al., 2007; Doernberg et al., 2006) (Figure 4.13).

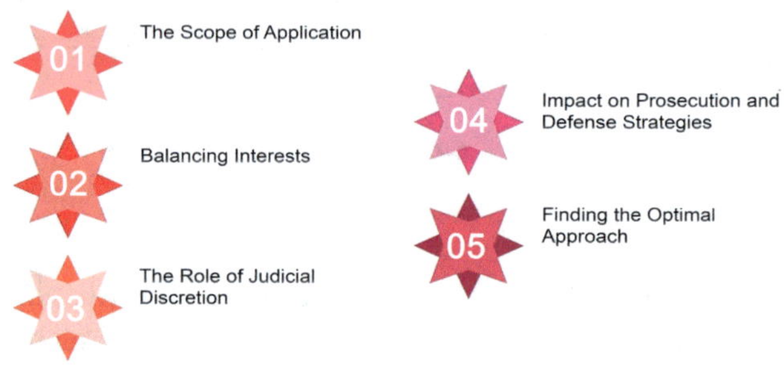

Figure 4.13. Key cases establishing the exclusionary rule.

Source: https://fastercapital.co/i/The-Broad-Evidence-Rule--An-Exception-to-the-Exclusionary-Rule--Exclusionary-Rule-vsBroad-Evidence-Rule.webp.

4.4.3. Limitations and Exceptions to the Exclusionary Rule

The exclusionary rule is a valuable device designed to deter illegal conduct on the part of law enforcement officials by excluding illegally derived evidence based on the Fourth Amendment. While loopholes and exceptions have been judicially created to some extent, enabling certain kinds of evidence to be admissible even in cases of procedural violations,. A prominent exception is the good faith exception, enunciated in United States v. Leon, which permits the admission of evidence obtained by officers who reasonably believed they were acting in accordance with a valid warrant, although the warrant proves to be defective. This exception captures a pragmatic reaction by judicial circles to balance the need for effective law enforcement against respecting constitutional rights at the expense of diluting the deterrent impact of the exclusionary rule. Further, the attenuation doctrine itself presents a significant restriction on what evidence can be admitted, and it provides that the evidence can be admitted if the illegal search and discovery of evidence relationship is distant enough or severed by intervening circumstances. Courts resolve issues of how close in time the illegal activity was and whether the defendant appeared voluntarily at the later discovery of evidence. The doctrine thus suggests judicial acceptability that the exclusionary rule should not be enforced absolutely, especially when the initial illegality is clearly distanced from the evidence. Such a judicial development suggests movement towards maintaining the effective functionality of law enforcement on occasions at the expense of the strict protection anticipated by the Fourth Amendment. In addition, the inevitable discovery doctrine allows for the admission of evidence if it can be established that law enforcement authorities would inevitably have learned of the evidence through lawful means. This exception, developed in Nix v. Williams, is based upon the belief that excluding evidence that otherwise would have been obtained lawfully does not further importantly the goals of the exclusionary rule. Through this method, the courts prioritize outcomes over procedural integrity, risking the abuse of authority in investigations. As these limitations illustrate, there is a sensitive balance between the protection of constitutional rights and ensuring law enforcement is effective, an environment increasingly determined by developing technologies and regulatory environments as referenced in the wider body of discourse on surveillance and investigatory procedures (Milligan et al., 2014; Solove et al., 2005).

4.5. SURVEILLANCE TECHNIQUES

Surveillance techniques have evolved dramatically through advances in technology, and the questions regarding concern over their effect on civil liberties have been paramount. Police weapons like electronic surveillance, data gathering, and social media spying generally operate in an arena where regulatory comprehension falls behind. This delay has the potential to create a scenario wherein government officials avail themselves of intrusive measures unregulated, essentially perpetuating a scenario wherein rules or the lack thereof permit great intrusions into privacy. This lag can be traced to various factors involving delay tactics by law enforcement institutions and legislative process challenges. The resultant environment often supports the massive application of harmful investigative methods, thus necessitating regulation that distinguishes what is permissible for surveillance practice within the context of constitutional liberties (Milligan et al., 2014). A major role of contemporary surveillance practices is that they can disrupt the core requirements of privacy as protected in the Fourth Amendment.

Figure 4.14. Surveillance techniques.

Source: https://www.aryaman.co.in/wp-content/uploads/2023/10/Surveillance-Investigations-Techniques-and-Technology-The-Art-of-Surveillance-Aryaman-Detective-Agency.jpg.

The social compact between government and citizens is founded on a commitment of a reasonable amount of privacy and protection against unwanted intrusions. Courts have always stressed the right of freedom from unreasonable searches and seizures, but there has been more recognition of needing to interpret that right more expansively. By framing it as a right to be "protected" against unauthorized surveillance, there emerges a compelling argument for a more proactive judicial approach to safeguarding privacy. Such an interpretation acknowledges the fears that arise from the unchecked deployment of surveillance technologies and aims to restore a balance between governmental interests in security and the individual's right to privacy (Milligan et al., 2014). Also, the new "mosaic theory" subverts traditional privacy concepts by calling attention to the combined effect of surveillance practices and data collection. It assumes that despite individuals' consent to sharing of separate pieces of information, assembling those points of information can reveal vast glimpses of their lives, ultimately invading their reasonable expectations of privacy. This paradigm shift in measuring privacy rights demands that the courts consider both quantitative and qualitative aspects in information collection, thereby facing the danger of an authoritarian surveillance state. The engagement with this theory not only underscores the nuances involved in today's surveillance practice but also recognizes the imperative of judicial prudence in policing modern-day surveillance technology to protect against overreaching governmental intrusion (Figure 4.14).

4.5.1. Types of Surveillance Used in Criminal Investigations

Surveillance is a core aspect of the criminal investigations' field and an invaluable weapon for criminal investigation agencies. Employing surveillance ranges from traditional to modern technologies from physical surveillance and tapping, to computerized surveillance and social media analysis. Physical surveillance involves officers observing suspects in the present moment to gain insight into their activities. Wiretapping, however, allows investigators to intercept individual communications through the use of telephonic or electronic means. As much as the methods have assisted in numerous cases, they pose unavoidable constitutional concerns regarding privacy rights and due process under the Fourth Amendment. Balance between institutional demands of proper law enforcement and protection of rights of citizens is always a contentious issue with which courts must cope in evolving legal landscapes. Technology has significantly transformed the realm of criminal investigation surveillance. Police forces increasingly employ sophisticated tools such as drone technology, facial recognition software, and mobile-based tracking. These innovations are supplementary to traditional means, facilitating better data collection and crime monitoring. However, these innovations also come with substantial ethical implications as well as controversies regarding legal regimes under which such conduct takes place. For instance, while such technologies as GPS tracking can be valuable tools for investigations, they can intrude on someone's reasonable expectation of privacy. As courts decide cases involving such technologies, it is pertinent to consider the recommendations made by scholars such as Professor Orin Kerr, who suggest exercising caution in embracing Fourth Amendment protections in adapting to evolving technology (Solove et al., 2005). Caution must be exercised to ensure a balancing and differential approach is adopted in the application of methods of surveillance. The scope of surveillance is not limited to the boundaries of a country, particularly when it comes to seeking digital evidence stored outside of the country. The Stored Communications Act mirrors the legal difficulty of international data access, in that it falls short of the digital age's sophistication. Current law fails to keep pace with the nuances involved when U.S. law enforcement officers issue warrants for information held in foreign countries. United States v. Microsoft is the classic case for the urgent need for the Supreme Court to define the parameters of this legal challenge and whether present legislation can be extraterritorially applied (Kirschenbaum et al., 2018). A legislative approach has been proposed to provide clearer directives on law enforcement practices, seeking distinct domestic and international processes to respect foreign sovereignty while addressing contemporary surveillance methods' issues. The reconciliation of law enforcement interests with individual privacy protection remains a challenging problem in criminal procedure.

4.5.2. Legal Standards Governing Electronic Surveillance

The Fourth Amendment, which protects citizens from unreasonable search and seizure, is the legal requirement that essentially outlines the guidelines of electronic monitoring. The challenge has been created with increasing technology since courts are finding it challenging to determine what constitutes a search in today's cyber era, particularly with the ability to aggregate data and conduct surveillance expanding. This is compounded by legislation that sometimes lacks the clarity and comprehensiveness the court system prefers. Academics like Orin Kerr call for judicial restraint in interpretation and suggest that legislatures play a more prominent role in making rules that tackle new technologies. Kerr's view recognizes a fundamental tension of constitutional law, under which courts and Congress tend to disagree on how to respond to the out-of-sync rate of technological advances (Solove et al., 2005).

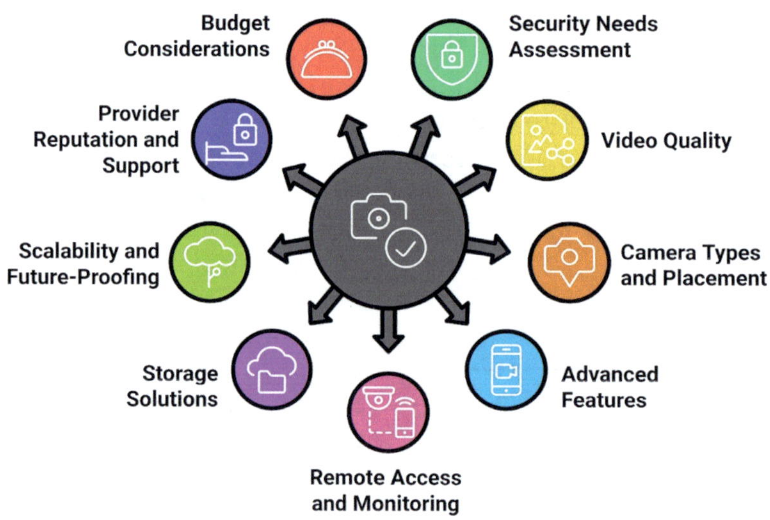

Figure 4.15. The legal standards governing electronic surveillance.

Source: https://www.sibservices.in/wp-content/uploads/2023/12/how-to-choose-the-right-electronic-Surveillance-company.png.

Mosaic theory has been at the forefront of recent legal debate, with particular relevance to whether an aggregation perspective towards surveillance can be viewed as a violation of privacy. The Supreme Court decision in United States v. Jones suggests that monitoring a person's movements over time arguably amounts to a search within the meaning of the Fourth Amendment. If the courts accept mosaic theory, the potential effect on judicial standards for electronic surveillance is profound. This shift could lead to a reconsideration of reasonable expectation of privacy by appreciating that seemingly innocuous data points—when aggregated—can form a vast picture of an individual. As courts argue about how this theory should be applied most effectively, the necessity to construct firm statutory standards is essential (Slobogin et al., 2012). Legislative frameworks of electronic surveillance must be regularly updated to keep pace with new technology and address the deficiency of existing law. As Kerr contends, legislatures possess unique capacities for formulating rules that are more sensitive to technological change, but these are weighed against the patchwork character of current protections. History attests that legislatures are behind judicial innovations, with the consequence being a patchwork of legislation which places citizens at risk. Moreover, whereas courts attempt to place contemporary surveillance methods within outmoded legal frameworks, technological misconceptions act to amplify constitutional risks. Therefore, a conciliatory approach that balances legislative action and judicial vigilance is necessitated to formulate robust legal standards that adequately protect privacy interests in a networked world (Solove et al., 2005) (Figure 4.15).

4.5.3. Impact of Technology on Surveillance Practices

Technological progress has dramatically transformed surveillance practices, reconfiguring the machinery through which law enforcement gathers data on private and public space. Technologies such as closed-circuit television (CCTV), drone technology, and facial recognition technology have amplified the capability of police forces to collect information and monitor individuals, apparently for purposes of crime prevention.

However, these technologies have also produced tremendous controversies regarding privacy rights and civil liberties. For instance, in Florida's city of Tampa, the implementation of the FaceIt facial recognition system was protested by privacy activists who accused the use of such technology as a rights violation by taking photographs of individuals without their consent. This controversy highlights the conflict between apparent public safety benefits and the danger of unregulated surveillance practice encroaching on privacy, suggesting that the mass adoption of technological surveillance has a tendency to overwhelm public debate and regulatory controls (Taslitz et al., 2002). The argument that "use precedes regulation" in surveillance also highlights the necessity for control in the era where technology outpaces the law. This principle contends that before the identification of useful regulation, law enforcement agencies tend to misuse new surveillance tools in the absence of requisite guidelines or limits, paving the way for the social costs of invasive investigation techniques being mainly unfathomable. During the interim between bringing in such techniques and subsequent regulation, law enforcement officials enjoy a functional impunity, normally resulting in inappropriate and arbitrary surveillance. The lengthened delay in regulation stems from a variety of reasons, including bureaucratic delaying tactics and political maneuvering complexities within law enforcement, which are likely to defer necessary debate on the ethics of technology in surveillance (Milligan et al., 2014). Additionally, the argument surrounding the Fourth Amendment's protection reflects the complexities of balancing individual rights against surveillance technological advancements. Traditionally interpreted as a shield against unreasonable searches and seizures, the language of the Fourth Amendment has also been used to cover other protection rights from intrusive surveillance behavior that inspires fear among the public. More expansive interpretations of the Amendment, however, require more than the government avoiding unreasonable searches but also ensuring citizens are free from random surveillance tactics. This strategy provides a framework for judicial action prior to the implementation of regulations, thereby enabling persons to challenge invasive surveillance tactics as unconstitutional. Therefore, reexamination of the Fourth Amendment's meaning in the context of modern surveillance technologies can be applied to create a more robust protective regime sensitive to the evolving landscape of privacy rights and state power in criminal procedure (Milligan et al., 2014).

4.6. BALANCING SECURITY AND PRIVACY

The balancing act between privacy and security is vivified so intensely in the Fourth Amendment case against unreasonable searches and seizures. The constitutional protection is one of a fundamental value in society meant to preclude random government intrusions into individuals' personal lives. High-tech surveillance capabilities complicate this balance, however. Law enforcement authorities argue that more surveillance authority is essential to preserve public safety and effectively combat crime. Citizens, however, have a valid concern regarding their right to privacy and the potential for government overreach. This tension is rendered quite apparent in cases involving digital data, where expansive definitions of search power threaten to destroy the very privacy that the Fourth Amendment purports to safeguard.

Figure 4.16.

Source: https://www.uscybersecurity.net/wp-content/uploads/2016/04/23Technology-and-the-Tension-between-Security-and-Privacy-1.jpg.

The consequences of technological innovations on privacy rights have prompted legal minds and legislators to reevaluate existing structures that govern surveillance. Laws such as the Stored Communications Act currently provide a paradigm under which law enforcement's access to online information is justified. Nevertheless, as the commentary makes clear, legislation like this does not keep pace with high-speed technological advances, particularly on foreign data storage and access. This imbalance raises inherent questions about the adequacy of current legal protection aimed at weighing individual privacy against successful law enforcement. As a response to such deficiencies, a likely legislative solution is the establishment of independent legal processes that distinguish between domestic and extraterritorial access to information. By proposing such frameworks, interests may try to respect foreign sovereignty and provide exact guidelines for law enforcements investigatory power in an effort to advance security as well as privacy. Secondly, modern legal theory has placed a big emphasis on the requirement of a mosaic theory approach, realizing that the assembly of seemingly innocuous information can provide a broad-encompassing portrait of an individual's life that needs protecting with the Fourth Amendment. It is this perspective that highlights the importance of courts not only looking at specific instances of surveillance, but also balancing the broader effect of data collection overall. As witnessed through the Supreme Court non-decision, there is growing recognition that the citizen is entitled to a reasonable expectation of some privacy as it relates to their collective information. While doing so, one should remember the law enforcement legitimate interests in using surveillance technology to address serious public safety concerns. Achieving the balance between the two will require advanced policies that safeguard individual liberties but still allow law enforcement agencies to perform their tasks appropriately (Citron et al., 2013; Kirschenbaum et al., 2018) (Figure 4.16).

4.6.1. Tensions Between Law Enforcement and Individual Rights

This integration of law enforcement action and personal rights has become more emotionally charged with tension, particularly in the fields of search, seizure, and monitoring. Advances in technology have allowed law enforcement agencies to carry out extensive digital forensics, including numerous methodologies tracing the online activities that might be symptomatic of crime. Though these features enhance anti-cybercrime, they have serious ethical problems relating to privacy violations and individual rights. With the governments embracing the developments, the danger of untrammeled investigations heightens, violating individuals legal right to privacy. The challenges cut across multiple levels, and calls have been made for a balanced means of dealing with the balancing act between privacy protection and effective law enforcement. The paradigm itself necessitates governments to balance on a tightrope, allowing them investigatory rights to avoid unfairly encroaching on the freedoms afforded to citizens without compromising democratic society's foundational values. As digital forensics evolves, the ethical complexities of its use become increasingly evident. Monitoring and extracting employees, justifications as measures needed to stop crime, could in themselves violate organizations' rights over their intellectual capital. The pressure placed on forensic examiners to secure convictions puts them under a conflict between attaining law enforcement objectives and adherence to ethical standards that honor individual and organizational rights. The conflict is amplified within the criminal justice arena, where investigative efforts aimed at securing evidence can compromise both legal entities and suspect privacy rights. As noted in the discussion regarding the proposed PRECEpt framework, it is essential to establish standards that not only guarantee efficient investigations but also eliminate the risk of perceived injustice to stakeholders, thus restoring the confidence in law enforcement processes while still ensuring individual rights and organizational interests (Ferguson et al., 2020). In addition, the implications of poor controls in digital investigations extend beyond the privacy of the subject. The overall social impact of perceived lack of justice can foster public distrust of police conduct, ultimately working against the very aims these investigative methods are designed to achieve. If the public feels that its rights are being withheld or that investigations are not equitable, the foundation of cooperation between the public and the police is eroded. This scenario highlights the inherent need of possessing a consonant legal framework to keep up with expectations and rights of stakeholders across the board. Implications drawn from varied practices in alternative jurisdictions, e.g., harmonization exercises witnessed in the context of intellectual property rights in Gulf Cooperation Council States, can be utilized in developing equitable legal standards in the field of digital forensics (Alfadhel et al., 2016). Consequently, a remedy which finds equilibrium between the requirements of law enforcement and the unalienable rights of the public is not only in demand but necessary to the preservation of justice and public trust.

4.6.2. Public Perception of Surveillance and Privacy

Public perception of surveillance and privacy is a controversial issue in contemporary society, particularly as it relates to criminal procedure. As technology advances, the threat of government agencies collecting, analyzing, and storing great amounts of personal information grows. This has contributed to increased public concern regarding erosion of Fourth Amendment protection of privacy rights. Fourth Amendment case law has historically grown in a patchwork manner to accommodate evolving governmental methods of intrusion, producing a congruently uneven legal landscape with emerging public expectations of privacy. The critics argue that the courts have traditionally overstated the notion of one reasonable expectation, not considering the complex nature of privacy expectations in the age of the Internet, and with it creating a gap between legal safeguards and what the public views as surveillance (Doernberg et al., 2006). The applications of advanced surveillance technologies, such as facial recognition and live monitoring, have caused immense controversy at the intersection of security and civil liberties. While the proponents refer to how such technologies enhance public safety, the privacy campaigners raise the threat of unchecked surveillance power. In cities like Tampa, municipal governments adopted installations like FaceIt due to their ability to combat crime, but such a strategy found itself at odds with citizens who perceived that the undermining of privacy and lack of consent in information collection were concerns (Taslitz et al., 2002). These demonstrations are reflective of a broader public skepticism, with citizens increasingly recognizing that good government cannot be at the cost of fundamental rights to privacy and personal freedom, and therefore calls for stricter controls on surveillance methods. In addition, the perception of the public is not only determined by short-term response to surveillance, but also by mounting concern with its effect on democratic freedoms and social trust. As cases of surveillance become common, the general sentiment shifts towards suspicion, with individuals feeling that they are always being watched. This kind of environment breeds suspicion in state institutions purportedly committed to safeguarding citizens' rights. The two conflicting narratives of security and privacy pose significant questions about the legitimacy and transparency of the surveillance practice in criminal proceedings. So, as the world struggles with the intricate balance of surveillance and privacy, it is important to review the legal framework behind these practices so that they continue to uphold values and public opinion in today's age (Doernberg et al., 2006) (Figure 4.17).

Figure 4.17. Public perception of surveillance and privacy.

Source: https://theincmagazine.com/wp-content/uploads/2022/10/Surveillance-Technologys-Impact-on-Privacy.jpg.

4.6.3. Legislative Responses to Privacy Concerns

Legislatively, the landscape of privacy issues has changed considerably in recent years due to increased sensitivity towards governmental surveillance. In the face of expanding capabilities of law enforcement to collect information, legislatures have begun to examine how to safeguard personal privacy rights without unduly compromising public safety. Such a prominent case here is the Supreme Court decision in United States v. Jones, which effectively opened up the possibility of a mosaic theory of Fourth Amendment law. Such a theory suggests that the aggregate of discrete bits of information taken through surveillance could equal a search and thus need a warrant and probable cause. As a result, there are efforts from lawmakers to enact the guidelines into public legislation as the rate at which technology is changing tends to outpace existing legal frameworks (Slobogin et al., 2012). Apart from the above shifts in judicial interpretations, some municipalities have enacted privacy acts voluntarily to ease tension on surveillance technology. For instance, the implementation of the FaceIt system, which improves public safety through the use of facial recognition technology, in Tampa, Florida, was met with strong resistance from privacy rights activists. The critics maintained that the adoption of the technology without the consent of people infringes on the right to privacy. This instance signals the paradox between security policies advocated for by law enforcers and the civil rights question raised by the public, highlighting the imperative to have serious deliberations between local governments and community stakeholders before presenting surveillance technology. Legislative responses, therefore, must maintain a delicate balance that is sensitive to issues of privacy while being instrumental to the efficacy of law enforcement (Taslitz et al., 2002). In addition, the necessity of strong data protection law has gained ground as public sensitivity towards surveillance issues expands. Policymakers are increasingly being called to consider measures that place responsibility and transparency requirements on the surveillance practices of law enforcement bodies and private corporations both. These may be through mandatory reporting of the use of surveillance technology, well-defined data retention requirements, and effective mechanisms of oversight and redress. Through policymaking which ensures accountability on the part of the authorities in their use of surveillance equipment, parliamentarians are able to establish public trust while protecting simultaneously the privacy rights of people. As privacy law develops further, legislators have to apply a looking-forward approach in enacting legislation that is capable of keeping up with emergent technology and addressing the subtleties of privacy in the age of information.

SUMMARY

The interdynamic push-and-pull between search, seizure, and surveillance in criminal process serves to underscore the significant role that legal regimes have to adapt to keep up with technological advances. The strengthening of surveillance methods calls for re-examination of existing legislation to ascertain that they indeed achieve the balance between law enforcement interests and the protection of citizen liberties. As observed in recent decisions, such as the United States v. Microsoft landmark case, flaws in the Stored Communications Act demonstrate a clear need for legislative measures that reflect the complexity of data privacy transnationality. These models must not only elaborate on legal remedies available to law enforcement, but also serve to maintain the sovereignty of foreign jurisdictions, thereby achieving a more equitable legal arena in today's globalized world (Kirschenbaum et al., 2018). Moreover, the use precedes regulation principle illustrates the challenge of keeping government actors accountable for their investigatory practices. The lag in time between early surveillance practices and eventual regulation usually leads to ubiquitous practices that could violate citizens' rights. The resulting regulatory lag undermines public trust and poses ethical questions about the validity of evidence produced through unregulated surveillance. Through the study of the consequences of qualified immunity and the good faith exception, it is apparent that reform is necessary for creating strong safeguards for people against unjustified state encroachment. These aspects compel us to reflect on more assertive judicial frameworks that are able to neutralize adverse social effects of slowdowns in regulations, particularly safeguarding the Fourth Amendments core principles (Milligan et al., 2014). Ultimately, an entire-brain method of reforming search, seizure, and surveillance legislations must aim at establishing stronger judicial review and redefining appropriate government behavior. By shifting legal interpretations towards the broad rights of citizens to be safe and free from unreasonable searches, we can foster a constitutional climate respectful of personal freedom but allowing for reasonable law enforcement initiatives. The broader reading is in consonance with historical conceptions of the Fourth Amendment, thereby fostering a climate of law that fosters security and freedom. Giving judicial access early on to challenge government practices will both empower individuals and render the interaction between state interests and civil freedoms healthier, resulting in a more just legal system in criminal procedure (Milligan et al., 2014).

The subtleties of search, seizure, and surveillance in criminal procedure demand a careful examination of existing legal frameworks and their adaptation to new technology. One of the arguments presented by Professor Orin Kerr is that Fourth Amendment protections erode steadily with evolving policing practices and new technology. In his view, courts should be cautious and provide legislative branches room to establish specified rules for investigation using new technologies. Specifically, Kerr contends that legislatures can come up with more advanced and adaptable rules than can the courts, rules which can yield more specific guidelines for police. This perspective is nevertheless open to intense questioning about legislatures' capacity to keep pace with speeding technology and the potential for loopholes in protections that come from utilization of statute-based methods (Solove et al., 2005). The existing system of surveillance has also highlighted the intrinsic antagonism between public power and private privacy. As discussed, the principle of use before regulation shows a problematic dynamic whereby investigation mechanisms are usable without prior inspection, providing an opening for abuses during periods of regulatory hiatus. This delay in regulation provides a platform for the police to employ tactics that remain untested and unregulated for extended periods. The penalties for such stasis can be significant and have the result of creating a wide array of privacy violations that remain untested in the courts. The need to reexamine such delay is further exacerbated by the potential that more robust understandings of the Fourth Amendment might generate earlier standing for court review of these invasive techniques, thereby balancing the societal costs of such regulatory delay (Milligan et al., 2014). The balance controversy between enforcement and civil liberties protection is a reflection of how the reconsideration of the interpretation of the Fourth Amendments is timely and needed. Through examination of the broader implications of the Amendments wording, particularly the concept of security in reference to protection from unreasonable searches and seizures, courts and scholars could redefine their understanding of constitutional rights. The move towards the acknowledgment of an extended right to be protected and in safety can work proactively as a protection to citizens from unwarranted intrusions by the state. This change could lead to the creation of judicial benchmarks upon which legal objections to surveillance operations are made sooner, working under a constitutional climate that places preference on civil rights while compromising with the need for establishing public security (Milligan et al., 2014).

KEY TERMS

- CCTV Surveillance
- Electronic Surveillance
- House Search
- Interception of Communication
- Panch Witnesses
- Search and Seizure Memo
- Search without Warrant
- Telephone Tapping
- Chain of Custody
- Forensic Analysis
- Illegally Obtained Evidence
- Inventory of Seized Items
- Personal Search
- Search Warrant
- Seizure
- Tracking Devices

A LOOK TO THE FUTURE

FUTURE IMPLICATIONS FOR SEARCH, SEIZURE, AND SURVEILLANCE

The search, seizure, and surveillance world is evolving at a rapid rate due to technology advancements that are testing the existing legal frameworks to the extreme. As law enforcement agencies more and more use sophisticated surveillance methods, an individual's right to privacy is increasingly tested. The principle that use comes before regulation is the inevitable analytical lens under which to view this dynamic; governmental players probe and exploit with little or no oversight until formal regulations converge. This creates a foul gap where harmful practices can be employed with impunity and establish abuses of power that whittle away at civil liberties. The social costs of such regulatory lag run deep, and worthy of reconsideration of the way Fourth Amendment protection against unreasonable search and seizure is interpreted and applied, as new technologies become part of the investigative tool kit for police. In the shadow of the continuing technological revolution, surveillance law's future may be shaped by judicial interpretations of rights to be protected and free from fear. This broader use of the Fourth Amendments to be secure clause could urge earlier litigation to challenge unregulated surveillance practices. Specifically, creation of a judicial rule against government appropriation of investigatory techniques that are unregulated will spur an active strategy in defending constitutional rights. Courts can potentially provide a deeper examination of the constitutionality of surveillance methods prior to their being widely used, thereby lessening the window for government players to exploit the lack of regulation. These actions by courts would not only encourage accountability but also establish an important balance framework between law enforcement requirements and individuals' rights to privacy. But there is still ongoing debate about the appropriate balance between legislatures and courts in regulating these new technologies. Scholars like Professor Orin Kerr advocate a restrained judicial style that allows legislatures to pass precise and adaptive rules governing law enforcement practice. But question is raised whether Congress can execute this role, as history shows legislative lag after technological leap. Critics argue that Congress has a tendency to create a piecemeal and incomplete framework that does not provide effective protection against searches and surveillance. Legislative supervision is thus called for, but the delicate interplay between technology and constitutional rights might necessitate a more affirmative role by the judiciary in monitoring state power in surveillance practice, so the Fourth Amendment continues to be robust and relevant in a more technologically oriented society.

REFERENCES

1. Alfadhel, L. N. M. (2016). TRIPS and the rise of counterfeiting: A comparative examination of trademark protection and border measures in the European Union and the Gulf Cooperation Council. https://core.ac.uk/download/77040683.pdf (accessed on 13th August 2025).
2. Burton, A. (2006). Fixing FISA for long war: Regulating warrantless surveillance in the age of terrorism. https://core.ac.uk/download/72052791.pdf (accessed on 13th August 2025).
3. Castiglione, J. D. (2007). *Hudson* and *Samson*: The Roberts Court confronts privacy, dignity, and the Fourth Amendment. https://core.ac.uk/download/76622134.pdf (accessed on 13th August 2025).
4. Citron, D. K., Rinehart, L. C., & Gray, D. C. (2013). Fighting cybercrime after *United States v. Jones*. https://core.ac.uk/download/56359684.pdf (accessed on 13th August 2025).
5. Citron, D., Cloud, M., Colbert, B., Cuddihy, T., et al. (2017). Brief of scholars of the history and original meaning of the Fourth Amendment as *amici curiae* in support of petitioner, *Carpenter v. United States*, No. 16-402 (U.S. Aug. 14, 2017). https://core.ac.uk/download/132075613.pdf (accessed on 13th August 2025).
6. Doernberg, D. L. (2006). Can you hear me now? Expectations of privacy, false friends, and the perils of speaking under the Supreme Court's Fourth Amendment jurisprudence. https://core.ac.uk/download/46714108.pdf (accessed on 13th August 2025).
7. Donohue, L. K. (2019). Customs, immigration, and rights: Constitutional limits on electronic border searches. https://core.ac.uk/download/213035841.pdf (accessed on 13th August 2025).
8. Dripps, D. A. (2010). The "new" exclusionary rule debate: From "still preoccupied with 1985" to "virtual deterrence." https://core.ac.uk/download/144227629.pdf (accessed on 13th August 2025).
9. Ferguson, R. I., Irons, A., Renaud, K., Wilford, S., et al. (2020). PRECEPT: A framework for ethical digital forensics investigations. https://core.ac.uk/download/288653619.pdf (accessed on 13th August 2025).
10. Kirschenbaum, A. (2018). Beyond *Microsoft*: A legislative solution to the SCA's extraterritoriality problem. https://core.ac.uk/download/216957567.pdf (accessed on 13th August 2025).
11. Milligan, L. (2014). The forgotten right "to be secure." https://core.ac.uk/download/186332456.pdf (accessed on 13th August 2025).
12. Plourde-Cole, H. (2010). Back to *Katz*: Reasonable expectation of privacy in the Facebook age. https://core.ac.uk/download/144228588.pdf (accessed on 13th August 2025).
13. Slobogin, C. (2012). Making the most of *United States v. Jones* in a surveillance society: A statutory implementation of mosaic theory. https://core.ac.uk/download/62560000.pdf (accessed on 13th August 2025).
14. Solove, D. J. (2005). Fourth Amendment codification and Professor Kerr's misguided call for judicial deference. https://core.ac.uk/download/144222388.pdf (accessed on 13th August 2025).
15. Taslitz, A. E. (2002). The Fourth Amendment in the twenty-first century: Technology, privacy, and human emotions. https://core.ac.uk/download/62568511.pdf (accessed on 13th August 2025).

Chapter 5

BAIL AND REMAND PROCEDURES IN CRIMINAL PROCEDURE

Contents

Introduction....143
5.1. Historical Context of Bail....147
5.2. Types of Bail....151
5.3. Factors Influencing Bail Decisions....155
5.4. Remand Procedures....159
5.5. Rights of the Accused....163
5.6. Criticisms and Challenges....167
Summary....171
References....174

INTRODUCTION

The topic of bail and remand procedures in criminal justice is a matter of core concern with extensive implications for the justice system and personal liberties. The very nature of the institution of bail is contained in its role to uphold the presumption of innocence, allowing accused persons to be at liberty until their trial. But the road from arrest to trial can be sullied with nuances, most particularly where judges must make decisions on bail or remand. In essence, such decisions are not administratively but cumulatively significant to defendants, most times setting the tone for the judicial process that follows. Therefore, examining policies and structures governing bail and remand is central to understanding more general socio-legal processes, with respect paid to varying responses adopted by jurisdictions worldwide. The comparative examination of custodial remand and alternatives to it, such as electronic monitoring (EM) bail, is a core part of the evaluation of bail practice. Research has sought to explain the impacts of such alternatives, considering whether they reduce custodial remands without compromising public safety. For instance, one such study that included cross-stakeholder involvement by law enforcement officers and judicial staff has indicated the importance of evidence-based consideration when determining appropriate conditions of bail (Barry et al., 2007). These dynamics represent a changing trend in criminal procedure, which highlights the call to sensitivity as jurisdictions face trying to balance risk assessment and rights. Furthermore, the debate surrounding reforming bail practice is continually pertinent in discussions of systemic inequalities that can disproportionately affect marginalized groups. Targeting groups of young people injects further complicating influence into bail and remand practice. With regard to international obligations, including those in other UN instruments, there is a requirement for jurisdictions to balance the sensitive issue of keeping young people in custody settings. Minimizing the duration of unnecessary remand is a priority, particularly for young individuals, who stand to be long-term impacted by any form of detention. A comprehensive report on bail trends among Australian youths reveals alarming trends in remand custody, which reflect the need for specialized interventions toward ensuring fairer outcomes (Richards et al., 2025). As the law continues to evolve, being aware of these factors is imperative in the development of evidence-based policies that can keep pace with contemporary standards of law and morality.

Definition of Bail and Remand

The bail and remand principles are central to the criminal procedure framework, serving as a balancing mechanism between the right to be presumed innocent and protecting the public. Bail refers to the release on conditions of an accused individual from detention, typically pending their return to face further legal proceedings. The foundation for bail is that pre-trial detention can be prejudicial without eradicating the presumption of innocence until conviction. Remand, however, pertains to cases where individuals are detained pending trial for various purposes like the perceived risk of flight, potential interference with evidence, or the risk of harm to the community. An understanding of the definitions is important as they highlight the efforts of the legal systems in dealing with issues that are intricate surrounding public interest and individual rights. Legislative reforms and criminal justice attitudes toward punishment and crime largely shape the dynamics of bail and remand. For example, stricter policies, i.e., those that have been implemented through the Crime Package Bill, are a reflection of a shift towards stricter punishment of certain crimes, especially of young people. Significantly, these reforms have caused controversy surrounding their effectiveness and effectiveness within the justice system. Critical, such measures may not only fail to deter their intended effect, but, more significantly, may perpetuate an indiscriminate use of detention without adequate consideration being paid to alternative rehabilitative measures. This tension is a reminder of the need to periodically scrutinize procedures vis-a-vis bail and remand to ensure that they form part of a balanced and fair system of justice responsive to changing values in society (Woods et al., 1980). For the purpose of enhancing the efficiency of bail and remand processes, recent evaluations took into perspective new alternative practices such as electronic monitoring (EM) bail. It aims at replacing traditional custodial remands with an alternative that allows individuals to remain in the community during trial. Studies that quantify the use of EM bail indicate it has the potential to reduce the use of custodial remand, thereby addressing issues on cost-saving and recidivism. Data collected from different sources, for instance, stakeholder interviews and quantitative data, offer comparison of outcomes among those set on EM bail and those detained in custody. These estimates are crucial in assisting policymakers in making sense of the complexities of the criminal justice system and attempting to streamline processes surrounding bail and remand (Barry et al., 2007) (Figure 5.1).

Figure 5.1. The concepts of bail and remand.

Source: https://www.cycj.org.uk/wp-content/uploads/2015/10/young-people-524513_640-640x320.jpg.

Importance of Bail in the Criminal Justice System

The significance of bail in the criminal justice system cannot be overemphasized as it has a crucial role to reconcile the presumption of innocence with the need to ensure public safety and the integrity of the judicial process. Through enabling defendants to purchase their release ahead of trial, bail reduces the punishment that people experience before guilt or innocence is determined. Freedom during the pretrial period is a critical factor in maintaining individual rights and eliminating stigma toward those who are not yet convicted. This is particularly relevant in the case of custodial remands, when consideration would need to be taken in the giving of bail so as not to impose unreasonable hardship on the defendants pending trial. In jurisdictions where bail provisions exist, it can effectively reduce prison overcrowding and thus address systemic issues in the criminal justice system. Empirical evidence is available to support the notion that effective bail practice can be good for both individuals and the system as a whole. Research has shown that alternatives such as electronic monitoring (EM) bail can be used in lieu of custodial remand, in that there is a realizable alternative that neither has the negative consequences of imprisonment nor does not make concessions to judicial pressures. Evidence from reviews of EM bail shows how it performs in keeping risks of release prior to trial at bay while delivering a more humane method of confinement.

Figure 5.2. The importance of bail in the criminal justice system.

Source: https://www.leadindia.law/blog/en/wp-content/uploads/2024/07/Reform-of-Criminal-Justice-System-%E2%80%93-Bail-Trial-Delays.jpg.

Apart from that, the alternatives save public funds and also decrease the psychological and social impacts of wrongful imprisonment. In this context, the bail decision-making process gains an urgency dimension that touches not just the accused but also the larger community and the institutions respect for fair justice procedures (Barry et al., 2007). Also, bail is particularly significant for vulnerable offenders, like young offenders, who may be disproportionately affected by custodial remand. The doctrine of detention as a matter of last resort has international commitments within the area of juvenile justice in a series of UN instruments. It needs to be appreciated that while custodial remand has important contributions to make, there are significant costs for young people whose lives can be permanently ruined by even short periods of detention. Research into the use of remand among Australian youth underscores the significance of examining why it is being used and recognizes trends most likely to explain its increase. These can guide policy reform to promote bail practice, thus keeping unnecessary remand to a minimum and maximizing a justice system that is both accountable and rehabilitative (Richards et al., 2025) (Figure 5.2).

5.1. HISTORICAL CONTEXT OF BAIL

Historically, bail has been an integral part of the criminal justice system, and its background traces back to English common law. Bail originally came into use to ensure the appearance of defendants in court but gave them freedom from detention during trial. The bail institution was a progressive step away from pre-trial punitive detention to more equitable policy, aware of the innocence presumptions. Over time, though, the complexities concerning bail became increasingly deep, particularly with regard to developments in society and growing concerns over crime levels. Such a background explains not merely the struggle for equal treatment of defendants but also the concern of states with effective judicial processes, a concern that continues to influence contemporary controversies surrounding remand and bail. As societies developed, particularly through the transition from agrarian to industrial economies, the use of bail came under severe criticism. The rise in crime in urban areas meant additional demands on the bail eligibility, even unfairly targeting poor groups. Standard practices often reflected the contemporary biases in society, with economic and social status dictating the right to bail. For instance, wealthier individuals could afford to be released, while the poor would languish in pre-trial detention, questioning the system of justice and fairness. The evolution of bail law thus mirrors social sentiment and records contemporary debates on justice, particularly across youth systems, in which custodial remand is also under serious challenge, as reported in recent research on youth detention practice in Australia (Richards et al., 2025). To reverse previous unfairness, recent bail reforms place emphasis on making sure that remand remains a final option for young offenders. Custodial remand reliance has created enormous ethical concerns as it has a tendency to worsen situations of vulnerability for young people and denies them the opportunity to reform and reintegrate into society. The United Nations instruments are demanding states take action that minimizes detention among young people, and this is compelling jurisdictions to reconsider their bail systems. Discussions about these reforms are key to understanding how legal systems can be enhanced to balance public safety more equally with the rights of pretrial detainees. This development highlights ongoing carryovers of historical injustices on current bail practice and requires persistent activism for equitable treatment within the criminal justice system (Bartkowiak-Theron et al., 2025).

5.1.1. Evolution of Bail Laws

The evolution of bail laws has significantly transformed the approach to pretrial release, reflecting broader societal changes in perceptions of justice and individual rights. Historically, bail practices were often arbitrary and heavily biased, with wealthy defendants easily securing release while indigent individuals languished in detention. As awareness grew regarding the inequities embedded within such a system, reforms began to emerge in the late 19th and early 20th centuries. These fresh laws aimed to stabilize bail decisions according to the justice of fairness. Consequently, states were moving towards guidelines curtailing judges' discretion and arguing that bail was an inclusive right of all people irrespective of economic conditions. This shift not only reflected a growing understanding of justice but also gave rise to debates on the need to balance public safety with rights of the accused. Parallel to these reforms, the 1960s saw a turning point in the evolution of bail law, fueled by an outburst of civil rights movements. Reformers advocated for legal systems that recognized the presumption of innocence and sought to eradicate discriminatory patterns of decision-making in the bail process. High-profile cases and legislative reforms defined the rights of the defendants, culminating into attempts that dissuaded high bail amounts and promoted the use of non-monetary conditions of release. For example, pretrial services dominated this era, emphasizing the mandate that risk assessment rather than ability to pay should be employed to set bail levels. These trends drew on more universal human rights standards, implying that holding someone solely on the basis of their inability to pay was an impairment of individual freedom and diminished the moral credibility of the judicial process. Even so, these forward steps notwithstanding, recent debates over bail legislation suggest persistent difficulties and complexities. Current cases have exhibited tension between public safety on the one hand and proper treatment of the defendants, particularly with increasing crime rates in various jurisdictions. It is basic Supreme Court rulings, such as Cheff v. Schnackenburg, that illustrate the sensitive balance that courts must strike in determining the limits of pretrial release and conditions of bail. The decision stressed the requirement for equitable treatment while underlining legislative loopholes that continue to guarantee disparities in the system. As the law regarding bail is evolving, it will be vital to address the current inequalities that remain such that the system not only symbolizes the essence of justice but actually operates in a way that enhances the fairness and effectiveness of bail and remand procedures within criminal procedure (Bartkowiak-Theron et al., 2025; N/A, 1967) (Figure 5.3).

Figure 5.3. The evolution of bail laws.

Source: https://leppardlaw.com/wp-content/uploads/LL-Image-Evolution-of-US-Federal-Bail-Laws-From-1966-to-Present-FE.webp.

5.1.2. Key Legal Cases Influencing Bail Practices

Bail practices have been shaped quite deeply by a series of key legal cases that instill the importance of balance in balancing public safety and protecting the rights of the accused. A key case is that of the U.S. Supreme Court decision in *United States v. Salerno*, which upheld the Bail Reform Act of 1984 as constitutional. The decision established precedent that preventive detention was valid if it furthered an important governmental interest, namely public safety. Thus, this decision has impacted discretionary power of judges to refuse bail on perceived threats to specific defendants. The implications of such judicial determinations still reverberate in the criminal justice system, creating an atmosphere under which bail is no longer regarded as a mere formality but as a consequential decision that affects human rights and public safety. In the field of youth detention and bail processes, current significant research is on the impact of international legal obligations on domestic processes. The Australasian Juvenile Justice Administrators-commissioned report identifies the importance of minimizing custodial remand for young people to the barest minimum required, consistent with UN instruments which advise against detention as a last resort option. This is done by cases that have underscored the importance of having a legal framework that prioritizes rehabilitation over punishment, particularly for juvenile defendants. As a result, many jurisdictions have revised their bail policy along these terms, considering not only the alleged offenses but also the social and family history of youth defendants. Such cases are paramount to inform reforms that aim to balance justice to the accused with broader social obligations. Another groundbreaking area that impacts bail practices is the administrative reforms in England and Wales' lower criminal courts, as achieved by contemporary criminal justice literature. This change is characterized by the greater role of the police in prosecution decisions and the development of virtual courts along lines of dependence on technology for hearings. The administration's emphasis on haste, as characterized as a move towards 'rapid justice,' provokes the problem of due process of procedure, which remains central to fair treatment of defendants. Judicial decisions in such matters elaborate on conflicts between justice and efficiency, bringing with them consideration for the impact of such reforms on the right to bail. Procedural processes within the judiciary evolve with time, and the impact of such legal institutions does not just represent current conceptions of justice but also precedes to influence subsequent bail hearings and the overall criminal law climate.

5.1.3. Historical Perspectives on Remand Procedures

The origin of remand proceedings traces back to the underlying concepts of justice and social order in the earliest legal frameworks. Remand was originally punitive and preventive with priority given towards keeping society safe by preventing the presence of presumed culprits as a danger to society in the pre-trial process. The early detainment policies used to heavily rely on the subjective discretion of magistrates, who made their judgments based on how dangerous in their assessment a defendant is to society. This subjectivism used to lead to inconsistencies across jurisdictions and cases. As society developed, the legal system began focusing more on formalized procedures and cut-and-dried standards to ensure fairness and accountability. This background informs current controversy surrounding bail and remand, announcing the conflict between public safety and individual rights which continues to inform criminal process today. In the latter half of the 20th century, profound changes in the topology of remand procedures began to appear, motivated almost exclusively by mounting public anxiety regarding crime and perceptions of judicial leniency. Parliamentary reforms, such as those seen in the Crime Package Bill in New York, introduced stricter parameters for pre-trial detention, particularly for juveniles accused of serious offenses. The intention was to protect society as well as to respond to public sentiment demanding harsher treatment of perceived threats. But others argue that such measures not only proved ineffective but were even injurious in effect, widening the evils of existing in an already unfair system. The critique of such legislative history illustrates how remand policy comes to reflect public fears and the tension between justice and public safety (Woods et al., 1980). In contemporary debates on remand processes, it is necessary to examine the legacy of reforms in the past and how they have had a lasting impact on the judiciary. Events like the 2012 Australian and New Zealand Critical Criminology Conference help to perpetuate ongoing debates surrounding justice, e.g., the need to turn back the clock and reassess traditional customs that shaped the current. Scholars point out that shifts in perspective regarding issues such as gender, vulnerability, and social justice necessitate critical scrutiny of entrenched remand practices that may no longer be serving their intended purposes. The importance of this historical context should not be overstated, as it frames major debates regarding legal reform and the future of remand and bail policy, and thus the functioning of justice in respect of marginalized and vulnerable groups (Bartkowiak-Theron et al., 2025) (Figure 5.4).

Figure 5.4. Historical perspectives on remand procedures.

Source: https://thelaw.institute/wp-content/uploads/2024/03/An_oil_painting_of_an-1.png.

5.2. TYPES OF BAIL

The concept of bail is the foundation of the criminal justice system, providing mechanisms whereby defendants are able to secure their release prior to trial while assuring their appearance in court. There are several types of bail distinguished on the basis of conditions and purposes, and the most common of these are cash bail, surety bail, and recognizance bail. Cash bail is the payment of a monetary amount by the defendant, which will be returned upon their making the mandatory court appearances. It is a monetary incentive for the suspect to appear in court for hearings scheduled. The second is surety bail, in which a third-party surety, most often a bail bondsman, posts an amount for the defendants' release, with a fee in return.

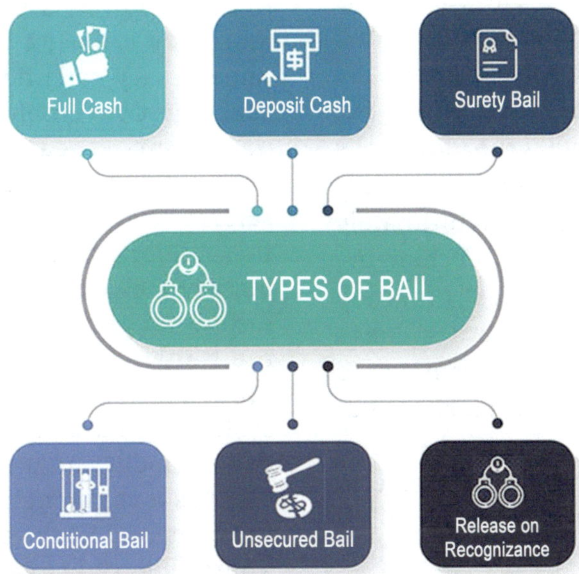

Figure 5.5. Types of bail.

Source: https://www.vpslawfirm.com/wp-content/uploads/2019/06/TYPES-OF-BAIL2.jpg.

Recognizance bail, traditionally given to minimal-risk defendants, releases defendants on their promise to come back to court, highlighting judicial discretion in the assessment of flight risk and public safety. Electronic monitoring (EM) bail is a modern form of the different forms of bail, attempting to strike a balance between public safety concerns and the rights of the accused. This form of bail makes use of technology to track the movement of an individual, allowing them to remain in the community and adhere to conditions imposed by courts. Studies to test the effectiveness of EM bail have demonstrated its potential to replace custodial remands, signaling a shift in how judicial systems handle pretrial release. According to Barry et al. (2007), qualitative and quantitative analysis were employed to establish the impact of EM bail on criminal proceedings with considerable cooperation among stakeholders in the criminal justice system. These involve interviews with professionals such as police officers, social workers, and members of the judiciary that provided insights into the ability of electronic monitoring as a valid form of alternative to imprisonment. Another categorical classification is conditional bail, and this is in the form of specific conditions that defendants must comply with while released on bail. Conditions may involve travel restrictions, curfew, or frequent check-ins with police officers. Such provisions are purposed to mitigate risks implicated in releasing individuals who might pose a threat to public safety or those who tend to be non-compliant. The conditions set by the court, here, are reflective of a good sense of each case's individual situation, the power to make individualized bail strategies. The nature of bail also highlights the judiciary's role in striking a balance between individual liberty and protecting society, which ultimately means more extensive discussions on changing the bail system. While this area of study grows, it is vital that policymakers balance the effectiveness and equity of alternatives to traditional remand processes, as referenced at the 2012 Australian and New Zealand Critical Criminology Conference, a recurring theme in criminal justice (Bartkowiak-Theron et al., 2025) (Figure 5.5).

5.2.1. Cash Bail

Cash bail is a controversial topic in discussions of criminal procedure, particularly with regard to its implications for social justice and equity access. Cash bail programs allow suspects to secure their release from incarceration by providing a predetermined amount of money, purportedly to ensure their appearance in court. However, this procedure disproportionately impacts low-income individuals who lack the economic means to pay bail and thus face pretrial detention based on their inability to pay, irrespective of guilt or innocence. This payment requirement creates a two-tiered system of justice where liberty is based on wealth, in violation of the mandate of equal treatment under the law. Advocates assert that any justice system must prioritize fairness, necessitating a reexamination of cash bail practices to reduce the disparity faced by economically disadvantaged defendants. Further examination of bail and remand procedures reveals a growing awareness among lawmakers regarding the adverse effects of cash bail, leading to reform initiatives across various jurisdictions. The majority of reformers call for alternatives that eliminate reliance on monetary bail altogether and foster systems employing risk assessment to identify pretrial release eligibility. This non-monetary criterion works towards minimizing unnecessary detention while maintaining public security. Conversely, however, as highlighted in recent research, including Australia's observations into custodial remand practices, reform has to be pursued cautiously. Having these reforms inadvertently replicate existing biases is of critical relevance, particularly for disadvantaged groups such as youth, who have their own circumstances and stresses that influence their engagements with the justice system (Richards et al., 2025). Furthermore, the development and utilization of risk assessment tools as a component of bail reform have been the center of fiery controversy in recent years. These actuarial models are supposed to provide a more neutral basis for bail determinations, perhaps reducing the impact of discriminatory human discretion. While the trend toward such tools presents a promising avenue of reform, there are serious concerns about how they will be used. If left unregulated, these models could reinforce existing racial biases and other prejudices in the criminal justice system. For instance, studies have indicated that algorithms can have the ability to perpetuate long-standing biases based on past data and therefore should be seriously regulated and ethically scrutinized in use (Dalakian et al., 2018). In trying to control the magnitude of cash bail reform challenges in jurisdictions, they should aim to balance innovation and protection of constitutional rights so as to ensure an equitable and just legal process (Figure 5.6).

Figure 5.6. Cash bail.

Source: https://filtermag.org/wp-content/uploads/2019/11/judge-gavel-handcuffs-and-money-1461289328PKy.jpg.

5.2.2. Surety Bail

Surety bail is the concept that manifests as a key element of the bail and remand process in general, exercising protective and regulatory functions in the criminal justice system. Surety bail involves a third-party agent who agrees to forfeit an amount of money in case of default on the part of the accused to appear for hearings at court. This system is intended to ensure that such individuals who otherwise would prove flight risk are released pending trial without harm to the public. Through levying financial undertakings by sureties, the justice system strives to enhance responsibility, compelling defendants to maintain the judiciary-assigned expectations. The deployment of surety bail, thus, articulates the reasonable balancing between upholding the presumption of innocence and safeguarding the integrity of judicial processes, particularly in jurisdictions where the threat of non-compliance is higher. In examining the use of surety bail, there must be consideration for its effect on vulnerable groups, particularly young people. As suggested in research commissioned by the Australasian Juvenile Justice Administrators, a need exists to cut back on unnecessary custodial remand, especially for trial or conviction waiting young ones. The research examines trends in custodial remand usages and the determinants of such usages and concludes that excessive use of surety arrangements can disproportionately affect socio-economically disadvantaged groups. In addition, the hardships placed on juveniles may also inadvertently have negative effects like further entrenchment in the criminal justice system.

Figure 5.7. The concept of surety bail.

Source: https://lh3.googleusercontent.com/proxy/RJ4a-87bi75ukPX1TwwV5V_IFoewehGu8W8KFa1jsbbCOLdr6NUA_Xyl9KDBhjPAtHfpx4MCM_jvyl8mjaPGNU0m9xDrec4Q1zsH92GbkEIEPqNsEH3o35l8pHb2Rcxpp-9hJMkUSi-PDFQ6El2r.

A thorough grasp of such dynamics becomes important for reforming bail practices that seek to provide equal treatment while taking into account the special concerns faced by youth involved in criminal processes (Richards et al., 2025). The interconnectedness of legal representation and bail outcomes also serves to demonstrate the intricacy of practice in surety bail and its application. Research from Western Australia indicates that access to quality legal representation can influence decision-making at bail, potentially diminishing age and race-based discrimination. Such data provides an understanding of how the structural inequities of the justice system can impact the experiences of individuals in acquiring bail. With adequately represented conditions, defendants have a better chance of putting their side of the story in a manner that not only pleads for them in terms of release but also addresses the issues of interest to the court more meaningfully. Hence, enhancing legal representation access is a critical supplement to mechanisms for surety bail to ensure equal treatment in line with the themes of justice and fairness (Allan et al., 2003) (Figure 5.7).

5.2.3. Personal Recognizance

Personal recognizance, a pre-trial release, permits defendants to secure their freedom without the expense of paying monetary bail. This method relies on faith that individuals will return for their court appearances, premised on the presupposition of innocence until guilt is determined. By employing personal recognizance, the criminal justice system attempts to relieve overcrowded jammed jails and prevent unnecessary detention, particularly of persons who may pose little threat to public safety. Whether a defendant qualifies for release on personal recognizance often hinges on a consideration of the defendant's community ties, past criminal history, and the nature of the current charges. Lastly, the application of personal recognizance is not only to uphold the presumption of innocence but also to convey a more modest system of justice, which conforms to the values of a fair and equitable legal process. Risk assessment tools have become central in the application of personal recognizance. Judicial authorities increasingly are using quantitative evaluations to decide whether a defendant poses a significant flight risk or threat to public safety. The combination of these tools, however, raises serious questions about their validity as well as possible bias that can be made effective in court decisions. As argued by Garrett et al. (2020), the criminal justice system process of risk assessment is not only empirical but also an articulation of subjective judgment by decision-makers. Despite the intention of such measures to enhance objectivity, it has become increasingly feared that they instead perpetuate original bias in the legal system, with a requirement for enhanced scrutiny and refinement of these assessment tools. Further, personal recognizance development aligns with broader trends of restorative justice, which attempts to balance the interests of offenders, victims, and the state. According to Fadeyi et al. (2016), the goals of contemporary criminal justice are keeping communities secure while enabling offender rehabilitation. Personal recognizance can be a key component of this restorative practice, allowing one to have more mature reactions to harm-inducing offenses without resorting to punitive bail procedures. This kind of preference for restorative remedies represents a new awareness that re-integration of offenders is significant, not merely for their own well-being but for society's well-being as well. The crossroads of recognizance and restorative justice demonstrate a move towards a fairer system that recognizes the dignity of all stakeholders involved.

5.3. FACTORS INFLUENCING BAIL DECISIONS

The determination to bail or refuse bail is affected by numerous determinants that represent the general principles of criminal justice and safety. Judges will usually consider the severity and nature of suspected offense, taking into consideration whether it would be deemed violent or not. Offenses that are potentially harmful to victims or the public often result in tighter bail conditions or outright denial. Secondly, the criminal history of the defendants is considered; repeat offenders tend to be under more scrutiny compared to first-time offenders. Flight risk potential is also a central consideration being weighed, as courts analyze the likelihood of a defendant absconding from trial.

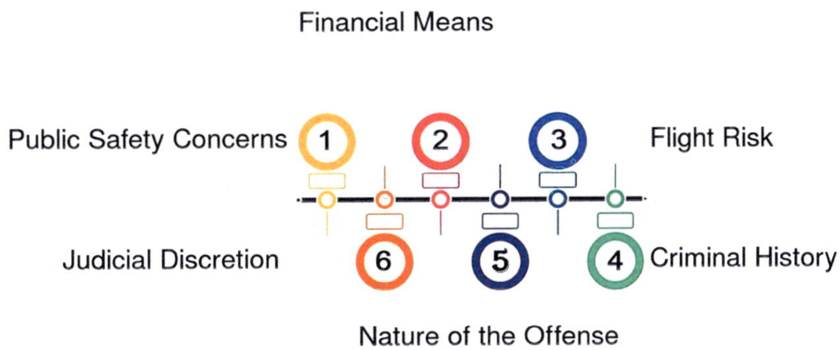

Figure 5.8. Factors influencing bail decisions.

Source: https://fastercapital.co/i/Felony-arraignment--Understanding-the-Gravity-of-the-Charges-update--Factors-that-Influence-Bail-Decisions.webp.

These nuanced considerations comprise an advanced framework that shapes judicial discretion upon bail determination, characterizing the balance between individual rights and public security. In addition to offense character and criminal history, individual characteristics of the defendant can play an important role in bail decisions. Variables such as age, employment, and marriage are the factors that determine stability and willingness to observe conditions of bail of defendants. Youthful defendants, especially those in remand for trivial offenses, can be treated leniently given their potential for rehabilitation, as in arguments over juvenile justice (Richards et al., 2025). Conversely, defendants with poor community attachments are more likely to have higher bail amounts or incarceration with more restrictive conditions, mirroring concerns over their propensity to flee. Ultimately, incarceration and judicial standards combined interface with incarceration supporting the understanding that bail decisions are not solely dependent on the offense itself but rather becoming familiar with the defendant as someone in society. Also, systemic factors such as socioeconomic status and systemic disparities should not be overlooked in bail decisions. Marginalized defendants typically face more stringent bail conditions that reflect the broader social biases within the criminal justice system. These disparities have far-reaching implications in terms of the equitable enforcement of justice because defendants who lack the ability to pay bail spend more time incarcerated, impacting their eventual participation with the legal system. Studies have shown that the presumption of innocence right can be undermined when economic limitations hamper access to release, which necessitates that reforms be implemented to provide fair bail practices (Bartkowiak-Theron et al., 2025). In-depth consideration of the factors influencing bail determinations should hence include these imbalances to provide an improved fairer system sustaining the philosophy that justice is for all, regardless of socio-economic position (Figure 5.8).

5.3.1. Flight Risk Assessment

Flight risk assessment is a vital component of bail and remand procedures in the criminal justice system. The determination of whether or not an individual will appear in court hearings is of significance to judges and lawyers, directly impacting pretrial release. This typically is based on a multi-dimensional interaction of factors, including history of offense, community ties, and severity of offense. In the past, these were determined primarily by judicial discretion; however, the variability and potential prejudices inherent in individualized decision-making have triggered a need for more institutionalized mechanisms, like risk assessment tools. These actuarial models aim to standardize evaluation, whereby the ability to predict the likelihood of a defendants flight is facilitated while at the same time targeting the long-term effects of mass incarceration (Dalakian et al., 2018). Risk assessment tools present opportunities and challenges in responding to flight risk. Advocates argue that the technology can enhance the sagacity of bail determinations through allowing empirical evidence potentially leading to wiser, more equitable decisions. Again, however, prudence is to be exercised, as highlighted in criminal justice reform debates. Without adequate controls, such devices might inadvertently exacerbate existing racial and socio-economic prejudices. This alert emphasizes the importance of jurisdictions developing systems that not only evaluate risk objectively but also protect the rights of individuals and neutralize any prejudice that might be generated by algorithmic assessment (Dalakian et al., 2018). Therefore, while flight risk evaluations might cement judicial discretion, they have to be integrated into existing bail practice with caution. Also, the research on flight risk evaluations extends beyond the individual case to encompass broader systemic consequences. A comparative analysis of pretrial detention across different jurisdictions, such as Europe, shows a mixed pattern of responding to flight risk. Expose reports of excessive pre-trial detention highlight reform efforts to ensure that defendants are treated fairly, as well as concerns over public safety. As states grapple with adopting or refining risk assessment models, domestic and international experience will be especially instructive. Ultimately, the goal must be to create a system of bail that does not unjustly burden defendants yet does not undermine the integrity of the judicial process, to create a more just climate in the world of criminal procedure.

5.3.2. Severity of the Offense

The gravity of the offense is an essential factor in bail and remand process determination in the criminal justice system. Graver offenses, typically involving violent crimes or great loss of money, typically result in more severe bail conditions or remand in custody until trial. This preference for remand comes as a result of public safety interests and the need to ensure that high-risk offenders are not a menace in society. For instance, serious charges may cause judges to consider the likelihood of the accused offender reoffending if released. In jurisdictions of high violence, such as New York City, and their reaction and punishment have shifted toward heavier measures; reacting to social pressure for deterrence and accountability (Woods et al., 1980). Consequently, the subjective severity of a crime is a key factor in shaping judicial decisions prior to pre-trial release. The gravity of the charges also has a tendency to shape the legal system on bail and remand. Courts set varying bail amounts based on the seriousness and stakes of the offense for which an individual is charged, suggesting an enlightened assessment of risk. More serious crimes will command higher bail because the stakes for the accused significantly affect both the judicial process and public perception. For example, a felony defendant who is accused of inflicting physical injury could be presumptively disqualified from bail, even stronger, to affirm the reality that certain crimes are too serious to allow early release. This is done to protect not only prospective victims but also the integrity of the judiciary process, which is brought into jeopardy by defendants who can self-administer if subjected to harsh punishments. Severity of the offense, thus, plays a crucial role in balancing individual freedom and community safety. The implementation of bail reforms in jurisdictions is proof of the debate over the seriousness of offenses and its implication on pre-trial release. Legislative reform, informed by popular opinion and demands for criminal justice reform, has seen the re-evaluation of the application of severity in the exercise of bail discretion. Reforms intended to reduce unnecessary pre-trial detention focus on low- vs. high-risk offending and thereby address issues of severity and its impact directly. However, in the midst of such reforms, concerns about potential implications on public safety remain, particularly with respect to legislative interventions such as New Yorks Crime Package Bill. Although designed to address juvenile offenses, it arguably upholds a belief that the more serious the crime, the more stringent the approach should be overall (Woods et al., 1980). Therefore, the seriousness of the crime remains a significant yardstick in bail and remand considerations, reflecting the two subtleties of justice and public safety (Figure 5.9).

Figure 5.9. The severity of the offense.

Source: https://fastercapital.co/i/Sentencing-guidelines--Considering-Consequences-at-Arraignment--Severity-of-the-Crime--Criminal-History--and-Victim-Impact.webp.

5.3.3. Criminal History of the Accused

The criminal record of the accused is also significant in determining bail conditions and the remand process in criminal procedure. Upon a keen examination of the history of crimes of an individual, it is possible to acquire information regarding the likelihood of re-offending, whether the individual poses a threat to society, and flight risk. Judges and lawyers consider various factors of a defendant's previous encounters with the justice system, including the nature and type of violation, compliance with previous bail stipulations, and general conduct in previous court proceedings. Background information is essential because it informs judicial decisions in juggling between public safety and the accused's rights. Giving a fair assessment of criminal history helps in curtailing unjustified detention and facilitates intelligent decisions regarding bail, ultimately promoting the spirit of justice and due process. In Australia's courts overall, studies have brought up the concern about the disproportionate impact of remand processes on juveniles, where an appropriate understanding of their criminal history is necessary. As exemplified by recent national studies, custodial remand of young accused persons should be approached with caution and applied only when absolutely necessary, following international obligations to use detention as a last resort (Richards et al., 2025). Vulnerability and youth render the prior offense challenging to interpret as most youths could be lacking the maturity to fully understand the implications of their offense. This sophistication underscores the need for specialized treatment of juvenile crime, particularly in bail alternative decisions. The risk-aversive approach acknowledges the demand to identify young offenders as in need of rehabilitation over punishment and therefore emphasizes the need to take criminal history into context. The release of alternatives to custodial remand, such as electronic monitoring (EM) bail, underscores the dynamic nature of criminal justice to an accused's criminal past. Research analyzing the utilization of EM bail has pointed toward it as a viable substitute for custodial remand, particularly for those with less severe historic offenses and signs of compliance potential. Qualitative and quantitative data gathered showed the capacity of EM bail to reduce unnecessary detention without jeopardizing public safety (Barry et al., 2007). The ability to monitor accused individuals in the community can relieve the pressures on the demands made on the justice system and create a balanced approach that considers both the criminal history and circumstances of a person. The more developed remand and bail practice becomes, the more the consequences of an accused's history need to be a primary focus in well-informed decision-making.

5.4. REMAND PROCEDURES

Remand processes are critical within the criminal justice system, in this instance, in handling suspects who are charged but not yet brought to trial. Upon arrest of a suspect, police can opt to hold such a suspect on remand, in effect depriving them of bail until the conclusion of the case. Such a procedure is crucial in maintaining the safety of the public and the integrity of the judicial process. All the same, remand must be applied judiciously in order not to commit the unwarranted detention of individuals, particularly vulnerable individuals such as young people. Remand stakes are high and extend beyond freedom of accused persons to their psychological health and reintegration into society upon trial. Assessing, thus, the setting in which remand is used assumes added significance in deciding upon fairness and effectiveness of pre-trial procedure in the overall criminal procedure framework. Variations have been observed in remand practice in recent studies, e.g., that funded by the Australasian Juvenile Justice Administrators, in the case of juvenile offenders.

Figure 5.10. Remand procedures.

Source: https://litigatinghand.com/wp-content/uploads/2023/03/Remand.jpg.

The research documents that a high percentage of young individuals are being taken into custodial remand, at times as an automatic presumption, regardless of the seriousness of the alleged offense. While the custodial remand is viewed as suitable for certain situations, it is now widely appreciated that its use should be avoided and only utilized as a last resort in line with Australia's international human rights treaty obligations. This not only highlights judicial discretion but also requires large-scale alternatives to detention, such as community programs, that might serve to mitigate negative impacts of pre-trial detention on families and young people (Richards et al., 2025). The remit of remand procedures exceeds individual cases, necessarily crossing over mass-scale human rights issues. Most detainees are not convicted offenders, and the potentiality for serious concern regarding how they are treated and what principles pre-trial procedures should be based on (Hausler et al., 2025). The threat of human rights violations underscores the importance of proper scrutiny and reform in custodial remand policy. Reform may involve implementation of international standards of law and re-evaluation of the guidelines governing bail decisions. Maintaining that pre-trial detention is founded on principles of justice and equity remains essential in ensuring the integrity of the criminal justice system as a whole and public compliance and trust in norms of justice (Figure 5.10).

5.4.1. Definition and Purpose of Remand

The remand is a central theme in the criminal justice system, not least for purposes of bail and remand procedures. Remand is the judicial order to hold an accused individual in custody until trial or other proceedings before a court. Keeping the public safe and maintaining the integrity of the judicial process are necessary. There are three reasons for remand: to avoid potential flight risk, protect victims and witnesses, and decrease re-offending by the accused in the community. Consequently, the decision to remand has to balance individual rights and public interests in safety and make the justice system operate effectively and fairly. Remand decisions in reality are based on various considerations, including the seriousness of charges, defendants' criminal records, and the likelihood of flight. Courts look at each case separately, weighing the evidence against them and considering the consequences of keeping the accused free until the day of trial. For instance, where there is violent offending or high risks of recidivism, remand is a necessary judicial response. Remand can also reveal underlying deficiencies in the criminal justice process, including overcapacity detention facilities and the impact on the psychological health of those in custody. Such issues underscore the need for reform in the handling of pre-trial detentions and of the processing of potential remandees, as the enhancement of these can be of benefit to the overall effectiveness of the criminal justice system. The application of remand also has other socio-legal implications, considering the rehabilitation of offenders in the criminal justice process. While the short-term objective of remand is to have the accused present for trial, the long-term consequences to the person's life are immense. Many individuals on remand suffer hardship, for example, loss of employment, family dislocation, and stigmatization within the community, which complicates rehabilitation upon release. This aspect is, in turn, highly emphasized in contemporary literature addressing the psychosocial effect of detention on family and society integration (Adèle Jones et al., 2013; Alexander, 2013). Remand is therefore not merely by definition and purpose confinement; it entails social responsibility towards treating pre-trial persons in a manner that protects the community while offering avenues of rehabilitation as well as reintegration.

5.4.2. Legal Standards for Remand

In criminal procedure, there are legal prerequisites to remand that have significant bearing in safeguarding the rights of accused persons and in harmonizing public interests. Remand is the incarceration of a defendant during the pre-trial stage, and the application of remand is controlled by prevailing legal standards. The foremost concerns are risk of flight, risk of further offences, and necessary protection of public security. Judges would use a pattern of risk evaluation to determine whether or not an individual must be remanded. Laws also demand a particular rationale to be expressed, where remand is actually not utilized for punitive purposes but aligns with the concepts of justice and due process, thus conforming to the common goals of equitable treatment within the legal system. Evaluating the adoption of alternative measures, such as electronic monitoring (EM) bail, reveals significant trends in how jurisdictions have been approaching remand practices. In accordance with many studies, the implementation of EM bail has been touted as a likely alternative to custodial remand aimed at reducing overpopulation of correctional facilities without diminishing public safety. Barry et al. (2007) identifies that these evaluations demand large-scale data collection and qualitative examination, balancing the benefits of alternative measures against traditional remand processes. Judicial criteria for remand should hence develop to address these alternative techniques, with provisions to ensure the safety and welfare of the suspect and the community at large. The law on unnecessary pre-trial detention is brought to light by scrutiny from national and international bodies. There have been reports that in some European Union nations, pre-trial detention practices have been giving notice of the risk of human rights violations due to excessive and unjustified imprisonment. Heard et al. (2011) is referring to the case studies, which indicate how such practices tend to violate individual rights, necessitating reconsideration of legal principles surrounding remand. This examination calls for harmonization of detention law to prevent arbitrary deprivation of liberty while bringing to the fore the importance of speedy and fair legal procedures. With the jurisdictions set to reform their remand procedure, inclusion of these guidelines will ultimately enhance legal accountability and protection of civil rights (Figure 5.11).

Figure 5.11. Legal standards for remand.

Source: https://edulaw-free-content.s3.ap-south-1.amazonaws.com/88/banner_image.png.

5.4.3. Differences Between Remand and Bail

The remand and bail difference is significant in the criminal justice system, determining the handling of pretrial detainees in the law's eyes. Remand is the incarceration of an accused person in custody pending trial, typically where found to be a risk of flight or danger to the public. That is such placement after arrest and before trial, essentially restricting freedom during a critical period. Bail, however, permits the accused to remain at liberty awaiting legal proceedings, where conditions can be imposed, such as appearing in court or limiting travel. Remand use, particularly among young people, has raised a lot of concern, and greater interrogation into its impact within various jurisdictions has been called for, as evident through custodial practice studies in Australia that emphasize limiting unnecessary remand (Barry et al., 2007). The procedural impact of remand and bail weighs significantly on defendants' experiences and outcomes within the justice system. On the one hand, bail attempts to weigh presumption of innocence against public safety and provide a more compassionate approach to pre-trial liberty. On the other hand, the process of remand has the potential to cause a multitude of negative effects, such as stress and potential collateral damage to family and intimate relationships. The pre-trial utility of bail is ambivalent, with developments like electronic monitoring (EM) applied to provide alternatives to custodial remand. Research examining EM bail has found advantages, which point to it being a useful replacement for standard custody in certain instances, and is enhancing personal freedom without compromising public safety (Barry et al., 2007). The social impact of remand and bail extends past individual cases, and has effects on the manner in which overall perceptions of justice and equity are viewed in the system. Custodial remand tends to be interwined with considerations of racial and socio-economic inequalities, the latter producing ethical concerns regarding the fairness of policies of pre-trial detention. In addition, because states are normally not able to meet international law standards, e.g., the UN's standards concerning the rights of children, the indiscriminate application of remand is put under focus. Balancing need for security against the imperatives of justice is an ongoing challenge to legal systems, demanding ongoing examination and reform to render pre-trial practice fair and equitable. As testified in research based on countries, use of custodial remand trend suggests the crucial part strategic evaluation plays in the system of justice (Richards et al., 2025).

5.5. RIGHTS OF THE ACCUSED

The rights of the accused individual are at the heart of guaranteeing the integrity of the judicial process, particularly in the context of bail and remand proceedings. Central to this issue is the principle of the presumption of innocence, the cardinal idea that states that individuals must not be assumed guilty until being proven so. This presumption necessitates the use of remand, or pretrial detention, only where risk of flight or potential danger to the public is evident and sparingly. With increased jurisdictions becoming aware of the ills of excessive remand, there remains an imperative need to evaluate the effectiveness of alternatives, such as electronic monitoring (EM) bail. The research into EM bail practice, as testified in pilot studies, identifies the advantages of such practices in alleviating unnecessary custodial remands and thereby the upholding of the rights of the accused in accordance with public safety concerns (Barry et al., 2007).

Figure 5.12. Rights of the accused.

Source: https://i.scdn.co/image/ab67616d0000b273aebf840ef6903a9e261ca22b.

Resolving the rights of the accused in special consideration to young people is increasingly significant within the criminal justice system. Research conducted on young Australians' bail and remand reveal ominous trends that signal the effects of custodial remand. Young individuals are increasingly being detained before they have even been able to make a plea, which is troubling in terms of concerns about the appropriateness and fairness of such practice. The obligation under various United Nations instruments to reserve the use of detention of young people as the last resort heightens concerns regarding the disproportionate impact of custodial remand on vulnerable groups. Attempts to reform the remand and bail processes as responses to these commitments only show the growing appreciation for ensuring the protection of the rights of accused persons to ensure that youth detention only remains an essential part of the criminal justice process and not a routine procedure (Richards et al., 2025). In addition, it is pertinent to critically assess the application of bail and remand procedures against the backdrop of socioeconomic indicators that impact disproportionately on outcomes for the accused as well. Minority groups typically experience structural barriers to ensuring they are not able to obtain bail, which is indicative of discriminatory access to justice. For instance, inadequate legal counsel or a lack of access to post-release requirements to be bailed out can lead to unreasonably lengthy detention periods at the expense of the protections that the legal system purportedly holds dear. By creating comprehensive studies of remand processes and how they overlap with concerns such as race, economics, and community resources, stakeholders are able to work together toward developing more equitable solutions. Lastly, closing such gaps is not only important for the latter's sake of the rights of the individual but for the attainment of a more equitable and efficient criminal justice system that recognizes the dignity of each accused individual (Figure 5.12).

5.5.1. Right to a Fair Hearing

The hearing right is a key assurance of making sure justice be served in the criminal process, particularly in bail and remand hearings. This is guaranteed in a number of human rights documents by way of expressing that everyone accused of a crime has the right to an impartial scrutiny of the case against them. In terms of bail, that translates to a court forum where the defendants are afforded a chance to present their case for why they ought not to be detained before trial. Thus, the right of a fair hearing safeguards not only the individual's liberty but also guarantees that the law has purity of process. Through the facilitation of adequate examination of conditions under bail applications, courts play an important role in preventing arbitrary detention and, in the process, enhancing public confidence in judicial processes and defense against potential abuse of power. Additionally, through the implementation of electronic monitoring (EM) as a custodial remand option, it is clear that reasonable hearings are required in fixing suitable conditions for defendants. The evaluation of EM bail efficiency has emphasized the facilitation of public security and private freedoms. Quantitative and qualitative evidence from empirical studies demonstrates the viability of EM bail as a viable mechanism in deciding whether to release on bail or not (Barry et al., 2007). These evaluation systems call for hearings where defense and prosecution can present evidence and arguments relating to the appropriateness of EM measures. By critically analyzing these hearings, judicial officers can make informed decisions that uphold a commitment to the fair treatment of accused persons while appreciating remand and bail practice implications for society as a whole. Finally, judgments such as Kaley v. United States typify the ongoing legal discourse on the right to a fair hearing in the context of bail. This Supreme Court case will address whether defendants are entitled to appeal a grand jury's ruling in an attempt to maintain resources necessary in legal defense (Fine et al., 2014). These types of decisions have ramifications beyond individual cases, affecting the manner in which bail hearings are conducted throughout the nation. Assuming that defendants are provided with solid reasons to challenge pre-existing conditions, not only does it maintain constitutional protections, but it also plays an important role in general credibility of judicial rulings. In the midst of continued contest regarding the right to a fair hearing, they are increasingly essential to protecting the rights of the accused and thereby public trust in the system's ability to adhere to fairness and due process in bail and remand procedures (Figure 5.13).

Figure 5.13. The right to a fair hearing.

Source: https://ksandk.com/wp-content/uploads/8442199.jpg.

5.5.2. Right to Legal Representation

Right to legal representation is a foundational requirement from the bail and remand procedures point of view under criminal law. The right to legal representation has assurances for the accused by allowing them access to defend themselves through the services of an experienced lawyer, thus increasing an equal legal process. In the majority of jurisdictions, this is enshrined in law, accepting that legal procedures are intimidating for individuals without access to professional advice. Legal advice at bail hearings can make a significant difference in the decision reached, particularly concerning bail terms or the issue of remand, as solicitors may be able to compellingly argue against custody. Inadequate legal representation not only undermines the fairness of the judicial process but may also lead to unfair outcomes, including unnecessary detention prior to trial. Inclusion of adequate legal representation in bail matters is particularly important among vulnerable populations, such as those with poor access to legal resources. Marginalized people often face systemic obstacles that tend to discourage their right to access legal counsel, and thus they are treated unfairly in the criminal justice system. Empirical studies have consistently demonstrated that represented defendants are more likely to secure favorable bail conditions and even escape being remanded.

A critical review of electronic monitoring (EM) bail programs, as put forth in Barry et al. (2007), exemplifies the contribution of legal representation in addressing custodial remand options, which exemplifies that knowledgeable defendants possess an enhanced capacity to safeguard their rights. Providing legal representation is therefore not only preferable but imperative in upholding justice and equity in bail and remand practice. Furthermore, the implications of the right to counsel go far beyond the bail hearing situation, influencing the general landscape of criminal justice. When defendants are properly represented by legal experts, the chances of acquiring decisions that uphold the ideals of justice and rehabilitation are greater, not just punishment. This is especially so in cases where other options exist, e.g., community punishment or electronic monitoring, that can be used for particular offenders. The legislational framework behind bail and remand practices, as outlined in Bean et al. (2016), exists to underline the value of legal representation access, so it reflects its role in helping to achieve more equality. Finally, the right to counsel is a keystone for an equitable and balanced judiciary, affirming every person's right to a fair opportunity within the criminal justice system.

5.5.3. Right to Appeal Bail Decisions

The right to appeal bail decisions is an essential element in the grand scheme of criminal procedure, weighing the interests of justice with individual liberties. When bail is denied by a court, the results for the defendant are serious, usually resulting in pretrial detention that can disrupt their private and professional life. The process of appeal is a safeguard against potential judicial error or abuse of discretion that allows defendants to appeal unfavorable decisions that may unnecessarily prolong their time outside society.

Figure 5.14. The right to appeal bail decisions.

Source: https://leppardlaw.com/wp-content/uploads/LL-Image-Bail-Decision-Appeals-in-Federal-Court-FE-2.webp.

This appeal right not only fosters judicial accountability but also upholds the presumption of innocence principle, a fundamental principle in the justice system that states individuals should not be subjected to excessive punishments before they are convicted. Appeal procedures of bail decisions are also an important aspect of ensuring defendants enjoy meaningful access to justice. Appeals typically require the presentation of new evidence or a misapplication of the law in the initial ruling, which is oftentimes challenging for defendants lacking adequate legal resources. This reality underscores the necessity of legal representation for bail appeals because properly prepared motions can effectively spot defects within the initial ruling. As seen through studies on custodial remand options, such as electronic monitoring bail systems, a comparative analysis of results illustrates the multifaceted consequences of bail decisions, further testifying to the viability of robust appeal processes to guarantee fair treatment under the law (Barry et al., 2007). The developing character of bail and remand processes requires regular re-examination of the appeal right in light of the emerging standards of contemporary legal doctrine and societal expectations. Recent legislative changes have sought to clarify and accelerate the appeal process, addressing the former obstacles confronting defendants. These innovations, as outlined in comparative law studies, call for a better system that does not just balance the accused's rights but also the needs of public safety and judicial efficacy (Bean et al., 2016). As courts continue to weigh these competing interests, the right of appeal remains an essential method of guaranteeing justice both served and perceived to be served, maintaining public confidence in the rule of law (Figure 5.14).

5.6. CRITICISMS AND CHALLENGES

In elaborating on the criticisms and challenges surrounding bail and remand procedures under criminal procedure, there is a requirement to elaborate on the socio-economic impact felt by those exiting the prison system. The majority of released individuals are confronted with an acute housing shortage, continue their vulnerability to reoffending or recidivism. This issue is highlighted by studies that establish a strong correlation between recent imprisonment and homelessness, adding that numerous individuals get trapped in a cycle of socio-economic disadvantage once released (Centre PIA). Legal submissions on behalf of such individuals indicate that short of addressing the housing crisis for recently released prisoners, bail and remand procedures risk inadvertently generating a cycle of disadvantage, re-arresting rather than rehabilitating. The shortcomings of generalist homeless services to serve this population specifically make the issue more complex, and a sophisticated approach needs to be taken to reform bail that considers the broader socio-economic context. Furthermore, application of risk assessment tools in bail decisions confronts a complicated landscape of ethical as well as practical challenges. While these actuarial models are designed to reduce use of judicial discretion and curb possible bias, their critics argue that they can have the indirect consequence of entrenching current inequalities within the criminal justice system (Dalakian et al., 2018). In particular, algorithms can reinforce racial and socio-economic differences if the data that inputs them reflect systemic differences. The need for protection in the use of such tools is paramount, since they have the ability to erode personal constitutional rights unless subject to tight control. Policymakers should exercise caution lest the objective of reducing discrimination in bail processes ends up with the unintended outcome of augmenting marginalization of such groups. Finally, the existing legislative framework of bail and remand processes is yet another obstacle in achieving effective reform. Several jurisdictions have laws that are hopelessly out of date and unaligned with contemporary views on criminal justice reform, often emphasizing punitive rather than rehabilitative strategies. Such stick-to-what-we-know approaches pose monumental barriers to the implementation of new strategies, such as holistic support services for individuals who are dealing with post-incarceration challenges (Centre PIA). In addition, there is fear of opposition from communities seeing bail reforms as being lenient on crime. This public sentiment can breed political opposition, draining the momentum for change. Meeting these criticisms and challenges requires an integrated strategy with legal professionals, social services, and community stakeholders to develop a balanced, effective bail system grounded in equity and justice.

5.6.1. Inequities in Bail Practices

The current bail system in the United States is full of injustices that overwhelm marginalized communities, particularly racial and socioeconomic minorities. Despite the doctrine of innocence until guilt, pretrial imprisonment of a person on grounds of inability to pay bail is supportive of inadvertent punishment. It creates a system that makes wealth become a determining factor of freedom, thereby expanding extant inequalities. Those who are unable to afford bail may be detained, which can result in job loss, family disruption, and a heightened risk of further legal penalty.

This phenomenon, therefore, not only fuels the mass incarceration crisis but also persistently perpetuates cycles of poverty and disadvantage, undermining the foundational ideals of fairness and justice in the criminal legal system. As a response to such disparities, a number of reforms have been advanced and implemented in a number of jurisdictions that consist of the utilization of tools of risk assessment that are aimed at injecting a more objective measure of evidence for bail determination. These actuarial models aspire to reduce the application of judicial discretion, which is prone to personal bias, and hence provide a pathway to equitable pretrial practices. The use of such models is not, however, devoid of considerable challenges. Critics argue that the devices will reinforce existing biases unintentionally unless properly calibrated and tested because they depend on historical data which can reflect systemic discrimination. One example case study that illustrates these complexities is New Jersey's bail reform initiative, which addresses the necessity of putting proper measures in place to optimize the potential of risk assessment not to continue perpetuating discriminatory patterns by the justice system (Dalakian et al., 2018). Additionally, widespread reforms must also consider broader socioeconomic factors of bail inequalities, especially in connection to indigent populations. Reports indicate that differences along racial lines are not just present in the arrest rates but also in how individuals are treated once they are arrested within the bail system. The Closing the Gap Clearinghouse highlights methods of bridging the disadvantage by illuminating how necessary a well-rounded approach to criminal justice reform is. This involves investing in community resources that provide early intervention and support systems, so as to address the risks that trigger criminal behavior in the first instance. Addressing the causes of disadvantage is critical to achieving a system that promotes equity and accessibility, ultimately resulting in safer and more just communities (N/A, 2025) (Figure 5.15).

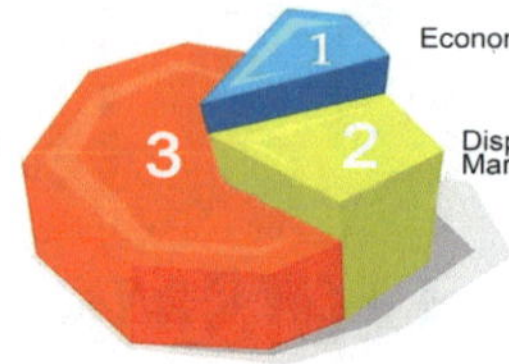

Figure 5.15. Inequities in bail practices.

Source: https://fastercapital.co/i/Bail-bond-reform--Advocating-for-fair-and-equitable-bail-practices-update--The-Consequences-of-Unfair-Bail-Practices.webp.

5.6.2. Impact of Bail on Marginalized Communities

The impact of bail on marginalized communities is a consideration in the broader context of criminal justice reform. All too often, the inability to secure bail leads to a larger percentage of marginalized individuals being pretrial detained, which creates the cycle of poverty and criminalization. Most members of these groups lack the economic means to post bail and, as a result, are incarcerated before trial. This detention not only disrupts their personal lives but also exacerbates underlying socioeconomic disparities. The economic effects of pretrial detention can be profound, including lost jobs, disruption of family life, and reduced access to essential services. Hence, the current bail system's reliance on financial resources perpetuates disparities, entrenching the marginalization of vulnerable groups in the criminal justice system. Moreover, the overrepresentation of marginalized populations in jails reflects the inherent issues in accordance with the bail process itself. The deployment of imprisonment as an inadequate offender deterrent and frequently recidivism-inducing apparatus, in particular for marginalized communities who can perceive imprisonment as an extension of society's rejection, is illustrated by studies. Also, the subtleties of the bail system are also a reflection of broader race, class, and privilege issues that see the privileged individual released while the less privileged counterpart is in detention. This disparity creates an unequal system of justice where the system serves those who can afford it at the cost of those already laden with insurmountable hurdles due to societal inequalities already in place. Lastly, such discriminatory treatment only widens already existing gaps in communities and indicates a pressing need for reform in criminal justice processes. The nuances implicated with the incarceration of marginalized groups also call for deeper understanding of the socio-cultural drivers in play.

As has been observed in the discourse on imprisonment, the life of the convict entails demonstrating that not only is prison a space of exclusion but also a space of administrated interpersonal relations and survival mechanisms. The social dynamics of interactions in prison settings have the capacity to influence the way marginalized individuals interpret their conditions and interact with the outside environment. These realities need to guide resistance against the punitive practices of the justice system, meaning that such efforts at reforming bail and remand practices should be cognizant of these lived realities. Through targeting the causes of the dependence on bail and remodifying policies that are equity-pro, stakeholders have the ability to battle to end the structural barriers that perpetuate the cycle of incarceration, therefore fostering more constructive interactions between marginalized communities and the criminal justice system (Kelly et al., 2015; Schneider et al., 2020).

5.6.3. Calls for Reform in Bail and Remand Systems

Bail and remand reform has grown in popularity throughout the world as there is recognition of the adverse consequences of unnecessary custodial remand, especially among vulnerable populations. Young offenders is one sector that takes precedence when it comes to prioritization. Research underscores the need to minimize unnecessary remand because it has a detrimental effect on children, such as increased susceptibility to mental illness and potential criminalization. Youth who are in remand not only forfeit freedom but are also disadvantaged in the sustenance of family relationships, which are essential to their emotional and social development. In light of Australia's international obligation to utilize youth detention as an ultimate measure, reform proposals advocate the development of alternatives to remand that prioritize rehabilitation and community-based support plans with the ultimate objective of aligning practice with evidence-based practices within youth justice (Richards et al., 2025).

The adverse impact of an enforcement bail and remand system is not confined to individual young offenders but extends to the broader society. Incidents of pre-trial custody have been linked to increased recidivism, particularly among young people and children. Studies have found that the custodial remand environment can be harmful to existing psychological conditions, disrupt educational opportunities, and establish a cycle of offending that is costly not only on a societal level but also to the state. The Prison Reform Trust illustrates these concerns by elucidating how child imprisonment tends to be self-defeating, producing worse outcomes than to rehabilitate young crime. These outcomes contribute to calls for root-and-branch change in the system with a focus on preventative work, community intervention, and mental health services to break such a cycle and enhance outcomes in society (Barry et al., 2010). Moreover, closer insight into the systemic pressures underlying the use of bail and remand holds the possibility of significant reform. Research indicates that stringent legal conditions imposed on young offenders, supplemented by rising rates of remand

and short sentences with low rehabilitation, contribute to rising numbers of young people in custody. Policymakers must tackle these issues if they are to reform successfully by enhancing alternative sanctions and support systems favoring rehabilitation over punishment. This involves evaluating the grounds on which bail eligibility is determined and formulating new benchmarks according to restorative justice. Bail and remand mechanisms need reforming through analyzing fully how policy decisions interact with societal beliefs, with the end result of creating a more balanced and effective justice system which contributes to better lives rather than excluding them (Barry et al., 2010).

SUMMARY

The quest for bail and remand processes within the criminal justice system depicts a complex interplay of legal principles, public perception, and administrative practice. The research indicates that the effectiveness of such processes often hinges on bail-granting standards that reflect systemic shortcomings inherent in the judicial system. As pointed out in numerous case studies, including the utilization of EM bail as a custodial remand option, the need for constant review and reform remains imperative. Notably, qualitative and quantitative data-based research studies among stakeholders in the law enforcement and judicial systems, for example, point to the great potential for EM bail to be used as an equitable alternative to traditional remand, hence being cost-saving as well as having the safeguarding of community interests (Barry et al., 2007). Moreover, identification of public policy implications of legislative reform, such as those established in New Yorks Crime Package Bill, illustrates the tension between public interest in safety and the accused's rights. The proposed changes in the juvenile system indicate a shift towards more punitive punishment as a move towards addressing passionate public outcry. But this reactionary phenomenon actually leads to inefficiencies and failure of the system, which destabilizes the justice system itself (Woods et al., 1980). Thus, reform must be guided by consideration of not only short-term public outrage but also long-term effects for offenders and the effectiveness of the justice system in rehabilitating. Lastly, bail and remand processes must be examined in a balanced manner that upholds the presumption of innocence while ensuring community protection. As idealistic as such policies as EM bail may sound, they must be implemented with stringent monitoring and stringent scrutiny to avoid abuse. The integration of stakeholder feedback and evidence-based information will be paramount in shaping successful bail reforms that address evolving times in criminal justice. While the world grapples with these concerns, it is paramount that conversations are fostered that facilitate the attainment of justice and fairness, ushering in a new, fairer system for all parties to criminal proceedings.

The sophistication of bail and remand procedures is an integral component of criminal justice systems worldwide, a reflection of general social orientations toward crime and punishment. By examining the principal concerns regarding these procedures, it may be observed that their effectiveness relies upon an equilibrium approach, inclining towards maximizing public safety and individual rights. The application of EM as an alternative to custodial remands has been a mainstream field of study. Studies have demonstrated the potential of EM bail in replacing custodial remands with a more humane and flexible pre-trial release option. The evaluation of the application of EM bails has involved intensive collection of qualitative and quantitative data, illuminating its impacts on various stakeholders, including law enforcers and judiciary institutions (Barry et al., 2007). In addition, the need to reduce unnecessary custodial remands is also driven by global commitments, especially in youth justice. The search for bail and remand trends discloses pertinent patterns, particularly regarding young offenders. For example, youth detention is to be used as a last resort in Australia, in line with UN requirements. This guideline brings into focus the pressing need for alternatives to avoiding the negative impact of formal prisonization on youth, such as stigmatization and re-entry into society. Research in this area provides essential details on the effect of custodial remands on adolescents' interactions with the justice system and further reveals the complexities through which variables such as socioeconomic status and experience with the law might have a disproportionate effect on remand decisions (Richards et al., 2025). In general, understanding bail and remand procedures entails an inter-disciplinary process with consideration of many intervening variables including legal prerequisites, social effects, and detention options. Interjurisdictional integration of data forms a comprehensive overview of bail practice and reform in harmony with modern notions of justice and rehabilitation. With the progression of technology, the use of such innovative steps as EM bail has wonderful prospects in making the pre-trial system even more just. Continuous monitoring and upgrading of these processes are necessary, the ultimate goal of which is a justice system that can safeguard the rights of the accused without losing public confidence in its efficacy (Barry et al., 2007; Richards et al., 2025).

KEY TERMS

- Bailable Offence
- Bail Bond
- Anticipatory Bail
- Bail Application
- Police Custody
- Production before Magistrate
- Extension of Remand
- Custodial Interrogation
- Non-Bailable Offence
- Surety
- Discretion of Court
- Judicial Discretion
- Judicial Custody
- Remand Application
- Magisterial Review
- Transit Remand

A LOOK TO THE FUTURE

THE FUTURE OF BAIL AND REMAND PROCEDURES

The future of bail and remand procedures is being defined increasingly in terms of arguments about their effectiveness and fairness, especially for vulnerable populations such as young people. There is increasing evidence that custody and remand practices harm more young people, usually providing adverse psychological and social outcomes. For instance, the Prison Reform Trust notes that not only are children's imprisonment cruel and not effective but also can exacerbate underlying mental illness through the stresses of imprisonment and the disruption of family relationships. Therefore, policies that reduce the number of young people on remand will be essential to guarantee that the criminal justice system not only punishes but also reintegrates the offenders. Wiser utilization of bail discretion is vital in preventing the incarceration of youths and addressing its complex drivers, which are deeply intertwined with socioeconomic and policy factors. Furthermore, technological advancements and evolving legal systems will redefine bail and remand procedures towards more individualized risk and need determinations. With jurisdictions attempting to identify custodial remand alternatives, the integration of comprehensive pre-bail assessment tools can provide judges with the intelligence needed to make sound decisions.

A national survey of young people bail practice reveals pressing matters related to custodial remand increases, emphasizing the need for alignment with international standards that mandate detention as a measure of last resort. Emphasis on avoidable remand reduction will propel reforms that not only safeguard the rights of an individual child but further promote community safety through reducing recidivism via therapeutic intervention. This shift recognizes that there is urgency in ensuring remand fulfils its role as designated without sacrificing the futures of young offenders. As public values evolve, society's desire for reform in the bail and remand procedures will continue to gain momentum based on public pressure and campaigning organizations. Continued debate regarding concerns over fairness, rehabilitation, and reintegrating offenders into society will play crucial roles in shaping future policies. Advocacy groups, such as the Prison Reform Trust, are actively identifying structural issues within the current system and calling for evidence-based changes that prioritize rehabilitation over punishment. Thus, when policymakers are arguing over the future of these procedures, they must consider the multifactorial determinants behind both youth and adult incarceration. Addressing these issues holistically will not only enhance the integrity of the justice system but also ensure that it addresses contemporary notions of social justice and human rights.

REFERENCES

1. Alexander, J. (2013). Militarization and state institutions: 'Professionals' and 'soldiers' inside the Zimbabwe Prison Service. *Journal of Southern African Studies, 39*(4), 807–828. https://doi.org/10.1080/03057070.2013.858536 (accessed on 13th August 2025).
2. Allan, A., Allan, M. M., Drake, D., Giles, L., et al. (2003). The relationship between bail decision-making and legal representation within the criminal justice system. https://core.ac.uk/download/151083682.pdf (accessed on 13th August 2025).
3. Barry, M. (2010). Youth custody in Scotland: Rates, trends and drivers. https://core.ac.uk/download/9026844.pdf (accessed on 13th August 2025).
4. Barry, M., Malloch, M., Knapp, M., Moodie, K., et al. (2007). An evaluation of the use of electronic monitoring as a condition of bail in Scotland. https://core.ac.uk/download/9026853.pdf (accessed on 13th August 2025).
5. Bartkowiak-Theron, I., & Travers, M. (2025). Changing the way we think about change: Shifting boundaries changing lives. https://core.ac.uk/download/pdf/30677431.pdf (accessed on 13th August 2025).
6. Bean, D., Cooper, P., Creaby-Attwood, A., Grubin, D., et al. (2016). *Unfitness to Plead. Volume 1: Report.* https://core.ac.uk/download/41075001.pdf (accessed on 13th August 2025).
7. Dalakian, G. J., II. (2018). Open the jail cell doors, HAL: A guarded embrace of pretrial risk assessment instruments. https://core.ac.uk/download/216958634.pdf (accessed on 13th August 2025).
8. Fadeyi, I. (2016). Restorative justice: A means to reduce imprisonment, instigate and implement rehabilitation and reintegration (a comparative study of Canadian and Nigerian criminal justice system). https://core.ac.uk/download/644031086.pdf (accessed on 13th August 2025).
9. Fine, A. J. (2014). *Kaley v. United States*: The right to counsel of choice caught in the wide net of asset forfeiture. https://core.ac.uk/download/62560401.pdf (accessed on 13th August 2025).
10. Garrett, B. L., & Monahan, J. (2020). Judging risk. https://core.ac.uk/download/213021325.pdf (accessed on 13th August 2025).
11. Hausler, K., & McCorquodale, R. (2025). Re-trial detention and human rights in the Commonwealth: Any lessons from civil law systems? https://core.ac.uk/download/33336802.pdf (accessed on 13th August 2025).
12. Heard, C., & Mansell, D. (2011). Detained without trial: Fair Trials International's response to the European Commission's Green Paper on detention. https://core.ac.uk/download/96659201.pdf (accessed on 13th August 2025).
13. Jones, A., Gallagher, B., Manby, M., Robertson, O., Schützwohl, M., Berman, A. H., Hirschfield, A., et al. (2013). Children of prisoners: Interventions and mitigations to strengthen mental health. https://doi.org/10.5920/cop.hud.2013 (accessed on 13th August 2025).
14. Kelly, M., & Tubex, H. (2015). Stemming the tide of Aboriginal incarceration. https://core.ac.uk/download/61305103.pdf (accessed on 13th August 2025).
15. N/A. (1967). Constitutional law: The Supreme Court constructs a limited right to trial by jury for federal criminal contemnors. https://core.ac.uk/download/62551699.pdf (accessed

on 13th August 2025).

16. N/A. (2025). What works to overcome Indigenous disadvantage: Key learnings and gaps in the evidence 2011–12. https://core.ac.uk/download/pdf/30675455.pdf (accessed on 13th August 2025).
17. Public Interest Advocacy Centre. (2025). Beyond the prison gates: The experiences of people recently released from prison into homelessness and housing crisis. https://core.ac.uk/download/pdf/30675879.pdf (accessed on 13th August 2025).
18. Richards, K., & Renshaw, L. (2025). Bail and remand for young people in Australia: A national research project. https://core.ac.uk/download/pdf/30675576.pdf (accessed on 13th August 2025).
19. Schneider, L. (2020). Degrees of permeability: Confinement, power and resistance in Freetown's Central Prison.
20. Ward, J. (2014). Transforming 'summary justice' through police-led prosecution and 'virtual courts': Is 'procedural due process' being undermined? https://core.ac.uk/download/42488327.pdf (accessed on 13th August 2025).
21. Woods, J. P. (1980). New York's Juvenile Offender Law: An overview and analysis. https://core.ac.uk/download/144227546.pdf (accessed on 13th August 2025).

Chapter

6

INITIATION OF PROCEEDINGS AND CHARGE FRAMING IN CRIMINAL PROCEDURE

Contents

Introduction 177
6.1. The Concept of Initiation of Proceedings 181
6.2. The Role of the Police in Initiating Proceedings 185
6.3. The Role of the Prosecution in Charge Framing 189
6.4. Legal Standards for Charge Framing 193
6.5. Judicial Oversight in Charge Framing 197
6.6. Challenges in Initiation of Proceedings and Charge Framing 201
Summary 205
References 208

INTRODUCTION

Proceedings initiation in criminal cases marks a milestone event in the judicial process since it transforms a potential crime into an enforceable case of law. The first step of this process oftentimes begins with the filing of a complaint or the issuance of a police report, putting the machinery of law enforcement and the judiciary in motion. It is critical to understand how this process unfolds because, in addition to impacting the accused and victim themselves, it impacts the overall societal perception of justice and responsibility. The relationship between the initiation of proceedings and the rights of the accused and victims underscores the delicate balance the system must maintain. On this score, lessons learned from a range of historical and recent cases can provide a glimpse into how justice systems adapt to shifting social needs and expectations. Charging is another very important step in the criminal procedure that directly affects the ways cases are prosecuted and adjudicated. It involves the formal characterization of the alleged criminal offense against the defendant, which plays a conclusive function in defining the limits of the following legal discussion. Interestingly, the phrasing of the accusations may have consequences for the public's perception of innocence or guilt, often before the trial begins. This period is significant not only for determining the baseline of the prosecution case but also for ensuring legal standards are met to safeguard defendants' rights. As Davies describes, this evolution of such framing practices has been influenced by more general legal maxims, some of which perhaps diverged from the original intent of the Bill of Rights' Framers (Davies et al., 2010). And so, the charge framing significance extends beyond legal niceties to the social justice sphere. Gender-based crime cases, for instance, are framed in a manner that reflects the complexities involved in charge framing and lodging of charges. Legal responses to such a case can conveniently affect the pursuit of justice for a victim, particularly in societies where cultural narrative may have a tendency to continuously downplay the seriousness of such offenses. Accounts of women's lives in contexts of violence demonstrate that the legal system frequently fails with its inadequacies in addressing their needs. These are a signal of the ongoing challenges of the victims and the imperative of legal structures sensitive to the multifaceted complexities of gender-based violence, as seen in the discussion of Indian legal responses (Chatterji et al., 2015). By identifying these factors, a more comprehensive framework to decide criminal procedure can be created, which in turn leads to a fair judicial outcome.

Definition of Criminal Procedure

The definition of criminal procedure is the rules and methods through which criminal law is enforced by the state. Essentially, it outlines how criminal cases are initiated, investigated, and prosecuted. The initiation of proceedings typically begins with law enforcement consideration of evidence and potential culpability and then charging by a prosecutor. This elaborate process is not only bureaucratic but also has constitutional implications since it serves the purpose of safeguarding defendants' rights as well as allowing state interests to take precedence in pursuing justice. Thus, criminal procedure knowledge involves examination of the delicate balance between public security and individual freedom. In fact, as Davies argues, the establishment of criminal procedures, particularly the invention of probable cause, constitutes a landmark achievement in this equilibrium, pointing to a drift from earlier standards that the Bill of Rights Framers endeavored to preserve (Davies et al., 2010). Framing charges in the criminal process is a significant step that translates investigations into tangible legal accusations. Prosecutors are required to exercise meticulous weighing of the evidence, determining whether there are sufficient grounds for prosecuting a case against a suspected criminal. This significant decision-making involves exercising elements of discretion and judgment, where the reliance on evidence possesses the ability to direct the trajectory of justice. The consequences are deep; a charge can generate pre-trial motions, the possibility of plea bargains, and ultimately trial proceedings. Therefore, charging is not merely the inception of litigation but expresses the prosecutions view of the defendants action. As has been noted in various contexts, including those the Special Rapporteur on Violence Against Women has identified, nuanced understandings of charge framing may disproportionately accrue to marginal groups, and this implies that there is a need for a fair application of criminal procedure to ensure access to justice for all (Chatterji et al., 2015). Criminal procedure encompasses more than technicalities and statutes. It is inextricably intertwined with social dynamics and the ethical ramifications of police actions. The initiation of criminal procedure has to consider broader society effects, namely toward marginalized groups who may be subjected to systematic biases. The very procedure that serves to uphold the law also perpetuates discriminatory patterns when not exercised judiciously. This serves to emphasize the need for openness and accountability in criminal process. As legal systems evolve, so must the frameworks that govern them, leaving space for reforms that center on justice and equitable treatment. The real challenge lies in executing these procedures fairly and effectively, with a guarantee that the accused as well as the victims receive their rights throughout the judicial process.

Importance of Initiation of Proceedings

The commencement of proceedings plays a critical function in the criminal justice process, serving as the nexus between the investigative stage and official charges. It is necessary for a number of purposes, such as protecting the rights of the accused and maintaining the integrity of the judiciary. It sets the formal framework in which further action, like arrest and questioning, occurs, thus setting precise parameters for due process. The establishment of likely cause, a fundamental doctrine established long after the drafting of the Bill of Rights, underscores the significance of an intelligent and thorough initiation process (Davies et al., 2010). By insisting on proper evidence at this stage, the courts can prevent unjust or capricious treatments of citizens and, concurrently, enable law enforcement to effectively address criminal activity. Furthermore, starting proceedings has wide-scale implications for the public perception of justice and policing procedures. Media reporting of criminal cases typically centers on the initiation phase, when it is seen as the moment at which justice is being done or denied. Such a representation has implications for public awareness and attitude towards policing and the judicial process in general.

Figure 6.1. Initiation of proceedings.

Source: https://i0.wp.com/lawbhoomi.com/wp-content/uploads/2023/04/Lawyer.webp?fit=600%2C400&ssl=1.

Although the medias focus can bring illumination to matters of ultimate concern about child abuse and intervening actions, it is also problematic. Sensationalizing a particular case is capable of skewing the general context of criminal behavior and undermining trust in the professionals who work within these complex legal contexts (Lonne et al., 2014). Consequently, understanding the process of initiation becomes crucial not only for legal practitioners but also for society as a whole since it encourages informed conversation regarding justice and responsibility. Finally, initiation of proceedings goes closely hand in hand with charging the case, which lies at the heart of ensuring justice through a fair trial. This stage primarily involves determining the precise charges the accused will be prosecuted on, and thereby the entire prosecution as well as defense legal strategy. Proper initiation and statement of charges need to be effected in order to avoid confusion and inform all parties involved on the nature of accusation being made. It allows the defense to effectively prepare and mount a successful challenge to the prosecution's case, and hence encourage the right to fair trial. For this purpose, the quality of the primary investigation and accuracy of given information lay down the effectiveness of legal proceedings. A rigorous and well-documented initiation process is therefore necessary for an equitable and balanced criminal justice system that enhances the rule of law and encourages public trust in judicial outcomes (Figure 6.1).

Overview of Charge Framing

Charge framing in the criminal justice system constitutes a critical first step that determines both prosecution strategy and defense response. The charge framing process involves the careful selection and construction of legal charges against a person, requiring attorneys to navigate statutory language along with the overall case context. Effective framing of charges not only determines official charges, but also the direction for subsequent legal actions, which influence how juries view cases and the progression of a trial. Owing to the intricacies of legal doctrine, framing of charges can play a significant role in shaping the parties involved. Therefore, this early stage of criminal process may end up having varied outcomes, and hence an understanding of framing of charges is not only vital for legal professionals but also scholars. The intricacy of charge framing is further augmented by the social and moral issues that lawyers must navigate through in this first stage. Lawyers are often faced with the challenge of balancing their duty to pursue justice and representing clients' interests appropriately. Such conflict raises some major questions: To what extent should charges be specifically expressed? To what extent must the potential for public scrutiny help determine how charges are framed? Furthermore, fresh waves in law schools require that curricula involve not only field knowledge but also experiential learning to equip students with the skills to cope better with such dilemmas (Hall et al., 2018). The integration of inquiry-based learning paradigms is increasingly being observed as essential, equipping future attorneys with the tools to problematize and negotiate the complexity of charge construction within the broader judiciary (Hall et al., 2018). Charging framing can be seen applied practically by using solid legal frameworks that outline the way charges may be framed based on jurisdictional demands and precedent law. Delimitation of functions between legal actors in this instance, as by the attorneys, is essential. For example, in practice areas such as property law, the fiduciary duty responsibility is reflected in the obligation attorneys have in charging framing. Legal representatives must accord due regard to all matters of procedure and ensure that charges meet statutory and ethical standards. The implications of poorly drafted charges are long-lasting and can result in not just miscarriages of justice but also loss of public confidence in the legal system. As has been confirmed by trust accounting fraud analysis, negligence can be expensive and far-reaching in its effects, and thus there is a necessity for correct and honest charging to provide the judicial process with integrity (Antoniades et al., 2013).

6.1. THE CONCEPT OF INITIATION OF PROCEEDINGS

The initiation of proceedings represents an essential phase of the criminal justice process upon which the future legal journey of an action is established. This phase involves formal acknowledgment of criminal charges, which can be initiated from various sites such as police investigations, complaints by victims, or prosecutorial initiative. If the jurisdiction's prosecutorial agency determines that sufficient evidence exists to prosecute, it begins the formal process by filing charges. This step not only marks a transition from investigation to prosecution but also brings far-reaching implications to the accused's rights. How proceedings begin can reflect legal norms and ethical standards which are the building blocks of criminal justice and therefore influence judgments as to fairness and transparency in the system.

Figure 6.2. The concept of initiation of proceedings.

Source: https://legalvidhiya.com/wp-content/uploads/2023/05/image-16.png.

Moreover, the beginning of proceedings underscores the need for a prudent balance between legal authority and freedom of the individual. Rights of defendants, which include the right to be informed and to respond adequately to charges made against them, are crucial in ensuring a fair legal process. While courts are engaged in scrutinizing the grounds under which proceedings are being held, they similarly incline to investigate how law enforcement and prosecution agents have acted in carrying out investigations. This analysis is particularly important in the aftermath of precedents established by cases such as Crawford v. Washington and Davis v. Washington, which have charted the legal landscape for hearsay and testimonial evidence. Such reflection contributes to a principle of initiation of proceedings that promotes a justice system that is not only effective in pursuing accountability but also attuned to the rights of defendants as well as due process. Furthermore, the framing of the charge during the initiation of proceedings plays a pivotal role in perceptions and handling of the cases by courts. Charge framing is the articulation of the specific offenses and the statute under which they are charged, and this establishes the legal basis for prosecution. Effective charge framing matters because it influences resource allocation, the prospects of plea bargaining, and the overall strategy pursued by the defense. The intricacies involved in how charges are constructed can also be quite different based on the habits of jurisdiction, type of crime suspected, and what evidence exists. Therefore, making an informed charge framing guarantees that the prosecution can make a strong case while providing for fair treatment of defendants. Lastly, the dynamics between commencing proceedings and charging in framing a basis ensure a foundation of responsibility in that it also protects enshrined principles within the criminal justice system (Figure 6.2).

6.1.1. Legal Framework Governing Initiation

The legal framework controlling initiation of proceedings in criminal procedure provides fundamental guidelines and protocols which are a vital part in the protection of the rights of the accused as well as the interests of justice. This framework typically consists of various legal statutes, procedural rules, and case laws that determine when and how a criminal case may be initiated. The primary function of such legal provisions is to ensure that all actions taken at the initiation phase observe principles of due process, thereby shielding people from arbitrary arrests and unfair prosecutions. At the heart of this process is the requirement for law enforcement agencies to secure sufficient evidence before charging, which imposes a degree of accountability within law enforcement processes and encourages public confidence in the criminal justice system. As central within the legal system is the role of prosecutors, whose discretion has a significant influence on initiating criminal prosecutions. Prosecutors must evaluate evidence against law and public interest and determine if a case should be pursued. It calls for a delicate balance between public policy and ethics, as highlighted by arguments about the effect of prosecutorial discretion on community trust and the legitimacy of the criminal justice system. Incorporation of inquiry-based approaches into legal education emphasizes the importance of understanding this process of decision-making in the context of the general society, as expressed by the experiential learning approach arguments towards methodologies being included within legal curricula (Hall et al., 2018). The procedural demands of initiating charges therefore not only reflect legal doctrine but are also consistent with the general societal consequences underlying criminal justice. Furthermore, the influence of media representation and legal framework that governs initiation is an essence of the complexity of public perception of criminal cases. While media are essential to the public's awareness of criminal justice, they also distort information. This sensationalism is potentially a multiplier of problems in the initiation process since sensationalized media coverage can influence public opinion, and often lead to prescriptive stereotypes against the accused, or even the justice system. These portrayals compromise the integrity and reputation of criminal justice professionals, creating tension between public accountability and fair treatment of individuals accused of crimes (Lonne et al., 2014). This intricate interdependence among media, law, and public opinion necessitates familiarity with the legal context of starting proceedings, a necessity to have objective reporting and informed discussion toward enhancing the integrity of the criminal justice system.

6.1.2. Types of Proceedings in Criminal Law

The beginning of criminal proceedings is a multifaceted process that varies extensively from one jurisdiction to another but normally takes the form of a structured sequence of progress from investigation to formal charging. Police have a central role to play in investigating and in procuring evidence in most cases. This stage may culminate in an arrest when there is sufficient probable cause. After a person is taken into custody, the prosecution must review the evidence to determine whether it will justify indicting the individual for a crime. The determination of whether or not to pursue charges and what type of charges to pursue can significantly influence the direction of the case as well as the final disposition for the defendant. A thoughtful consideration at this initial stage is essential because it will determine the context for either successful prosecution or potential legal objection of violation of rights or un lawful procedure. Charge framing is also a central aspect of the criminal law process, exercising a strong influence upon the context of surrounding law of a case. Prosecutors must navigate a number of factors, including the severity of the crime and the evidence that they have, in order to bring forward charges which best represent the actions taken by the accused. This framing not only determines the legal strategy adopted, but it also influences public opinion and the media reporting on the case. For instance, the way charges are framed can determine media coverage, perhaps sparking public outrage or indifference, hence shaping the social environment of the trial. According to one analysis, the media framing of such cases reflects a tendency towards sensationalism, warping the common citizen's understanding of the issues before court, thwarting the search for justice, as in Lonne et al. (2014). Furthermore, going types under criminal law extend beyond charge framing to include other hearing forms, e.g., preliminary hearings and plea bargains. Each has various functions and implications for justice provision. Preliminary hearings allow for earlier judicial determination of whether there is probable cause to pursue prosecution. Depending on the outcome, this could result in charges being dropped or a decision to pursue formal litigation. Alternately, the most frequent, plea bargaining, could give defendants a chance to plead guilty to lesser charges in exchange for lesser sentences, affecting case resolution timetables significantly. While these proceedings enhance judicial processes by making them more efficient, they also raise ethical concerns of coerced confessions and justice within judicial process. The effectiveness of such proceedings in resolving crimes also becomes enmeshed with social issues of victim rights, which calls for continuous reform of the legal system, as discussed in Chatterji et al. (2015) (Figure 6.3).

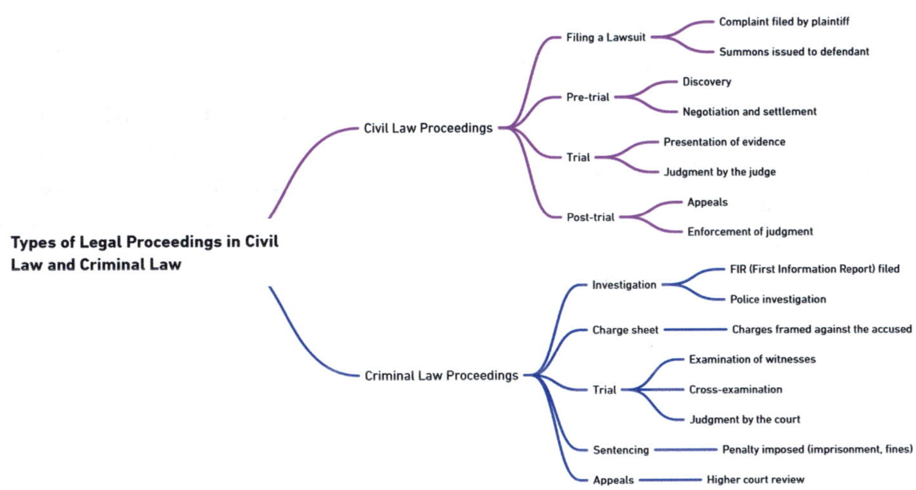

Figure 6.3. Types of proceedings in criminal law.

Source: https://legalfly.in/wp-content/uploads/2024/08/Types-of-Legal-Proceedings-in-Civil-Law-and-Criminal-Law-Summary-Mindmap.webp.

6.1.3. Role of Law Enforcement in Initiation

Law enforcement's role in commencing criminal proceedings is central, being the portal through which cases first enter the system. Law enforcement agencies are most instrumental in collecting evidence and determining probable cause, which is the key standard for making arrests and bringing charges. The actions of law enforcement at such an early point in a case have a significant bearing on where a case is headed, including on defendants' possibilities and on the overall efficacy of the justice system. By adhering to stated standards of law, such as those outlined in the Bill of Rights, law enforcement can help uphold the initial intent behind American democracy. Davies discloses a history that has been virtually totally overlooked: that the currently accepted doctrine that probable cause alone can justify a criminal arrest or search did not arise until many years after the Bill of Rights was drafted in 1789 and was a radical departure from the criminal-procedure standards that the Bill's Framers thought they had preserved intact (Davies et al., 2010). Moreover, cooperation between the police and the people is also vital to successful policing as well as filing of cases. Effective law enforcement lies in an intricate relationship with the community it serves, whereby the community can be utilized as a source of intelligence and also as the starting point for legitimacy. If the people are engaged and secure to report crime, then the police are able to identify and act against crime with ease. But the fine line between maintaining public confidence and defending the law is hard to maintain. Mistakes by law enforcers—say, abuse of authority or biased police practices—can erode community collaboration as well as the legitimacy of subsequent legal proceedings. Law enforcement agencies have to provide transparency and accountability so that the public will be assured of a joint responsibility in bringing criminal cases. The impact of judicial interpretation on the standing of law enforcement cannot be overstated. Throughout history, the legal climate has become altered by seminal decisions of the Supreme Court that chart the parameters to which law enforcement is held accountable. Such as, for instance, the Court's determinations regarding environmental regulation illustrate the ways in which judicial attitudes can shape public mechanisms of enforcement. Action by the police in many different contexts is frequently evaluated against more general constitutional principles, such as the separation of powers. As such, the clarity of law enforcements operating limits can increase or limit their efficiency in filing proceedings. Supreme Court decisions not only reflect prevalent legal standards but also influence police officers' engagement with citizens and building charges, detailing the complex relationship between police practices and judicial oversight (Miller et al., 2012).

6.2. THE ROLE OF THE POLICE IN INITIATING PROCEEDINGS

The police have a central role in the initiation of criminal cases, that of being both first responders to crime and gatekeepers to the judicial system. When a crime is perpetrated, it is usually the responsibility of law enforcement to gather evidence, conduct interviews, and ultimately decide whether to refer a case for prosecution. This first stage is critical, as police officers' actions have the potential to greatly influence the course of a case, the direction of charges, and the ensuing legal story. By their own investigative work, police decide not just who gets charged but also the gravity of the charges that are imposed, thus exercising a pivotal influence on justice provision. Their assessment and categorization of evidence necessarily indicate their conception of public safety and community trust, situating their actions in broader context within the criminal justice system.

Figure 6.4. The police play a crucial role in the initiation of criminal proceedings.

Source: https://legalmaestros.com/wp-content/uploads/2025/03/DALL%C2%B7E-2025-03-11-17.38.14-An-infographic-style-digital-illustration-representing-initiating-legal-proceedings-under-Bharatiya-Nagarik-Suraksha-Sanhita-2023.-The-image-includes.webp.

In addition, police presence and decision-making have far-reaching implications beyond the courtroom. When people are arrested, they are often faced with a range of collateral consequences that extend well beyond the criminal process itself. Arrests can be followed by hard-hitting consequences such as deportation, job loss, or homelessness, as some of the systemic impacts that have been reported in legal writings. Police behavior in the initial procedures can inadvertently set off a chain of civil consequences that alter the arrested individuals' lives. Police, therefore, need to weigh their responsibilities against an acute awareness of the potential ripple effects of their response. The relative lack of attention devoted to the civilian repercussions of arrests, as seen in discussions of the overlap of law enforcement and other regulatory bodies, necessitates more nuanced consideration of the polices role in instituting proceedings and charge framing. Of specific interest, the trend of police discretion is a key part of their function as initiators of criminal action. Police officers are often confronted with various situations that necessitate immediate judgment, and their decisions can alternatively influence not only enforcement of law but also the potential destiny of the parties. Police discretion is a reflection of society's values and beliefs regarding enforcement of law and crime. Also, since they collaborate with organizations such as housing authorities or prosecutors, their determinations of arrests get linked to other regulatory systems, which can strengthen or undermine the integrity of the criminal process. These interactions call for close examination of the system dynamics at play and also underscore the need for accountability and regulation of police practices, particularly where charge initiation is at stake and the emergent narratives that transpire in the justice system, as this has been explained in the literature on the meanings of arrests (Jain et al., 2015; Sekhon et al., 2020) (Figure 6.4).

6.2.1. Investigation and Evidence Collection

Investigation and collection of evidence is a central component in the criminal process and directly influences the initiation of proceedings and charges framing. This stage primarily involves collection of factual and physical evidence supporting police allegations. The complexity of the process is underscored by the need to adhere to accepted legal standards, which require that evidence that is collected not just be pertinent but also admissible as evidence in court. In addition, the method of gathering evidence can significantly impact its integrity; coercive methods of interrogation or excessive handling can compromise not just the evidence itself but the credibility of law enforcement agencies as a whole. Therefore, emphasis should be put on educating investigators into doing thorough and ethical investigations, keeping in mind the legal implications of their methods of evidence collection. The role played by media in bringing out criminal investigations to the public cannot be overstated. While media attention can bring forth child maltreatment issues and other social concerns, it is also able to manipulate public understanding by focusing on the sensationalized aspects of cases rather than their depth. The media presentation, according to the research in Lonne et al. (2014), deflects attention away from the most salient features and causes of criminality. This distortion may be brought to the investigative phase as public opinion, influenced by sensationalized media reports, may put pressure on authorities to prioritize certain evidence or leads favoring presently popular narratives. Thus, the investigators must be cautious within these external pressures and remain committed to their pursuit of a fair, reasonable course in the collection of evidence that does justice to the case facts. Involving inquiry-based and experiential learning in the preparation of law enforcement officers can lead to a more efficient method of investigation and evidence collection. As stated by Hall et al. (2018), employing diversified learning experiences makes sure that professionals learn not only legal concepts but also how to use them practically in real situations. This integration of progressive approaches to education can endow law enforcement agents with the competencies to manage the challenges they encounter in the field, due consideration to following proper process while investigating. With improved knowledge of investigative techniques in real-world settings, field workers are better placed to gather evidence judiciously, hence strengthening the system for the ensuing legal actions. Overall, an integrated process bringing theoretical acumen to the mix with practical application is the order of the day for enhancing the quality and integrity of evidence gathering in criminal investigation.

6.2.2. Filing of First Information Report (FIR)

The filing of the FIR is a legendary mechanism of initiating criminal prosecution under Indian law. FIR is the first document that captures the information reported to the police about a cognizable offense. It is significant as it triggers the criminal justice process, and compelled involvement and investigation by police. The FIR has to be filed in time because delays can jeopardize the credibility of evidence and recall of witnesses, which are critical for ensuring justice. Besides, formal filing of an FIR acts as a protective measure that offers victims the formal acknowledgment of complaints and ensures the police become statutorily obligated to take action (Chatterji et al., 2015). It is noted that initial state response can have a deep influence on the case trajectory, including charge framing later on and legal issues. The procedural sanctity of FIR registration has important implications for victims, particularly gender-based violence. Women, who disproportionately suffer from such crimes, are confronted with institutional barriers in the FIR mechanism that discourage them from pursuing justice. The Special Rapporteur on Violence Against Women observes that gender-based violence in India constitutes a particular continuum which is much in need of urgent attention. The law mechanism, e.g., the FIR, consequently reinforces this continuum unintentionally if not managed and enforced correctly (Chatterji et al., 2015). Hence, the FIR process is more than simply a procedural matter but an integral part of an essential element of a victim-centered approach to justice. As FIRs serve as the pillars of criminal prosecution, they must be developed to empower victims by giving them both protection and voice within the justice system. Additionally, the FIR filing challenges can also affect charge framing effectiveness in later legal processes. A defective FIR—either because of faulty collection of facts, failure to follow legal procedures, or reporting prejudices—may result in tainted investigations and reported charges. Consequently, this may result in a failure to prepare correct charges, ultimately dissuading the ability of the judicial system to deliver justice and punish the guilty. It is therefore essential that police departments are adequately trained and equipped to hurdle through these obstacles, such that FIRs are filed accurately and rightfully. These measures must be taken to enhance public confidence in the legal system and implement a change of culture towards accountability and supporting victims, particularly in such ghastly incidents of violence against women (Figure 6.5).

Figure 6.5. The filing of a First Information Report (FIR).

Source: https://blog.ipleaders.in/wp-content/uploads/2019/03/ffir.jpg.

6.2.3. Discretionary Powers of Police

Police discretionary powers are of most importance in triggering criminal proceedings and laying charges. Under the exercise of discretion, police officers have the power to choose whether or not to investigate, arrest, or warn individuals, based on their perception of the case. Though crucial for policing to be effective, this power comes with the inherent risk of arbitrariness and inconsistency. For instance, the norms that influence an officer's judgment in creating probable cause can vary widely among people and bureaus. The variations may lead to unequal treatment of suspects as well as challenges in serving justice, particularly to minorities. It is therefore essential that police bureau's create robust frameworks to govern discretionary decision-making to ensure it meets legal demands and moral ramifications. This constitutional and historical background of discretionary police power also makes their exercise in reality even more controversial. The Fourth Amendment, as originally contemplated by the Framers, was intended to prohibit unreasonable searches and seizures and require that whatever was done by law enforcers had to be justified (Davies et al., 2010). Obscurity still exists in the Amendments provision under which warrants are required, making it vulnerable to various interpretations. Courts continually expanding definition of reasonableness has provided broad discretion, sometimes more latitude than intended to law enforcement. Legal theorists say that the polices own judgment of what constitutes probable cause undermines restraints on government overreaching the constitutional designers sought to achieve (Davies et al., 1999). This tension underscores the necessity of ongoing discussion of establishing more precise parameters for the exercise of police discretion in the context of the overall constitutional rights framework. Accountability mechanisms are required to balance the risks of police discretion in charging initiation and charge framing. Implementing strong supervision and open reporting mechanisms can serve as checks on police practice, and a culture of accountability may result. The agencies must accord high priority to training on the significance of constitutional protections, and the moral considerations of discretionary decisions in policing. Policing may enhance the legitimacy of police operations by engaging with the community, and bringing diverse social settings and community values into consideration. Furthermore, new technology devices, such as body cameras, can provide tangible records of police encounters, allowing for unbiased reviews of officer discretion and strengthening public trust. By structuring the discretionary power of police in an organized way, legal frameworks can transform to allow for fair and equitable application of the law.

6.3. THE ROLE OF THE PROSECUTION IN CHARGE FRAMING

The prosecution's role in framing charges is an essential component of initiating criminal proceedings, with serious implications for the direction of a case from the outset. Prosecutors possess wide discretion over which charges to file, frequently dictating the severity and character of allegations. That use of discretion is not merely a product of the evidence on hand but also an expression of prosecutorial policy and priorities. In a majority of instances, decisions made here establish a catalyst of legal responses that end up defining the final result for the defendant, showing the thin line between interests in justice and the prosecutor's authority.

Figure 6.6. The role of the prosecution in charge framing.

Source: https://framerusercontent.com/images/8OGF2uw4vbub97rW2YDUiOiXeLI.png.

Thus, it is of the essence for criminal lawyers and scholars who want to provide opinions on the broader implications for the criminal justice system at large to comprehend the nuances of charge framing. In addition, the process of charge framing has a crucial role in defining the boundaries of a case, hence impacting the rights of victims and defendants. Prosecutors also serve to represent the state, and with ensuring that justice is dispensed, which, of course, sometimes means weighing the impact of the charges on society. Such a dual mandate causes tension, as pursuing a victory may, occasionally, take precedence over a fair trial and presumption of innocence. For instance, problems of overcharging have created controversy in terms of ethical standards in prosecution. In this case, legal scholars emphasize the importance of transparency and accountability in the system of prosecution in order to safeguard against potential abuses of authority, ultimately resulting in an effective system that is both fair and unbiased. The process of prosecution is also made complex with evolving legal norms about what constitutes legitimate charges. Historically, the belief that probable cause suffices to justify such action has been widely questioned, as embodied by legal minds who argue that the intended meaning of the Bill of Rights' Framers has over time been watered down (Davies et al., 2010). This transformation underscores the necessity for ongoing debate regarding the limits of permissible charge framing, especially in cases concerned with vulnerable populations. For instance, study on prosecuting gender-based violence indicates that charge framing is prone to distortions on the basis of systemic biases that impact justice to victims who are female (Chatterji et al., 2015). Such facts point to the importance of considering the ethical aspects of charge framing and policy reforms aimed at fostering a fair criminal justice system (Figure 6.6).

6.3.1. Responsibilities of the Prosecutor

Prosecutor's office is the focal point of initiating criminal prosecution and charges' framing thereafter, serving as the guardian of justice in the criminal justice system. It is not merely about the mere filing of charges but also involves balancing the evidence, legal standards, and ethical responsibilities with carefulness. Prosecutors must balance the pursuit of justice with their duty to uphold the law and charges that reflect the nature and seriousness of the offense. Failure to do so can result in overcharging or faulty prosecution that undermines public confidence in the legal system. Besides, when prosecutors relinquish their ethical functions, they become a cause of miscarriages of justice, questioning their position as defenders of the legal requirements they are under oath to uphold, which is a pivotal aspect of a fair legal process. While exercising their functions, prosecutors also owe it to themselves to assess the sufficiency of proof before charging a case. This evaluation is critical, as it serves as the foundation upon which charges are brought. Prosecutors must exercise their discretion judiciously, such that they do not prosecute cases based on prejudice or for their own convictions. The prosecutor's role thus extends beyond the mere filing of charges; it entails moral obligations which call for due management of evidence as well as uprightness of the judicial process. These are also compounded by mental heuristics that may have the unintended ability to affect decision-making. As reinforced by prosecutorial decision-making research, cognitive biases such as confirmation bias can lead to distorted assessment of evidence and consequently on charge allegations and even on wrongful convictions, highlighting the need for increased monitoring and ethics in the role of the prosecutor (Burke et al., 2006).

Figure 6.7. Responsibilities of the prosecutor.

Source: https://karnavatiuniversity.edu.in/wp-content/uploads/2025/05/Public-Prosecutor-vs.-Defense-Lawyer-Roles-and-Responsibilities-in-Criminal-Trials.webp.

Ultimately, the prosecutor's work must be seen within a system committed to accountability and ethical behavior. This framework is important in generating a system of criminal justice based on fairness, not conviction rates. The transformation of prosecutors' roles with societal expectations and the measure of the law means that increased transparency and accountability could eliminate the risks of misconduct or prejudice. Reforms acknowledging and addressing cognitive biases used in prosecutorial decision-making can also enhance the integrity of delivered justice. These reforms are essential, since they strive not just to fix already present flaws but also to establish a climate under which the prosecutors duty is held in respect with integrity. Consequently, the two mandate to pursue justice and safeguard defendants' rights remains a central component of the prosecutorial role, shaping the character of criminal proceedings and framing of charges (Miller et al., 2012) (Figure 6.7).

6.3.2. Evaluation of Evidence for Charge Framing

The charge framing procedure in criminal procedure relies heavily on the process of evaluating evidence, which is vital in deciding the overall direction the prosecutors pursue at the outset. Prosecutors are tasked with going through the enormity of evidence gathered during the investigation phase to compile charges that not only state the facts but also satisfy the requirements of the statute. The necessity for a critical analysis of such evidence arises from the convention that the charges leveled must be proportionate to the seriousness of alleged criminal conduct and that the accused must be accorded a fair trial. Where legal systems are based upon precedents such as Crawford v. Washington, the constitutionality and admissibility of evidence, especially hearsay, are rigorously tested. Next, the effective framing of charges must consider how various types of evidence—testimonial and non-testimonial—will invoke varying legal standards at trial, and thereby potentially influence outcomes in profound ways (Mosteller et al., 2007). Furthermore, the changing context of charge framing is reflective of broader transformation in the justice system, including the increased embedding of legal doctrines designed to protect defendants' rights. The crossover between rules of evidence and doctrines of procedure has important implications for phrasing charges as well as subsequent prosecution strategy. Most pertinent to the discussion in this case are the Confrontation Clause implications, which demand that certain statements, particularly those of vulnerable witnesses such as children, be subjected to more rigorous standards of admissibility. Neglect of properly evaluating the context of such words undermines the soundness of charges preferred, leaving prosecutions vulnerable to dismissal. This sensitivity highlights the need for legal practitioners to be sensitive to seeing that charge framing is not a technicality but an integral part of a proper working justice system (Glover et al., 2012). The evaluation of evidence in charge framing also raises serious issues about the motivations of legal actors. A systematic analysis of how evidence is evaluated can reveal much about political, social, and institutional pressure on prosecutorial offices. For instance, the tendency to prioritize obtaining convictions might have an unintended effect of charge framing based on weak or marginal evidence. It may undermine confidence in the justice system among citizens, making it crucial to have a balanced approach that targets both the integrity of legal institutions and justice values. When these dynamics are examined by legal scholars and practitioners, it becomes clear that effective and appropriate analysis of evidence in charge framing will not only influence individual cases but also enhance the broader criminal justice system infrastructure (Mosteller et al., 2007).

6.3.3. Decision-Making Process in Charge Framing

Charging decisions lie at the heart of initiating criminal cases because they decide the basis on which cases are constructed and interpreted within the legal process. Prosecutors play a pivotal role in making such decisions—facing the simultaneous challenge of acting in justice while sustaining the values of due process. They examine the evidentiary basis of the charges, not only considering the weight of evidence but also the overall implications for the accused's rights. Furthermore, this exercise of discretion requires balance, as prosecutors must mediate available precedents in law while attempting to uphold community standards of justice. Such subtlety is a testament to the richness and complexity of the criminal justice system itself, where prosecutorial decisions can directly influence case outcomes and affirm the perception that charge framing is not merely an administrative act but an inherently moral one. The developmental history of charge framing only serves to emphasize the intricacies of this decision-making process. Historically, the rules governing probable cause and the right to bring charges have undergone a deep transformation, as in the transformation of judicial interpretations subsequent to the coming into being of the Bill of Rights. It illustrates that the Framers of the Constitution wanted to keep some checks against the fancies of government procedures, but judicial procedures have at times gone away from fundamental ideas. As noted, the prevailing doctrine at the time now widely held to permit probable cause to be the sole foundation for criminal arrest or search only emerged decades of years later after the Bill of Rights drafting in 1789, highlighting a major departure from conceived original standards (Davies et al., 2010). Being aware of this context deepens research on charge framing today, illustrating the ongoing struggle between constitutional innovation and the preservation of original values within the constitution. Further, consistency in judge-made law remains a core feature in the decision-making process at the charge framing stage. Judges are continually faced with cases that test the limits of the existing legal frameworks, particularly where doubt is present in the law. As so characterized by Benjamin Cardzzo, the decisions in such cases have far-reaching implications that can propel or deter legal development and popular trust in the judiciary (Friedman et al., 2014). Judicial decision-making in frame charging therefore transcends legal meaning alone; it even incorporates general implications of legal congruence as well as the perceived legitimacy of the judiciary itself. As both prosecutors and the courts make their way through this complex system, the framing of charges is more than mere face value, affecting a people's outlook on justice and law enforcement in a constitutional democracy (Figure 6.8).

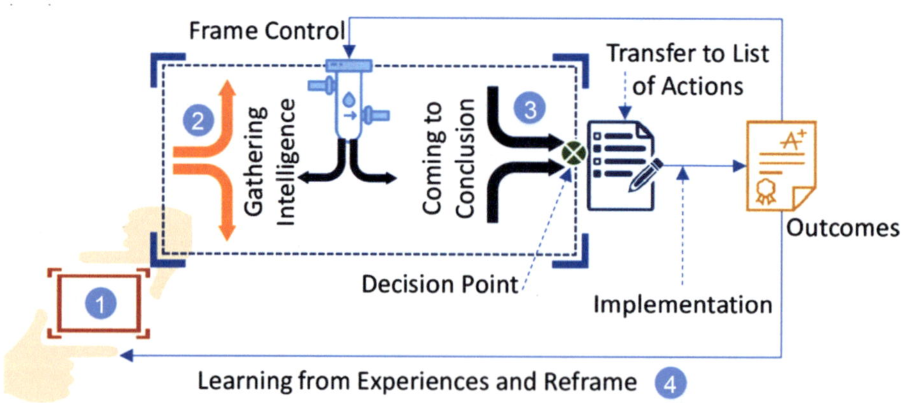

Figure 6.8. Decision-making process in charge framing.

Source: https://www.researchgate.net/profile/Caesar-Wu-4/publication/364689982/figure/fig3/AS:1143128109193055O@1666668789990/Decision-Framing-A-Good-Decision-Making-Process.png.

6.4. LEGAL STANDARDS FOR CHARGE FRAMING

The legal standards of charge framing in criminal procedure are at the core of the provision of fair justice. Charge framing is the initial step taken to describe the charges leveled against a defendant, which decides the subsequent course of legal proceedings. At the heart of this system is the doctrine of probable cause, which demands that a charge needs to be founded on evidence as strong as would warrant further legal action. This theory was never based on justice systems but evolved over a period of time.

Figure 6.9. The legal standards for charge framing in criminal procedure.

Source: https://blog.ipleaders.in/wp-content/uploads/2021/01/Criminal-Law.jpg.

Notably, Davies uncovers a story that has been largely overlooked: that the now-established principle that mere probable cause is sufficient to justify an arrest or criminal search did not emerge until many years after the Bill of Rights was drafted in 1789 and was a radical departure from the criminal-procedure practices that the Bill's Framers thought they were leaving undisturbed (Davies et al., 2010). Alongside probable cause, specificity and clarity of charges are essential in safeguarding the rights of the accused and providing due process. Legal requirements stipulate that charges should explicitly state the nature and elements of the offense for which a suspect is being held, so that the defendant will have an adequate amount of information to mount an effective defense. This demand is serving a number of purposes; it reduces the likelihood of unsubstantiated allegations to arbitrary prosecutions and helps ensure trials integrity. Charging also aids judicial case management by enabling courts to determine the merits of claims prior to trial. Disregard for these expectations can result in miscarriages of justice, eroding public trust in the criminal justice system. Therefore, charge framing must strike a balance between the needs of expeditious judicial proceedings and the needs of justice and transparency. Furthermore, the current reality of charge framing must also consider sociocultural settings influencing legal proceedings. Gender-based violence is one such aspect that demonstrates the complexities within charge framing in certain jurisdictions. In India, for instance, the delicacy of the female experience in sexual violence points to the importance not just of legal norms but also of societal norms that inform them. The Special Rapporteur on Violence Against Women's 2014 report on gender-based crime describes the Indian female experience as a continuum of violence from womb to tomb. This highlights the manner in which legal standards may prove weak in coping with the realities of vulnerable populations. Including sensitivity to the same in charge framing is essential to a fair and equitable legal process, further underscoring the need for continuous scrutiny of legal standards in line with societal changes (Chatterji et al., 2015) (Figure 6.9).

6.4.1. Threshold for Framing Charges

The threshold for framing charges in criminal procedure is a significant milestone that significantly influences the legal process. It is the dividing line between suspicion and the necessity for formal charges to effectuate due process. One of the key elements of this boundary is the concept of probable cause under which it's contended that police should have sufficient evidence to reasonably suggest that a crime has occurred before charges can be prepared. The requirement is a gauge of how to balance the rights of accused with society interests in deterring and punishing criminal behavior. Above all, the emergence of this idea demonstrates a fundamental departure from earlier procedural necessities, as is pointed out by current scholarly criticism. According to Davies, the modern concept of probable cause emerged much later after the Bill of Rights draft, demonstrating an improvement in the legal situation in terms of safeguard against capricious action on the part of the state (Davies et al., 2010). In addition, charging also necessitates an interdependence between prosecutorial discretion and judicial discretion. Prosecutors must consider evidence submitted by law enforcement agencies and decide whether the evidence justifies a threshold for charges. This discretion not only establishes the nature of charges but also dictates the direction of criminal proceedings. The complexities involved in this process of making decisions underscore the importance of having strict guidelines and a standard approach to evaluating evidence. In some jurisdictions, the test has evolved to incorporate elements of judicial review, whereby a judge is allowed to subject evidence to the test of adequacy before charges are laid. This judicial interference is a restraint on prosecutorial discretion and emphasizes the fair trial entitlement principle, and it contributes to the integrity of the judicial process. The test for charge drafting in international criminal law has introduced layers of complexity in relation to the diversity of legal traditions and the specialized international tribunal mandates. The Rome Statute of the International Criminal Court (ICC) provides for a system of addressing crimes against the administration of justice, such as the requirements for initiating cases against individuals for serious crimes. As thoroughly detailed in relevant legal commentary, Rome Statute articles 70 and 71 establish procedures for the prosecution of offenses such as tampering with witnesses and false testimony, which form part of the discussion on legal thresholds. As the ICC Commissioner remains to test the limits of having many investigations on its plate and the evolving landscape of international jurisprudence, the benchmarks set in the Rome Statute demand ongoing discussion about effective legal interpretation and policy choices, informing future practices in terms of forming charges (Kayuni et al., 2016).

6.4.2. Types of Charges: Felonies vs. Misdemeanors

The classification of criminal offenses between felonies and misdemeanors is a key aspect of the criminal justice process, deciding whether to institute proceedings and charging. Felonies are basically more serious offenses, mandating possible sentences of prison for over one year or, in some cases, death. Murder, armed robbery, and violent sexual offenses are a few examples of felonies. These serious charges demand a sophisticated judicial process, including preliminary hearings and grand jury indictments, that reflect the seriousness of the crime at issue. Misdemeanors, however, condense less serious crimes, typically punishable by fines or jail time for a term shorter than a year. Their comparatively lesser seriousness often leads to a streamlined beginning of proceedings, allowing quicker terminations. This categorization of crimes serves as the basis for comprehending how charges under the umbrella of felonies and misdemeanors have different impacts on legal consequences and defendants' experience within the criminal justice system.

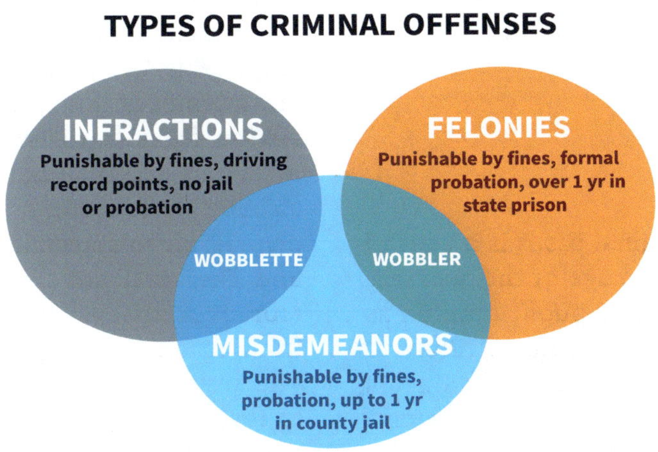

Figure 6.10. The classification of criminal offenses into felonies and misdemeanors.

Source: https://cdn-jgfil.nitrocdn.com/gxjrNoavFwVFpoQiaPtshWLsYZgHunAj/assets/images/optimized/rev-a2faa61/toplawyer.law/wp-content/uploads/2021/07/Misdemeanor-vs-Felony-vs-Infraction-Wobbler-Comparison-Chudnovsky-Law.png.

Differences between misdemeanors and felonies are crucial in analyzing charge framing and subsequent legal consequences for defendants. Felonies have severe long-range effects, such as a loss of voting rights, employment opportunities, and civil rights, making it all the more important to have effective legal representation. The initiation of criminal cases for felonies must not only entail an increased level of evidence, typically being a matter of probable cause, but also protective procedures to prevent unjust convictions. Misdemeanors, although less serious, nonetheless endanger the personal and professional well-being of individuals. The complexities of these charges underscore the significance of precise charge invocation and the resulting implications for defendants. Significantly, the difference between the two types of crime defines the direction of legal process, guiding strategies used by defense attorneys and prosecutorial strategy. Discussion of felony and misdemeanor crimes is extended to significant constitutional rights based on prior and current practices. The Sixth Amendment provides defendants a right to a fair trial, but how it is applied varies enormously between felonies and misdemeanors, particularly in the right to a jury trial. While felonies ensure a jury decision, misdemeanors, also known as petty offenses, might escape this process and leave individuals exposed to the summary judgment of a magistrate.

Jurists believe that this conduct contravenes guiding principles behind the right to a jury trial as stipulated under Article III and the Sixth Amendment. The disparate treatment of misdemeanor cases raises questions as to whether there is fairness and justice in the criminal justice system. Therefore, it is essential to comprehend these differences not only for the sake of understanding proceedings initiation but also because the broader picture of charge framing and criminal procedure must take cognizance of what safeguards are essential for all defendants in this new legal landscape (Figure 6.10).

6.4.3. Impact of Charge Framing on the Accused

The charge frame in criminal cases is a central process to construct the image of the accused, and generally, this influences public opinion as well as the judgment. Charge framing refers to the manner allegations are framed against a defendant, and this can construct the narrative of the case. A case, for instance, depicted with the background of violence or social unrest, may result in certain emotional responses from jurors and the people. This impact is specifically experienced in instances of gender-sensitive matters such as gender-based violence, where social biases are bound to color the narrative surrounding the accused in advance. Empirical evidence in India documents alarming rates of sexual violence that place instances in the context of a broader discourse of institutional gender-based offenses, where the accused is likely to be viewed through a lens of societal hostility and suspicion, thereby affecting the fairness of the proceedings (Chatterji et al., 2015). The implications of charge framing extend beyond the public impression; they do have real impacts on legal methods employed during the trial. Charges' clarity and specificity can be to blame for divergent perceptions of the accused's intent and culpability. For example, specific and accurate allegations may limit available arguments to a defense team, while vague and general charges can lead to broader interpretations in favor of the accused. Also, the framing can determine admissibility of evidence, particularly in situations involving vulnerable witnesses, say children. The Supreme Court decisions in Crawford v. Washington and subsequent decisions such as Davis v. Washington emphasize the significance of the perception of statements and their categorization within charge frames, particularly whether they are or are not testimonial in nature (Mosteller et al., 2007). Therefore, the framing takes on a pivotal role in determining the limits of evidence and the final conclusions in criminal trials. Moreover, the psychological impact of charge framing on the suspect cannot be overstated. The way charges are framed has the capacity to instigate stigmatization, emotional distress, and powerlessness among defendants. Guilty individuals internalize the narratives constructed around their charges, and this internalization plays a significant impact on their behavior during trials and their receptiveness to legal strategies. This process is particularly important in cases involving allegations of sexual violence, as the social storytelling entirely stigmatizes the defendants of such type of charges. The enduring implications of charge framing can have long-term consequences on the accused beyond the walls of the court house into their lives and mental health. By understanding the tri-fold impact of charge framing, the judiciary could identify ways to minimize bias and optimize the integrity of the criminal justice system (Chatterji et al., 2015).

6.5. JUDICIAL OVERSIGHT IN CHARGE FRAMING

Judicial oversight is a necessary element of criminal procedure charge framing, which maintains prosecutors decisions in check. Judicial oversight is crucial in upholding the pillars of fairness and justice in the law. By judicial review of accusations against the accused, potential abuse of authority is prevented. This analysis is especially relevant where the separation of powers doctrine is analyzed in terms of the implications it has towards ensuring that there is no abuse of authority by any branch of government. Judicial review, in this case, acts as a check on the prosecutorial role to ensure that charges not only reflect the facts of the case but also safeguard the constitutional rights of the people.

Figure 6.11. Judicial oversight is a fundamental aspect of charge framing in criminal procedure.

Source: https://i0.wp.com/lawbhoomi.com/wp-content/uploads/2023/04/law21.webp?fit=600%2C400&ssl=1.

This type of approach provides a platform wherein the legitimacy of charges can be ascertained within the confines of law and established norms. In addition to that, charge framing and judicial supervision have gained much attention in recent legal thought, particularly with regard to the consequences of poor supervision. Where judicial supervision is inadequate or non-existent, consequences can prove to be fatal and may result in wrongful conviction or wrongful punishment. Criminal procedure must have robust mechanisms subjecting prosecutorial discretion to controls and holding prosecutors accountable, and maintaining public trust. The role of the judiciary here is not only to examine the sufficiency of the evidence but also to ensure that the motive to charge is appropriate. Through a principled analysis of charge framing in the judicial framework, issues surrounding prosecutorial conduct can be addressed with a balance to ensure constitutional safeguards to reinforce the integrity of the criminal justice system. Furthermore, the issues of judicial control over charge framing are demonstrated by way of case studies that shed light on the complexities involved. For instance, judicial decisions on environmental law have enlightened the broader implications of judicial dispositions toward private enforcement in law.

The Supreme Courts skepticism of citizen suits also poses critical questions on the part of judicial intervention in altering prosecutorial practice. Where corruption and exploitation are the charges, like when the issues border on natural resources management in Africa, judicial oversight is most vital to prevent abuse that would undermine democratic control. An in-depth examination of judicial supervision of charge framing, therefore, brings its crucial role in ensuring the rule of law, ensuring that the prosecutorial behavior is maintained to ethical levels, and protecting the rights of suspects of crimes as stipulated under (Lucky et al., 2005; Miller et al., 2012) (Figure 6.11).

6.5.1. Role of the Courts in Reviewing Charges

The role of the courts in reviewing charges is a critical check within the criminal procedure mechanism. The review by the judiciary ensures that charges brought against an individual are not only prudent but also meet constitutional protections and due process. This oversight is particularly critical in the early stages of criminal proceedings, where the danger of mistaken convictions or arbitrary charges jeopardizes justice significantly. Through an analysis of evidence put forward by prosecuting agencies, the courts are in a position to decide if there is reasonable cause to justify charges made. This parallels developments in criminal procedure in history, given that the courts have become more active in protecting rights enshrined in the Bill of Rights, in the wake of speculations that earlier doctrines will not adequately protect individuals against government overreach (Davies et al., 2010). Additionally, the task of the courts is not only to scrutinize probable cause; they also decide the implications of charge framing for the right to a fair trial. Judicial oversight is a crucial element in making sure that the charges are prepared in a form that facilitates adequate defense. General or imprecise charges can bring about ambiguity that limits the defendants ability to respond appropriately. By careful judicial scrutiny, courts can insist on specificity in charging documents, thus maintaining the integrity of the judicial process. Such diligence eventually serves the interests of public trust in the justice system since defendants and the community themselves realize the value of a rational and fair approach to criminal cases. In serious crime cases, such dedication is particularly warranted, since the effects of mediocre charge framing disproportionately hurt minority communities and further reinforce social imbalances (Chatterji et al., 2015). Additionally, the courts are also tasked with addressing any claimed biases or institutional injustices that may occur in the process of reviewing the charges. This entails not only looking at the evidence generated but also looking at the broader social and legal environments that frame criminal charges. For instance, the court is able to analyze patterns of framing of charges that disproportionately affect specific demographic groups and thus determining discrimination problems within the justice system. As the courts consider these underlying disparities, they contribute to creating more equitable criminal processes. The mandate of courts to advance justice is not only in discrete cases; it is a duty to ensure that all individuals are treated alike under the law. This strategy serves not just individual defendants, but also stands for a wider criminal procedure reform, an acknowledgment of the realization that justice must access everyone, especially where vulnerable groups are involved (Chatterji et al., 2015).

6.5.2. Pre-Trial Hearings and Their Significance

The significance of pre-trial hearings in the criminal procedure system cannot be overstated, particularly where the initiation of proceedings and the charging occur. These hearings are the turning point when the prosecution must present adequate evidence to establish probable cause of the charges against the defendant. Not only does the process safeguard the rights of the accused, but it also heightens the integrity of the judicial system. By requiring the prosecution to substantiate its accusations before proceeding to trial, pre-trial hearings in fact eliminate bad cases of insufficient evidence and thus spare unnecessary court pressure and ensure that only genuine charges proceed. As seen in reports of criticisms against standard procedures, the ability to accelerate or reject cases at this stage minimizes the risk of false convictions, an issue which is increasingly pertinent in more recent judicial debate (Dession et al., 1932). Furthermore, pre-trial hearings have profound implications for the power balance between the prosecution and defense. This phase gives defendants an opportunity to dispute the case of the prosecution prior to being heard in full trial settings. Challenges can be in forms like disputing the legality of evidence that has been procured or challenge of issues of the investigation as being wanting. This pre-trial hearing aspect imposes the adversarial character of the criminal justice system, giving place to both sides to assert their positions and broker terms that can bind subsequent plea bargains or trial results. The role of these hearings is therefore more than a matter of procedural courtesy, being a constructive aid to a larger openness and equity in the legal process. Additionally, their significance comes out in other research on justice in context, identifying system reform for proper handling of specific crimes as well as enhanced victim care (Chatterji et al., 2015). Apart from their procedural impact, pre-trial hearings are crucial in shaping the broader narrative of the court regarding cases, particularly where issues such as gender violence are at stake. Such offenses usually generate strong social responses, and how they are constructed during hearings has the potential to shape public opinion as well as policy discourse. For example, in sexual violence offenses, the outcomes at hearings have implications not just for the parties involved but also provide reference points for what society does or does not demand of the justice system. As pointed out in gender-based violence discussions in India, how such issues are handled in pre-trial proceedings affects victims in their pursuit of compensation as well as the credibility of the legal system as a whole. The value of pre-trial hearings, in this case, thus transcends individual case particulars to encompass broader social narratives, enhancing their status as pillars of justice (Chatterji et al., 2015) (Figure 6.12).

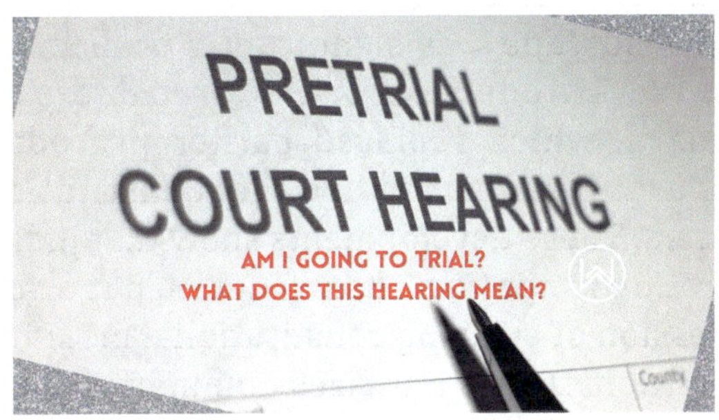

Figure 6.12. The significance of pre-trial hearings within the framework of criminal procedure.

Source: https://wittlegal.com/wp-content/uploads/2022/06/4b9f9da50cf2f358abdcd4a4321104f9.jpg.

6.5.3. Judicial Discretion in Charge Framing

Judicial charge framing discretion is a critical element in prosecutorial framework formulation in criminal procedure. Discretion by the judges and prosecutors in initiating criminal proceedings has a considerable impact on not only the charges brought but even the resulting legal outcomes for accused individuals. This discretion allows legal professionals to craft charges to fit the unique facts of each case, aligning the interests of justice with the nuances of criminal behavior. Furthermore, charge form variation may be an instrument of broader societal values and legal meaning, illustrating the role of judicial discretion in brokering between law and context. For instance, there is a thin line between exercising discretion wisely to attain justice and embedding systemic prejudices that can result in disproportionately influencing charge decisions against marginalized communities, thus attracting ethical concerns in the administration of justice. The background of judicial discretion traces its evolution and the principles governing practice today. Historically, criminal search and arrest standards established by the Bill of Rights have experienced a gargantuan reinterpretation. For instance, the court landscape was significantly transformed with the introduction of the probable cause standard, which replaced earlier procedural standards established by the Constitution's Framers. These developments show that judicial discretion is not just a handy device but also an expression of evolving constitutional meanings. In addition, Davies criticizes dominant criminal procedure doctrines to the point that the Framers' initial purpose of upholding lofty standards of justice have often been breached by judicially sanctioned policies that prioritize expediency over fairness. This analysis suggests discretion's implications require constant discussion in the framing of charge. Further, judicial discretion is not merely a legal interpretation function; it incorporates deeper ethical analysis that defines the role of judges and prosecutors. The balancing between prosecutorial discretion and judicial review becomes questionable with respect to criminal case integrity in charge framing. Prosecutors are also privileged with significant power in deciding which charges to bring, often depending on a plethora of considerations like public safety, available evidence, and potential societal implications. The discretionary use of this power can result in differing prosecutorial approaches, which can in turn reinforce or counter existing legal disparities. Similarly, the role of the courts in reviewing such a decision is underpinned by arguments over separation of powers and the appropriate degree of judicial intervention. This intersection of ethics, power, and discretion reveals the complexity built into charge framing that governs the initiation of criminal proceedings, thus demanding wise conversations regarding judicial responsibility in a democracy.

6.6. CHALLENGES IN INITIATION OF PROCEEDINGS AND CHARGE FRAMING

Initiation of proceedings and charge framing in criminal process is plagued by a number of challenges, impacting heavily on the pursuit of justice. Among the principal challenges is the inherent intricacy involved in gathering evidence, particularly in sensitive cases of gender-based violence. The Special Rapporteur on Violence Against Women, for instance, identifies with the rampant gendered crimes committed within India where victims struggle to cope with a judicial system that will not offer protection or compensation (Chatterji et al., 2015). This breakdown in adequate response by state authorities may discourage victims to report, thereby undermining the principle of public safety and the rule of law.

Figure 6.13. The initiation of proceedings and charge framing in criminal procedure is fraught with various challenges.

Source: https://legalseva.net/wp-content/uploads/2023/08/Framing-of-Charges-Challenged-in-High-Court-Revision-.jpg.

Failure to initiate proper proceedings, therefore, does not only affect individual victims but also undermines general public trust in the criminal justice system and its ability to address violence and discrimination. Additionally, charging an offense is sometimes a special challenge that poses its own obstacles for early stages of the judicial process. Prosecutors have to carefully weigh on one hand the desire to properly represent the seriousness of an offense and on the other whether there is enough evidence to support it. The media is also an integral component of this dynamic, as public interest in high-profile cases has the ability to pressure prosecutors into acting in ways that do not necessarily adhere to ethical or legal standards (Lonne et al., 2014). This can lead to charges being made hastily or the wrong charges being filed, ultimately compromising the integrity of the legal process. The stress to respond to heightened public scrutiny can drive charge framing further on the basis of popular expectations and not on solid legal grounds, further complicating the quest for justice. The obstacles in initiation and charge framing extend beyond isolated cases and reveal systemic defects in the legal system. For instance, bureaucratic inefficiencies. In addition, an inability on the part of inter-agency coordination could retard proceedings and also ensure that effective case handling is not achieved. Most often, the police are burdened by resource weaknesses that limit their capacity to carry out stringent investigations, hence making charge framing challenging (Chatterji et al., 2015). Where evidence is in short supply, there is a greater risk of mistaken charges, which puts the rights of the accused directly at risk while simultaneously denying justice to victims. Hence, meeting these challenges necessitates an approach that is multi-dimensional in nature and involves legal reforms, more training for police officers, and improved public awareness campaigns so that proceedings and framing of charges ensure the rule of law and protect the rights of all the parties to the process (Figure 6.13).

6.6.1. Issues of Misuse of Power

Misuse of power in criminal procedural context often manifests itself at the stage of initiation of proceedings and framing of charge, the processes which are critically dependent on the honesty and objectivity of police and judicial officials. When the people in power misuse power for themselves, public confidence in the system of justice is eroded and the foundations of justice itself are shaken. For instance, police forces can engage in selective enforcement or focus on a certain population based on prejudice or political pressure, hence leading to erroneous charges. Not only does this undermine the rights of the accused, but it also reflects a society's issue whereby the marginalized are more prone to experience the impact of systemic injustices. The effects of such behavior are likely to seep into society, creating a cycle of mistrust between the populace and the authorities that can interfere with effective policing as well as erode the social compact that permits the delivery of justice. The impact of media on how criminal cases are understood by the public further complicates issues of abuse of power. While the media might be helpful in focusing public attention on situations of injustice and calling for change, it can also be used to sensationalize, and therefore create biased reports and a citizenry that would demand retribution based more on passion than truth. This process, as shown in child maltreatment media coverage research, illustrates how media depiction is capable of distorting public opinion and influencing legal process through creating an atmosphere of fear or anger. This fierce scrutiny has the likelihood of subjecting attorneys to too much pressure to frame charges in language appealing to popular sentiment rather than the proportionality and justice requirements. Charges therefore have the tendency at times to lack alignment with the evidential base, further solidifying differences in the criminal justice system (Lonne et al., 2014). Lastly, the balance of power between the judiciary, police, and the press illustrates the frail nature of power within criminal proceedings. There needs to be protection against abuse of power at the stage of framing charges and initiating prosecution. The judiciary plays an important role in ensuring responsibility, acting as a check on potential excesses on the part of the police machinery. However, that balance can be disrupted when prosecutorial discretion is used unjudiciously to allow personal preferences to decide which cases are prosecuted and how the accusations are to be laid out. Additionally, the intersection of law and emerging sciences, like regenerative medicine, demonstrates the worth in being tied by ethical principles and in being careful with the exercise of power. Lastly, correcting the issue of abuse of power calls for a critical examination of institutional practices and a readiness to reform focusing on transparency and accountability within the criminal process (Abounit et al., 1966).

6.6.2. Impact of Public Opinion and Media

The relationship between public opinion and media representation plays an important role in defining attitudes around criminal proceedings and defining charges. The media can carry with it certain problems to the public sphere, as in the situation of child maltreatment and criminal justice. For instance, the media have emerged as significant actors in political and public agendas regarding child protection in the past 50 years through documentation of scandals and tragedies around such cases. However, such a portrayal has the potential to inaccurately characterize complex circumstances and divert attention from their roots. Consequently, criminal justice system professionals, particularly those in child protection, can erode trust and credibility as the media increasingly prioritize sensationalism over balanced reporting. Thus, the charging framings can be impacted by public opinion, spurred on by media coverage, impacting both final results and proceedings initiation. Additionally, the medias framing of gender crimes deeply impacts public opinion and the related criminal process. Studies have indicated that women in India undergo a continuum of violence and as such are very vulnerable to sexual violence, especially in conflict zones. The framing of such crimes in media reports significantly impacts the way gender violence is understood, public opinion, and policy-making on such issues. Media reports of these crimes bring them into focus and can reinforce calls for justice as well as perpetuate unintendedly stigmas and myths that obstruct effective charge framing. The contrast in the presentation of these cases can influence public opinion, and consequently, the readiness of legal institutions to respond effectively against such crimes. To this effect, it is evident that media reports not only inform public opinion but also reflect and present the legal and procedural techniques used in criminal justice systems. Along with this, the complexities of public opinion in criminal issues are also added to by the character of media to sensationalize and not thoroughly analyze. Even though the media have brought issues like child abuse up for debate, they tend to focus on the most sensationalized cases, a fact that blurs the general picture of such social evils. Such differential attention has the potential to generate mass hysteria about crime that compels police and judicial authorities to respond proportionally to popular fear rather than responding to the crime rates and preventive concerns. Proceeding with proceedings and laying charges can then become reactive, with the immediate need to satisfy public and media demand for justice rather than being guided by meticulous legal assessments. In this regard, public opinion and media representation also play a more general influence, not only on individual cases, but on the workings and legitimacy of the criminal justice system as a whole (Figure 6.14).

Figure 6.14. Impact of public opinion and media.

Source: https://skchildrenfoundation.org/wp-content/uploads/2023/07/blogpost-1-2.png.

6.6.3. Legal Reforms and Recommendations

The initiation of criminal proceedings and the charging of cases are at the forefront of law enforcement and civil rights, highlighting the significant necessity for legal reforms. The reforms are necessitated so that the mechanisms in use for the initiation and continuation of criminal cases are effective as well as fair. For instance, the legislation that governs this practice has to consider the public opinion role played by the media, as the media sensationalize cases by highlighting scandals and hence potentially undermining trust in legal processes and professionals. Such representations have the tendency to manipulate the public's understanding of the issues involved in cases of child abuse, seeking to create cries for revenge without adequate regard for motives or systemic factors at stake. An initial proposal for legal change would therefore involve measures for raising the objectivity and transparency of the medias role in criminal cases, facilitating more informed public discourse (Lonne et al., 2014). Moreover, legal reforms must also speak to the gendered character of gender-based crimes and, in those countries where cultural and system discrimination denies women justice, address the distinctive needs that women have in accessing justice. The lamentable reality that a woman is raped in India every 20 minutes underscores the necessity for legislative solutions. The procedural framework that commences proceedings on cases of gender-based violence must be reformed to enable seriousness with which gender-based crimes are prosecuted. This involves the engagement with lobby groups to integrate survivor voices within the legal system to gain a more victim-sensitive approach. Suggested reforms must also involve training law enforcers and legal professionals on how to handle sensitive cases to ensure that ad hoc bias does not influence charging of suspects. These measures would provide a more balanced legal response to crimes of gender, significantly increasing the effectiveness of the judicial system (Chatterji et al., 2015). Finally, the impact of legal reforms extends beyond procedural reforms in fact-specific reforms; it demands a shift of culture in the legal establishment. This is to create a culture that guarantees justice and equality in every facet of criminal procedure. Inclusion of stakeholders such as legal aid societies and community groups in policymaking can initiate this transformation. In mutual efforts at the level of changes, the stakeholders can bring on-the-ground experience to complement legal recommendations on charging and instituting cases and make them more effective and responsive. In addition, constant training and education programs can create a sense of responsibility among legal practitioners so that they can keep themselves updated about the needs and issues of the community. Lastly, such legal reforms and collaborative initiatives can establish a more participatory and responsive legal framework, connecting ideals of justice with realistic needs of social issues (Chatterji et al., 2015; Lonne et al., 2014).

SUMMARY

The initiation of proceedings and charge determination in criminal procedure, it is essential to consider the sensitive interplay between legal rules and their practical effects. Probable cause, a cornerstone in safeguarding individual liberties, has evolved a great distance since its inception. Davies accounts for how the probable cause used today, warranting arrest and search, moved away from the traditional standards envisioned by the Bill of Rights' Framers. This evolution signifies that as the justice system adapts in order to maintain pace with developments in society, it becomes crucial to note how such evolutions impact the rights of individuals accused of offenses, resulting in an overall understanding and faith in the system. These reappraisals thus disentangle the underlying tensions in criminal justice, which must be sustained through constant debate by legal players and academics. Also, the role of outside agencies, namely the media, cannot be excluded when considering charge formulation and the initiation of criminal proceedings. Public perception is shaped by the media's description of criminal behavior and thus can end up affecting court decisions. As noted, the media have played a pivotal role in placing child abuse and protection on the political agenda historically, but in doing so often contributes to simplifying and overgeneralizing their complexities. This sensationalism not only risks compromising the reputation of professionals in the field but also poses the threat of overwhelming systemic issues. Hence, it is important to comprehend how the narrative of media changes in order to set up suitable charges and initiate fair prosecution procedures, allowing the legal process to operate within the parameters of popular expectations without sacrificing fairness and justice for all concerned. Lastly, the conclusion of a search into the initiation of proceedings and charge framing in criminal procedure emphasizes the necessity of a responsive legal system that conforms to shifting societal values but remains unyielding in its quest for justice. With changing systems, increasingly greater demand for openness and responsibility in the legal process emerges. Deviation from the origin principles, as Davies defines, demands careful reevaluation of current practice to maintain it consistent with constitutional protection. Further, the twin influence of social narratives conveyed by representation in the media has both an educative and a warning function for legal practitioners. As we navigate these complexities, the continuous development of legal standards and procedures is essential to maintain public trust and guarantee the integrity of the criminal justice system as a whole.

The initiation of proceedings in criminal procedure is, in effect, a pivotal stage that sets the tone for the direction of the legal process. It involves a variety of mechanisms including police inquiries, charging, and initial hearings that serve to safeguard the rights of the accused while advancing the interest of the state in criminal law. These initial stages are not procedural ritual; they set the context by which the case will be resolved. Therefore, understanding the sensitivity of how such proceedings are initiated becomes crucial in any examination of their impact on the future of the accused. The quality of evidence garnered, what the police do, and prosecutorial discretion can significantly influence judicial determinations, and thus, the established procedure of initiation is greatly necessary. Properly charging the accused is equally crucial as it establishes the legal setting, determining the precise charges upon which the accused will be indicted. This stage entails meticulous consideration by prosecutors with a balance to be struck between the need for responsibility and the potential consequences for the accused. Charge framing entails significant legal acumen, with it centered on construing statutory definition and aligning facts with relevant laws. This technical component serves not only for the sake of justice but also to maintain public confidence in the judicial process. By making charges precise and clear, prosecutors uphold the sanctity of the legal process, making the charging phase a vital area of focus for procedural law understanding. In addition, the interplay between media portrayal and criminal proceedings cannot be discounted because it greatly affects public opinion and policy formulation. Here, the media coverage of cases can affect the initiation of proceedings because public opinion might cause authorities to move more aggressively or, conversely, bring about indecision. The framing of criminal cases, particularly those dealing with sensitive issues, can be converted into social pressure that complicates an already arduous process. Here, the media is a double-edged sword, bringing forth such vital issues while also posing the risk of misrepresentation of key characteristics and causes of crime. Considering this dynamic is essential to the legal professional's capacity to address the complexities involved in the charging and ensuing legal battle that comes with it, as noted within determinations of the public and political response to matters of justice (Hall et al., 2018; Lonne et al., 2014).

KEY TERMS

Amendment of Charge	Charge
Cognizance	Complaint
Discharge	First Information Report (FIR)
Framing of Charge	Investigation
Joinder of Accused	Joinder of Charges
Magistrate's Jurisdiction	Material Evidence
Police Report	Prima Facie Case
Summons Case	Trial Commencement

A LOOK TO THE FUTURE

FUTURE DIRECTIONS IN CRIMINAL PROCEDURE

The evolution of criminal procedure is marked by a variety of influences that chart its course into the future. As society becomes more advanced, there is a greater emphasis on the need for reform that provides for efficiency and justice in the commencement of proceedings and charge framing. Future possibilities include using technology to streamline these processes through automation, such as the establishment of online platforms for charging and managing case files. The shift not only has the potential to reduce delays but also aims to render the process transparent and accessible to all concerned. Apart from that, ongoing engagement between the judiciary and parliament will also be instrumental in ensuring reforms are followed by both judicial precedents and public pressure, ultimately The intertwined role of media and public opinion will also continue to influence the manner in which criminal proceedings are initiated and delineated in the future, requiring responsive measures. Furthermore, greater awareness of system discriminations in the criminal justice sector necessitates a reexamination of charge framing procedures. Future changes on this note may be focused on applying standards of equity and fairness to ensure fair targeting of marginalized communities. Cases that are scrutinized can be determined by legal professionals more effectively through evaluation to establish potential biases in a prosecuting environment. The policymakers and researchers must collaborate to develop standards that focus on fair charge framing and address the deep-rooted problem of discrimination within society. The debate regarding these reforms must be guided by different stakeholders, including advocacy organizations and jurists, to establish a shared framework that keeps justice as the focus. It is important that reforms not only correct current imbalances but also discourage future injustices and make way for a legal system that reflects the mores of society and enforces human rights. Finally, as criminal procedure changes to keep pace with the realities of today, public participation and education can serve no larger purpose in shaping future directions. More public visibility, often amplified by the media, can significantly influence legal proceedings. Public opinion can compel reform efforts, pushing parliamentarians to address issues such as transparency, accountability, and ethically charging. As noted in recent research, while the media brings critical issues to the fore, it could also warp the complexity of child protection and criminal process (Lonne et al., 2014). Thus, facilitating informed debate among the public, legal practitioners, and the media will be paramount. Encouraging responsible reporting can help to achieve an educated citizenry that in turn can hold the justice system to task for future actions and decisions, and ensure that future criminal proceedings adhere to the maximum possible standards of justice and diligence.

REFERENCES

1. Abounit, M., Armstrong, J., Auernheimer, L., Bae, J., Banito, A., Bao, S., et al. (1966). Controlling the bureaucracy of the antipoverty program. https://core.ac.uk/download/62556020.pdf (accessed on 13th August 2025).
2. Antoniades, H. (2013). White collar crime and property agents: A selection of convictions involving trust accounting fraud. https://opus.lib.uts.edu.au/bitstream/10453/23670/1/20120021890K.pdf (accessed on 13th August 2025).
3. Burke, A. S. (2006). Improving prosecutorial decision making: Some lessons of cognitive science. https://scholarship.law.wm.edu/wmlr/vol47/iss5/3 (accessed on 13th August 2025).
4. Chatterji, A. P., Fletcher, L. E., Kaur, M., & Altholz, R. (2015). Access to justice for women: India's response to sexual violence in conflict and social upheaval. https://core.ac.uk/download/75783197.pdf (accessed on 13th August 2025).
5. Davies, T. Y. (1999). Recovering the original Fourth Amendment. https://core.ac.uk/download/232714894.pdf (accessed on 13th August 2025).
6. Davies, T. Y. (2010). How the post-framing adoption of the bare-probable-cause standard drastically expanded government arrest and search power. https://core.ac.uk/download/62553055.pdf (accessed on 13th August 2025).
7. Dession, G. H. (1932). From indictment to information—Implications of the shift. https://core.ac.uk/download/72833635.pdf (accessed on 13th August 2025).
8. Friedman, L. (2014). Common law decision-making, constitutional shadows, and the value of consistency: The jurisprudence of William F. Batchelder. https://core.ac.uk/download/72052736.pdf (accessed on 13th August 2025).
9. Glover, J. M. (2012). The federal rules of civil settlement. https://core.ac.uk/download/74539279.pdf (accessed on 13th August 2025).
10. Hall, J. (2018). An integrated law curriculum: Balancing learning experiences to achieve a range of learning outcomes. https://core.ac.uk/download/159106099.pdf (accessed on 13th August 2025).
11. Haq, K. A., Khadka, S. S., Pradhan, R., Spiertz, H., et al. (2025). *Water Rights, Conflict and Policy: Proceedings of a Workshop Held in Kathmandu, Nepal, January 22–24, 1996*. https://core.ac.uk/download/pdf/6843901.pdf (accessed on 13th August 2025).
12. Jain, E. (2015). Arrests as regulation. https://core.ac.uk/download/70375362.pdf (accessed on 13th August 2025).
13. Kayuni, S. W. (2016). *Quis Custodiet Ipsos Custodes* (Who is guarding the guardians)? –Decision processes in the ICC's offences against the administration of justice. https://core.ac.uk/download/46523856.pdf (accessed on 13th August 2025).
14. Lonne, B., Chenot, D., Corby, B., Gilbert, R., Krugman, R., Laming, H., et al. (2014). Portrayals of child abuse scandals in the media in Australia and England: Impacts on practice, policy, and systems. https://core.ac.uk/download/30729800.pdf (accessed on 13th August 2025).
15. Lucky, C., Tamm, I., & Humphreys, S. (2005). Legal remedies for the resource curse: A digest of experience in using law to combat natural resource corruption. https://core.ac.uk/download/71348086.pdf (accessed on 13th August 2025).

16. Miller, J. G. (2012). The constitutionality of citizen suit provisions in federal environmental statutes. https://core.ac.uk/download/46713657.pdf (accessed on 13th August 2025).
17. Mosteller, R. P. (2007). Testing the testimonial concept and exceptions to confrontation: "A little child shall lead them." https://core.ac.uk/download/62562789.pdf (accessed on 13th August 2025).
18. Roth, A. (2022). The lost right to jury trials in all criminal prosecutions. https://core.ac.uk/download/543836296.pdf (accessed on 13th August 2025).
19. Sekhon, N. (2020). Representative defendants. https://core.ac.uk/download/323062030.pdf (accessed on 13th August 2025).

Chapter 7

CRIMINAL TRIAL PROCESS

Contents

Introduction....211
7.1. Pre-Trial Procedures....215
7.2. The Role of Key Participants....219
7.3. Jury Selection....223
7.4. Trial Phases....228
7.5. Deliberation and Verdict....231
7.6. Post-Trial Procedures....235
Summary....239
References....242

INTRODUCTION

The criminal trial process is a fundamental component of the larger judicial system mechanism consisting of the principles of justice, due process, and rule of law. To understand such a sophisticated process is to examine its procedures, which go from arrest, to arraignment, to trial, and perhaps appeal. Each procedure is a fulcrum upon which teeters the scales of defendants' rights and interests of the state. Throughout the trial process, the doctrine of innocence is a benchmark to guarantee defendants are presumed innocent until found guilty. This fundamental right, particularly pertinent during media coverage, is applicable to the question of any potential public opinion-formed prejudices that can be brought into the judicial process, which need protection under the judicial process to uphold neutrality and fairness (Resta et al., 2008). Besides, the criminal trial process is also dominated by procedural laws aimed at regulating the admissibility of evidence and case presentation. At the center of these processes is the relationship between the rights of a defendant and the obligation of the police and prosecutors, who must operate within established legal frameworks in order to provide justice. For instance, the complexity of holding corporate organizations to account highlights the need for simplified definitions of responsibility and accountability, as the law exposes criminal liability not only to people but also corporate entities (Doyle et al., 2013). The twain makes it challenging for the trial to proceed, as juries must contend with intricate legal standards while considering the effect of corporate behavior on public interest and legal accountability. Finally, the outcomes of criminal cases have long-term repercussions, not only affecting the parties involved, but society itself as well. Sentencing can be employed to prevent crime and maintain societal mores, thereby impacting the public perception of justice and morality. The balancing act between trial outcomes and societal values encapsulates the broad context of punishment, reform, and potential rehabilitation in the criminal justice system. As criminal justice reform discussions continue to play out, understanding the complexities of the criminal trial process becomes increasingly important. Carefully analyzing each component enables one to appreciate more fully how justice is administered—or withheld—within specific cases and within system structures (Figure 7.1).

Figure 7.1. Illustration of courtroom.

Source: https://selfhelp.courts.ca.gov/sites/default/files/styles/768x/public/2020-10/illustration-courtroom-jury.png?itok=DmHpnxcb.

Definition of the Criminal Trial Process

The criminal trial procedure is a significant means through which legal systems dispose of allegations of criminal conduct and obtain justice and order in society. In general, the procedure has various steps like arrest, preliminary proceedings, arraignment, trial, and potential appeals. Essentially, the criminal trial seeks to establish the guilt or innocence of the accused based on evidence presented by the prosecution and defense. The process of the trial is designed to ensure that due process is followed, which includes allowing defendants the opportunity to mount a strong defense. All stages of the trial are overseen by laws and jurisprudence, which collectively decide the very basis upon which justice is delivered in criminal proceedings. At the core of this definition is that the criminal trial process must find a balance between the public and victims' interests and the accused's rights. It is essential in understanding the criminal trial process dynamics to consider the context in which reforms have been created to render it more effective. New legislations have sought to address some of the deficiencies and setbacks suffered by different stakeholders, particularly crime victims. For instance, it has been evidenced that biased perceptions of legal norms can negatively affect the integrity of trials, leading to results that diverge from the legislature's objective of simplifying processes and fair trial conduct (Vlasova et al., 2022). These findings support the ongoing need for close scrutiny of prevailing practices and adoption of reforms to increase legal transparency and victim support to better overall functioning of the criminal justice system. Rehabilitation of the criminal trial process also involves focused attention to victims experience in this intricate system. In Australia, a number of major reforms have been instituted to address the disadvantage faced by victim/survivors of sexual assault during the criminal justice system, for example, specialized police service and support advocacy intervention (Fileborn et al., 2014). These reforms reflect heightened recognition of the value of a victim-focused approach, an approach that addresses not only the procedural concerns of trials but also the emotional and psychological needs of concerned parties. Through viewing and applying successful practices from the perspectives of victims, the criminal justice system is able to encourage more equitable processes that respect the interests and rights of all parties. Modifying the criminal trial procedure is thus not a legalistic exercise but concerning the institutionalization of the ethics of responsibility, justice, and compassion (Figure 7.2).

Figure 7.2. The criminal trial process.

Source: https://criminal-justice.iresearchnet.com/wp-content/uploads/2023/12/Trial-Process.jpg.

Importance of Understanding the Trial Process

Understandability of the process of a trial is also vital among practitioners of law and members of the public because it creates the platform for ensuring justice in criminal trials. The process of a trial entails complicated procedures to protect the rights of defendants even as it offers a platform where victims claim compensation. Understandability creates informed discussions concerning fairness, impartiality, and the various roles each actor takes in the justice system, including judges, lawyers, and jurors. By knowing how these factors are interconnected with each other, stakeholders can better advocate for changes that promote the victim-focused approach, particularly on sensitive issues such as sexual assault. As indicated under existing reforms, giving prominence to the experiences of victim-survivors can lead to a more compassionate justice system and ensure that their voices are heard throughout the whole judicial process (Fileborn et al., 2014). Apart from this, understanding the trial process clearly enhances juror decision-making, an integral component of determining outcomes. Jurors play an important role in translating testimonies and implementing law without prejudice. The complexity of levels of evidence, coupled with the emotive essence of testimonies, necessitates clear instructional guidance towards guiding jurors in their functions. For example, the effect of expert witness testimony on jurors' perceptions of mitigating circumstances, such as child abuse, goes a long way in shaping sentencing decisions. Whether or not jurors receive a solidly based overview of trial processes and legal instructions' subtleties, their ability to deliberate fairly improves, leading to more equitable results and reinforcing public confidence in the justice system (Konstantopoulou et al., 2014). Finally, the broader importance of understanding the trial process transcends the individual cases; they set society's perception of justice and accountability. Public awareness of trial functioning can de-mystify courts to make them open up, reducing thresholds of access, and making it a culture of openness. Educating the public about the trial process enables citizens to engage with court processes, as jurors, defendants, or victims. Secondly, once the citizenry is aware of how trial proceedings are conducted, they are in a better position to advocate for reforms that dwell on systemic flaws, and the judicial system will grow to accommodate the needs of the contemporary society. Such grassroots awareness is crucial in promoting a just and equitable legal system that, in the long run, benefits the broader community.

7.1. PRE-TRIAL PROCEDURES

The pre-trial phase in the criminal trial procedure is necessary to safeguard the rights of the accused as well as obtain a fair trial. Following arrest, the accused will typically proceed to an initial appearance before a judge, which is intended to inform them of the charge and their rights. It also offers the possibility of setting bail as well as conditions of release. A glaring problem identified by the Deason Criminal Justice Reform Center in their report on the initial appearance crisis is that the majority of individuals spend a long time incarcerated in jail before they ever arrive at this significant meeting, leading to significant breaches of due process rights, particularly for indigents.

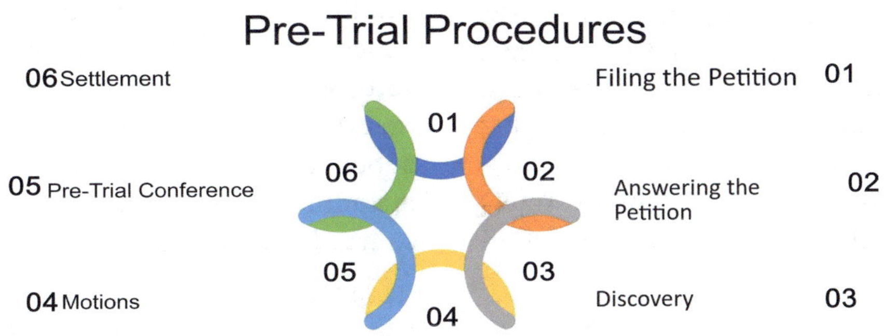

Figure 7.3. Pre-trial procedures.

Source: https://fastercapital.co/i/Tax-Court--Appealing-a-Notice-of-Deficiency-Decision--Pre-Trial-Procedures.webp.

Thus, these initial appearances ought to be timely and allow access to counsel to reverse the ill effects of unlawful detention (Brink et al., 2022). Additionally, pre-trial processes include the discovery process, where defense and prosecution exchange information regarding the case. Discovery has a role to play in that it ensures that both sides of the case are adequately prepared for the upcoming trial, keeping on an even keel upon which an equal trial must be based. Discovery not only serves to promote openness but also supports plea bargaining, whereby the defendants plead guilty to lesser charges in exchange for more lenient sentences. However, issues tend to arise at the discovery phase, particularly between the prosecutions obligation to offer evidence and the strategic interests of case building. Legal systems must ensure that there are incentives for complete discovery procedures to prevent compromising defendants' rights irrespective of the interests of justice (Doak et al., 2005). The complexity of the pre-trial processes is also underscored by the ongoing evolution of the victims roles within the criminal justice system. Traditionally viewed as mere witnesses, contemporary debates are increasingly recognizing the merit of the role of victims at the trial. This evolution is an indication of sensitivity to the social and emotional dimensions of criminal trials, particularly for victims seeking justice and reconciliation. Discussion of the rights of victims has, in turn, moved toward enhancing their active role, such as that which has occurred in a number of jurisdictions that have made reforms allowing the contribution of victims within trials. This provision has the twofold effect of legitimizing victims experience and evidencing a broader rethinking of the criminal trial processes nature, reconciling the defendants' rights with victims so that justice is better understood and administered holistically (Doak et al., 2005) (Figure 7.3).

7.1.1. Arrest and Booking

The initial phase of the criminal trial cycle, arrest and booking, is a crucial juncture in the justice system. The arrest typically occurs whenever police officers have probable cause to suspect that an individual committed a crime. This critical action initiates judicial proceedings and underscores the safeguarding of the rights of the accused. Secondly, the arrest is not only a detentive function but also involves a range of procedural steps to act as a guarantor of accountability.

Figure 7.4. A man arrested by police.

Source: https://upload.wikimedia.org/wikipedia/commons/5/52/ICE.XCheckII.3cops1arrest.jpg.

For instance, in an arrest, individuals should be informed of their rights, which is the bedrock of due process. These procedures are inherent to prevent abuse of power within the criminal justice system. As Maryland v. King demonstrates, the constitutionality of certain investigative methods, such as the taking of DNA samples at the arrest stage, raises significant questions regarding the balance between public security and individual privacy interests (Witanachchi et al., 2013). Once the suspect has been arrested, the process of booking also produces an official record of the crime suspect. This process involves documenting essential information, including the identity of the suspect, the nature of the offense suspected, and any personal property with them at the time of detention. Moreover, the booking process can also lead to initiating the identification of conditions such as drug abuse or mental illness, which are critical to consider in criminal justice settings. A pre-arraignment survey indicates that the detection of these problems at the time of booking can lead to appropriate intervention, including diversion to mental health or drug courts (Broner et al., 2003).

It is an argument for a less obtrusive method of booking, in which police officers and legal professionals can collaborate to treat the causes of criminality. The significance of the arrest and booking procedure is wide-ranging, both for the individuals who are arrested as well as for the system as a whole. As the first phases of the criminal trial process, they pave the way for what ensues, i.e., arraignment and trial. Data that emerges during the booking is in a position to influence bail determinations, potential charges, and even defense strategy. In addition, effective handling of this initial step might contribute to averting troubles like recidivism by considering the social and psychological matters that typically define criminal matters. Court systems must regularly reassess and refine procedures that are used throughout arrest and booking in a bid to make them align with dictates of justice, equity, and rehabilitation support. Thus, understanding the nuances and complexities of these initial steps is significant to establish an equitable criminal trial process (Figure 7.4).

7.1.2. Initial Appearance and Bail Hearings

The initial appearance is the most important moment in the criminal trial process since it is the initial interaction of defendants with the judiciary after being taken into custody. During the hearing, defendants learn about the charges that have been preferred against them and are explained their rights. It is also here that the issue of bail is addressed particularly, whether or not the accused should be released prior to trial. The immediate consequences of this decision can be profound, as pretrial detention can have broad personal, social, and economic ramifications on the defendant. Academics argue that these initial hearings must be accorded greater legal significance, as they determine the tone of defendants treatment throughout the remainder of the judicial process, including provision of counsel and protection against self-incrimination (Reynolds et al., 2019). Bail hearings have a vital function not merely of preventing defendants from suffering disproportionate punitive action before trial but also protecting the integrity of the central premise of due process. The determination of bail generally relies on a number of factors, such as the seriousness of the charges, defendants prior criminal history, and risk of flight. Notably, legislative reforms and recent landmark court decisions, such as Senate Bill 407 in Georgia, have stoked controversy regarding the adequacy of current bail practices. While there has been some improvement in some jurisdictions in providing prompt hearings and effective representation, there remains considerable disparity in how effectively these standards are met across various counties. In most counties, for instance, there is a lack of compliance with legal standards regarding bail hearings within 48 hours of arrest, raising questions about fairness of treatment for defendants (Armstrong et al., 2020). Furthermore, the evolving face of bail reforms highlights glaring disparities in the implementation of equitable bail practices, most notably in states like Georgia. Mixed-methods research on misdemeanor bail practices indicates that some counties have made significant strides in meeting legal guidelines, yet the majority of them lag behind. Alarming as this appears, a substantial proportion of misdemeanor arrestees still await jail for more than the mandated period, which threatens to undermine the effectiveness of existing reforms. These delays can potentially overburden social inequalities, with those lacking the means to pay bail being functionally punished prior to trial, which demands increased advocacy and reform movements in bail processes. Closing these gaps is significant because they indicate broader systemic issues across the criminal justice system that must be addressed and reformed immediately (Armstrong et al., 2020) (Figure 7.5).

Figure 7.5. Initial court appearances.

Source: https://www.hoganeickhoff.com/wp-content/uploads/2020/09/Untitled-design-66.png.

7.1.3. Preliminary Hearings and Grand Jury Indictments

Preliminary hearings and grand jury indictments play very significant roles in the criminal trial process as key determinations in deciding whether there is sufficient evidence to proceed to trial. A preliminary hearing, a mini-trial of sorts, permits a judge to balance the prosecution's evidence against the accused. This hearing provides the defense with some opportunity to challenge the evidence and arguments presented by the prosecution. The integrity of the process is important because it not only ensures the protection of the accused's rights but assists in determining whether the state is making an unwarranted charge. The significance of preliminary hearings thus lies in their dual role as safeguard to the accused and as filters to keep the court system from being overwhelmed with unsubstantiated cases. Grand jury indictments, on the other hand, act as an additional pretrial filtering level but with other process dynamics. A grand jury composed of citizens balances evidence presented by the prosecution without defense representation. This process is flawed with respect to openness because defendants are not provided an opportunity to deny the prosecutions account. Yet grand jury indictments are intended to protect citizens from unfounded criminal accusations by requiring more evidence before charges are formally made. The grand jury also serves as a public restraint of prosecutorial discretion and plays a crucial role in a critical element of the accusatorial system of American justice. Most strikingly, the practice of using grand juries has been questioned, with people questioning whether or not they are effective at providing defendants with fair treatment. The intersection between preliminary hearings and grand jury indictments is a representation of the shifting patterns of pretrial hearings against the backdrop of an increasingly plea-bargaining-oriented legal environment. In the modern criminal justice system wherein plea bargains could replace traditional trials, such pretrial processes become milestones of the highest significance to the legal status of the defendant. A note should be taken that the outcome of preliminary hearings and grand jury decisions could settle whether the case would reach trial or be resolved through plea. Because theorists posit that replacing plea-bargaining with the criminal trial mandates a reconsideration of pretrial screening procedures because these hearings are the only independent review processes of guilt in an over-reliance on negotiated pleas system (Arenella et al., 1980), an understanding of these processes is significant in appreciating the intricacies and challenges embedded within the criminal trial process (N/A, 1974) (Figure 7.6).

Figure 7.6. Preliminary hearings and grand jury indictments.

Source: https://i0.wp.com/nemiss.news/wp-content/uploads/2020/10/grand-jury-2.jpg?fit=1030%2C468&ssl=1.

7.2. THE ROLE OF KEY PARTICIPANTS

The criminal trial process is significantly dictated by the roles the various key players assume, each introducing their own expertise and opinions into the mix as they construct the process. Central to this framework is the judge, whose function extends beyond mere adjudication; they ensure the trial is lawful and safeguard the rights of all participants. Judges apply the law, interpret it, supervise court procedure, and often control jury selection. Judges' approach to work, as per recent reforms, can significantly improve the victim/survivor's experience in the justice system. This entails the integration of trauma-informed practices that are attuned to the multiple challenges faced by victims, with the ultimate aim of changing judicial practices to be more inclusive and supporting (Fileborn et al., 2014). Additionally essential to the process are attorneys representing the prosecution and defense, whose strategies and advocacy direct much of the trial's result. Prosecutors present the case of the state against the accused, with a duty to establish guilt beyond a reasonable doubt. Their role is not only the collection of evidence but also dealing with victims, ensuring that their voices are heard during the course of the trial. Alternatively, defense attorneys protect the rights of suspects, advocating for fair treatment and challenging the prosecution's evidence. The manner in which these champions engage the courtroom is seen through specialized court settings, where problem-solving innovations become increasingly common, affirming the need for performance measures that go beyond typical benchmarks (Mansky et al., 2010). This collaboration and reformative practices articulate how these legal representatives seize the balance of justice. Victims and witnesses also play a crucial role in the criminal trial process, serving as valuable sources of information for bringing justice. Victims must undergo significant trauma, and testifying in court can be a trying experience. This has prompted the judiciary to introduce reforms aimed at minimizing the risk of re-traumatization, for instance, by providing victims with the ability to provide evidence in a less confrontational manner. The shift to victim-focused approaches signals the direction towards the recognition of their rights and needs, in the expectation of a more sympathetic court environment. Moreover, as research highlights, the ability to offer advocacy services and alternative provisions has provided for a more favourable environment for victims, highlighting growing perceptions of the necessity of overhauling entrenched culture to enhance their experience and participation in the criminal justice process (Fileborn et al., 2014).

7.2.1. The Judge's Responsibilities

The role of the judge in the criminal trial procedure is much more nuanced than merely hearing cases in court. Judges have the duty of ensuring that trials are fair, impartial, and according to the law. One aspect of this is determining paramountly whether evidence is admissible or not, a duty it has for upholding the integrity of the legal process. Judges must be vigilant to maintain procedural justice at all times, balancing the accused's rights with the interests of justice at all times. Ongoing education and professional development are emphasized in most jurisdictions, such as with programs including cooperative efforts of the China Trial Advocacy Institute. This institution demonstrates the way in which evolving legal systems necessitate judges and attorneys remaining current with procedural advancements and the adversarial process, and thus become more effective courtroom practitioners

(Lancaster et al., 2006). Additionally, judges play a critical role in managing courtroom dynamics and ensuring all parties comply with established legal procedures. They bear the responsibility of instructing juries regarding legal standards and evidence relevance, a factor that significantly determines the jury's understanding of the case at hand. In addition to this, judges have the responsibility to exercise discretion in maintaining order in the courtroom while upholding the defendant's, victim's, and attorney's rights equally.

This becomes very difficult to manage when considering ethical challenges surrounding defense strategy. Certain judges struggle with the consequences of permitting defense lawyers to offer fictitious defenses for culpable defendants, where there is a conflict between maintaining the adversarial system's principles and guaranteeing truthfulness in court. Therefore, judges need to navigate such ethical challenges to maintain the integrity of the judicial process and meet their obligation to protect individual rights (Liebman et al., 2016). Moreover, judges are custodians of the law, relying on statutes and precedents in making decisions. The interpretive role is not theoretical; it has real-world implications for trial outcomes. Judges need to apply concepts of law with care and in a similar fashion, their findings in line with legislative intention as well as societal mores.

This requires a judicious understanding of the law, combined with awareness of the general public sentiment regarding justice and fairness. In addition, the judge's role transcends sentencing, where balancing the rehabilitative intent of the justice system with appropriate punishment for offenses must be considered. A judge's decision can create vital protections, influencing not only the case immediately before it but also subsequent application of the law. Thus, the role of a judge is central to the legitimacy and effectiveness of the criminal trial process, which decides its outcome and people's perceptions of justice in society (Figure 7.7).

Figure 7.7. The role of a judge in the criminal trial process.

Source: https://becomingthis.com/wp-content/uploads/2023/11/important-skills-for-a-county-judge.jpg.

7.2.2. The Prosecutor's Role in the Trial

The prosecutor is also a central figure in the criminal trial process, highly influential in the process. Their primary mandate is the representation of the federal or state government in criminal matters, where they seek to uphold the law while ensuring that justice prevails. This role is a difficult balancing act, in which prosecutors must advocate for the public interest without violating the rights of the defendants. In all these obligations, prosecutors are entrusted with sweeping powers, for example, discretion for deciding whether to charge, negotiate plea agreements, and direct the course of a case. The context here requires comprehension of the consequences of such choices, since they have the potential to affect outcomes of trials and, ultimately, public view of justice in the system (Montana et al., 2012). Second, the role of the prosecutor is not merely presenting evidence and witnesses. They also have to establish the legal framework under which a trial will be held, which takes a detailed knowledge of procedural and substantive law. During the trial, prosecutors have to frame lucid narratives that resonate with jurors, presenting the strengths of the case while counteracting the defenses argument. This involves planning, for example, gathering and preparing evidence to present a strong case. In addition, their role involves upholding codes of ethics, as they are not only required to secure convictions but also ensure that justice is just in the course of the judicial process. The prosecutor's conduct and strategies are, thus, instrumental in the way justice is received and dispensed in criminal trials (Doak et al., 2005).

Figure 7.8. The prosecutor serves as a central figure within the criminal trial process.

Source: https://www.shutterstock.com/image-photo/court-law-trial-session-charismatic-260nw-2056433804.jpg.

As the criminal justice environment evolves, so too does that of the prosecutor. Recent reforms have created controversy regarding the inclusion of victim voices within the trial, challenging prevailing assumptions about their role as solitary witnesses. This evolution signals a broader movement toward placing victim justice at the forefront and providing greater voice to victims in trials. These changes necessitate prosecutors to internalize victim interest factors along with their legal duty, thereby achieving a more harmonious pursuit of justice. The dynamic character of the role of the prosecutor underscores the need for continuous accommodation in the criminal trial process since legal cultures and social norms continue to change. Therefore, the prosecutor has to reconcile these complexities without undermining their fundamental duty to serve justice (Montana et al., 2012) (Figure 7.8).

7.2.3. The Defense Attorney's Duties

In the complex process of the criminal trial, the role of a defense attorney is imperative to ensuring the fairness and integrity of the judicial system. Fundamentally, the defense attorney bears the duty of clients advocate and zealous defense of the charges. This calls for the responsibility to procure evidence, take statements from witnesses, and make a case that reasonably counters the prosecutions claims. As established by the tenets of the adversary system, the attorneys are not only entrusted with the duty of protecting individual rights but also ascertaining the truth in accordance with ethically sound practices. The delicate equilibrium between such duties is best illustrated by the current controversy over whether knowingly inaccurate defenses are acceptable, as highlighted in contemporary judicial discourse (Liebman et al., 2016). This situation, wherein the lawyer tightrope-walks along lines of law, best illustrates the complexity of their duties. Defense attorneys' professional obligations go beyond the fervor of the advocate; they must also navigate the complexity of confidentiality and client competency. When they are representing individuals who might not have the mental capacity to comprehend the charges against them, lawyers experience formidable ethical challenges that are linked with their professional responsibilities. Such circumstances demand lawyers to evaluate their clients' capacity to make informed decisions and, if so, raise competency concerns while not violating confidentiality. Current standards of ethics impose limitations on disclosure, typically putting defense attorneys in a precarious position where they have an ethical duty to protect client confidences while, all the while, ensuring the preservation of the rights of potentially incompetent defendants (Cohen et al., 1997). This is not just a representation of the nature of their profession but also of the necessity to safeguard an equitable legal process which is sensitive to clients' heterogeneity. Furthermore, the defense attorney's mandate is fundamentally based on the pursuit of aggressive representation while being obligated by professional ethics. They have an obligation to see that all clients receive a complete defense regardless of what the public will believe or their opinion regarding the clients guilt. The aggressive representation plays a crucial role in ensuring the adversarial character of the trial process is maintained, whereby both sides get a chance to fairly advance their case. Even though the legal profession grapples with defense methods in general, including at times objectionable means, the commitment of lawyers towards maintaining their professional duties remains a pillar in the criminal trial system. The challenges that defense attorneys face in dealing with these issues are symptomatic of the complexity of the justice system, where the calibration between ethical obligation and defense strategy continues to evolve with novel legal precedent and societal demand (Liebman et al., 2016) (Figure 7.9).

Figure 7.9. The defense attorney's duties.

Source: https://www.mbfc.com/wp-content/uploads/2023/02/Defending-the-Accused-The-Role-of-Criminal-Defense-Lawyers.jpg.

7.3. JURY SELECTION

The jury selection is a critical turning point in the criminal trial process because it more or less determines the personality and significance of trial outcomes. Defense and prosecution lawyers examine potential jurors closely here, not only looking at their background but also their tendencies and inclinations. The analysis is critical, as the impartiality of the jurors is directly related to the fairness of the trial. In addition, strategic juror selection can play a significant role in the jury's final decision. Courts have recognized the importance of an impartial jury, evidenced by trials throughout history in jurisdictions where prejudices led to unpopular or unjust rulings. Therefore, the process of selecting a jury is not procedurally neutral; it is one expression of broader values concerning justice and impartiality in the administration of law. During jury selection, due process and equal protection values are essential to ensure that all sections of society are represented on the jury roll. Criminal defendants have decried the exclusion of certain demographic groups from juries that can undermine the legitimacy of the trial. Cases like Labat v. Bennett illustrate how the exclusion of particular racial or socioeconomic groups invokes constitutional questions on the representativeness of juries.

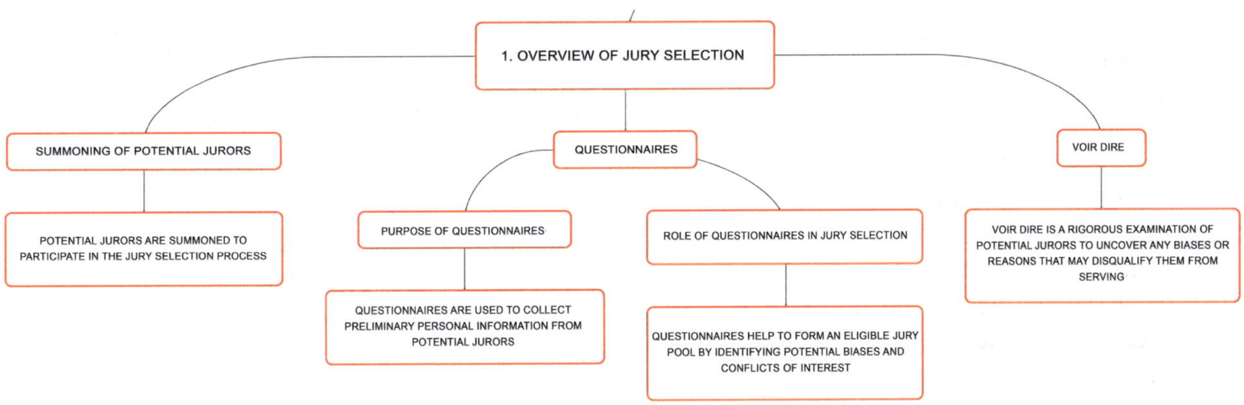

Figure 7.10. Jury selection.

Source: https://cards.algoreducation.com/_next/image?url=https%3A%2F%2Ffiles.algoreducation.com%2Fproduction-ts%2F__S3__07547c45-6310-4044-beab-848137ffd0f3&w=3840&q=100.

The significance of these exclusions does not end with the case itself but instead symbolizes larger systemic injustices within the criminal justice system. While states grapple with the problem of how best to obtain diverse jury panels, they also grapple with the cost of the jury trial system, trying to balance efficiency with the fundamental right to a fair trial emphasized in many court decisions and legal reform initiatives (Chesterman et al., 1999). In addition, the intervention of the high courts in the issue of jury composition reflects a persistent conflict between efficiency on the one hand and traditional values regarding jury trials on the other. Such values favor the protection of an jury that is representative of a cross-section of the community, a requirement in ensuring public confidence in the justice system. Pointedly, the need to minimize costs attributable to jury trials can result in some legislative interventions that threaten such values. The insistence of the High Courts to have a representative jury points to the commitment towards a process that has a success rate based on diversity and neutrality. It is thus imperative that jury selection conforms to legal standards in order to uphold the integrity of the criminal trial process. In this way, jury selection serves as a window through which the complexities of justice, representation, and procedural fairness can be viewed and commented upon (N/A, 1967) (Figure 7.10).

7.3.1. Importance of an Impartial Jury

The unbiased jury is a cornerstone of the criminal trial process, encapsulating the essence of fairness and justice in a democratic society. An unbiased jury, as established in the Sixth Amendment to the U.S. Constitution, must be representative of a cross-section of society, ensuring that different viewpoints and experiences are included in the decision-making process. This variety is particularly valuable in community cases with their own specific cultural heritage, as it maximizes the jury's ability to understand the nuances of an individual case. The effects of failure to achieve impartiality can be wide-ranging, both in ensuing miscarriages of justice and in public views of the legal system as not being balanced and trustworthy. This then erodes the confidence of society in judgments and the law, highlighting the need for a system that closely follows the ideal of impartiality. The Alvarado v. State case highlights the need to ensure juries are made up of members of the area where the crime has taken place, especially in remote regions. The Alaska Supreme Court ruling emphasized that a jury should consist of people who are representative of the community in which the trial is being conducted. This is especially relevant in cases such as Joseph v. State, where the trial of the defendants was conducted far from his residence village. The lack of jurors who understand or share the accused's cultural background can cause a huge disconnect in terms of the societal values and norms that may have led to the crime in question. As set forth in Criminal Rule 18, it becomes the imperative that defendants, especially those from marginalized communities, are provided an opportunity to be tried by a jury that indeed represents their peers and can place themselves in their shoes.

Figure 7.11. The concept of an impartial jury serves as a crucial pillar of the criminal trial process.

Source: https://cdn-iibfh.nitrocdn.com/cKVyddlMCBddgISAvTByKkHUTEYmSzoY/assets/images/optimized/rev-192385a/wolflawcolorado.com/wp-content/uploads/2021/11/jury.jpg.

Secondly, the consequences of failing to recognize the right to an unbiased jury could be more far-reaching than in the courtroom. It could yield systemic injustices that further marginalize such communities in society. In Joseph v. State, the failure to inform the defendant of his right to make a motion for change of venue illustrates the potential defect that may arise in the legal process. If defendants are not well informed about their rights, or their rights are not made effective, the integrity of the legal process is disrupted. This necessitates reforms to ensure that not only defendants be informed, but also actively participate in decisions affecting their trials. Lastly, the pursuit of justice necessitates vigilance in upholding the right to an impartial jury because this right is a safeguard against prejudice and unfair verdicts, sustaining the cornerstones of an impartial judicial process (Figure 7.11).

7.3.2. The Voir Dire Process

The voir dire process is an extremely critical component of the criminal trial process, serving primarily as a preliminary examination of potential jurors. Through this process, the prosecution and defense attorneys perform questioning of potential jurors in order to assess their suitability and impartiality. This stage is important as prejudices and biases of jurors can influence the outcome of trials to a great extent. Skilled attorneys use voir dire to identify such jurors who may harbor prejudgmental mindsets toward the case so that the selected jury is unbiased and representative of society. The ability to strike jurors on the basis of challenges for cause and peremptory challenges is at the heart of this process, allowing parties to build a jury that is congruent with their legal strategies and assumptions regarding the case, thereby increasing the probability of a successful verdict. Voir dire's seeming advantages apart, their application of peremptory challenges has implications for jury impartiality. While the system allows attorneys to strike jurors seen as unfavorable for no reason, studies have shown that this contributes to inadvertent biases that misshape the makeup of the jury.

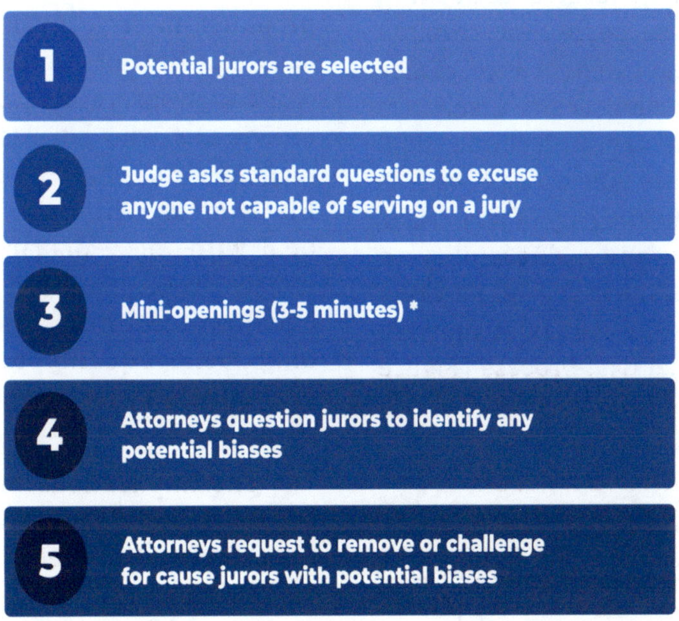

Figure 7.12. Voir dire process.

Source: https://cdn.prod.website-files.com/63b02cb683088c54455df892/63b84e4f56f82280d99d727b_voir-dire-process-980x813.png.

That is, peremptory challenges discriminate against jurors who hold median positions, and in so doing, tend to break up the diversity of viewpoints required for an effective deliberation.

As noted by existing empirical studies, such systemic biases can actually end up increasing the probability of conviction, particularly in cases involving serious offense where prejudices among jurors will incline the verdict to an inherent inclination towards guilt. Thus, while the purpose of voir dire is to acquire a fair jury, the pragmatic effect of peremptory challenges demonstrates that the process can undermine its intention (Ford et al., 2010). In addition, the jury lottery effect, whereby randomness in jury selection could have a pronounced influence on trial outcomes, demonstrates the harsh reality of the voir dire process. Research has confirmed that defendants who are assigned less desirable juries—most notably Black defendants—have very high conviction rates, placing the intersection of race and impartiality at the heart of jury selection (Kostyshak et al., 2019). This numerical information generates unsettling questions regarding the fairness of the criminal justice system and to what extent chance, rather than the merit of a defendant or the excellence of evidence generated, can determine trial outcomes. Thus, while the voir dire process is intended to guarantee the integrity of jury trials, its inherent complexity and vulnerability to systemic prejudice necessitate careful scrutiny and reform to promote the values of fairness and justice in the criminal trial process (Figure 7.12).

7.3.3. Challenges and Strikes During Jury Selection

In the broader framework of the criminal trial procedure, jury selection is one of the key phases where defense lawyers as well as prosecuting lawyers can encounter a big problem, primarily through the use of peremptory strikes. Peremptory strikes allow lawyers to strike a juror without giving a reason, thereby enabling them to shape the jury composition in their favor. However, such use has been contested on the premise of fairness and impartiality of the justice system. Notably, strategic peremptory attacks can produce racial imbalances in jury composition as an disproportionate impact on minority groups. In line with empirical evidence, criminal defendants who receive lower juries indicated by the exhaustion of peremptory strikes suffer higher conviction rates. This disturbing trend highlights the intersection of jury selection mechanisms with structural inequalities that can disqualify the veracity of the trial process, particularly among marginalized groups (Kostyshak et al., 2019). Moreover, the policy framework regulating jury selection is defined by twists that impede equitable representation of multicultural groups.

The Supreme Courts demand for a colorblind interpretation of the Equal Protection Clause often does not make up for the subtle ways in which the composition of juries can express prejudice in society. This rigid doctrine seeks facial equality but overlooks structural issues that work to preserve inequality, such as excluding individuals who have felony convictions from jury service, which disproportionately harms Black men. While the judiciary attempts to deal with these disparities, there is growing debate on the necessity for a more principled equal protection doctrine than one that seeks only facial equality to address substantive inequalities in jury representation (Nordmark et al., 2013).

The implications of these jurisprudential norms indicate the strong need for reform in the process of jury selection so that there can be an equitable trial for all defendants. Lastly, the challenges in juror selection illustrate a broader criticism of the criminal justice system's ability to deliver equal results. The manipulation of peremptory strikes through institutional bias raises a fundamental ethical challenge about the values upon which the trial process is conducted. Because juries bear the whiz-bang responsibility for determining guilty or innocent parties, skewed jury compositions resulting from such challenges can potentially redefine trial outcomes entirely. This underscores the necessity of procedural and legislative reform that aims to reduce the adverse effects of jury selection practices. Addressing such issues not only facilitates the trial's fairness but also re-affirms the primal tenets of justice that are pre-requisites to a healthy democracy. As the debate on jury selection proceeds, it becomes increasingly imperative to map these complexities to a fairer criminal trial process.

7.4. TRIAL PHASES

In the criminal trial procedure, one should be aware of the particular phases of a trial so one can discern how justice is administered. The phases of a trial begin typically with the selection of the jury when the intention is to have an impartial panel. This is followed by the defense and prosecution opening statements, where both sides present the summing up of their case and set forth the issues that will direct the remainder of the debates. Having made these statements, the prosecution initially presents first and calls witnesses and presents evidence to establish the guilt of the defendants beyond a reasonable doubt. Each of these phases is important, as they create the groundwork for developments and strategic action that follow, giving both sides a fair opportunity to argue their case effectively. After the prosecution has completed its case, the defense is given an opportunity to refute the accusations. This is a phase that typically entails the introduction of rebuttal evidence and statements from witnesses that will undermine the credibility of the prosecution case. The defense may also not prefer to produce its own evidence but instead capitalize on the fact that the prosecution has not proved its case beyond reasonable doubt. The closing arguments follow, where both sides once more recap their positions and bring to the forefront significant evidence or witness testimony supporting their position. Surprisingly, the subtleties of this phase can seriously distort juror impressions, typically leaning toward the final verdict. The climax of these events leads to the jury's deliberation, the turning point before making a decision that will determine the defendant's life. The trial phases do not exhaust with the conviction; the post-trial phases are also in need of significant attention. Especially, prosecutorial discretion plays a key role after conviction, namely in sentencing and criminal record expungement. This emphasizes the perpetual pressure on prosecutors to balance justice with the defendant's rights even after a trial. For example, a recent controversy raises the need for deliberation of prosecutorial discretion to extend beyond pre-trial judgments to include judgments after conviction. These deliberations are important as they affect not just the convicted but also the public perception of fairness in the judicial system. Implications are important, highlighting the necessity of continued debate concerning the ethical function of prosecutors throughout all trial stages, as noted in argument about case law and judicial precedent (Lahey et al., 2010; Murray et al., 2018).

7.4.1. Opening Statements

The opening statement in a criminal trial is a basic component, providing each party with the chance to outline their case for the court. This opening speech has significance because it will decide the tone of the entire proceedings, allowing both prosecution and defense to set out their version of events as they see it, and lay down the key themes and evidence that will be introduced throughout the trial. A successful opening speech has a powerful influence on how jurors will see a case, giving an indication of the general direction of the case. Secondly, it is also crucial that the opening statement is concise, persuasive, and founded on the evidence to be brought forward later, as jurors are likely to utilize the groundwork laid here in an effort to form their initial impressions (Rothstein et al., 2015). A proper opening statement should also refrain from arguments or appeals to emotion and rather focus on factual portrayal. It intends to inform the jury regarding what they can anticipate in the form of evidence and testimonies of witnesses that will confirm or negate the charges brought by either side. For the prosecution, this involves expressing how the defendant is implicated in the crime, while the defense is tasked with indicating discrepancies and presenting alternative explanations of the evidence that would acquit the accused. This narrative element is crucial, as jurors respond well to coherent narratives which are logically consistent. Remaining focused on facts and logical arguments in the opening statement, as emphasized in landmark cases such as Williams v. Illinois, underscores the importance of speaking to the jury without engaging in argumentative debate (Djerf et al., 1990). The opening statements are also crucial for establishing the legal and ethical questions at the core of the trial. By establishing clearly the fundamental arguments of the case, the parties can take their stance on key concepts of law that could determine the case. The statements establish limits on what will be considered relevant to jurors, focusing their attention as they sort through evidence and testimony. Additionally, a good opening statement can highlight the procedural aspects for the purposes of fairness, such as the right to confront witnesses, a safeguard augmented by landmark decisions throughout the Confrontation Clause. Hence, the opening statement is not just the prelude to the case in question, but a significant phase that impacts jurors' understanding of larger legal systems, ultimately shaping their deliberative process (Rothstein et al., 2015).

7.4.2. Presentation of Evidence

Evidence presentation in criminal trials forms a fundamental component ensuring the credibility and integrity of the judicial process. The effectiveness of a trial largely depends on the manner of presentation, interpretation, and evaluation of evidence within the trial courts. Various forms of evidence like testimonial evidence, documentary evidence, and physical evidence can be presented to prove the case of either the defense or prosecution. The expert witnesses' function is especially important since they present specialized information, which can help explain complicated issues to both the judge and jury. The need for this evidence, therefore, presents in both its relevance and credibility as well as reliability, which must be shown through its presentation. The process is stringent and is intended to guarantee that the verdict given will be on the basis of factual and sound information and not on speculation or prejudice. The dynamic of presentation of forensic evidence is vital to contemporary criminal proceedings, particularly those involving complex scientific testing. Forensic evidence, by its nature requiring expert examination, is increasingly relied upon to establish culpability or innocence. In cases involving mass graves, for instance, presentation of forensic findings—such as those determined from exhumations—can provide sound evidence connecting persons to crimes. This is clearly evident in the trials of the International Criminal Tribunal for the former Yugoslavia where forensic science has been important in determining forensic truth. This cautious presentation of such evidence demands not only its gathering but also an analytical knowledge of its meanings in the legal system so that the courts can differentiate its utility and worthiness in establishing pivotal facts to the determination process (Klinkner et al., 2008, 2009). Moreover, the method of presenting forensic evidence frequently determines its validity in the legal system. Courts tend to utilize a mixture of cross-examination and offering counter-expertise in responding to methodological problems with forensic findings. The court system permits an exact examination of expert evidence, in that any scientific evidence offered is sound and applicable to the case being adjudicated. This interplay between legal provisions and scientific integrity is most critical in that it actually influences the perceived legitimacy of the presented evidence. For instance, through careful examination of expert witness testimony, the courts can navigate their way through complex science issues and arrive at an informed decision that makes a token of balance between facts and law. Through this, the presentation of evidence not only adds credibility to charges but also supports the entire model of justice in the criminal trial procedure (Figure 7.13).

Figure 7.13. The presentation of evidence in criminal trials.

Source: https://wolfvision.com/uploads/media/x1220/06/386-Swiss-Knife_VZ-8.jpg?v=2-0.

7.4.3. Closing Arguments

The final argument is a significant milepost in the criminal trial process, representing a culmination of evidence presented and theories presented by the defense and prosecution. Lawyers are able to sum up jumbled case facts at this point, pointing to key arguments in support of their side. A solid closing argument not only strives to solidify the jury's understanding of the facts but also tries to appeal to their hearts and moral conscience. This is particularly significant in cases where high stakes are involved and members of the jury must make basic, life-altering decisions. Accordingly, the success of closing arguments can literally control the outcome of a trial, illustrating how important they are to finding justice, as their impact can literally spill over beyond the courtroom to shape public opinion of the justice system in general. As it relates to implicit bias, the wording and delivery of closing arguments can literally have a snowballing impact on fairness in jury deliberations. Studies have shown that implicit racial prejudice, which many of these jurors are not necessarily aware of, can influence their perception when they are exposed to racially charged terminology in prosecution. For example, as the prosecution uses racial issues in their closing arguments, they expose themselves to the possibility of invoking these biases, which eventually result in unequal treatment for defendants, especially Black defendants.

Such a dynamic not only underscores the necessity of lawyers being extremely sensitive to their choice of words but also signifies that there should be a more in-depth examination of closing addresses in the jurisprudential perspective so that inherent prejudices are not sullied in the principles of justice, as analyzed in the context of Prasad et al. (2018). Also, the judicial process has resorted to steps to prevent prosecutorial misconduct from affecting closing arguments, especially in high-stakes trials such as capital trials. Various studies have identified the importance of subjecting the jury to particular judicial instructions meant to counteract the effect of suggestive arguments. Such warning instructions have been found to significantly reduce the chances of excessive punitive recommendations, as argued by Platania et al. (2010). By informing jurors of the potential effects of overzealous but inappropriate rhetoric, courts can preserve constitutional protection. This is the reason why caution is still required in overwatching prosecutorial behavior during closing arguments and thus preserving the integrity of the criminal trial process while trying to deliver fair verdicts on the basis of evidence and not on emotional or biased persuasion.

7.5. DELIBERATION AND VERDICT

The deliberation process in a jury is an important step in the criminal trial process, the point at which individual judgments meet to form one judgment. It is the stage where jurors thoroughly discuss each other's opinions as they make sense of the evidence brought out at trial and translate the law as directed by the judge. Deliberation's success hinges on the ability of the jurors to open their mouths and share their different perspectives, and in the process, it not only provides a comprehensive grasp of the case but also assists in the suppression of prejudice. Deliberation is geared towards being the melting point where individual perceptions and presumption of guilt or innocence are cleansed, converting individual perceptions into a unified verdict. This process manifests the inherent position of the jury, for their deliberations ultimately make sense of the judicial process, making their decisions being significant portions of the process to justice (Akers et al., 2018). The jury's decision, which is the result of deliberation, is a reflection of the judgement of the evidence and testimonies put before them.

Figure 7.14. The process of deliberation within a jury.

Source: https://lh5.googleusercontent.com/proxy/04f7lkKZ6b_-arOZJoObpblXOqVa5bo9HN69FbVszNXFuex9dYgsge-hs02G55n6bG3CsOibvZqZ2yfykpD7lM1PJ1Tvemb8QoIfti-LcB4SlEJcMrzqgjRVNe3yUXJ-y3T1ONWPH2bqlu7ExEoH1w.

This selection is often seen as a distillation of the morality and values of society and a visualization of the combined expectation of the prosecution and defense. Jurors must navigate complicated legal requirements while being confronted with the emotional weight of their duty—the duty of deciding another individual's fate. The verdict can have a profound impact not only on the accused but also on victims, families, and society in general, raising issues of equality and justice. Understanding the reasons behind this process, including extraneous influences, the jury's level of understanding of the law, and their own prejudices, is significant. Understanding the consequences of these verdicts brings the discourse on legal reforms to improve the jury system (Chalmers et al., 2016) more informed. Further examination of the deliberation and verdict process illustrates underlying flaws that are in a position to hamper the efficacy of jury decision-making. Study has illustrated that certain prejudices, especially those involving preconceptions of culpability, can effectively taint juror deliberation. Most critically, issues like the presence of groupthink can lead to the control of strong personalities in a deliberation group, which might suppress dissident opinions. Existing debate about jury research, particularly in Scotland and analogous jurisdictions, demands an investigation into whether jury decision-making and reasoning could be enhanced. Proposals for reforming procedures like simple majority verdicts may address some of these issues, so there are suggestions that systemic reforms would yield fairer results. By fostering an understanding of the complexity in jury deliberation and verdict formulation, legal stakeholders can be in a position to encourage that the systems employed promote justice and equity (Akers et al., 2018; Chalmers et al., 2016) (Figure 7.14).

7.5.1. Jury Deliberation Process

The jury deliberation process is an essential process of the criminal trial process and is the stage where a group of jurors examine the evidence presented to court and decide on a verdict. The process is characterized by collective decision-making where the jurors deliberate, share opinions, and weigh the merits and demerits of the prosecution and defense arguments presented. During deliberations, jurors also grapple with varied perspectives of evidence due to their backgrounds and experiences. The diversity of thought among jurors can make it easier to discuss but also likely to cause tension as individuals promote varied conclusions. It is worth knowing this process because not only does it reflect the values of the legal system but also highlights the potential for bias that is likely to unconsciously influence the final conclusion. During the past decade, the traditional role and worth of the jury have been attacked, particularly over their presence in civil cases. Of special mention is the presence and role of the civil jury, which has plummeted in the majority of states to a near-absence, exemplified by reforms in states such as New Zealand whereby the civil jury is virtually non-existent. This fall results in rethinking the function of the jury in the criminal sphere with specific consideration for the implications of issues like public opinion, jury competency, and the dynamic nature of the legal norms. With increased legal question sophistication, jury competency in their ability to deal with intricate details is crucial, with the need for adequate jury direction and instruction during the process of deliberation. These developments undermine the traditional assumptions of jury effectiveness to fulfill their fundamental role of meting out justice. Secondly, the nature of jury deliberation is more often to negotiate among jurors, particularly when the verdict options render a position of non-consensus. Empirical research shows that jurors do compromise, the need to agree making a desire to find a verdict that may not always accord with their own assessment of the merits of the cases. This phenomenon runs counter to the widespread assumption that criminal verdicts should be a product of unanimous and factual conclusion by all of the jurors. Instead, intrajury negotiations exhibit a complex dance of viewpoints that can mirror the endemic negotiation present in plea bargaining situations. By embracing a new understanding of compromise verdicts, as shown in the definition of plea negotiations, the criminal trial system can evolve, providing improved jury results and more sophisticated utilization of the deliberation process.

7.5.2. Types of Verdicts (Guilty, Not Guilty, and Hung Jury)

Throughout the criminal trial process, the jury's verdict determination is critical to determining legal trial outcomes. Of all verdicts, a guilty verdict means that the jury has found evidence substantial enough to conclude that the defendant in fact committed the crime for which they were indicted, and this results in penal sanctions. This depiction of mass judgment illustrates both the seriousness of the evidence presented and the jury's interpretation of the defendants actions and intent. A conviction not only marks the conclusion of the trial but also serves to validate social norms and laws, ensuring that justice has been served. Hence, such a judgment can have long-term implications for the parties concerned, impacting future legal hearings, sentencing procedures, and popular perception towards justice delivery within the judicial system (Akers et al., 2018). Alternatively, a not guilty verdict is rendered when the jury finds that the prosecution has been unable to establish its case, leading to the acquittal of the defendant. This belief reflects the principle that an individual is innocent until proven guilty, the cornerstone of the criminal justice system guarding against wrongful conviction. In the majority of instances, a finding of not guilty indicates flaws in the prosecution's case, including lack of evidence or inconsistency of witness testimony, finally highlighting the jury's role as a significant evaluation body within the trial process. Notably, a not guilty verdict does not mean the innocence of the defendants but rather hints at the lack of sufficient evidence against them so that the bar for conviction remains high. This aspect is reflective of the subtle role of jurors, who must fend off the social pressures and focus on what evidence comes before a court (Chalmers et al., 2019). In some instances, the jury will be unable to reach a consensus, resulting in a hung jury. Such a circumstance occurs when jurors cannot agree on a unanimous or required majority decision, typically due to the existence of deep divisions of opinion regarding the case. The consequence of a hung jury can lead to a wide array of legal solutions, as the prosecution can request a retrial, which can lead to more court wars. This kind of verdict also displays the complexities involved in juror deliberations and points to the inherent uncertainty of the jury system. It compels the courts to question their jury selection and deliberation system because jurors have to navigate the vast expanse of evidence, legal rationale, and their biases. As such, an understanding of the dynamic of a hung jury is relevant to the overall criminal trial process and its problems that follow (Akers et al., 2018).

7.5.3. Impact of the Verdict on the Defendant

The result of a criminal trial represents the highlight in the lives of defendants as the verdict of the jury carries very great consequences. A conviction can lead to many sanctions, including imprisonment, fines, or other penal sanctions, that can cause a recurring cycle of hardship for the individual and his/her family. Moreover, social stigma associated with a conviction typically affects the defendant's reintegration into society, his/her employment opportunities, social relationships, and mental well-being. Several defendants are confronted with collateral consequences, such as loss of civil rights, which can further isolate them from society. The effects of a verdict extend beyond punishment; they can alter a defendants self-perception, leading to shame and having long-lasting psychological effects as they exist in a world that tends to see them from the view of their conviction as identified in the findings highlighted in the study published in the current thesis (Curley et al., 2018). In looking at how jury's make decisions, it is clear that verdict-influencing factors can lead to unequal outcomes among defendants. It has been shown that jurors tend to use many different cognitive biases, including confirmation bias, whereby they tend to accept information favorable to their prior beliefs and conclusions regarding a case or defendant. Such a bias has the potential to create a skewed perception of innocence or culpability on the basis of flawed or prejudiced evidence, thus giving the prosecution an undue advantage. The availability of different verdict options also alters the inclinations of the jurors, with empirical research indicating that a three-verdict system could increase the likelihood of a guilty verdict compared to systems that have a very few choices (Curley et al., 2018). Thus, the verdict of the jury has a significant impact on the future of the defendant and hence the reforms must be introduced to ensure a fairer trial process for the accused. Moreover, the trial process serves to reinforce existing social biases, discriminate against marginalized defendants, and unfairly target those who are already marginalized. Pre-trial biases have been found to influence jurors' guilt judgments, and as a result, trial verdicts reflect social biases and not objective evidence determinations. For instance, race, socioeconomic status, and public opinion can skew juror frames and render the interaction between the legal process and the defendants fate even more challenging. Such externalities do not merely influence outcomes but challenge the criminal justice systems legitimacy. When verdicts are based on prejudice rather than facts, the very foundations of equity and justice are compromised, and the defendants are open to unjustified repercussions (Curley et al., 2018). Hence, consideration of the impact of the verdict on the defendant illuminates broader issues of equity and justice in the criminal trial process (Figure 7.15).

Figure 7.15. Impact of the verdict on the defendant.

Source: https://cdn-copkk.nitrocdn.com/YltYtAKgPcLedXEEgYFqpFzrZUtcEffn/assets/images/optimized/rev-d4ad741/www.aerlawgroup.com/wp-content/uploads/2020/05/How-Does-a-Guilty-Verdict-in-a-Criminal-Case-Affect-a-Civil-Case.jpg.

7.6. POST-TRIAL PROCEDURES

Post-trial procedures are at the core of the criminal trial procedure with an emphasis on dealing with outcomes subsequent to a verdict having been rendered. Following a trial, a convicted defendant is entitled to have some rights in order to gain redress by way of appeal and motions for post-conviction relief. These procedures are imperative as they provide a mechanism through which the validity of a verdict or the procedure adopted in a trial can be challenged. The appeal process is also time-consuming and may involve many levels of review, including state courts and potentially the federal courts. Yet it is important to recognize that the focus on the finality of criminal convictions makes it very challenging for defendants to assert innocence due to newly discovered evidence, as evidenced by the restrictions on post-trial claims of innocence in many legal systems, merely a symptom of a larger systemic deficiency within the justice system (Garrett et al., 2017). Post-trial proceedings have come to the forefront in the context of wrongful convictions. The setting up of innocence commissions and associated agencies is a significant development for fixing historic miscarriages of justice. These agencies are likely to examine cases post-trial for the specific purpose of establishing factual innocence and for correcting procedural mistakes that might have resulted in wrongful convictions. The supporters argue that such policies not only serve to provide justice to the wrongly accused individuals but also increase public confidence in the criminal justice system as a whole. The institutional adoption of broader remedies to support innocence claims demonstrates a shift towards a more active approach to justice, where the identification of wrongful convictions is a priority for legal reforms across jurisdictions (Garrett et al., 2017). In addition, dynamic post-trial process environment also includes aggregation methods through which cases involving systemic issues within the criminal justice system are merged. Cases are also considered in batches by courts at the appellate level in order to ascertain that equivalent allegations of injustices are addressed and determined en masse. For instance, this might involve addressing systemic violations, e.g., in poor indigent defense or forensic manipulation. Aggregative procedures may thus be employed as an effective tool to increase fairness and efficiency in the judicial process. The re-examination of due process protections in light of these aggregative procedures is essential to ensure that defendants do not lose their constitutional protections, which could lead to significant institutional changes to enhance the integrity of the system of justice.

7.6.1. Sentencing Options and Considerations

The sentencing phase of the criminal trial process is a critical juncture, transforming the convicted judgment into tangible retribution for the defendant. A variety of sentencing options are present, which can range from incarceration and probation to community service and economic retribution. The primary goal of these options is typically multi-faceted, encompassing punishment, deterrence, rehabilitation, and protection of society. For instance, the use of prison time can effectively incapacitate violent criminals, while others like probation can be applied for less severe crimes and allow rehabilitation away from prisons. Besides, considerations such as the severity of the crime, defendants past criminal history, and special circumstances are central in the decision-making regarding appropriate sentencing options, in a way that the justice system addresses the demands of both the offender and society. Part of the central aspect of the concept of sentencing is the debate around the practice of capital punishment, and it remains extremely contentious in the majority of jurisdictions, including the State of New York. The complexities of the capital punishment pose serious legal and moral matters involved in the sentencing process. Proponents argue that capital punishment serves as a deterrent and responds to the perpetuity of the most heinous crimes, while opponents pose doubts regarding its ethical issues and potentiality of erroneous executions. In 2004, the New York State Court of Appeals held the death penalty law in the state to be unconstitutional under the state's own constitution, and this threw capital punishment open to debate within the state. As the next set of legal arguments that involve legislative responses shows, legislative responses can render capital punishment moot and illustrate how sentencing choices are intensely influenced by sociocultural perceptions of justice (Huffman et al., 2008). In the federal criminal jurisdiction, case heterogeneity further complicates the sentencing context, particularly that of white-collar crime. Although federal courts receive fewer cases compared to state courts, the impact of sentencing in corporate fraud and financial deception cases presents unique challenges. These cases are the ones that best demonstrate the challenge of imposing appropriate penalties since the crimes typically involve intricate networks of fraud that can harm larger economic structures significantly. Importantly, numerous additional federal cases involve drug and violent crimes, which flood the dockets. While the courts grapple with the need for effective deterrence in white-collar offenses, the nuances of sentencing decisions have to be balanced carefully so that justice is not only sensitive to the seriousness of the violation but also to the context in which it was perpetrated (Richman et al., 2012) (Figure 7.16).

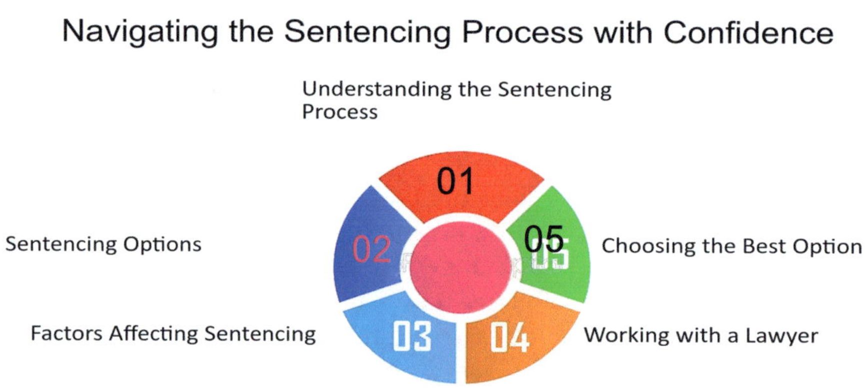

Figure 7.16. The sentencing phase of the criminal trial process.

Source: https://fastercapital.co/i/Sentencing-options--Exploring-Sentencing-Options-Following-an-Arraignment--Navigating-the-Sentencing-Process-with-Confidence.webp.

7.6.2. Appeals Process and Grounds for Appeal

Appeals process is a crucial element of the criminal trial process because it offers a platform to review the trial courts' decisions for legality and fairness. Once a verdict has been delivered, both sides can appeal on specific grounds, including in law errors, insufficiency of evidence, or on the issue of constitutionality of trial process. The appellate court typically reviews the record of trial, but mainly to determine whether law was duly applied and whether defendant's rights were protected in the trial process. This function is not a secondary one; it is vital to maintaining public confidence in the judicial process through the correction of injustice and the promotion of the rule of law, thereby maintaining the integrity of the legal process and providing a process of accountability. One of the prominent issues within the appeals process concerns wrongful convictions, particularly in sensitive contexts such as historical allegations of sexual abuse. The procrastination in such cases undermines credibility of witness testimony and admissibility of evidence, exposing defendants to harsher examination in appeals. As indicated by recent research, there is a critical need to reform how such cases are handled in appellate courts. Recommendations include expanding the jurisdiction to appeal to serve better the unique issues of late claims, particularly where evidence unavailable at the trial period deprives the trial of equity. Implementing procedural safeguards within the trial, as recommended by Greenwood et al. (2024), would enhance the appeal system so that cases sullied by delay are handled equitably without jeopardizing the rights of defendants. Alongside this, the interaction between appellate review and procedural protections creates a complex landscape within which legal practitioners have to operate. The courts are likely to grapple with the balance between vindicating defendants' rights and upholding the integrity of the judicial process, particularly in those situations where much time is involved after the initial trial. The substance of this challenge is that of the doctrine of abuse of process upon which one can stay cases where delay effectively frustrates the possibility of a fair trial. Such considerations support the necessity for a formulated framework in the appeals process that is attuned to each case's individuality. Although there is potential for reform, as analyzed in Greenwood et al. (2024), the path towards a more equitable appeals process is still contingent upon sound judicial discretion and the regular application of established procedural safeguards.

7.6.3. Role of Post-Conviction Relief

The post-conviction relief institution is essential to ensuring that the criminal trial process is just and fair, particularly in an environment where finality of convictions is at times more important than the truth. In the event of new evidence or newly emerging legal arguments subsequent to a trial, post-conviction relief provides opportunities for individuals to appeal their convictions on the grounds of ineffective assistance of counsel, prosecutorial misconduct, or newly discovered evidence. This protective role not only rectifies miscarriages of justice but also preserves the integrity of the judicial process. As described in various legal debates, the possibility of aggregation through procedures throughout the appeal process demonstrates the ways in which courts have the ability to address systemic faults leading to wrongful convictions, affirming the vital role of post-conviction remedy in safeguarding constitutional rights (Garrett et al., 2007). In addition, the evolving reality of post-conviction relief means emphasizes increasing importance of global opinion regarding wrongful convictions. Historically, the interest in ensuring finality to criminal convictions has limited avenues for defendants to appeal innocence after trial. Nevertheless, recent trends herald a striking change in attitude, and most jurisdictions now are moving towards broader remedies to allow for case reopening on the basis of newly discovered facts. As has been noted in recent discussion on the subject, this trend recognizes a growing recognition of the necessity for legal systems to provide meaningful avenues by which exoneration and assertions of innocence can be lodged and thus enhance trust in justice processes (Garrett et al., 2017). The role of post-conviction relief is thus that of a significant safeguard of judicial rulings, preventing mistakes from being irreversible and ensuring the protection of the accused's rights. Furthermore, existing post-conviction relief mechanisms are of utmost significance in maintaining transparency and accountability in the criminal justice system. Applications of innocence commissions and specialized judicial reviews are new ways of responding to systemic weaknesses with full investigation of particular cases becoming possible. These measures can lead to systemic changes, thereby heightening the procedural fairness of trials and post-trial procedures equally. Interestingly, the synergy of these processes is able to minimize wrongful convictions to make the legal system fairer. With these shifting systems, post-conviction relief not only corrects individual injustice but also assists in altering institutions overall, thus putting its vital significance in the criminal trial process as a whole (Garrett et al., 2007) (Figure 7.17).

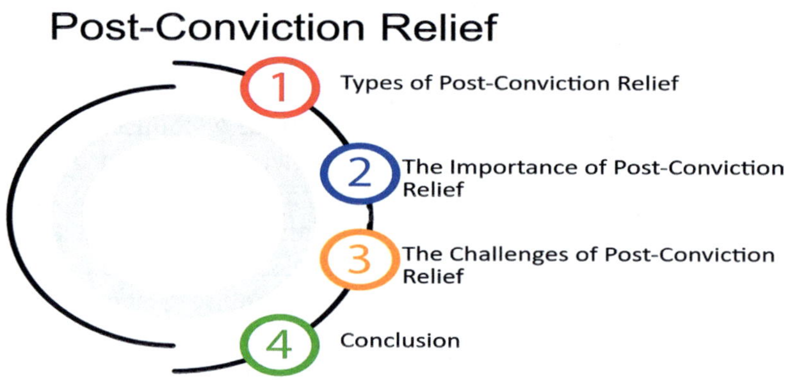

Figure 7.17. Post-conviction relief.

Source: https://fastercapital.co/i/Post-Conviction-Relief--The-Road-to-Redemption--Introduction-to-Post-Conviction-Relief.webp.

SUMMARY

The criminal trial process is a central device within the broader framework of justice systems, exhibiting the subtle balance between safeguarding individual rights and promoting public safety. Through the vigilant application of legal norms and procedural fairness, trials not only seek to establish the guilt or innocence of suspects but also maintain the concept of due process. Observing the nuances of trial process—from jury selection to the presentation of evidence—witnesses the numerous layers committed to upholding justice. In addition, all these pieces contribute to shaping public perception of the credibility of the legal system so that citizens continue to have faith in judicial consideration. As society evolves, so does the tradition underlying the criminal trial process, adapting to stay current with contemporary challenges while remaining ever-watchful in seeking equal justice. Also, the integration of forensic science and technology innovation into the trial process is a demonstration of ongoing interest in optimizing accuracy in legal conclusions. Utilization of DNA testing, video evidence, and expert opinion proves heightened reliance on empirical data to substantiate judicial conclusions. Such innovations not only validate the evidence presented but also discredit traditional assumptions of guilt or innocence. As these technologies filter into the courtroom, the criminal trial process must evolve to make sure legal professionals are equipped with the tools and data they will need to manage the subtleties of evidence in today's world. This constant evolution refines the trial process to ensure a system that not only incentivizes ill behavior but also works to deliver just results to an increasingly complex society. Finally, the consequences of the criminal trial process carry over to the world at large, influencing public policy and legislative reform. With trends from trial outcomes and procedure efficiency being studied, policymakers have to contend with the justice system's inherent weaknesses. This closed-loop system discloses the necessity of a dynamic legal system responsive to social needs and directed by trial outcomes. The role that community engagement has in shaping such reforms—whether in the form of advocacy, public opinion, or social movements—justifies the idea that justice is neither a static but a dynamic construct shaped by shared societal values and aspirations. Lastly, there is a keen vision of the criminal trial process emphasizing the requirement for a continuous discourse among legal practitioners, academics, and society as a whole to acquire a more equitable and just legal system for all, as noted in Chambers et al. (2016) and Sanders et al. (2016).

The criminal trial process is a complex and methodical series of events that seeks to deliver justice while following the defense and prosecution legal rights. The trial begins by choosing the jury where the jurors are chosen to decide impartially as judges of the evidence and render a verdict. The prosecution presents first, describing the charges against the defendant and presenting evidence to establish guilt beyond a reasonable doubt. The defense presents second, with counterarguments and evidence that may give rise to reasonable doubt. The adversarial system attempts to provide a balanced view, one however determined by the parties' dynamics themselves. The strict examination of evidence, witness accounts, and legal arguments all contribute to strengthening the judicial process as a whole. Throughout the progression of the trials, roles of victim and witness come to the forefront and, more frequently than not, finally decide the fate of the trials. Common law victims have historically held the position of private party in that they are primarily found in the role of witnessing without participatory rights. Nevertheless, this is changing, with recent reforms placing greater emphasis on victim-centered models in the criminal justice system. Indeed, new measures introducing advocate services and police training specifically for addressing violence against women and gendered violence are designed to make victim/survivor experiences shape the trial process more effectively (Fileborn et al., 2014). These reforms highlight a transformation of society in the direction of accepting victim rights and the significance of their involvement in pursuing justice, in order to fortify the essential values of justice and equity within criminal proceedings. The incorporation of these reforms is complementary to a broad development towards the reconstruction of victims' roles in criminal cases. Long perceived as passive players, victims are now being dealt with as essential stakeholders whose rights need to find their space within the legal system. This emergent paradigmatic shift has led to effective uses of victimology practices that guarantee active participation and advocacy for crime victims. In these jurisdictions where such reforms are being implemented, as in Australia, there is now greater understanding of the harmful effect past structural barriers had on victims' experiences in courts, hence the need for legislative and procedural reform to demolish such barriers (Doak et al., 2005). This shifting landscape within the criminal trial process not only encourages more inclusive speech, but it also serves to empower victims, leading ultimately to a more equitable and balanced judicial process.

KEY TERMS

- Acquittal
- Burden of Proof
- Conviction
- Documentary Evidence
- Final Arguments
- Judgment
- Plea of Guilty
- Presumption of Innocence
- Appeal
- Charge Framing
- Cross-Examination
- Examination-in-Chief
- Hostile Witness
- Opening Statement
- Plea of Not Guilty
- Re-examination

A LOOK TO THE FUTURE

WITNESS TESTIMONY

The future of witness testimony in criminal proceedings is about to be revolutionized by technology, evolving standards of law, and a widening emphasis on safeguarding and authenticating witnesses. Traditionally, witness testimony has lain at the very core of the justice system, typically deciding the fate of cases. However, gaps in memory, threats, and coercion have created alarms about its validity and usability. In the coming years, more technology-based alternatives will probably be embraced by courts for authenticating the truthfulness and safety of witness testimony. Perhaps the most promising innovation is virtual testimony, by which witnesses can testify remotely through secure video conferencing, reducing the risk of intimidation and enabling access even from distant or safe places. It may be particularly important in sensitive cases dealing with vulnerable or at-risk witnesses. Voice identification software and artificial intelligence (AI) can even be used to assess witnesses' emotional and intellectual patterns, allowing courts to identify inconsistencies or coercion. Video recording of initial witness statements and real-time transcription in trial hearings will even make the process more precise and tamper-proof. Augmented reality (AR) could in the future be used to recreate crime scenes, which would help witnesses remember incidents more clearly and help jurors understand complex testimonies.

More stringent witness protection schemes and trauma-informed approaches will also be put in place by the legal system, specifically for survivors of child and gender-based violence. With increasing cross-border crimes, international criminal laws for witness cooperation and testimony may become standardized as well. In short, the future of witness testimony will strive to find a balance between technological progress and human rights so that justice becomes efficient but not unjust. The technologies will not replace the human voice in the courtroom but will significantly authenticate the voice's credibility and integrity.

REFERENCES

1. Akers, H. (2018). Aspects of the jury in criminal proceedings. https://core.ac.uk/download/158970350.pdf (accessed on 13th August 2025).
2. Arenella, P. (1980). Reforming the federal grand jury and the state preliminary hearing to prevent conviction without adjudication. https://core.ac.uk/download/232717787.pdf (accessed on 13th August 2025).
3. Armstrong, G., Mayson, S. G., Potts, A., Sudeall, L., et al. (2020). Boots and bail on the ground: Assessing the implementation of misdemeanor bail reforms in Georgia. https://digitalcommons.law.uga.edu/context/glr/article/1228/type/native/viewcontent (accessed on 13th August 2025).
4. Brink, M. N., Metzger, P. R., & Yu, J. (2022). Grading injustice: Initial appearance report cards. https://core.ac.uk/download/541421340.pdf (accessed on 13th August 2025).
5. Broner, N., Karopkin, M. G., Lamon, S. S., Mayrl, B., et al. (2003). Arrested adults awaiting arraignment: Mental health, substance abuse, and criminal justice characteristics and needs. https://core.ac.uk/download/144228613.pdf (accessed on 13th August 2025).
6. Cameron, N., Potter, S., & Young, W. (1999). The New Zealand jury. https://core.ac.uk/download/62568669.pdf (accessed on 13th August 2025).
7. Chalmers, J., & Leverick, F. (2016). How should we go about jury research in Scotland? https://core.ac.uk/download/42373258.pdf (accessed on 13th August 2025).
8. Chalmers, J., Leverick, F., Munro, V., Murray, K., et al. (2019). Scottish jury research: Findings from a large-scale mock jury study. https://core.ac.uk/download/296224369.pdf (accessed on 13th August 2025).
9. Chambers, D. A., & Norton, W. E. (2016). The adaptome. *American Journal of Preventive Medicine, 51*(1), S124–S131. https://doi.org/10.1016/j.amepre.2016.05.011 (accessed on 13th August 2025).
10. Chesterman, M. (1999). Criminal trial juries in Australia: From penal colonies to a federal democracy. https://core.ac.uk/download/62568664.pdf (accessed on 13th August 2025).
11. Curley, L. J. (2018). Is the jury still out? The decision-making processes of jurors. https://core.ac.uk/download/520511466.pdf (accessed on 13th August 2025).
12. Djerf, H., & Hy, J. (1990). Rights of the criminally accused. https://core.ac.uk/download/62554233.pdf (accessed on 13th August 2025).
13. Doak, J. (2005). Victims' rights in criminal trials: Prospects for participation. https://core.ac.uk/download/30635564.pdf (accessed on 13th August 2025).
14. Doyle, C. (2013). Corporate criminal liability: An overview of federal law. https://core.ac.uk/download/19958992.pdf (accessed on 13th August 2025).
15. Fileborn, B., & Bluett-Boyd, N. (2014). Victim/survivor-focused justice responses and reforms to criminal court practice: Implementation, current practice and future directions. https://core.ac.uk/download/pdf/30674908.pdf (accessed on 13th August 2025).
16. Ford, R. A. (2010). Modeling the effects of peremptory challenges on jury selection and jury verdicts. https://core.ac.uk/download/72052017.pdf (accessed on 13th August 2025).

17. Garrett, B. L. (2007). Aggregation in criminal law. https://core.ac.uk/download/213020497.pdf (accessed on 13th August 2025).

18. Garrett, B. L. (2017). Towards an international right to claim innocence. https://core.ac.uk/download/213020519.pdf (accessed on 13th August 2025).

19. Greenwood, H. (2024). Responding to the danger of wrongful conviction for historical sexual abuse: A case for resurrecting abuse of process for delay? https://core.ac.uk/download/603348845.pdf (accessed on 13th August 2025).

20. Huffman, D. N. (2008). To act or not to act: Will New York's defeated death penalty be resurrected? https://core.ac.uk/download/144227799.pdf (accessed on 13th August 2025).

21. Klinkner, M. J. (2008). Proving genocide? Forensic expertise and the ICTY. https://core.ac.uk/download/4897043.pdf (accessed on 13th August 2025).

22. Klinkner, M. J. (2009). Forensic science expertise for international criminal proceedings: An old problem, a new context and a pragmatic resolution. https://core.ac.uk/download/4897045.pdf (accessed on 13th August 2025).

23. Konstantopoulou, F., & Platania, J. (2014). Evaluating evidence of childhood abuse as a function of expert testimony, judge's instructions, and sentence recommendation. https://core.ac.uk/download/56706384.pdf (accessed on 13th August 2025).

24. Kostyshak, S., & Sukhatme, N. U. (2019). Down to the last strike: The effect of the jury lottery on criminal convictions. https://core.ac.uk/download/213035844.pdf (accessed on 13th August 2025).

25. Lahey, E. (2010). *State v. Burgess*: A limitation on a defendant's right to remain innocent. https://core.ac.uk/download/72052615.pdf (accessed on 13th August 2025).

26. Lancaster, R., & Ding, X. (2006). Addressing the emergence of advocacy in the Chinese criminal justice system: A collaboration between a U.S. and a Chinese law school. https://core.ac.uk/download/144226114.pdf (accessed on 13th August 2025).

27. Larsen, A. O. (2011). Bargaining inside the black box. http://scholarship.law.wm.edu/cgi/viewcontent.cgi?article=2210&context=facpubs (accessed on 13th August 2025).

28. Liebman, J. A. (2016). Dishonest ethical advocacy? False defenses in criminal court. https://core.ac.uk/download/144231813.pdf (accessed on 13th August 2025).

29. Mansky, A., Rempel, M., & Porter, R. (2010). What makes a court problem-solving: Universal performance indicators for problem-solving justice. https://core.ac.uk/download/71361439.pdf (accessed on 13th August 2025).

30. Marshall, P. D. (2011). A comparative analysis of the right to appeal. https://core.ac.uk/download/62547246.pdf (accessed on 13th August 2025).

31. May, J. D. (2011). *Alvarado* revisited: A missing element in Alaska's quest to provide impartial juries for rural Alaskans. https://core.ac.uk/download/62546141.pdf (accessed on 13th August 2025).

32. Montana, R. (2012). Adversarialism in Italy: Using the concept of legal culture to understand resistance to legal modifications and its consequences. https://core.ac.uk/download/9559363.pdf (accessed on 13th August 2025).

33. Murray, B. M. (2018). Unstitching scarlet letters? Prosecutorial discretion and expungement. https://core.ac.uk/download/216957629.pdf (accessed on 13th August 2025).
34. N/A. (1967). Constitutional law: State jury selection procedure held a violation of the Fourteenth Amendment. https://core.ac.uk/download/62551722.pdf (accessed on 13th August 2025).
35. N/A. (1974). *Rhode Island Report on the Judiciary 1974*. https://core.ac.uk/download/56384312.pdf (accessed on 13th August 2025).
36. Nordmark, S., & Nyström, S. (2013). Equal dignity and unequal protection: A framework for analyzing disparate impact claims. https://core.ac.uk/download/213021369.pdf (accessed on 13th August 2025).
37. Platania, J., & Small, R. (2010). Instructions as a safeguard against prosecutorial misconduct. https://core.ac.uk/download/56706391.pdf (accessed on 13th August 2025).
38. Prasad, P. (2018). Implicit racial biases in prosecutorial summations: Proposing an integrated response. https://core.ac.uk/download/216959163.pdf (accessed on 13th August 2025).
39. Resta, G. (2008). Trying cases in the media: A comparative overview. https://core.ac.uk/download/62553225.pdf (accessed on 13th August 2025).
40. Reynolds, A. M. (2019). A "critical" question of state law: Georgia's ambiguous treatment of initial appearance hearings and implications of bail reform. https://digitalcommons.law.uga.edu/cgi/viewcontent.cgi?article=1168&context=glr (accessed on 13th August 2025).
41. Richman, D. (2012). Federal white collar sentencing in the United States: A work in progress. https://core.ac.uk/download/62559791.pdf (accessed on 13th August 2025).
42. Rothstein, P. F. (2015). Unwrapping the box the Supreme Court justices have gotten themselves into: Internal confrontations over confronting the Confrontation Clause. https://core.ac.uk/download/70375288.pdf (accessed on 13th August 2025).
43. Sanders, G. D., Neumann, P. J., Basu, A., Brock, D. W., Feeny, D., Krahn, M., Kuntz, K. M., et al. (2016). Recommendations for conduct, methodological practices, and reporting of cost-effectiveness analyses. *JAMA, 316*(10), 1093–1093. https://doi.org/10.1001/jama.2016.12195 (accessed on 13th August 2025).
44. Vlasova, G. (2022). Procedural features of the pre-judicial investigation of criminal offenses. https://core.ac.uk/download/551314590.pdf (accessed on 13th August 2025).
45. Witanachchi, S. V. (2013). *Maryland v. King*: The Fourth Amendment spirals down the double helix. https://core.ac.uk/download/62560368.pdf (accessed on 13th August 2025).

Chapter

8

EVIDENCE: MEANING, TYPES, AND ADMISSIBILITY IN CRIMINAL PROCEDURE

Contents

Introduction.....245
8.1. The Concept of Evidence.....249
8.2. Types of Evidence.....253
8.3. The Rules of Evidence.....259
8.4. Admissibility of Evidence.....263
8.5. Exclusions and Exceptions.....267
8.6. The Role of Judges and Juries.....271
Summary.....275
References.....278

INTRODUCTION

The idea of evidence is central to criminal procedure, as it acts as the key to determining facts in legal scenarios. It embodies a variety of materials, conduct, and witness statements that together seek to authenticate assertions heard in a court of law. This principle extends beyond physical objects; it includes other types of testimonies and expert witness testimonies, which differ in terms of credibility and impact on case outcomes. With every shift in legal dynamics, so does the deployment and meaning of evidence-based standards. In order to understand the context of evidence—from its definition to admissibility—there has to be a critical examination of legal precedents, statutory codes, and judicial decisions that constitute the criminal justice system. This essay assumes an investigation of these dimensions, noting how much evidence is crucial in the determination of judicial outcomes. Admissibility of evidence is a complex concept, regulated by numerous considerations including the character of the evidence put forward and the legal doctrine that prescribes its admission into court. Historically, courts have been vexed by applying scientific validity measures to various categories of evidence, as reflected in the present criticism of the admissibility of forensic evidence. In particular, Kaye et al. (2018) outlines how terminological uncertainty and the lack of rigorous scientific validation have allowed some of the forensic methods to sidestep close judicial examination. Furthermore, the jurisprudence established in cases such as United States v. Scheffer works to underscore the balancing effect that occurs in determining what constitutes admissible evidence. The Supreme Court ruling in the case reaffirmed that certain exclusionary rules are justified even when a defendant would prefer to proffer evidence possibly favorable to their case, further clouding the waters of evidentiary admissibility. Moreover, this discussion will examine the multifaceted meanings of such terms as reliability and validity, which play a focal role in the vocabulary of expert testimony and evidence standards. Since courts increasingly determine the evolving definition of scientific evidence, implications for criminal procedure are becoming increasingly significant. The law profession must confront the ethical as well as practical considerations of the submission of expert evidence, especially in the context of findings provided by reports such as the PCAST report, which is concerned with a request for objective confirmation of subjective testimony. Lastly, the essay will offer a framework that reiterates the admissibility of evidence in such a manner that courts use standards that, besides proving rigorous scientific examination, also respect the defendants' constitutional rights to provide a holistic defense premised on legal precedents established in landmark cases like those named in Gershman et al. (1998).

Definition of Evidence in the Context of Criminal Law

Evidence in criminal law is basically the means by which facts are established or negated in court. It is a broad category of materials including testimony of witnesses, documents, physical items, and expert opinions, all aimed at establishing or negating charges brought up in court. Evidence, both in the nature of its kind but also admissibility in the legal process, is the meaning that stresses that information must be precise and proper to uphold the integrity of the legal process. An equilibrium between the accused's rights and the quest for justice compels courts to scrutinize evidence presented closely, ensuring it meets strict criteria of evidence. Therefore, understanding of the intricate nature of evidence is crucial for legal professionals and ordinary individuals since it automatically dictates the fate of criminal cases. Character evidence plays a significant role in characterizing and admissibility of evidence under criminal law. In the past, admission of character evidence has been rigorously controlled with the aim of preventing undue prejudice to the defendant. However, modifying legislative enactments, as seen in the Federal Rules of Evidence, indicate a progressive trend toward admitting such evidence in specific situations. For instance, Rules 413–415 reflect a disposition towards complying with social and political pressures by permitting character evidence in certain situations in cases involving sexual crimes. But this concession puts a high value on strong empirical basis for any evidentiary rule changes, as stakes for the right to a fair trial and presumption of innocence run deep. Shifting dynamic of evidence admissibility highlights the inherent tension between developing societal norms and legal traditions in criminal justice (Leonard et al., 1995). Judicial discretion plays a pivotal role in reviewing expert testimony within the field of criminal law. Unlike in civil trials, where expert testimony admissibility may encounter fewer nuances, criminal courts tend to encounter new challenges that need to be extensively deliberated upon. The role of judges in such instances is crucial, as they have to ensure that expert testimony is relevant and credible to the jury according to standards laid down. The significance of this role is also enhanced in addressing issues related to forensic methodology or psychological assessment, where subjective interpretations can influence jury perception. Effective approaches, as suggested in legal theory, can enhance judicial decision-making on expert evidence and its effect on the formation of jury verdicts. Robust scrutiny of expert evidence not only influences the fairness of trials but eventually reflects the overall principles of justice that constitute the criminal legal system (Grimm et al., 2018) (Figure 8.1).

Figure 8.1. The evidence in the context of criminal law.

Source: https://advocatetanwar.com/wp-content/uploads/2024/06/Untitled-design-2-900x600.png.

Importance of Evidence in the Judicial Process

The significance of evidence cannot be overstated, since it forms the basis of legal judgment. Evidence helps establish facts in a case, guide judges and juries during their deliberations, and ensure that the verdict is rendered on justified claims and not on conjecture. In criminal proceedings, the prosecution bears the burden of proof and must establish guilt beyond reasonable doubt. This appeal has heightened the requirement for high-quality evidence because the effects of wrongful convictions are devastating and irreversible. Moreover, the recognition of the significance of evidence made people try to make legal professionals better educated in the analysis and presentation of such evidence and the growing consensus among judicial scholars that specialized expertise in this area is essential to guarantee justice in the judiciary system (Davies et al., 2016). The complexity surrounding the admissibility of evidence also underscores its importance in the justice system. The rules governing what constitutes admissible evidence exist to guarantee that only credible, relevant, and probative evidence is considered during trials, thereby protecting defendants' rights and integrity of the justice system. Courts make very thorough examination to determine evidentiary admissibility, often referring to legal precedents to guide their interpretation. These rules of procedure, in addition to enhancing trial equity, also assist in mitigating the danger of wrongful convictions, particularly in cases that have expert evidence involved. The need for effective and robust training of legal practitioners on how to value such rules of evidence is further highlighted by controversy among legal authorities, whereby inadequate knowledge leads to mishandling or misinterpretation of significant evidence (Davies et al., 2016). Moreover, the function of evidence in determining judicial outcomes goes beyond simple factual determination; it shapes the emotional and psychological aspects of the legal process. The introduction of victim impact evidence during capital trials, exemplified in the Payne v. Tennessee case, demonstrates how emotional testimony can powerfully influence sentencing determinations. Such evidence attunes legal process to the lived experience of human beings and points to the human cost of a defendant's actions. Alternatively, the deployment of such emotional evidence within the judicial narrative raises questions of the congruence of justice to the victim and fair treatment for the accused. Dealing with such more nuanced considerations sets out the complexities of the evidentiary landscape, requiring an informed and reflective response to the use of evidence throughout the judicial process (Figure 8.2).

Figure 8.2. The significance of evidence in the judicial process.

Source: https://i0.wp.com/www.skepticalraptor.com/blog/wp-content/uploads/2017/05/hierarchy-of-scientific-evidence.jpg?fit=768%2C432&ssl=1.

8.1. THE CONCEPT OF EVIDENCE

The principle of evidence is the cornerstone of legal practice, particularly of criminal procedure, wherein it forms the basis for the determination of the merit of charges. Evidence is in a variety of formats—testimony, documents, physical objects, and electronic data—and all contribute separately to the larger quest for knowledge within legal mechanisms. For the criminal justice system, evidence not only helps to prove narratives, but it also significantly aids in safeguarding the rights of the accused. The requirement of admissibility states that evidence must be pertinent and credible so that it neither predisposes the jury unduly nor sways the judgment on the basis of inadmissible facts. This evidence analysis is a reflection of the balance between obtaining justice and preserving procedural correctness for behaviour in trials, which must outweigh in a democratic society. There are numerous different types of evidence looked into in criminal procedure, each being classified by nature and the way it is obtained. Direct evidence, such as that given by an eyewitness, provides direct proof of a fact, while circumstantial evidence relies upon inference and the building of an infrastructure of facts culminating in a conclusion. The growing significance of digital evidence, particularly in the aftermath of technological innovations, has transformed the manner cases are dealt with. Digital forensics, for instance, allows one to retrieve evidence from gadgets such as smartphones and computers, but it presents complex privacy and admissibility of data in court issues. The variety of sorts of evidence points to the necessity of strong legal systems that are quite able to adapt to evolving technological settings, making way for justice as well as ensuring individual rights. Admissibility of evidence is regulated by legal norms that prescribe whether or not to present evidence before a court. Courts usually refer to determinate rules, such as the Federal Rules of Evidence, that set standards for relevance, reliability, and prejudicial impact. The nuances of hearsay, expert opinion, and chain of custody compound these requirements and make them increasingly difficult to meet, requiring highly critical analysis by legal specialists. As emphasized by authors, the interplay of procedural concerns and rules of law creates a need for ongoing debate to understand evidences role within evolving legal systems. Also, with the advent of the Internet of Things (IoT) and its associated complexities of digital evidence, as reflected in Stoyanova et al. (2020), there is an immediate appeal made to legal professionals to also adapt their strategy and methodology towards such advancements while ensuring the integrity and admissibility of evidence without any detriment.

8.1.1. Historical Background of Evidence in Legal Systems

The etiological background of evidence in legal systems reflects a multidimensional evolution influenced by cultural, societal, and ideological transformation. The ancient Mesopotamian and Egyptian civilizations formulated evidence on testimony and divine belief, with religious conviction central to the process of legal procedure. As civilizations grew, so did their idea of evidence; the establishment of written codes, like the Code of Hammurabi, was a significant step toward more formalized ways of gathering and evaluating evidence. This transition laid the groundwork for modern legal systems, wherein evidence must meet certain requirements to be admissible in court. The intersection of shifting social norms and legal practice affected contemporary understandings of the characteristics of good evidence, and with it, the debates on admissibility that persist in contemporary criminal practice. The history of legal evidence was further transformed by the development of common law practice in medieval England, altering the paradigm from reliance upon divine authority to legal principles based on human reason. The trial by jury institution during this period was representative of the increasing embrace of evidence as a means of establishing truth rather than divine intent. The jury began to consider evidence not just on the witness statement but also physical objects and written documents. This shift was groundbreaking in establishing the concept of legal truth as a possibility through a systematic examination of evidence, paving the way for today's evidence standards. Procedural rules, with time, established a more standardized way of approaching evidence, derived from previous decisions and product of a combined perception of justice. This evolution evidences a continuous refinement of what constitutes admissible in the legal sphere, consistent with changing values in society. Evidence in contemporary law plays a central role in ensuring justice through the utility of its function in trial proceedings. The legal system now prizes the evidence's integrity and quality, with rigorous requirements for admissibility aimed at minimizing bias and error. The application of narrative theory in legal proceedings has been significant in pointing out the importance of the presentation and interpretation of evidence, and that the jurors will create other narratives from the information presented. This understanding provokes continued debate regarding the usefulness of legal rules and procedures in providing actual outcomes. Legal brains argue that a holistic evaluation of the manner in which narratives converge with evidentiary norms can unveil prejudice and point toward improvement to trial mechanics. Efforts to formalize evidentiary rules, as elaborated by Bazerman's reading of intertextuality in judicial process, illustrate the increase in focus on how evidence operates within the broader narrative structure of legal process (Bazerman et al., 2009; Griffin et al., 2013) (Figure 8.3).

Figure 8.3. Historical background of evidence in legal systems.

Source: https://www.centurylawfirm.in/blog/wp-content/uploads/2023/11/The-Role-and-Admissibility-of-Forensic-Evidence-in-the-Indian-Criminal-Justice-System-Indian-Evidence-Act.png.

8.1.2. The Role of Evidence in Establishing Facts

The practice of analyzing evidence is critical when establishing facts in the criminal justice process because evidence provides the basis for judicial decision-making. Evidence enables the testing of accusations brought by both the defense and prosecution and informs judges and juries how to establish guilt or innocence. The relationship between the different types of evidence—e.g., physical, testimonial, and documentary evidence—can decide the outcome of a case. The process of evidence, therefore, advocates a systematic process for the pursuit of truth, whereby opinions from facts of reality are allowed. Furthermore, the admissibility of evidence is also significant, as it determines what can be presented in court, thereby influencing the factual setting of the legal argument. Consequently, the role played by evidence cannot be overstated; it is part of the foundation upon which legal proceedings are built. In criminal procedure, the relationship between facts and evidence is more a function of underlying legal principles than procedure per se, as an outflow of such more fundamental principles that govern the system of justice. The admissibility of evidence is challenged using various standards of law, which, as argued by Bazerman, pre-condition the introduction of scientific literature into a court. The judiciary's minimal citing of extraneous documents underscores a highly integrated system that largely relies on established laws and precedents to guide its functions (Bazerman et al., 2009). This intertextual nature of legal argumentation gives emphasis to the need to adhere to rules of evidence since they ensure pertinent, trustworthy, and legally obtained evidence to the court. Hence, the standards of admissibility justify the need for efficiency in the collection and presentation of evidence, which indirectly affects the formation of factual accounts in legal arguments. Comparative analysis of evidence working in adversarial and non-adversarial systems enhances our understanding of the contribution of evidence to establishing facts. An investigation into the handling of forensic DNA evidence by American versus Swiss legal systems, for instance, reveals considerable variation between approaches employed by criminal defense lawyers (Thompson et al., 2016). In an adversarial system like that of the United States, the focus on competition can lead to challenge in the delivery of unprejudiced evidentiary accounts. By comparison, systems in Switzerland can arguably be conducive to a more collaborative approach to evidence appraisal, which can advance a refined understanding of facts. These distinctions demonstrate that the context in which evidence is brought can make a significant difference to its interpretation and weight, again illustrating that evidence's role in establishing facts is inherently subject to ordinary influence not only by its nature but also by the procedural imperatives in which it is contained.

8.1.3. Distinction Between Direct and Circumstantial Evidence

In criminal procedure, understanding the distinction between direct and circumstantial evidence is vital for court officials and jurors alike. Direct evidence refers to information that directly establishes an item of fact, typically in the form of testimony from a witness who narrates first-hand information of an occurrence. For instance, if the witness actually saw the commission of a crime being done, the evidence becomes direct testimony that can easily establish the defendant's guilt. Circumstantial evidence, however, entails inferential reasoning in its interpretation because it entails indirect observation whose implication indicates a fact but does not necessarily establish it directly. For example, finding defendants fingerprints at the scene of a crime may not necessarily establish their culpability but can contribute to a story that ends in conviction when combined with other circumstantial evidence. Circumstantial evidence derives its intricacies from its requirement that the background of an event must stand up and so special scrutiny is afforded by the jury. While direct evidence has the capacity to make a strong impact since it is so obviously fact-based, circumstantial evidence often compels jurors to balance numerous factors—motivation, availability of opportunity, and behavior, for instance—potentially connecting a suspect to the crime. The interpretive nature of such evidence underscores the necessity for jurors to become thoroughly immersed in the evidence that stands before them. Besides, as emphasized by recent discussion regarding how in such evidence in court proceedings should be put forward, circumstantial evidence success is in many instances largely dependent on juror comprehension and the competence of legal practitioners at crafting rational narratives in linking the dots in front of the jurors, and therefore they are inalienable factors in the process of assessment (Chesterman et al., 2008). In spite of its inferential nature, circumstantial evidence may be highly persuasive and usually constitutes the foundation of most legal judgments in the absence of direct evidence. The legal systems across the globe are challenged with reconciling the admissibility of circumstantial evidence in a way that promotes justice without compromising the fairness of a trial. In nations such as the UK and Australia, recent judicial rulings emphasize the need for a more refined approach to the evaluation of circumstantial evidence, with a detailed emphasis on gaining an insight into patterns of behavior and their relevance in cases involving serious allegations, i.e., sex offenses (Gerry et al., 2013). This emerging controversy not only demonstrates the distinctions among types of evidence but also broader dynamics in how evidence of this nature is applied across different legal systems, finally a reminder of the intricate relationship between evidence, juror perception, and the pursuit of justice (Figure 8.4).

Figure 8.4. The distinction between direct and circumstantial evidence.

Source: https://keydifferences.com/wp-content/uploads/2021/05/direct-vs-circumstantial-evidence-thumbnail.jpg.

8.2. TYPES OF EVIDENCE

The concept of evidence is central to the criminal process decision-making, where various categories are employed to provide support for statements by both the prosecution and the defense. In its primary manifestations, evidence constitutes mostly three: testimonial, physical, and demonstrative evidence. Testimonial evidence consists of what witnesses testify, stating what they know relative to the case. Physical evidence, however, is concrete items such as documents or firearms that may be collected and analyzed.

Figure 8.5. Types of evidence.

Source: https://legodesk.com/wp-content/uploads/2020/05/Evidence-Act-India-IG-LD-xb0-643x1024.jpg.

Demonstrative evidence, in turn, is employed as a visual aid to help jurors better understand complex elements of a case such as charts or diagrams. All types of evidence play a great role in finding the truth and safeguarding the cause of justice, highlighting the need for judges to exercise due judgments while admitting such evidence in criminal trials. Particularly in the case of expert evidence, the plight of judges while considering admissibility is great and deserving serious attention. While other forms of evidence are straightforward, expert evidence can be infused with technical information that is not generally accessible to the jury. This has caused immense judicial discretion in determining whether the expertise of the experts, their methods, and the materiality of their testimonies adhere to set standards of law. Judges must navigate through the intricacies created by expert evidence while pitting its probative value against prejudice. As Grimm et al. (2018) states, this situation becomes more complex in criminal proceedings, with a tendency to result in adversarial fights regarding the admissibility of expert testimony. Training attorneys and judges on expert evidence management is thus crucial in making just decisions but also based on an adequately developed understanding of the involved scientific theory. Moreover, the link between expert training quality and miscarriages of justice risk highlights systemic flaws that have the potential to undermine judicial verdicts. The both House of Commons Science and Technology Committee Report and Law Commissions 2011 report attest to the glaring need for adequate education regarding expert evidence in the legal practice. As reflected in Davies et al. (2016), there is a huge imbalance between current training frameworks and the level of evidence provided in criminal cases, which indeed raises critical questions regarding whether legal professions are ready to handle such cases appropriately. Correcting these training deficiencies is needed not only for the integrity of the judiciary but also to foster a culture of enlightened legal practice that minimizes the risks of wrongful convictions. Enhancing the training of the judiciary as well as legal practitioners may make an enormous difference in the evaluation process of expert evidence, thus ensuring the fundamental rights of defendants and upholding the integrity of the justice systems (Figure 8.5).

8.2.1. Physical Evidence and Its Significance

Physical evidence is at the core of criminal procedure because its physical nature provides the police and the courts with concrete facts that corroborate or refute accusations made through investigations. Compared to testimonial evidence, which relies on human memory and is subject to potential error or bias, physical evidence is an objective opposite in the pursuit of truth. The usefulness of this type of evidence is that it can link a suspect to a crime scene, establish timelines, or even exonerate the innocent. Particularly in light of modern forensic technology, the importance of physical evidence has increased, and there is a need for careful examination and strict adherence to procedures for its collection and examination so that it can be admissible as a valid means of analysis in court. However, physical evidence is not controversy-free as legal procedures provide for the fact that such evidence needs some benchmarks to render it acceptable. Courts are often tasked with balancing its probative value against potential prejudices it can introduce into a jury. The technicalities of physical evidence require judicial scrutiny to ascertain its authenticity and relevancy, which can be directed by many legal precedents and rules. For instance, Federal Rule 702 of the Federal Rules of Evidence underscores the fact that expert witnesses' testimony should be grounded on relevant facts or data and must satisfy a standard of reliability. This problem is also echoed in the area of forensic science, where variability and subjective nature of certain classes of evidence can contaminate the validity of expert conclusions, say Kaye et al. (2018). Standards of admissibility also serve, therefore, to guard against the introduction of potentially misleading information. In criminal justice physical evidence study, it is clear how its standards and practice are continuously debated so as to maintain integrity for legal proceedings. Advancing developments in forensic science continue to stretch evidentiary traditions beyond the line, prompting lawmakers and legal scholars to review current norms. The appearance of the character evidence amendments reflects a widening view of the effect of context on the evaluation of evidence, but with more scrutiny around its use in specific instances, as discussed in Leonard et al. (1995). As legal frameworks lag behind the requirements of scientific advancements, the necessity for a balanced approach towards physical evidence is increasingly evident, emphasizing that solid procedures and accessible guidelines are vital in attaining the ideals of justice (Figure 8.6).

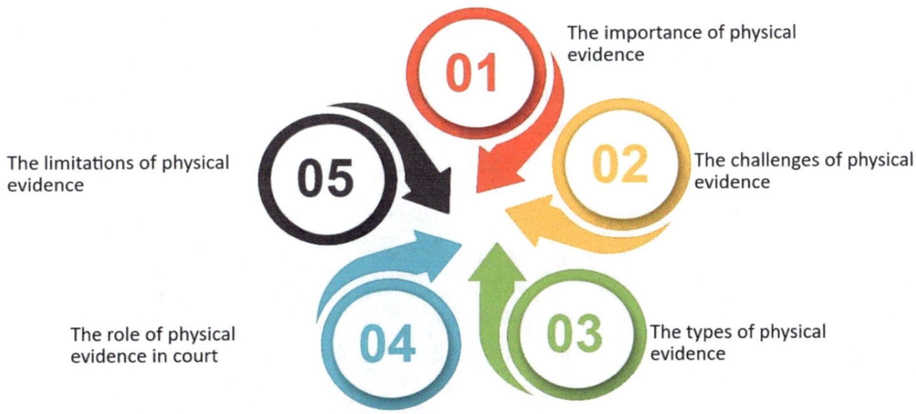

Figure 8.6. Physical evidence and its significance.

Source:

8.2.2. Testimonial Evidence and Its Reliability

Testimonial evidence is an intrinsic element of criminal procedure, particularly with regard to the immediate consequences on a defendants rights. Admissibility of such evidence can prove crucial to legal outcomes, and the issues surrounding its admissibility are significant. Traditionally, courts employed the standard of Ohio v. Roberts, which admitted hearsay if it was deemed reliable and apt to pre-established exceptions. The watershed moment arrived in the landmark case of Crawford v. Washington. The Court ruled that reliability is not the same as adequate constitutional protection, although it is vital. Instead, the Confrontation Clause prohibits testimonial statements from being introduced except when the defendant is given a chance to cross-examine the witness, thus placing the focus on the testifying evidence process and not raw reliability. The shift places greater emphasis on ensuring defendants' rights through a formal cross-examination process such that there can be a more substantial questioning of testimonial credibility. Moreover, the Williams v. Illinois decision reinforces the evolving idea of testimonial evidence by establishing tight boundaries where it is admissible. Since the Crawford decision, it has been increasingly important to recognize differences between statement types and their roles in legal cases. Testimonial statements, as Crawford would define them, are statements uttered with an expectation that they can serve as evidence in a formal situation, typically with representatives of the state. The implication of the distinction is quite profound; it is not sufficient for testimonial evidence to meet a threshold of reliability. Instead, the potential for cross-examination enters as the anchor of the scheme of testimonial evidence. This not only constitutes a defense of rights for defendants, but it also results in a more detailed examination of the evidence presented with respect to reliability and context, ultimately resulting in a more equitable legal process. The testimonial evidence argument is further complicated by differing positions of judicial systems, particularly when comparing the U.S. and European judicial systems of law. The European Court of Human Rights (ECHR) encourages a broader admissibility standard that is looking for a balance between the rights of the defendant against effective administration of justice. This has resulted in periodic tensions between the strict U.S. confrontation rights and pragmatic European standards. Adherents to the ECHR paradigm are against the rigid confrontation requirement, suggesting it could damage justice when the evidentiary integrity—its probative value—is otherwise determinable. In that case, a more flexible approach that is consistent with the best evidence principle could lead to better legal outcomes without compromising an element of defendant protection. The debate surrounding these divergent models draws attention to the necessity for continuing discussions concerning how testimonial evidence, and its credibility, needs to be weighed in an international forum so as to ensure that the essential rights are protected while the legitimacy of the legal process is maintained (Figure 8.7).

Figure 8.7. Testimonial evidence and its reliability.

Source: https://www.alsolaw.com/wp-content/uploads/2018/05/witness-testimony-e1551824015923.jpg.

8.2.3. Documentary Evidence and Its Role in Court

The utility of documentary evidence to the court is its ability to confirm facts through tangible documents. Documentary evidence is almost any material ranging from documents and official documents to reports and emails. Admissibility of documentary evidence is crucial in criminal trials as it tends to buttress the case of the prosecutions. The court relies on the reliability and validity of these documents in determining whether they are pertinent or not to the case at hand. The system of courts, however, as observed by Bazerman, operates under a system that shuts the door against entering scientific literature, and thereby limiting the type of document to be heard on evidence. The importance of this limitation is evident in the fact that it helps to maintain the legal context precise yet simultaneously raises issues regarding the extent of information available to support or contradict submissions made under trial (Bazerman et al., 2009). In criminal procedure, documentary evidence might be made difficult by hearsay admissibility. Despite the tendency of hearsay evidence to be inadmissible due to reliability issues, exceptions to its admissibility have grown, particularly in federal courts. As described in Douglass et al. (2000), the legal framework of handling hearsay demonstrates unevenness regarding how the evidence is treated in criminal cases as compared to civil cases.

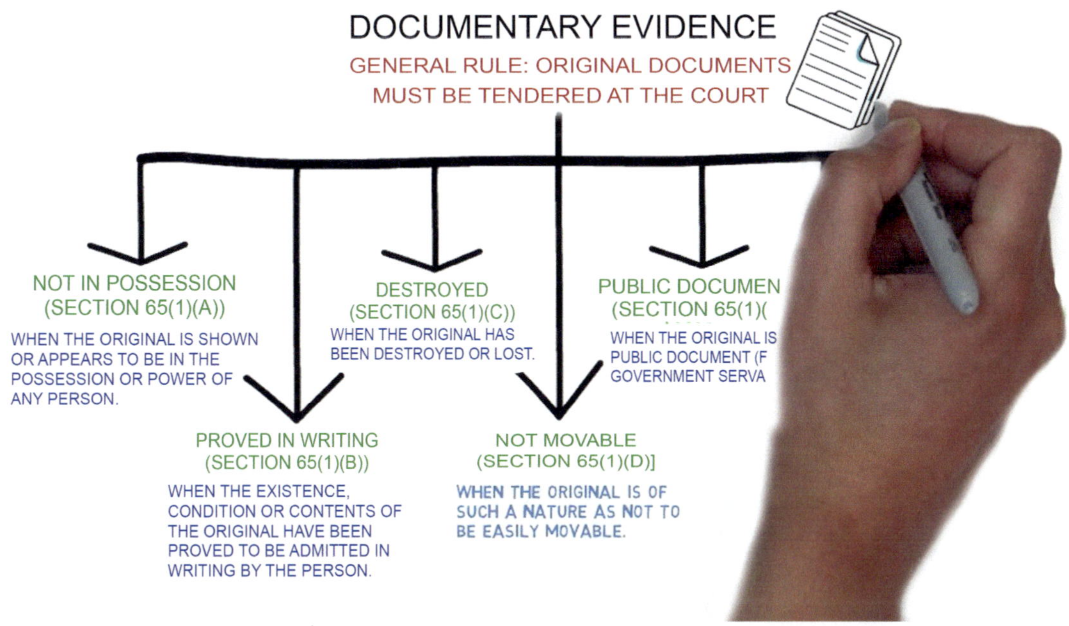

Figure 8.8. Documentary evidence and its role in court.

Source: https://i.ytimg.com/vi/0H7ggob3JUg/maxresdefault.jpg.

Defendants typically encounter a litigation culture where minimal discovery occurs, and thus it becomes challenging to be able to challenge hearsay-based claims effectively. With this in mind, documentary evidence is even more critical because it can indeed be the bedrock layer on which the credibility of questionable hearsay is decided. Documentary evidence, explained clearly, can not only make the prosecutions version stronger but also give defendants invaluable chances to rebut the validity of charges leveled against them. The effectiveness of documentary evidence further relies on the procedural rules according to which it is admitted. Courts impose rigorous requirements to ensure that any document produced meets requirements of relevance, authenticity, and materiality. The requirements serve to ensure integrity in the judicial process by averting the filing of misleading information. With changing judicial understanding, so does the interplay between documentary evidence and other types of evidence, such as expert testimony and hearsay. The balancing required to adjudicate the admissibility of documentary evidence underscores its stabilizing effect in the courtroom. Through discussion in Bazerman et al. (2009), the evolution of the understanding and admission of evidence over time in criminal courts attests to the ever-present conflict between the need for full information and the legal regime that governs its admission as evidence. Thus, an understanding of the role of documentary evidence is needed to truly recognize its meaning for fairness and justice in the criminal justice system (Figure 8.8).

8.3. THE RULES OF EVIDENCE

The Rules of Evidence serve a key role in shaping the landscape of criminal procedure, determining what types of information get admitted into court. In particular, such regulations delineate the boundaries of acceptable evidence, which is vital for the intent of carrying out a fair trial. Of special concern among such regulations is prohibition against character evidence, whose aim is to maintain the focus on specific controversial facts and not on a defendant's behavioral record. However, reforms implemented in recent times have made provision for certain exception from this rule, which testify to the developing reality susceptible to sociological as well as political influences. The union of conservatism and compromise within the Federal Rules of Evidence is indicative of the need to exercise cautious evaluation before changing rules that can tarnish the integrity of trials. As previously stated, Congress must ensure that recommendations for new changes are grounded on solid empirical evidence in order not to institute dramatic shifts without a basis (Leonard et al., 1995). In criminal cases, the complexity of admissibility for expert testimony adds a further layer of scrutiny under Rules of Evidence. Judges are typically presented with special circumstances that have a significant impact on the trial result, particularly when deciding if expert testimony is permissible in terms of reliability and relevance. In civil litigation, where evidence can be comparatively lower, criminal trials require stricter adherence to rules of evidence because there is more on the line when it comes to convictions. This requires a pragmatic knowledge of scientific processes and principles. Expert testimony cannot be dismissed; it can sway the jurors' perception and make or break the narrative of a case. Addressing such issues in a workable way is crucial in order to preserve the integrity of legal process and ensure justice being dispensed in an equitable way (Grimm et al., 2018). Lastly, the Rules of Evidence contain both admissibility principles and procedural protections aimed at protecting the accused's rights. As the law community wrestles with current debate on reforming rules of evidence, it is important to take into account both the historical background and the practical consequences of such reforms. Reforms that make character evidence a priority or lower the standards of expert testimony threaten to undermine the pillars of the adversarial process. It is essential that admissibility decisions remain free from legislative whim or public fashion but from regard to due process and equity. Any subsequent amendments, in consequence, must balance the need for creative solution in relation to advances in modern times with the established principles that have as yet governed criminal procedure. The delicate balance between these factors will determine the efficiency of evidence rules to generate unbiased results in criminal trials.

8.3.1. Overview of the Federal Rules of Evidence (FRE)

The FRE are the fundamental guidelines that regulate the admissibility of evidence in U.S. federal courts, ensuring consistency and fairness in judicial proceedings. Passed in 1975, the FRE regulations stipulate the types of evidence permitted to be presented during trials in the form of witness testimony, documentary material, and tangible exhibits. The keystone of the FRE is evidence relevancy, which must not only bear on something at trial but also pass the test of potential prejudice against probative value. This emphasis on relevance opens the door for judges to critically examine the sheer amount of presented evidence, particularly in criminal cases when so much is at stake. By providing clear guidelines, the FRE strives to render the judicial process more equitable, and utilizing these rules proves difficult, most importantly when dealing with complex expert witness testimony (Grimm et al., 2018). Of particular significance, expert evidence is particularly scrutinized for admissibility under the FRE, especially after significant judicial constructions such as the landmark Daubert v. Merrell Dow Pharmaceuticals, Inc. ruling. The ruling held that not only did expert evidence need to be relevant but also had to be reliable, with judges now required to assess methodologies applied by experts along with their application to the facts of a particular case. However, despite these protections, Rule 702 has been faulted to be practiced in such a way that judges still allow dubious expert evidence, particularly in criminal cases. The disparity can find admission of deceptive forensic techniques that have, in some cases, caused the wrongful conviction of innocent individuals, making justice more difficult to seek. Recurring controversy over the admissibility of evidence brings to the foreground the necessity to meet guidelines that guarantee accuracy and fairness in the judicial process (Fabricant et al., 2018). Moreover, use of Federal Rules of Evidence demonstrates glaring variations in how evidence is treated differently in various jurisdictions, that can affect criminal case decisions. For example, while federal courts are governed by the FRE, state courts have developed their own codes that sometimes diverge from the federal rules. Such divergence perhaps leads to confusion among practitioners and makes it more difficult for defendants' rights, since evidence disqualifiable in a particular jurisdiction may be admissible in another. The varying uses of rules of evidence underscore the necessity for a full familiarity with the FRE and any applicable state rules in an attempt to deal with the complexities of judicial proceedings. Lastly, as courts keep grappling with the evolving nature of evidence and admissibility, continuous review of the FRE is vital in driving a just and equitable justice system that defends the rights of individuals accused of offenses (Grimm et al., 2018) (Figure 8.9).

Figure 8.9. Overview of the federal rules of evidence.

Source: https://www.legalbites.in/wp-content/uploads/2020/10/Federal-Rules-of-Evidence.jpg.

8.3.2. State-Specific Variations in Evidence Rules

The landscape of rules of evidence in the United States legal environment is one of wide state-to-state variation because of the decentralized criminal procedure. State-to-state variation in rules affects what can be admitted as evidence during trials and has a tendency to lead to varied outcomes for the defendant. For instance, admission of character evidence, typically restricted under the Federal Rules of Evidence, would be more acceptable in certain jurisdictions. This discrepancy is due to a mix of precedence in history, local legal tradition, and court interpretation which impacts both prosecution and defense strategies. Therefore, attorneys are required to navigate these complexities well in order to have their cases laid down on tolerable evidence, which further influences trial equity and the pursuit of justice

(Leonard et al., 1995). In addition to character evidence, the rules governing forensic evidence, such as fingerprint identification, also vary state-to-state regarding rules of admissibility. It is reported through a study that various terminology is used by fingerprint examiners to assess the reliability of the matches that can make a significant difference to lay jurors' perceptions regarding such evidence. Different states have the ability to apply diverse standards of what would constitute valid forensic evidence, typically in turn impacting the way juries balance the weight of such evidence when they deliberate. For example, some states can include fingerprint evidence to be presented without rigorous scientific testing standards, while others can require exhaustive means of evidence analysis before admissibility into a trial. These variations highlight the necessity for standardized guidelines to provide fairness among jurisdictions (Garrett et al., 2013). Moreover, states' procedural variants can make it easier to deviate in the use of evidentiary rules, particularly in criminal procedure. Some states would be inclined to follow the Federal Rules of Evidence, while others have permissive or restrictive standpoints depending on local policy and legal theory. This makes not only the defense strategy but also the prosecution efforts to build a workable case more complicated, leading to a patchwork of court practices. For these reasons, it is very crucial that legal professionals remain sensitive to the specific rules governing their state so that they are sufficiently equipped to argue for or against the admissibility of evidence. Lastly, such state-to-state variations indicate the complexities inherent in the American criminal procedure system such that rules of evidence carry profound implications for criminal case outcomes.

8.3.3. The Purpose of Rules Governing Evidence

Rules controlling evidence play a natural role in criminal procedure whose main aim is to ensure the integrity of the judicial process. These rules establish the types of evidence that may be brought to court and thereby avoid admitting inadmissible or prejudicial facts. Character evidence, for instance, which will pervert juries unfairly, is generally barred so that the accused's right to a fair trial can be preserved. The application of evidence according to predefined rules reduces the likelihood that emotive appeals will come to dominate factual findings, making the judicial process more rational and equitable. Further, the observance of such rules ascribes to a larger aspiration for justice, upholding the principle that determinations must be grounded in credible and ascertainable information, and not in speculation or prejudice, making it easier for people to trust the legal system. In addition to preserving equity, rules of evidence also facilitate effective administration of justice through evidentiary standardization. By their establishment of clear admissibility rules, the rules are able to eliminate chaos in trial proceedings and enable judges and lawyers to navigate complex legal territory with ease. The Federal Rules of Evidence illustrates this success by having created a combination of conservativism and political accommodation that has influenced American court procedures. Some of these amendments, for example, those regarding the admissibility of character evidence, illustrate continuing issues in litigation that emerge as a result of shifting social values and increased sensitivity to the consequences of evidentiary requirements. Therefore, such rules not only shape courtroom operations but also respond to the need for an efficient legal scheme that can cope with developing issues of criminal law (Leonard et al., 1995). Judges are presented with special difficulties when ruling on the admissibility of various sources of evidence, particularly expert testimony in criminal trials. The complexity of evaluating expert evidence sometimes renders judging rather difficult, as standards of admissibility must balance legal precedent with the requirement that expert opinions be based on good methodology and relevant facts. Moreover, the danger of expert testimony influencing jurors pre-judicially has generated more judicial oversight, calling for an appropriate examination of the qualifications and the legitimacy of the proposed evidence. Overcoming all these barriers is critical in ensuring the integrity of the trial process and making presented evidence not only suitable but also for the purposes of truth-finding (Grimm et al., 2018). Therefore, the laws that control evidence are crucial for the establishment of an efficient and equitable system of judiciary in the context of criminal procedure (Figure 8.10).

Figure 8.10. The purpose of rules governing evidence.

Source: https://info-savvy.com/wp-content/uploads/2020/07/Rules-of-Evidence-infosavvy.jpeg.

8.4. ADMISSIBILITY OF EVIDENCE

Admissibility of evidence in criminal procedure is heavily influenced by a number of legal standards and principles that ensure that there is a fair trial. Central to these discussions is the principle of relevance, which ensures that proof presented is immediately connected to facts that are disputed within a case. This standard operates towards the avoidance of the admission of irrelevant information that could mislead the jurors or hide the truth. Besides, evidence must also pass the reliability test, which is largely determined in relation to available judicial precedents. The courts conduct rigorous examination in determining whether the processes of gathering evidence adhered to legal procedures, ensuring the rights of the defendants while maintaining the integrity of the judicial process. It is against such a backdrop that the service of representation by attorneys becomes indispensable, where experienced attorneys deal with the complexities of admissibility to advance the interests of their clients. Apart from relevance and reliability, probability of evidence to cause unfair prejudice is another significant consideration in admissibility in criminal proceedings. Courts must weigh the probative value of the evidence against the risk that it could unjustly sway a jury's conclusion with inflammatory or emotional facts. Such weighing is essential to maintaining the integrity of the judicial process, since the law seeks to uncover not only the truth but also to protect from the unjustified application of facts that could lead to erroneous verdicts. In addition to this, procedural rules regulate how evidence is to be obtained, as well as the significant detail of the chain of custody. A continuous chain guarantees evidence has not been altered or tampered with and thus remains authentic and admissible to court upon judicial examination. Finally, the advent of technology and digital evidence introduces further complexity to evidence admissibility criteria. With the explosion in smart devices and the Internet of Things, law enforcement agencies increasingly rely on digital evidence that, as dense in potential evidentiary value as it is, poses special challenges. Privacy, data security, and jurisdictional legal concerns arise, particularly in the case of cloud storage systems where data can be stored in many jurisdictions. The need to satisfy varied legal requirements, including the standards outlined in international human rights instruments, accentuates the intricacy of evidential admissibility in a world of increasing digitalization. As discussed in recent discourse, for example, in Stoyanova et al. (2020), such advancements call for reconsideration of traditional principles of evidence to apply with evolving technology-dependent evidence while ensuring cardinal rights in the process of justice.

8.4.1. Criteria for Admissibility in Criminal Trials

In criminal trials, admissibility criteria play a pivotal role in ensuring equitable and fair proceedings. With the relevancy of evidence being the central focus of such criteria, the evidence should not only relate distinctly to the case being tried but also be of considerable value in proving or disproving a material fact. This principle is enshrined in legal precepts, according to which irrelevant data, no matter how persuasive, are not admissible. This underpinning serves to protect against unwarranted prejudice that might obscure the minds of judges and jurors both. In addition, judicial discretion is also crucial in admitting evidence as judges have the responsibility of examining with care and accuracy whether admitting certain evidence will be justifiable in taking the risk of confusing or prejudicing jurors and impacting the credibility of the trial process. The other significant criterion for admissibility is the reliability of the produced evidence. Courts require evidence not only to be pertinent but also to be inherently reliable, particularly if presented in the form of expert witnesses. Credibility of experts is questioned because miscarriages of justice become a greater probability when the evidence of experts is not examined to high standards or well-educated within legal circles. The nexus of expert evidence and sufficient legal education was strongly promoted in the House of Commons Science and Technology Committee Report, highlighting the urgent need for legal practitioners to enhance their insight into matters with regard to evidence related to expert witness (Davies et al., 2016). The Law Commissions follow-up report did little more than again identify the important role of appropriate training and advocate changes to improve the reliability of expert evidence in criminal trials. Beyond the requirements of relevance and reliability, the procedural standards of admitting evidence also create demands for consideration. Admissibility is generally managed by specific regulations and rules, which vary by jurisdiction but generally operate the function of promoting procedural fairness. The reception of victim impact evidence, sanctioned by the Supreme Court ruling in Payne v. Tennessee, is a procedural development towards their incorporation into trials without undermining its risk of prejudice (Forster et al., 2005). Such paradigmatic rulings demonstrate an evolving understanding of the landscape of evidence that allows courts to take into account the effect of the emotional aftermath of a crime on sentencing. Therefore, evolving standards of admissibility reflect legal mandates as well as the values of society and the intricacy of human life, demonstrating an active interaction between ethics and law in criminal proceedings (Figure 8.11).

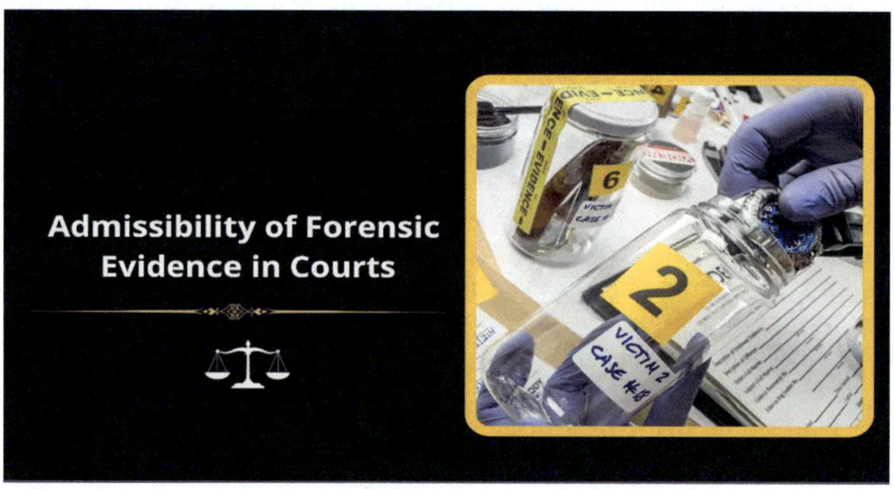

Figure 8.11. Criteria for admissibility in criminal trials.

Source: https://www.legalbites.in/h-upload/2024/05/06/1325129-lb-admis-forensic.webp.

8.4.2. The Role of Relevance and Materiality

The doctrines of relevance and materiality are basic concepts in determining evidence in criminal procedure. Relevance is a threshold test, determining whether or not evidence is somehow relevant to the facts of the case. In the Federal Rules of Evidence, relevant evidence is evidence tending to make the existence of a fact more or less probable than without the evidence. Materiality, on the other hand, is the significance of a fact to the legal matters in dispute in the case. The interconnection of materiality and relevance is that evidence which is relevant to a case can be excluded if it lacks appropriate materiality to impact the outcome of a trial. It is against this delicate balance that only evidence which will assist the jury in reaching findings of relevance directly related to the case being heard is presented. Where the Criminal Procedure and the Classified Information Procedures Act are concerned, relevance and materiality become a still more paramount stake when it comes to the issue. CIPA demonstrates how the cause of national security may prevail over the right of the individual to a fair defense in some cases as the Act limits the discovery process where cases involve classified information. Where the government seeks to protect sensitive information, the defendant's right to make an effective defense must be preserved. Materiality is then tried, as evidence relevant to the defendant's case can be abridged by superior national interests. This raises basic questions regarding how to properly balance these competing interests while honoring constitutional mandates requiring fair process. By examining these cross-currents, one has an appreciation for the broader implications of relevance and materiality on criminal justice outcomes. Furthermore, the nature of hearsay evidence adds a yet another layer of complexity regarding relevance and materiality. Recent developments in law of evidence have begun to reflect a trend in favor of more blanket permission of hearsay in criminal cases, thereby creating a disproportion between the admissibility of hearsay and the defendants' rights to effective discovery. As federal courts continue to allow greater hearsay evidence, the challenge increasingly lies with the defendants to contest such admissions without prior knowledge of the material they are facing. In such instances, the very essence of relevancy is lost if defendants are not able to employ resources to counter allegations leveled against them. This disparity underscores that there must be a reform in the manner in which criminal discovery operates, with particular focus on aligning the discovery process even further so that it can accommodate within itself the realities of modern-day standards of admissibility and the central role of relevance and materiality in this new standard.

8.4.3. The Impact of Prejudicial Versus Probative Value

In criminal process, the delicate balance between prejudicial and probative value of evidence is a significant role in guaranteeing fair trial rights. Probative value is the ability of evidence to prove something relevant to the case, whereas prejudicial value refers to the potential that such evidence could unfairly taint the jury's perception. Courts are also likely to wrestle with ruling on the admissibility of evidence likely to have significant prejudicial impact and dominate its fact relevance. This problem is particularly noted when character evidence arises since it is likely to elicit emotional responses and thus biased judgments. These are relevant thoughts in light of the fact that character evidence is introduced under special amendments to earlier rules, an implication of the progressive trend in evidentiary practice. Courts must act carefully to be in a position to determine that probative value is not secondary to its prejudicial effect, thus ensuring the purity of the legal process (Leonard et al., 1995). Effects of admissibility decisions are realized in rules-governed cases, particularly where management of sensitive evidence enters the scene, such as in sexual assault. For instance, application of Rule 412, better known as the Rape Shield Rule, seeks to limit prejudicial character evidence in court. But the question is how courts determine and weigh interpreting and assessing the probative value of such evidence against its inherent prejudice tendency. Inconsistencies in judicial decisions throughout history demonstrate how difficult courts are in using such a rule, as conclusions of probative significance change significantly depending on jurisdiction and case specifics. The balancing test utilized by courts on a regular basis brings about contradictory interpretations, which may undermine the original purpose of the Rape Shield Rule and may give courts an arena where unintentionally prejudice influences decisions (Aiken et al., 2002). While legal analysts are analyzing the consequences of the rules of evidence, the necessity of greater specificity in the balancing of prejudicial versus probative value also becomes increasingly imperative. The tendency must be to give courts more explicit guidance to narrow discretionary power that leads to inconsistency of judgments. It would enhance fairness by making the probative value criteria more stringent in order to circumscribe evidence's power to raise disproportionate prejudice. In assuming revisions serving uniformity, courts would be better equipped to protect against arbitrary influence by prejudicial evidence. Lastly, creating a comprehensive system that rigidly tests both the prejudicial and probative value of evidence will result in an even-handed and equitable judicial system, maintaining the ideal that justice must prevail above all else (Aiken et al., 2002) (Figure 8.12).

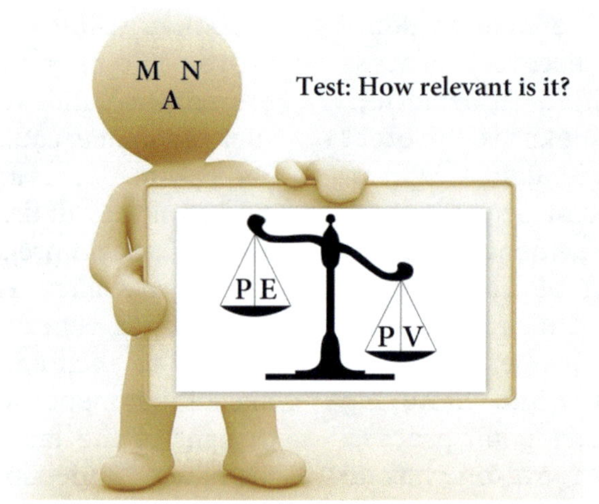

Figure 8.12. The impact of prejudicial versus probative value.

Source: https://amicuscuriaeco.weebly.com/uploads/2/4/0/3/24031391/802607.jpg?715.

8.5. EXCLUSIONS AND EXCEPTIONS

Exclusion and exceptions are very crucial in criminal procedure in regard to evidence, defining boundaries for what is acceptable in court. Such mechanisms are required due to the need to balance the interests of justice against the rights of the person. Exclusionary rule is a case in point, where illegally obtained evidence is excluded from use in court as a Fourth Amendment violation of protection against unreasonable search and seizure. This rule is an expression of a fundamental notion that evidence should not only be committed to truth-seeking but also comply with constitutional imperatives to preserving the integrity of the judicial process. By establishing boundaries on admissibility, the law seeks to deter illegal police conduct and preserve the integrity of the judicial system, thereby sustaining exclusions as essential to the safeguarding of public and private interests. Aside from the blanket exclusions established under the exclusionary rule, there are some exceptions under which particular evidence can be allowed into court despite being gathered under questionable circumstances. One exception is the good faith doctrine, which states that evidence gathered by law enforcement under an objectively reasonable assumption that their activity was legal can be deemed admissible. Such an exception shows an interest-balancing style of evidence, where it is recognized that adherence to exclusion too rigidly can undermine the efficacy of criminal prosecutions. In addition, exceptions such as the inevitable discovery rule posit that illegally procured evidence can be admitted if one can prove that it would have been discovered in due course of time legally. This flexibility indicates the legal systems ongoing struggle to balance the demands of effective enforcement of the law with the need to protect constitutional liberties. Argument over exclusions and exceptions is exacerbated by a shifting legal landscape and prevailing ethics. Rulings of the courts often overshadow what is considered acceptable evidence, as the courts periodically revisit existing doctrines to bring themselves in line with prevailing norms. As an eminent judicial scholar explained, the subtle issues surrounding the employment of legal jargon and the tendency for the legal community to resort to historical precedents can conceal the functional implications of these rules and emphasize the significance of simplicity and clarity within legal interpretations (Posner et al., 2016). Moreover, the fate of such exclusions and exceptions is now being determined by modern arguments regarding privacy, technology, and policing practices that contradict traditional admissibility understandings (Posner et al., 2015). Thus, comprehension of exclusions and exceptions covers not just current legal practice but also dictates potential reform in the field of evidence admissibility.

8.5.1. Overview of Hearsay and Its Exceptions

The hearsay doctrine is at the center of the evidence field in criminal procedure, involving a statement not made at court, which is offered as evidence to prove the truth of the matter asserted. Hearsay is typically excluded because it calls into question its reliability as the original speaker is unavailable for cross-examination, a pillar of the adversarial process. This type of evidence compromises the integrity of the judicial process, and courts are therefore required to adhere strictly to rules admitting it. However, the dynamic evolution of evidentiary law has witnessed recognition of various exceptions to the rule against hearsay to accommodate cases where such statements have indicia of reliability that are adequate to warrant admission into the judicial process. These exceptions should be understood by defendants and prosecutors to navigate criminal trials. Among the most robust hearsay exceptions are those that aim at declarations relying on certain situations that reflect trustworthiness. Excited utterances, for example, which are declarations made while in the process of being excited, are usually admissible due to the spontaneity and contemporaneity in time that they reflect. Likewise, present sense impressions statements are also admissible since they are the perception of the speakers in an occurrence that is unfolding. Lastly, admissions on the part of an opponent of a party allow a party to produce statements made by the opposing party against one's interest, and these are an acknowledgment that facts can be elicited out of statements made in circumstances where one will be speaking the truth. Use of such exceptions focuses on the judiciary's understanding of circumstances under which hearsay can be in the interests of justice while being inimically problematic to evidentiary purity. The balancing act between hearsay admissibility and criminal defendants rights remains a crucial area of judicial inquiry. Recent changes in the law of evidence have resulted in a redefinition of the tension between hearsay and discovery since federal courts increasingly grant greater admissibility of hearsay in criminal proceedings. It has created a perceptible dichotomy where defendants are often left with a litigation environment of limited rights of discovery harmonized with an inundation of possible inculpatory hearsay evidence. To cure this imbalance, the researchers and scholars have called for greater procedural means that would offer defendants a reasonable opportunity to contest hearsay evidence presented against them, offering a more equitable legal process that honors both the pursuit of the truth and the protection of individual rights. The reform call demonstrates a growing awareness of the complexity of hearsay, as well as the ever-evolving criminal procedure landscape (Douglass et al., 2000; Posner et al., 2016) (Figure 8.13).

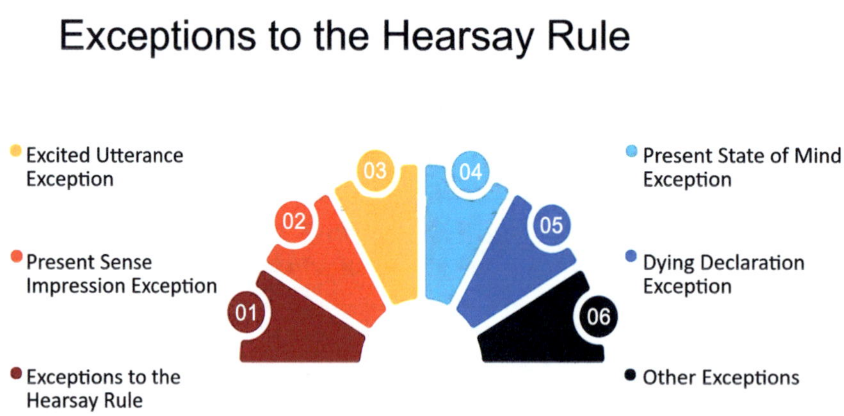

Figure 8.13. Overview of hearsay and its exceptions.

Source: https://fastercapital.co/i/Hearsay-or-Not--Understanding-the-Broad-Evidence-Rule--Exceptions-to-the-Hearsay-Rule.webp.

8.5.2. The Exclusionary Rule and Its Implications

The exclusionary rule is a key component of the American criminal procedure model, providing protections for defendants as well as the integrity of the justice process. Excluding the admissibility of evidence obtained by unconstitutional means such as illegal search and seizure, the rule serves to deter the police from engaging in violations of rights. This principle is in concordance with the Fourth Amendment's protection against unreasonable searches, reiterating an inherent trust in individual privacy and liberty. Thus, the exclusionary rule not only protects individual rights but also maintains public faith in the judiciary system, with the guarantee that convictions are founded on valid evidence. Critics argue, however, that the rule has the potential to exclude good evidence, with guilty individuals escaping, raising very important questions on how to balance protecting rights and efficient law enforcement. The exclusionary rule has profound extensions that stretch beyond the courtroom to touch law enforcement practices, judicial processes, and the general perception of justice. Law enforcement officers may use more stringent methods of collecting evidence in order to avoid the risks of exclusion, leading to an advancement in training and practices. This improvement can produce a culture of accountability, with officers more conscious of constitutional boundaries while conducting investigations. However, this adjustment can also cause increased tensions between the police and society if methods that are seen as overly restrictive result in decreased effectiveness in preventing crime. In addition, the possibility of vital evidence being excluded from court because of procedural errors can create frustration on the part of law enforcers and victims as well, making it more difficult to obtain justice in an already complex legal system. The literature on the exclusionary rule is often intersected with broader evidentiary admissibility issues, for instance, the intricate relationship between character evidence and constitutional protection. For instance, while traditionally character evidence has been subject to strict rules of admissibility, recent trends indicate the erosion of these rules over time as an aspect of general shifts in the attitude of society towards the standards of evidence. Supporters of reconsidering the balance of rules of evidence believe that a more utilitarian approach, similar to what has been proposed under European law, can give indications for optimizing the best evidence principle and maintaining essential rights. This constructive dialogue highlights a central conflict: the requirement to maintain judicial integrity within the exclusionary rule within a highly evolved legal context that necessitates effective enforcement as well as fastidious compliance with constitutional standards (Leonard et al., 1995; Redmayne et al., 2010).

8.5.3. Exceptions to the Exclusionary Rule

Exclusionary rule is one of the fundamental principles in American criminal procedure aimed at safeguarding defendants against unconstitutionally gathered evidence. There are, nonetheless, certain exceptions that allow otherwise inadmissible evidence to be admitted under this rule. Prominent among such exceptions, however, is the good faith doctrine, whereby evidence procured pursuant to a subsequently determined invalid warrant if law enforcement officials reasonably believed their conduct to be lawful. This exception attempts to reconcile the need for a fair trial with the necessity of enforcing the law, as not all police error will necessarily be corrupt or intended. The inclusion of such exceptions underscores a paradox of criminal procedure: safeguarding personal rights in tandem with preventing effective law enforcement, thus shaping the evidence admissibility environment of courts. The inevitable discovery rule is another significant exception to the exclusionary rule, stipulating that illegally acquired evidence must be admitted if it would inevitably have been found through legal avenues in the future. This doctrine operates based on the premise that evidence would have eventually been found by law enforcement agents had there not been any unusual behavior. When giving such evidence, the courts aim to prevent exclusion of probative and relevant information that otherwise would have hugely impacted the final judgment in the case. This exception is a constant judicial concern for the integrity of the criminal justice system as a whole, and it reflects a concern for balancing the protection of citizens' rights with a need to see that truth and justice are served. The evolving nature of these exceptions constitutes a constant discussion about the application of legality and ethics in evidence collection and admission. In addition, the incident of criminal procedure is also constantly revised by shifting statutes and judicial precedents that may further broaden or limit such exceptions. For instance, amendments of rules of evidence can reflect the culture's perceptions of a specific category of offenses, for instance, offenses of sexual abuse where liberal interpretations of the rule of admissibility of evidence are allowed in courts to address contestants' patterns of conduct in a string of cases. These adjustments reflect a response to the evolving legal standards and necessity for public safety in light of moving societal values. In the context of international legal systems, these variations in the handling of character evidence show the nuances of admissibility as evidence. Effective reforms should seek a more rational path, such as the recent controversies over how jurisdictions may learn from one another in a quest to attain a balance that serves justice efficiently but still honors individual rights, particularly in sensitive issues of child abuse and trauma (Gerry et al., 2013; Leonard et al., 1995) (Figure 8.14).

Figure 8.14. The exclusionary rule serves as a fundamental principle in American criminal procedure.

Source: https://i.ytimg.com/vi/Q3GVRMlqZNw/maxresdefault.jpg.

8.6. THE ROLE OF JUDGES AND JURIES

Judges and jurors have pivotal roles in the dispensation of criminal justice within the judicial process. Judges are interpreters of the law, as they interpret the statutes and ensure that due process is provided to all parties during trials. One of their roles involves ruling on admissibility of evidence, which has a significant impact on the determination of a case. In this, judges evaluate every type of evidence, including physical, testimonial, and electronic evidence, in terms of their relevance and reliability. This evaluation process is crucial as inadmissible evidence can corrupt the integrity of the judicial process and cause miscarriages of justice. By having standards for admissibility, judges not only protect the rights of the defendants but also ensure public confidence in the justice system. Consequently, the role of the judges is central in the formation of an even trial environment where evidence can be examined properly. Unlike the role of the judges, juries are ordinary citizens who express the conscience of society. Their one function is to assess the given evidence in trial and render a verdict based on facts discovered. Whereas judges do not weigh the credibility and persuasiveness of evidence but rather interpret the law, juries give consideration to just these aspects. This serves to highlight the crucial function of juries in their function as embodiments of society's norms and values, especially in weighing diverse types of evidence such as eyewitness testimony and expert opinions. Juries are required to measure evidence reliability against their own life experiences and community perspectives. Their rulings are important in restoring a level of justice to victims and defendants alike by highlighting the necessity of public engagement with the criminal justice system and ensuring that the rulings align with the norms of society. The dynamic between judges and juries is vital to preserving the procedural purity of trials. Judges not only guide juries in matters of law, but they ensure that jury instructions set forth the procedures for determining evidence. These advisories have the potential to shape the understanding of a jury about admissibility's nuances, particularly in the context of high-tech forms of evidence, such as electronic data in modern cases. The dangers are self-evident here, since emerging technology gives birth to new means of evidence, not least those deriving from the Internet of Things (Stoyanova et al., 2020). Besides, when cultural dynamics control a defendants actions, the jury must consider these nuances without an official cultural defense (Volpp, 2017). Judges and juries collectively navigate the complexities of evidence, trying to balance legal mandates with the very demands of justice, thus embodying the collaborative nature of the justice system.

8.6.1. Judges' Responsibilities in Determining Admissibility

The role of judges with regard to admitting the evidence is the central element of ensuring a fair trial in the criminal justice system. Judges have to determine whether the evidence meets established legal standards before its use in court. This duty emanates from principles such as the Federal Rule of Evidence 702, which stipulates that expert testimony shall be based on trustworthy principles and methods, and shall be reliably applied to the facts of the case. The dilemma comes from the subjective character of reliability, where judges have to harmonize their discretion with judicial precedents. In recent years, the immediate emergence of instances of substandard forensic practices has placed in the limelight the necessity for cautious judicial scrutiny to prevent wrongful convictions, putting the judges' gatekeeping function to evidence in pursuit of justice into sharp relief. The importance of the decision-making process of the judges is also highlighted by the implication that it has for the uprightness of the legal system. As described in the context of expert evidence admissibility, judges are seen not to always enforce the stricter standards contemplated by Rule 702, with a result being the admission of unreliable evidence. This leniency is criticized to be able to lead to miscarriages of justice on a very large scale, in which innocent persons are convicted on the basis of erroneous forensic information. Judges have to, therefore, strike the balance of impartial arbiters on the one hand and uphold evidentiary standards for the integrity of judicial process. They have immense pressure both from defense as well as prosecution but need to make sure that they give the topmost priority to a rigorous examination of evidence so that public trust in the system is maintained. Comparatively, examining what other legal systems' judges do can educate American judges a lot about what their own responsibilities are. The Swiss legal system, for example, has an inquisitorial model that differs significantly from the adversarial approach utilized in the United States. Here, judges play a greater role in scrutinizing evidence and questioning witnesses, potentially bringing stricter scrutiny of admissibility prior to trial. This is directly opposed to the American system, where judges are apt to render decisions on admissibility following consideration by adversary parties of arguments. Variations such as these are interesting to arguments ongoing regarding whether or not the American system is successful in ensuring the reliability of evidence, and thus demands new measures. Lastly, as emphasized by comparative research, judges' roles in admissibility of evidence decisions play an important role to further ensure criminal proceedings' integrity in any legal system, including those characterized by adversarial values, such as the United States (Thompson et al., 2016) (Figure 8.15).

Figure 8.15. Judges' responsibilities in determining admissibility.

Source: https://slideplayer.com/slide/17434897/101/images/2/Responsibilities+of+the+Judge.jpg.

8.6.2. Juries' Role in Evaluating Evidence

The duty of juries to evaluate evidence is given the utmost importance in the criminal justice system. The task of interpretation and evaluation of the evidentiary worthiness and credibility of the submitted evidence before the court falls on the shoulders of juries. This task is particularly important while deciding on expert evidence, involving complex scientific analysis, and that can act as a determinant factor in the resolution of a trial. The essence of a jury's function lies in its ability to exclude such evidence, judging the relevance and coherence of such against precedent set within law. However, their capacity for this function relies effectively upon their understanding of the nature of presented evidence and legal professionals' training in the assessment of such material. House of Commons Science and Technology Committee Report and the Law Commission findings point to the necessity of widespread training concerning expert evidence, which is usually of vital importance in avoiding miscarriages of justice (Davies et al., 2016). Secondly, the grounds used by jurors in evaluating evidence, particularly expert testimony, are not always set out, with the result that consistency is lacking in their process of conclusion. Effective evaluation is based on the assumption that expert evidence has to be at a standard level of reliability if it is to be admissible in court. Such evidence has to meet a standard of potentially safely reliable, especially regarding the totality of the evidence within a case. The implications of this norm reinforce the ability of jurors to believe what they are presented with. Their belief in expert testimony and to what extent they consider it to support the prosecution's case define the ease at which they can give a verdict. As juries navigate the complexities of evidence relationships, a competent expert testimony with sufficient legal instructions is significant to their judgmental assessment (Ward et al., 2020). Lastly, juries must contend with burdens of proof and rational deliberation requirement. In criminal trials, prosecutors are required to prove defendants' guilt beyond a reasonable doubt, a high threshold that requires jurors not just to balance evidence but to consider competing explanations consistent with innocence. The act of making such a choice calls for a subtle interpretation of factual evidence and contextual background by expert witnesses. Misinterpretation or overreliance on expert opinion can lead juries to unsafe conclusions, thus the imperative need for cautious investigation under such circumstances. By correctly identifying the effects of the evidence produced, jurors are in a better position to engage in a more competent process of deliberation that has profound effects on the pursuit of justice within the judicial system. Thus, their evaluative role is not merely procedural but also pivotal to the integrity of criminal justice.

8.6.3. The Impact of Judicial Decisions on Jury Perceptions

Judicial decisions impact jury perception substantially, particularly with regard to admitting and interpreting evidence presented at trial. In making decisions on what evidence can be introduced, judges not only regulate the flow of information, but also have an impact on jurors' perception of the case. It is particularly robust in the case of vulnerable witnesses, such as children, where judicial practice centers on protecting them from potential trauma. For example, judges are likely to employ specific guidelines in an effort to minimize the psychological impact on child witnesses, knowing that their testimony can be instrumental but possibly traumatising. The subsequent judicial decisions, intended to secure witnesses, unwittingly shape the jury's own notions of credibility and reliability, addressing the intersection of legal safeguards and juror constructions in the courtroom context (Björk et al., 2002). In addition, the specificity and detail of judicial guidance have a significant impact on the manner in which jurors process evidence. Jurors have to translate vague legal standards and the tipping point of the evidence, which can be elusive and emotionally draining. Research indicates that detailed instructions regarding victim impact can restrain juror sentiments, particularly in death penalty trials where the stakes are extremely high. For instance, the use of accurate victim impact instructions has been discovered to direct jurors towards more lenient sentences than broader instructions (Berman et al., 2006). This goes to demonstrate that the specificity of judicial language not only enhances juror comprehension but also directly affects their sentencing recommendations, illustrating the extensive influence of judicial decisions on jury verdicts. Finally, the judicial role is more than merely ruling on admissible evidence; it is stewardship of the entire procedural integrity of the trial. Judicial decisions can legitimize the function of the jury's by enhancing their level of participation and quality of their deliberation. Insofar as judges define the boundaries of acceptable evidence with clear and authoritative decisions, they impose the duty of the jurors to judge the presented facts in an impartial manner. On the contrary, ambiguous or perceived-unfair judicial decisions might lead jurors to doubt judicial integrity, and thus by implication the trial's outcome, thus eroding their faith in its result. The intersection between judicial power and jury perception is hence a critical element in the criminal procedure matrix, influencing not just the specific case in hand, but broader public faith in the justice process.

SUMMARY

It is critical to appreciate the wide-ranging implications of evidentiary admissibility on the legal process. The standards for admitting various types of evidence—particularly scientific and forensic evidence—have undergone rigorous scrutiny. Above all, cases like Kumho Tire Co. v. Carmichael demonstrate the necessity for courts to maintain a high standard of scientific validity, in which such evidence should not be admitted merely because it is expert testimony. The built-in impreciseness of existing standards of evidence creates a precarious arena for justice, with the tendency to add spurious but unreliable evidence to cases, potentially undermining the integrity of judicial decisions. Rethinking standards of admissibility is thus necessary to uphold the principles of fairness in the administration of justice. Moreover, PCAST report debate has served to underscore the requirement to establish clearer and more rigorous standards for the generation of scientific evidence. The diversity of technique and knowledge of reliability and validity between disciplines complicates the forensic testifying environment. It is the responsibility of courts to ensure discrimination between anecdotal expert opinion and conclusions based on science to avoid miscarriage of justice. By adopting more stringent requirements, courts can heighten the probative value of evidence adduced at trials, ultimately leading to jurors being more competent and knowledgeable to render judgments which accurately reflect the facts on each case. As noted in argument following the PCAST proposals, an evolved approach to Rule 702 can fortify the very pillars of the judicial system. Lastly, the ultimate goal of raising evidence standards is to fortify the credibility and reliability of the judiciary. Confronting challenges and disparities in the admissibility of forensic evidence is not merely a procedural update; it is proof of devotion to justice and to safeguarding individual rights. The deliberations aroused by the Standing Advisory Committee on Evidence Rules is a progressive initiative toward better court processes and outcomes. It is imperative that the law evolves according to the expanding knowledge of scientific principles and the changing environment of expert witness. In doing so, the court can ensure that the principles of justice are ensured and standards of evidence are reconciling empirical validity with and demands of society in general, as testified by continuing refinement of legal practice and discourse (Kaye et al., 2018; Lander et al., 2018).

In acknowledging the nature of evidence in criminal procedure, it is imperative to clarify its multiple meanings and connotations. Evidence forms the basis of the adjudicative process, providing the information necessary to substantiate legal conclusions. Its relevance and reliability play a critical role in the determination of criminal cases, ensuring that justice is served. Although various types of evidence exist, including testimonial, documentary, and physical evidence, how each of them is evaluated for admissibility is crucial. Evidence rules have pre-established guidelines so that the judicial community can determine what evidence can be presented before the court and under what conditions, ensuring the integrity of the justice system. Additionally, evidence admissibility is guided by several rule-based principles, prominently the rules of relevance and materiality. Not only must evidence be relevant to the case at hand, but it must also be sufficiently strong to affect the decision of the court. Criminal procedure emphasizes highly stringent evidentiary standards as a means of avoiding miscarriages of justice. One such example is expert evidence controversy, whereby various reports have given accounts of how expert evidence is associated with wrongful convictions. Such questions place emphasis on the necessity of better training in legal experts, something which is central to deconstructing complex evidentiary documents, something referred to in the House of Commons Science and Technology Committee Report Expert Evidence on Trial (Davies et al., 2016). Lastly, reforming legislative guidelines that inform the admissibility of evidence still place an impact on its real-world application within courts. Amendments to the Criminal Procedure Rules maintain the focus on improving fairness and accuracy in court proceedings. Discussion of the amendments also focuses on whether they facilitate a cultural shift for legal professionals towards greater understanding and control of different types of evidence. The amendments are the foundation for issues, especially as legal professionals contend with more complicated evidentiary environments in contemporary trials. Thus, with evolving research and practice, ongoing dialogue on the nature of training to address dealing with evidence is required, anticipating future challenges for the criminal justice system (Tigar et al., 1994).

KEY TERMS

- Admissibility
- Character Evidence
- Confession
- Documentary Evidence
- Expert Evidence
- Illegally Obtained Evidence
- Oral Evidence
- Best Evidence Rule
- Circumstantial Evidence
- Direct Evidence
- Dying Declaration
- Hearsay Evidence
- Judicial Evidence
- Presumptions

A LOOK TO THE FUTURE

JUDICIAL EVIDENCE

Judicial evidence in the future will be decidedly influenced by technological advance, shifting legal norms, and mounting pressure for justice and transparency within the justice system. With increasing courts adopting digitization, electronic documents, digital footprints, surveillance data, and artificial intelligence-generated evidence are assuming prominence in courts. This development erodes the traditional notions of authenticity, dependability, and admissibility, and necessitates new legal frameworks and judicial training. Perhaps the most significant change will be the use of blockchain technology to validate the integrity and tractability of evidence documents. Blockchain is able to provide tamper prevention and chain-of-custody assurances that are critical in criminal cases. Likewise, ever-greater reliance on AI and machine learning-based software for forensic analysis and predictive profiling must be tightly regulated to avoid prejudices, offer explainability, and protect constitutional rights. Moreover, expanding utilization of remote testimony, especially post-pandemic, presents the test of challenging problems with regard to credibility assessment and confrontation rights. Virtual reality recreations and 3D modeling of crime scenes can also be admissible as demonstrative evidence, delivering juries immersive and realistic visuals.

The future also requires a re-examination of hearsay exceptions and the handling of digital evidence, particularly in light of the ubiquity of social media, metadata, and cloud storage. Ensuring that these sorts of evidence are of fixed quality without compromising privacy and due process will be a delicate balance. International cooperation will become ever more important as more crimes and evidence flow across international borders, requiring harmonization of evidentiary rules and procedures and mutual legal assistance rules. Judicial evidence is, in fact, moving into a new era—one defined by technological convergence, ethical sensitivity, and reform of procedure. Courts need to be able to respond positively to ensure that the administration of justice is both effective and fair in a digital age.

REFERENCES

1. Aiken, J. H. (2002). Protecting plaintiffs' sexual pasts: Coping with preconceptions through discretion. https://core.ac.uk/download/70373474.pdf (accessed on 13th August 2025).
2. Bazerman, C. (2009). How does science come to speak in the courts? Citations intertexts, expert witnesses, consequential facts, and reasoning. https://core.ac.uk/download/62553212.pdf (accessed on 13th August 2025).
3. Berman, G., & Platania, J. (2006). The moderating effect of judge's instructions on victim impact testimony in capital cases. https://core.ac.uk/download/56704928.pdf (accessed on 13th August 2025).
4. Björk, D., Blomqvist, A., Elander, L., Engblom, H., et al. (2002). Child witness policy: Law interfacing with social science. https://core.ac.uk/download/62568554.pdf (accessed on 13th August 2025).
5. Chandran, A. (2015). The Classified Information Procedures Act in the age of terrorism: Remodeling CIPA in an offense-specific manner. https://core.ac.uk/download/62567389.pdf (accessed on 13th August 2025).
6. Chesterman, M., Cunneen, C., Duff, R., Findlay, M., et al. (2008). Juror comprehension and the hard case–Making forensic evidence simpler. https://core.ac.uk/download/50973.pdf (accessed on 13th August 2025).
7. Davies, G., & Piasecki, E. (2016). No more laissez faire? Expert evidence, rule changes and reliability: Can more effectively training for the Bar and judiciary prevent miscarriages of justice? https://core.ac.uk/download/74228540.pdf (accessed on 13th August 2025).
8. Douglass, J. G. (2000). Balancing hearsay and criminal discovery. https://core.ac.uk/download/144223519.pdf (accessed on 13th August 2025).
9. Fabricant, M. C., & Garrett, B. L. (2018). The myth of the reliability test. https://core.ac.uk/download/213020569.pdf (accessed on 13th August 2025).
10. Forster, P. H. (2005). An argument for the admissibility of execution impact evidence in Pennsylvania. https://core.ac.uk/download/12214738.pdf (accessed on 13th August 2025).
11. Garrett, B. L., & Mitchell, G. (2013). How jurors evaluate fingerprint evidence: The relative importance of match language, method information, and error acknowledgment. https://core.ac.uk/download/213020463.pdf (accessed on 13th August 2025).
12. Gerry, F., Sjölin, C., & Urbas, G. (2013). Patterns of sexual behavior: The law of evidence: Back to the future in Australia and England. https://core.ac.uk/download/30650425.pdf (accessed on 13th August 2025).
13. Gershman, B. L. (1998). Lie detection: The Supreme Court's polygraph decision. https://core.ac.uk/download/46714156.pdf (accessed on 13th August 2025).
14. Griffin, L. K. (2013). Narrative, truth, and trial. https://core.ac.uk/download/62565963.pdf (accessed on 13th August 2025).
15. Grimm, P. W. (2018). Challenges facing judges regarding expert evidence in criminal cases. https://core.ac.uk/download/216957556.pdf (accessed on 13th August 2025).

16. Kaye, D. H. (2018). How *Daubert* and its progeny have failed criminalistics evidence and a few things the judiciary could do about it. https://core.ac.uk/download/216957558.pdf (accessed on 13th August 2025).

17. Lander, E. S. (2018). Fixing Rule 702: The PCAST report and steps to ensure the reliability of forensic feature-comparison methods in the criminal courts. https://core.ac.uk/download/216957559.pdf (accessed on 13th August 2025).

18. Leonard, D. P. (1995). Federal rules of evidence and the political process. https://core.ac.uk/download/144228540.pdf (accessed on 13th August 2025).

19. Posner, R. A. (2016). On hearsay. https://core.ac.uk/download/144231424.pdf (accessed on 13th August 2025).

20. Redmayne, M. (2010). Confronting confrontation. https://core.ac.uk/download/17328.pdf (accessed on 13th August 2025).

21. Rothstein, P. F. (2015). Unwrapping the box the Supreme Court justices have gotten themselves into: Internal confrontations over confronting the Confrontation Clause. https://core.ac.uk/download/70375288.pdf (accessed on 13th August 2025).

22. Stoyanova, M., Nikoloudakis, Y., Panagiotakis, S., Pallis, E., & Markakis, E. (2020). A survey on the Internet of Things (IoT) forensics: Challenges, approaches, and open issues. *IEEE Communications Surveys & Tutorials, 22*, 1191–1221. https://doi.org/10.1109/comst.2019.2962586 (accessed on 13th August 2025).

23. Thompson, W. C., & Vuille, J. (2016). An American advantage? How American and Swiss criminal defense attorneys evaluate forensic DNA evidence. https://core.ac.uk/download/287622730.pdf (accessed on 13th August 2025).

24. Tigar, M. E. (1994). Pretrial case management under the amended rules: Too many words for a good idea. https://core.ac.uk/download/62565119.pdf (accessed on 13th August 2025).

25. Volpp, L. (2017). (Mis)identifying culture: Asian women and the "cultural defense." In *Routledge eBooks*. https://doi.org/10.4324/9781351157728-18 (accessed on 13th August 2025).

26. Ward, T. (2020). Explaining and trusting expert evidence: What is a 'sufficiently reliable scientific basis'? https://core.ac.uk/download/305121486.pdf (accessed on 13th August 2025).

Chapter

9

EXAMINATION OF WITNESSES IN CRIMINAL PROCEDURE

Contents

Introduction....281
9.1. Types of Witnesses....285
9.2. The Role of Witnesses in Criminal Trials....289
9.3. Pre-Trial Procedures....293
9.4. Examination Techniques....297
9.5. Challenges in Witness Examination....301
9.6. Legal Standards and Guidelines....304
Summary....308
References....311

INTRODUCTION

Witness questioning in criminal process is a pinnacle of the pursuit for justice, summarizing the ideals of truth-discovery and procedural justice. Witnesses are the linchpin to uncovering the subtleties of a case, providing firsthand accounts that can singly sway juries and judges. Consequently, understanding the mechanics and methods of questioning witnesses is of utmost concern. Legal systems struggle to balance the rights of the accused against the necessity to verify factual reality through testimony of witnesses. Each jurisdiction develops its own unique model of witness examination based on its own legal traditions and culture. Comparative analysis of witness examination technique, therefore, can provide telling insights into the values and structures of different legal systems. Investigating the nuance of witness questioning entails an awareness of varying categories of witnesses and their role in criminal proceedings. Eyewitnesses, character witnesses, and expert witnesses all contribute distinct perspectives that may or may not hold water for a case. Of particular interest is managing expert witnesses to illustrate various strategies legal systems have employed. For instance, the adversarial model of trials is greatly relied upon by the American legal system, with both parties seeking to try and verify expert witness evidence.

This can be seen in comparative analyses such as those demonstrated by Kötz et al. (2009), in which the tension between advocacy and impartiality in judicial processes is highlighted. As the examination of witnesses continues, it is apparent that the practices employed are not only indicative of procedural norms but also reflect the inherent social values contained within the administration of justice. Furthermore, the examination of witnesses is also infused with credibility and reliability concerns, which challenge legal practitioners to navigate the complexities of human testimony. Memory, perception, and prejudice are just some of the things that can significantly influence a witnesses testimony and hence raise fundamental questions regarding the fairness of the trial process. Lawyers and academics are left to wonder how to obtain the witness testimony as believable and as relevant as possible. The application of procedural safeguards such as pre-trial hearings and cross-examinations is one attempt at balancing potential prejudices and enhancing judicial process integrity. Each action taken in the examination of witnesses is all part of the general pursuit of justice, underscoring the need for sensitive consideration in every step of the witness examination process, as with the overall discourses of this topic in criminal procedure.

Definition of Witness Examination

Witness examination is the characteristic idea to the functioning of criminal procedure as an intensive process where witnesses are interrogated to gather fact evidence in relation to the case. It is a systematic conversation that occurs in court and typically comprises two distinct phases: direct examination and cross-examination. During cross-examination, the witness is questioned by the attorney who called the witness in order to obtain useful evidence, allowing the witness to describe what happened and what they saw regarding the case. This is a critical phase since it impacts the judge and jury and reveals the story built around the evidence. Conversely, cross-examination serves as a check on this process, allowing opposing counsel to challenge the credibility of the witness and the credibility of their evidence, hence being a fundamental element of the adversarial system of justice. Witness examination is more than superficially complex in terms of extracting information; it entails planned questioning with the aim of discovering inconsistencies and bias. Effective cross-examination is thus a work of art, and attorneys have to be well-prepared to capitalize on any contradictions in a witness testimony. Notably, the process of examination itself has also to be sensitive to the witness's background, e.g., age and psychological condition. As a case in point, where child witnesses are used, the judicial system has to adjust its process to be aware of their emerging abilities. This is in support of the request for children to be considered as individuals with rights, as they are considered to have levels of understanding and reasoning (Tomey-Alleyne et al., 2015). As such, the process of examination applies sensitive consideration of a number of factors that can influence the credibility of a witness's evidence. Besides this, witness examination is accompanied by legal protections, particularly regarding witnesses immunity under criminal law. The present controversy on the extent of witness immunity under section 1983 mirrors the delicate balance between safeguarding witness testimony and encouraging accountability for unlawful conduct on the part of law enforcement. The evolution of history of the Supreme Courts stance on the issue attests to the necessity of safeguarding witnesses against retaliatory litigation, especially when they risk inculpating governmental misdoing (Kaufman et al., 1987). Lastly, witness examination is a living combination of legal skill, ethical issues, and system measures, all of which must be maintained to uphold the integrity of criminal trials (Figure 9.1).

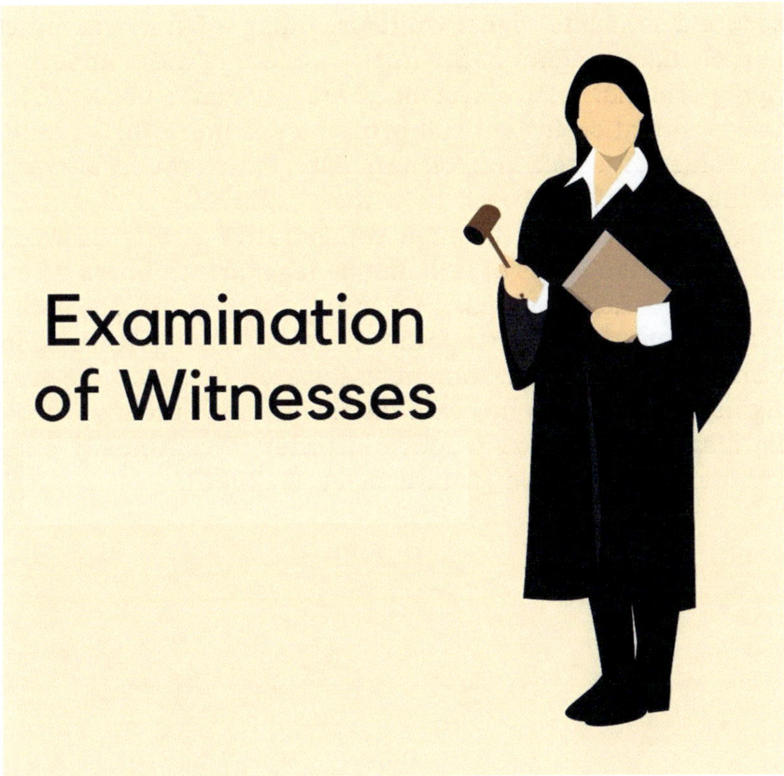

Figure 9.1. The witness examination.

Source: https://i1.wp.com/bnwjournal.com/wp-content/uploads/2020/05/Examination-of-Witnesses.jpg?fit=1024%2C1024&ssl=1.

Importance in Criminal Procedure

The role of witnesses in criminal process cannot be overstated, as their evidence constitutes integral elements that determine trial outcomes. Witness examination is the foundation of evidence brought into the courtroom, allowing juries and judges to decide whether what has occurred is or isn't true. In an optimal adversarial system, witnesses give testimony based on first-hand experience that provides the case story. However, witness testimony is always tested for credibility, and much inquiry into how examination techniques have the capacity to influence the truth and utility of such testimony follows. Notably, procedural reforms to enhance the integrity of witness examination can help towards a more just legal system, as can be seen in emerging practices within various jurisdictions, including those reported by the China Trial Advocacy Institute, focused on imparting legal professionals with needed competencies (Lancaster et al., 2006). Furthermore, the examination of vulnerable witnesses, such as children and intellectually disabled individuals, is particularly problematic in criminal proceedings. The traditional adversarial approach, particularly cross-examination, has the potential to enhance the trauma and fear of such witnesses. Empirical evidence indicates that direct cross-examination can provide suspect information and lead to miscarriages of justice. Consequently, the need for reform has become increasingly prominent. For instance, proposals to end direct cross-examination and utilize video-recorded sessions by neutral third parties have emerged as viable options. Such reform would not only protect vulnerable witnesses but also secure defendants' rights while providing a fairer trial process for everyone. A balance between the defendant's rights and witness welfare is most important and may require re-evaluating underlying criminal justice system practices (Plater et al., 2014). In this case, the importance of witness examination in criminal procedure is more than simply finding facts; it is an embodiment of the values of justice and fairness upon which the legal system is founded. With the changing face of the law, the approach to witness interactions also has to change. Greater interdisciplinary thought, as developed through collaborative efforts between legal institutions, can significantly contribute to the levels of skill among legal practitioners who are tasked with the examination of witnesses. By placing emphasis on training that addresses both the confrontational nature of trials and the requirement of empathetic and effective witness engagement, the legal system is poised to ensure that an environment is fostered in which the truth prevails without compromising the dignity of all parties involved. As this is done, the legal profession is motivated to draw lessons from local and overseas practice in order to continually enhance procedures in the management of witness examination (Lancaster et al., 2006).

9.1. TYPES OF WITNESSES

Criminal procedure witness examination is sophisticated, mirroring the different roles that various modes of witnesses have to play in the justice process. Of primary concern among these is the eyewitness category, the individuals who observed a crime and can provide helpful information regarding what occurred. Eyewitness testimony is often decisive, as it may establish important facts and corroborate other testimony presented at a trial. But it is also susceptible to error on the basis of sources like stress, leading questions, or forgetting over time. Such vulnerabilities require careful scrutiny of eyewitness accounts, prompting the justice system to look for means of rendering them secure, particularly in cases of capital punishment where recollections are personal. Also, expert witnesses form another significant group of witnesses, offering special knowledge that could explain complex aspects of a case.

Figure 9.2. The examination of witnesses in criminal procedure.

Source: https://eitherview.com/wp-content/uploads/2022/04/witness.jpg.

They tend to be specialists in fields such as forensic science, psychology, or medicine and can assist the court to understand technical information that would be beyond the reach of a regular juror. Their testimony can shed light on the conditions under which a crime was committed, for example, the cause of damage or the state of mind of the defendant when he or she committed the crime. Proper utilization of expert evidence can significantly influence a jury's verdict, but it also generates issues about the qualifications and prejudices of such witnesses. Consequently, the courts must examine expert witnesses rigorously, ensuring that their evidence is scientifically acceptable and relevant to the case at hand. Within the broader framework of witness cross-examination, character witnesses are a unique and occasionally deciding type of evidence in criminal proceedings. Character witnesses do not provide direct evidence of the crime but rather provide evidence regarding the defendant's character, reputation, or history. Most commonly used in sentencing proceedings, their evidence can significantly influence the attitudes of a judges or jury's, possibly minimizing sanctions by revealing insights into the defendants lives that may evoke sympathy or empathy. The use of character witnesses can, though, introduce subjectivity into the proceedings, and considerations based upon considerations of the fairness and efficiency of invoking personal opinion in an objective legal system are thus complicated. In addition, the setting in which character evidence is presented needs to be treated cautiously so as not to cause undue prejudice, and hence the role played by these witnesses becomes both essential and challenging in obtaining justice (Figure 9.2).

9.1.1. Eyewitnesses

Eyewitness testimony becomes a focal part in the context of criminal procedure, summarizing the intricacies and complexities of the justice system. The eyewitness has long held a sacred position within the criminal justice system on the basis that contemporaneous memories will be the lifeblood of key evidence for criminal offenses. But empirical research verifies that eyewitness testimony is stunningly unreliable. Stress levels, levels of illumination, and weapons' visibility can all significantly hinder an eyewitness's detail memory. Furthermore, the suggestibility of questioning and line-up procedures contributes to the reliability problem of eyewitness identifications. This raises a paramount issue regarding wrongful convictions based on unreliable eyewitness evidence, thus making them a center of focus in the criminal justice debate. Solutions that work to mitigate the harmful consequences of eyewitness misidentifications need a multi-faceted approach involving all actors in the criminal justice process. Judges are also significant in the role of issuing juries with certain instructions regarding the limitations and potential fallibilities of eyewitness testimony. Such actions are necessary for verifying that jurors consider the validity of eyewitness evidence with care before rendering a verdict. Prosecutors are also obligated to perform impartial investigations of the credibility of eyewitnesses, with regard to the significance of ethical principles in seeking truth. By scrutinizing the credentials of eyewitnesses and withholding likely-to-lead-to-miscarriage-of-justice testimonies, the prosecution process can be greatly enhanced. This systemic improvement highlights an increased awareness at the system level of the risk of eyewitness testimony and the protection of the accused's rights. This recent trend in procedural safeguards for eyewitness identification evidence is also indicative of the continued evolution of criminal procedure. Methods such as double-blind line-ups and standardized interviewing protocols have been created in the light of irrefutable evidence exposing the flaws of standard identification procedures. Minimizing suggestibility, these processes aim to enhance the validity of eyewitness identification, thereby enhancing the integrity of the judicial process. Commentary on law has also underscored the importance of expert witness on the cognitive and psychological underpinnings of memory recall within the courtroom. This method guarantees a knowledgeable jury that is able to assess the reliability of eyewitness evidence in the context of current research-based evidence. As these procedural reforms become more widely implemented, they are a dynamic response to the decades of witness centrality that have been found to have played a significant role in generating a high proportion of wrongful convictions. The integration of legal practice and scientific understanding of memory is essential in overcoming the complexities of issues related to eyewitness testimony (Gershman et al., 2009; Roberts et al., 2025) (Figure 9.3).

Figure 9.3. Eyewitness testimony remains a pivotal element in the context of criminal procedure.

Source: https://www.newjerseycriminallawattorney.com/wp-content/uploads/2023/06/JFM_600x314_EyeWitness.jpg.

9.1.2. Expert Witnesses

Expert witnesses in criminal process play a critical role in interpreting advanced technical or scientific issues that lie outside the comprehension of the average juror. Experts provide technical professionalism that assists the court in making decisions based on well-informed decisions, particularly where forensic science, psychology, or engineering cases are in question. However, the efficacy of expert testimony relies significantly on the qualification and training of the witness. Misuse and misinterpretation of expert evidence by experts themselves can lead to significant legal errors, which can result in miscarriages of justice. This was particularly reinforced by the House of Commons Science and Technology Committee Report, which placed emphasis on the need for enhanced training of the legal community in the assessment of expert evidence (Davies et al., 2016). When experts fail to communicate their findings effectively and accurately, they can risk misleading the jury and undermining the integrity of the legal process. Education and certification standards for expert witnesses are essential in providing assurance that their testimony is maintained at the level of reliability and validity necessary in legal proceedings. Law Commissions 2011 Report recognized the importance of providing standardized guidelines for expert evidence, noting that the majority of legal practitioners may not possess the necessary knowledge of scientific principles necessary to adequately evaluate an expert's contribution. The amendments to Part 19 of the Criminal Procedure Rules and Part 19A of the Criminal Practice Direction serve to acknowledge some recognition of this issue; however, there remains an urgent need for formal training programs within legal education (Davies et al., 2016). The implications of failing to thoroughly screen expert witnesses may not only have individual cases fall short of justice, but may also present more significant systemic problems to public confidence in the judicial system.

Beyond the challenges posed by qualifications of expert witnesses, the different legal traditions of jurisdictions also influence the role and treatment of expert testimony. For example, the American legal system's reliance on juries to determine facts affects the way expert evidence is presented and utilized in the process of court trials. As noted by Professor Kötz, this reliance may give rise to special procedures in connection with presenting such testimony, affecting various aspects of the trial, including discovery and judges' roles. By contrast, other jurisdictions may be more inquisitorial, with judges taking an active role, questioning experts more directly. Such comparative perspectives direct attention toward the complex interplay between legal systems and the use of expert evidence, underlining the necessity for a comprehensive appreciation of the procedural context against which such witnesses operate within criminal trials.

9.1.3. Character Witnesses

The character witness role in criminal cases lies at the heart of establishing the defendants moral character, trust, and overall credibility. The witnesses whose testimony pertains to a defendants behavior and characteristics directly influence the jury's impression of the defendant on trial. While their testimony itself is not direct evidence of guilt or innocence, it does carry important context, shading jurors' emotions toward defendants by showing them a portrait of character. However, jurors' biases and assumptions can invalidate the validity of character witnesses. Consequently, the credibility of such a witness raises questions about the impartiality of the judicial process and the standards of admissibility governing character evidence in court. The presence of character witnesses in court also goes to reinforce the controversy surrounding the victims role and its greater implications for the justice system. There has been a significant change in recent years regarding how the presence of victims in criminal trials is perceived, as highlighted in recent discussions regarding their attendance in hearings. This change in perspective prioritizes thinking of trials not only as adversarial confrontations between prosecution and defense but as comprehensive narratives. By allowing character witnesses to individuate defendants and, by analogy, validate victims' accounts, the judicial process can be rendered more representative and inclusive. This approach resists the traditional boundaries that, as discussed in present debates on victims' involvement (Doak et al., 2005), isolate public and private interests in criminal justice. In addition, credibility and training of persons providing testimony as character witnesses cannot be ignored. A growing body of evidence focuses on the need for rigorous training in areas such as expert testimony and reliability of witnesses, arguing that it is imperative to minimize opportunities for miscarriages of justice (Davies et al., 2016). Given that character witnesses are often not formally qualified, it is the duty of the law to give lucid guidelines around their qualification and the nature of testimonies. Enhancement in training and awareness not only enhances character witnesses' roles but also the integrity of the criminal process in general. Through adherence to such enhancements, the criminal process can deliver more reliable verdicts, thereby sustaining public trust in its work (Figure 9.4).

Figure 9.4. The role of character witnesses in criminal proceedings.

Source: https://www.lisastrausslaw.com/wp-content/uploads/2024/11/Importance-of-Character-Witnesses-in-Criminal-Cases-1024x683.jpg.webp.

9.2. THE ROLE OF WITNESSES IN CRIMINAL TRIALS

Witnesses are a critical focus in criminal trials, supplying the prevailing means of information guiding judicial decisions. Their testimony can affirmatively or negatively substantiate or deny allegations against accused defendants by elucidating the fact pattern of a crime. Historically, there have been two broad categories of witnesses: fact witnesses, who give first-hand descriptions, and expert witnesses, who give specialized information relevant to a case. The credibility of the witnesses plays a huge role in the jury's perception and ultimately, the verdict of the trial. The use of victim testimony has evolved in recent years; whereas the victims were previously relegated to being bystanders within the courtroom, their testimonies are now being recognized more and more as something that is needed for a restorative justice agenda. This movement focuses on the importance of making victims' voices heard during the criminal trial process against the notion of criminal disputes belonging only in the public arena (Doak et al., 2005). The witness cross-examination process is nevertheless fraught with intricacies, particularly regarding handling vulnerable witnesses, such as children or the disabled. The initial remedy within the adversarial system has typically been in the form of cross-examination, intended to question a witness's evidence. Unfortunately, this may result in traumatic experiences for vulnerable witnesses, which can distort their evidence and revive the trauma surrounding their experiences. As evident in critiques of existing frameworks, direct cross-examination can potentially indirectly grant an illegitimate benefit to the defendant by intimidating witnesses (Plater et al., 2014). This is a testament to the systemic deficits of the trial structure, where debate has continued over how reforms are to improve the protection of vulnerable witnesses while maintaining fairness in the trial for both sides. The emerging witness function discourse gives highest priority to a potential shift towards non-confrontational and more inclusive examination practices. Reforms such as third-party facilitation and pre-recorded evidence are under the limelight as these may diminish the adversarial pressures placed on witnesses while providing consistent and reliable evidence. These reforms acknowledge the emotional and psychological strain that confrontations in the courtroom can place on witnesses. Empirical evidence from courts that have adopted parallel practices show a twofold benefit: witnesses suffer less trauma, while the integrity of their testimonies is maintained. As social attitudes change towards a more humane jurisprudence, systemic reforms should embrace such new ideas so that the marginalized voices, like the victims, receive the due notice in criminal trials (Doak et al., 2005; Plater et al., 2014).

9.2.1. Establishing Facts of the Case

Fact creation in criminal cases is a fundamental part of the investigation of witnesses; it determines the direction of the judicial process and the trial verdict. Fact creation begins with the collection of evidence, which may consist of eyewitness testimonies, expert testimonies, and material facts. All these are essential in creating a comprehensive story of what occurred in relation to the crime. In particular, witness testimonies are critical because they provide first-hand information that can corroborate or contradict established facts. Effective cross-examination allows one to get detailed and accurate information that can clarify ambiguous situations in the case. Hence, the tactic of legal professionals in questioning witnesses can have a significant bearing on facts established and in what manner facts are considered in law. Furthermore, the reliability and credibility of witnesses are established by testing them during the questioning process to ensure that facts established have a solid basis. The witness's closeness to events, objectivity, and clarity of recollection may make his/her evidence of such great significance to the weight that is assigned to it. This analysis is even more relevant in forensic evidence matters, such as exhumations of mass graves, where expert testimony declarations can provide facts that could shift the course of the cases. Whence there is a requirement for cautious handling of the intersection of forensic science and witness testifying to determine the validity of both. For instance, the International Criminal Tribunal for the former Yugoslavia has placed particular importance on forensic evidence in trials, as in the Krstic trial. Such cases highlight how forensic knowledge can affect the interpretation of the facts of grave crimes, including war crimes and genocide (Klinkner et al., 2008). Finally, there is a serious cross-examination of witnesses that must be conducted in the resolution of methodological issues and constructing the evidentiary context of the case. The judicial process does not usually give clear-cut guidelines on the application of expert testimony, which calls for a tailored approach in trials. Cross-examination is employed to challenge the veracity and relevance of expert opinion so that it is made subject to judicial scrutiny. This problem-solving dialogue is of the essence in an environment of mixed systems where principles of national and international law blend together. Courts must navigate these complexities to determine the credibility of witness evidence and forensic evidence, in order to establish a fact-based platform for judgment. Adopting a pragmatic approach that applies cross-examination and counter-expertise, trial chambers can significantly enhance the process of fact-finding, leading to more informed and unbiased verdicts in criminal proceedings (Klinkner et al., 2009) (Figure 9.5).

Figure 9.5. Establishing facts in criminal cases.

Source: https://www.legalbites.in/wp-content/uploads/2018/10/Facts-Which-Need-Not-Be-Proved.jpg.

9.2.2. Influencing Jury Perception

Shaping jurors' perception is a critical component of the criminal trial process, significantly affecting the outcome of cases. Jurors bring their own bag of biases and assumptions into the courtroom, which are likely to be shaped by the appearance of witnesses and the manner in which they are questioned. A witness's credibility will usually rest on demeanor, consistency of testimony, and how they respond to lawyers. Effective witness interrogation strategies, therefore, seek not only to generate factual clarity but also to impact the jurors' affective and cognitive response, creating trust and credibility in the induced testimony. Lawyers must therefore exercise care when asking questions and within which setting, since witnesses tend to read behavior through several facets of understanding that emanate from incident occurrences in their lives and social commonplaces. The psychological character of witness testimony cannot be exaggerated in the context of jury perception. For instance, child witnesses present special difficulties, primarily in the sphere of emotional integrity to assuage their fears while in court. The courts wrestle with the dual imperative of formulating a true testimony while protecting such young witnesses from harm through potential trauma, particularly confrontations directly with defendants who in certain instances may have injured them beforehand. As the law that circumscribes child testimony suggests, steps such as provision for alternative forms of testimony, e.g., the use of closed-circuit TV, have been developed to minimize unnecessary distress. These formats not only protect vulnerable witnesses but also have the potential to enhance the credibility of the testimony in the eyes of the jury, to produce a more nuanced understanding of the described events (Björk et al., 2002). Besides, the impact of witness interrogation styles goes beyond mere presentation of facts to affect jury stories that decide case outcomes. A lawyer's ability to tell good stories is often complemented by shrewd witness selection and rigorous questioning. Witnesses are not mere fact transmitters; they carry the emotional gravity of a case. Effective witness interrogations create compelling stories that appeal to jurors both intellectually and emotionally, thereby affecting their perception and verdicts. According to studies on courtroom dynamics, a well-organized witness who can provide their account genuinely is highly capable of shaping juror perceptions. By placing greatest importance on those aspects appealing to jurors and by offering testimonies eliciting sympathy, attorneys are capable of constructing a strong narrative that is concurrent with the higher purposes of justice and truth (Graham et al., 2002).

9.2.3. Providing Credibility to the Prosecution or Defense

Credibility built in court is a prime aspect of the prosecution and defenses efforts at persuading juries about the honesty of testimony. Witness testimony is a major means through which both sides attempt to build their case. Through summoning witnesses who appear credible and professional, both sides can heavily influence jurors' impressions. Furthermore, how witnesses are questioned can give confidence in the words of witnesses. An effective analysis places a witness's credentials and the integrity of what they are saying at center stage, lending weight to what is being said. This credibility is not necessarily an attitude issue with a witness as it is with the legal rules about evidence and confrontation, particularly around hearsay, which has undergone a shifting status across the past decades (Douglass et al., 2000). The right to confront witnesses is enshrined under the Sixth Amendments Confrontation Clause, which provides defendants with the opportunity to challenge witnesses testifying against them regarding their credibility. This efficacy could be undermined as witnesses exhibit memory deficits in their testimonies. This inconsistency could introduce skepticism about their accounts' reliability, thus their credibility provided to both sides of the prosecution and defense. For example, if a witness attempts to recount an event but is experiencing difficulties with recall, it raises severe doubts regarding the authenticity of their statement and defendants ability to effectively confront such a statement. The Supreme Court has not clearly ruled on the effect of memory impairments on defendants confrontation rights, leaving a cloud of doubt regarding the resultant effects on trial results (Coleman et al., 2020). Finally, the intersection of witness credibility and law standards at examination can significantly impact the balance of a trial. As the evidence law evolves and expands, it must adapt to the realities found in the courtroom, particularly when dealing with hearsay and the defendant's right to challenge it. The imbalance between the admissibility of hearsay and limited rights of discovery for defendants calls for reforms that would make the process more equitable. With greater access to information that would allow a defendant to be able to effectively counter hearsay evidence, the judicial system can deliver a better experience of fairness during trials. This would not only guarantee the dignity of confrontation rights but would also reinforce the believability of all the testimonies that would be offered, ultimately to a more level playing field judicial arena for both sides (Douglass et al., 2000) (Figure 9.6).

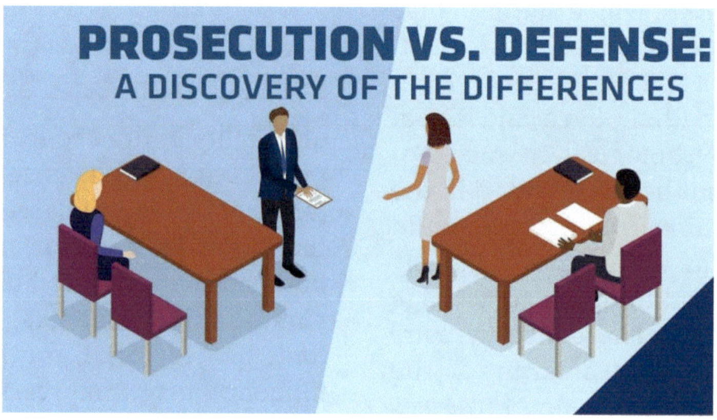

Figure 9.6. Providing credibility to the prosecution or defense.

Source: https://www.rasmussen.edu/images/rasmussenlibraries/admissions/prosecution-vs-defense-(1).jpg.

9.3. PRE-TRIAL PROCEDURES

Pre-trial procedures play a significant role in shaping the direction of a case within criminal proceedings, often impacting cross-examination significantly. Pre-trial procedures identify the foundation of the trial by putting in place relevant evidence, standards of law, and procedural rules via preliminary hearings and motions. Both the defense and prosecution at this stage prepare their lines of action, determine witness credibility, and determine case viability. Preparation is particularly important considering the complexities involved in vulnerable witnesses. As seen, the ability of cross-examining such witnesses cannot only affect the credibility of their testimonies but also the perpetuation of trauma, thus laying stress on how careful attention must be drawn to how witnesses of this nature are treated during pre-trial processes (Doak et al., 2005).

Figure 9.7. The pre-trial procedures.

Source: https://criminal-justice.iresearchnet.com/wp-content/uploads/2023/12/Pre-Trial-Procedures.jpeg.

In addition, pre-trial procedures emphasize the importance of the victims engagement within the criminal justice system. Historically, victims have existed on the periphery, viewed essentially as witnesses whose input is secondary to the underlying legal battle between the prosecution and defense. However, recent movements in legal thought call for a reevaluation of such status, with writers arguing that victims require more participatory rights in all trial procedures. This trend is consistent with broader reformations throughout many jurisdictions as victim-oriented approaches place greater emphasis on the value of their evidence and experiences. These changes reflect an emerging legal culture designed to equilibrate the interests of justice as well as emotional and psychological requirements of victims (Doak et al., 2005). Finally, pre-trial procedures impact the criminal justice system generally. Effective pre-trial arrangements ensure not only a fair trial for defendants but also equal treatment for witnesses and victims. The challenge lies in how to modify existing adversarial systems that can inadvertently damage vulnerable individuals. As argued in some recent arguments, the elimination of face-to-face cross-examination for such witnesses will prevent them from suffering possible trauma and questionable testimony (Plater et al., 2014). Courts can offer more certainty of accurate evidence while still retaining a defendant's right to a fair trial by employing other procedures, such as pre-trial video-recorded statements from experienced professionals. This subtle approach promotes more balanced examination of witnesses, resulting in a fairer legal process as a whole (Figure 9.7).

9.3.1. Witness Interviews

Witness interviews are an important component in criminal procedure that significantly contribute to the quality and reliability of evidence prior to trial. Collecting statements of witnesses is conducted at pre-trial stage, building a narrative which may confirm or deny the testimony of the accused's. Effective interviewing of witnesses involves understanding witnesses psychological and emotional condition because they may be traumatized or under stress, particularly where vulnerable populations such as children or intellectually disabled individuals are concerned. The way interviewers interact with such witnesses can contribute significantly to the accuracy of information gathered. The approaches in the various jurisdictions strive to balance the need for comprehensive information against ethical considerations that emphasize the welfare of witnesses during such critical examination. Considering criminal trial proceedings are adversarial, witness interviewing is particularly challenging, specifically in the matter of ensuring information being given is credible and communicated without compulsion. The intrinsic pressure of direct cross-examination, particularly on vulnerable witnesses, has the potential to lead to the danger of unreliable evidence and further psychological harm. For instance, it has been suggested to abolish direct cross-examination of vulnerable witnesses and instead utilize pre-trial interviews conducted by trained third parties and video-recorded, subsequently being used in court. Such a strategy not only minimizes the psychological distress for witnesses during the trial, it also eliminates any unjust benefit that can be taken by the defense through conventional adversarial means (Plater et al., 2014). The possible advantages of embracing such reformed procedures should be highlighted as central to maintaining the purity of the judicial process. Moreover, giving the victim's voice a platform in criminal justice processes is a departure from typical expectations under common law systems, where their participation has typically been restricted. This departure toward greater participation is reflective of growing recognition of victims as active participants within the criminal justice process, rather than passive spectators whose role is reduced to witness testimony (Doak et al., 2005). By examining the legal and structural barriers which have restricted victims to secondary roles, it is apparent that reform that allows for greater active participation has the potential to develop a more sympathetic and responsive system of law. Allowing the victim to be more directly engaged with their case could strengthen the prosecution's case while having the added benefit of ensuring their experiences and perspectives are adequately represented in the process. Thus, the interaction between witness interviews is a basic step toward making the overall criminal justice system more effective and fair.

9.3.2. Subpoenas and Legal Obligations

Subpoenas in criminal procedure are vital legal instruments that compel witnesses to testify or supply evidence critical for investigation and trial. These records serve as a link between the judicial system and witnesses so that relevant information is presented to facilitate the pursuit of justice. Legal requirements accompanying subpoenas place a burden on parties and organizations to abide by the requests, thus adding to the integrity of the judicial process. Failure to comply with a subpoena can result in harsh legal penalties, including contempt of court, making it clear how important this obligation is. Effective management of the intricacies of subpoena compliance is essential as it demands good understanding of legal rights and responsibilities, not only of witnesses but legal professionals as well who deal with these intricacies in their bids to ensure criminal justice. The service of a subpoena is not without its intricacies, particularly under the strain of legal necessity and individual rights. For instance, common witnesses may have legitimate apprehensions about self-incrimination or breach of confidentiality, thereby rendering their legal necessity complex.

Figure 9.8. Subpoenas and legal obligations.

Source: https://nickheimlichlaw.com/wp-content/uploads/2024/10/Ahandfillingoutasubpoenaformwithape-1024x576.jpeg.

The courts are inclined to arrive on a case-by-case scenario to reconcile the tensions, as evidenced in most decisions weighing the exigency for evidence against potential harm to the witness's rights. On this count, courts can utilize protective measures, thus enabling the witnesses to assert their rights without compromising their responsibilities under law. Since this is a balancing act, it not only guards individual liberties but also the fulfillment of the legal systems to ensure that all available evidence for criminal proceedings is considered, thereby enhancing the pursuit of truth and justice in court (Crabb et al., 1996). The nuances of subpoenas are common to their crossings with inherent legal concepts such as the work-product doctrine, which establishes the boundaries of what can be required in legal cases. This doctrine articulates some protections for documents prepared with anticipation of litigation in mind, thus determining the extent of information accessible under subpoenas. Scholars have been engaged in debating the meaning of this doctrine, referencing its pivotal role in securing the adversarial system of justice (Cohn et al., 1984). As the courts continue to refine the application of the work-product doctrine with subpoena authority, the debate remains consistent with the dynamic nature of legal duties in criminal procedure. Thus, lawyers must be careful in a way that their cooperation with subpoenas does so under existing standards of the law while safeguarding the rights and interests of their clients, thus ensuring the overall integrity of the criminal justice system (Figure 9.8).

9.3.3. Disclosure of Witness Information

Open disclosure of witnesses is a basic aspect of the criminal procedure with close affinity to the rights of the defendants and the integrity of the judicial process. Recent developments in the hearsay rules have underscored the requirement for open witness disclosure so that defendants may adequately prepare for defense. Traditionally, the asymmetry of the adversary system has favored the prosecution, with the advantage of being able to utilize the admissibility of hearsay evidence without any corresponding transparency. As outlined in recent research, asymmetry must be addressed to ensure that defendants are provided with the devices to effectively respond to hearsay accusations leveled against them. Existing criminal discovery rules, particularly in federal trials, are short of addressing the heightened admissibility of hearsay evidence. In order to harmonize discovery practice with these advances, progressive procedural norms are in order, thus promoting fair access to witness testimony at the time of trial (Douglass et al., 2000). The Supreme Court's decisions, most notably in Dennis v. United States, have indicated a trend towards more permissive standards of disclosure, namely for grand jury testimony. The Court had held that defendants might secure access to such critical information on demonstrating a particular need, but left no procedure in place for detailing full criteria for such requests. Consequently, lower courts have interpreted the mandate in different ways, and now there is a fragmented world when it comes to disclosing standards to defendants. Some of the states have embraced permissive disclosure policies, whereas others have retained stricter requirements, creating inconsistencies that make it difficult for defendants to effectively present a case. A shift towards a norm of consistency on the basis of doctrines of constitutional due process would minimize such inequalities and ensure that every defendant, irrespective of jurisdiction, operates under transparent and equitable criteria concerning disclosure of witness information (N/A, 1968).

The enhancement of standards for witness information disclosure would also help to consolidate the fundamental rights of defendants as well as promote an improved judicial process. Implementation of some of the legislative reforms could lend more heft to existing discovery regimes, such as the Brady doctrine and Rule 16, governing access to evidence. More robust versions of such rules would require prosecutors not only to provide exculpatory evidence but also information regarding potential witnesses, including prior statements and testimony. This active disclosure measures would allow defendants to construct well-informed defenses that directly address the prosecution's case, facilitating fairer trials. Lastly, a realignment of the balance between the use of hearsay by the prosecution and the defenses access to witness information would reflect both the evolving world of evidence law and the ageless principles of justice at the heart of criminal procedure (Douglass et al., 2000) (Figure 9.9).

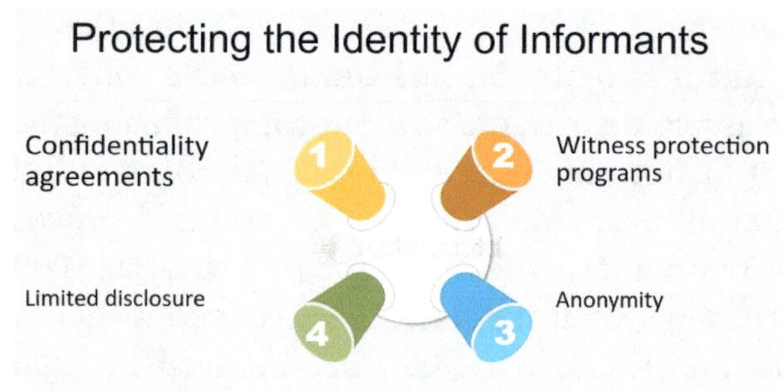

Figure 9.9. The practice of disclosing witness information.

Source: https://fastercapital.co/i/Inside-Information--How-Informants-Aid-in-Breaking-Syndicates--Protecting-the-Identity-of-Informants.webp.

9.4. EXAMINATION TECHNIQUES

Methods of examination of criminal procedure are essential in getting truthful testimonies and ascertaining witnesses' credibility. Organization is essential while carrying out examination-in-chief and cross-examination procedures to ensure that the information gathered is not only relevant but also credible. In examination-in-chief, the primary objective is to enable the witness to present their account in an uncluttered manner so as to minimize opportunities for confusion or misunderstanding. It is a skill that requires professional questioning ability in enabling the witness to recount events without compromising spontaneity and emotional veracity. Lawyers resort to a more combative style under cross-examination with the aim of discrediting the witness's credibility, finding inconsistency, and bringing out biases. This adversarial dynamic emphasizes the necessity for careful preparation and an understanding of psychological principles to skillfully navigate witness testimony subtleties. The evolution of examination techniques has also been influenced by significant advances in the broader context of criminal justice, particularly during the era of the Warren Court. The standards of this period demanded more humane treatment of defendants and witnesses, and the attention was now directed towards the preservation of constitutional rights. Methods of examination thus have to be employed with regard to legal consequences, so that they do not breach the rights of witnesses or lead to coercion. The adoption of these more ethical approaches illustrates the ongoing commitment to upholding the integrity of the judicial process. Through the adoption of these evolving standards, legal practitioners can conduct examinations that maintain fairness as well as try to provide honest and true recollections of witnesses. The meeting of legal and ethical concerns thus creates practice in examination techniques in criminal process. In addition, examination techniques can also be more effectively understood by means of a critical assessment that considers the social settings in which they are being used. The Fairbanks Four case example, highlighted by systematic flaws leading to wrongful convictions, highlights the consequences of bad examination procedures and the necessity for firm questioning strategies (Hill et al., 2014). Unless witnesses are adequately interrogated or their testimony left unexplored, the risk of wrongful convictions is significantly increased. Furthermore, disparities in witness treatment across different classes of individuals contaminate the results of judicial processes, meaning practitioners have to deal with examinations in an integrated manner. In addition, examining these approaches against the background of historical advancements shows how shifting legal requirements call for ongoing modifications in trial procedures. This is in order to ensure the provision for the assurance that the cross-examination of witnesses will fulfill its role constructively in the search for justice in the criminal trial process (Pye et al., 1968).

9.4.1. Direct Examination

Direct examination is a significant feature in the criminal trial process, wherein the prosecution or defense seeks to tell its story through the evidence of witnesses. During this phase, the attorney poses open-ended questions intended to give factual testimonies for the case. The style of direct examination is significant since it constructs the narrative of what happened before and during the crime. Done right, it can best convey the credibility of the witness and the gravity of their testimony. But its value can be lost if the testimony is subsequently subjected to forceful cross-examination, and thus places direct examination firmly in cooperation with effective evidence presentation. Generally speaking, the value of direct examination has a powerful impact on criminal case outcomes by shaping jurors' impressions and understanding of presented evidence. Although direct examination is essential, several problems persist, most significantly in cases against vulnerable witnesses, such as children or persons with disabilities. The adversarial nature of the trial process produces conditions under which such witnesses are unable to present clear and credible evidence, raising doubts about the sufficiency of direct examination in such cases. The procedure has been faulted on the basis that it unwittingly places vulnerable witnesses at a disadvantage as the direct examination does not necessarily shield them from the intimidating environment of the courtroom. The reform debates have signaled towards adjustments that maintain the equilibrium between ensuring fair trial to the defendants and protecting witnesses' rights and welfare. In this framework, the removal of direct cross-examination for vulnerable witnesses has been advocated, instead suggesting other means through which the trauma experienced during trial procedures can be minimized (Plater et al., 2014). Also, the admissibility of learned treatises on direct examination adds another complicating factor to the realm of criminal procedure. The vast majority of American jurisdictions adhere to strict hearsay rules that limit the admission of expert evidence derived from published works, on the basis that the evidence could taint the reliability of the testimony. Alabama and like jurisdictions have been less strict, though, and permitted the learned treatise to be admitted as direct evidence. This reform sheds light on the broader implications of rules of evidence to direct examination, with the suggestion that reconsideration of rules on hearsay will enhance information quality put forward during periods of testimonies. Such enhancement would not only make the evidentiary climate within criminal trials stronger, but also further the objectives of attaining honest and credible outcomes in the justice system (N/A, 1967) (Figure 9.10).

Figure 9.10. Direct examination.

Source: https://blog.ipleaders.in/wp-content/uploads/2019/09/111-1.jpg.

9.4.2. Cross-Examination

Cross-examination is a fundamental aspect of the criminal process that serves a number of very critical functions within the system of justice. Central to the pursuit of truth, cross-examination allows attorneys to challenge witnesses' credibility and the validity of their testimonies. This adversarial process is particularly crucial in criminal cases where the stakes are high and the rights of the defendant must be zealously guarded. By questioning witnesses, attorneys can highlight inconsistencies in their statements, seek clarification on ambiguous points, or introduce alternative narratives that may influence the judge or jury's perception. The effectiveness of cross-examination can impact a case in a significant manner, highlighting its significance as a pillar of equitable trial standards in the justice sector, as outlined in recent legal studies of numerous procedural statutes, such as inferences drawn in the comparison of cross-examination regulations across jurisdictions (Guo et al., 2022). Furthermore, the process of cross-examination is more of a cultural manifestation of the law rather than a strategic practice that signifies the importance of witness credibility in the evidence process. Cross-examination in most jurisdictions, and those modelled after Anglo-American law, is regarded as a key process to ensure testimony before courts can withstand thorough scrutiny. It not only buttresses the validity of the witness's testimony but also generates a sense of responsibility. Indeed, criminal procedure codes, as applied in its uses in Brazil, include cross-examination methodically since legislative reforms; one cannot help but reach this conclusion. The application of these practices across different procedural systems demonstrates an international acknowledgment that a reasonable adversarial procedure is necessary in court, such as through changes in practices around witness examination (Cardoso et al., 2021). Albeit crucial to criminal proceedings, cross-examination has its own challenges and limitations.

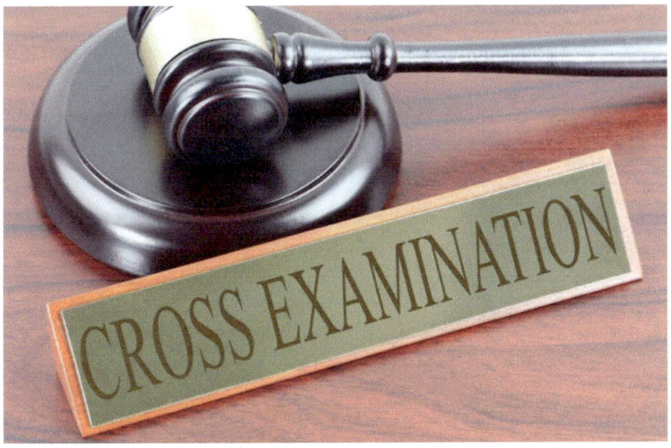

Figure 9.11. Cross-examination.

Source: https://forensicexpertinvestigation.com/wp-content/uploads/2024/04/cross-examination-1024x683.jpg.

The effectiveness of this process can be defined by the competence of the attorney undertaking it, and by legal standards of permissible questioning. In certain jurisdictions, the lack of strict cross-examination standards could lead to prejudiced techniques or vulnerability to witness intimidation and hence compromise the trial process. The evolving nature of legal reform in countries like China makes it a priority to push for more concise guidelines that provide for fair cross-examination practice and protect the rights of witnesses. Through ongoing examination of these aspects by scholars and practitioners, the call for a more standardized procedure for cross-examination is a concern as there are increasingly demands for enhancing legal frameworks governing witness testimony (Guo et al., 2022) (Figure 9.11).

9.4.3. Re-Direct Examination

Re-direct examination is one of the most important procedures involved in a criminal trial. Through re-direct examination, a party is given a chance to explain or expand on testimony volunteered during cross-examination. Following cross-examination, the party that first called a witness has a chance to return to the witness's stand and correct some of the mistakes or wrong impressions that may have been introduced to the jury during the cross-examination. This is important for a balanced presentation of evidence as clarification may dampen the harm done in the form of aggressive cross-examination practices. The ability to perform re-direct examination preserves the integrity of witness testimony, thereby minimizing the possibility of wrong assumptions that might negatively influence the perception of the jury. By adding more clarity to a witness's testimony, re-direct examination helps make the judicial process more just. While presentation techniques in criminal procedure are important for thorough and fair examination, the techniques used by attorneys can be particularly determinative of the outcome of a case during a re-direct examination. The re-direct questions generally aim at issues raised under cross-examination, enabling the lawyer to reaffirm the witness's coherence and credibility. It is especially crucial in cases of vulnerable witnesses, e.g., children or disabled people, where there is a greater risk of misunderstanding. This process attorneys should tread with care lest they introduce new issues or exhibits, because re-direct is only a clarifier of matters addressed during the cross. The need for the variously skilled advocacy during re-direct exhibition emphasizes the interactive relationship between witnessing testimony and legal strategy toward ensuring the fairness and justness of judicial processes for parties on either side of the dispute. It mirrors the general challenges that exist in procedural reforms intended to safeguard witness integrity while respecting defendants' rights. The re-discussion of re-direct examination is also placed in context within the changing criminal procedure environment across the globe. With jurisdictions increasingly considering the efficiency of classic adversarial process, some professionals propose other approaches to witness examination in a bid to mitigate inherent disadvantages involved in direct and cross-examinations in adversarial systems. For example, some reforms in the likes of Australia suggest amendments to restrict cross-examinations' potentially adverse impacts on vulnerable witnesses, offering methods that would ensure fairness while increasing evidentiary reliability. Such changes reflect the continuous challenges observed in locations such as China, wherein legal professionals are shifting their methods towards greater acceptance of the adversarial orientation of contemporary trials (Lancaster et al., 2006). These interactions signal a growing recognition of a need for greater balance between the fair treatment of defendants and the interests of witnesses, ultimately leading to further wider goals of justice in criminal procedure concerning the examination of witnesses.

9.5. CHALLENGES IN WITNESS EXAMINATION

Witness examination during criminal litigation is faced with a broad variety of obstacles that can heavily impact the integrity of the judicial process. Among the most urgent concerns are those that emanate from the confrontational nature of court hearings, where witnesses, especially vulnerable ones, are subjected to increased stress and intimidation under cross-examination. Children and those with intellectual disabilities are particularly at risk, whose testimonies, when put through intense scrutiny, render uncertain proof and introduce further psychological injury. Recent advocacy for reform underscores the importance of protecting these vulnerable witnesses, suggesting that direct cross-examination in its current form may unfairly advantage defendants, thereby compromising the overall fairness of criminal trials (Plater et al., 2014). Such dynamics illuminate the complexities inherent in assessing witness credibility and the need for a more supportive framework within which examinations occur. In addition, the historical position of the victim as only passive actor in criminal cases further complicates witness examination. Traditionally, victims have been given the status of private parties and therefore their involvement has been curtailed and their invaluable contribution to the judicial narrative suppressed. This disconnection creates a gap between victim experiences and justice processes and precipitates alienation and powerlessness. Recent changes in attitudes have led to a re-examination of victims' roles, encouraging greater involvement within trials. Enabling victims to take a direct role in their cases could not only improve the quality of witness evidence but also affirm the public nature of the criminal justice system (Doak et al., 2005). Redressing this imbalance is a challenge to convention but has the potential to enhance overall witness examination effectiveness. The call for reform in witness examination must therefore also consider alternative methodologies to the current adversarial practices. A potential solution involves employing a third-party neutral to conduct witness examinations prior to trial, which could diminish the stress associated with courtroom confrontations and allow for more reliable testimonies. Such a scenario has been applied in countries, for instance, Norway, and has had prospects to reduce the harsh effects of direct cross-examination on vulnerable witnesses. It protects the integrity of witness evidence and upholds the right of defendants to a fair trial by ensuring that evidence is gathered in less adversarial environments. Finally, reassessing the procedures of witness examination is a vital process towards solving the complex issues involved in the criminal procedure (Plater et al., 2014).

9.5.1. Memory Reliability

The issue of memory reliability is central to the examination of witnesses in criminal procedure because the reliability of recollections plays an important role in the judicial process. Eyewitnesses are a major factor in determining narratives about a crime, but most research has demonstrated that human memory far from perfect. The passage of time, suggestive questions, and stress can all distort memories, adding in potentiality for inaccuracy. Moreover, the repercussions of those manipulations of memory may be vast, particularly in cases involving court where a verdict might rest on one eyewitness account. The researchers emphasize that understanding the malleability of memory must be crucial for legal practitioners since it not only affects the credibility of the witness but also the integrity of the judicial process in totality. Vulnerable witnesses, such as children, increase the sense of urgency in the reliability of their memories. The ability of the child to process and retain memories of the trauma depends on the emotional status of the child when disclosing their experiences, together with the environment in which disclosure is made. The courts often face difficulties in balancing the value of witness testimony with the anticipated psychological harm as a result of deep interrogation and confrontation with the defendants. In particular, there is an imperative necessity to know the developmental cognition of children and how it affects their capacity to testify with accurate recall. In light of the possibility of trauma, courts have to put measures in place to protect child witnesses without undermining the truth-finding goals of criminal trials, which constitutes a difficult yet unavoidable endeavor for the judicial apparatus (Björk et al., 2002). In addition, the dependability of memory is of utmost importance in determining the ability of witnesses in court. Psychological findings have repeatedly demonstrated that memory is susceptible to different external and internal influences, resulting in the so-called misinformation effect. According to this effect, it is possible to distort witnesses memories using information they are exposed to after the incident, which concerns the validity of their testimony. These concerns are important in crafting efficient interrogation methods that do not compromise suggestibility and further distort the memories of those testifying inadvertently. Legal practitioners should remain aware of these forces, ensuring that witness interrogations do not undermine the validity of their memories while protecting the search for justice (Graham et al., 2002). Evaluating the credibility of a witness therefore requires a more fundamental understanding of cognitive psychology because it affects the court's process.

9.5.2. Witness Bias

Witness bias is an important concern in the voir dire process in criminal trials. Witness bias describes how people, while testifying, tend to give evidence tilted by interest, belief, or any other form of affinity. This prejudice may be caused by a number of different factors, for example, social relationships with a party to the case, preconceived assumptions regarding the situation leading up to the offense, or sometimes even personal experiences which tint a witness's worldview. These predispositions make the judicial process more complex since the law depends a great deal on the integrity and validity of witness testimony in order to maintain justice. Consequently, it becomes imperative for courts to apply stringent measures to evaluate and curb the effects of witness bias, such that the evidentiary value of testimonies does not get compromised during the trial process. The issues of witness bias become acutely discernible in vulnerable witnesses, including children. The court system has to work around the challenges of obtaining credible witness statements from child witnesses, who can be prone to suggestion or manipulation. The psychological burden of reliving experiences of trauma also blur a child's recollection and perception of the facts, supplementing personal interests in causing layers of bias that can undermine the credibility of their testimony. As explained in Björk et al. (2002), children's evidence can be tainted by the emotional trauma of facing an accused perpetrator, making it difficult to determine the truth objectively. Thus, using specialized techniques for the interrogation of child witnesses is of highest priority in order to reduce biases and safeguard their welfare without jeopardizing their testimonies for criminal courts. Aside from personal biases, the legal professional training of legal professionals has an important role in managing witness bias in criminal proceedings. There is a significant amount of evidence to show that a lack of training and sensitization on the intricacies of witness testimony can result in miscarriages of justice. The House of Commons Science and Technology Committees report, as quoted by Davies et al. (2016), elucidates the connection between expert evidence, legal education, and wrongful convictions. It is thus essential that legal experts, including lawyers and judges, should receive comprehensive training on identifying and understanding witness bias and psychological aspects involved in the testimony. Improving this training is not simply an intellectual exercise; it is necessary to develop a justice system that values fairness and accuracy, limits the perils of prejudiced testimony, and makes its legal process more equitable (Figure 9.12).

Figure 9.12. Witness bias.

Source: https://i0.wp.com/www.trialpracticetips.com/wp-content/uploads/2017/01/cross-examination.jpg?fit=600%2C343&ssl=1.

9.5.3. Legal Objections During Examination

Legal objections made during examination of witnesses within criminal procedure are fundamental checks to ensure that the judicial process is maintained with integrity. Such objections occur when a party feels that the other counsels line of questioning contravenes set legal rules or principles. Typical grounds for such objections are irrelevance, hearsay, leading questions, and speculation. Every objection is raised to prevent admitting prejudicial or inadmissible evidence that might distort the jury's perception or corrode the trial's fairness. The judge plays a pivotal role here, as they must find whether the objection has merit and issue rulings that comply with the rules of evidence. Thus, the role and nature of these objections is most critical because they significantly influence admissibility of evidence and finally decide criminal case outcomes. The change of legal objections in examination of witnesses also illustrates broader societal change, namely the role of victims within the criminal justice system. Victims historically are defined as simply witnesses whose role is limited to their evidence. However, as outlined in contemporary terminology, this vision is presently being reconsidered on broad grounds. As increasingly recognized, victims are not merely considered witnesses but also as active contributors to the justice process, implying calls for changes that would involve them as active participants in hearings. This progression might carry implications with respect to the nature of objections taken on examination, since victim involvement might complicate the evidential context. With differences between public and private roles in the courtroom reducing, implications of such changes have to be scrutinized cautiously to ensure a fair and equitable judicial procedure (Doak et al., 2005). Furthermore, the use of legal technicalities and technical legal arguments remains controversial among legal professionals and commentators. There is growing the sense that the law ought to strive to be understandable and transparent, particularly in the cross-examination of witnesses where crucial choices are arrived at out of closely matched arguments. Reformers desire lawyers and judges to prioritize simplicity and transparency over technical language, aligning courtroom procedures with the broader social necessity for justice to be understandable to all players. This is also evidenced by the rationale that law not only requires to deal with precedents but also evolves to adapt to contemporary challenges and social needs. In establishing a platform whereby objections and responses are articulated simply, the judicial process itself becomes more transparent, which is bolstered by increased public trust and confidence in the efficacy of criminal trials (Posner et al., 2016).

9.6. LEGAL STANDARDS AND GUIDELINES

Rules of law and procedure governing witness interrogation in criminal process play a crucial role in establishing the effectiveness and integrity of legal processes. Central to these rules is the doctrine of adversarial testing, where all parties have a right to test evidence brought against them. The tradition, however, also yields opportunities of complexity, particularly in the situation of vulnerable witnesses such as children and those with intellectual impairments. The current system would, nonetheless, potentially grant defendants an unfair advantage at cross-examination, tainting the credibility of the ensuing evidence and the trial process overall. To address such issues, researchers propose reforms that would allow for other means of witness examination, such as pre-recorded examinations by independent persons, which would minimize the trauma alongside safeguarding the defendants' rights (Plater et al., 2014).

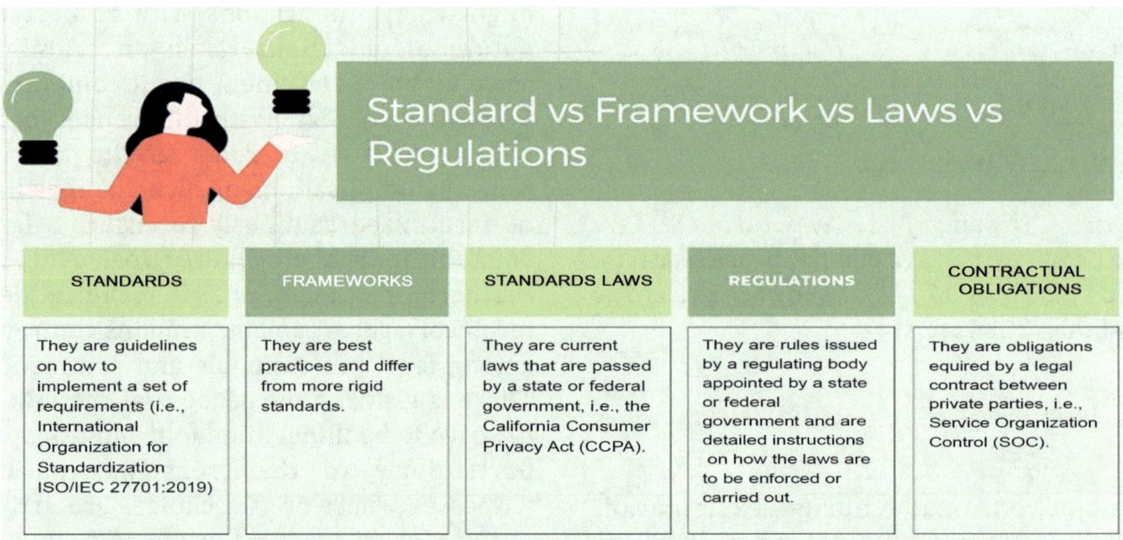

Figure 9.13. The legal standards and guidelines governing the examination of witnesses in criminal procedure.

Source: https://community.trustcloud.ai/kbuPFACeFReXReB/uploads/2022/11/Standard-vs-Framework-vs-Laws-vs-Regulations.jpg.

Furthermore, the requirements of the law concerning effectiveness in defense representation bring to light an overarching issue in the criminal justice system. Defendants' access to effective counsel is critical to the delivery of fair trials and equitable verdicts. Nevertheless, it has long been documented that numerous attorneys have trouble overcoming the constraints of their caseloads, as well as personal and ethical dilemmas, to deliver competent representation. In the majority of instances, the only recourse for defendants denied effective counsel is through direct appeals or post-conviction examination. Variance within judicial opinions concerning the purpose and standard of the reviews impedes effective reforms. This ambivalence underlines a basic dilemma: whether the focus is to be on gaining a fair verdict for the individual defendant, or whether it is to be on compelling attorneys to perform more effectively in their responsibilities (Tague et al., 1977). As a whole, the interrelation of legal requirements, witness examinations, and the right to competent defense representation helps to underscore the multifaceted nature of criminal procedure. While the adversarial system is designed to ensure justice and fairness, at times it requires radical examination and reform to prevent prejudice and ensure equity for all the players. The calls for reforms in witness questioning, particularly with vulnerable groups, are a growing acknowledgment of the necessity for a reform of the legal system so that the interest of witness protection is balanced with defendants' rights. Alongside, the issue of incompetent defense representation must also be addressed, which necessitates clear guidelines and expectations for attorneys to perform their duties properly. Drawing attention to these primary areas ensures a balanced approach towards justice, where legal standards and guidelines are aligned with the underlying principles of equity and due process (Figure 9.13).

9.6.1. Rules of Evidence

The rules of evidence are a core aspect of the criminal procedure process of questioning witnesses because they make it fair and reliable. The rules of evidence are based on the doctrines of admissibility and relevance, which dictate what is allowed to be offered as testimony in court. Admissibility is concerned with whether or not evidence can be introduced pursuant to prevailing legal standards, while relevance is an assessment of whether the testimonial evidence in fact relates to the case in question. The balancing in close proximity of allowing relevant evidence with a protection from misinformation is essential; overly nebulous rules can have prejudicial outcomes, thereby destabilizing the integrity of the justice system. Furthermore, rules of evidence always evolve, as society evolves and progresses, as well as in accordance with progress in theory of law, showing the necessity of ongoing scholarly and pragmatic scrutiny to ensure that such rules function their role as well as they potentially can. In the field of vulnerable and intimidated witnesses (VIWs), rules of evidence do include specific provisions seeking to accommodate the unique challenges such witnesses pose in the courtroom environment. The YJCEA, 1999, remedies this situation by putting in place special measures such as the availability of video recorded evidence and the visibility of screens. They aim to eliminate the fear and anxiety VIWs normally experience when giving evidence, thus allowing for a better atmosphere in which to give evidence. Moreover, the addition of video recorded cross-examination under s.28 is a big leap forward, reducing delay in the justice process and enabling the ability of courts to deliver timely justice. However, there is an observation of identification of the occurrence of substantial research gaps into effective usage of such provisions with an emphasis on continued evaluation and development in such a field of criminal procedure (Evans et al., 2018). Furthermore, the new landscape of questioning witnesses necessitates a careful analysis of how the special measures taint the integrity of evidence being brought before the court. As noted, while the YJCEAs innovations, such as the Intermediary service, are of essential aid to VIWs, there are inherent complexities within identifying persons who would require such support. This continuing issue suggests a need for interdisciplinary research that can expand not only the practical application of special measures but also the theoretical framework to witness credibility and reliability within the courts. The future research direction may consider the intersection of linguistic psychology and best evidence principles, thereby improving the debate on witness examination techniques. Completion of such shortcomings may introduce material improvements to criminal procedure, eventually ensuring that the evidence law delivers on its critical function in advancing fairness and justice (Ewin et al., 2018).

9.6.2. Admissibility of Witness Testimony

Admissibility of witness testimony is a critical component in the face of criminal procedure, as a foundation in establishing facts in court. It operates under an evidence regime based on rules of evidence to ensure that only relevant and reliable information underpins the deliberation. In criminal cases, whether or not testimony should be admissible is a function of balancing the rights of the accused with justice. The problem created by hearsay evidence illustrates this dilemma, where the Federal Rules of Evidence are focused on the value of direct witness testimony but at the same time also recognize the problems caused by indirect statements. Year after year, as the trend of evidentiary law has inclined more and more toward an expansive provision allowing hearsay evidence, the legal environment for witnesses has become even more complicated, working against defendants in advance of trial (Douglass et al., 2000). Aside from hearsay, witness credibility and trustworthiness also rest heavily on the qualifications of the testifying individuals. The use of expert witnesses has gained wider usage, particularly in specialized knowledge cases, for instance, forensic science. Expert witnesses can provide insightful analysis, but admissibility typically requires rigorous examination to ensure that their particular skill is relevant to the case. The courts must filter out the validity and relevance of expert testimony, often through cross-examination, in order to avoid prejudice or mistakes in their research methodologies (Klinkner et al., 2009). The procedural safeguards on expert testimonies thereby help ensure the purity of the judicial process while safeguarding the rights of the defendants. The establishment of standards for what constitutes proper expert testifying thus remains a valid issue in the realm of admissibility. Lastly, the admissibility of evidence by witnesses is not merely a legal formality but a delicate balancing act between law, practice, and human rights. The law surrounding witness evidence evolves ever further, prompted by public views of fairness, openness, and justice. As criminal trials increasingly involve sophisticated scientific evidence and evolving standards of admissibility, the prospect of a gap between legal provision and court reality becomes increasingly evident. These inconsistencies can be resolved by reform in procedure rules to level the playing field for defendants, especially where hearsay predominates and where expert evidence is determinative. Thus, the ongoing controversy surrounding witness evidence must be on enhancing legal frameworks that support contemporary issues in criminal trials, to ensure fair administration of justice to all parties (Douglass et al., 2000; Klinkner et al., 2009) (Figure 9.14).

Figure 9.14. Admissibility of witness testimony.

Source: https://blog.ipleaders.in/wp-content/uploads/2019/06/1000w_q95_7.jpg.

9.6.3. Ethical Considerations for Attorneys

When cross-examining witnesses in criminal trials, ethical implications for lawyers are at the forefront of maintaining the integrity of the legal process. Lawyers are bound by the duty to represent their clients zealously while also adhering to the ethical provisions set by legal regulating bodies. This dual responsibility occasionally poses tensions, particularly when attorneys must serve quasi witness functions in some instances. Here, attorneys must balance their loyalty to the client and their responsibility to the court, which poses challenging ethical problems. Maintenance of this balance is important, as breaches of ethical duties might lead to tainted attorney-client relationships and the possible erosion of the defendants interest, illustrating the great power of ethical standards in the pursuit of justice, a cornerstone for the criminal justice system (Slater et al., 2016). Furthermore, the attorneys role as a moral advocate is highlighted when interviewing witnesses. Lawyers should guarantee that their questioning tactics do not provoke fabricated stories or unfairly manipulate testimonies. It is not only a responsibility of lawyers in the court, but it is also an ethical responsibility lawyers have to prepare clients well on how to respond accordingly as per the defense strategy. Lawyers should reinforce the value of honesty while counseling clients on how to respond under cross-examination accordingly. By encouraging a culture of transparency and honesty, attorneys can uphold ethical standards alongside forming a solid defense, ensuring the right of defendants is aggressively safeguarded throughout the proceeding (Rhode et al., 1995). Beyond that, however, are the complexities of ethical implications in the broader context of attorney abuse cross-examining witnesses. When attorneys engage in unethical activities, such as subornation of perjury or alteration of testimony by witnesses, they jeopardize not only their own credibility but the public's faith in the legal process as well. Ethics guidelines for attorneys emphasize the attorneys role as a protector of justice, putting them on a moral pedestal that calls for responsibility and answerability in what they accomplish. The effects of ethical misconduct can last for a long time, for instance, unjust convictions and marginalization of the public from the judiciary. Consequently, attorneys must be vigilant and committed to practicing with ethics because the achievement of justice is greatly connected to their ability to traverse the ethical labyrinth present in witness examination within criminal practice (Slater et al., 2016).

SUMMARY

The Summary of an essay on testing witnesses in criminal process serves the function of summarizing the key arguments and determining the implications of the testing process in the justice system. There is a need to acknowledge the fact that while the adversarial system has impacted the practices in trials, there have been serious doubts raised concerning how vulnerable witnesses, e.g., children or intellectually disabled individuals, are handled. Such witnesses can be cross-examined such that not only is the credibility of their evidence jeopardized but they also suffer emotional trauma. Therefore, as has been argued, reforms such as eliminating direct cross-examination of the use of pre-trial procedures by qualified third parties may counteract these challenges, hence avoiding the rights of the defendant from overshadowing the need for fair treatment of victims and witnesses in court (Plater et al., 2014). Aside from examining the procedural aspect of witness testimony, expert witnesses and their cross-examination are the singular point of utmost significance. The technicality of expert testimony, especially in forensic matters, necessitates that the courts exercise extreme care when deciding on the credibility and admissibility of such evidence. The hybrid system of legal procedure in international tribunals, as an example, illustrates the issues arising from the convergence of scientific evidence into a legal system. Resolution of methodological concerns in this instance generally hinges on vigilant examination and cross-examination of expert witnesses confirming their pivotal role in validating presented evidence (Klinkner et al., 2009). Thus, expert witness management must be as rigorously checked as lay witness management to ensure the integrity of the legal process. Lastly, criminal procedure's method of questioning witnesses reveals a fine balance between the preservation of adversarial rights and the protection of vulnerable witnesses within the legal system. As the discussion about potential reforms continues, it becomes increasingly clear that revision of the existing procedures is necessary in order to create a more balanced environment for all the interested parties. This entails not only enhancement of the witness examination methods but also the broader concern of the eliciting and use of evidence in the court. As the awareness of the psychological impact of witness interrogation and the value of expert testimony increases, legal systems are better able to situate themselves within paradigms of justice that balance the rights of the accused with the traumatic pasts of the victims (Klinkner et al., 2009; Plater et al., 2014).

Cross-examination of witnesses in criminal trials is at the heart of both preserving the integrity of the legal process and the soundness of verdicts that are handed down. Evidence of witnesses has the potential to profoundly influence juror impressions, decisively determining the outcome of a case. Standard procedural guidelines regulate how witnesses are examined and cross-examined in order to guarantee that their evidence is not just relevant but also credible. This is particularly on display in adversarial systems, in which cross-examination of witnesses is central to developing inconsistencies or biases in what they say. Success in such procedures depends greatly upon the legal representatives' ability to employ rigorous questioning strategies that reveal seminal information while finding potential weaknesses in the witness's testimony. As the legal climate evolves, particularly in international environments, there is an increasing requirement for successfully prepared witnesses. For instance, developments in co-operative legal education have emphasized the significance of studying complicacies of witness examination by legal professionals. The China Trial Advocacy Institute is a perfect model of how reforms in education and procedure can enhance the functioning of the judiciary. Through the development of judges, prosecutors, and defense counsel with advanced levels of adversarial process skills, such programs seek to enhance the existing levels of witness examination skills that contribute to improved and fairer criminal trials. The emphasis on developing such skills is in itself an expression of a broader recognition of the need for specialized training in the emerging legal systems of the globe (Lancaster et al., 2006). Among forensic evidence, the intricacy of expert witness testimony has been prominent. The convergence of law and science in criminal investigation cases involving mass graves demonstrates the intricacy of ensuring expert knowledge sits well within the legal framework. Forensic science—a discipline classically defined by depth of method—represents the need for systematic investigative procedures. Traditionally, trial chambers resolve the admissibility of the above expert evidence through the lens of cross-examination and the introduction of counter-expertise. This not only resolves methodological disputes, but it also maximizes the integrity of offered evidence. The judicial process therefore must see to it that the scientific input is properly scrutinized through strict examination in the instance of witness testimony, especially expert witnesses (Klinkner et al., 2009).

KEY TERMS

- Child Witness
- Corroboration
- Demeanor of Witness
- Hostile Witness
- Perjury
- Refreshing Memory
- Witness Protection
- Contradiction
- Cross-Examination
- Expert Witness
- Leading Questions
- Re-Examination
- Tutored Witness
- Witness Summons

A LOOK TO THE FUTURE

FUTURE CONSIDERATIONS IN WITNESS EXAMINATION PRACTICES

The future of criminal procedure witness examination practice will undoubtedly be influenced by new technology and innovative methodology aimed at enhancing the reliability and effectiveness of witness evidence. Among these is the application of video-recording techniques as part of the witness examination process. Documentation evidence indicates that video statements can provide a visual testimony that often complements written testimony, thereby overcoming memory recall and bias. Intriguingly, jurisdictions that adopted such practices are said to witness increased victim participation as well as overall management of cases. Enforcing video-recording procedures necessitates precise understanding and coordination among prosecutors, law enforcement, and victim advocates to ensure the integrity of evidence collected while being sensitive to witnesses' privacy and confidentiality. As a result, future consideration must be given priority in legal and moral policies for these technological applications. In addition, innovations in online communication platforms offer ways to improve remote witness testimonies, which can be indispensable when conventional examination proves to be challenging. As online court proceedings become more prevalent, the inclusion of remote examination tools provides extended access to witnesses who cannot or will not appear in court.

This approach not only is adaptable to logistical constraints but also expands the selection of witnesses by enabling participation from a geographically dispersed distribution of locations. But it also raises severe problems with security and integrity of testimony, technical malfunction at pivotal stages of questioning. Strong guidelines around remote testimony will be vital in ensuring that the advantages of this approach are balanced against the necessary need to maintain procedural integrity. Therefore, creating a robust digital examination framework will be a critical factor in framing future legal standards. Apart from technology updates, the ethical implications of witness examination practices should always remain at the forefront of future deliberations. The complex nature of witness interactions with potential biases and inaccuracies gives rise to a re-evaluation of the ethical standards that underpin existing practices. Legal stakeholders are challenged with managing issues on the authority of examination techniques on testimonies and implications for trial outcomes. With every new technology that emerges, like inquisitorial approaches applied in various legal contexts, there are ethics standards that scrutinize conduct of examiners into prominence. Development of a tailored code of ethics is needed to minimize actual and perceived abuse in witness examinations such that the rights of witnesses are safeguarded and an even legal process is promoted. These ethical issues will thus play a key role in determining the future of witness examination within criminal procedure.

REFERENCES

1. Backes, B., Grau, K., Kammer-Kerwick, M., LaMotte, A., et al. (2019). Recording victim video statements as evidence to advance legal outcomes in family violence cases (ReVEAL). https://core.ac.uk/download/286367667.pdf (accessed on 13th August 2025).
2. Björk, D., Blomqvist, A., Elander, L., Engblom, H., et al. (2002). Child witness policy: Law interfacing with social science. https://core.ac.uk/download/62568554.pdf (accessed on 13th August 2025).
3. Bussel, D. J. (2016). Ethics for examiners. https://core.ac.uk/download/144231470.pdf (accessed on 13th August 2025).
4. Cardoso, O. V. (2021). Direct examination and cross-examination no Código de Processo Civil. https://core.ac.uk/download/490592622.pdf (accessed on 13th August 2025).
5. Cohn, S. L. (1984). The work-product doctrine: Protection, not privilege. https://core.ac.uk/download/70375594.pdf (accessed on 13th August 2025).
6. Coleman, R. J., & Rothstein, P. F. (2020). Confronting memory loss. https://core.ac.uk/download/287923482.pdf (accessed on 13th August 2025).
7. Crabb, B. B. (1996). Judicially compelled disclosure of researchers' data: A judge's view. https://core.ac.uk/download/84098837.pdf (accessed on 13th August 2025).
8. Davies, G., & Piasecki, E. (2016). No more laissez faire? Expert evidence, rule changes and reliability: Can more effectively training for the Bar and judiciary prevent miscarriages of justice? https://core.ac.uk/download/74228540.pdf (accessed on 13th August 2025).
9. Djerf, H., & Hy, J. (1990). Rights of the criminally accused. https://core.ac.uk/download/62554233.pdf (accessed on 13th August 2025).
10. Doak, J. (2005). Victims' rights in criminal trials: Prospects for participation. https://core.ac.uk/download/30635564.pdf (accessed on 13th August 2025).
11. Douglass, J. G. (2000). Balancing hearsay and criminal discovery. https://core.ac.uk/download/144223519.pdf (accessed on 13th August 2025).
12. Evans, J., Khan, H. T. A., & Kubascikova, J. (2018). Video recorded cross-examination or re-examination: A discussion on practice and research. https://core.ac.uk/download/158372846.pdf (accessed on 13th August 2025).
13. Ewin, R. (2018). Video recorded cross-examination or re-examination: A discussion on practice and research. https://core.ac.uk/download/158372846.pdf (accessed on 13th August 2025).
14. Garrett, B. L. (2013). Validating the right to counsel. https://core.ac.uk/download/213020469.pdf (accessed on 13th August 2025).
15. Gershman, B. L. (2009). The eyewitness conundrum: How courts, police and attorneys can reduce mistakes by eyewitnesses. https://core.ac.uk/download/46713877.pdf (accessed on 13th August 2025).
16. Guo, Z. (2022). Cross-examination of witnesses in Chinese criminal courts: Theoretical debates, practical barriers, and potential solutions. https://core.ac.uk/download/560343379.pdf (accessed on 13th August 2025).

17. Hill, M. (2014). The Fairbanks Four: Hopeless innocence and the flawed system that escorted them to stagnant wrongful convictions. https://core.ac.uk/download/187434644.pdf (accessed on 13th August 2025).
18. Kaufman, J. (1987). Section 1983: Absolute immunity for pretrial police testimony. https://core.ac.uk/download/144228082.pdf (accessed on 13th August 2025).
19. Klinkner, M. J. (2008). Proving genocide? Forensic expertise and the ICTY. https://core.ac.uk/download/4897043.pdf (accessed on 13th August 2025).
20. Klinkner, M. J. (2009). Forensic science expertise for international criminal proceedings: An old problem, a new context and a pragmatic resolution. https://core.ac.uk/download/4897045.pdf (accessed on 13th August 2025).
21. Kötz, H. (2009). Civil justice systems in Europe and the United States. https://core.ac.uk/download/62565990.pdf (accessed on 13th August 2025).
22. Lancaster, R., & Ding, X. (2006). Addressing the emergence of advocacy in the Chinese criminal justice system: A collaboration between a U.S. and a Chinese law school. https://core.ac.uk/download/144226114.pdf (accessed on 13th August 2025).
23. N/A. (1967). Learned treatises as direct evidence: The Alabama experience. https://core.ac.uk/download/62551621.pdf (accessed on 13th August 2025).
24. N/A. (1968). Defense access to grand jury testimony: A right in search of a standard. https://core.ac.uk/download/62551554.pdf (accessed on 13th August 2025).
25. Plater, D., Bowden, P., & Henning, T. (2014). Balancing fairness to victims, society and defendants in the cross-examination of vulnerable witnesses: An impossible triangulation? https://core.ac.uk/download/pdf/30674727.pdf (accessed on 13th August 2025).
26. Posner, R. A. (2016). On hearsay. https://core.ac.uk/download/144231424.pdf (accessed on 13th August 2025).
27. Pye, A. K. (1968). The Warren Court and criminal procedure. https://core.ac.uk/download/62565423.pdf (accessed on 13th August 2025).
28. Rhode, D. L. (1995). Annotated bibliography of educational materials on legal ethics. https://core.ac.uk/download/62553709.pdf (accessed on 13th August 2025).
29. Roberts, A. J. (2025). Eyewitness identification evidence: Procedural developments and the ends of adjudicative accuracy. https://core.ac.uk/download/48622.pdf (accessed on 13th August 2025).
30. Slater, E. (2016). A legal and ethical puzzle: Defense counsel as quasi witness. https://core.ac.uk/download/144231816.pdf (accessed on 13th August 2025).
31. Tague, P. W. (1977). The attempt to improve criminal defense representation. https://core.ac.uk/download/70374459.pdf (accessed on 13th August 2025).
32. Tomey-Alleyne, M. (2015). A critical assessment of how effective the criminal courts are when examining the child. https://core.ac.uk/download/30731207.pdf (accessed on 13th August 2025).

Chapter

10

CONFESSIONS, STATEMENTS, AND BURDEN OF PROOF IN CRIMINAL PROCEDURE

Contents

Introduction....................313
10.1. The Role of Confessions in Criminal Procedure....................317
10.2. The Admissibility of Confessions....................321
10.3. Statements vs. Confessions....................325
10.4. The Burden of Proof in Criminal Cases....................329
10.5. The Impact of Coerced Confessions....................334
10.6. The Role of Technology in Confessions and Statements....................338
Summary....................342
References....................345

INTRODUCTION

The intricate world of criminal procedure is all about the balance between confessions, statements, and the onus of proof, all confluencing in the pursuit of justice and protecting individual rights. As juridical systems evolve, the value of understanding how confessions are elicited and subsequently analyzed cannot be overemphasized. Miranda v. Arizona is the landmark case that demonstrates the delicate equilibrium between law enforcement's right to get people to confess and the obligation to safeguard a person's rights. With this judgment, among others, criminal procedure direction has been guided by a requirement to ensure that suspects are informed of their rights before interrogation so as to provide an environment of law where coercive practices are addressed and contained (N/A, 1966). In this context, interrogations are carried out with a sharp awareness of the ethical and legal concerns surrounding the involuntary nature of confessions. As the juridical controversies move further, the privileged role of exculpatory statements becomes most prominent in the context of criminal evidence standards. Defendants traditionally rely on the expectation of presenting evidence which may absolve them, exculpatory evidence, highlighting the doctrine that it is the burden of the prosecution. The connection between the prosecution's duty and the defense's right is aggravated by the intricacy of measuring any judicial process flaws. Hindsight bias, on the other hand, is particular challenges because it tends to make the evaluation of trial-related judgments biased, with a preference for applying current judgment to historical events rather than looking at the proceedings themselves (Griffin et al., 2016). Hence, examining confessions and exculpatory statements is crucial in understanding the broader issues surrounding ensuring fair trials within the framework of criminal procedure. In the study of the relationship between confessions, statements, and the burden of proof, it is clear that an interdisciplinary perspective must be adopted. The convergence of law, psychology, and ethics informs our understanding of the processes by which confessions are obtained and the pitfalls to which trial evaluations fall prey. In addition, scrutiny of past convictions, tainted by involuntary confessions or inadequate defense, enhances the need for reform in standards of evidence assessment. In re-evaluating existing paradigms in the system, legal professionals and scholars can suggest better assurances against dilution of individual rights and ensure that neither confessions nor statements compromise the integrity of the judicial process. It is only through a serious debate on such issues that the complexity of criminal procedure may be addressed, paving the way for an even more just legal system.

Definition of Key Terms: Confessions, Statements, and Burden of Proof

The word confession in criminal procedure carries much weight, being predominantly a turning point in proving guilt. A confession typically refers to a statement of culpability on the part of a person for committing a crime. However, the integrity of such confessions has come into doubt, precisely because postconviction DNA testing has acquitted many innocents who, either coerced or duped, provided false confessions. The phenomenon emphasizes the necessity for careful examination of confessional evidence in the judicial system. As observed in the majority of studies, even confessions presented in minute details do not always indicate the actual culpability of a subject but questions the validity of confessions made under high-stress conditions like interrogations. It is therefore crucial to discover the dynamics of confessions to guarantee justice is served in the proper way and that innocent individuals are safeguarded against unlawful convictions, according to Garrett et al. (2010). Under criminal procedure, the testimony of an individual can extend to a wide variety of statements aside from a confession. Statements are any words spoken or written that convey information pertaining to an investigation regardless of whether they reflect an individual's perception of an event, character, or intention. The admissibility and meaning of these statements rely to a large extent on context and the circumstances under which they were spoken. Of significance here is the distinction between coercively obtained statements and voluntary statements in order to guarantee the integrity of court proceedings. The consensus of legal scholarship is that the context in which statements are gathered is of utmost significance because coercive means can lead to tainted or unreliable evidence. Efforts that ensure that statements are consistent with the principles of justice demand keen examination of the circumstances that envelop their collection, which is essential to maintain the level of equity in trials, as discussed by Griffin et al. (2016). The proof beyond a reasonable doubt is a fundamental doctrine in criminal law, and the duty rests with the prosecution to devise sufficient evidence to demonstrate the defendant's guilt beyond any reasonable doubt. This judicial requirement safeguards the rights of citizens and prohibits them from being convicted based on circumstantial evidence or insufficient evidence. Not only do the prosecution need to gather evidence in the form of confession and statements, but they must also present such evidence in a manner that meets or surpasses the statutory level. In addition, the onus of proof necessarily shapes the nature of legal processes, deciding how evidence is perceived and weighed by judges and juries. With judicial systems grappling with the outcome of erroneous evidence, from contaminated declarations or suspect confessions, calls for change become increasingly relevant. Emphasizing the purity of the burden of proof is significant to the integrity of the criminal justice system and serves as a safeguard against miscarriages of justice in the guise of wrongful conviction, to ensure not just that justice is done, but that it is seen to be done (Figure 10.1).

Figure 10.1. Key terms: confessions, statements, burden of proof.

Source: https://www.rostrumlegal.com/wp-content/uploads/2023/04/Admissibility-of-Confession-Evidence-Law-in-India.jpg.

Importance of Confessions and Statements in Criminal Law

Confessions and statements play a vital role within the criminal law paradigm, and they serve as effective evidence during trial hearings. They often provide the basic source of information upon which individuals are prosecuted, as magistrates and juries generally treat confessions as conclusive proof of guilt. The impact of a confession can even prevail over other types of evidence, and it can significantly alter the conclusions of cases. As dictated in historical rulings, such as Miranda v. Arizona, it is important to protect individuals' rights to ensure confessions are legally and ethically attained rather than through coercion tactics. The addition of constitutional confession protections shows an ongoing commitment to justice in identifying the balance necessary between the effectiveness of law enforcement and the preservation of civil liberties (N/A, 1966).

But the meaning of confessions must be taken with great scrutiny, particularly in the presence of prevalence of false confessions in the criminal justice system. Innocent individuals can admit to non-crime activities they did not commit under extended psychological pressure of the interrogation process. This tragic reality shows the complex dynamics that could result in coercive but false claims of guilt. Research has revealed that such false confessions contain exhaustive and veracious descriptions of the offense, creating an aura of credibility to substitute for credibility. As in studies of miscarriages of justice through wrongful convictions, such confessions can result in serious miscarriages of justice if not subject to procedural control (Garrett et al., 2010). For this reason, the procedures by which confessions are obtained and put before courts need to be reexamined. The implications of confessions being the strongest source of evidence in criminal trials demand an immediate overhaul of criminal procedure, particularly regarding the management of interrogation methods. The establishment of procedures such as complete videotaping of interrogations can guarantee that the circumstances surrounding the extraction of confessions are well defined and open to examination. Changing approaches of testing the reliability of confessions within trials could possibly feature a better balance of justice. Lacking such reforms, confession taint remains a threat, with the possibility of wrongful convictions as well as public erosion in confidence in the criminal justice system. Thus, such issues not only justify the legitimacy of legal process but also public confidence that justice is indeed being delivered, serving a substantial convergence of law, ethics, and human rights (Garrett et al., 2010).

10.1. THE ROLE OF CONFESSIONS IN CRIMINAL PROCEDURE

The significance of confessions within criminal procedure cannot be overemphasized as they can become key parts of evidence in the prosecution's case. Confessions have the power to shift the burden of proof substantially, effectively resulting in a confession of guilt that can powerfully affect juries. The past shows how there is a change in the means by which confessions are obtained and interpreted. Prior to watershed holdings like Miranda v. Arizona, confessions obtained through coercive methods of interrogation were permitted by law, raising serious voluntariness and reliability issues. The Miranda ruling not only guaranteed individual rights but also reaffirmed the importance of making sure that confessions are obtained with consideration for constitutional protections. This evolution in jurisprudence reflects an ongoing effort to balance the quest for justice with safeguarding civil liberties, with particular emphasis on the indispensable role that confessions play in criminal procedure (N/A, 1966).

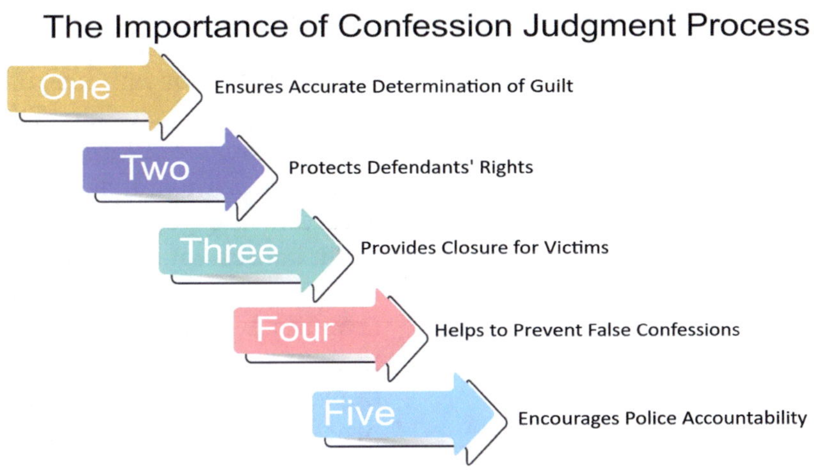

Figure 10.2. The Role of confessions in criminal procedure.

Source: https://fastercapital.co/i/Confession-Judgment-Process--A-Step-by-Step-Guide--The-Importance-of-Confession-Judgment-Process.webp.

The interrogation process, particularly its psychological aspects, is central to comprehending the role of confessions in criminal procedure. Police officers have created tactics aimed at evoking confessions that, in most cases, lead to false confessions of guilt. Cognitive psychology shows how individuals can be rendered susceptible to coercion, leading to coerced false confessions, without the presence of coercion. The findings of this phenomenon raise questions of ethics on the police procedures and the reliability of confessions as evidence. Further, the ongoing empirical research on wrongful convictions sheds light on the prevalence of such cases, indicating a failure in the examination process of confessions. As the legal system is developing to incorporate research on social sciences, it is important that the confession assessment process is also adapting correspondingly to lead towards a more pragmatic approach that acknowledges the intricacy in human decision-making (Griffin et al., 2016). Also, the effect of confessions on the overall judicial process is beyond their admissibility. When a confession is introduced, it is of extraordinary strength in the eyes of jurors, overshadowing any other evidence or lack of evidence. This psychological aspect can be potentially to blame for an unconscious prejudice, wherein jurors decide validity of confession as an intrinsic fact regardless of conditions under which it was extracted. These biases can prejudice fairness of trials, leading to potentially unjust convictions. Moreover, the burden of proof is also contingent upon the nature of confession. The prosecution owes it to prove guilt beyond all reason to doubt, but a confession facilitates this for them, so the defense must then strive to disprove it. Therefore, the role of confessions is not only as a piece of evidence but as a critical aspect defining criminal cases' paths, which leads to more scrutiny and revamp in interrogations and standards of proof (Griffin et al., 2016; N/A, 1966) (Figure 10.2).

10.1.1. Legal Definition and Types of Confessions

The legal conception of a confession is central in determining its ramifications within the criminal justice system. A confession is essentially defined as a statement of guilt in relation to a criminal offense. It can be either formal in that a suspect voluntarily admits their wrongdoing in the presence of law enforcers or informal in that it can be made during a routine conversation when one unwittingly discloses his or her criminal actions. The significance of confessions is not merely in their application as concrete evidence of crime but also in the capacity to minimize the prosecution burden of proof. Confessions are thus able to alter the trajectory of a criminal trial completely, to plea bargaining, mitigated sentencing, or, in some instances, to wrongful convictions due to coercion and circumstances under which an individual confessed. Such dynamics bring into perspective the importance of understanding the legal framework governing confessions and their role in criminal procedure. In the case of confessions, there are various types each with varying evidentiary value and legal significance. A confession in the proper sense is a confession that comes with elaborate details of the crime including the circumstances or means employed. On the other hand, a false confession tends to occur under duress, coercion, or psychological pressure, where a person admits guilt in the absence of guilt, and this usually comes from intense interrogation methods. There are also implied confessions that may happen when the suspect behavior implies guilt without verbally confessing to the crime. The variety of forms of confessions outlines the complexities of the judiciary, with judicial scrutiny necessary to ascertain the genuineness and legal status of such confessions. A deep understanding of these variations is important, particularly since lawsuits by alleged victims, as substantiated in the Fairbanks Four case, arise as a result of improper processes of confession collection and processing (Hill et al., 2014). Additionally, legal handling of confessions relies on fundamental procedural safeguards for ensuring fairness and preserving the integrity of the judicial process. Use of the Fifth Amendments Due Process Clause comes into play, bringing into focus the necessity of protection against self-incrimination and coercive obtaining of confessions. Courts have traditionally upheld the argument that certain rights need to be extended to people during confession procedures, and they have buttressed the argument that procedural protections are needed in situations for protecting defendants, particularly in immigration proceedings that involve criminal convictions (Traum et al., 2011). In doing so, the judicial system grapples with balancing the efficacy of confessions as tools for prosecution with the expansive need for having ethical standards in their procurement. This tension is apparent in argument over mistaken convictions and demonstrates the significant position that legally defined confessions have within the broader spectrum of criminal procedure and justice.

10.1.2. Historical Context and Evolution of Confession Laws

The history of confession laws reveals an extensive transformation as a result of social, legal, and political concerns throughout centuries. Initial confessions were usually brought about by coercion, threats, or torture and therefore came to be used extensively in legal cases without respect for individual rights. The process of moving toward protection for suspects began in the 20th century, beginning with recognition of the issue of confessional unreliability. Gradually, courts began questioning the circumstances under which confessions were procured, with the pinnacle being reached in milestone cases such as Miranda v. Arizona. This case established key safeguards, ensuring that individuals are informed of their rights before providing statements to the police, a stark difference to previous practice that, more often than not, led to involuntary admissions of guilt (N/A, 1966).

With these developments, modern confession laws now ensure a balancing act between the requirements of law enforcement and individuals' rights under the constitution. The importance of reforming confession law is beyond the immediate criminal trial, impacting policies concerning the treatment of defendants in the justice system. Recognition of the rights of the accused individuals played a crucial role in changing legal principles as courts began to emphasize the requirement for voluntary and informed answers. The shift was characterized by the introduction of protection from self-incrimination, necessitating explicit standards for police officers. Following widespread judicial responses, including those stated in subsequent holdings after Miranda, police practice began to incorporate these safeguards into their methods of questioning. This development is a reflection of an even broader commitment to ensuring confessions are not only valid but also reflective of people's voluntariness when under questioning. With increasingly expansive protections, arguments over the burden of proof also became more salient, with a focus on the need to obtain confessions that advance credibility required in criminal proceedings. The historical models of confession statutes are also intertwined with the evolving notion of due process, particularly regarding habeas corpus. Following such watershed occurrences as those regarding the 9/11 detentions, application and enforcement of due process rights came increasingly under critical examination.

The fusion of Suspension Clause and habeas corpus demonstrated how procedural protection could be enriched in line with evolving constitutional standards, specifically for the detention of individuals without charge. In landmark cases like Boumediene v. Bush, the Court enforced that core due process protections cut across citizenship status, reshaping the concept of legal rights in detainees (Garrett et al., 2012). This evolution reflects a persistent debate of the balance between individual rights and national security, further securing the foundation for the existence of modern confession legislation. Through ongoing evolution through history informing modern practice, the intersection of confessions, statements, and the standard of proof continues to be an abiding component of the debate of criminal procedure (Figure 10.3).

Figure 10.3. The historical context of confession laws.

Source: https://criminallawstudiesnluj.wordpress.com/wp-content/uploads/2018/09/hqdefault.jpg?w=480&h=300&crop=1.

10.1.3. Impact of Confessions on Case Outcomes

The impact of confessions on case outcomes cannot be overstated, in that they tend to play as turning-point evidence that decides the trajectory of legal cases. In current judicial practice, a confession can greatly advance the prosecution's case, overshadowing other factors such as witness statements and circumstantial evidence. This such dependency on confessions is of concern, particularly matters relating to coercion and the voluntariness of such statements. False confessions, which can be due to psychological pressures or misleading interrogation techniques, point to the requirement for judicial interference. In a number of instances, the confessions have led to false convictions because of the inherent prejudice in the legal system. Therefore, an understanding of these dynamics is essential in order to prevent miscarriages of justice and ensure confessions operate to reinforce the fact-finding function of courts rather than hide it. Furthermore, the evidential weight that has become associated with confessions has profound implications for the burden of proof in a trial situation. The reliance on confessions can strip the requirement that the prosecution establish guilt beyond a reasonable doubt of its core emphasis. When confessions dominate accounts of law, they can promote a culture in which jurors may unintentionally equate confession with guilt and dismiss legal standards of evidence. This can shape a hindsight bias culture that leads courts to wrongly assume confessions are infallibly reliable, thereby perpetuating wrongful convictions upon the occurrence of mistakes. The courts' retrospective assessment of the confessions can reflect blindness that undermines judicial review integrity to the extent that it becomes difficult to chase justice in the criminal justice system (Griffin et al., 2016). The consequences of confessions do not just exist within single cases but reach out into broader societal constructions of justice and police practice. In most jurisdictions, patterns of coercive practice, particularly among vulnerable groups, highlight the structural nature of how confessions are obtained. Problematics such as the militarization of police increase the likelihood of undergoing coercion, leading to involuntary confessions that can significantly influence case outcomes (Magaloni et al., 2020). The intertwining of coercive tactics and confession validity further exacerbates existing imbalances in the legal process, ultimately undermining public confidence. A more empathetic criminal justice approach that prioritizes protection of suspects rights is critical in alleviating these issues. Shift in focus towards ensuring fair interrogation practices and truthful confessions could not only enhance case outcomes but also further promote the development of a more just legal system.

10.2. THE ADMISSIBILITY OF CONFESSIONS

The admissibility of confessions within criminal procedure has an intimate relationship to the protections afforded by the Miranda decision, which mandates that individuals under custodial interrogation be informed of their rights. The landmark Supreme Court case was a response to the widespread fear of coercion of police interrogations, which routinely led to false confessions. The Court aimed to safeguard against the self-incriminating aspect involved in confession-making, thus ensuring that suspects are made aware of their right against silence as well as their right to counsel. The implications of Miranda v. Arizona extend beyond individual cases; they establish a significant legal precedent and highlight the necessity for clear procedure in obtaining statements from suspects. By insisting on a more open and rights-based approach, the ruling is intended to improve the credibility of confessions as evidence to courts without undermining the accused's constitutional rights (N/A, 1966).

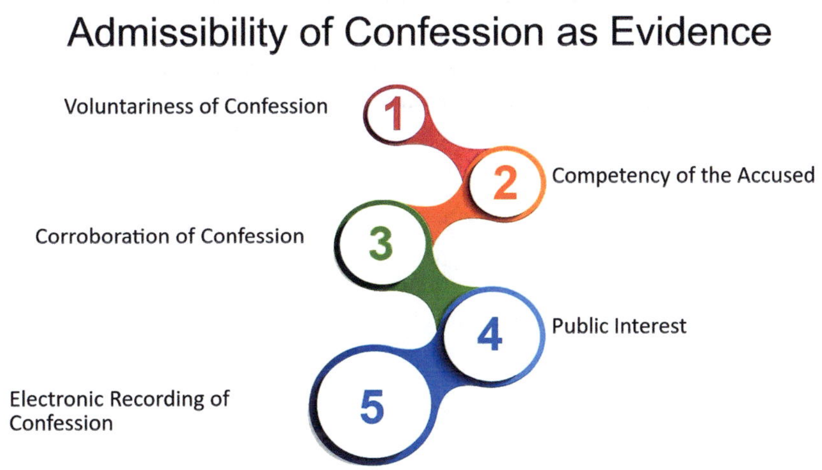

Figure 10.4. The admissibility of confessions in criminal procedure.

Source: https://fastercapital.co/i/Legal-Confession-Judgment--Understanding-the-Basics--Admissibility-of-Confession-as-Evidence.webp.

In addition to the original criteria established by Miranda, the admissibility of confessions is increasingly evolving as courts use subtle tests to evaluate their voluntariness. Legal scholars mention that it is important to examine the environment in which a confession is obtained, particularly when looking at factors such as suspects' ages, mental abilities, and sensitivity to how interrogations are handled. The treatment of youths in the criminal justice system reveals striking differences in addressing confessions because their vulnerabilities lead to lower levels of understanding and higher levels of coercion. This distinction demands a more strenuous application when ascertaining admissibility of confessions of child suspects against adults. Thus, courts can implement supplementary measures to ensure that statements attributed to vulnerable members meet the requisite levels of voluntariness and reliability (Chiu et al., 2009). The consequences of inadmissible confessions may lead not only to wrongful convictions but also to broader impacts on public faith in the criminal justice process. If coercive confessions are admitted as evidence, they are damaging to the integrity of the system and may result in miscarriages of justice. Additionally, the psychological impacts on those wrongly convicted might be profound, often to lead to long-term emotional and social difficulties. Adopting rigid criteria of admissibility of confessions is, thus, essential in designing a legal environment that is concerned with moral questioning methods. Popular conception of justice hinges on the access of the judicial process and demands that the courts examine strictly circumstances of the taking of confessions. By ensuring only confessions gained under equitable and fair conditions are admissible, the justice system can enhance its legitimacy as well as compliance with the virtues of justice it professes (N/A, 1966) (Figure 10.4).

10.2.1. Legal Standards for Admissibility in Court

The standards of admissibility in law are part of the judicial process and play a direct role in determining criminal cases. At the focal point of these standards is the exclusionary rule, through which evidence procured in disdain of a defendant's rights under the constitution cannot be heard in court. This doctrine has its origins in the desire to discourage police from performing illegal acts, thereby bolstering a system of justice that values personal liberty. At the center of this argument is the landmark case of Miranda v. Arizona, wherein the Supreme Court compelled warnings for suspects being read their rights prior to custodial interrogation.

Figure 10.5. The legal standards for admissibility in court.

Source: https://fastercapital.co/i/Admissible-evidence--Prima-Facie--The-Quest-for-Admissible-Evidence--Rules-and-Standards-for-Admissibility.webp.

This decision emphasized the importance of protecting against coerced confessions and set a precedent that remains at the heart of deciding whether words spoken under police interrogation are admissible (N/A, 1966). Another key component of legal admissibility criteria is evidence credibility and reliability. Courts generally use a twofold analysis: not just must the evidence be legally acquired, but it must also possess sufficient probative value to be helpful in the present case. All of this hinges on the burden of proof, in which the prosecution must demonstrate the defendant's guilt beyond a reasonable doubt. The emphasis on this burden is a safeguard against unfair convictions, ensuring legal standards not only comply with procedural standards but also seek justice. Lastly, the consistency and integrity of the evidence presented is a test of its admissibility, reinforcing the broad principle of equity and fair process in criminal trials (Pye et al., 1968). The evolution of such standards of law in the context of criminal process has been significant, most notably between the years of the Warren Court, which brought about pioneering reforms to the protection of defendants' rights. The decade was a revolutionary new model for criminal justice, commonly described as a revolution in the handling of confessions and statements by the courts. The decisions delivered over this time have been pivotal in shaping current practice around evidence and defendant's rights, further stoking ongoing debate on balancing effective law enforcement with protecting individual freedoms. The legal admissibility requirements thus not only outline the procedural landscape but also reflect society values of justice, equity, and enforcement of the law in America (Pye et al., 1968) (Figure 10.5).

10.2.2. The Role of Miranda Rights in Confession Admissibility

Miranda rights have a fundamental role to play in the admissibility of confessions under the criminal process. From the seminal case of Miranda v. Arizona, Miranda rights ensure police-custody suspects are informed of their right to remain silent and their right to an attorney. The value of these rights is that they can protect one from self-incrimination and thus support the rule that confessions be voluntary as well as informed. Failure to provide these warnings could lead to exclusion of any statements or confessions made by the accused during interrogation, which would significantly impact the prosecution's case and uphold the integrity of the judiciary process. Further, the psychological elements involved in police interrogation reinforce the need for Miranda rights. The evidence indicates that there exists a susceptibility to coercive strategies open to inducing false confessions as well as tainting confession evidence. Where jurisdictions have incorporated safeguards of equivalent quality, e.g., those being considered in Canadian case law, there is an effort to counteract such psychological coercion. Aiders recognize the usefulness of psychological coercion in influencing confession admissibility, creating a safeguarding legal setting whose mission is to neutralize the risks presented by interrogation techniques likely to elicit false confessions of guilt, as identified in discussion on averting wrongful convictions (Smith et al., 2010). Finally, application of Miranda rights is more than a legal formality but a necessary protection against potential abuses of the criminal justice system. By making sure individuals are adequately advised of their rights, law enforcement agencies are held to a standard that stresses due process. The observance by the courts of these rights indicates respect for the thin line between the imperatives of proper law enforcement and the constitutional rights entitled to the accused. In the ever-evolving law, as it changes with the times, emphasis on procedural integrity and scrutiny of admissibility of confession will continue to be important, between justice and protection of freedoms (Bodini, 2011).

10.2.3. Exceptions to the Exclusionary Rule

In criminal procedure, the exclusionary rule serves as a pivotal protection designed to keep law enforcement agencies from using unconstitutional means when they are collecting evidence. The rule is optional and has several exceptions that impact greatly on its enforcement. One prominent exception is the good faith exception created in United States v. Leon, under which evidence obtained by a technically defective warrant can be admissible even if police officers acted in good faith, relying on the belief that the warrant was valid. This exception emphasizes a balance between the punitive purpose exclusionary rules and the practical necessity for law enforcement to have the ability to be able to effectively carry out their work without punishing the judicial system for good faith mistakes. Circumstances whereby evidence may be introduced in defiance of procedure defects complicate the legal framework on confessions, statements, and criminal cases' burden of proof further. The inevitable discovery doctrine is an essential exception to the exclusionary rule. Under this doctrine, if it can be demonstrated by the police that the available evidence would have inevitably ended up being discovered through legitimate means, then such evidence may be admissible in court even if there was a constitutional mishap during procuring it. For example, if police illegitimately obtain a confession but are able to demonstrate that they would have obtained the same information from a legitimate investigation, such a confession may not be excluded. This doctrine provides an access way for the truth to come out through judicial procedures and hence highlights the risk of excluding evidence that may prove highly probative. The foreseeability of discovery validates the idea that certain confessions or utterances, while tainted with procedural missteps, remain indispensable to the pursuit of justice in the criminal justice system. Additionally, harmless error doctrine forms the core of exceptions to the exclusionary rule. When a court determines that a procedural mistake, such as the admission of evidence in an inappropriate manner, did not significantly affect the outcome of the trial, then the mistake is deemed harmless. This rationale has particular relevance in wrongful convictions, wherein the onus turns to correcting the system breakdowns that led to the injustices. The courts grapple with the fact of allowing some confessions or assertions to take hold over against violations of rights, particularly in view of the argument that violations of rights in some cases may serve to further cover up evidence of innocence. The existence of error doctrines harmless to the accuse, as seen in most arguments regarding fair trials, demonstrates the persistence of a historical tension in the legal system that seeks to reconcile individual rights with the pursuit of truth and justice in criminal trials and therefore suggests the need for continuous change and re-examination of established principles in light of evolving judicial standards (Garrett et al., 2005) (Figure 10.6).

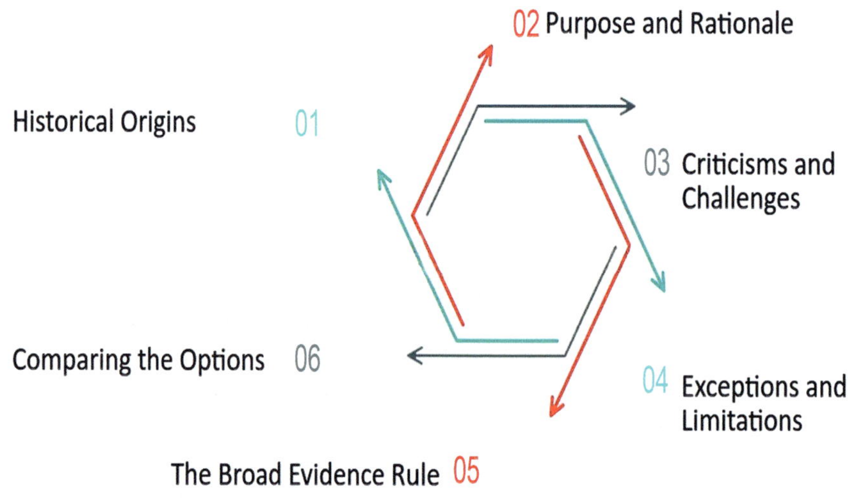

Figure 10.6. Exceptions to the exclusionary rule.

Source: https://fastercapital.co/i/The-Broad-Evidence-Rule--An-Exception-to-the-Exclusionary-Rule--Understanding-the-Exclusionary-Rule.webp.

10.3. STATEMENTS VS. CONFESSIONS

In criminal procedure, the distinction between statements and confessions is of a general significance within the legal framework. A statement, frequently volunteered by a suspect, is any admission of fact pertaining to a case without necessarily admitting the individual to a criminal offense. In contrast, a confession is characterized by the acknowledgement of guilt, in which an individual admits committing the crime in question. This is an important distinction as confessions are quite strong evidence, and their introduction can shift the direction of a criminal case. The potential for false convictions advanced in several scholarly analyses is a problem related to the elicitation of confessions under coercive conditions, which produce involuntary admissions of guilt that taint the legal process and undermine the integrity of the judiciary (Garrett et al., 2012). The burden of proof in criminal offenses is largely based on the character of the evidence led, particularly that of confessions over statements.

Figure 10.7. The distinction between statements and confessions.

Source: https://framerusercontent.com/images/6EcXfU2wPQC6mncAOjXH4YkLqTc.png.

Whereas statements are often challenged on facts and conditions, confessions can be given a presumption of truthfulness for being outright admissions of guilt. The aforementioned presumption is, however, riddled with challenges. For instance, psychological compulsion while being questioned can lead individuals to confess to crimes they did not commit, a highly controversial issue in legal scholarship. In addition, the law of confessions is shaped by cases emphasizing the need to safeguard defendants from exercising their rights fully, and in particular, the right against self-incrimination. The resulting legal framework attempts to balance the need for confessions as a way of finding the truth with the requirement to prevent miscarriages of justice that undermine public confidence in the justice system (Garrett et al., 2005). The implications of confessions and statements move beyond their definitions into the ethical considerations of how they are used in trials. The rules treatment of these two types of evidence often reflects broader societal attitudes toward fairness and due process. Confessions may quicken legal proceedings, but they must be subjected to close questioning to guard against possible abuse of police power. Scholars have argued for reform to prevent pressures on suspects to make confessions that increase the likelihood of coercive confessions leading to miscarriages of justice. By promoting a legal culture of strictly assessing the conditions under which confessions are given, the system of justice upholds its integrity to truth and justice while reiterating the constitutional requirement of the presumption of innocence until guilt (Garrett et al., 2012) (Figure 10.7).

10.3.1. Distinction Between Statements and Confessions

The distinction between statements and confessions in the context of criminal procedure is multifaceted and determinative to an understanding of the legal framework governing the admissibility of evidence. A statement usually describes a broad category of oral or written assertions made by an individual, and these could either incriminate or not incriminate such individual in criminal activity. On the other hand, a confession is a type of statement where the subject confesses to being involved in a crime, in effect acknowledging guilt. The implications of these differences are immense, in that confessions are typically treated with more distrust at trial. The rationale for this distrust emanates from issues relating to the validity and voluntariness of confessions, especially in the face of the danger of coercion or misperception in police interrogation (N/A, 1966). Thus, the law tries to make a distinction between confessions and statements to safeguard personal rights while making sure that the justice process is not compromised. The way confessions and statements are dealt with is also greatly influenced by such landmark cases as Miranda v. Arizona. This decision imposed major requirements for advisement of rights to the person being held in custody, emphasizing voluntary and informed waivers of the rights as a necessary prerequisite to the admissibility of a confession. Here, the distinction is not semantic but axiomatic in that legal jurisprudence recognizes that pressures inherent in custodial settings have the potential to yield unreliable confessions, which themselves can skew the burden of proof (Griffin et al., 2016). This has led to a significant change in the way that police carry out interrogations and take statements, necessitating an elevated level of vigilance to ensure what is written actually accurately interprets the person's intention and understanding. In addition, the criminal standard of proof complicates the confessions and statement situation. Although a confession is strong evidence, it does not have to result in a conviction without other supporting evidence. Statements from defendants may require more information or additional support to establish their legitimacy and relevance within the court.

The courts are confronted with the fallacies of hindsight bias, which contaminate the evaluation of evidence, particularly in establishing whether the confession is coerced or is a true depiction of events engaged (Griffin et al., 2016). These intricacies highlight the persistent need for criminal procedure reform to ensure that confessions and statements both undergo tests that place precedence on justice and fairness in pursuit of truth (Figure 10.8).

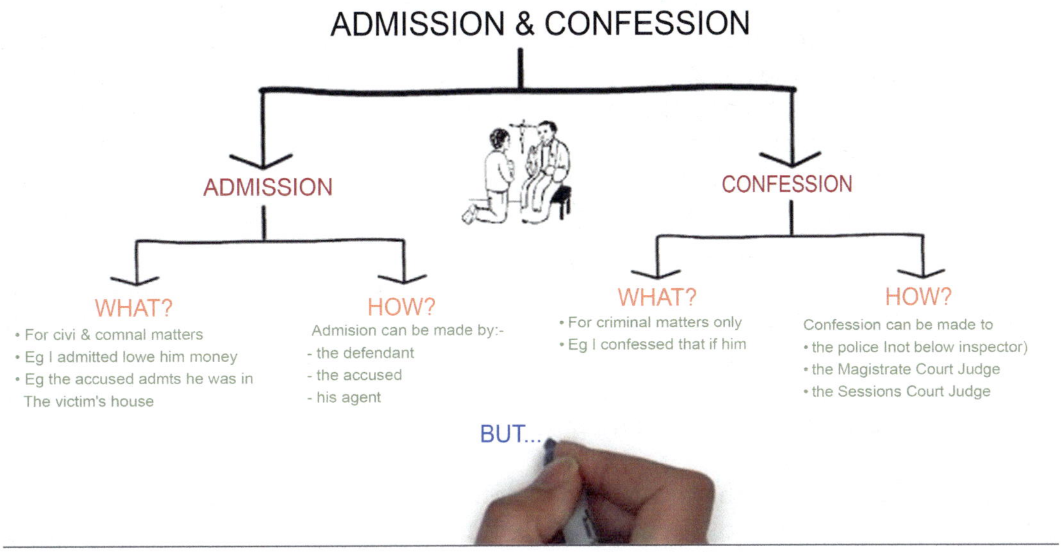

Figure 10.8. Distinction between statements and confessions.

Source: https://i.ytimg.com/vi/3ewEBe1d9vo/sddefault.jpg.

10.3.2. Legal Implications of Each in Criminal Cases

Confessions and defendants' statements in criminal procedure carry grave legal consequences associated with constitutional rights. The inherent importance of safeguarding individual freedoms in police interrogation is shown in the landmark case Miranda v. Arizona, where it was held that suspects have a right to be made aware of their rights prior to custodial interrogation. In the case, the Supreme Court emphasized knowing one's rights in a bid to avoid coercive techniques resulting in coerced confessions. The ruling went one step further to highlight the protection against self-incrimination and tightened the procedural safeguards that are required by the justice system, thus impacting the way law enforcement interacts with suspects. All confessions should be critically analyzed regarding voluntariness so that procedural integrity is upheld and confessions are reliable and admissible in court (N/A, 1966). The criminal standard of proof also has a grave legal consequence, as it directly impacts the prosecutions obligation to establish guilt beyond a reasonable doubt. Such a standard is a primary safeguard for defendants since it maintains that convictions be based on sound and reliable evidence rather than unsubstantiated claims. The presumption of innocence remains the cornerstone of the justice system; hence, the prosecution must present solid evidence to reach the burden of proof. Falling short in satisfying this level can result in acquittal, a show of the need for evidentiary standards to help maintain trials as equitable. Further, the interconnection between confessions and the burden of proof takes on an additional importance when examining situations in which a suspects confession of guilt is questioned, necessitating scrupulous judicial scrutiny in order to determine both the validity of the confession and its impact upon the totality of provision of evidence (Garrett et al., 2012). Habeas corpus and the interrelationship to defendants' due process rights also clarify the complexities of legal significance in criminal cases. As the courts examine the underlying fairness of the detentions and subsequent legal processes, the intersection of the habeas corpus, the Due Process Clause, and constitutional rights becomes more applicable. In cases such as Hamdi v. Rumsfeld and Boumediene v. Bush, the courts set that habeas corpus is a necessary protection against abusive detention, providing even noncitizens some measure of protection under due process. These cases are part of a broader vision of how procedural rights should control treatment of those in the criminal justice system and how it operates within the larger system of legal protections. As courts navigate these complicated relationships, they reiterate the necessity for accountable and open legal processes, particularly when cases rely on confessions as primary evidence in securing convictions (Garrett et al., 2012).

10.3.3. Examples of How Statements Can Influence Investigations

The influence of statements on criminal investigations is quite substantial, typically guiding the direction of the investigation itself. As illustration, for instance, at the interrogation phase, a suspect's word can serve as a turning point, which can direct an investigator to pivotal evidence or accept confessions that make a case against a person stronger. The judicial precedent in Miranda v. Arizona reveals the delicate balance between law enforcements role to obtain information and an individual's constitutional rights. The Supreme Court ruling necessitated suspects to be informed of their rights, thereby acknowledging the fact that coerced or uninformed confessions not only test the credibility of investigations but can also cast doubts on the validity of the confessions elicited. The statements, thus, not only record the reactions of the suspects but also inform investigative techniques that rely essentially on the validity and the context of the statements (N/A, 1966). Moreover, the psychological nuances of what is being interpreted in statements directly affect the investigative process. Suggestibility, police question wording, and interrogative context all can lead people to provide false or misleading information. The research on wrongful convictions further emphasizes the susceptibility with findings that most convictions were heavily based upon un credible testimonies. Researchers like Simon Cole and Elizabeth Loftus have contributed to this literature through identifying evidence coherence in criminal investigations and how, through cognitive bias or pressure, misleading statements can be made. These results not only enlighten on the complexities of testimonial evidence but also reiterate the need for careful scrutiny of how statements are obtained and used in the judicial system, further supporting the effects they have on the defective construction of criminal cases (Garrett et al., 2012). In addition, the effects of statements extend far beyond mere confession; they play a significant role in shaping public opinion and informing judicial outcomes. In celebrity prosecutions, media depictions of statements made by suspects can enhance preconceived opinion and bias, ultimately affecting the rulings of juries. Public opinion engagement with judicial proceedings provokes ethical concerns regarding the representation of such statements. Statement-centric investigation can provide a confirmation bias for the investigating process and the societal context of the case as well. This aspect highlights the importance of law enforcement and judiciary to maintain objective criteria that safeguard against societal narratives interfering with them, thereby ensuring assertions are subjected to examination on their actual evidentiary worth rather than popularity (Garrett et al., 2012).

10.4. THE BURDEN OF PROOF IN CRIMINAL CASES

The criminal beyond reasonable doubt evidence is the underlying foundation of the justice system that establishes who has the duty to prove the truth of claims. The burden during criminal proceedings rests with the prosecution itself, and it must establish the defendant's guilt beyond a reasonable doubt. This very high standard is critical in that it reflects the inherent principle that it is better for one guilty person to escape than for an innocent person to be wrongly convicted. This principle is excellently established in the judgments of pioneering cases, e.g., Miranda v. Arizona, affirming the necessity of protecting individual rights within the criminal justice system. The complexities inherent in the burden of proof not only affect trials but the direction in which confessions and statements are investigated within the overall view of criminal procedure (N/A, 1966). Confessions play a considerable role in determining the burden of proof because they are considered a conclusive indicator towards guilt.

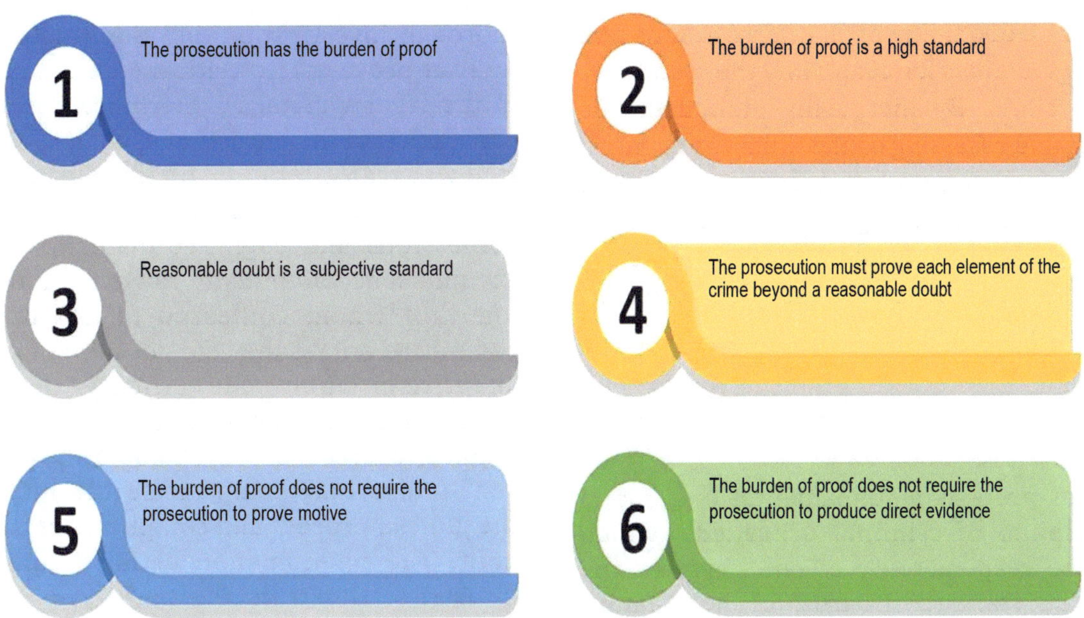

Figure 10.9. The burden of proof in criminal cases.

Source: https://fastercapital.co/i/The-Anatomy-of-Reasonable-Doubt--Understanding-the-Legal-Standard--The-Burden-of-Proof-in-Criminal-Cases.webp.

However, the intricacy of the reliability of confessions poses severe challenges to the prosecution. False confessions, either brought about by psychological pressure or coercive methods, complicate the narrative presented in court. Experiments have proved that suspects can confess freely to crimes they never committed, raising core concerns about the reliability of the evidence presented before court. As pointed out by recent legal literature, the problem of false confessions illustrates the urgency for reforms that guard against suspect statements contaminating the evidence base. A recognition of such subtleties facilitates a re-evaluation of mechanisms governing the elicitation and use of confessions in light of the burden of proof in criminal proceedings (Garrett et al., 2010). The consequences of the burden of proof extend beyond mere guilt or innocence; they involve more abstract issues with justice and civil liberties. For instance, the police interrogation process and confession procedure in court can bolster or undermine the integrity of the judicial process. Once the burden of proof is proven by questionable means, particularly in the case of false confessions, there is an increased risk of miscarriages of justice. It is therefore crucial to institute systemic changes such as mandatory videotaping of all interrogations and rigorous guidelines for evaluating the credibility of confessions. By increasing standards for obtaining and assessing confessions, the criminal justice system can ensure that the burden of proof is a formidable safeguard against wrongful convictions, ultimately enhancing public trust in the criminal justice process (Garrett et al., 2010) (Figure 10.9).

10.4.1. Definition and Significance of the Burden of Proof

Burden of proof is a fundamental concept in the discipline of criminal procedure, which means the responsibility of one party or the other to substantiate the truth of their claims. In criminal trials, the prosecution has the duty to establish the defendant's guilt beyond all reasonable doubt. This high demand is the immunity from false accusation, so that no person is unjustly punished except where evidence presented meets the essential test of certainty. The burden of proof is more than merely procedural in nature; it includes the principle of presumption of innocence, an elementary maxim of criminal law. This principle demands a defendant to be innocent until proven guilty, therefore placing the onus squarely on the state to establish its allegations, a dynamic that protects personal rights in an adversarial system. The burden of proof also impacts the tactics employed by prosecution and defense during trial proceedings. Because the prosecution must go through this elevated standard of proof, it has a tendency to lead to the production of solid evidence and appealing arguments to persuade the jury. In failing to fulfill this obligation, it can lead to acquittal, stressing the great risk for the prosecution. Conversely, the defense can utilize the burden of proof to create effective countering arguments on grounds of reasonable doubt or inconsistency of case in prosecution. In the dynamic, not only does the burden of proof impact decisions during trials but it also highlights the importance of thorough investigation and the sanctity of the judicial process as a critical element of justice in the legal system. Furthermore, the modern conception of the burden of proof has prompted renewed consideration of its impact in light of recent studies of such phenomena as false confessions and cognitive distortion. In fact, the innocence of unjustly convicted individuals many of whom confessed falsely to having committed crimes they did not commit provokes skepticism about the efficacy of existing procedural safeguards. As testified by current studies, coerced or psychologically pressured confessions may compromise the integrity of the judicial process and complicate establishing guilt. The phenomenon of false confessions is used to illustrate the pervasive impact of investigative procedures on the burden of proof because the content of confessions has to be scrutinized for credibility (Garrett et al., 2010). Thus, understanding these complexities paved the way for reforms favoring the scrutiny of evidence and credibility of confession ultimately making the pillars of justice and accountability stronger in the criminal justice system (Figure 10.10).

Figure 10.10. The significance of the burden of proof.

Source: https://i0.wp.com/jpassociates.co.in/wp-content/uploads/2025/01/9.png.

10.4.2. Differences Between Civil and Criminal Burden of Proof

The distinction between civil and criminal burdens of proof lies at the heart of the legal system, largely determining the outcome of court cases. In criminal cases, the burden of proof is on the prosecution to establish the defendant's guilt beyond a reasonable doubt. This strict standard is applied to make sure that individuals do not get wrongly convicted, which maintains the adage that it is better for an innocent person to go free than for a guilty person to be wrongly convicted. Civil suits make use of the standard of preponderance of the evidence, where the plaintiff must make a showing that their claims are more than likely than not. This split emphasizes the varying stakes of civil and criminal cases, criminal cases having large sanctions, such as imprisonment, whereas civil cases typically involve monetary damages or specific performances. There is another substantial split regarding the procedural impacts of these burdens of proof. In a criminal case, the rule of the presumption of innocence plays a central impact, wherein the defendant is innocent until he/she is proven otherwise. This fundamental idea not only teaches the burden placed on the prosecution, but also allows the defense to present evidence without necessarily proving guilt wrong. Civil actions, however, require the plaintiff to both verify their complaint and often respond to defenses of the defendant, possibly including a more active responsibility in procuring and presenting evidence. The dynamic processes in each case type reflect their varying nature and evidence the prioritizing by the legal system to protect individual rights against the backdrop of the criminal process. The variations further explain the complexities of confessions and statements in court processes. The stringent demands of the criminal burden of proof necessitate strict examination of confessions for ensuring that they are lawfully and voluntarily made, ensuring thereby the rights of the defendant. In civil cases, evidence and testimony presented can be from any source at all, such as affidavits or hearsay, which can have even broader impacts on the manner of case argument and resolution. In addition, the focus of whether new evidence can substantiate innocence or guilt assertions—especially subsequent to trial—has yielded shifting legal perspectives regarding such burdens. Nations are increasingly considering the sufficiency of their systems to respond to such allegations in order to support a proper debate concerning the balance of justice and the role of evidence in the case of civil and criminal situations (Chiu et al., 2009; Garrett et al., 2017).

10.4.3. The Presumption of Innocence and Its Implications

The presumption of innocence rule is a fundamental principle of criminal procedure, whereby an accused individual is presumed innocent until they are established to be guilty. This is a vital safeguard in guaranteeing that the prosecution must bear the burden of proof. In putting the responsibility on someone else instead of the defendant, the criminal justice system is adhering to the principle that it is preferable to release a possibly culpable individual than to convict an innocent one. Through the principle of presumption of innocence, a climate is established where confessions and assertions of defendants are made with skepticism to prevent wrongful convictions, hence preserving the integrity of the judicial process. Importantly, breaches of this principle potentially result in systemic injustices, demonstrating the fine balance between a defendants rights and legal authorities obligations in prosecutorial behavior.

Figure 10.11. The presumption of innocence and its implications.

Source: https://fastercapital.co/i/Burden-of-proof--The-Burden-of-Proof--Understanding-Prima-Facie-s-Dilemma--Presumption-of-innocence.webp.

The effect of the presumption of innocence is deep-reaching, having ramifications on both legal practice and public attitudes towards justice. Where the legal process enforces this principle consistently, it instills public confidence in the justice process and reduces the risk of mass bias against defendants. Moreover, the doctrine of innocent until proven guilty supports the inherent importance of evidence to determine culpability; without sufficient and persuasive evidence, charges against a person are no more than accusations. The courts, made up of judges and jurors, must guard against the force of public opinion or emotional response that would vitiate this principle. By doing so, the protection of the presumption of innocence safeguard the rights of the accused and ensures an atmosphere of fairness in the legal process, reinforcing the importance of due process to criminal justice. There are challenges in applying the presumption of innocence, particularly considering today's judicial challenges and pressures within society. For instance, cases of media sensationalism can create a prejudicial climate where defendants are pre-judged guilty in the eyes of the public before their case's determination. This pre-judgment can influence jury selection and trial outcomes, emphasizing the significance of unbending adherence to the presumption of innocence. Furthermore, treatment of confessions and statements thereof in this respect emphasizes the need for procedural protection against manipulation or coercion. Legal precedent also upholds the voluntariness of confessions as the most significant, as noted in landmark cases that examine statements made under duress. Thus, upholding the presumption of innocence not only protects individual rights but also increases the overall legitimacy of the criminal justice system such that justice is not only done, but also seems to be done (Figure 10.11).

10.5. THE IMPACT OF COERCED CONFESSIONS

The phenomenon of coerced confessions comprehensively ruins the credibility of the criminal justice system, upsetting fundamental principles addressing confessions, statements, and proof. The confessions, which are typically done under duress or fraudulent tactics, create an irreversible mark on the court process. When such statements are brought in the process of trials, the presumption of guilt becomes the overwhelming rider on rational investigations to make an unbalanced presentation favoring confession over fact. The institutional reliance on such confessions can lead to wrongful convictions and carry on a chain of injustice against marginalized groups. It then becomes vital to examine the way coerced confessions not only infringe the accused's rights but also assault the generalized principles of fair trial assurances in criminal procedure. Moreover, coerced confession implications are not limited to the specific case and indicate systemic defects among judiciary and law enforcement practices.

Figure 10.12. The phenomenon of coerced confessions significantly undermines the integrity of the criminal justice system.

Source: https://fastercapital.co/i/False-Confessions--The-Perils-of-Misjustice--The-Impact-of-False-Confessions-on-the-Justice-System.webp.

It is revealed through research that vulnerable populations such as juveniles and the mentally challenged are particularly vulnerable to abuse during interrogation. This vulnerability not only presents ethical challenges but also strains procedural safeguards against coercion. This is according to arguments in the context of wrongful convictions, having procedural rights as these cases unfold normally leads to significant misinterpretations in courts. For instance, the harmless error approach is brought in; errors caused by coercive practice can be dismissed as nonsubstantial even if they adversely affect the trial's outcome, thereby perpetuating an unfair process (Garrett et al.,

2005). Lastly, the legal framework governing coerced confessions requires re-examination of procedures governing their admissibility in courts. Current paradigms in the judiciary struggle to address the effects of coercive interrogation tactics. Failing to effectively differentiate between involuntary and voluntary confessions can result in huge misapplications of justice, as the right to a fair trial under the constitution is violated. The implications of such misapprehension are grave, since coerced confessions hence may go unproven and lead to an avalanche of unjust convictions that overwhelm public faith in judicial uprightness (Greabe et al., 1994). A thorough examination of these procedural flaws is crucial as society grapples with the implications of coerced confessions and their ability to dictate case outcomes, thereby making a strong case for the reform of police practices and legal standards (Figure 10.12).

10.5.1. Psychological Factors Leading to Coerced Confessions

Psychological factors intrusively impact the process of coerced confessions, thus serving as part of the intricate elements involved in criminal interrogations. Vulnerability, particularly among teen defendants, is a central element of the issue. Adolescents, often lacking the intellectual sophistication to appreciate the long-term consequences of their confessions, can be coerced into confessing to crime. Research indicates that jurors struggle to identify the unreliability of such confessions, assuming that a confession equates to culpability. Such a phenomenon is particularly problematic in the case of juvenile defendants, who are at their most susceptible to coercive tactics (Dobrowolski et al., 2018). The psychological manipulation inherent in the process of interrogation, thus, not only warps facts but also compromises the integrity of the justice system, resulting in wrongful convictions. It is important to recognize these psychological frailties in order to promote fair outcomes within the criminal justice system. The interaction between social influence strategies and elicitation of confessions demonstrates the psychological variables that cause coercive confessions. Law enforcement's methods, including the Mr. Big operation, are dependent on manipulation of suspects' psychological states that create a setting conducive to conformity. This method employs social principles like authority and reciprocity to create circumstances when individuals feel they are under pressure to meet standards anticipated by authorizers. The new Supreme Court of Canada ruling presents the requirement for assessing the prejudicial effects of these confessions, as it illustrates how psychological pressure can transgress due process rights (Luther et al., 2016). By acknowledging the social dynamics involved in interrogations, legal systems can better be designed to limit the risk of coerced confessions and enhance respect for standards of fair trials. In addition to short-term psychological ploys employed in interrogations, structural issues in the criminal justice system also contribute to the prevalence of coercive confessions. Conditions such as racial biases and economic disparities exacerbate the vulnerabilities of certain groups, leading to coerced admissions of vulnerable groups. The intersectionality of the conditions is apparent in the jurors' assessment of confessions as seen from the variation in how members of the jury perceive the credibility of confessions based on the race of the defendant (Dobrowolsky et al., 2018). Subsequently, the indigent and other minority defendants may be exposed to greater scrutiny, sometimes reinforcing stereotype-perpetuating validation that may influence jurors' perceptions. Bolstering such systemic issues is central to the development of a more equitable legal system, ensuring equal treatment for all defendants by demographic and reducing the incidence of wrongful convictions on the basis of coerced confessions.

10.5.2. Legal Ramifications of Admitting Coerced Confessions

The legal effects of their admissibility as evidence are multifaceted and extensive, typically endangering the very foundations of the criminal justice system. Coerced confessions undermine the integrity of the judicial process, as they are not results of genuine voluntary choice but consequences of manipulation or coercion on the part of law enforcement officers. When such confessions are presented in trials, they distort the justice that is required to an even-handed legal system. They can lead to mistaken convictions, as evident through empirical research that shows numerous examples where innocent individuals have been mistakenly convicted on the basis of confessions. Courts are faced with the burdensome task of ascertaining where a confession comes from, as coercion undermines the credibility of a defendant's confessions and opens up a dangerous precedent, which can justify the use of improper methods. The use of coerced confessions also raises valid questions regarding the burden of proof in criminal trials. While the prosecution is likely to have the onus of proving guilt beyond reasonable doubt, the presence of a coerced confession merely exacerbates the matter. The inherent bias resulting from an advertisement under duress can skew the evidence into a wrong direction, resulting in misinterpretations of guilt that are not indicative of objective reality. While legal standards maintain that confessions need to be voluntary, the cognitive biases and hindsight blindness as described in existing literature have the potential to weaken the effective assessment of coerced confessions in court. The aforementioned biases are capable of causing courts to fail in adequately questioning the context of a confession and subsequently reinforcing inherent flaws within the adjudicative process (Griffin et al., 2016). Furthermore, the trend towards active participation by defendants in their trials has complicated the scene in terms of coerced confessions. With the evolution of legal systems, the consequences of penalizing non-cooperation have emerged, leading to more calls for defendants to cooperate in the criminal process. This pressure can unknowingly expose individuals to coercive practices as they struggle to demonstrate compliance or innocence, which can affect their own judgment and lead to innocent confessions of guilt. Critics argue that coercively engaging defendants negates their right to a fair trial, where the state's obligation to establish its allegations is compromised when confession thresholds are influenced (Owusu-Bempah et al., 2016). Therefore, it is important to analyze these legal consequences in order to determine the implications of coerced statements on the criminal procedure system's overall fairness and effectiveness (Figure 10.13).

Figure 10.13. The legal ramifications of admitting coerced confessions.

Source: https://cdn.lawlytics.com/law-media/uploads/1814/327267/large/coerced-confession.jpg?1744989661.

10.5.3. Case Studies Highlighting the Consequences of Coercion

Case study analysis demonstrating the impact of coercion in criminal procedure presents basic details about aspects pertaining to the integrity of statements and coerced confessions. A classic case is that of Miranda v. Arizona, which highlighted protecting the rights of individuals during custodial questioning. The Supreme Court ruling established that any confessions made in ignorance of one's rights are by definition vulnerable to coercive pressures, underlining the need for procedural protection. The landmark ruling not only reformed the image of American criminal law, but also underlined the psychological impact of coercion, where vulnerable suspects stood likely to be coaxed into confessing crimes for which they are innocent. Therefore, Miranda v. Arizona highlights the extensive consequences of coercive methods, stressing the thin line between police objectives and the fundamental rights of the accused (N/A, 1966). Yet another sad case highlighting the consequences of coercion is the use of torture and degrading techniques of questioning, particularly in democratic countries where these techniques are meant to be otherwise regulated. Research has determined that the militarization of police operations and inadequate protection of suspects' rights explain the persistence of such violent methods. For instance, a poll of Mexican prisoners revealed that coercive treatment, including torture, are alarmingly prevalent due to inadequate institutional protection. The general prevalence of these practices is concerning in terms of accountability and the legitimacy of confessions obtained under coercion. They not only make up a violation of human rights but also undermine the credibility of the criminal justice system as a whole. The research brings to the forefront the pressing need for transformational changes to rid the system of outdated practices and increase the rights of accused persons to mitigate the effects of coercion (Magaloni et al., 2020). The implications of these case studies extend beyond the specific cases to point towards systemic breakdown in the criminal justice system. Harsh interrogation techniques often lead to wrongful convictions, which reflect the overall societal consequence of disregarding proper procedure. Cases of coerced confessions later being withdrawn or found to be false further suggest dire implications for the accused and the integrity of the justice system. Besides, such cases illustrate an urgent necessity for ongoing legal and social reforms to enhance accountability among police officers. Knowledge of the impacts of coercion can help stakeholders better advocate for a shift to more humane and fairer practices in criminal procedures. Finally, the treatment of coercion not only legally vindicates wrongly accused individuals but also enhances public faith in the legal system as a protector of rights and justice (Magaloni et al., 2020; N/A, 1966).

10.6. THE ROLE OF TECHNOLOGY IN CONFESSIONS AND STATEMENTS

The application of technology in the context of confessions and statements has transformed the criminal process landscape to a large degree. Not only does technology enable the recording of statements through various media, such as digital audio recordings and web interrogations, but it also brings extra integrity and authenticity to confessions. The operation of audio and video recording equipment ensures that there is the assurance of all communications by law enforcers with suspects being written down, and this promotes openness and reduces pressure or misrepresentation. This innovation provides a higher quality benchmark upon which the voluntariness of confessions may be measured, since the tape version can be examined for signs of psychological coercion or undue influence that can corrupt the defendant's statement. Technology is thus at the heart of the guarantee that confessions are not mere products of duress but instead accurate representations of an individual's perception of facts.

Figure 10.14. The role of technology in confessions and statements.

Source: https://static.wixstatic.com/media/f721f3_1700a95db8fd474184e15b466d43db95~mv2.webp/v1/fill/w_568,h_568,al_c,q_80,usm_0.66_1.00_0.01,enc_avif,quality_auto/f721f3_1700a95db8fd474184e15b466d43db95~mv2.webp.

No less significant is the capacity of technology to aid in substantiating what is being said during the investigating process. Forensic kits and data analysis allow police to substantiate confessions through physical evidence as well as credible eyewitness accounts. For instance, DNA testing, the game-changer, can provide tangible proof either to corroborate or contradict a confession. The ability to cross-examine electronic data, such as mobile phone location or internet search history, can enhance the probative value of a confession by associating disparate strands of information that point toward or away from the suspicion of guilt of an accused. While this technological interconnectivity heightens the efficiency of investigations, it also raises ethical issues regarding privacy and misuse of information gathered, hence necessitating moderation in its use.

Furthermore, the implications of technological advancement go beyond the mere collection of evidence; they chart the story of wrongful convictions and the burden of proof. As the judiciary becomes more aware of its own errors, often spurred by deficient procedural protections, the acknowledgement of the power for change that technology can deliver grows. The legal landscape that has existed around wrongful convictions, in which exculpatory evidence used to be disregarded or where confessions were found to be coerced, is shifting. Exoneration cases, often aided by the revelations of scientific strides like DNA evidence, are evidence of the shortfalls within conventional investigative methods. The development of wrongful conviction law introduces a rigorous analysis of how confessions are analyzed within the framework of procedural safeguards, emphasizing that technology should be harnessed not only for effective investigation but to ensure justice in a way that minimizes the risk of error within the judicial process (Garrett et al., 2005; Griffin et al., 2016) (Figure 10.14).

10.6.1. Use of Recording Devices and Their Legal Implications

The use of recording devices in law enforcement has transformed the means used to record confessions and statements of suspects. The technology, aside from magnifying the accuracy of the recorded transaction, serves as a critical legal safeguard against coercion and misrepresentation. Recording equipment keeps a clean record of interrogations, thereby guaranteeing that the confessions, if any, are obtained under rightful conditions. Following the precedents established, led by the landmark case of Miranda v. Arizona, the Supreme Court placed great importance on these recordings in order to protect an individual's right against self-incrimination. The existence of recording devices thus becomes a critical component in determining criminal procedure validity, allowing confessions to be verified for authenticity as well as complimenting the burden of proof laid on the prosecution to establish guilt beyond a reasonable doubt (N/A, 1966). The legal implications of recording devices are both applicable to procedural justice and requirements of evidence. The courts increasingly rely on recorded evidence to ascertain confessions' voluntariness according to set legal standards. Recording devices minimize the occurrence of "he said, she said" scenarios that serve to undermine testimonies as evidence in court. Furthermore, the effects of utilizing such devices are particularly crucial in maintaining the defendants' rights during interrogations. As evidenced in instances where taped confessions later provided evidence of coercive means, the tapes are both a measure of safety and verification of words spoken during the process of trials. This action towards taping translates to a change from subjective examination of confessions towards more objective analysis of evidence, thus making the commitment to justice and transparency within the legal process even more secure (Griffin et al., 2016). But the use of the recording tool is also not controversy-free and trouble-free. Admissibility concerns as well as privacy rights always arise, particularly regarding storage and collection of the records as well as where and how they are being done. The legality of observation methods, especially without prior consent, raises fundamental issues regarding the rights of a person in the judiciary. For instance, laws in various jurisdictions concerning recording of conversations differ, and it ends up providing complicating elements in trials. In addition, selective editing or manipulation of recorded evidence remains a concern; unless courts can entirely ensure the integrity of these recordings, the entire foundation for utilizing them as credible evidence is compromised. Thus, while recording technology enhances confessional descriptiveness in criminal proceedings, the legal community must navigate the entangled ethical dilemmas and present robust paradigms to ensure that such technology serves to enhance justice and not undermine it (Griffin et al., 2016).

10.6.2. The Impact of Social Media on Confessions and Statements

The sudden development of social media sites has totally transformed the character of confessions and statements under criminal procedure. Individuals are routinely posting their ideas, emotions, and everyday experiences on the web at such a pace that they do not even consider the legal implications of what they are sharing. This pervasive virtual world witnesses spontaneous confessions of guilt by the accused who may believe that they are merely unburdening themselves or merely seeking sympathy from their virtual community. Such actions end up being unwittingly contributory to a legal process, as detectives will search social media posts in order to locate potential confessions or clues. The implications of such online statements not only complicate understanding conventional notions of consent and coercion, but it also complicates the credibility and validity of social media as hearsay presented in court, which is problematic for the burden of proof demands at criminal trials. With the evolving character of confessions during the times of digital communication, the legal system must address moral concerns regarding the admissibility of social media evidence during court proceedings. Unlike traditional confessions typically received during a direct police questioning, social media words are expressed in informal settings and have no juridical supervision. This jeopardizes the voluntariness of these confessions, particularly in light of the psychological motivations of social media persuasion, i.e., peer pressure or desire for public approval. Social media confessions can have most impact in wrongful conviction cases, where attitudes on the part of the jury and the seriousness attributed to them decide a defendants fate. Legal commentators have noted that the public's growing familiarity with the platforms can also have biases that affect juror interpretation and blur the line between valid evidence and damaging misinformation. The research on wrongful convictions is particularly definitive in highlighting that there is inherent overlap between social media utterances and the justice system's persistent failure to deal with confessions and the burden of proof. Research indicates that the majority of wrongful convictions are a result of misapplied or misinterpreted evidence, as a rule augmented by the spread of misinformation on social media. Social media thus plays a dual function: it can bring to light loopholes in evidence as well as solidify bad news narratives which are likely to lead to miscarriages of justice. The scholarly debate further involves the legal consequences of such occurrences, discussing cases in which social media confessions presumably led to miscarriages of justice. For instance, the research into wrongful conviction pinpoints a need for reform regarding admissibility of social media evidence in court as highlighted by recent controversies surrounding rights of the defendant and legal professionals' responsibility for maintaining the integrity of the process (Garrett et al., 2005, 2012) (Figure 10.15).

Figure 10.15. The impact of social media on confessions and statements.

Source: https://schoolyears.org/wp-content/uploads/2023/04/impact-of-social-media.jpg.

10.6.3. Emerging Technologies and Their Influence on Evidence Gathering

Emerging technologies are transforming the landscape of evidence gathering in criminal procedure, with the potential to bring both challenges and opportunities to lawyers. Conjoining advanced data analysis, artificial intelligence, and machine learning capabilities facilitates the assembly of extensive data sets, significantly expanding the ability of police forces to detect patterns and potential criminal activity. For instance, predictive policing software can utilize historical crime information to forecast the areas in which crimes are most probable to occur and more effectively target resource allocation. However, such reliance on technology is open to criticism on grounds of bias—following the Algorithmic Jim Crow phenomena, whereby systems can perpetuate existing discriminatory means of rulemaking by claiming objectivity (Hu et al., 2017). Thus, while technological advancements can strengthen the law enforcement toolkit, they also need to be monitored to ensure continued adherence to norms of justice and fairness in the criminal justice system. Moreover, the arrival of digital forensics has revolutionized the process of collecting and interpreting evidence. Cloud computing, social media examination, and mobile device extraction tools allow examiners to obtain important information from various electronic sources. This not only enhances the volume of potential evidence but also allows for more precision in proving or disproving criminal allegations. But the use of such technologies is filled with privacy concerns and ethical dilemmas, particularly regarding the admissibility of evidence obtained from private devices without explicit consent. Courts are forced to contend with ensuring that suspects' and defendants' rights are not sacrificed in the process of gathering incriminating evidence because such intrusions would undermine the integrity of the judicial process (McGarity et al., 2013). Additionally, the use of new technologies for evidence collection similarly necessitates reevaluation of the standards for confessions and statements in criminal procedure. Since technology bestows law enforcement authorities with the ability to influence suspects—i.e., interrogation facilities with AI analysis of verbal and nonverbal cues—there is the inherent potential for coercion. The very environment within which confessions are squeezed, complemented by the potentiality of technology, can warp the authenticity of those statements rendered by individuals. This is the kind of complexity that puts into question the burden of proof and how much technology should be allowed to intervene in assessing the validity of confessions. Legal practitioners, therefore, have to fight for strict standards that guarantee technology serves to augment, and not undermine, the pursuit of justice in the criminal arena.

SUMMARY

The complexities surrounding confessions, speech, and the burden of proof within criminal process ultimately identify a necessity for ongoing reform in the criminal justice system. Modern criminal justice increasingly grapples with the psychological forces behind interrogations that may lead the innocent and guilty to give false confessions. False confessions have disproportionate value in trials, usually tilting the burden of proof and misleading juries. The implications of this issue were made starkly apparent by seminal legal decisions, such as Miranda v. Arizona, where the Supreme Courts emphasis on the protection of individual rights was a paradigm shift within the criminal justice setting (N/A, 1966). By making these issues ongoing, legal professionals and policymakers are tasked to focus their energies on the authenticity of confessions to ensure justice. It is important to address the reality of false confessions in order to protect the integrity of the legal system. The sad truth is that postconviction DNA testing has freed many individuals who were wrongly convicted, and many of these wrongful convictions have been the result of false confessions obtained through coercive tactics of interrogation (Garrett et al., 2010). The frequency with which these wrongful convictions occur is a cause of concern about the efficacy of existing practices of interrogation and their far-reaching implications for the lives of innocent people. The judicial system has to evolve to incorporate practices such as tape recording of interrogations in detail and steps that test the credibility of defendant statements. These are important measures to ensure that miscarriages of justice do not recur and that confidence in the criminal justice system is restored. Lastly, it is incumbent upon the legal community to make a serious reconsideration of how confessions are processed in the courtroom. Because the intersection point between confession validity and victim rights remains a battlefield with a great deal of strife, there must be a more advanced approach. By pointing out the need to tighten control over the process of interrogation, the justice system might eliminate risks for confessions that are laden with outside contamination. Scholars and practitioners must fight for reforms that not only recognize the psychological nature of confessions but also ensure that considerations of due process and fairness are accorded priority in criminal procedure. In the long term, it is only through reformed practices that take into consideration these many variables that the legal system can aspire to bring true justice and protect the rights of all concerned.

The intersection of confessions, statements, and the need for proof in criminal procedure constitute immediate ethical and legal issues. Perhaps the most relevant piece that has been written is the classic case of Miranda v. Arizona that established the right to counsel and the advisement of rights requirement to suspects prior to interrogation. This decision underscored the need to safeguard the rights of the individual in the legal process, while responding simultaneously to the potent influence of confessions on the process of adjudication. The decision has provoked extensive debate regarding its scope and effectiveness in bringing about justice, with scholars offering varied perspectives that enrich our understanding of its influence on law enforcement practice and defendants' rights (N/A, 1966). Further, the phenomenon of false confessions brings to the fore the complexities that attend the eliciting of genuine admissions of guilt. The instances of the wrongly convicted who have made admissions of guilt to offenses they did not commit give us grounds to suspect the interrogation tactics of the police. Psychological coercion inflicted on suspects might result in spurious admissions of guilt that taint the reputation of the judicial system. This has become a priority, particularly with postconviction DNA exonerations, that indicate the alarming prevalence of false confessions in capital cases. Researchers are focusing more on how some interrogation strategies give rise to this uncomfortable phenomenon, and they emphasize the necessity for reforms to maintain the validity and reliability of confession evidence (Garrett et al., 2010). Conforming to the threats presented by false confessions and the possibility of contamination of statements, it is increasingly argued that a rethinking of current criminal procedural rules is called for. There seems to be a need for radical reforms, particularly with respect to the rules that govern interrogation procedures. Suggestions include requiring videotaping of entire interrogations as a means of ensuring accountability and transparency. Furthermore, the concept of reformulating judicial review processes to investigate under what circumstances confessions are obtained is imperative in eliminating the prospect of wrongful convictions. By the identification of such areas of focus, the justice system will be capable of serving to protect the rights of the innocent more effectively while ensuring the viability of confessions in order to continue building a fairer and more just criminal justice system.

KEY TERMS

Admissibility
Custodial Confession
Evidentiary Value
Extra-Judicial Confession
Judicial Confession
Presumption of Innocence
Reverse Burden
Voluntariness
Confession
Dying Declaration
Exculpatory Statement
Inculpatory Statement
Onus Probandi
Retracted Confession
Standard of Proof

A LOOK TO THE FUTURE

FUTURE CONSIDERATIONS FOR LEGAL REFORMS AND PRACTICES

On account of constant controversies regarding the truthfulness of confessions and statements during criminal trials, future legal reforms need to address the scrutiny and regulation of interrogation strategies. Psychological pressure compelling innocent people to make false confessions has long been a cause for worry, and there is increasingly a need for comprehensive policy reforms. Police interrogations are often founded on coercive tactics that can deceive vulnerable suspects into making false confessions for crimes they have never committed. By enacting reforms that mandate the complete videotaping of interrogations, policymakers can create an open record of the interrogation process that can possibly stem abusive tactics and promote accountability. In addition, these actions would further allow courts to look at the circumstances surrounding confessions being given, so that each of those possibly tainted statements could be scrutinized to ensure defendants' rights as well as the integrity of the judicial process. In addition to revising interrogation techniques, the justice system must also confront the challenge of confession contamination, a severe attack on criminal proceedings' validity. False confession experiments have shown that a large proportion of people unwittingly incorporate information from the interrogation process into their confessions, creating determinations of credibility as problematic. As noted, with two exonerees excluded from consideration, all of them provided comprehensive confessions that appeared to incorporate information outside of their access independently of external influence.

The disturbing phenomenon reveals a clear need for change in how confessions are tried and prosecuted postconviction. By prescribing procedures for rigorously testing the credibility of confessions, the courts can make a concerted effort towards preventing miscarriages of justice. Parliaments may also introduce benchmarks for testing the probative value of confession material, which would further discourage contamination and practically implement the doctrine of fairness in court proceedings. Moving forward, reforms are not limited to bureaucratic reform; rather, a total transformation of the mindset of the criminal justice system when it comes to confessions and evidence is needed. Since civil rights complaints arise out of cases involving wrongful convictions, they attempt to redefine conventional concepts of criminal procedure rights. The implications of federal cases of wrongful conviction suggest a reforming potential for transforming the manner in which the system responds to trial violations. Recent examination maintains that the emancipatory model of civil action may dissolve the pernicious error insulation that has sustained prosecutorial abuse in criminal cases, opening new channels of accountability and disclosure. Through the acceptance of this change, the judiciary can strive towards a renewed model that is focused on seeking the truth and justice, eventually safeguarding against future injustices while ensuring the basic tenets of adequate fair trial rights.

REFERENCES

1. Bodini, S. P. (2011). Fighting maritime piracy under the European Convention on Human Rights. *European Journal of International Law, 22*, 829–848. https://doi.org/10.1093/ejil/chr052 (accessed on 13th August 2025).
2. Chiu, W. K. (2009). Criminal interrogation and the right to remain silent: A study of the Hong Kong Customs Service. https://core.ac.uk/download/38038910.pdf (accessed on 13th August 2025).
3. Dobrowolsky, L. (2018). Are jurors' judgments about confessions affected by juvenile defendant race? https://core.ac.uk/download/230543474.pdf (accessed on 13th August 2025).
4. Garrett, B. L. (2005). Innocence, harmless error, and federal wrongful conviction law. https://core.ac.uk/download/213020502.pdf (accessed on 13th August 2025).
5. Garrett, B. L. (2010). The substance of false confessions. https://core.ac.uk/download/213020483.pdf (accessed on 13th August 2025).
6. Garrett, B. L. (2012). Habeas corpus and due process. https://core.ac.uk/download/213020472.pdf (accessed on 13th August 2025).
7. Garrett, B. L. (2012). Introduction: Symposium on 'Convicting the Innocent.' https://core.ac.uk/download/213020532.pdf (accessed on 13th August 2025).
8. Garrett, B. L. (2017). Towards an international right to claim innocence. https://core.ac.uk/download/213020519.pdf (accessed on 13th August 2025).
9. Greabe, J. M. (1994). Spelling guilts out of a record? Harmless error review of conclusive mandatory presumptions and elemental misdescriptions. https://core.ac.uk/download/72054425.pdf (accessed on 13th August 2025).
10. Griffin, L. K. (2016). Criminal adjudication, error correction, and hindsight blind spots. https://core.ac.uk/download/62571288.pdf (accessed on 13th August 2025).
11. Hill, M. (2014). The Fairbanks Four: Hopeless innocence and the flawed system that escorted them to stagnant wrongful convictions. https://core.ac.uk/download/187434644.pdf (accessed on 13th August 2025).
12. Hu, M. (2017). Algorithmic Jim Crow. https://core.ac.uk/download/144232642.pdf (accessed on 13th August 2025).
13. Luther, K., & Snook, B. (2016). Putting the Mr. Big technique back on trial: A re-examination of probative value and abuse of process through a scientific lens. https://core.ac.uk/download/76962673.pdf (accessed on 13th August 2025).
14. Magaloni, B., & Rodriguez, L. (2020). Torture as a method of criminal prosecution: Police brutality, the militarization of security and the reform of inquisitorial criminal justice in Mexico. https://core.ac.uk/download/322310836.pdf (accessed on 13th August 2025).
15. McGarity, T. O., Shapiro, S. A., Shudtz, M., Steinzor, R., et al. (2013). Workers at risk: Regulatory dysfunction at OSHA. https://core.ac.uk/download/211386891.pdf (accessed on 13th August 2025).
16. Murray, J. (2010). Assessing allegations: Judicial evaluation of testimonial evidence in international tribunals. https://core.ac.uk/download/234118271.pdf (accessed on 13th August 2025).

17. N/A. (1966). Interrogation of criminal defendants—Some views on *Miranda v. Arizona*. https://core.ac.uk/download/144225689.pdf (accessed on 13th August 2025).

18. Owusu-Bempah, A. (2016). Introduction: Participatory requirements and rights. https://core.ac.uk/download/82917151.pdf (accessed on 13th August 2025).

19. Pye, A. K. (1968). The Warren Court and criminal procedure. https://core.ac.uk/download/62565423.pdf (accessed on 13th August 2025).

20. Smith, S. M., Stinson, V., & Patry, M. W. (2010). Confession evidence in Canada: Psychological issues and legal landscapes. *Psychology Crime and Law, 18*, 317–333. https://doi.org/10.1080/1068316x.2010.486380 (accessed on 13th August 2025).

21. Traum, A. R. (2011). Constitutionalizing immigration law on its own path. http://scholars.law.unlv.edu/facpub/684 (accessed on 13th August 2025).

Chapter

11

APPEALS, REVISIONS, AND POST-TRIAL REMEDIES OF CRIMINAL PROCEDURE AND EVIDENCE

Contents

Introduction..347

11.1. The Appeals Process..351

11.2. Standards of Review..356

11.3. Revisions in Criminal Procedure...................................361

11.4. Post-Trial Remedies..365

11.5. The Role of Defense Attorneys.....................................369

11.6. The Impact of Technology on Appeals 373

Summary 377

References 380

INTRODUCTION

The criminal procedure landscape is greatly defined by the mechanisms of appeals, revision, and post-trial relief, all of which are designed to correct possible miscarriages of justice in the judiciary. In a world where wrongful convictions are under mounting scrutiny, the relevance of these mechanisms has become more focal. Historically, many legal systems have given precedence to the finality of criminal conviction, often trumping innocence claims based on new evidence. The outcome has been defendants in limbo with limited ways for relief, demonstrating the need for a more equitable post-trial system for claims, particularly in light of evolving international norms. Countries are beginning to enact more extensive remedies to allow defendants to effectively assert innocence, challenging traditional beliefs that have held criminal law for decades (Garrett et al., 2017). Examining the complicated coexistence of appeals and revisions highlights the distinct yet connected legal processes involved in pursuing justice. Appellate courts are significant tribunals where factual and legal errors are thoroughly examined, with the power to overturn or alter lower court judgments. However, the success of such procedures is inherently dependent upon the standard applied, for instance, the standard of miscarriage of justice. This rule calls not only for a sophisticated understanding of the accurate mistakes made at trial but also for a reasonable prospect that different results might have occurred with optimal conditions. By doing this, such proceedings weigh the inherent rights of defendants against the implicational constraints of finality that characterize much of the law (Aleklett et al., 2009). The evolution of post-trial remedies is necessarily reflective of broader social attitudes regarding justice and accountability. As new evidence and technology develop, so too must the legal community adapt to maintain the integrity of the judicial system. Most jurisdictions are considering reforms that create increased ability to attack wrongful convictions through multiple judicial avenues, a step that is essential to preserving public trust in the rule of law. These developments not only impact individual cases but also work to promote systemic reform, engaging argument about how process may more effectively incorporate pursuit of truth and fairness. As contemporary discussions continue to locate the importance of vindicating innocence claims, the question of appeals, revisions, and post-trial remedies becomes pressing in redefining justice within the criminal procedure domain.

Definition of Criminal Procedure

Criminal procedure refers to the laws and regulations that govern procedures under which the state enforces criminal law. It defines how trials, arrests, investigations, and appeals are to be conducted so that there is balance between the rights of the accused and the interests of justice. Criminal procedure has its main objective as protecting the constitutional rights of individuals while following ideals of a fair trial and due process. This system not only provides for the administration of justice but also serves as a necessary check on government power in preventing unjust convictions. By procedural safeguards, criminal procedures offer established routes for remedy and adjustment, hence the way for appeals, revision, and post-trial corrective actions which are indispensable in an equitable legal system. The importance of these processes is underscored by historical precedents and international standards, which describe the evolving nature of the criminal justice system. For instance, despite advancements, the majority of legal systems still grapple with the impact of wrongful convictions, preferring to maintain the finality of convictions over justice. The predicament of pleading innocence post-trial only serves to highlight the necessity for firm appeal procedures, which tend to reverse convictions with the introduction of new evidence. This predicament has its echo in the widespread application of general remedies across jurisdictions, allowing a more nuanced approach to claims of innocence. Last but not least, the evolving situation of criminal procedure represents a growing appreciation for the need to correct miscarriages of justice in modern legal practice (Garrett et al., 2017). Perhaps most importantly, the complexity issue regarding sentencing errors poses tremendous challenges within the field of criminal procedure and appeals. Sentencing is susceptible to a range of errors, yet their rectification remains primarily plagued by challenges, particularly in the context of appeals. Where the courts scrutinize these errors, they must consider whether they would be a miscarriage of justice and therefore impact the viability of a claim. The introduction of the miscarriage of justice test by the Supreme Courts makes this even more difficult, as various types of claims will arise from sentencing errors. As the law develops, there is an increasing need for a universal standard on claims of innocence due to sentencing errors. Adjustments to sentencing standards or procedures may be a reflection of deeper ethical issues over fairness and accuracy in the justice system (Aleklett et al., 2009).

Importance of Appeals and Revisions

Revisions and appeals are a vital process for ensuring justice under the premises of criminal procedure and evidence. Wrongful convictions would lead not just to individual tragedy but also public shame in the entire legal system. The appeal process allows review of convictions, rectification of procedural errors, misapplication of law, or the production of fresh evidence that may support a claim of wrongful conviction. This is a necessary remedy in the maintenance of fairness and accuracy in judicial decisions, balancing human frailty inherent in legal proceedings. In doing so, the emphasis on appeals serves to underscore the dedication of the legal institutions to undoing mistakes and incorporating a measure of accountability within its institutions, so that justice is not a platonic ideal but a lived reality for all those affected by the criminal justice system. In addition, the emergence of appeals as a post-trial remedy for wrongful convictions also reflects a shift in societal orientation towards post-trial remedies.

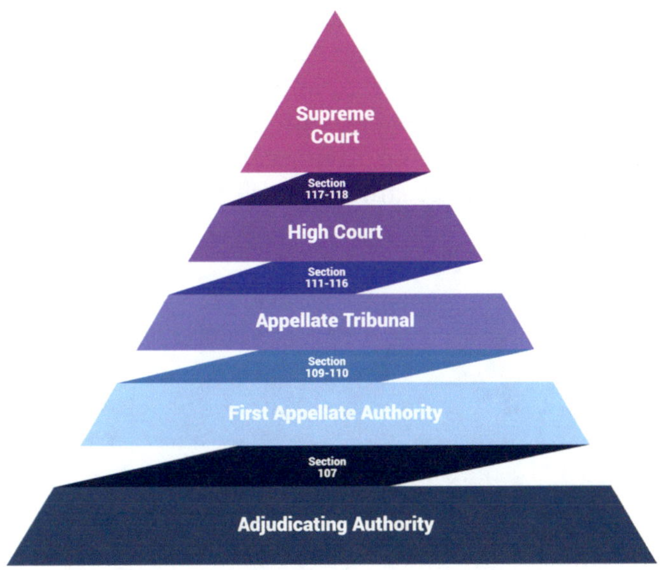

Figure 11.1. The system of appeals and revisions.

Source: https://irisgst.com/wp-content/uploads/2019/09/Pyramid-Blog-inside-image-1024x882.png.

Overview of Post-Trial Remedies

Post-trial criminal procedure encompasses a number of remedies intended to correct injustices that may have befallen during the trial. The remedies are critical mechanisms for ensuring the integrity of the legal system, where defendants are allowed to appeal convictions and claim redress on the basis of newly discovered evidence or procedural defects. In all jurisdictions, the organization of post-trial remedies includes motions for new trials, appeals, and post-conviction relief. Each remedy is characterized by unique rules and practices that regulate their application, testifying to the complexity of criminal procedure. The evolution of the said remedies reflects growing recognition of the need to foster access to justice and also to remedy miscarriages of justice, with particular regard for standards measuring the impact of any misstep which occurred subsequent to the trial. A key aspect of post-trial remedies is the appeal mechanism, through which convicted criminals may challenge the legality of their conviction or the fairness of their trial. Appeals may be made on any number of grounds such as errors in the law on substance, incompetent counsel, or admitting evidence that was supposed to be suppressed. Interestingly, the standard of review on appeal varies depending on the nature of the claim, often in line with strict rules of procedure. Harmless error rule is applied in some jurisdictions whereby convictions will be sustained if the appeals court believes that the error had no significant bearing on the outcome. This raises some pertinent issues regarding the nature of finality in criminal justice, particularly in light of the fact that injustice may still prevail despite a trial and conviction. The availability of post-trial relief applies as well where defendants attempt to assert innocence on the grounds of recently discovered evidence. Although there have always been some legal systems that have been reluctant to entertain allegations of innocence on grounds of finality, there has actually been a considerable shift towards accepting such allegations in recent years. This is consistent with an understanding that miscarriages of justice do and can occur, and that access to remedies is important in correcting such mistakes. The engagement of standards like miscarriage of justice, as a precondition to the exercise of the merits of an application post-trial, undermines the subtle character of these remedies. These requirements not only examine the authenticity of innocence claims but also compel courts to reexamine their treatment of errors caused by the trial and sentencing processes, evidenced by drastic shifts in both procedural and substantive law (Aleklett et al., 2009; Garrett et al., 2017).

11.1. THE APPEALS PROCESS

The appeals process is a critical element of the criminal justice system, allowing defendants to appeal the outcomes of their trials. The process is premised on the reality that errors can occur in trials and acknowledges the necessity of safeguarding against unjust conviction. Defendants can, after conviction, allege error in procedural law, evidence rulings, or jury instructions that prejudiced the trial's outcome. Thus, the process of appeals provides a formal means through which such claims can be heard by more authoritative courts. This tiered judicial review is required in order to ensure fairness and justice within the system so that convictions are indicative of a fair determination of the facts and law of the case. As dynamics within the appeals arena evolve, controversy over how to balance finality with the pursuit of justice remains ever more heated. Perhaps most critically, the test for obtaining an appeal too often hinges on the legal definition of errors committed during the conduct of trial proceedings.

Figure 11.2. The appeals process.

Source: https://fastercapital.co/i/Taxpayer-Rights--Protecting-Yourself-Against-a-Notice-of-Deficiency-update--Understanding-the-Appeals-Process.webp.

The character of this test can range broadly between jurisdictions, with some courts inquiring as to whether the particular errors constitute a miscarriage of justice. In deciding such claims, the courts must weigh the impact of allowing the appeal against society's need for criminal convictions to be final. The Supreme Courts miscarriage of justice test gives a persuasive perspective to this consideration, in that it requires an exception subject to the condition that the procedural hurdles are surmounted where grave doubts taint the integrity of a conviction. This quiet standard not only highlights the tension between justice's interest and the principle of finality but also foreshadows future controversies regarding the appropriate application of law in the appeals process. In recent years, international sentiments toward wrongful convictions have significantly influenced national policies on the appeals process because they demand that defendants be afforded the right to appeal on grounds of new evidence. Historically, most legal systems were interested in the finality of judgments and were disposed toward minimizing post-trial pleas of innocence. However, there has emerged a sense of unanimity that the administration of justice is best served when the legal system provides for the reconsideration of cases that may have been subject to procedural idiosyncrasies or fresh revelations. As suggested by current tendencies, most countries have begun adopting broader redress options for individuals who plan to rectify unjust convictions and therefore get more involved in the appeals process. This evolution towards a more open post-trial claims regime not only contributes to a more just legal landscape but also constitutes a significant safeguard against potential miscarriages of justice in criminal law (Aleklett et al., 2009; Garrett et al., 2017) (Figure 11.2).

11.1.1. Types of Appeals in Criminal Cases

In criminal law, appeals play a pivotal role in ensuring justice and correcting court errors. Appeals can be categorized into a number of types, primarily direct appeals, collateral attacks, and post-conviction relief petitions. Direct appeals occur following a conviction where the defendant can appeal against overturning the legal rulings of trial courts or appropriateness of the sentence. The appellate court examines the case record to determine if the trial conformed to legal guidelines and due process procedures. Collateral attacks, on the other hand, allow defendants to challenge more general allegations of erroneous convictions, typically based on novel evidence or procedural missteps in the first trial. Moreover, post-conviction relief petitions provide for remedies in cases not raised during the direct appeal process, once more displaying the sophistication of appeals within the criminal justice system.

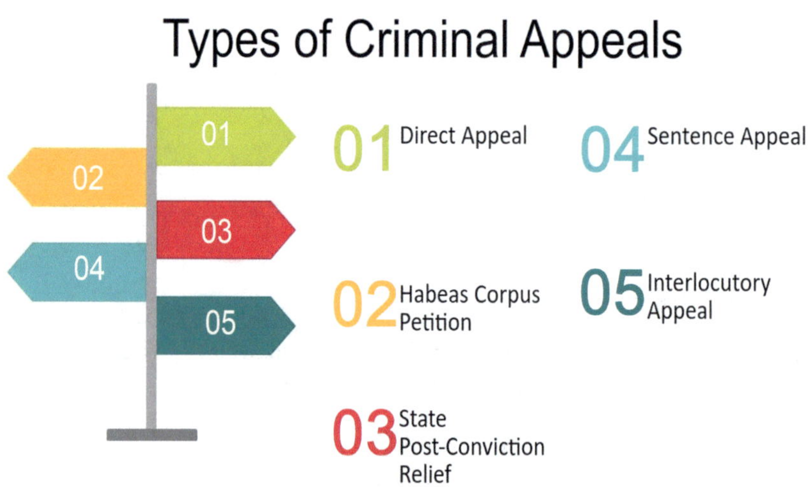

Figure 11.3. Types of appeals in criminal cases.

Source: https://fastercapital.co/i/Criminal-Appeals--Fighting-for-Freedom--Types-of-Criminal-Appeals.webp.

Appeals are more than the absence of procedural correctness; they are vital to the whole enterprise of fairness and justice within the legal system. Appellate courts in most jurisdictions possess the authority to overturn convictions or modify sentences whenever they hold that errors of law occurred during the trial. This rule is cardinal in situations where the integrity of the legal process is at stake. Mechanisms for appeals develop as society changes regarding its importance on justice and human rights. Notably, greater awareness of wrongful convictions has led to reexamination of the way courts handle claims of innocence, particularly where new evidence is discovered. This shift points to growing recognition of the need for greater flexibility within legal processes, particularly as global human rights standards continue to emphasize protecting the rights of the accused and the guarantee of fair trials (Garrett et al., 2017). Individual landmark decisions have also further shaped the criminal appeals environment by challenging the boundaries of legal redress available to defendants. In civil rights law, holdings in Georgia v. Rachel and City of Greenwood v. Peacock have emphasized the function of judicial review as a means of enabling redress for procedural injustice. These cases have caused the Supreme Court to re-examine long-standing interpretations of civil rights statutes, a renewed concept of justice in light of previous injustices. As courts revisit these provisions, they are likely to be faced with a delicate balancing act between upholding the rule of law and heeding the call for reforming legal standards so that individuals can truly combat wrongful convictions. These developments point to the interconnectedness of criminal appeals with more broad civil rights concerns, a reminder that everybody's rights need to be safeguarded through continuous reexamination of legal doctrine (N/A, 1967) (Figure 11.3).

11.1.2. Grounds for Filing an Appeal

In analyzing the grounds for filing an appeal, regard must be taken of the legal principles that form the basis of a defendant's right to seek redress in appeal courts. At the forefront of this regard is the matter of ineffective assistance of counsel, where a defendant feels that his attorney did not deliver professional standards of care and thereby influenced the verdict of his case. As determined in the 2012 case by the United States Supreme Court, defendants are entitled to bring claims of ineffective assistance through a writ of habeas corpus under specific circumstances, particularly where they can establish that prior representation was below standard because of a second incompetent lawyer or complete absence of legal representation at trial or on appeal (Bambach et al., 2014). This legal precedent is a primary foundation for defendants to argue that they had their rights violated due to incompetent legal representation during critical phases of their trial. Other grounds for appeal in addition to ineffective assistance of counsel will be procedural errors, recently discovered facts, and violation of constitutional rights. For instance, an appeals court may overturn a verdict where it finds trial procedures were flawed or where evidence had been improperly admitted, and which might have inappropriately influenced the jury's decision. Also, the revelation of new evidence capable of exonerating a defendant will often make a good appeal case, especially if the new evidence was not available to be used during the initial trial. Of most interest is whether such claims are capable of being relevant to habeas corpus proceedings, where defendants may raise that conditions surrounding their trial did not provide an authentic opportunity to defend effectively against a charge (Malani, 2025). These grounds for appeal cumulatively emphasize the multi-faceted nature of post-trial remedies within the legal system. Lastly, whether or not to appeal is a function not only of the merit of claims but also the strategic interests of the defense counsel. Attorneys must weigh the potential benefits of an appeal against the risk of prolonged legal process or additional obstacles. The concept of habeas bargaining has emerged as a popular trend whereby the defendants bargain away their habeas rights for more favorable sentencing terms. While these transactions are less common than regular plea bargains, they demonstrate the importance of capturing all available remedies. By including habeas claims as part of the discussion about post-trial remedies, defendants and their lawyers can seek a more comprehensive consideration of legal remedies that could be effective for their case within the framework of the larger criminal justice system (Malani, 2025) (Figure 11.4).

Figure 11.4. Grounds for filing an appeal.

Source: https://www.taxscan.in/wp-content/uploads/2023/09/Death-of-Father-of-CA-Delay-in-Filing-Appeal-Before-Tribunal-Appeal-Before-TribunalCovid-Relaxation-Period-ITAT-Dismisses-Appeal-taxscan.jpg.

11.1.3. The Role of Appellate Courts

Appellate courts are an important part of the judicial system, and their primary duty is to review judgments given by the lower courts. Reviewing trials according to established legal principles and guarding the rights of the interested parties is what the process ensures. Appeal courts look at the case record and the case on both sides and, in a bid to ascertain if there was or not any mistake of law which would have a significant impact on the outcome of the trial. By enforcing the standards of law and maintaining even application of the law, appeal courts play an important role in ensuring sustained reliance on the justice system. The process not only offers the correction of possible judicial errors but also ensures that legal interpretations evolve in regard to evolving circumstances and expectations in society, thus serving to reinforce the call for justice and impartiality in criminal proceedings. Apart from correcting errors, appellate courts serve a crucial function of creating legal precedents to guide future cases. Appellate decisions through statutory and constitutional interpretation contribute to the shaping of crime law to create a more consistent and robust regime. This is particularly the case in instances of systemic violation of criminal procedures, as judicial decisions there can catalyze broader reforms. In the instance of wrongful convictions or subpar representation that taints the judicial system, appeals courts can rectify the same. Such decisions can inspire reform at the legislative level or initiate new procedural norms that enhance defendants' rights. The role of appellate courts extends far beyond one case; their decisions shape the overall criminal justice context and reiterate the fundamental requirement of due process for everyone in the system. Moreover, the evolving relationship between aggregate issues of litigation and appellate courts mirrors their leading position in addressing system problems in law. Unlike civil courts, where a variety of aggregation procedures is allowed, appellate courts have increasingly ventured into aggregative techniques in order to rectify mass procedural mistakes. These involve merging multiple cases before trial or appeal, thereby streamlining the handling of the same problem. For instance, instances related to wrongful conviction, poor legal representation, or fraud through forensic science can be helped through stacked proceedings that enhance judicial efficiency and equity. Through creative aggregative procedures, appellate courts not only attempt to remedy isolated injustices but also bring their authority to bear on institutional reforms that aim to make the criminal justice system as a whole more efficient and equitable, as argued in contemporary scholarship of these complex legal confrontations (Garrett et al., 2007, 2017) (Figure 11.5).

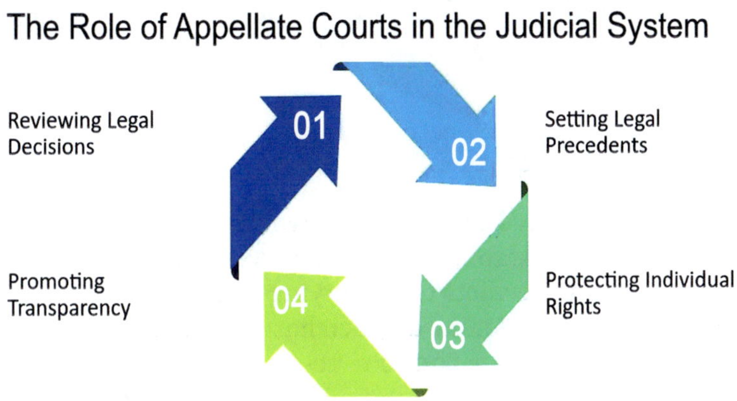

Figure 11.5. The role of appellate courts.

Source: https://fastercapital.co/i/Appellate-Courts--Reviewing-Adjudication-Decisions--The-Role-of-Appellate-Courts-in-the-Judicial-System.webp.

11.2. STANDARDS OF REVIEW

The role of Standards of Review is pivotal within the world of appeals and trial-after-remedies in criminal procedure. The standards establish how courts review errors, perhaps made at trial, in determining baselines for reversing verdicts or modifying sentences. Generally categorized as clear error, de novo, and abuse of discretion standards, each has distinct applications for legal process. For instance, a de novo review allows appellate courts to re-examine legal issues once again independent of the judgment of the trial court, while an abuse of discretion standard requires a high degree of evidence to prove that a trial court has acted wrongly in a serious way. Ultimately, the chosen standard can greatly influence the outcome of an appeal, acknowledging the significance of these review functions within the justice system. In considering the appellate standards of review, it is important to see how wrongful convictions correlate with appellate practice. Traditionally, the law has prioritized finality of criminal convictions, thus making it difficult to advance claims of innocence based on evidence uncovered after trial.

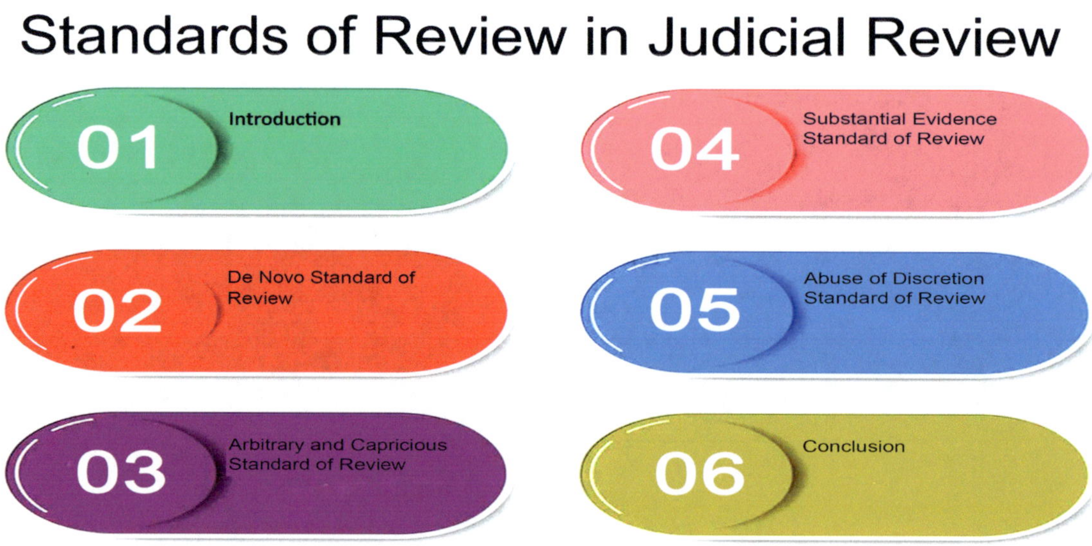

Figure 11.6. The concept of standards of review.

Source: https://fastercapital.co/i/Judicial-Review--Beyond-De-Novo--A-Comprehensive-Guide-to-Judicial-Review--Standards-of-Review-in-Judicial-Review.webp.

This inflexibility is reflected in the standards applied on appeal, where there is a tendency to affirm trial results except for major or egregious errors. The inefficacy of existing legal instruments to vindicate unjustified convictions has necessitated reform, as defendants who are bogged down by procedural obstacles fail to present claims of innocence effectively. This evolving situation emphasizes the need for a more flexible application of review standards capable of addressing emerging evidence, thereby upholding legal processes' integrity and safeguarding the rights of the accused, as evidenced through controversy on post-trial remedies (Garrett et al., 2017). Besides, the Supreme Courts standard of miscarriage of justice shows itself to be an essential building block in informing relevant standards of review, particularly in the context of sentencing errors. This standard asks whether a rational decision-maker would reach the same result or verdict and sentence, thus opening the door to the correction of patent mistakes that might otherwise go uncorrected due to procedural barriers. But the use of this standard for sentencing errors remains controversial and sometimes unresolved. While some argue finality does not rule out correcting sentence errors, others advocate keen adherence to procedural requirements. The conflict about the miscarriage of justice standard clearly mirrors essential issues of how to reconcile judicial efficiency and the quest for justice and therefore is a significant topic of debate in discourse on standards of review in criminal appeals (Aleklett et al., 2009) (Figure 11.6).

11.2.1. De Novo Review

One of the key elements of the appellate process, De Novo Review is a fundamental mechanism by which appellate courts examine lower court decisions without regard to deference to the lower court findings. The standard is particularly pertinent in controversies involving issues of law where the appellate court decides the merits and applicability of legal principles from first principles. De Novo Review is distinct from other standards such as abuse of discretion, where appellate courts give some respect to the findings of the lower courts. Giving new review of issues primacy, De Novo Review ensures that the law is properly interpreted and applied consistently among cases, hence upholding the integrity of the judicial process and reaffirming the distinct roles of trial and appellate courts.

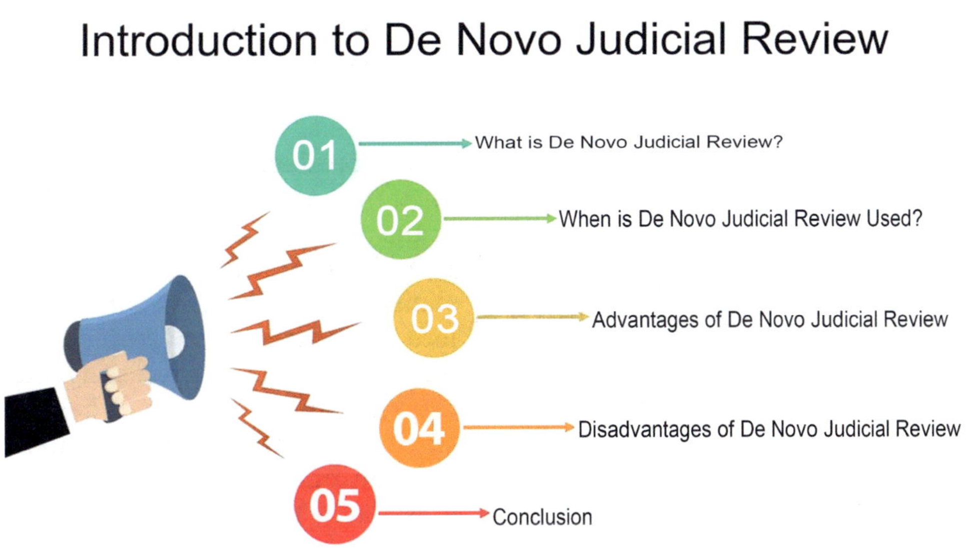

Figure 11.7. The essential components of the appellate process.

Source: https://fastercapital.co/i/The-Role-of-Appellate-Courts-in-De-Novo-Judicial-Review--Introduction-to-De-Novo-Judicial-Review.webp.

The use of De Novo Review is especially relevant in the case of post-trial remedies, such that when legal mistakes contained in an appeal can clearly influence the result of a case. In the event of a party claiming the trial court incorrectly applied the law, an appellate court will use De Novo Review to ascertain whether the interpretation of the lower court was actually in error. This level of scrutiny is not only necessary to rectify errors but also for the sake of maintaining public confidence in the justice system. In addition, the possibility of disparity in judgments due to variations in interpretation of law necessitates that appellate courts provide clarification. This leads to the formation of legal precedents that guide subsequent cases, thus making the legal landscape fairer for all the parties involved. However, excessive dependence on De Novo Review raises a significant issue regarding the efficacy and workload of appellate courts, particularly as they struggle to address an increasing case load. The emphasis on prudent reconsideration is likely to result in congestion of the appellate system since judges have to sort through complex legal issues without the advantage of the trial courts contextual conclusions.

Contextually, such a problem gains salience in cases of indigent litigants whose lives are primarily stuck within the appellate stage. As is evident in the literature, the growing frequency of unpublished decisions may cultivate a below-par level of legal justice that contradicts the purpose of De Novo Review (McAlister, 2020). In addition, the relationship between federal and state courts in dealing with appeals tends to mirror standards that are different from one another and may hinder the application of De Novo Review from one jurisdiction to another (Grimm et al., 2019). These considerations call for an effective debate on procedural reforms with a view to balancing the requirements of careful legal examination with the realities of operating an appellate justice (Figure 11.7).

11.2.2. Abuse of Discretion Standard

The Abuse of Discretion Standard is a cornerstone doctrine in the criminal appeals context, a necessary insurance against judicial abuse of power. The standard is invoked where appellate courts examine whether a trial judge has acted by making an arbitrary or capricious use of his or her discretion having a substantial effect on the case. The discretion concept means that the judges have some level of independence in determining issues based on the facts and the case circumstances. However, this discretion is not complete; it must be within well-established legal principles and criminal procedural legislation. Abuse of discretion — in the sentencing sphere, for example — can produce outcomes that appear arbitrary and unjust, and hence warrant review on appeal to ensure fairness and consistency in the judicial process. When addressing cases of purported abuse of discretion, particularly in sentencing, the courts invoke the miscarriage of justice standard. This standard of review encourages judges to look beyond the technical criteria of a decision and ask whether the choice rendered might produce a very substantial injustice, including an inappropriately harsh sentence or the nonapplication of vital mitigating factors. The Supreme Court's formulation of this standard has extended far beyond sentencing into many areas of law, essentially highlighting the importance of protecting the integrity of the judiciary, especially in delicate areas such as sentencing. In such a context, the courts have an obligation to decide whether or not it is likely that a reasonable decision-maker would find themselves arriving at the same conclusion, thus upholding fair practices of sentencing. Its application is necessary, and it significantly contributes to the debate regarding the limits of judicial discretion as well as the reasonable interests of justice. In addition, a thorough understanding of the Abuse of Discretion Standard is significant in deciding its application to post-trial relief and appeals in criminal procedure. The standard not only navigates the process of appellate review but also emphasizes the reconciliation of judicial independence and accountability. Where sentencing errors have been ascertained, finding those errors as a miscarriage of justice can enable the re-examination of penalties that might disproportionately target defendants. Judges have struggled with whether finality ought to preclude correction of genuine errors, so judges have proposed a standard miscarriage of justice test to use for all sentencing applications. These suggestions will harmonize the approach to judicial review, ensuring that justice is served amidst the complex interplay of legal doctrine and sentencing guidelines (Aleklett et al., 2009; Garrett et al., 2014) (Figure 11.8).

Figure 11.8. Abuse of discretion standard.

Source: https://encrypted-tbn0.gstatic.com/images?q=tbn:ANd9GcS7TbAJDmTBIvrwvcD7HTJ7qDEmM0ckZEn1kw&s.

11.2.3. Harmless Error Analysis

Harmless Error Analysis plays a crucial role with regard to criminal procedure, particularly appeals and post-trial remedies. This analysis attempts to determine whether a specific error that had happened during trial substantially affected the verdict or the rights of the defendants. The premise that drives this analysis is the fact that not all errors necessitate the reversal of a conviction, but rather it is necessary to assess if such mistakes may have probably had a material effect on the outcome of the trial. The incorporation of harmless error doctrine enables appellate courts to maintain judicial efficiency by refusing to hold retrials in situations where the errors are discovered to be inconsequential to the final decision. This clause satisfactorily balances defendants' rights against the need to maintain the integrity of judicial proceedings and save court resources, thus ensuring a fair approach towards administering justice. In sentencing, harmless error analysis becomes even more complicated. The majority of the sentencing errors, particularly those concerning misapplication of guidelines or misinterpretation of law, can make the process of determining if they might have affected a defendant's sentence even more complicated. When judges are faced with possible sentencing errors, they will usually be guided by the Supreme Courts test of miscarriage of justice, and whether a reasonable decision-maker would have arrived at the same sentence despite the errors. The test is controversial concerning the role of finality in criminal proceedings since it challenges the boundary line between those errors that effectively affect a defendants rights and those that do not. Hence, in the application of this analysis, the courts must consider the broader implications of their conclusions because the interface between harmless error and miscarriage of justice tests can have a profound effect on a person's case post-conviction (Aleklett et al., 2009). Essentially, harmless error analysis relies on the courts' capacity to appreciate the intricacies of each case without ignoring procedure rules as well as substantive justice. With the law evolving further, particularly in the context of appeals and post-trial remedies, there is a pressing need for enhanced clarity in the application of harmless error doctrine. The ever-changing nature of cases involving sentencing errors invites legal practitioners and scholars to engage in more detailed examination of the way such guidelines can be implemented equally across various contexts. Therefore, the implementation of a standard framework for harmless error determinations can empower courts to handle issues regarding innocence and justice more effectively, especially when they are faced with challenges against the integrity of the sentencing decisions. By encouraging a unified framework of this analysis, the judicial system can manage the objectives of safeguarding defendants' rights in a better manner while ensuring efficient and equitable judicial processes (Garrett et al., 2014) (Figure 11.9).

Figure 11.9. Harmless error analysis plays a pivotal role in the context of criminal procedure.

Source: https://federal-criminal.com/wp-content/uploads/2025/03/F-C-Image-Harmless-Error-Analysis-in-Federal-Sentencing-Appeals-FE.webp.

11.3. REVISIONS IN CRIMINAL PROCEDURE

Given the realities of legal systems bearing the brunt of wrongful convictions, criminal procedure reforms are inevitable to enhance the integrity of judicial verdicts. Finality in criminal convictions has, hitherto, been a mainstay of most legal regimes, rendering post-trial claims of innocence insurmountable barriers. The tide is turning towards the availability of such claims, gaining momentum globally as more and more recognition is accorded to the reality that wrongful convictions have to be remedied. Against this, states are resorting to broader solutions, enabling those found guilty to appeal their convictions on the grounds of new evidence. These changes are significant because they not only advance the principles of justice and fairness but also ensure that some of the most fundamental rights—such as the presumption of innocence—remain protected beyond the initial-trial stage (Garrett et al., 2017).

Figure 11.10. Revisions in criminal procedure.

Source: https://www.centurylawfirm.in/blog/wp-content/uploads/2023/02/review-revision-appeal-cpc-crpc.jpg.

As procedural reforms become a reality, they challenge the entrenched attitudes toward finality and correctness in criminal justice processes. The role of sentencing errors introduces a subtle aspect to the controversy over changes in criminal procedure, particularly concerning the handling of such errors on appeal. The Supreme Court's creation of the miscarriage of justice standard is a valuable weapon for addressing procedural obstacles in the realm of federal habeas corpus review.

It invites judges to query whether a reasonable decision maker would be more likely than not to have arrived at the same conclusion in the absence of the cited errors and whether to think in terms of a more nuanced conception of justice at sentencing. Nonetheless, its application is still controversial, particularly regarding the differentiation between generalized claims of error and those specifically addressed in claims of innocence (Aleklett et al., 2009). The disparity in the manner sentencing errors are categorized and assessed calls for an evaluation of current procedures. While legal scholars demand far-reaching reforms in this sense, the discussion is sure to turn towards creating a standard that will approach such complexities more evenly. Ultimately, the ongoing struggle between justice and procedural finality is ensured by the ultimate necessity for criminal procedure reform at the end of the day. The evolution of these procedures acknowledges that errors, either on trial or sentencing, may undermine public confidence in institutions of justice. In moving towards the application of revised frameworks permitting post-trial remedies on more open grounds, legal systems may recommit themselves to having fair outcomes. This has implications not only for the individual defendants but also for both the perception and reality of fairness within a criminal justice system that all too often values finality over accuracy. As recognition of wrongful convictions continues to shape legal contexts, systemic reforms must be accorded highest priority to significantly enhance the fidelity of criminal procedure and evidence (Aleklett et al., 2009; Garrett et al., 2017) (Figure 11.10).

11.3.1. Legislative Changes and Amendments

The criminal procedure and evidence environment has, to a great degree, been influenced by legislative reforms and amendments, with the aim of enhancing the fairness and efficiency of legal process. Such reforms usually stem from outcry regarding miscarriage of justice or seeming injustices within the justice system. Juries, judges, and lawyers frequently must navigate the complex web of statutory provisions regarding the administration of appeals and post-trial remedies. The conflict between federal and state laws creates a battleground for legal interpretation, where amendments can make as well as confuse procedural standards. For instance, certain legislative changes have sought to empower defendants by streamlining the appeal process so that innocent parties may enjoy a realistic means of redress against miscarriage of justice. This directs attention to the need for continuous scrutiny of legislative intent in the context of criminal justice. In appeals and post-trial relief, legislators have come to realize more and more the need to respond to the limitations posed by traditional procedural models. Historical emphasis on the finality of judgments has served to obscure the necessity for processes through which convictions may be reconsidered with new evidence. As recent developments have made clear, the majority of states have rewrote their laws to provide more fruitful avenues of post-conviction claims of innocence. These reforms acknowledge shifting public attitudes towards wrongful convictions and the reality that justice isn't merely about securing a conviction, but also guaranteeing that people's rights are preserved throughout. Whilst these legislative gains have been seen, problems persist, namely in relation to equality of access to legal information that can detract from defendants' ability to cope with the changed procedures effectively. Legislative evolutions also appear in the increase in administrative discretion awarded to prosecutorial agencies with regard to forum choice. As noted in the study of administrative hearings, Commissions extending powers raises questions at the root of fairness and accountability. With its power to select forums over which it has jurisdiction, the potential for skewed perception or an institutional advantage is palpable. These dynamics call for continued scrutiny of legislative amendments that define the administrative landscape, particularly those that come with appeals and post-trial processing. By actively promoting reforms that are more attuned to openness and balance, legislatures can move to allay the specter of potential institutional bias and assist in the crafting of a more equitable justice system. Appreciating these complexities is fundamental to further legislative efforts toward reform of criminal procedure because it has a direct impact on defendants' rights and the general notion of justice in society (Garrett et al., 2017; Grundfest et al., 2016).

11.3.2. Judicial Interpretations and Precedents

Judicial interpretations and precedents are significant determinants of the landscape of criminal procedure and evidence, particularly where appeals and revisions are at stake. Precedent, obtained through earlier rulings by the judiciary, is both a guiding principle and source of constraints for judges in legal hearings. This established law not only determines how new cases can be interpreted but also enforces the rule of consistency within the legal process. When a court must make a decision on accepting or not accepting evidence or a post-trial relief, it considers highly previous judgments that may be in harmony with the case at hand. Thus, the reliance on judicial precedents creates a systematic approach to justice, thereby promoting fairness and predictability of the law. Furthermore, the interaction of legislative action and judicial interpretation makes it more difficult to apply justice systematically. Legislatures respond to court decisions by overriding or underwriting those decisions and thereby influencing the interpretive context. Legislative underwrites, in which legislatures indeed grant validity to judicial interpretations, can reinforce some precedents and thereby influence future judicial consideration. The argument about judicial precedents and interpretations is particularly pertinent when one considers those situations wherein the courts may have to navigate ambiguity of statutory language, a field wherein Brudney et al. (2017) finds legislative underwrites to enhance collaborative dimensions of interbranch discourse. Because courts enforce criminal procedure legislation, the foundation writings of the legislation assist in explaining legislative intent and thus constitute a solid basis on which judicial decisions are rendered in the appellate environment. In addition, shifts of judicial deference, particularly in areas such as immigration law, recognize the dynamic nature of judicial interpretation and its effect on criminal procedure. The Supreme Court has been refining the boundaries of judicial review of administrative law, and this has implications for the broader criminal appeal context.

Figure 11.11. Judicial interpretations and precedents.

Source: https://media.licdn.com/dms/image/v2/D4D12AQHwpS8QFAQB_Q/article-cover_image-shrink_720_1280/article-cover_image-shrink_720_1280/0/1694019661496?e=2147483647&v=beta&t=QtYNb5ZbE8pIz0YNK1ziXJcYRiIAtYEr_y3m0JXPKVw.

As discussed in Rana et al. (2012), this trend of increased deference to agencies diminishes the courts' role in statutory construction, particularly where agencies gain new powers over significant legal matters. For criminal procedure, this is a step-by-step development whereby courts can bestow greater power on administrative agencies, disregarding the centuries-old checks which judicial review provided. This making real these modifications is therefore necessary in order to understand how judicial decisions and precedents function under domains of appeals, revisions, and post-trial recourse, for they not only decide direct judicial outcomes but also the underpinning principles which rule the legal landscape (Figure 11.11).

11.3.3. Impact of Revisions on Case Law

In criminal procedure, the impact of revisions on case law is important, particularly in light of shifting societal sentiment regarding wrongful convictions and post-trial relief. Historically, wrongfully convicted defendants faced a formidable regime of finality that severely limited appeal on the basis of newly discovered evidence. Modern developments mirror a growing awareness of such issues, as broader solutions to those alleging innocence upon conviction are being progressively applied throughout jurisdictions worldwide. This shift does not only signify judicial evolution but also a moral imperative to move against the rampant issues surrounding wrongful convictions, which erode stringent dogmas previously slowing justice. With countries embracing reformative measures, the appeals and revision dynamics are practically redefined, forming a culture that is more sensitive to the dictates of justice as well as the presumption of innocence (Garrett et al., 2017). The miscarriage of justice idea has dominated the terrain of sentencing errors, providing an essential context for case law revisions. The U.S. Supreme Courts application of this requirement is now an important legal mechanism that allows for reconsideration of sentences that otherwise otherwise would be final. The threshold questions—whether an objective reasonable decision-maker most likely would make the same finding—increase the complexity, particularly when sentencing mistakes are weighed with these questions in mind. The successive controversies regarding the application of the miscarriage of justice standard prove its specific pervasive influence across various legal situations, setting a precedent on how courts address systemic flaws (Aleklett et al., 2009). As case law continues to evolve, the implications of this standard ensure that amendments are not merely procedural but are inherently connected to ideas of fairness and equity within the judicial process. In addition, the revamps affecting case law also make clearer the need for a more precise definition of what precisely constitutes a sentencing error, essentially reimaging the realm of appeals. The demands for more uniformity in the way different types of claims involving sentencing are handled are increasing in intensity, potentially drastically streamlining the appeals process. Proponents make the point that all errors in sentencing must be governed by a single miscarriage of justice test, rather than away from the incoherent approach it has today. In encouraging such clarity, the justice system may be better able to promote genuinely just outcomes for all defendants, at least removing the risks introduced by finality in wrongful convictions. As case law is reformed through these debates, it can be seen that amendments are not merely called for to rectify historical injustices but also play a crucial role in ensuring a judicial system that is resilient, responsive, and most importantly, fair (Aleklett et al., 2009).

11.4. POST-TRIAL REMEDIES

The domain of post-trial remedies in criminal procedure has grown increasingly important as the legal environment adapts to remedy wrongful convictions and advance defendants' rights. Such remedies are vital vehicles that allow for the pursuit of redress after conviction at trial, particularly where new evidence is available or due to errors of procedure. Historically, concern for the finality of convictions has restricted the avenue through which defendants can appeal innocence post-trial. However, contemporary trends towards broader avenues for appealing convictions have led to developments in the law that recognize the importance of reasserting justice. These reforms are guided by the fact that persistent issues, such as unjustified convictions, necessitate a more responsive judicial system that acknowledges the fallibility of the law (Garrett et al., 2017). Post-trial remedies are thus now established as central aspects in promoting justice and safeguarding the rights of suspects (Garrett et al., 2017).

Figure 11.12. The realm of post-trial remedies in criminal procedure.

Source: https://prolegalminds.com/wp-content/uploads/2024/02/judgment.jpg.

With these evolving practices, claims of innocence based on newly discovered evidence have become increasingly significant in criminal procedure. While jurisdictions go about granting persons to present such evidence after their trial, the judiciary grapples with its implications. There is an increasing acknowledgment that post-trial relief must expand beyond appeals to encompass a wider spectrum of legal options. The likelihood of fresh evidence exonerating wrongly accused individuals is a direct contradiction to the general belief that finality precedes the pursuit of truth. Therefore, legal scholars and attorneys propose more extensive mechanisms that empower defendants to vindicate themselves. Such enhancement in post-trial remedies serves not only as a vital check on the justice system but also aligns with international norms of human rights that emphasize fairness and due process (Garrett et al., 2007). Moreover, the incorporation of aggregation in the context of post-trial remedies presents a promising avenue in addressing systemic issues in the criminal justice system. Recent studies have spoken about new methods of allowing criminal case consolidation and hence the scope of remedies for defendants. These include designing innocence commissions and prosecutorial oversight mechanisms that expand the capacity for correction of wrongful convictions. These models enable the courts to respond effectively to series of procedural errors without infringing basic constitutional safeguards. Through enhancing such aggregative processes, the criminal justice system is able to make itself more effective, accurate, and fair. Accordingly, as post-trial remedies continue to evolve, they can help play a key role in constructing a new type of legal system that not only does justice for discrete grievances but also corrects systemic flaws that compromise the integrity of criminal adjudication (Garrett et al., 2007) (Figure 11.12).

11.4.1. Motion for a New Trial

The new trial motion is a central vehicle in the realm of post-trial remedies in criminal procedure. The motion for a new trial allows defendants to move for retrial on some grounds, such as newly discovered evidence, prosecutorial or juror misconduct. These motions emphasize the dedication of legal systems to the assurance that justice is well served, even in the case of a verdict. By providing a legal avenue to protest the validity of the initial trial outcome, this motion safeguards against miscarriages of justice. It works within the restraints of procedural law, keeping in mind the necessity to be cautious when it comes to the defendants' rights while safeguarding at the same time the integrity of the judicial process. The significance of this procedural tool ought not be exaggerated, since it is the nicety of court procedure between finality and a necessity for correction of possible serious errors after conviction. One of the most distinguishing features of motions for a new trial is their potential to cure egregious judicial miscarriages that may have arguably prejudiced trial results. These kinds of errors can include improper admission of evidence, ineffective representation, or issues regarding jury instruction. When these problems occur, the potential for filing a motion for a new trial offers an important check on the judicial process, permitting the court to reconsider the facts leading up to the original verdict. This mechanism is particularly important in ensuring that the whole process of the trial is in conformity with the standards of justice and due process. Moreover, the motion for new trial can expose disparity in the application of law, supporting the need for retrial in order to protect the rights of the accused and maintain public confidence in the judicial process. E effectively, too, the motion for new trial is also a vehicle for how systemic issues within the criminal justice system can be identified and addressed. The ideals expressed in the motion are consonant with broader legal concepts, such as the concept of miscarriage of justice, which is well embedded in appeals review processes. For instance, the guidelines of the Supreme Courts on what constitutes a miscarriage of justice do not merely seek to ascertain innocence but also whether granting post-conviction relief is necessary in instances of sentencing errors. In navigating these highly legal waters, courts must ensure that defendants receive a meaningful chance to appeal their verdicts when gross injustices are committed against them, thus protecting the core belief in fair trial standards and equal representation in the judicial system (Aleklett et al., 2009; Bambach et al., 2014).

11.4.2. Writs of Habeas Corpus

The writ of habeas corpus is the most significant instrument in the framework of appeals, revisions, and post-trial recourse in criminal process. It is a judicial remedy that affords individuals under detention the chance to challenge the lawfulness of their incarceration. The strength of habeas corpus rests in its ability to act as a bridle on illegal or arbitrary detention and to establish the principle of freedom of the person over the coercive might of the state. Historically, the development of habeas corpus has been shaped by landmark judicial constructions, most significantly regarding the jurisdictional limits that delineate its availability. As succinctly described in scholarly literature, the period from the mid-20th century to the enactment of the Antiterrorism and Effective Death Penalty Act (AEDPA) in 1996 was a watershed moment for state prisoners, who were generally entitled to de novo review of legal matters determined against them by state courts, thereby ensuring a check on state power and enhanced due process entitlements (Vázquez et al., 2016). Although the writ of habeas corpus is theoretically a post-conviction remedy, its application is circumscribed by some procedural limitations that can make it challenging for defendants to pursue grievances. That is, defendants are usually not permitted to raise new grievances with the exception of as they establish that such grievances could not have been raised previously due to valid reasons, such as ineffectiveness of counsel. In 2012, the U.S. Supreme Court introduced an equitable exception to this rule, namely allowing defendants to plead habeas corpus on the grounds of ineffective assistance claims if they were able to prove that their inability to present these claims in the past resulted from the attorney's failures (Bambach et al., 2014). This exception acknowledges the subtleties entailed in the attorney-client relationship and the right to meaningful legal representation, thus attempting to reconcile the interests of procedural integrity and the pursuit of justice. The evolution of habeas corpus jurisprudence reflects a pervasive interest in maintaining the integrity of legal processes and yet ensuring that justice is attained. Specifically, the Courts subsequent expansion of the equitable exception highlights the difficulties of defendants with weak representation, particularly in states with restrictive procedural rules. In recognizing the need for "meaningful opportunity" for defendants to challenge their convictions, the Court has asserted the importance of competent and conflict-free legal representation at pivotal stages of a case. As habeas corpus continues to adapt to address new legal concerns and societal expectations, however, it remains necessary to examine and clarify its enforcement so that it remains a viable protection of individual rights within the criminal justice system (Bambach et al., 2014) (Figure 11.13).

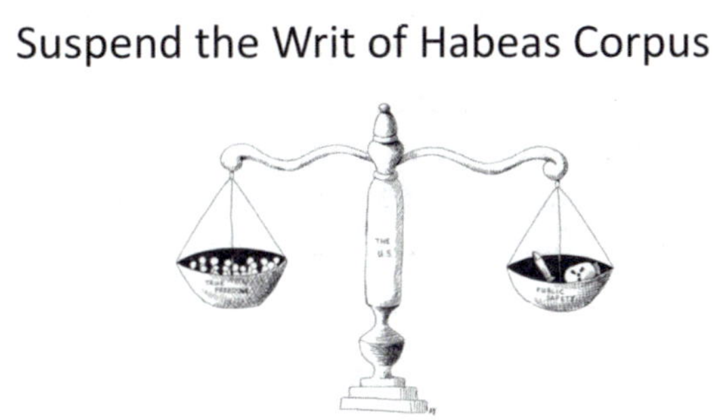

Figure 11.13. Writs of Habeas Corpus.

Source: https://image1.slideserve.com/2257310/suspend-the-writ-of-habeas-corpus-l.jpg.

11.4.3. Sentencing Modifications

In criminal procedure, sentencing reforms are critical to the operation of the justice system itself in adapting to evolving standards of fairness and efficacy. The changes can be brought about by a variety of various causes, including the appellate courts, legislative reforms, or the existence of newly found evidence significantly altering the dynamics of a case. When an appellate court reviews a sentence, it may have grounds to reduce a sentence or rule that it is invalid in total, thereby imposing a new penalty that better reflects standards of today. This review by the judiciary is consistent with a broader devotion to justice, particularly when the original sentence could have been excessively harsh or predicated on archaic laws. Therefore, sentencing power underscores the fluid nature of the judicial system, with a focus on continuous reconsideration and revision in the cause of just outcomes. One of the significant vehicles of challenge to imposed sentences is the provisions of 28 U.S.C. § 2255, which allow federal inmates to attack their sentences by motion to "vacate, set aside or correct" them. This new legal framework seeks to enhance judicial efficiency in handling collateral reviews, simplifying the process under which convicts are allowed to appeal their conviction or sentence. However, the usefulness of this remedy depends on the interpretation of the "savings clause," which permits writs of habeas corpus to be invoked whenever § 2255 motions fail. The differences in interpretation by the circuit courts create disparities in access to justice since, based on circuits, inmates may use new law precedents to appeal their sentences or be subject to stricter restrictions. The difference makes the argument for reform in the application of the savings clause to enhance prisoners' rights protection and provide avenues for changing sentences across all jurisdictions (Casale et al., 2019). Furthermore, sentencing modifications comprise the increasing investigation of corporate criminal liability, particularly foreign corporations. As federal prosecutors grow more ambitious in pursuing massive foreign corporations, the impact of sentencing corporate crime has come to the surface. The evolution of corporate criminal liability has lent itself to heightened expectations of the punishment imposed on foreign firms, typically in the guise of high fines and responsibility beyond the norm for domestic firms. This asymmetry is a mirror to the advanced sophistication of the process of sentencing in the corporate environment, and whether these developments are reasonable or are creating unreasonable and unfair equivalence. In this evolving legal landscape, sentencing analysis in corporate prosecution recognizes the precarious balance between effective deterrence and justice, cementing the importance of clear standards governing the imposition of sanctions (Garrett et al., 2011).

11.5. THE ROLE OF DEFENSE ATTORNEYS

In the criminal trial process, defense lawyers play a focal role in safeguarding accused persons' rights, such that legal representation is something more than a mere process but an essential aspect of a fair trial. Their role is not merely to deny evidence; they must become proficient with complex legal frameworks to plead forcefully on their clients' behalves. This exchange is particularly crucial in appeals, where defense attorneys expertise of procedural nuances can be a difference maker. The function of defense attorneys is even more urgent in vulnerable groups cases, i.e., minors who commit crimes, as shown by Dohrn et al. (2007). To this end, the caliber of defense can have a direct impact on both immediate legal ramifications and long-range impacts on the accused, highlighting the ethical and professional obligation of defense attorneys to provide capable representation.

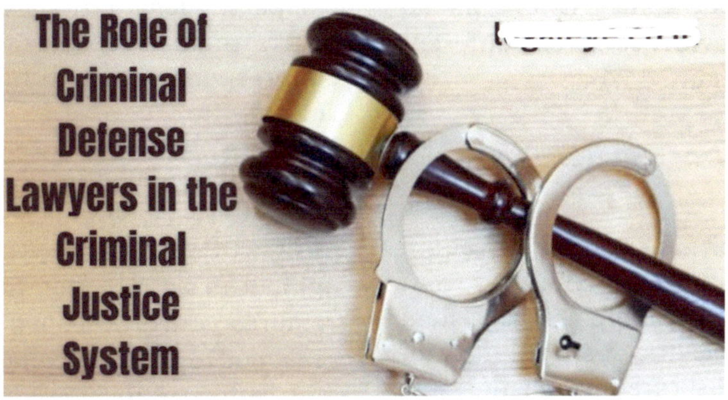

Figure 11.14. Role of defense attorneys.

Source: https://legaleye.co.in/wp-content/uploads/2024/04/The-Role-of-Criminal-Defense-Lawyers-in-the-Criminal-Justice-System-1-1024x576.jpg.

Moreover, defense attorneys are not only obligated to represent their clients in trial courts but also must get engaged substantially with post-trial remedies. These kinds of solutions typically involve retrials of trial outcomes via appeals or amendments due to errors in legal representation or procedural irregularities. The defense attorney's responsibility during this period is the identification of reversible mistakes, such as ineffective assistance of counsel or violations of due process that will lead to a retrial or an altered sentence. This is their work that underscores the defense lawyers essential role as a firewall against miscarriages of justice, facilitating the repair of potential injustices that should never have been committed in the first place. Prosecutors suspicion of the defenses ethical practice, as observed by Green et al. (2012), can further complicate the lawyers role in advocating for justice, emphasizing the importance of unyielding commitment and proficiency in post-trial scenarios. Aside from their technical functions, defense attorneys also serve the important role of ethical guardians in the criminal justice system. Their commitment to the rights of their clients instills public trust in the legal system, particularly in the midst of systemic biases and inequalities. By refusing demands that may come from a number of stakeholders, including prosecutors and regulatory agencies, defense attorneys instill a balance within courtroom dynamics. As is discussed in the case of juveniles, the additional defender services are capable of enhancing the overall quality of justice for disadvantaged groups, sustaining the argument that adequate legal representation is an essential right. The relationships between the defense attorneys' task and the broader judicial system highlight the critical task of such professionals to protect the integrity of criminal procedure as well as evidence across different stages of litigation (Figure 11.14).

11.5.1. Responsibilities During the Appeals Process

The appeals process of the criminal procedure has several important responsibilities that hold various stakeholders of the justice system accountable. First, it is the responsibility of examining trial records carefully on the part of appellate courts to ensure both procedural justice and legal requirements were upheld in the initial trial. This entails the review of the decisions of the lower courts, determining if there were errors made that could have influenced the outcome of the case. The appellate judges also have to perform a critical analysis of the applicable law vis-a-vis facts presented. Such cautious review not only preserves the legitimacy of legal judgment but also safeguards the rights of the accused so that justice can be dispensed impartially throughout the entire process of appeals. No less significant are the responsibilities imposed on the defendants and their lawyers when appealing. Defendants must be proactive and persistent in engaging the judicial process, often being forced to make good arguments on possible errors of law or injustice in the trial process. Defense attorneys have the critical mandate to investigate and expound on such issues, pointing out to the court errors in application of law or evidentiary issues meriting re-visitation. Such research is usually based on a clear understanding of case law and statutory provisions under case dynamics and thus illustrates the impact of effective legal representation in safeguarding defendants against violation of their rights to due process. In particular, the complexities involved in navigating the landscape of appeals underscore the paramount role of seasoned legal counsel, who have to effectively convert trial experience into valid grounds for appeal and stabilize the appeal process through compelling legal rationale. Lastly, the appellate courts themselves must keep in check their own responsibilities in the articulation of their rulings.

All decisions issued by an appellate court have effects extending beyond the case itself, in that they establish precedent which will be applied in subsequent cases. Such a mandate requires courts to construct properly written, reasoned opinions explaining their decisions and rationale for them. Furthermore, as the landscape of legal norms continues to evolve, courts must still be attentive to the overall ramifications of their decisions in terms of defendants' rights, and nuances such as those put in place in controversies over federal habeas corpus policies and practices. In particular, examinations of the American Bar Associations stance regarding habeas corpus in death penalty cases reveal where complexity lies in appellate review (Dohrn et al., 2007; Yackle et al., 1998). The broad mandate of appellate courts, thus, is to see that justice prevails while in doing so contributing to a robust legal system that is amenable to evolving societal needs and legal ethics.

11.5.2. Strategies for Effective Representation

Effective representation in appeals, amendments, and remedies after trial in criminal process and evidence entails a multi-dimensional strategy. Attorneys must develop a deep understanding of procedural rules and substantive law so that they can meaningfully navigate the complexities involved in post-conviction claims. This involves, in addition to full awareness of statutory regimes, expertise in the application of judicial precedents most likely to influence the outcome of appeals. The application of the miscarriage of justice test is particularly significant. This test, founded upon the identification of whether a reasonable decision-maker would be likely to come to the same conclusion, is a critical fulcrum upon which lawyers can argue against unjust convictions. By striving to bring about such standards, attorneys are in a position to create sound arguments that compel courts to consider claims that, otherwise, would have been lost owing to procedural abandonment, upholding justice at the top of A criminal process (Aleklett et al., 2009). Building strong narratives that appeal to judges and jurors is another integral aspect of good representation. Legal representation should strive to argue their clients' positions within a context of compassion and human experience, centering the fallibility of the justice system and the need for careful scrutiny in post-trial situations. This involves not only arguing the factual errors which might have produced wrongful convictions but also including newly discovered evidence that may exonerate the defendant. With the transformed justice climate, where haste for finality tends to derail pleas of innocence, lawyers must battle for reconsideration of such pleas in earnest. This aligns with growing recognition that erroneous convictions are not unusual missteps but, instead, organizational mistakes, necessitating a turning on its head of traditional methods of appeals and post-trial consideration (Garrett et al., 2017). Finally, efficient legal defense entails proactive engagement with evolving laws and court decisions that may affect post-trial relief viability. Criminal defense attorneys must keep themselves informed about legislative updates relative to the appeals process and the application of the miscarriage of justice test across jurisdictions. By advocating for reforms that facilitate greater access to post-trial remedies, legal practitioners can maximize the potential for the reversal of wrongful convictions. This may include challenging prevailing norms supporting the finality of conviction over a quest for justice. Remaining engaged with stakeholders, including policymakers and advocacy organizations dedicated to criminal justice reform, is essential to creating an environment in which effective representation is not only possible but valued. Such collaborative efforts provide the possibility for more robust legal frameworks to facilitate genuine presentation of post-trial claims of innocence (Aleklett et al., 2009).

11.5.3. Ethical Considerations in Appeals

Ethical considerations in appeals are crucial in criminal procedure in the pursuit of justice and maintenance of the integrity of the judicial system. Appeals are a significant avenue for the review of potential miscarriages of justice, providing defendants an opportunity to appeal convictions in respect of errors committed in trial proceedings. Notably, the ethical obligations of lawyers, such as defense attorneys and prosecutors, are called into question in these processes. Prosecutors, for instance, owe a duty to secure convictions but also to uphold justice; their fight against regulatory frameworks that foster ethical disclosures is capable of eroding public trust and undermining the integrity of judicial proceedings. The ongoing debate regarding prosecutors attitudes towards professional regulation underscores the need for a system push for ethical standards that enhance the basis upon which appeals and revisions are made in criminal process (Green et al., 2012).

In addition, where the representation of vulnerable sections is brought into the equation, ethical issues on appeals are even more heightened. As an example, defense of suspected minors accused in juvenile court calls for the highest sensitivity to ethical concerns as the child defendants are often disproportionately disenfranchised. Unequal access to quality legal defense services for children raises significant questions about justice and fairness in the judicial system. Ethical issues must transcend representation itself; they must transcend access to adequate resources and training for defense attorneys who represent children. Enhancing defender service can offer assurances that ethical obligations will be met, making the process more equitable for all defendants, including juveniles navigating the technicality of appeals (Dohrn et al., 2007). Finally, the ethical dimensions of appeals also intersect with broader societal consequences, most notably regarding public trust in the justice system. The validity of post-trial corrective justice relies on the assumption that appeals are more than meaningless formalities of procedure but a necessary component of a fair legal process. When prosecutors or defense attorneys fail to adhere to ethical norms during appeals, their conduct undermines the legitimacy of the process generally. Such corrosion of confidence can be a reason behind public disillusionment with the judicial process and creating an attitude in which citizens tend to feel that their rights are not being adequately protected. Therefore, reenforcement of ethical dimensions in appeals is not merely concerned with conformity to law but is also important for the restoration of confidence in a system that is supposed to protect the rights of both parties in criminal cases (Figure 11.15).

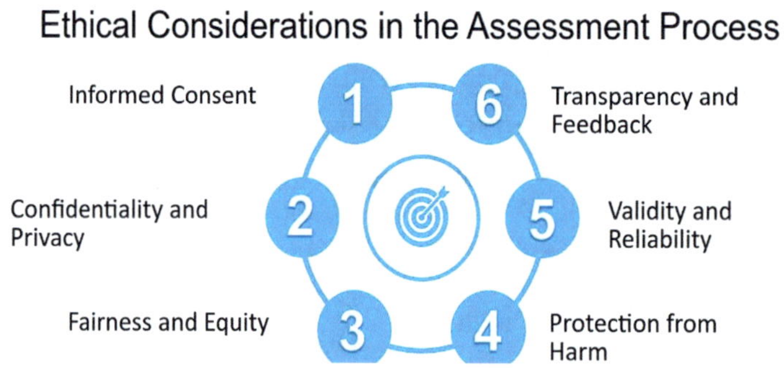

Figure 11.15. The ethical considerations in appeals.

Source: https://fastercapital.co/i/The-Ins-and-Outs-of-the-Assessment-Process--Ethical-Considerations-in-the-Assessment-Process.webp.

11.6. THE IMPACT OF TECHNOLOGY ON APPEALS

Technology in the criminal justice system has transformed the fabric of appeals significantly by making the appellate process more efficient and accessible. Legal professionals are empowered by the utilization of computer technologies that enable them to easily handle case files and evidence. For instance, electronic filing systems allow for on-time filing of appeal records, whereas data analytics allows attorneys to cull insight from vast collections of case law. Not only does this technological advance quicken the appellate review process but also optimizes opportunities for successful appeals by avoiding the omission of key evidence. The greater the number of jurisdictions that adopt these technologies, the clearer it becomes that the barriers traditionally encompassed by post-trial remedies are being dismantled, thereby providing defendants more effective means of vindicating their rights and objections against wrongful convictions based upon newly discovered evidence or transgressions which might have escaped notice in the past. In addition, the shift in social media and web dynamics has influenced public engagement with criminal appeals, establishing a new paradigm for awareness and advocacy. The rapidity of information communication on these sites enables heightened examination of conviction cases, which may influence both public opinion and judicial attitudes. High-profile cases that attract mass media coverage tend to put pressure on higher courts to re-examine rulings in view of new evidence or on grounds of ethical principles. Thus, using digital communication campaigns as part of advocacy efforts has played an essential role in rallying community action on the subject of wrongful convictions. This is indicative of a wider trend where the sentiment of the masses, enthused by technology, pressures courts to adopt less stringent reconsideration or retrial standards based on newly arising evidence, thus cementing the foundations of justice following the trial as more jurisdictions realize responsiveness to extrinsic societal pressures as essential. Finally, the introduction of forensic technology has radically transformed the standards of evidence to be applied in cases of appeals. Scientific breakthroughs in DNA analysis and other forensic methods have introduced possibilities of exoneration unheard of in recent decades. These defendants who initially accepted their convictions can today get a chance to present new scientific information from DNA analysis or technological comparison that may not have been present at their time of trial. As cited in the research, procedures and methods of claims of innocence via newly acquired evidence are changing because more states have adopted broader remedies for convicts to claim innocence (Garrett et al., 2017). These trends not only enhance bases for appeals but also an increasing awareness by the justice system of trial evidence flaws and the merits of technological verification. Therefore, the role played by technological innovation in forensic science cannot be overstated since it forms a crucial tool through which miscarriages of justice are reversed and the integrity of the judicial process is improved.

11.6.1. Digital Evidence and Its Implications

During the last few decades, the advent of digital technology has fundamentally changed the arena of criminal evidence, significantly affecting prosecution and defense strategy. Computer information, cellular information, and data from the Internet create challenging issues in constitutional law, most significantly under Fourth Amendment's protection against unreasonable searches and seizures. The courts have to balance law enforcement interests with individuals' privacy interests articulated in a line of appellate decisions. The inherently dynamic nature of digital evidence necessitates conclusive directives in terms of how and when digital evidence can be collected, preserved, and verified in a courtroom. This balancing act is particularly pertinent in the post-trial context where appeals are based on the integrity and admissibility of digital evidence. The impact of digital evidence has spillover consequences into the appeal process, where the admissibility of such evidence can significantly influence verdicts and subsequent remedies. For instance, if the digital evidence is ruled to be obtained in a wrongful way, it may result in suppression of crucial information that can turn the course of a trial. In recent trials, where the validity of digital evidence has been challenged, courts have to examine carefully the methodology used to extract and analyze the data. Thus, the danger of wrongful convictions or unjust acquittals presents a persuasive argument in favor of legal standards regarding admissibility of electronic evidence. Appeals are generally a significant check on the decisions of lower courts, particularly where new technology places conventional evidentiary practices under challenge and the rights of the accused in jeopardy. In addition, the potential of electronic evidence to cause inequalities within the justice system cannot be overlooked. Access to sophisticated technology and forensic laboratories can disproportionately favor well-resourced defense teams over their less affluent counterparts. Such inequality raises questions about the fairness of trial outcomes and credibility of appeals based on electronic evidence. As legal precepts keep evolving, it is crucial for judicial systems to ensure equitable access to expert examination of electronic data. Further, as evidenced in significant rulings and recent legal texts, there is a critical need for periodic training and standardization in the handling of digital evidence by legal practitioners. Resolving these concerns is pivotal to ensuring the equitable legal process and the future admissibility of appeals containing digital evidence, particularly as technology keeps evolving (Utah Supreme Court, 2018a, 2018b) (Figure 11.16).

Figure 11.16. Digital evidence and its implications.

Source: https://www.sifsindia.com/assets/front/img/blogs/1712129756.jpg.

11.6.2. Online Resources for Legal Research

Legal research has been transformed by the introduction of digital technology, and online resources are an essential part of practitioners who handle appeals, revisions, and post-trial remedies within criminal procedure and evidence. Legal databases such as Westlaw, LexisNexis, and Bloomberg Law contain enormous collections of court cases, statutes, and secondary legal material. Such websites are offering advanced searching facilities to enable lawyers to effectively browse precedent-setting cases and thus enable them to adopt a more strategic defense in appeals. Particularly when convictions in the past are appealed on grounds of new evidence in some jurisdictions, access to relevant case law in advance is very important. These online sources enhance the ability to overturn wrongful convictions or seek post-trial relief, aligning with contemporary discussions of procedural justice and access to justice (Garrett et al., 2017). Furthermore, online legal research tools have democratized access to legal information, from seasoned attorneys to law students, pro se litigants, and self-represented individuals. Websites like FindLaw and Justia offer clear-cut summaries of legal principles, practices, and case summaries required in understanding criminal appeal complexities. Such access is essential in courts where legal representation may be limited, allowing individuals to better manage the intricacies of post-trial procedures and issues of evidence. With heightened reliance on the net sources of law, there arises the call for users to critically evaluate the reliability of sources and the timeliness of information. Such discrimination is critical, especially in the face of changing legal standards and emerging doctrines affecting post-trial remedies (Garrett et al., 2011). In addition to traditional legal databases, the role of government websites and public interest organizations toward providing online legal content cannot be overstated. All but a few states have large collections of online legal materials, such as appellate court rulings and procedural manuals on post-conviction claims. Organizations dedicated to criminal justice reformers typically bring together and disseminate resources with newly enacted legislation and new jurisprudence impacting appeals and post-trial relief. These materials are valuable tools to legal practitioners, lawyers, and researchers exploring the constantly evolving landscape of law. As recent happenings illustrate, for instance, the shifting response to claims of wrongful conviction and the growth of remedies for proving innocence, continued engagement with diverse online legal materials remains at the core of effective legal practice in criminal procedure (Garrett et al., 2017).

11.6.3. Virtual Courtrooms and Remote Hearings

The innovation of virtual courts and virtual hearings is a dramatic shift in legal proceedings, serving to necessitate the development of the judiciary in sync with contemporary technological platforms. With the challenges occasioned by the COVID-19 pandemic, United States courts transitioned to video teleconferencing (VTC) as a primary platform for hearing proceedings. This change calls into doubt whether remote adjudications are effective, and equitable in this instance, in determining witness credibility. Referring to arguments in asylum and immigration hearings, judges' ability to accurately discern a witness's demeanor is compromised in an online setting, where technological distortion may intervene in evaluating credibility and truthfulness. Therefore, a review of the standards used to determine credibility in virtual hearings is needed to maintain the integrity of judicial decisions in an age that is progressively characterized by technological advancement (Bradley et al., 2022). The effects of virtual courtrooms go beyond merely redefining procedural standards; they also have a complex interplay with the very core legal principles of due process and fairness. The interface of technology with judicial proceedings requires careful attention, since diminished physical presence of defendants and witnesses might impact the adjudicative process. Legal philosophers argue that the transformation calls for a protective system designed to ensure that rights of all participants are preserved even in remote places. The need for robust legal safeguards becomes increasingly pertinent, particularly in such a context as habeas corpus, where the legitimacy of detentions is subject to high-stakes examination. With increasingly popular virtual hearings, the challenge becomes how to prevent substantive rights being undermined by procedural experimentation without adequate judicial and academic surveillance of the ways in which virtual forums can be balanced with due process principles (Garrett et al., 2012). Moreover, as virtual hearings become a standard part of judicial practice, discussion regarding the long-term implications of virtual hearings for post-trial remedies and appeals is warranted. The restrictions inherent in virtual systems, including the potential for failures in communication and the challenge of providing a balanced and equitable courtroom experience, looms large over the potential for unequal results. The judicial community must meet these challenges head-on, with a focus on developing policies that can successfully integrate technology while upholding the values of justice. The current review and subsequent recommendations against barring adverse credibility determinations based solely on demeanor determinations made through VTC underscore the compelling need for close examination of current practices. Lastly, encouraging a model which centers on flexibility in the framework of changes in technology will help ensure that the key postulates of criminal procedure and evidence remain intact even in the new climate of legal practice (Bradley et al., 2022).

SUMMARY

The complicated mesh of appeals, revision, and post-trial remedies in criminal procedure and evidence, it is apparent that an effective justice system must achieve a balance between the need for finality in convictions and a need to correct miscarriages of justice. The miscarriage of justice standard plays a central role in this balancing act, acting as a vehicle of re-examination of wrongful sentencing and claims of innocence. As noted, this standard empowers courts to ask themselves whether a reasonable decision maker would most likely reach the same conclusion, thereby demarcating when courts can revisit an individual's sentence. This model raises important questions about legal finality and the quest for justice, which should warrant ongoing debate between legal scholars and practitioners about enhancing redressal mechanisms in cases of potential injustices (Aleklett et al., 2009). Contributing to this debate is the evolving global conceptualization of wrongful convictions, where there is a shift from viewing them as isolated local miscarriages. In the past, the rigidity of finality in criminal convictions discouraged the acknowledgment of post-trial claims of innocence, in effect disenfranchising defendants who might otherwise attempt to overturn their convictions based on newly discovered evidence. As noted, international law guarantees the right to a fair trial as well as the right to a presumption of innocence, but does not necessarily mandate states to allow defendants to make effective post-trial claims. The trend towards the adoption of broader remedies by a number of states is a growing recognition that there needs to be a response to the realities of wrongful convictions and that there needs to be a more robust model for post-trial innocence claims, thereby enhancing the credibility of the judiciary as a whole (Garrett et al., 2017). Lastly, complete understanding of appeals, amendments, and post-trial relief demonstrates the nexus between legal processes and the quest for justice. While the law continues to grapple with the consequences of wrongful convictions, the controversy surrounding the standard of miscarriage of justice and the rights of accused individuals to advance claims of innocence will be at the center of reform. There needs to be reconciliation between the requirement of finality in legal proceedings and avenues for significant correction to safeguard individual rights while still ensuring public trust in the justice system. The ongoing evolution of such legal standards, particularly in response to new evidence and changing public attitudes, is crucial in fostering a more equitable and equitable legal system that balances the rights of the criminal with the integrity of the rule of law (Aleklett et al., 2009; Garrett et al., 2017).

In criminal procedure, appellate processes, revisions, and post-trial remedies are the central mechanisms that are all about the nature of justice. Appeals give defendants a chance to challenge the verdicts of their trials by requesting a reviewing court to revisit the decision so that errors—both procedural and substantive—are not left to stand. This overarching layer of scrutiny is not only essential for immediate parties, but also in establishing public trust in the justice process. Furthermore, revisional powers, traditionally reserved for appellate courts, serves to reinforce the need of judicial accountability and precision in legal rulings, reflecting sentiments articulated in legal scholarship on the need for high standards in judicial review processes (Callander et al., 2017). The landscape of post-trial relief is broader than mere appeals and involves a number of mechanisms that are intended to resolve potential miscarriages of justice that happen after a verdict is reached. These remedies can be in the form of motions for a new trial, which are oftentimes predicated on the discovery of fresh evidence or procedural error that might have prejudiced the trial's outcome. Additionally, the rules of procedure guiding such remedies are well-crafted to avoid abuse and see justice in good time for genuine grievances. As can be observed from studies in court proceedings, effective post-trial remedies form an essential element in reversing wrongful convictions and miscarriages of justice, hence upholding the criminal justice system's integrity (Grundfest et al., 2016). The subtleties concerning appeals, amendments, and post-trial relief reflect the age-old tension between finality and justice in criminal trials. On the one hand, victims and society need closure; on the other, the risk of miscarriages of justice demands a robust system of checks and balances. It is this dualism which is then overlaid by socio-legal factors that may affect both the availability and efficacy of these legal remedies. Consequently, an understanding of this interconnection between these variables is central to any thoughtful criminal law debate. The arguments that were triggered by appeals and post-trial remedies are deeply resonant within the general backdrop of legal reform, calling forth further argument regarding the pursuit of a more equitable judicial process (Callander et al., 2017).

KEY TERMS

- Acquittal Appeal
- Appellate Court
- Conviction Appeal
- Double Jeopardy
- Error of Law
- Interlocutory Order
- Leave to Appeal
- Post-Conviction Relief
- Review
- Appeal
- Bail Pending Appeal
- Doctrine of Finality
- Enhancement of Sentence
- Extraordinary Remedy
- Judicial Discretion
- Miscarriage of Justice
- Remand
- Revision

A LOOK TO THE FUTURE

CRIMINAL PROCEDURE AND APPEALS

Criminal procedure and appeals are on the verge of a dramatic transformation as continuing technological progress continues to redefine the judicial process. These technologies can potentially make processes more efficient, provide greater access to justice, and render outcomes more precise. For instance, artificial intelligence software can help to review case law and precedence, making it easier for legal practitioners to identify relevant arguments. Further, virtual hearings, which became popular during the COVID-19 pandemic, could go on to become the new normal, obviating travel and time barriers. This change would democratize access to the appeals process, so that litigants in far-flung regions of the country have an equal chance to put their cases before them. Despite these advantages, it is important to balance technological integration with measures against possible disparity, thus maintaining the fundamental principles of justice in the criminal process while conforming to contemporary requirements. The future of criminal appeals also raises issues pertaining to the efficacy and structure of existing remedies. Post-trial remedies such as motions for a new trial and appeals are central aspects to reversing judicial errors and correcting miscarriages of justice. The complexity, however, of these proceedings will often keep them from being highly effective, particularly for marginalized groups who are apt to be faced with systemic impediments. As discussion of criminal procedure further evolves, there is greater emphasis placed on refashioning such post-trial remedies to position them in a more accessible and equitable form of correction. For example, jurisdictions may adopt standard procedures to further streamline the appeals process so that it can be more quickly resolved and thereby decrease defendant and judicial workload. A reimagined process of appeals can allow for a more fair legal system with more review of trial-stage rulings while being aware of the realities facing those who have to navigate the criminal justice system. The use of data analytics in reviewing appeal outcomes can support efforts towards transparency and accountability for the systems. By systematically analyzing trends in appeal decisions, legal scholars and practitioners can identify disparities or biases to be addressed through reform. This analysis can illuminate systemic shortcomings in the appellate process and inform legislative reform to improve procedural justice. Ultimately, considering the implications of demographic and geographic variation in appeal outcomes can further guide policy readjustment towards providing a more equitable judicial setting. As jurisdictions embrace these data-based wisdom, the possibility arises for recalibration of the criminal procedure system that not only addresses short-term demands of appeals but also goes a long way to contribute to the longer-term integrity of the criminal justice system. In this context, knowledge of how new technologies, institutional change, and data's role interconnect becomes essential in architecting a more effective future in criminal procedure and appeals.

REFERENCES

1. Aleklett, K., Höök, M., Jakobsson, K., Söderbergh, B., et al. (2009). Accuracy in sentencing. https://core.ac.uk/download/213020452.pdf (accessed on 13th August 2025).
2. Bambach, M., Bleck, W., Stieben, A., Wirths, M., et al. (2014). Giving meaning to "meaningful enough": Why *Trevino* requires new counsel on appeal. https://core.ac.uk/download/144230271.pdf (accessed on 13th August 2025).
3. Bradley, L., & Farber, H. (2022). *Virtually incredible*: Rethinking deference to demeanor when assessing credibility in asylum cases conducted by video teleconference. https://core.ac.uk/download/519804527.pdf (accessed on 13th August 2025).
4. Brudney, J. J., & Leib, E. J. (2017). Legislative underwrites. https://core.ac.uk/download/216959302.pdf (accessed on 13th August 2025).
5. Callander, I., Campbell, K., & Leverick, F. (2017). Post-conviction review: Questions of innocence, independence, and necessity. https://core.ac.uk/download/145642309.pdf (accessed on 13th August 2025).
6. Casale, L. (2019). Back to the future: Permitting habeas petitions based on intervening retroactive case law to alter convictions and sentences. https://core.ac.uk/download/216959285.pdf (accessed on 13th August 2025).
7. Dohrn, B., Crawford, C., Moss, M. B., Puritz, P., & Geraghty, T. F. (2007). Illinois: An assessment of access to counsel & quality or representation in delinquency proceedings. https://core.ac.uk/download/71352113.pdf (accessed on 13th August 2025).
8. Garrett, B. L. (2007). Aggregation in criminal law. https://core.ac.uk/download/213020497.pdf (accessed on 13th August 2025).
9. Garrett, B. L. (2011). Globalized corporate prosecutions. https://core.ac.uk/download/213020480.pdf (accessed on 13th August 2025).
10. Garrett, B. L. (2012). Habeas corpus and due process. https://core.ac.uk/download/213020472.pdf (accessed on 13th August 2025).
11. Garrett, B. L. (2014). Accuracy in sentencing. https://core.ac.uk/download/213020452.pdf (accessed on 13th August 2025).
12. Garrett, B. L. (2017). Towards an international right to claim innocence. https://core.ac.uk/download/213020519.pdf (accessed on 13th August 2025).
13. Green, B. A. (2012). Prosecutors and professional regulation. https://core.ac.uk/download/144231089.pdf (accessed on 13th August 2025).
14. Grimm, D., Wendel, M., & Reinbacher, T. (2019). European constitutionalism and the German Basic Law. In *T.M.C. Asser Press eBooks*. https://doi.org/10.1007/978-94-6265-273-6_10 (accessed on 13th August 2025).
15. Grundfest, J. A. (2016). Fair or foul? SEC administrative proceedings and prospects for reform through removal legislation. https://core.ac.uk/download/144231809.pdf (accessed on 13th August 2025).
16. Huq, A. Z., & Ginsburg, T. (2017). How to lose a constitutional democracy. *SSRN Electronic Journal*. https://doi.org/10.2139/ssrn.2901776 (accessed on 13th August 2025).

17. Malani, A. (2025). Habeas bargaining. https://core.ac.uk/download/pdf/7158663.pdf (accessed on 13th August 2025).
18. McAlister, M. (2020). "Downright indifference": Examining unpublished decisions in the federal courts of appeals. *Michigan Law Review*. https://doi.org/10.36644/mlr.118.4.downright (accessed on 13th August 2025).
19. N/A. (1967). Federal jurisdiction: The civil rights removal statute revisited. https://core.ac.uk/download/62551751.pdf (accessed on 13th August 2025).
20. Peel, J., & Lin, J. (2019). Transnational climate litigation: The contribution of the Global South. *American Journal of International Law, 113*, 679–726. https://doi.org/10.1017/ajil.2019.48 (accessed on 13th August 2025).
21. Rana, S. (2012). *Chevron* without the courts? The Supreme Court's recent *Chevron* jurisprudence through an immigration lens. https://core.ac.uk/download/56355735.pdf (accessed on 13th August 2025).
22. Utah Supreme Court. (2018). *State of Utah, Plaintiff/Appellee, v. Calvin Paul Steward, Defendant/Appellant: Brief of Appellant*. https://core.ac.uk/download/387912835.pdf (accessed on 13th August 2025).
23. Utah Supreme Court. (2018). *State of Utah, Plaintiff/Appellee, vs. Calvin Paul Steward, Defendant/Appellant: Brief of Appellant*. https://core.ac.uk/download/519808104.pdf (accessed on 13th August 2025).
24. Vázquez, C. M. (2016). Habeas as forum allocation: A new synthesis. https://core.ac.uk/download/70375675.pdf (accessed on 13th August 2025).
25. Yackle, L. W. (1998). The American Bar Association and federal habeas corpus. https://core.ac.uk/download/62568583.pdf (accessed on 13th August 2025).

Chapter

12

EMERGING ISSUES AND REFORMS IN CRIMINAL PROCEDURE AND EVIDENCE

Contents

Introduction 383

12.1. Technological Advancements in Evidence Collection 388

12.2. The Role of Artificial Intelligence (AI) in Criminal Justice 392

12.3. Reforms in Search and Seizure Laws 397

12.4. The Right to Counsel and Access to Justice 401

12.5. Issues of Racial and Socioeconomic Disparities 405

12.6. Legislative Changes and Policy Reforms 409

Summary 413

References 416

INTRODUCTION

The criminal procedure and evidence terrain is also constantly evolving as a result of pressures from society for justice, fairness, and transparency. Emerging issues in the field are typically caused by changes driven by technology, societal values, and growing awareness of civil rights. As a way of responding to these advances, legal systems must undergo grand reforms to counter inefficiencies and injustices that have also detracted from the judicial process over the years. These reforms are not so much aimed at making the evidence more reliable that can be brought before a court of justice but are also aimed at ensuring every party an equal treatment, placing confidence in the integrity of the judiciary. Judicial practice, particularly that of expert evidence, stands at the focal point of such reforms. Recent trends in various jurisdictions like Australia prove so, wherein judges have led the reforms for the presentation of expert evidence. In using approaches like concurrent evidence, there is a move to reduce expert partisanship and moderate the conflict that too often occurs in adversarial settings. This is one element of a broader movement towards the use of scientific principles in legal processes. However, as Edmond observes, the effectiveness of such reforms could be compromised if they are based on traditional scientific practices that may not be suitably responsive to contemporary problems in the legal system (Edmond et al., 2009). The confrontation between new challenges and necessitated reforms throws significant questions about the future of evidence and criminal procedure. As social norms evolve, the courts need to tread carefully between the intricacy of precedent within the law and innovative methods that are optimized for procedural efficiency and access to justice. Additionally, integrating scientific norms into legal practice is a departure from traditional adversarial methods, and it suggests a change in judicial philosophy towards cooperation and transparency. But as evidenced by the current controversy surrounding expert evidence reform in Australia, making this transition is fraught with complexities, necessitating cautious consideration of current scientific ethos and its ramifications for the advancement of justice (Edmond et al., 2009).

Definition of Criminal Procedure

Criminal procedure refers to the principles and procedures through which the state enforces criminal statutes, and those objectives are primarily ensuring justice and safeguarding defendants' rights. This complex process involves several steps such as arrest, charging, trial, and sentencing, and is backed by constitutional protections, most importantly the right to due process and the right to counsel. Throughout this process, there is a precarious tension between effective law enforcement and protection of personal liberties to be negotiated on an ongoing basis. As the world evolves, so do the criminal procedure systems have to address emerging issues, such as the evolution of cybercrime and assuring equitable treatment of vulnerable sections. These changes not only form the core of enhancing justice, but they also form a basic role in achieving public confidence in the system of justice. At the center of criminal procedure is its relationship to evidence law, which regulates the admission and presentation of evidence before the courts. The integrity of the justice system relies on rules that authenticate evidence as being properly collected and handled, but existing challenges like the proliferation of digital evidence pose novel challenges. For example, increased use of technology has raised debate over privacy rights and the implications of data gathering on the judicial process. Furthermore, the need for evidence law reform, such as how to treat vulnerable witnesses and admitting hearsay evidence in specific cases, is taking traction. As highlighted in a number of academical controversies, including those calling for the integration of human rights issues in police operations, the formation of these legislations is required to provide fair trials while addressing the demands for security by the public (Arican et al., 2025; Hepworth et al., 2011). New challenges facing criminal procedure are increasingly calling for revolutionary reform policies that match evolving values in society and technology. For instance, the criminal justice response to addressing trafficking and gender-based violence illustrates the importance of employing more subtle utilization of processes which consider special nuances of those affected. Rehabilitation-based policies as opposed to punishment for non-violent offenders are gaining traction, illustrating an increasing trend towards restorative justice practices. Furthermore, the increased inter-agency collaboration in the provision of community services would further assist victims by bridging gaps in service delivery that otherwise exacerbate their trauma. Therefore, ongoing reform is needed to privilege not only the intricacies of procedural justice but also the substantive rights of individuals so that the system responds to the diverse needs of a population (Arican et al., 2025; Hepworth et al., 2011).

Importance of Evidence in Legal Proceedings

The role of evidence in the legal practice cannot be overstated, as the foundation upon which justice is grounded. Admissibility, relevancy, and credibility of evidence shape the path and the verdict of criminal and civil cases. With changes in society and the development of new techniques, the practice in the collection, presentation, and analysis of evidence must also evolve. Increased challenges such as the risk of evidence tampering and unfair convictions necessitate reforms that aim at maintaining integrity in the judicial system. The interaction of such challenges underscores the necessity for not merely the traditional rubrics of evidence—such as testimonial and documentary evidence—but also the newer advancements such as digital evidence and expert testifier input, which need to be rigorously tested to prevent bias and ensure maximum fairness. Recent tendencies in judicial proceedings indicate a growing realization of the weaknesses of traditional adversarial styles of giving expert testimony. In an effort to make trials less complex and ensure unbiased handling of evidence, innovations like the concurrent evidence system have found application in countries like Australia. In this system, expert witnesses give their evidence together in a single sitting so that less adversarial content that inclines to overwhelm their testimonies is presented. These changes reflect a wider trend towards integrating scientific values and norms into the legal system. Judges have begun to challenge excessive partisanship and expert witness conflicts that can shift the jury's perception and deliberation. By building a more cooperative culture among the experts, the legal system is heading towards procedural efficiency as well as addressing the public's call for justice based on factual integrity (Edmond et al., 2009). Additionally, the importance of evidence does not stop within the courtroom but seeps into public trust in the judiciary. If the judicial process is perceived as fair and based on reliable evidence, it acts to reinforce the belief that justice can prevail and hence create more harmony in society. But situations of abused or manipulated evidence can lead to severe repercussions such as false convictions and erosion of public faith in legal institutions. With shifts in the crime environment, such as the development of technology, the problem of adapting evidentiary standards hangs over the horizon. Reforms must target the inclusion of cutting-edge scientific methods that uphold rigorous standards of reliability without sacrificing accessibility and comprehensibility to juries. Ultimately, the constant evaluation and reform of evidentiary practices are essential to deliver justice equitably and impartially across jurisdictions (Edmond et al., 2009) (Figure 12.1).

Figure 12.1. The role of evidence in legal proceedings.

Source: https://globallitigationnews.bakermckenzie.com/wp-content/uploads/sites/50/2019/10/symbols-of-law-scale-hammer-and-themis-AMT9YPE.jpg.

Overview of Emerging Issues and Reforms

Ongoing evolution of criminal procedure and evidence is increasingly driven by reform initiatives aimed at combating newly emerging issues in the judiciary. The reliability and integrity of expert testimony has been one of the areas of focus that has come under attack for its susceptibility to partisanship. Current Australian reforms reflect an emerging convergence of common-law judges in efforts to enhance the procedural tightness and transparency of expert evidence. Judges across various civil jurisdictions are motivated by ensuring reduced bias and adversarial stands in expert witness testimonies. The institution of concurrent evidence hearings enables witnesses to demonstrate their findings together, providing an environment that is less confrontational and more objective, thus improving the overall quality of expert observations related to legal processes (Edmond et al., 2009). These reforms are a collective movement to align legal practice with evolving scientific standards and norms, thereby redressing embedded inefficiencies in the justice system. In pursuing reforms, it is necessary to consider the broader ramifications of these new issues in criminal procedure.

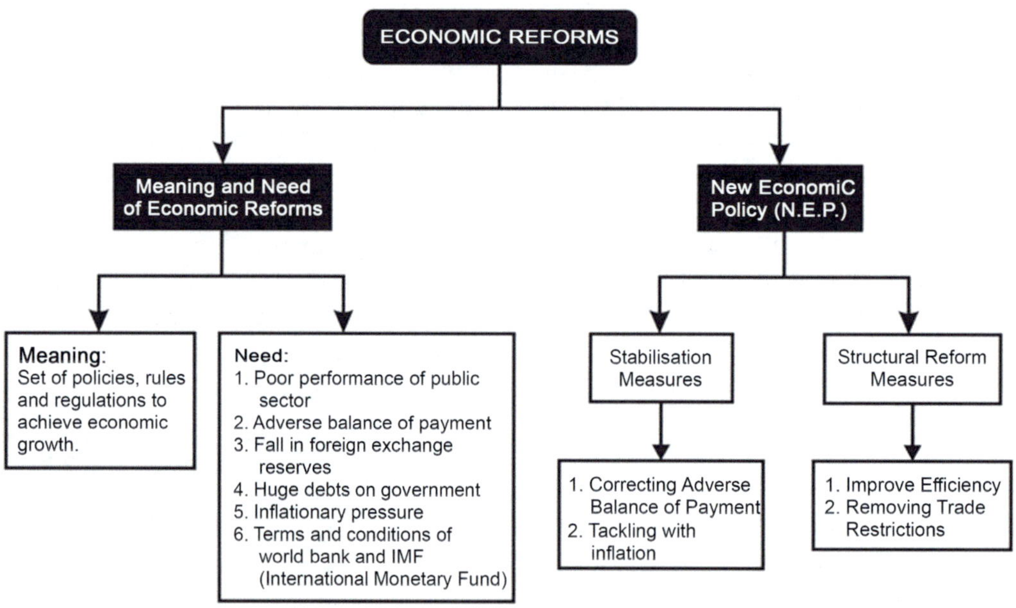

Figure 12.2. An overview of emerging issues and reforms.

Source: https://cdn1.byjus.com/wp-content/uploads/2019/06/economic-reforms.png.

The shift to collaborative expert testimony not only improves the credibility of expert evidence but also significantly affects access to justice. By encouraging a more cooperative setting in the courtroom, these reforms have the potential to combat the disproportionate cost and complexity of formal adversarial systems. In addition, enhancing procedural effectiveness is a vital role in assisting marginalized individuals who might otherwise be powerless to deal with the complexity of court proceedings. The reforms illustrate the manner in which judicial frustration with bias and lack of cooperation has created legal innovations to democratize access to justice (Edmond et al., 2009). Such a reform movement represents a departure from entrenched adversarial traditions, a welcome response to shifting expectations of litigants and the broader community. Finally, the embracement of these new issues and reforms forms the basis of a fairer and more effective legal system in criminal procedures. The growing emphasis on scientific principles and interdisciplinary collaborations demonstrates a legal system responsive to the requirement of adjusting to modern realities. As court systems undertake the task of redefining expectations for expert testimony, continued focus on reducing partisanship and collaborating can help reinforce public faith in the legal process. The reforms are designed not only as process changes but as essential shifts that bring the legal process more in line with scientific integrity and candor. These advancements only serve to demonstrate an embracing of the reality that conventional practices are bound to adapt to the dynamism of social expectations and the evolution of technology. The future research and practice will only continue to explore the implications of these reforms, ensuring the justice system continues to be responsible and responsive to societal needs (Figure 12.2).

12.1. TECHNOLOGICAL ADVANCEMENTS IN EVIDENCE COLLECTION

In the past couple of years, the adoption of technological innovations in evidence gathering has transformed criminal procedure significantly by making traditional mechanisms more straightforward and enhancing the overall effectiveness and dependability. The advent of technologies such as DNA analysis, electronic forensics, and body-worn cameras has provided law enforcement agencies with more sophisticated tools to gather and analyze evidence. Not only do these technologies facilitate accelerated investigation, but they also improve the credibility of the evidence that is presented before the court, thus even further establishing the integrity of the judicial process. For example, DNA evidence has emerged as a pillar in exonerating wrongly accused persons and catching culprits. In addition, the use of digital technologies for the collection of evidence corresponds to modern communication patterns, making it necessary that legal systems adapt accordingly to ensure procedural justice and protection of individual rights as provided under basic legal norms, like those under Article 21 of the Indian Constitution (Dr. Kushwah et al., 2024).

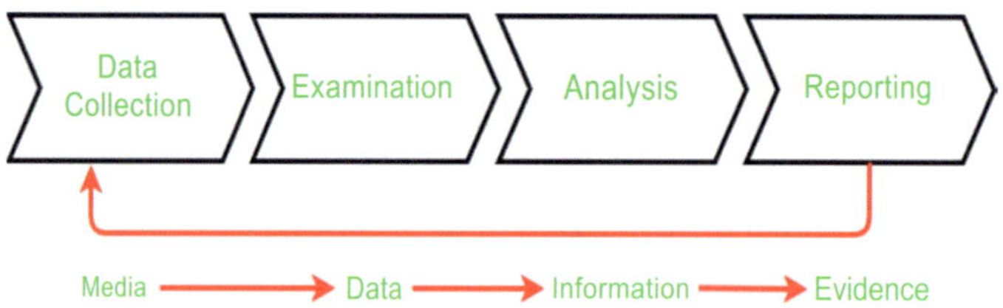

Figure 12.3. Technological advancements in evidence collection.

Source: https://media.geeksforgeeks.org/wp-content/uploads/20220303221354/DigitalEvidenceCollectionProcess.jpg.

Moreover, the digitalization of evidence collection raises pertinent issues regarding the ethical ramifications and legal norms of privacy and protection of data. With the increased use of digital resources by law enforcement agencies, such as collecting data from personal devices and cloud storage, the prospects of infringing on the privacy rights of citizens are greater. Achieving equilibrium so that these technologies do not erode constitutional protections is a substantial challenge. New reforms, such as recent legislation on the handling of electronic data, emphasize the necessity for stringent procedures to direct admissibility and evidence protection of digital evidence. These procedures need to balance the needs of law enforcement bodies in combating crime and the inherent privacy rights of citizens, hence the need to develop a mature understanding of technological evidence and its implications to privacy rights in the overall context of criminal procedure and evidence reform (Marshall et al., 2011). Finally, access and utilization of new technologies have the promise of broadening public engagement and capability within the judiciary. Lawyers and law enforcement agents must be ready to be transformed by these technological innovations through continuous education and training, which will equip them to use appropriately technology resources while delivering due process. Apart from this, public education campaigns can encourage informed discussion about the interconnection between technology and evidence collection so that communities are informed about how their rights and freedoms will be impacted by such developments. With the continuous progress at the nexus of technology and law, the success of new reforms in criminal procedure and evidence also hangs in the balance, to a significant extent, on combined efforts towards integrating these developments responsibly for enhancing delivery of justice without corroding the foundations of civil liberties (Dr. Kushwah et al., 2024) (Figure 12.3).

12.1.1. Use of Digital Evidence in Criminal Cases

The application of digital evidence in criminal cases has turned into a double-edged sword, promising hope for justice along with threats to civil rights. The facile availability of digital technology has enabled the law enforcement agencies to tap vast amounts of information which are precious for investigations. Facilities such as emails, SMS, and web surfing logs enable one to look into criminal motivation and activities that would otherwise be invisible. But the utilization of electronic evidence raises a very serious ethical problem, particularly in regards to privacy rights and misuse by the authorities. Weak institutional protections of criminal suspects' rights are, as they have been identified in recent research, typically exacerbating these issues and producing a kind of environment where digital evidence can be indiscriminately harvested and infringe on the civil liberties that the criminal justice system is intended to protect (Magaloni et al., 2020). In addition, the digital world is constantly evolving, and this creates unique problems for the legal system that governs the use of the same evidence. Computer evidence is readily fabricated or destroyed, necessitating strict procedures to ensure its integrity and authenticity. The absence of standardized protocols for gathering and analyzing computer evidence may affect its admissibility in court. Additionally, the complexity of digital platforms poses challenges to law enforcement as well as the judiciary when interpreting the evidence correctly. As the society remains to be confronted by such issues, it is necessary to concentrate on developing comprehensive reforms in criminal processes to address technological evolution. By the enforcement of policies to increase transparency in how digital evidence is procured and utilized, the justice system can minimize wrongful conviction based on misleading or misinterpreted digital forensic results.

Figure 12.4. Use of digital evidence in criminal cases.

Source: https://a.storyblok.com/f/198504/2896x1092/b041f01262/justice-lifestyle-laptop-and-gavel-header.jpg/m/3840x0/filters:quality(75):format(webp).

At a broader level, the use of digital evidence intersects with prominent issues surrounding international law and accountability. For instance, resistance to bodies like the ICC can contribute to the way in which states pursue prosecution of crimes with digital evidence. States politicize their request for digital capacity while undermining international legal systems that work towards ending impunity at the same time. By examining the efforts by the Kenyan government to counter ICC prosecutions, one is able to draw parallels in how digital evidence can be weaponized as part of broader political agendas (Helfer et al., 2017). This shift in criminal procedure and global standards of law further emphasizes the imperative to rethink the use of digital evidence in courts so it promotes justice, not widens imbalances and injustices in the criminal justice system (Figure 12.4).

12.1.2. Impact of Surveillance Technology on Privacy Rights

The advent of surveillance technology has transformed the privacy rights landscape, creating a balance between security demands nationally and individual freedom. With the reach of facial recognition technology, drone surveillance, and biometric data collection, citizens are under constant surveillance, prompting the query: at what cost do these technologies ensure public safety? The alleged reason for stepped-up surveillance is frequently presented in terms of combating crime and terrorism; yet this justification is usually employed to circumvent basic privacy safeguards. Additionally, the hidden character of such technology usually makes it impossible for people to know when they are subject to its effects and the possible ramifications regarding their right to privacy, and thus there are serious ethics questions regarding consent and autonomy. As governments step up the use of these technologies, there is a growing threat to interfering with personal freedoms, aggravating citizens' fears of the erosion of civil liberties in the name of security. The concept of an Algorithmic Jim Crow, forwarded in recent scholarship, sheds light on the risk of surveillance technologies to establish systemic discrimination. Compared with the blatant segregation of earlier times, modern surveillance regimes claim to be founded on principles of equality; however, the algorithms governing these technologies often have inherent biases that disproportionately burden marginalized communities. For instance, the data samples used to train such systems may lack diversity representation, leading to amplified surveillance and monitoring of specific groups. Consequently, as the technology promises assistance in public security, they also reinforce existing social disparities since they encourage unequal treatment for the sake of objective data analysis. This paradox of technological progress requires careful scrutiny of the legal guidelines that govern the use of surveillance technologies to ensure that they do not establish a new form of societal segregation, since all stakeholders should be given equal protection under the law (Hu et al., 2017). Since police departments increasingly utilize digital forensics in their operations, the balance between effective crime fighting and privacy rights is tenuous. The rapid development of cyber-supported crimes compelled government agencies to apply advanced forensic techniques to chase suspects online. However, such extensive investigations raise concerns regarding violation of individual privacy rights and furthermore involve ethical issues in surveillance policy.

Figure 12.5. Impact of surveillance technology on privacy rights.

Source: https://bhattandjoshiassociates.com/wp-content/uploads/2025/01/the-intersection-of-data-privacy-laws-and-digital-surveillance-in-india.png.

Citizens grow wary of law enforcement's ability to reap and scrutinize their personal data without adequate control or justification. This reality necessitates a reformist approach in criminal procedure and evidence for closer congruence between investigative activity and privacy rights. The requirement of developing ethical guidelines for digital forensics examinations to facilitate transparency, secure the public's trust, and safeguard individuals' rights but allow law enforcement to effectively execute their mandate (Ferguson et al., 2020) (Figure 12.5).

12.1.3. Challenges of Cybercrime and Digital Forensics

The changing cybercrime landscape presents a range of multifaceted challenges for law enforcement and legal practitioners to overcome. One of the primary concerns is the rapid growth of digital technologies, which typically comes before developing the corresponding legal norms. After this technology growth, cybercriminals exploit vulnerabilities in digital systems, and it becomes increasingly difficult for law enforcement agencies to investigate and prosecute these crimes effectively. Such a challenge is particularly prevalent in nations like Nigeria, whose rise in cybercrime has been abetted by weak legal responses and inadequate law enforcement resources. The convergence of traditional criminal behavior with contemporary technology tends to make it all the more challenging for the climate of criminal procedure and evidence, and there is a requirement to re-engineer the legal system to help it effectively address the threats emerging from cybercrime and help provide public safety (Enebeli et al., 2024). Digital forensics has become a crucial component in the fight against cybercrime but is facing tremendous challenges inherent in the nature of digital evidence. Preservation and integrity of digital evidence are of prime interest. Data is manipulated or destroyed using sophisticated techniques by cybercriminals, which may taint the evidence for prosecution. Law enforcement agencies typically do not have the technical expertise to effectively collect, process, and present electronic evidence during prosecution. Furthermore, the complexities that come with issues of jurisdiction and cooperation between nations add layers of sophistication in performing successful prosecutions. This also raises admissibility concerns and evidentiary standards of practice, compelling recurring debates and revisions of criminal procedure to harmoniously enfold these emerging elements into the justice system (Urbas G et al.). Combating the cybercrime and forensic issues requires not only legislative reforms but increased training and equipment for judicial and law enforcement agencies. As cases involving technology become more prevalent, the judicial system needs to understand the accompanying digital ideas and technical terms that characterize such cases. Enhanced training programs might assist prosecutors and judges in addressing the complexity of cyber-crimes so that they can process such cases with expertise. Furthermore, it is essential to promote international coordination, particularly in cases that cross borders. Enacting standard legal frameworks and cooperation agreements will enhance the global effort to fight cybercrime and improve digital forensic investigations as part of an overarching approach to criminal procedure and evidence reform in the new challenge context (Enebeli et al., 2024).

12.2. THE ROLE OF ARTIFICIAL INTELLIGENCE (AI) IN CRIMINAL JUSTICE

New technologies, particularly AI, have begun influencing various sectors, and the criminal justice system is among the key areas being touched. Through the integration of AI systems into law enforcement processes, decision-making can be streamlined and public safety guaranteed. Although the application of such technologies has the potential to prove highly beneficial, their application is of serious ethical issues, particularly with regards to civil liberties and accountability decision-makers would be faced with the aftermath of employing algorithmic tools that exacerbate and potentially even enhance underlying systemic biases. As cited in criticism of policing practice, AI has the ability to temper and enhance authoritarian tendencies in democratic societies, considering cautious and responsible implementation in criminal justice environments, especially considering how these practices are emerging due to growing demands for reform and accountability in light of historic injustices (Magaloni et al., 2020).

Figure 12.6. The role of artificial intelligence (AI) in criminal justice.

Source: https://media.licdn.com/dms/image/v2/D4D12AQGWPKdmbs-MIA/article-cover_image-shrink_720_1280/article-cover_image-shrink_720_1280/0/1718211984853?e=2147483647&v=beta&t=KG9H5F6T_xbv3xF4WM3Bm3Ef4H8uwr9ha679_9iauSI.

Another significant improvement in the use of technology in criminal justice is the use of AI-based risk assessment tools for pretrial decision-making. These are actuarial models that attempt to replace the deployment of judicial discretion, which has been found to be inconsistent and biased. By employing data-driven approaches, AI systems in theory can offer a more transparent and equitable system of evaluating defendants' likelihood of recidivism or failure to appear before court.

The risks inherent in these technologies notwithstanding, while the possibilities of reducing pretrial incarceration rates are high, the approach taken by organizations and jurisdictions towards these tools is one that must be taken with caution and appropriate safeguards. Unless subjected to rigorous scrutiny, the tools designed to yield more just outcomes actually perpetuate discrimination, perpetuating the same injustices they are designed to eliminate (Dalakian et al., 2018). Moreover, the entry of AI into criminal justice raises doubts about its long-term consequences on the common perception of justice and human rights. Algorithmic decision-making contributes to a depersonalized justice system in which traditional standards of responsibility get obfuscated. When AI systems scan huge amounts of data to shape police practices and judicial decisions, the risk of lost transparency and diminished essential due process safeguards becomes an immediate issue. Doing everything possible to see that these technologies are used to expand fairness, not undermine individual rights, is a top priority as reformers confront the challenges of criminal procedure and evidence modernization. Ultimately, a balance between innovation and protection of civil liberties will decide the role of artificial intelligence in developing a more humane criminal justice system within evolving societal expectations and demands for reform (Dalakian et al., 2018) (Figure 12.6).

12.2.1. Artificial Intelligence (AI) in Predictive Policing and Risk Assessment

The application of AI to predictive policing and risk assessment represents a fundamental transformation of criminal procedure, raising promises of innovation as well as profound ethical concerns. These AI-driven applications are designed to sift through vast databases to identify patterns, predict criminal conduct, and direct decision-making. But this reliance on algorithmic judgment raises enormous concerns about fairness and accountability. Predictive policing platforms have the tendency to perpetuate biases in historical data inadvertently, thereby propagating inherent racial disparities in policing. Scholars argue that policymakers must be cautious in mitigating these risks, particularly in the context of growing public concern regarding the implications of automated decision-making in policing platforms. The call for systemic transformation is present, with emphasis placed on protections that guarantee individual constitutional liberties while limiting predictive technologies from increasing entrenched disparities. As states continue to adopt risk assessment tools as a part of bail reform efforts, the discussion around their use must take center stage. In particular, AI technologies are generally admired as being capable of enhancing the pretrial process but with the proviso that, unless strictly regulated, the very same inequalities they aim to address might be reinforced. Empirical studies indicate that while actuarial models may prove useful, there is a very real risk that unregulated application of such technologies may lead to unfair treatment of minority groups. This is particularly a consideration in jurisdictions like New Jersey, where reform has called into question the relationship between risk assessments and at-risk populations. Reformers insist that their application be followed by rigorous evaluation models to guarantee that their impact on fairness and justice within the criminal process is monitored, both in terms of effectiveness as well as ethical bases to their use. Also, concerns about the ethical deployment of AI in policing remain at the heart of debate for police reform. Ethical guidelines that have been formulated expressly for predictive policing suggest an urgent need for ensuring AI systems are directed by rational principles with the aim of protecting the rights and dignity of individuals. Present discourses indicate general agreement on the development of a shared understanding that situates AI use in American policing, which struggles with ingrained issues of violence and discrimination. As such, the development of sound governance frameworks is critical to encouraging trust and accountability in these technologies. Interventions should involve community participation, open algorithms, and constant monitoring of AIs social impacts. Policy-makers and law enforcement officials are thus tasked with not just implementing the latest technology but with implementing it in a manner consistent with ethical necessities and public perceptions, making their respective contributions to the larger conversation of overhauling criminal process and evidence in response to impending technological challenges.

12.2.2. Ethical Concerns Surrounding Artificial Intelligence (AI) Decision-Making

The application of AI in criminal justice decision-making poses serious ethical challenges that must not be overlooked. With the growing role of AI in assisting law enforcement institutions with predictive policing and risk assessment, transparency and bias dominate the controversy. Babuta et al. (2020) highlights the alarming trend of algorithmic bias in police data analysis and analytics that is poised to perpetuate existing disparities in the criminal justice system. Lack of national direction, and the homogenization of algorithmic cultures further exacerbate these concerns. Ensuring that any framework established for AI usage in policing enhances existing legal as well as ethical principles and enhances a sense of dedication to fairness is imperative. Addressing these biases, thus, requires a value-led approach of policy-making with emphasis on making AI decision-making more transparent and accountable. In addition, ethical concerns extend beyond mere bias because the human-machine interface can impact the outcomes of judicial processes significantly. The application of AI in criminal procedures has the tendency to promote reliance on numerical assessment rather than human judgment, which might diminish multifaceted human discretion. The shift raises important questions about responsibility for false predictions and decisions made in response to algorithmic recommendations. The danger of exacerbating the digital divide in access to fair trials and justice has also been underscored by the learning through expert exchange on digitalization, particularly for vulnerable populations. Garcia et al. (2020) posits that the meaning of the different availabilities of benefits from digital advancements carries with it the requirement of inclusive methods for AIs use in criminal justice. Therefore, upholding an ethical and equitable ethos is crucial in addressing such disparities. Lastly, the need for far-reaching oversight mechanisms becomes clear as AIs role in the criminal justice system expands. The ethical implications of AI decision-making go far beyond specific cases, potentially transforming societal views of justice and accountability. The ethical guidelines and advice proposed for the application of AI need to be adaptive to the changing nature of technology and societal values to match the fluidity of changing developments. It requires multiple stakeholders to be engaged, such as legal professionals, community representatives, and technologists, in developing the guidelines so that the potential unintended consequences of algorithmic decision-making can be averted. Deploying AI systems without thorough examination and continuous monitoring risks creating a culture of systemic injustice rather than enhancing the efficiency and fairness of the criminal justice system. A methodical approach to these moral questions will chart the future course of AI in criminal procedure and evidence (Figure 12.7).

Figure 12.7. Ethical concerns surrounding artificial intelligence (AI) decision-making.

Source: https://s3.amazonaws.com/img2.copperdigital.com/wp-content/uploads/2023/08/10131515/Ethical-Concerns-in-AI-Powered-Manufacturing-1024x512.png.

12.2.3. Potential for Bias in Artificial Intelligence (AI) Algorithms

The use of AI algorithms in criminal justice processes has great potential for enhancement but also great risk of bias. The algorithms are increasingly being utilized for decision-making functions such as risk assessment pretrial detention. Through the implementation of actuarial models, jurisdictions anticipate an increased efficacy in tackling the traditionally subjective nature of judicial discretion. But as noted in the controversy surrounding these models, they don't necessarily free us of bias but instead go on and even exacerbate existing inequalities in the criminal justice system. Reformers are concerned with the necessity to establish guarantees to protect individual constitutional rights in the evolving context of AI. If not addressed, all these challenges may lead to consequences that entrench racial and social inequalities because the algorithms would have learned from existing data that reflect discriminatory practices, hence maintaining the cycle of injustice (Dalakian et al., 2018). Aside from the concerns raised around risk assessment tools, using AI in policing brings a new dimension of ethical concerns. Increasingly, there's an understanding that current guidelines for the application of AI in policing run the risk of overlooking the nuanced realities of policing. Reports and recommendations for responsible AI use have a tendency to offer broad principles that may not always meet the complex and context-dependent challenges faced by police forces in the United States. Such oversight can have the consequence of separating theoretical guidance and practice, with the potential for unaccountable use of AI technologies. The AI and policing debate, thus, demands a tailored perspective that takes into consideration the unique realities of the American policing system, and it has been contended that ethical principles should be reappraised and realigned in terms of these specific contexts (Joh et al., 2022). In addition, the ethics surrounding AI in criminal justice underscore the imperative of sweeping reforms. Because courts and legislators grapple with AI issues, there is a necessity for sparking a debate that promotes transparency and accountability in algorithmic decision-making. Policy-makers will need to contend with a broad range of stakeholders, including activists, technologists, and jurists, in order to develop an integrated framework that mitigates bias while enhancing public trust in such systems. This collaborative effort must also address how to regularly assess and improve AI tools so that they function in the service of justice without infringing on individual rights. Lastly, combating the specter of bias in AI algorithms is the solution to continuing criminal justice reform in an effort to make it equitable and just for all (Dalakian et al., 2018) (Figure 12.8).

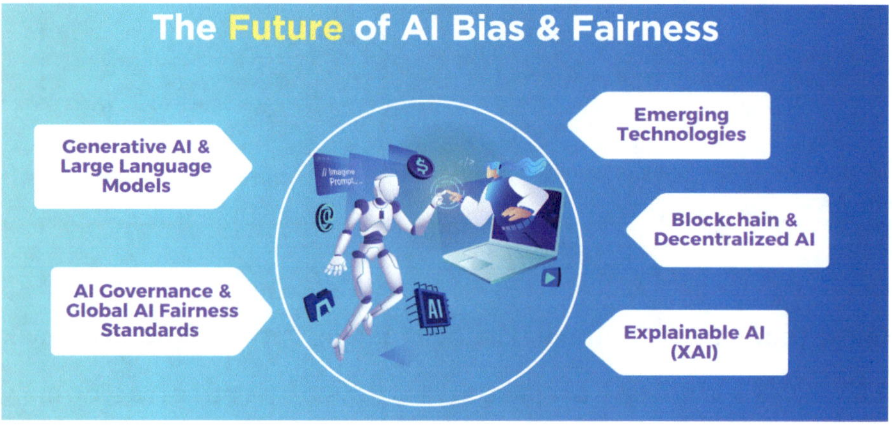

Figure 12.8. Potential for bias in artificial intelligence (AI) algorithms.

Source: https://smartdev.com/wp-content/uploads/2025/03/5-4.png.

12.3. REFORMS IN SEARCH AND SEIZURE LAWS

The area of search and seizure laws has been subjected to strong scrutiny over the last few years, specifically the effects of the exclusionary rule that prohibits the admissibility of evidence obtained in violation of the Fourth Amendment. In Hudson v. Michigan, the Supreme Court hinted that there may be a desirability to be rid of the exclusionary rule, since Justice Scalia indicated that the rule's usefulness may no longer be greater than its cost. This assertion encourages critical scrutiny of contemporary law enforcement practice and the wisdom of existing protections against illicit searches and seizures. In order to ensure reforms address these pressing matters, a comprehensive method that combines empirical knowledge and technological development is required (Harris et al., 2009). One field with potential for reform is the development of tracking systems for police search and seizure activity. Building on innovations routinely used to combat police abuse, such mechanisms can allow supervisory officers to effectively monitor adherence to the law. By providing oversight and accountability, these systems would ensure a culture of respect for constitutional protections by law enforcement agencies. Furthermore, instilling a culture in which individuals can appeal to federal courts for alleged police abuse would also be an incentive for officers to respect the Fourth Amendment. In particular, such reforms can help redress the prevalence of Fourth Amendment violations that result in evidence that is ruled inadmissible, thereby fortifying the integrity of law and law enforcement practice (Harris et al., 2009). Racial imbalance in the criminal justice system also enhances the debate over reforms in search and seizure law. Recent studies point out that entrenched social causes explain much of the racial imbalance in policing and broader judicial outcomes. These differences ought to be reduced by reforms that embrace an integrated approach and target not just procedural reforms to the law-enforcement role but also addressing root causes beyond the criminal justice system. Procedures supporting community alliances and enhanced public engagement can foster mutual respect and cooperation, thereby ensuring that search and seizure practice is fair and even-handed. By integrating these methods, pursuit of meaningful changes to search and seizure law can more closely align with the broader objectives of judicial fairness and public safety.

12.3.1. Changes in Legal Standards for Warrants

The evolution of legal standards for warrants has been influenced, in part, by the increasing technologizing of law enforcement culture. As the virtual world expands so does the concept of reasonable search and seizure. The Fourth Amendment tends to mandate warrants that are based on probable cause and detailed descriptions of the place to be searched and the items to be seized. However, such transparency becomes problematic in the digital evidence situation; the scale of information stored by cloud providers and internet service providers renders it challenging to support the classical warrant application paradigms. This shift challenges privacy rights and the adequacy of existing legal standards to accommodate new norms of surveillance and collection, particularly in counterterrorism, as explained by recent study on how surveillance technology influences individuals' privacy rights (Lachmayer et al., 2025). The conflict between national security needs and individuals' privacy has also had a shaping effect on warrant standards. Legislation passed in 9/11's aftermath signaled a shift toward broader interpretations of probable cause, oftentimes at the expense of highly cherished civil liberties. The USA PATRIOT Act, for example, provided for enhanced surveillance authority and included "sneak and peek" warrants that allowed police to delay notifying individuals when they are searched. This was a record deviation from the inherent underlying principles that lie in the Fourth Amendment, and one that incited controversy over the tension between the enforcement of law and the breakdown of civil rights. As many legal scholars have claimed, it is in the critical analysis of how changes in warrant standards can augment or dismantle democratic principles and human rights in the face of perceived security threats that this balance is achieved (Arican et al., 2025). Finally, the future of legal standards for warrants is in the dialectical interaction between legislators, judges, and advocates of civil rights. Reform calls emphasize the need for comprehensive legislative frameworks that recognize the evolving nature of technology and the need to protect fundamental rights. Proposals can vary from the application of open criteria for digital warrants to calling for more transparency and accountability of law enforcement authorities and ensuring judicial review is sufficiently robust. These reforms are not only responsive but an essential move towards enhancing public trust in the criminal justice system with increasing concerns about privacy and state oversight. With the changes that we witness taking place in legal standards, it is only fit that we guard the basic tenets of justice and rights of individuals in the context of new technologies (Lachmayer et al., 2025) (Figure 12.9).

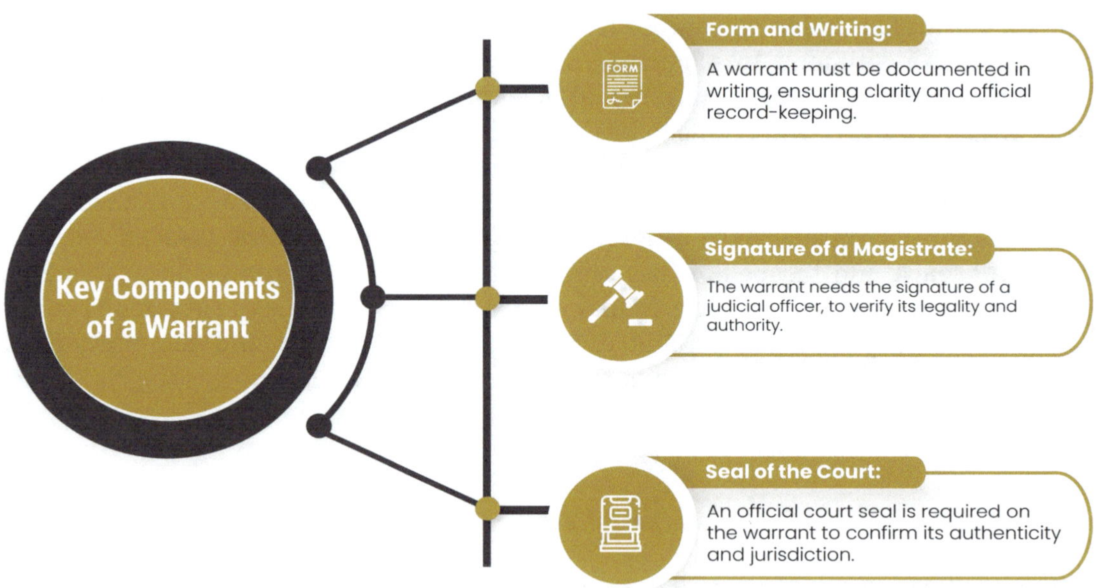

Figure 12.9. The evolution of legal standards for warrants.

Source: https://rtc-prod.s3.ap-south-1.amazonaws.com/7cf9f9b2-7c66-43b4-b903-28689e4a93bf.webp.

12.3.2. The Exclusionary Rule and Its Implications

The Exclusionary Rule is a valuable ally of the American criminal justice system, one designed to discourage illegal behavior on the part of law enforcement agencies and protect the constitutional rights of individuals. Founded on the basis of the Fourth Amendment, the Rule states that illegally seized evidence from seizures and searches cannot be used in a court of law. It is a fundamental principle in ensuring the purity of judicial process by holding a balance between the authority of the state and rights of the accused. The Exclusionary Rule excludes tainted evidence and acts as a safeguard against potential abuse of power, maintaining public trust in the justice system. As newer criminal procedure issues keep changing, the relevance of this Rule remains a prime focus of debate among scholars of law, legal practitioners, and policymakers about its effects on justice and due process. Also, the question of burden posed by the Exclusionary Rule has led to renewed controversy about potential reforms under criminal procedure. Critics argue that the Rule sometimes prevents justice from achieving its objective by allowing guilty persons to go free due to technicalities. The argument has been most prominent following high-profile cases where evidence critical in establishing guilt had been rendered inadmissible. Some legal scholars offer a response in the form of alternative methods, proposing the implementation of good faith exceptions, which permit evidence obtained in good faith reliance on a search warrant, even if that warrant is subsequently held to be invalid. These modifications are representative of an increasing trend towards the reexamination of classical legal axioms in an effort to harmonize the administration of justice with the safeguarding of individual rights. Discussion of these reforms is necessary for an evolving legal landscape that promises the promise of accountability and equity in enforcing the law. When considering the broader vision of the Exclusionary Rule, it is necessary to consider its interplay with state constitutional legislation. Federal courts' differing philosophy from that of many state courts makes up a richer brocade of legal vision, often having uneven applications of justice. Whereas state constitutions have historically duplicated the federal Bill of Rights protections, they sometimes give broader meanings concerning rights and liberties. This inconsistency raises fundamental questions about the role federal courts play in engaging state statutes when determining comparable constitutional issues, particularly in light of recent occurrences highlighting the role of police practices and the integrity of evidence collection. With legal professionals navigating these intricate issues, increased focus on the nuances of state constitutional law will be crucial, providing a comprehensive approach that amplifies the existing debate surrounding criminal justice reform and the Exclusionary Rule's function in safeguarding individual rights in the midst of evolving legal norms (Blocher et al., 2011) (Conway et al., 2019).

12.3.3. Impact of Recent Supreme Court Decisions

Holding of the Supreme Court in recent years has significantly changed the criminal procedure and evidence landscape, with significant implications for the justice system. The Court's decisions generally reveal a balancing between society's interest and individual rights, which is most frequently observed in Fourth Amendment protection against unreasonable search and seizure cases. Landmark judicial precedents have determined the scope of police powers in conducting searches and thus set precedents for police practice nationwide. As these precedents continue to evolve, they give rise to controversies over public safety, privacy, and the risk of government overreach, underscoring the need for constant scrutiny of the balance between these competing interests within the criminal justice framework. With regard to evidence standards, the recent Supreme Court decisions have also influenced shifts in direction towards examination of what constitutes admissible evidence in criminal trials. Expert opinion testimony is one of the areas that has been a focus point since it plays a dominant role in influencing jury attitudes and trial outcomes. More and more, it is becoming agreed upon that not only should expert evidence be scientifically acceptable but it should also be relevant and reliable. The Court has emphasized intense cross-examination of expert witnesses to reduce potential bias and enhance fairness in trials. The trend is aligned with parallel reforms within other courts where the aim has been to simplify expert opinion presentation and reduce partisanship. These reforms, for example, the use of concurrent evidence, highlight a wish for openness and responsibility in the judicial process with the ultimate goal of increasing access to justice while preserving the integrity of the judicial process (Edmond et al., 2009). Also, these decisions by the Supreme Court have generated debate concerning reform for criminal procedure and handling evidence in the future. Since the Court's rulings take meaning well beyond the cases, stakeholders in the criminal justice system are being called upon to innovate and adapt practices that remain current with changing times. The emergence of digital evidence, for instance, puts to challenge privacy rights and data protection, which in turn impacts the way evidence is being collected and presented in court. Moreover, as the courts grapple with addressing biases and systemic injustices, ongoing reform in criminal procedure and evidence are essential. Ongoing impact of these Supreme Court decisions not only marks a judicial response to current issues but also sets the stage for future legal practice and doctrine, demanding a continued adherence to justice (Edmond et al., 2009) (Figure 12.10).

Figure 12.10. Impact of recent supreme court decisions.

Source: https://www.legals365.com/legalblogimages/impact-of-recent-supreme-court-decisions-on-property-law.jpg.

12.4. THE RIGHT TO COUNSEL AND ACCESS TO JUSTICE

Right to counsel remains a pillar of access to justice, embodying the principle that all individuals are entitled to equal representation regardless of socio-economic status. The right to counsel under the Sixth Amendment is important to the degree that it allows defendants an adequate capability for dealing with the complexities of the criminal justice system. As emerging issues reveal systemic inequities, particularly for indigent defendants who cannot afford to hire private attorneys, the effects of less-than-optimal legal representation become glaringly clear. In many situations, public defense systems are overwhelmed, leading to inadequate preparation and lack of resources on behalf of the defendant. Consequently, this raises gigantic issues about conviction validity and the overall fair administration of justice. Eliminating these constraints calls for reforms that not only bring to the forefront the appropriations of adequate financial resources for the public defense but also invite new best practices to enhance the effectiveness of legal representation. Current debates on aggregation in criminal law outline how procedural reforms can further strengthen the right to counsel, particularly due to courts looking for new mechanisms to cure systemic violations. Traditional practices always ignored the interrelatedness of cases, and a number of defendants found themselves without a definite means to fairness and justice. With courts today considering the merging of cases before trial, aimed at mending such flaws as ineffective representation and wrongful conviction, the necessity for comprehensive due process protections remains paramount. These reforms can also potentially redefine the functioning of the criminal justice system in a manner wherein aggregation would become a system wherein rights would not only be acknowledged but even enforced in the affirmative.

This could lead to a more centralized functioning providing additional resources and representation for defendants charged with the same, thus transforming the face of criminal adjudication and access to justice for marginalized communities. The consequences of wrongful convictions also intersect with the debate around the right to counsel and the right to access justice. As recent legal literature has shown, people who have been wrongfully convicted tend to pursue remedies through civil actions after they have been released, and this basically defies the current paradigms of criminal procedure. The convergence of wrongful conviction cases and the right to effective counsel highlights an essential element of the possibilities for systemic reform. For instance, looking at wrongful convictions on the grounds of prosecutorial misconduct or ineffectiveness of counsel, it is found that remedies today fail to correct such injustices. Not only do such a shift away from civil rights claims eliminate the traditional harmless error rules, but it also invites broader systemic reforms, thereby revitalizing the constitutional guarantees in terms of a fair trial. Consequently, these advances herald a renaissance of legal responsibility in the criminal justice system, re-emphasizing the necessity of rigorous moral guidelines for all legal experts involved.

12.4.1. Challenges Faced by Public Defenders

Public defenders have an important role to play in the criminal justice system of providing fair trials to those who are unable to afford attorneys. However, such attorneys face numerous issues that undermine their ability to represent their clients adequately. One of the main issues is the overloading of cases by which the majority of public defenders are bogged down. Heavy workloads can lead to substandard preparation and reduced quality of representation, further contributing to the shortage of incompetent counsel. This is especially concerning considering that appeals on grounds of inadequate representation tend to cause procedural obstacles in their path, rendering redress complicated for convicted defendants. The systemic pressures therefore experienced by public defenders therefore not only affect their clients but also highlight overarching inadequacies in public defense systems, pointing to the necessity of reforms in guarantees of fair access to justice (Tague et al., 2001). Additionally, the lack of funds allocated to public defense offices turn into barriers for the exhaustive inquiries and availability of expert witnesses for the public defenders. For the majority of jurisdictions, the public defenders operate with shoestring budgets that limit their ability to acquire evidence or challenge effectively the prosecutions' claims. As a result, convincing pieces of evidence that can be employed to exonerate innocent clients are not being taken into account, and this has resulted in wrongful convictions. This imbalance of resources raises serious ethical concerns within the legal profession by leaving public defenders at a disadvantage in a system that claims fairness and justice as its guiding ideals. Besides, the increasing public awareness of wrongful convictions, fueled by innocence movements, shows how imbalances in the system may yield extreme injustices, highlighting the greatest necessity for institutional reform that addresses these imbalances directly (Smith et al., 2010). Furthermore, the public defenders are usually victimized by stigma and misinformation about the nature and extent of their advocacy. These attitudes are at times based on social opinion that equates being a public defender to representing the guilty or undermining the justice system. Such stereotypes place extra pressure on these attorneys, many of whom are passionate about their work and working to safeguard the rights of marginalized clients. Such stigma can only increase difficulty in public defenders work in maintaining energetic motivation for their work, and may lead to burnout and turnover at public defense offices. Debunking these myths requires a concerted effort in attempting to enlighten the public regarding the indispensable role played by public defenders to defend civil liberties and provide a fair legal process to everyone regardless of their economic status (Smith et al., 2010) (Figure 12.11).

Figure 12.11. Challenges faced by public defenders.

Source: https://www.lomtl.com/wp-content/uploads/2022/08/public_defender.jpg.

12.4.2. Innovations in Legal Aid and Representation

Innovations in legal aid and representation are critical to addressing systemic imbalances in the criminal justice system. The innovations are usually driven by empirical evidence that offers insights to guide procedural and policy reforms to enhance access to justice. The evolution of legal aid in the last couple of years has incorporated technology-based interventions into it, such as internet platforms for legal information and representation. This is intended to enhance the gap for marginalized communities by providing them with information, advice, and assistance on the critical issues without the normal barriers experienced in formal legal services. This progression toward accepting technology not only puts legal aid within everyone's reach but also encourages broader participation in the legal system, which is vital to realize a fair and equitable process of justice. In addition, the adaptability of legal aid systems toward adopting consumer-oriented approaches represents an essential paradigm shift in legal representation. As highlighted by recent debate, a cafeteria-style civil justice system can offer consumers greater autonomy in choosing legal services, and it may produce superior results for clients. Such innovations as cost capping and risk-sharing agreements are essential in this context, allowing clients to make informed decisions regarding their representation while encouraging collaborative engagement between legal representatives and clients. These changes could make more effective the distribution of resources in the legal aid system so that the service is more responsive and tailored to address directly the various needs of people going through the criminal process. The importance of empirical research in piloting these innovations cannot be overstated. It not only quantifies the effectiveness of reforms but also identifies loopholes in service delivery. For instance, patterns of litigation have been shown to significantly impact accessibility and efficiency in criminal procedure. Analysis of these patterns assists stakeholders in developing strategies for rationalizing processes in a bid to enhance the operation of legal aid systems as a whole. Furthermore, ongoing critical examination of mechanisms of civil justice, as quoted in relevant literature, highlights the requirement for ongoing innovation and reform. This approach provides an environment whereby legal aid can innovate, experiment, and refine, responding to the limitations of existing procedural conventions and dispense justice more equally across populations (Garth et al., 2010; Peacock et al., 2025).

12.4.3. The Role of Technology in Enhancing Access

Technology is increasingly a prime driver in criminal procedure of providing access to justice, particularly by bringing on board digital platforms that become channels of making judicial processes easier. Online case management systems become empowering for legal professionals as well as members of the public by providing them with ongoing access to relevant information. These advancements enable attorneys and defendants to search case files, file motions, and review courtroom calendars without going physically. Not only does this decrease logistical problems but it also facilitates an even more open legal system where everyone involved is better informed and ready for hearings. Increased access to information online can promote transparency and accountability in the judicial system, moving towards a more just legal landscape taking into consideration and addressing the barriers to accessing justice by marginalized groups. Further, technology's impact on expert testimony is a transformative shift in the perception and presentation of evidence in court. As demonstrated through recent reform in Australian civil procedure, the judges are now actually reforming the methodologies of preparation and presentation of expert evidence. The introduction of concurrent evidence allows the expert witnesses to present collectively in a more open way, thereby eliminating adversarial partisanship and facilitating cooperative understanding among experts. Such developments are evidence of a profound enthusiasm for improving procedural efficiency as well as improved access to justice. Through the minimization of disagreement among expert witnesses, courts enhance the trustworthiness of the evidence being presented, making the process more equitable to all. The practice is in line with the general aim of employing scientific values that can enhance confidence in judicial rulings, maintaining the central role of technology in current legal processes (Edmond et al., 2009). Additionally, the employment of technological instruments within court processes presents the promise of eliminating age-old inefficiencies to barriers to access to justice. By facilitating analysis of data and presentation of evidence electronically, courts can expedite case resolution with the confidence that procedure remains equitable. The use of technologies such as video conferencing and virtual hearing has become increasingly prevalent, particularly in the wake of the COVID-19 pandemic. These measures not only facilitate remote involvement of legal representatives and witnesses, but also reduce the economic cost of attending court in person. As courts incorporate these innovations, it is essential that it maintains equilibrium between technological advancements and protecting fundamental rights and protection of defendants. In general, the embracement of technological reforms is an innovative method of addressing emerging issues and enhancing access in the criminal justice system (Edmond et al., 2009) (Figure 12.12).

Figure 12.12. The role of technology in enhancing access.

Source: https://media.licdn.com/dms/image/v2/D4D12AQE8WKTg5nRLGQ/article-cover_image-shrink_600_2000/article-cover_image-shrink_600_2000/0/1660304127577?e=2147483647&v=beta&t=SRBBtL4D7OownguS11sxrAaqYIATE3E3zKiO3X4q8pE.

12.5. ISSUES OF RACIAL AND SOCIOECONOMIC DISPARITIES

The intersection of racial and socioeconomic disparities within the criminal justice system is one of the challenges that continues to erode public trust and equitable treatment. Research shows that practices such as police stops, pretrial detention, and sentencing disproportionately affect minority communities and low-income individuals. Not just do the disparities make cycles of poverty and disenfranchisement greater, but they also contribute to systemic flaws in the justice system. As seen in Rudovsky et al. (2015), identifying these procedural disparities and pressing for change is important for ensuring public safety while fostering fairness. Various effective reform initiatives elsewhere demonstrate how human rights-based review mechanisms can alleviate such disparities, reinforcing the need for legal systems with equity as a prime consideration over punitive action in human rights procedures. Examining the barriers to justice, socioeconomic status plays an important role affecting individuals opportunity to engage with human rights processes. Economically poor individuals are normally hesitant to seek legal aid, as is evident from alarming figures indicating that a high percentage of the poor, particularly poor Black individuals, completely avoid legal aid when they are confronted with matters of civil justice. This hesitancy stems from a variety of factors, including past bad experiences with the criminal justice system and loss of faith in its effectiveness, further augmenting inequalities. As emphasized in Greene et al. (2015), it is crucial to understand the described patterns of behavior in creating sound access-to-justice policy. By clarifying the complex interactions between socioeconomic status and civil justice use, policymakers are able to craft programs that can establish trust and provide individuals with a sense of confidence when accessing the system for assistance. Lastly, addressing racial and socioeconomic disparity in the criminal justice system is a two-pronged approach combining legal reform and community outreach programs. Trust-building initiatives are essential, particularly among victimized marginalized groups who perceive the system as being against them. The reforms must address both procedural reform in the criminal justice system and social conditions underlying such imbalances. As theorized in Rudovsky et al. (2015), community-based programs can serve as useful complements to formal legal systems, providing assets and support systems that can empower people. By convening lawmakers, community organizations, and affected groups, one can create a more equitable criminal justice system that actively confronts its role in dismantling the deeply ingrained barriers that fuel racial and socioeconomic disparities.

12.5.1. Disparities in Sentencing and Conviction Rates

Disparities in conviction and sentencing rates are severe issues within the criminal justice system, reflecting systemic bias that disproportionately targets vulnerable populations. Research has repeatedly demonstrated that racial and socioeconomic factors are prime determinants of outcomes at all stages of legal process, from arrest to sentencing. For instance, racial minority group members are punished more harshly than white offenders for similar offenses. The impact of these disparities extends beyond individual cases, leading to systemic overall societal problems such as eroding the public's trust in the justice system and increased perceptions of injustice among the communities affected. The reforms aimed at reducing these disparities are crucial, as they not only provide fairness but also try to enhance public trust in the legal process and the overall efficacy of justice. One particularly unsettling contributor to disproportionate sentencing is the utilization of pretrial detention. Conditions of pretrial release in most states are extremely inconsistent and usually based upon a defendant's socioeconomic status and not the character of their alleged crime. Those who are unable to afford bail may languish in jail for months, giving rise to a ripple effect where they are under more pressure to accept plea bargains, innocent or guilty. This is further exacerbated by actuarial-based risk assessment models that can reproduce inherent biases unless vetted with equity protocols (Risk and Advocacy Management Authority, 2018). According to the author of recent research, there have been some successes with innovative bail reforms in certain states aimed at minimizing the effect of these disparities, but the problems remain widespread and warrant ongoing attention and critique (Dalakian et al., 2018). Moreover, sentencing disparities frequently go along with the discretion of judges and prosecutors and create a context replete with uncertainty and possible unfairness. The disparity in application can lead to systematic under-prosecution or over-prosecution of particular groups on the basis of such factors as economic status and race. For example, the judicial discretion at sentencing has been found to have a significant impact, with studies having pointed to an unfavorable trend of judges meting out harsher sentences where minority defendants are concerned. Addressing this disparity is of vital concern, and reform has trended towards simplifying sentencing guidelines to avoid disparity and ensure more equitable treatment. These projects aim not only to contain inequalities but also to establish a more open and more dependable judiciary system reflecting the virtues of fairness and justice (Rudovsky et al., 2015) (Figure 12.13).

Figure 12.13. Disparities in sentencing and conviction rates are significant issues within the criminal justice system.

Source: https://static.archerdxp.io/cms/482f5461-000f-4331-a854-21ddf5248b95.jpg.

12.5.2. The Impact of Socioeconomic Status on Legal Outcomes

The intersection of socioeconomic status and legal outcomes is a critical subject matter in the criminal justice system. Members of the lower socioeconomic statuses are likely to experience more legal difficulties compared to their wealthier counterparts, primarily due to limited access to quality legal representation. This disparity creates a skewed playing field where one's financial status plays a significant role in determining how one will make it through the complicated legal procedures. Research indicates that legal costs and fines disproportionately affect poorer citizens, making it more challenging for them to engage with the legal system (Dahaghi et al., 2018). Thus, the impact of socioeconomic status extends beyond plain case outcomes to broader rule implications, reflecting system inequities that pervade the justice process. These inequities need to be rectified to create a more equitable legal system, where clients are dealt with fairly irrespective of their financial position. Further, recent legislative actions have become increasingly prone to utilizing fines and fees as punishment, a trend that has often been economically justified but with fatal implications for those already excluded. The revenues that accrue to the state under these policies disproportionately burden economically marginalized individuals, creating a debt cycle that can increase criminalization rather than prevent it. This legislative tradition has won bipartisan support, an ill-starred bipartisan agreement on penalizing instead of meeting the causes of poverty (Dahaghi et al., 2018). Legal debt as a social and financial punishment generates a specific kind of inequality that strongly contributes to legal outcomes and reinforces impediments to justice among the poor. Understanding how such policies arise from and loop back into socio-political processes is crucial to stakeholders advocating for reforms in an attempt to counter the negative impact of socioeconomic forces on legal proceedings. In regions such as the south of Italy, whose operations of organized crime enterprises intersect with socio-economic concerns, the consequences of ineffectual enforcement and socio-economic imbalances manifest themselves in disparate legal outcomes. Research indicates that criminal activity thrives where regulatory control is less, and the significance of equitable enforcement strategies is thereby underscored. Lower socio-economic status is often linked to fewer legal protections and less enforcement activity, leading to mixed criminal behavior. The reverse correlation between the level of enforcement and criminal activity underscores the complexity involved in addressing criminal activity based on socioeconomic vulnerabilities. The difference in legal results between areas underlines pressing imbalances that need specific reform in policies of enforcement—deterrents that must serve not just to combat organized crime but also to tackle the underlying socio-economic issues that fuel legal imbalances.

12.5.3. Reforms Aimed at Reducing Discrimination

Efforts to seek reforms decreasing discrimination within criminal procedures have become more intense, particularly with increasing recognition of structural inequalities. Discrimination generally comes in many diverse forms, including gender discrimination, racial profiling, and economic disadvantage, fundamentally derailing justice and equality ideals. Some measures towards curbing such biases involve re-tooling profiling policies and practices disproportionately affecting marginalized groups. For instance, conducting training sessions for police officers on implicit biases has had potential for encouraging fairer treatment of individuals irrespective of origin. In addition, reforms must offer provisions for mechanisms to guarantee that legal systems tackle not just the obvious discriminatory actions but also the oblique prejudice that may insidiously influence decisions within the judiciary. Such integrated strategies are imperative to create a platform that fosters equal rights in criminal justice and ultimately creates public trust in legal institutions. Knowledge of the pervasive prevalence of gender-based violence (GBV) indicates the necessity for focused reforms to protection and justice for all, but particularly for women. There is evidence that GBV is not an individual issue but a structural one that impacts health, economic security, and social welfare. Effective interventions require an approach that is multidimensional in nature, involving legal reform, institutional accountability, and community engagement. Those countries with advanced legal systems dealing with GBV have established policies that improve victims' access to justice and the accountability of offenders, thereby minimizing the ill effects of violence on society. Second, Bott et al. (2025) emphasizes that good law and policy practices, change at the institutional level, and community-level intervention are all critical in dealing with GBV comprehensively. This system-level reform does not only provide for the application of protective legislation but also promotes changes in societal attitude towards equality of the sexes. The arena of civil litigation, as portrayed by recent literature, highlights the ways in which procedural reforms may be reoriented to effectively combat discrimination. Procedures current at the time tend to perpetuate injustice by favoring results based on non-merit factors, which can misalign the neutrality of legal resolutions. Glover et al. (2012) argues that the Federal Rules of Civil Procedure need to be rethought in the light of the current society where settlements reign supreme compared to trials. By envisioning a new procedural landscape to prioritize substantive fairness, reforms can improve alignment between results and claim merits, thereby minimizing prejudice in legal outcomes. Formulating a new paradigm under which pretrial rules not only try cases but also impact equitable settlements is critical to reducing discrimination within the legal system. This alignment would guarantee that procedural integrity is consistent with the concept of justice and therefore optimize fairness and equality among everyone in the litigation process (Figure 12.14).

Figure 12.14. Reforms aimed at reducing discrimination.

Source: https://advocatebindu.com/wp-content/uploads/2024/08/Promoting-Equality-in-Indian-Constitution-Law.webp.

12.6. LEGISLATIVE CHANGES AND POLICY REFORMS

Legislative reforms and policy shifts are the primary vehicles in reshaping the criminal procedure and evidence landscape. As societies evolve, the challenge of legal systems that address the issues of our time becomes more pressing. Recent developments are often crafted to enhance the rights of defendants while balancing the necessity to protect public safety. For instance, shifts in rules of admissibility of evidence mirror a trend towards prioritizing fairness in trials. Policymakers are responding to calls for accountability and transparency in law enforcement practices, demanding reforms that enhance trust in cooperation among judicial organs and the communities they serve. Insistence on maintaining these frameworks leads to systematic injustices further undermining the foundations of justice and fairness that characterize democratic states. It is thus crucial that legislatures undertake complete reviews of existing legislation to establish whether or not it reflects current values and societal needs. One of the key areas of emphasis for recent legislative developments is the intersection of technology and criminal law. The introduction of digital evidence, particularly as an outgrowth of the development of cybercrime, necessitates a revisit of traditional rules of evidence. Courts and legislatures are faced today with grappling with issues surrounding digital privacy, monitoring, and proper collection and presentation of electronic evidence. Reforms in such concerns usually demand interagency collaboration from the stakeholders such as technology companies, attorneys, and human rights activists. By incorporating innovative solutions like establishing clear standards for digital evidence and further sophisticated training for the police, such reforms seek to make criminal procedures less complicated without detracting from the rights of individuals. Tackling these new issues is essential, as out-of-date legislative systems risk undermining public confidence and competence in the justice system. International views on legislative reforms also yield important lessons for policy reform in criminal procedure and evidence. Comparative examination of various legal systems shows divergent approaches to issues such as evidence gathering, prosecution discretion, and sentencing guidelines. For example, the intersection of criminal justice and security sector reform is a matter of urgent concern in post-conflict countries where trust needs to be re-established. In the cases of Turkey and the Occupied Palestinian Territories, SSR initiatives highlight the importance of integrating democratic control into the law enforcement practices in an effort to improve effectiveness and accountability (Arican et al., 2025). In addition, political forces also propel the evolution of legal systems to the same degree, and therefore, reforms have to be introduced that are sensitive to situational contexts and also protect investors and judicial integrity (Armour et al., 2025). Such inter-country dynamics validate the multiplicity of legislative reforms and underlines the necessity of adaptive context-based reforms in international criminal justice systems.

12.6.1. Recent Legislative Initiatives in Criminal Procedure

Within the criminal justice context, there has been growing prominence for recent legislative action seeking to fill systemic gaps in the justice system. Lead on the agenda has been legislation on responding to domestic violence and rape. Various jurisdictions have introduced comprehensive measures seeking to enhance response to these endemic issues, enhancing prevention and victim support measures. For instance, the broadened definitions of domestic violence that encompass psychological abuse as well as physical harm indicate a significant shift in the understanding of the complexities of such offenses. Such behavior is part of a broader push within society towards gender equality and empowerment of vulnerable groups, an indication that legislative reform can adopt a progressive policy with the potential to deliver enduring social gains, as outlined in the goals of the National Plan (Council of Australian Governments, 2025). Along with highlighting domestic violence, legislative initiatives also highlighted the establishment of standardized best practices for collecting and preserving evidence, particularly in sensitive cases of sexual offenses. Legislatures have come to realize the need for ensuring evidence is painstakingly collected so as to facilitate prosecution and make victims more credible. To that end, there are new codes mandating forensic technology in cases and emphasizing officers' specialization in handling sexual assault and domestic violence offenses. That commitment to having standard operating procedures makes it a more equitable space for victims, it being a root reform to the bigger criminal procedure narrative. As jurisdictions increasingly implement similar reforms, the need for having an informed and appropriately trained police force becomes stronger (Council of Australian Governments, 2025). Furthermore, there is greater awareness of criminal procedure and evidence collection through cross-jurisdictional collaboration. The latest legislative initiatives emphasize the need to integrate various responses to security sector reform and oversight by the judiciary within contextually suitable frameworks. The variations observed in countries such as Turkey and Palestinian states account for the challenges involved in developing a common policy in the presence of various political settings and levels of state development. This necessitates establishing clear guidelines that promote cooperation among the police, courts, and civil society bodies to facilitate comprehensive reform as well as monitoring mechanisms. As nations navigate these complex legislative landscapes, the very need emerges for consistency and transparency in the enforcement of provisions securing victims' rights and holding perpetrators accountable (Figure 12.15).

Figure 12.15. Recent legislative initiatives in criminal procedure.

Source: https://authbridge.com/wp-content/uploads/2024/07/New-Criminal-Laws-in-India.jpg.

12.6.2. The Role of Advocacy Groups in Reform Efforts

Advocacy groups play a central role in the ongoing reform process in the criminal justice system, specifically in relation to criminal procedure and evidence. These organizations often act for disadvantaged groups, calling attention to systemic inequalities and suggesting reforms of outdated legal systems. Through studies, public campaigns, and collaboration with legislatures, advocacy organizations implement reforms that correct particular injustices, for example, wrongful convictions, police misuse of power, and racial discrimination in prison sentencing. These organizations not only fight for change on a particular topic but also establish an ideal of a more equitable system. Furthermore, the activism of such groups is important in sustaining the pressure for reform because it keeps legislatures accountable to the communities they represent. Ultimately, advocacy groups are needed drivers of change within the generally conservative venues of legal systems. Throughout the recent years, legal aid debate has been mostly occupied by campaigning organizations whose primary concern is to revolutionize the Community Legal Service (CLS) in accordance with the achievement of social justice. Even though attempts have been made to restructure legal aid for improvement, the challenge remains one of integrating the fundamental principles of social justice into pragmatic legal services. The disjuncture evidenced in earlier reforms underscores the limitations of merely piling on new systems without strong commitment to equal access. Advocacy groups then become not merely champions for necessary reforms but critics of existing structures that prove detrimental to vulnerable groups. Their resolve compels a re-thinking of the CLS's mission, demanding an integrative strategy that harmonizes anti-poverty efforts, social inclusion, and human rights into the clinical practices of legal aid (Stein, 2025). This ongoing dialogue substantiates the role of advocacy in reshaping public policy and legal practice. Additionally, as procedural norms evolve to pressures from advocacy groups, the impact on legal education and practice cannot be overemphasized. The convergence of the inquisitorial and adversarial systems is the best example of this shift, particularly in Latin America where major procedural reform is in progress. This conversation is supported by advocacy groups, which underscore the need to educate legal practitioners who can work within and bring together these divergent systems. With these organizations placing focus on issues of discomfiture faced by foreign lawyers while undergoing this process of transition, they provide inputs leading to a better understanding of trial advocacy, particularly concerning procedural fairness and substantive rights. Proposed recommendations from such dialogue can ease the process of transition while actively addressing hurdles that are likely to hinder the process of consolidating new models of law (Cavise et al., 2006). Thus, the advocacy organizations are not just agents of change but also instructors in the evolving field of criminal procedure and evidence.

12.6.3. Future Directions for Policy Changes

Directions for future policy reforms in criminal procedure and evidence must be aimed at incorporating technology and data analytics. As the criminal justice system is grappling with the nature of digital evidence and cybercrime, policymakers must develop frameworks which not only address these challenges but also expedite legal processes. For example, the use of artificial intelligence in case management systems can also aid in the automation of evidence collection and assessment. Furthermore, the adoption of certain protocols for the acceptance and processing of digital evidence will reduce risks of errors and increase the integrity of judicial processes. This technology-driven transformation is crucial to making sure that the legal world does not lag behind rapidly changing social norms and criminality and, ultimately, retains public confidence in the administration of justice. Further, reforms must cater to the required need for improved training and education for legal professionals, specifically with respect to the interpretation of expert evidence. As the House of Commons Science and Technology Committee Report and subsequent findings by the Law Commission have highlighted, there is a significant interconnection between training covered by legal practitioners and miscarriages of justice caused by expert evidence. Closing this gap requires an overhaul of law school and continuing legal education courses such that both novice and veteran attorneys are well-grounded in scientific evidence. It is imperative to cultivate a culture of strict training within the legal system to prevent risks associated with faulty interpretations of expert testimony as well as further an enlightened judiciary (Davies et al., 2016; University of Nevada et al., 2013). Last but not least, future policy changes must pursue a more holistic approach toward criminal justice system reform, engaging community stakeholders in decision-making. A liberal approach that gathers inputs from diverse vested interests—of the form of community groups, victims' rights organizations, and law enforcement administrations—can bring greater transparency and public trust into judicial processes. Creating open forums for deliberation can highlight the practical consequences of rules of procedure and facilitate required modifications to the legal regime. In addition, this participatory mechanism increases the accountability of legal actors and can result in more inclusive outcomes for marginal groups. Emphasizing community involvement in policymaking will most likely lead to reforms that are more responsive to the needs of those most affected by criminal justice processes, bringing about an actually just system for all.

SUMMARY

In an attempt to condense the new issues and reforms of criminal procedure and evidence, it is evident that the landscape is shifting due to a combination of judicial innovations and legislative changes. These reforms have been driven mainly by the need to enhance access to justice, expedite judicial processes, and address the public dissatisfaction with the integrity of evidence. As observed in recent Australian legal practice, the use of concurrent evidence is a critical turning point in expert evidence. This shift not only encourages collaboration between specialists but also diminishes the dangers of partisanship—a weakness that has long eroded the credibility of evidence in court. In general, the ongoing shift in these disciplines is a response to the complexity of contemporary legal challenges, emphasizing the necessity for continuous adaptation in legal procedures. Furthermore, the role accorded to scientific norms and values, as seen in adoption of reforms such as concurrent evidence, signals a basic shift away from traditional adversarial models. Judges have increasingly come to understand that the assurance of fair trials involves promoting realistic debate among expert witnesses, and thereby preventing the prevalent prejudices associated with expert opinion. This transformation is crucial to outlining clearer paths for juries and judges to evaluate the evidence presented before them. But as noted by Edmond, the success of these reforms could be limited by the enduring conventions of the scientific community, which have long affected how expert evidence is presented. Understanding these limitations is crucial to inducing a more effective and fairer legal climate. Overall, the continued progress in criminal procedure and evidence mirrors a larger trend towards enhancing judicial results through creative reform. As various jurisdictions adopt more liberal practices, the movement toward a less adversarial system offers promising avenues for enhancing the quality and integrity of evidence presented to the court. However, lawyers and lawmakers must be cautious to ensure these reforms are well rooted in the legal system so that they will retain their desired effects. The experiment is in how to achieve efficiency and accuracy without compromising the essential canons of justice. Criminal procedure and evidence development is not an isolated phenomenon but a vital component of an evolving legal system attempting to uphold ideals of fairness and justice for all parties in the process.

The criminal process and evidence scene is being radically transformed by a range of new challenges and the passage of effective reforms. Treatment of sexual assault victims, among others, has been one of the pertinent issues in recent years. Reforms in Australia have attempted to address the specific disadvantage borne by victim/survivors of sexual assault under the criminal justice system, as noted by Fileborn et al. (2014). These initiatives involve the enhancement of advocacy services and specialist policing of sexual crimes, which allow for a more victim-centered approach to justice. Furthermore, alternative evidence presentation at trial and jury direction adjustments have been made to create a more equitable forum for victims. Collectively, these reforms signify a shared commitment to enhanced victim experience while, at the same time, restoring confidence in the justice process. Yet another essential reform has been the enhancement of custodial legal assistance, which is necessary because of the need to protect the rights of detainees. The Supreme Court's judgment in Cadder, which emphasized shortcomings in legal representation within the Scottish police custody, prompted a similar review of custodial rights in many jurisdictions. As explained in Giannoulopoulos et al. (2013), Scottish legal reforms were distinct from their French counterparts, offering valuable lessons regarding issues of complexity surrounding the issue of custodial legal aid. Such trends not only make arguments for the application of legal rights to everyone in custody but also emphasize an examination of what constitutes best practice in achieving effective legal representation. Hence, this section of the reform aims to reinforce the principles of due process and ensure that the legal system protects the accused's rights, and hence fosters a more level judicial landscape. It is through these reforms that an explanation of the broader institutional issues which have long held back change in the criminal justice system is needed. Problems of entrenched practices, institutionalized resistance to change, and systemic bias often make enforcing victim-focused and rights-oriented measures difficult. An examination of such obstacles is of immense value, given the fact that stakeholders like policy makers, campaigning organizations, and legal specialists collaborate for bringing considerable reforms. As pointed out in Fileborn et al. (2014), understanding the empowering or limiting factors that affect the adoption of reforms is crucial in the integration of victim-oriented approaches in court practice. With the dynamic changes in crime and societal needs, an ongoing debate and research must be conducted to provide effective support to an accommodating criminal justice system that not only meets changing societal requirements but ensures full protection of the rights of all concerned parties.

KEY TERMS

- Admissibility of Electronic Records
- Bail Reform
- Cybercrime Procedures
- Forensic Technology
- Plea Bargaining Expansion
- Presumption of Innocence
- Speedy Trial Mechanisms
- Video Conferencing in Trials
- Wrongful Convictions
- AI in Criminal Justice
- Chain of Custody
- Digital Evidence
- Judicial Transparency
- Police Accountability
- Restorative Justice
- Victim-Centric Justice
- Witness Protection Reforms

A LOOK TO THE FUTURE

FORENSIC TECHNOLOGY

The future of forensic technology will transform the profession of criminal investigations and courtroom evidence. As crime becomes increasingly sophisticated, so does the equipment used to probe and validate it. Emerging technologies like artificial intelligence (AI), machine learning, and genomic sequencing are already revolutionizing forensic science by rendering it more precise, faster, and analytically denser. At the forefront of the most promising developments is AI-driven forensic analysis, which can analyze vast quantities of data in the form of fingerprints, DNA, and digital crumbs with amazing accuracy. AI could detect patterns and anomalies that human analysts would overlook, improving rates of case closure and judicial efficiency. Next-generation sequencing is becoming increasingly easy to work with degraded or trace biological samples, promising hope for cold cases or multi-crime-scene investigations.

In digital forensics, the blockchain technology has the potential to safeguard the chain of custody, guaranteeing the admissibility and legitimacy of digital evidence. While it is occurring, the proliferation of cybercrime requires forensic tools that can monitor encrypted communications, follow cryptocurrency transactions, and reveal activity on the dark web. 3D crime scene reconstruction, driven by virtual and augmented reality, is another innovation that can revolutionize court presentations by enabling judges and jurors to engage with crime scenes for more informed assessments. Likewise, facial reconstruction and voice recognition software are projected to become more legal acceptable as their dependability increases.

However, such advancement sparks concerns about privacy, ethical use, algorithmic tool bias, and the requirement of standardized validation protocols. To safeguard justice, forensic science must be preceded and succeeded by stringent regulation, continuous education, and transparency of admissibility criteria. The forensic technology stands at the gateway of a revolution that will have the potential to enhance truth-finding in the criminal justice system. Its potential lies in responsibly harnessing innovation while preserving legal and ethical safeguards.

REFERENCES

1. Arican, M., Aytar, V., Collantes-Celador, G., et al. (2025). *Fostering an EU Strategy for Security Sector Reform in The Mediterranean: Learning from Turkish and Palestinian Police Reform Experiences.* https://core.ac.uk/download/9982956.pdf (accessed on 13th August 2025).
2. Armour, J., & Lele, P. (2025). *Law, Finance, And Politics: The Case of India.* https://core.ac.uk/download/pdf/7151395.pdf (accessed on 13th August 2025).
3. Babuta, A., & Oswald, M. (2020). Data analytics and algorithms in policing in England and Wales: Towards a new policy framework. https://core.ac.uk/download/305121462.pdf (accessed on 13th August 2025).
4. Blocher, J. (2011). Reverse incorporation of state constitutional law. https://core.ac.uk/download/62564097.pdf (accessed on 13th August 2025).
5. Bott, S., Ellsberg, M., & Morrison, A. (2025). *Addressing Gender-Based Violence in The Latin American and Caribbean Region: A Critical Review of Interventions.* https://core.ac.uk/download/pdf/6372976.pdf (accessed on 13th August 2025).
6. Cavise, L. L. (2006). When the inquisitorial and adversary systems collide: Teaching trial advocacy to Latin American lawyers. https://core.ac.uk/download/76623758.pdf (accessed on 13th August 2025).
7. Conway, V., & Daly, Y. M. (2019). From legal advice to legal assistance: Recognizing the changing role of the solicitor in the Garda station. https://core.ac.uk/download/286779063.pdf (accessed on 13th August 2025).
8. Council of Australian Governments. (2025). *The National Plan to Reduce Violence Against Women and Their Children 2010–2022.* https://core.ac.uk/download/pdf/30671574.pdf (accessed on 13th August 2025).
9. Dahaghi, K. (2018). Punishment and penal activity: The expansion of legal fines and fees in Texas from 1985 to 2015. https://core.ac.uk/download/211341177.pdf (accessed on 13th August 2025).
10. Dalakian, G. J., II. (2018). Open the jail cell doors, HAL: A guarded embrace of pretrial risk assessment instruments. https://core.ac.uk/download/216958634.pdf (accessed on 13th August 2025).
11. Davies, G., & Piasecki, E. (2016). No more laissez faire? Expert evidence, rule changes and reliability: Can more effectively training for the bar and judiciary prevent miscarriages of justice? https://core.ac.uk/download/74228540.pdf (accessed on 13th August 2025).
12. Edmond, G. (2009). Merton and the hot tub: Scientific conventions and expert evidence in Australian civil procedure. https://core.ac.uk/download/62553218.pdf (accessed on 13th August 2025).
13. Enebeli, V. N. (2024). *Evaluation of Emerging Trends in Nigerian Criminal Law Jurisprudence.* https://core.ac.uk/download/597470688.pdf (accessed on 13th August 2025).
14. Ferguson, R. I., Irons, A., Renaud, K., Wilford, S., et al. (2020). PRECEPT: A framework for ethical digital forensics investigations. https://core.ac.uk/download/288653619.pdf (accessed on 13th August 2025).

15. Fileborn, B., & Bluett-Boyd, N. (2014). Victim/survivor-focused justice responses and reforms to criminal court practice: Implementation, current practice and future directions. https://core.ac.uk/download/pdf/30674908.pdf (accessed on 13th August 2025).
16. Garcia, C. O., Cardona, D., Chesñevar, C., Collazzo-Yelpo, M., et al. (2020). *South American Expert Roundtable: Increasing Adaptive Governance Capacity for Coping with Unintended Side Effects of Digital Transformation.* https://core.ac.uk/download/286359460.pdf (accessed on 13th August 2025).
17. Garrett, B. L. (2005). Innocence, harmless error, and federal wrongful conviction law. https://core.ac.uk/download/213020502.pdf (accessed on 13th August 2025).
18. Garrett, B. L. (2007). Aggregation in criminal law. https://core.ac.uk/download/213020497.pdf (accessed on 13th August 2025).
19. Garth, B., & Menkel-Meadow, C. (2010). Process, people, power and policy: Empirical studies of civil procedure and courts. https://core.ac.uk/download/70375292.pdf (accessed on 13th August 2025).
20. Germani, A. R., Pergolizzi, A., & Reganati, F. (2015). Illegal trafficking and unsustainable waste management in Italy: Evidence at the regional level. https://core.ac.uk/download/54525861.pdf (accessed on 13th August 2025).
21. Giannoulopoulos, D. (2013). "North of the border and across the channel": Custodial legal assistance reforms in Scotland and France. https://core.ac.uk/download/13641681.pdf (accessed on 13th August 2025).
22. Glover, J. M. (2012). The Federal Rules of Civil Settlement. https://core.ac.uk/download/74539279.pdf (accessed on 13th August 2025).
23. Greene, S. S. (2015). Race, class, and access to civil justice. https://core.ac.uk/download/62571403.pdf (accessed on 13th August 2025).
24. Harris, D. A. (2009). How accountability-based policing can reinforce–or replace–the Fourth Amendment exclusionary rule. https://core.ac.uk/download/159569447.pdf (accessed on 13th August 2025).
25. Helfer, L. R., & Showalter, A. E. (2017). Opposing international justice: Kenya's integrated backlash strategy against the ICC. https://core.ac.uk/download/74513764.pdf (accessed on 13th August 2025).
26. Hepworth, J., Jones, M., Schofield, E., Schofield, T., et al. (2011). Health and community services for trafficked women: An exploratory study of policy and practice. https://core.ac.uk/download/10918153.pdf (accessed on 13th August 2025).
27. Hu, M. (2017). Algorithmic Jim Crow. https://core.ac.uk/download/144232642.pdf (accessed on 13th August 2025).
28. Joh, E. E. (2022). Ethical AI in American policing. https://core.ac.uk/download/617197499.pdf (accessed on 13th August 2025).
29. Kushwah, J. P., & Kushwah, S. P. S. (2024). *Examination of Procedure Safeguards Under the Indian Constitution (Article 21) and Specific Laws Like C.P.C., Bhartiya Nagarik Suraksha Sanhita, 2023 and Bhartiya Sakshya Sanhita, 2023.* https://core.ac.uk/download/643575229.pdf (accessed on 13th August 2025).

30. Lachmayer, K., & Witzleb, N. (2025). *The Challenge to Privacy from Ever Increasing State Surveillance: A Comparative Perspective.* https://core.ac.uk/download/pdf/30673640.pdf (accessed on 13th August 2025).

31. Lopez-de-Silanes, F. (2025). *The Politics of Legal Reform.* https://core.ac.uk/download/pdf/7043201.pdf (accessed on 13th August 2025).

32. Magaloni, B., & Rodriguez, L. (2020). Torture as a method of criminal prosecution: Police brutality, the militarization of security and the reform of inquisitorial criminal justice in Mexico. https://core.ac.uk/download/322310836.pdf (accessed on 13th August 2025).

33. Marshall, P. D. (2011). A comparative analysis of the right to appeal. https://core.ac.uk/download/62547246.pdf (accessed on 13th August 2025).

34. Peacock, A., & Main, B. G. (2025). *What Price Civil Justice?* https://core.ac.uk/download/pdf/7068340.pdf (accessed on 13th August 2025).

35. Rudovsky, D., Owens, E., Mayson, S., & Bibas, S. (2015). Improving fairness and addressing racial disparities in the Delaware criminal justice system. https://core.ac.uk/download/75761612.pdf (accessed on 13th August 2025).

36. Smith, A. (2010). In praise of the guilty project: A criminal defense lawyer's growing anxiety about innocence projects. https://core.ac.uk/download/70374631.pdf (accessed on 13th August 2025).

37. Stein, J. M. (2025). *The Future of Social Justice in Britain: A New Mission for the Community Legal Service.* https://core.ac.uk/download/pdf/7119323.pdf (accessed on 13th August 2025).

38. Tague, P. W. (2001). Faulty adversarial performance by criminal defenders in the Crown Court. https://core.ac.uk/download/70373764.pdf (accessed on 13th August 2025).

39. University of Nevada, Las Vegas–William S. Boyd School of Law. (2013). *Conference Bibliography: Juvenile Justice 1999–2013.* http://scholars.law.unlv.edu/jjc2013/1 (accessed on 13th August 2025).

40. Urbas, G., & Choo, K. K. R. (2025). *Resource Materials on Technology-Enabled Crime.* https://core.ac.uk/download/pdf/30688045.pdf (accessed on 13th August 2025).

INDEX

A

Acquittal 240
Acquittal Appeal 378
Admissibility 245, 246, 249, 250, 255, 256, 263, 264, 271, 276, 315, 321, 322, 323, 340, 343
Admissibility of Electronic Records 414
AI in Criminal Justice 414
Amendment of Charge 206
Anticipatory Bail 172
Appeal 236, 240, 353, 354, 378
Appellate Court 378
Arraignment 32
Arrest 32

B

Bail 32
Bailable Offence 172
Bail Application 172
Bail Bond 172
Bail Pending Appeal 378
Bail Reform 414
Best Evidence Rule 276
Beyond a Reasonable Doubt 32
Burden of Proof 32, 240

C

Case Diary 103
CCTV Surveillance 139
Chain of Custody 32, 139, 414
Character Evidence 276
Charge 177, 180, 181, 183, 189, 191, 193, 196, 197, 199, 201, 205, 206
Charge Framing 240
Charge Sheet (Final Report) 103
Child Witness 309
Circumstances 74, 88, 95
Circumstantial Evidence 32, 251, 276
Civil rights 383, 389, 398, 401
Cognizance 206
Cognizance of Offence 103
Committal Proceedings 103
Community 41, 47, 48, 51, 52, 53, 54, 59, 60, 62, 66, 71
Comparative analysis 281
Complaint 206
Confession 32, 276
Confessions 313, 314, 315, 316, 317, 318, 319, 320, 321, 322, 323, 324, 325, 326, 327, 328, 329, 330, 331, 332, 333, 334, 335, 336, 337, 338, 339, 340, 341, 342, 343, 344, 345
Confinement 145, 160

Constitutional rights 1, 9, 22, 25, 35
Contradiction 309
Conviction 237, 238, 240
Conviction Appeal 378
Convictions 347, 348, 349, 350, 351, 352, 353, 354, 356, 361, 362, 364, 365, 366, 367, 371, 373, 374, 375, 377, 378, 380
Correctional professionals 40, 62
Corroboration 309
Courts jurisprudence 110
Crime Scene Examination 103
Criminal justice 143, 144, 145, 147, 149, 151, 152, 153, 154, 155, 156, 157, 158, 159, 160, 161, 163, 164, 165, 167, 168, 169, 171, 173, 174
Criminal justice system 212, 213, 215, 216, 217, 218, 223, 226, 233, 235, 238, 239, 243
Criminal Justice System 39, 40, 43, 47, 69
Criminal offenses 2
Criminal procedure 109, 110, 111, 112, 118, 119, 120, 124, 125, 126, 127, 131, 133, 136, 138, 144, 148, 152, 156, 157, 159, 160, 166, 167
Criminal Procedure 1, 6, 11, 12, 25, 26, 27, 32, 33
Criminal prosecutions 2
Criminal trial procedure 212, 213, 215, 219, 226, 228, 230, 235
Criminal trial process 211, 212, 213, 216, 217, 218, 219, 220, 221, 223, 224, 225, 226, 227, 230, 231, 232, 233, 234, 235, 236, 237, 238, 239, 240
Critical function 179
Cross-examination 282, 284, 285, 289, 290, 293, 294, 297, 298, 299, 301, 303, 304, 305, 306, 307, 308, 309, 311, 312
Custodial Confession 343
Custodial Interrogation 32, 103, 172
Custodial remands 144, 145, 151, 163, 171
Cybercrime Procedures 414

D

Demeanor of Witness 309
Digital Evidence 389, 414
Direct Evidence 32, 276
Discharge 206
Discretion of Court 172
Doctrine of Finality 378
Documentary Evidence 240, 256, 276
Double Jeopardy 378
Due Process 32
Dying Declaration 276, 343
Dynamic interplay 41

E

Electronic device 110
Electronic monitoring (EM) 144, 145, 158, 160, 162, 163, 164, 165
Electronic Surveillance 132, 139
Enhancement of Sentence 378
Equilibrium 178
Equitable policy 147
Equity 40, 64
Error of Law 378
Evidence-based consideration 144
Evidence in criminal law 246
Evidentiary Value 343
Examination-in-Chief 240
Exclusionary Rule 19, 32
Exculpatory evidence 314, 339
Exculpatory Statement 343
Expert Evidence 276
Expert Witness 32, 309
Extension of Remand 172
Extra-Judicial Confession 343
Extraordinary Remedy 378
Eyewitnesses 282, 286, 301

F

Factual integrity 385
Fairness 383, 385, 393, 394, 395, 397, 400, 401, 402, 405, 406, 408, 409, 411, 413, 418
Federal Rules of Evidence 246, 249, 254, 259, 260, 261, 264
Final Arguments 240
First Information Report (FIR) 187, 206
Forensic Analysis 139
Forensic Evidence 103
Forensic Technology 414, 415
Framing of Charge 206

G

Growing awareness 383

H

Hearsay Evidence 276
Hearsay Rule 32
Hostile Witness 240, 309
House Search 139
Human testimony 282

I

Illegally Obtained Evidence 139, 276
Inculpatory Statement 343
Indictment 32
Instance 144, 145, 147, 152, 156, 159, 160, 164, 168, 173
Interception of Communication 139
Interlocutory Order 378
Inventory of Seized Items 139
Investigation 186, 206
Involuntary confessions 314, 320

J

Joinder of Accused 206
Joinder of Charges 206
Judgment 240
Judicial Confession 343
Judicial Custody 103, 172
Judicial Discretion 172, 378
Judicial Evidence 276, 277
Judicial Notice 32
Judicial Process 55
Judicial Transparency 414
Justice system 39, 40, 41, 42, 43, 45, 46, 47, 48, 49, 51, 52, 53, 54, 55, 56, 58, 59, 60, 61, 62, 63, 64, 65, 66, 67, 68, 69, 71
Juvenile justice 146, 155

L

Leave to Appeal 378
Legal accountability 212
Legal culture 74
Legal systems 383, 388, 389, 405, 407, 408, 409, 411

M

Magisterial Review 172
Magistrate's Jurisdiction 206
Material Evidence 206
Mechanisms of appeals 347
Miranda Rights 32
Miscarriage of Justice 378

N

Non-Bailable Offence 172

O

Offender rehabilitation mechanisms 40
Onus Probandi 343
Opening Statement 240
Oral Evidence 276

P

Panch Witnesses 139
Parliamentary powers 3
Perjury 309
Personal Search 139
Placing confidence 383
Plea Bargaining Expansion 414
Plea of Guilty 240
Plea of Not Guilty 240
Police Accountability 414
Police Custody 103, 172
Police Report 206
post-conviction claims 2
Post-Conviction Relief 378
Potential reform 41
Presumption 143, 144, 145, 148, 153, 154, 156, 159, 161, 163, 166, 171
Presumption of Innocence 240, 332, 343, 414
Pre-trial process 73, 83, 90, 91, 93, 95, 96
Prima Facie Case 206
Prima Facie Evidence 103
Production before Magistrate 172
Prosecutor 178, 189, 190

prosecutorial discretion 74, 91, 92, 102
Protections 384, 388, 389, 393, 397, 399, 401, 407
Psychological 145, 159, 160, 169, 173
Public confidence 74, 93
Public safety 144, 145, 147, 148, 149, 150, 151, 152, 154, 156, 157, 158, 160, 161, 162, 163, 166, 171
Punishment 41, 47, 49, 50, 53, 60, 61, 62
Pursuing justice 178, 187

R

Re-examination 240
Reform efforts. 40
Refreshing Memory 309
Relevance 264
Reliability 246, 249, 254, 255, 256, 257, 259, 261, 263, 264, 267, 268, 271, 272, 273, 275, 278, 279
Remand 378
Remand Application 103, 172
Restorative Justice 414
Retaliatory litigation 283
Retracted Confession 343
Retribution 40, 60
Reverse Burden 343
Revision 378
Risk assessment 144, 148, 152, 154, 156, 167, 168, 174
Robust training 248

S

Search and Seizure 23, 103
Search and Seizure Memo 139
Search Warrant 123, 139
Search without Warrant 139
Seizure 109, 110, 115, 139, 140
Sentencing 212, 235, 236
Societal changes 41
Societal norms 73, 92
Societal values 383, 394
Speedy Trial Mechanisms 414
Stakeholder interviews 145
Standard of Proof 343
Subjective testimony 246
Summons Case 206
Surety 153, 172
Systematic biases 179

T

Telephone Tapping 139
Tracking Devices 139
Transit Remand 172
Transparency 383, 384, 386, 389, 391, 393, 394, 396, 397, 398, 403, 409, 410, 412, 415
Trial 56, 57, 58
Trial Commencement 206
Trumping innocence 347
Tutored Witness 309

V

Validity 246, 254, 257, 275
Victim 70
Victim-Centric Justice 414
Video Conferencing in Trials 414
Voluntariness 343

W

Witness examination 282, 283, 301
Witness Protection 309
Witness Protection Reforms 414
Witness Statement 103
Witness Summons 309
Witness testimonies 245
Witness Testimony 241
Wrongful Convictions 414